The Three Wars
of
Lt. Gen.
George E. Stratemeyer

His Korean War Diary

Edited by
William T. Y'Blood

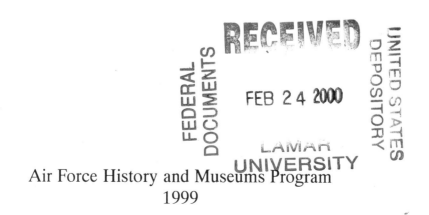

Air Force History and Museums Program
1999

Library of Congress Cataloging-in-Publication Data

Stratemeyer, George E., 1890-1970
        The three wars of Lt. Gen. George E. Stratemeyer:
His Korean War Diary/ edited by William T. Y'Blood.
        p. cm.
includes bibliographic references and index.
 1. Korean War, 1950-1953—Aerial Operations, American.
2. Korean War, 1950-1953—Personal Narratives, American.
3. Stratemeyer, George E., 1890-1970—Diaries. 4. Generals
—United States—Diaries. I. Title: 3 Wars of Lieutenant
General George E. Stratemeyer. II. Y'Blood, William T.,
1937- III. Title.

DS920.2.U5 S87 1999
951.904'2—dc21   99-041835

For sale by the U.S. Government Printing Office
Superintendent of Documents, Mail Stop: SSOP, Washington, DC 20402-9328
ISBN 0-16-050106-7

Lt. Gen. George E. Stratemeyer

Foreword

"The forgotten war." "The limited war." The Korean War has been called both of these and more. But if it all too quickly dropped from the front pages, it must nevertheless be remembered for what it was: the first major conflict between East and West, an important milestone in the formative years of the Cold War. Its outcome often subtly shaded and colored the thinking of both military and civilian leaders for many years thereafter.

Although some people see the Korean War as just a ground war, it was far more than that. It was the first war the United States Air Force fought as a separate service, and a war in which America's joint service air power team performed sterling work. Without the air dominance gained by Air Force F–86 Sabres against a numerically larger foe, the ground forces would have been left vulnerable to air attack with disastrous consequences. Without the close support and interdiction efforts of the Air Force B–26s, B–29s, F–51s, F–80s and F–84s, and Navy and Marine F9F Panthers, F4U Corsairs, AD Skyraiders and F7F Tigercats, the tasks of the ground forces would have been made immeasurably more difficult. Without the enormous exertions of the C–46s, C–47s, C–54s, and C–119s, supply, sustainment and evacuation of ground forces would have been virtually impossible. Without the men and planes of Lt. Gen. George E. Stratemeyer's Far East Air Forces and their naval and Marine colleagues, the war's denouement may have been entirely different.

This is a unique document. Throughout the years, although often officially frowned upon, officers and men alike have kept diaries. Some of these diaries, primarily from World War Two, have been published. Few, if any, from the Korean War have seen the light of day. Thus General Stratemeyer's diary of the first year of the war provides a unique look at the war from a high level. His diary is rich in the personalities, the operations, the problems and successes, and the behind the scenes maneuverings of the United States' military services in the Far East as they waged the war. Much of what he reveals in his diary is still valid today: proper force size and equipment; accurate and timely intelligence; coordination with the other services; a realization of the impact of media coverage on a war. Despite an organization possessing global capabilities well beyond what Stratemeyer could envision in 1950, these remain the concerns of the United States Air Force today, the centerpiece of America's joint aerospace team. Reading this work confirms one of the great lessons of twentieth century warfare, a lesson applicable to the conflicts of the twenty-first century as well: appropriate and timely use of aerospace power enables both the thwarting of an aggressor's will, and the minimizing of casualties to one's own surface forces.

RICHARD P. HALLION
Air Force Historian

Editor's Note

From June 25, 1950, to May 20, 1951, Lt. Gen. George E. Stratemeyer, the Far East Air Forces commander, kept a diary of his activities during the Korean War. A number of general officers kept such diaries during World War II, although the practice was generally frowned upon by higher headquarters and, in the Navy at least, was against regulations. In the Korean War, the writing of such works became less wide-spread. Surprisingly, however, three diaries written by senior Air Force officers (Stratemeyer, Maj. Gen. Earle E. Partridge, Commander, Fifth Air Force, and Maj. Gen. Edward J. Timberlake, Vice Commander, Fifth Air Force) exist from the Korean War. These three diaries view the war from different perspectives: Stratemeyer's from a high-level planning, strategy, and political viewpoint; Partridge's from a mid-level planning and operational plane; Timberlake's from a slightly lower operational level.

This book, however, deals only with General Stratemeyer's diary. It is a valuable document because his position as Far East Air Forces commander allowed him to observe the war and its personalities from a unique perspective. General Stratemeyer had his secretary type his diary entries onto 6 by 9 1/2-inch loose-leaf lined pages. Totalling some 750 pages, these were then placed into three large binders covering the periods June 25 - September 15, 1950, September 16 - December 16, 1950, and December 17, 1950 - May 20, 1951. The editor has changed this time division somewhat to conform to certain significant events and to make each section more or less equal in length. September 14 now ends the first section; the second section begins the following day with the Inch'ŏn landings and concludes on November 25 with the opening of the massive Chinese Communist offensive; the final section covers the period November 26, 1950, to May 20, 1951, the date of Stratemeyer's heart attack.

The reader should be aware that, although it was the intent of the editor to keep this diary as published as close as possible to the original, it is not the "raw" diary as Stratemeyer had it transcribed. By remaining close to the original, all messages have been retained even though some were word-for-word repeats of messages entered earlier, perhaps just a paragraph before. However, to prevent an overload of "*sics*," brackets or other such emendations, certain editorial changes have been made. This has been done primarily to make the text more readable.

As General Stratemeyer wrote the diary and his secretary typed it, punctuation tended to wander or be non-existent at times. Commas and other such punctuation were often omitted, resulting in words which ran together or created occasional odd sentences. Also, Stratemeyer (or his secretary) often used quotation marks randomly for no particular reason. He (or they) also tended to capitalize everything that had an "official" ring to it, regardless of whether it was necessary or not (*e.g.*, "Ground Force," "Border," etc.). In the case of place names, at times he capitalized the entire name but in the next sentence capitalized only the first letter of the name. Therefore, proper punctuation and capitalization has been inserted throughout the text.

Occasionally, individuals' names were misspelled in the diary, either because of a typographical error or because the general or his secretary were not familiar with the person's name (an example is Admiral "Strubel" instead of Struble). So, the editor has substituted the correct spelling of such names. Regarding Chinese names, the editor has used the old Wade-Giles system rather than the modern Pinyin, because the older method was in use during the Korean War and it was in this form that Stratemeyer identified Chinese individuals.

General Stratemeyer used many acronyms throughout his diary. Brackets have been used to spell out those acronyms when they are first encountered. Additionally, a listing of these acronyms has been added as an appendix. Closely associated with acronyms are military abbreviations. These abbreviations are sprinkled liberally throughout his diary, particularly in the numerous messages Stratemeyer recorded. Like the acronyms, these abbreviations are spelled out upon their first appearance. If the abbreviation is uncommon, it may also be bracketed again later in the diary. Unfortunately, Stratemeyer sometimes used abbreviations that could mislead the reader. An example of this is the use of "opr" for operation instead of its more common usage for operator. When instances such as this have occurred, the editor has changed the abbreviation (in this case, to "opn") to its normal usage. It is emphasized that changes such as these have in no way skewed the meaning in the passages in which they occur.

Although Stratemeyer noted the days of the month in his diary, he did not note the days of the week. Therefore, the week days have been added at the appropriate places. There is one other major change in the diary. Like the punctuation, General Stratemeyer was variable on the spelling of Korean place names. This is not peculiar to Stratemeyer, because Korean place names can be difficult for anyone. For consistency, however, these place names have been edited to conform to those of the United States Board on Geographic Names in *South Korea, Official Standard Names Gazetteer* (Department of the Interior, 1966), the *Gazetteer of North Korea* (Defense Mapping Agency, 1982), and on the excellent map of Korea in the U.S. Army's official history of the first six months of the Korean War, *South to the Naktong, North to the Yalu* (Washington, 1961).

Again, it is reiterated that neither intent nor meaning have been altered by these editorial emendations. However, for those who wish to compare the original "raw" diary with this published version, microfilm copies of the original (Air Force Historical Research Agency number 168.7018-16) are available at the Air Force History Support Office, Anacostia Naval Station (adjoining Bolling AFB), Washington, D.C., and at the Air Force Historical Research Agency, Maxwell Air Force Base, Montgomery, Alabama.

Biographical information on individuals mentioned in the diary was obtained from various sources — official service biographies, military records, Pentagon telephone directories, various editions of *Who's Who* (both American and British), other books and magazines, etc. Unfortunately, many individuals still cannot be identified. Stratemeyer often mentioned these people only by their last names with little other identification. Also, a disastrous fire a number of years ago at the National Personnel Records Center in St. Louis, Missouri, destroyed many records, including records pertaining to the period of the diary. So, regrettably, in a number of cases the editor has had to note these individuals as "unidentified" or "unknown."

Footnotes are used throughout this work to identify individuals; other footnotes are used to define terms and to describe important events. They have also been used to further explain or clarify situations that Stratemeyer believed important enough to include in his diary, but which he did not completely describe. For space reasons, air force designations in the footnotes are usually rendered in abbreviated form. For example, 5AF for Fifth Air Force.

Stratemeyer's comments reveal the Korean war, particularly the Air Force's role in that war, from the perspective of the top Air Force commander on the scene. These comments show the variety of problems that Stratemeyer encountered and that a high-level commander of today can face. Among these problems were a lack of materiel (both "metal" and "flesh"); a sometimes less-than-cordial relationship with the other services; a similar relationship, though more of the love-hate variety, with the press; and the continual problem of how to fight a war when the directives from above are often contradictory and conflicting.

These problems do not occur just in the conventional limited war that Stratemeyer fought in Korea but can crop up in all levels of combat from "low-intensity" guerrilla operations up to a nuclear war. Thus, General Stratemeyer's diary is not just a document of historical interest, but is one to be studied by officers of all ranks, as well as students of warfare, so as to better understand the problems of command in wartime.

A volume such as this is seldom the work of a single individual, and so it is with this endeavor. The editor would like to thank Ms. Nancy Carlsen, Ms. Diane Gordon, Mr. Jack Neufeld, Mr. David Chenoweth, Dr. Richard Wolf, and, particularly, Ms. Karen Fleming-Michael for their labors in bringing the diary to fruition. Their efforts are greatly appreciated.

Contents

Photographs

Maps.

Introduction

When the North Korean People's Army surged south across the 38th Parallel on June 25, 1950, Lt. Gen. George E. Stratemeyer had been commander of the U.S. Far East Air Forces (FEAF) since April 1949. However, on that fateful June day, he was in Washington for meetings at the Pentagon. Upon hearing of the attack, he immediately returned to Japan to resume control of FEAF. There he became involved in a war quite different from the one he fought five years earlier in the China-Burma-India (CBI) theater of operations. In Korea, George Stratemeyer found himself not only in a war against enemy forces, but warring with the other U.S. armed services and with the press.

Stratemeyer was born in Cincinnati, Ohio, on November 24, 1890, but spent most of his childhood in Peru, Indiana, where he graduated from high school. On March 1, 1910, he was admitted into the United States Military Academy as a member of the Class of 1914. A genial and handsome cadet, one of his claims to fame at West Point was his ability to imitate a steam calliope.[1] However, he was not a particularly good student and, because of problems with the subject of philosophy, was turned back to the Third Class (Sophomore) on April 7, 1913. He was granted a leave of absence, presumably to bone up on philosophy, "without pay or allowances," until August 28, 1913.[2] Stratemeyer then became a member of the Class of 1915, the "class the stars fell on," that produced Generals Dwight D. Eisenhower, Omar N. Bradley, and over 15 other generals. Still not the greatest student, Stratemeyer graduated 147 out of a class of 164. His best class ranking that final year was 80th in Drill Regulations—Hippology (the study of the horse) and his worst was last in Practical Military Engineering.[3] Following graduation, Stratemeyer was assigned to the 7th Infantry Regiment, and served with that organization in Texas and Arizona from September 11, 1915, to July 15, 1916. He then was with the 34th Infantry for just over a month before being detached in September for flight training at Rockwell Field in San Diego, California. The month before, Stratemeyer married Annalee Rix, a marriage that lasted until his death 53 years later.

Flying training took six months and on May 3, 1917, he became rated as a Junior Military Aviator.[4] Previously, in March, he received Federation Aeronautique

---

1. *The Howitzer, 1915* (West Point, N.Y. , 1915), p 178.
2. "Official Register of the Officers and Cadets of the United States Military Academy for 1915" (West Point, 1915), p 16.
3. Ibid., pp 16-18.
4. A rating of Military Aviator (MA) was established in 1912, and 24 aviators qualified for this rating. However, because it was not established by law, the MA designation was, essentially, one of semantics. In 1914, at (H.R. 5304) was passed in Congress establishing officially three aeronautical grades: Junior Military Aviator (JMA), Military Aviator, and Aviation Mechanician. A pilot had to serve three years as a JMA before he could be rated a Military Aviator. See Juliette A. Hennessy, *The United States Army Air Arm, April 1861 to April 1917* (Washington, 1985), pp 58-59, 107-112, 233-234, for a complete discussion of this subject.

Internationale (F.A.I.—the international organization that authenticated aerial flights) airplane pilot certificate No. 683. Stratemeyer later held ratings of Airplane Pilot (1920), Airplane Observer (1930), Military Airplane Pilot (1937), Combat Observer (1939), Command Pilot (1939), Aircraft Observer (1941), and Technical Observer (1943).

His first aviation assignment, with the 1st Aero Squadron at Columbus, New Mexico, lasted less than two weeks before he was sent to Columbus, Ohio, in late May 1917 to organize and command the School of Military Aeronautics at Ohio State University. Six months later, he went to Kelly Field in San Antonio, Texas, to serve as test pilot and executive officer at the field. Stratemeyer remained at Kelly Field until February 1921, the longest tour so far in his short career, before moving to Chanute Field, Illinois, to become its base commander for a brief period. In January 1918, Stratemeyer also organized, then commanded the Air Service Mechanics School at Kelly and at Chanute Field, a position he held until July, 31, 1921.

2d Lt. Stratemeyer during flight training at Rockwell Field, October 1916.

Flying has always presented a glamorous image to the public and none more so than during the years of World War I and immediately after. But flying was definitely dangerous then and many accidents had fatal results. Stratemeyer came close to becoming a fatality himself in early 1918. Taking off from Kelly in a SPAD for a routine hop, he was doing aerial acrobatics ("acrobacy" was Stratemeyer's term) at 3,500 feet when his propeller shattered. Hot oil and water spewed into the cockpit, burning and blinding Stratemeyer. The motor began vibrating and before Stratemeyer was able to shut off the ignition, the motor tore loose from its mounts and fell between the landing gear where it was held just by two drift wires.[5] Stratemeyer dove for the ground and landed without a scratch. Later, he reflected that he should have been more deliberate in his actions and descended in a shallow dive. He had been lucky that the motor had not fallen off completely or that its final position had not affected his plane's center of gravity more.[6]

While at Kelly, Stratemeyer was involved with the Air Service's contribution to the U.S. Government's Victory Loan campaign in 1919, the Victory Loan Flying Circus. The Flying Circus consisted of three flights — eastern, western,

---

5. A drift wire, also called a drag wire, is a cross-bracing wire or brace, designed primarily to resist drag.
6. Ltr, Maj Gen George E. Stratemeyer to Commanding General, Army Air Forces, subj: Narrow escapes from fatal accidents, Apr 14, 1942.

Stratemeyer (center) poses with members of the Middle Western Flying Circus.

and middle western (which Stratemeyer commanded). For 30 days beginning April 10, 1919, these three "circuses" put on air shows at 88 cities in 45 states.[7] It was also at Kelly in 1920 that Stratemeyer officially transferred to the Air Service. He was promoted to the permanent rank of major in December 1920 and served in this rank as the commanding officer of the Air Service Mechanics School, which moved to Chanute Field, Illinois, in February 1921.

From October 1921 to July 1924, he served in Hawaii in a variety of assignments. During this tour, he commanded both the 10th Air Park and Luke Field and was air officer and assistant air officer for the Hawaiian Department. In August 1924, Stratemeyer began a five-year tour at West Point as a battalion commander and instructor in tactics.

It was at West Point that Gen. Jacob E. Smart,[8] as a cadet, first met Stratemeyer. General Smart recalled Stratemeyer as sharp both intellectually and in appearance, an officer who made a great impression on Smart and influenced his decision to join the Air Corps. (The name was changed from Air Service in July 1926.) Their careers intersected several times in the following years. During World War II, they served together on the Air Staff and following the war, Smart became Stratemeyer's deputy for operations at Air Defense Command headquarters.

Following his tour at West Point, Stratemeyer attended the Air Corps Tactical School at Langley Field, Virginia, graduating in June 1930. More schooling

---

7. Maurer Maurer, *Aviation in the U.S. Army*, 1919-1939 (Washington, 1987), p 20.

8. Intvw, William T. Y'Blood, Charles J. Gross, and Richard H. Kohn, with Gen Jacob E. Smart, USAF (Ret.), at Ft. McNair, Washington, D.C., Nov. 6, 1986. General Smart graduated from the U.S. Military Academy in 1931. Following a series of flying assignments, in December 1941, he became Chief of Flying Training and then a member of Gen Arnold's Advisory Council. In March 1944, he became commander of the 97th Bomb Group, flying 29 missions before being shot down, wounded, and taken prisoner in May 1944. He remained a POW until April 29, 1945. After the war, Smart held several positions, including Secretary of the Air Staff; Deputy for Operations, Air Defense Command; Deputy for Operations, FEAF; Assistant Vice Chief of Staff, Headquarters USAF; Commander, Twelfth Air Force; Vice Commander, TAC; Commander, U.S. Forces, Japan and Fifth Air Force; Commander in Chief, PACAF; and prior to retirement in 1966, Deputy Commander in Chief, U.S. European Command.

followed, with Stratemeyer attending the Army's Command and General Staff School at Fort Leavenworth, Kansas, from August 1930 to June 1932. His work at the school impressed the leadership and he was asked to stay on as an instructor following graduation. Stratemeyer remained at Leavenworth the next four years.

At Leavenworth, Stratemeyer was involved briefly with the Civilian Conservation Corps (CCC). The Roosevelt administration established the CCC in April 1933 to provide temporary work for such disparate groups as young, single men, World War I veterans, and experienced woodsmen. These men then worked on government lands (both state and federal) doing reforestation, fire prevention, soil

As a Lt. Col., Stratemeyer was deputy commander, then commander of the 7th Bombardment Group from August 1936 to August 1938.

conservation, and other such projects. Although the Army did not supervise the work nor provide military training to the CCC members, it was intimately involved in the program. It inducted the men into the CCC, ran physical conditioning programs, set up and ran the camps, and provided food, shelter, and medical services to the CCC members.[9]

In the summer of 1933, Stratemeyer (along with many other officers at Fort Leavenworth) was ordered to temporary duty at the CCC camp at Leavenworth, and was placed in charge of a company of CCC inductees. There is no record of exactly what he did during this period, but it certainly must have been much different from what he was accustomed.

His tour as an instructor at Fort Leavenworth completed, and now a lieutenant colonel, Stratemeyer reported to Hamilton Field, California, in August 1936 to become deputy commander, then commander, of the 7th Bombardment Group. As commander of the 7th Group, Stratemeyer never seemed to lack ideas for the training of his crews. Almost every Saturday his squadrons flew a mission, each one involving different procedures or different sets of conditions to overcome.[10]

While at Hamilton Field, he had another close shave in an aircraft accident. Following a training mission, Stratemeyer was returning to Hamilton Field in his B–10B. Until beginning the approach for landing, the flight had gone well. The landing gear had been lowered and flaps extended when Stratemeyer noticed the right engine had lost some power and was indicating only about 1,000 RPM. The left engine still was operating normally, so Stratemeyer continued the approach.

Suddenly, as Stratemeyer started his turn to final, the left engine stopped.

---

9. Maurer, p 348.
10. Ibid., p 394.

Stratemeyer tried to raise his landing gear to stretch his approach, but quickly realized that he was not going to make the runway. The B–10 splashed into the waters of San Pablo Bay, throwing up a spray of dirty, brown water. The plane did not appear to be sinking when Stratemeyer and his crew left the plane, and they quickly discovered that this was because it had crashed into only about five feet of mud and water. Luckily, the only injuries suffered were slight bruises and cuts. A rescue boat soon appeared to pick up the crew and deposit them, wet, muddy, and bedraggled, on the Hamilton Field dock. Carburetor icing was believed to be the cause of this accident.[11]

Following his Hamilton Field tour, Stratemeyer's next assignment was as a student at the Army War College. Then, it was on to Headquarters, U.S. Army Air Corps, where he became head of the Training and Operations Division. This job involved not only overseeing the burgeoning training program of the Air Corps, but also being involved in a wide variety of important staff functions. In August 1941, Stratemeyer, now a full colonel, became executive officer to Gen. Henry H. Arnold, Chief of the Army Air Forces, the successor organization to the Army Air Corps. Shortly before the United States entered World War II, Stratemeyer received his first star and began a short tour as commanding officer of the Southeast Air Corps Training Center at Maxwell Field, Alabama.

With the rapid wartime expansion of all the services, Stratemeyer returned to Washington in June 1942 as a major general. His new job was Chief of Air Staff, Army Air Forces, a position he held until July 1943. Directly under General Arnold, he was in charge of the Air Staff, which during most of his tour, consisted of a policy level group made up of the chiefs of: A-1 (Personnel); A-2 (Intelligence); A-3 (Training and Operations); A-4 (Supply); and A-5 (Plans), the latter a later addition. The Air Inspectfor also was on this level.[12]

From April 8 to June 5, 1943, Stratemeyer made an extensive inspection trip to England, North Africa, the Middle East, and China. The latter stop proved to be very valuable to Stratemeyer because about two months later he was in India as the commanding general, USAAF, of the India-Burma Sector (IBS) of the China-Burma-India (CBI) Theater of Operations, his first combat command. This command was constituted on July 29, 1943, and was activated on August 20, 1943. While in the CBI, he held various other command positions, some simultaneously, including Commanding General, Eastern Air Command, which was an integrated AAF-RAF operational force (Tenth Air Force and Bengal Air Command), and Commanding General, Theater Air Forces, Southeast Asia.

Soon after taking command of Eastern Air Command on December 15, 1943, he told his troops, "We must merge into one unified force, in thought and in deed, neither English nor American, with the faults of neither and the virtues of both. There is no time for distrust or suspicion... We must establish in Asia a record of Allied air victory of which we can all be proud in the years to come. Let us write it now in the skies over Burma." [13]

The military and political situation in the region was ticklish, involving a varied collection of easily-bruised egos, including those of Brig. General Claire

---

11. Pilot's Statement, Nov 25, 1936.
12. Wesley Frank Craven and James Lea Cate, editors, *Men and Planes*, Vol. VI of *The Army Air Forces in World War II* (Washington, 1983), pp 34–35.
13. Headquarters, Eastern Air Command, GO No. 1, 15 Dec 1943.

L. Chennault, commander of the Fourteenth Air Force; Generalissimo Chiang Kai-Shek, the Chinese leader and head of the Kuomintang (Nationalist Party); Lt. Gen. Joseph W. Stilwell, U.S. theater commander and chief of staff to Chiang; and Lord Louis Mountbatten, Supreme Allied Commander, Southeast Asia. In a letter to Stratemeyer, General Arnold said, "The success of this complicated command setup depends in great measure on personalities. If a true spirit of cooperation is engendered throughout the command, it will work. If the reverse is true, it is doomed to failure. I know I can count on you to play your part and to pass the word right down the line." [14]

Success in this position took all of Stratemeyer's celebrated diplomatic ability, of which he was known throughout the AAF to possess in abundance, plus a great deal of additional tact and patience. In effect, Stratemeyer often acted as a quasi-ambassador. That Stratemeyer was able to organize his units into effective fighting forces, and that he was able to represent effectively at the highest levels in Southeast Asia both the AAF's and the United States' positions and concerns, despite the intrigues and Byzantine maneuvers that seemed to permeate the politics of the region, was a tribute to his skill.

Stratemeyer proved to be a consummate diplomat in the CBI, a theater replete with easily bruised egos.

When the CBI was divided into two theaters in October 1944, Stratemeyer retained command of the AAF forces in India-Burma. He was promoted to lieutenant general in May 1945, and from July 12, 1945, to January 1946, he was Commanding General, Army Air Forces, China Theater. In 1946, after his return to the United States and a brief stint at AAF Headquarters as Chief, Selection Branch, he became the first commander of the new Air Defense Command (ADC). During his tenure as ADC commander, Stratemeyer fought a valiant, albeit futile, battle to obtain command authority of the Air National Guard (ANG) units that made up the bulk of ADC. Jealous of their prerogatives, the various state National Guard commanders and the National Guard Bureau successfully applied strong political pressure to fend off Stratemeyer.[15] When the Air Defense Command and the Tactical Air Command (TAC) were reorganized into the Continental Air Command (CONAC) in November 1948, Stratemeyer became its commander. Finally, in April 1949, he came to Japan

---

14. Ltr, Gen H.H. Arnold to Maj Gen George E. Stratemeyer, Aug 28, 1943.
15. See Charles Joseph Gross, *Prelude to the Total Force: The Air National Guard 1943-1969* (Washington, 1985), pp 22-57, for a review of the highly-charged issue of control of National Guard units.

to become commanding general of the Far East Air Forces, the position he held on June 25, 1950.[16]

General Stratemeyer's rise in the Air Force to positions of power and responsibility generally had not been spectacular but steady. Like many of his peers, during the inter-war years he had remained in grade for a long time. For example, it took him 13 years to advance from major to lieutenant colonel, not uncommon for the time. With the approach of war, however, promotions came rapidly and Stratemeyer quickly demonstrated that he was ready for greater responsibilities.

Lt. Gen. Edward J. Timberlake,[17] who was Fifth Air Force vice commander in Korea until June 1951, remembered two routes on the promotion road during these years, excluding "luck." One was the active command route and the other via the management/administration route. Timberlake believed "the administrative route creates a more subtle and comprehensive mind" and that this was the route Stratemeyer followed.[18] Stratemeyer's abilities probably did lie more in administrative and staff work than in active command, but he did have experience in both roles. Primarily because of his high rank at the beginning of World War II and his efficient work at AAF Headquarters during the war, he never had the opportunity to command combat units at the operational level.

Generals Smart and Bruce K. Holloway[19] worked under Stratemeyer at Air Defense Command in the late 1940s and gained a good insight into their commander's methods and personality. Smart considered Stratemeyer an "intuitive" commander, one who did not necessarily make a decision through a logical process of analysis, but rather sensed when a decision was proper. He used this same approach in selecting subordinates. Though sometimes criticized by others for choosing individuals thought to be unproductive, Stratemeyer more often than not brought out the best qualities in his subordinates. This is not to say that only so-called "underachievers" found places on Stratemeyer's various staffs. Many top-flight individuals, such as Smart, Holloway, Laurence C. Craigie, J.V. Crabb (FEAF deputy for operations at the start of the Korean War) and Arthur C. Agan (at ADC under Stratemeyer and later Director of Plans, USAF) worked on Stratemeyer's staffs.[20] Stratemeyer commanded by delegating authority. General Holloway noted, "He trusted all subordinates unless they performed in a manner to discredit themselves of his trust." According to Holloway, "It was never the other way around. He did

---

16. Lt Gen George E. Stratemeyer official USAF biography; *Current Biography, 1951* (New York, 1952), pp 612-614.

17. During World War II, "Ted" Timberlake, (USAF Ret.) commanded the 93d Bomb Group, which became famous as "Ted's Flying Circus." One of its most renowned exploits was the August 1943 Ploesti mission. Timberlake later commanded the 2d Combat Wing and 20th Combat Bombardment Wing. After the war, he was Assistant Chief of Staff, Personnel, Headquarters Continental Air Forces, and Chief, Operations Division, Deputy Chief of Staff, Operations, Headquarters USAF. In September 1948, he was appointed commander of the 315th Air Division of the Fifth Air Force. He next became Chief of Staff, Fifth Air Force, until December 1949, when he became the Fifth's vice commander. When General Partridge became FEAF commander, Timberlake took over 5AF. Prior to his retirement in 1965, he was Commanding General, Continental Air Command.

18. Ltr, Lt Gen Edward J. Timberlake, USAF (Ret.), to William T. Y'Blood, Nov. 24, 1986.

19. General Holloway (USAF, Ret.) graduated from the U.S. Military Academy in 1937. As a member of the American Volunteer Group and later, the 23d Fighter Group, he shot down 13 enemy planes. After the war, among other assignments, he was Director of Operations, A-3, Air Defense Command in 1948-1949. Among his more important assignments before retirement in 1972 were: Deputy Commander in Chief, U.S. Strike Command; Commander in Chief, USAFE; Vice Chief of Staff, USAF; and Commander in Chief, SAC.

20. Smart interview.

not command with an iron hand, but there was no doubt that he was in charge. He was most forgiving of honest mistakes and never told his key staff officers or subordinate commanders how to do their jobs so long as they kept him informed and produced results in conformity with command policies." [21]

Lt. Gen. Laurence C. Craigie[22] agreed. "General Opie Weyland... was Vice Commander, Operations [of FEAF during the Korean War]. I was VC—everything else. Strat gave both of us strong backing and although he was well aware of all that was being done in our respective areas, he did not make us feel that we had to check with him before taking important actions." Craigie also stated that if Stratemeyer "didn't like something I did he told me so. We discussed it and that was the end of it." [23]

Regarding the relationship with his subordinates, both Holloway and Partridge believed that Stratemeyer may have been too easygoing, or tolerated certain individuals who were not performing up to their abilities. However, Stratemeyer trusted his officers to do a job without him having to look over their shoulders. Holloway also stressed that Stratemeyer was a good disciplinarian who could say "no" when appropriate.[24]

General Craigie recalled one incident where Stratemeyer never had the chance to say "no." Enroute to Japan to join FEAF, Craigie stopped at Hickam AFB, Hawaii, where he and his wife were to be picked up by a FEAF Headquarters C–54. While awaiting the plane's arrival, Craigie met two West Point cadets also trying to get to Japan. One was Eddie White, son of General Edward White and a family friend. Although there were many other people with higher priorities than the cadets awaiting transport to Japan, Craigie let the two cadets fill out the load for the trip. When the plane arrived at Haneda Airport near Tokyo, General and Mrs. Stratemeyer greeted it. Craigie saw Stratemeyer's "eyebrows raise perceptibly when he saw the two cadets get off the plane," but not a word was said. Later that afternoon, however, Stratemeyer stalked into Craigie's office.

"Bill," he blurted, "why in hell did you bring those two cadets with you when there were all those badly needed officers stacked up at Hickam awaiting rides?"

"Strat, I was wrong," Craigie replied, "but they were the first people we saw when we landed at Hickam. I promised them rides and didn't see fit to back away from my promise." The subject never came up again.[25] Years later, on June 3, 1965, Eddie White became the first American to walk in space.

Entries concerning social activities such as parties and golf appear frequently in Stratemeyer's diary. Although it may appear that these activities are frivolous, to Stratemeyer they were important duties for a senior officer.[26]

---

21. Ltr, Gen Bruce K. Holloway, USAF (Ret.), to William T. Y'Blood, Nov. 28, 1986.

22. General Craigie (USAF, Ret.) graduated from West Point in 1923. During World War II, he became the first member of the U.S. armed forces to fly a jet-propelled aircraft when he flew the XP–59A in October 1942. From March to November 1944, he was commander of the Twelfth Air Force's 63d Fighter Wing. Prior to his retirement in 1955, General Craigie was Deputy Chief of Staff, Development, Headquarters USAF, and commander of the Allied Air Forces in Southern Europe.

23. Ltr, Lt Gen Laurence C. Craigie, USAF (Ret.), to William T. Y'Blood, August 16, 1987.

24. Holloway letter; Ltr, Gen Earle E. Partridge, USAF (Ret.), to William T. Y'Blood, Nov. 26, 1986.

25. Craigie letter.

26. In this regard, it should be remembered that Japan, for its proximity to the war zone, never was attacked during the war, being accorded by the enemy something of a sanctuary status. Many dependents of U.S. military men remained in Japan throughout this period and many other individuals, military and civilian, continually visited Japan and Korea for a multitude of reasons.

General Smart believed that these activities show that to Stratemeyer "everything was important — not equally important — but important enough that everything should be done to a high order of perfection. Duty did not permit half measures or laxness in social or any other endeavors. Dress, politeness, timeliness, host-guest relationships, rectitude were all important to him." [27]

For a commander who found himself caught in a web of intrigues and personality clashes that seemed to permeate both the CBI in World War II and MacArthur's Far East Command during the Korean War, Stratemeyer remained remarkably level-headed and even-tempered, genial and outgoing. "You couldn't help but like him," commented General Timberlake, who placed Stratemeyer among the three top men he served under, only behind Generals Eaker and Doolittle.[28] Holloway thought Stratemeyer was "a naturally kind and friendly man with everyone," while Partridge judged Stratemeyer as a "gentleman of the old school, warm, generous, thoughtful, low key." [29] Craigie emphasized, "I felt fortunate to be on his team." [30] Nonetheless, as his diary reveals, there were moments when his easygoing nature was stretched to the breaking point.

Because he cared about his men and knew they could produce, a strong loyalty developed among Stratemeyer's subordinates, a loyalty which he reciprocated. One way this was evidenced was by his handling of medals for his staff. Craigie believed his boss was perhaps overgenerous in the awarding of medals but that Stratemeyer wanted his staff to know "that he appreciated what we as his staff officers were doing and didn't want us to feel that he was any less appreciative than General MacArthur," who had a tendency to give medals to his staff for almost anything.[31]

Stratemeyer was also intensely loyal to his superiors. In MacArthur's case, this loyalty was perhaps carried to an extreme, but Stratemeyer was neither the first nor the last to fall under the MacArthur spell. He was not one, however, to buckle under to whatever whims a senior officer might have. "He was anything but reticent in expressing his views," General Holloway remembered, "and pressed them with utmost sincerity and forcefulness, but always in a most courteous manner."[32] If his views were not accepted, Stratemeyer always obeyed orders to the best of his ability and never publicly complained.

Thus this was the man remembered by those who served under him, both in peacetime and wartime. But before considering Stratemeyer's role in the Korean War, it is important to look into Korea's past to understand the background of the war. It is also necessary to limn the strengths and weaknesses of those forces that faced each other in Korea during those last chaotic days of June 1950.

Looking somewhat like a mitten, fingers slightly curled, the Korean peninsula reaches almost 650 miles from the mainland of Asia toward Japan. This mitten, though, is not soft but hard and bony. Mountain peaks soar to 9,000 feet in the north; those along the east coast can reach 6,000 feet. These are just the highest peaks; much of the rest of Korea is covered with treeless lesser hills

27. Gen Smart manuscript comments, Sep. 19, 1988.
28. Timberlake letter.
29. Holloway letter; Partridge letter.
30. Craigie letter.
31. Ibid.; Smart interview.
32. Holloway letter

and mountain ranges. In between are steep gorges with cold rushing rivers. What flatland there is, is highly cultivated. Rice paddies are the dominant feature, especially in the south where there is relatively more level ground than in the north. Climatologically, Korea is a nation of extremes. Summers are generally hot and humid, while winters are cold and fairly dry. In winter, temperatures can drop below zero almost every night in the north, a fact brought home with brutal force to United Nations troops during the war, particularly during the winter of 1950-1951, which was one of the harshest on record. This was the arena where battle was fought and blood spilled.

Throughout much of its 2,000-plus years of recorded history, Korea has been an unfortunate country. Often caught between stronger powers, usually China and Japan, the Koreans contributed to their unfortunate situation by either fighting among themselves to establish various kingdoms or by maneuvering to be on the side of the winning outside power. For several hundred years, three Korean kingdoms vied for hegemony. One of these, the Silla kingdom, aided by the T'ang dynasty of China, eventually established control over the entire country in A.D. 676. This control, however, was obtained at a price. T'ang, as a suzerain nation, still dominated the Silla kings. The Koreans paid much tribute to China, but this was considered to be a small price in order to retain an autonomous government and some amount of freedom. Though China itself later came under Mongol influence, this suzerain relationship between Korea and China essentially remained intact (except for a period between 1254-1368 when Korea was under direct Mongol rule) until the Sino-Japanese War of 1894-1895. Peace was rare in Korea over these years. Chinese, Japanese, and Manchus fought many battles on or about Korean soil. In this, they were often joined by the Koreans who fought not only outsiders, but among themselves as well.

In 1894, the Tonghak (or "Eastern Learning"), a social and religious movement, reacted to what some Koreans saw as dangerous inroads being made in Korea by "Western Learning" (Catholicism) and by foreign commercial interests. Their rebellion was doomed to failure, however, because of a lack of leadership and because the movement was infiltrated by just those parties (primarily Chinese and Japanese) the Tonghak wished driven from Korea. Nevertheless, the uprising was bloody and forced the Korean government to request the help of Chinese troops. This request led to the intervention of Japanese forces and culminated in the Sino-Japanese War which the Japanese won.

Ostensibly a sovereign state following this war, Korea now was very much under Japanese influence, although this did not stop other countries from trying to supplant the Japanese in Korea. In particular, Russia (which was gaining control over large areas of northeast China) attempted to establish its own control over Korea. For a period, Korean governments came and went with disturbing regularity as first the Russians, then the Japanese, gained and lost positions of power. This situation could not continue and once again the flames of war were ignited in the region. To the surprise of the world, the Japanese were victorious in the Russo-Japanese War of 1904-1905. Korea became a Japanese protectorate and in 1910, was forcibly annexed to Japan. From that time until the end of World War II, Korea did not exist as a nation.

Japanese rule was harsh, for they viewed Korea as a second-rate nation and its people suitable only for menial labor. By edict, land which had traditionally

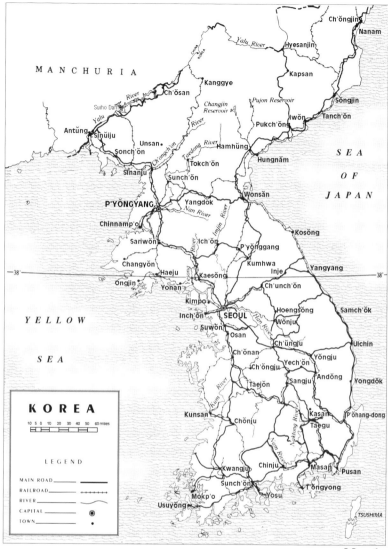

Map 1.

belonged to the peasants now belonged to the government which then sold it cheaply to various Japanese interests; dissent was brutally beaten down; what economic growth there was accrued to the benefit of the Japanese, not the Koreans. In the late 1930s, Japan even attempted to eradicate any Korean national identity by requiring that the Japanese language be exclusively used in schools and homes and compelling the Koreans to adopt Japanese style personal and family names. At the onset of World War II, Koreans were urged to volunteer for military duty, but this soon changed to conscription. Only with the defeat of Japan was Korea able to rise, slowly at first, and stand on its own feet again.[33]

---

33. Takashi Hatada, trans. by Warren W. Smith, Jr., and Benjamin H. Hazard, *A History of Korea* (Santa Barbara, Calif., 1969), pp 14-25, 98-126; Nena Vreeland et al, *Area Handbook for South Korea* (Washington, 1975), pp 7-21; Robert R. Simmons, *The Strained Alliance* (New York, 1975), pp 3-17.

United States interest in Korea had been slow to develop. In the mid-1800s, Americans went to Korea as missionaries and traders, but found that the Koreans wished to have little to do with those who they regarded as "barbarians." This attitude grew out of what the Koreans had seen happen to China when foreign interests had begun to make inroads in that country. Additionally, the Koreans feared Catholicism, which they believed would spread the contamination of Western ideas. Thus, Korea attempted to keep the door tightly shut to contact with the West. Well deserved was its nickname "The Hermit Kingdom."

An attempt by the U.S. Navy in 1871 to obtain a trade treaty with Korea failed, being more a show of military might (albeit very little might — just five small warships) than a true attempt at diplomacy. A later try was somewhat more successful. At the urging of China, which was concerned about Japanese interest in the country and saw it as a way to block further inroads by them, Korea signed a treaty of commerce with the United States in 1882. This was the first such treaty between Korea and a western nation, but little came of it. Because of its vast resources, China was the prize that most western nations coveted. This, along with the myriad political and social changes then taking place in the world, caused American interest in Korea, if not to lie fallow, to wane considerably.[34]

It was not until World War II that the United States again became actively interested in Korea. At the 1943 Cairo Conference, the United States, Great Britain, and China declared Korean independence as one of their objectives. In July 1945, the Potsdam Conference reaffirmed, among other things, the Allies' position on Korea. When the Soviet Union declared war on Japan on August 8, 1945, it stated that it would abide by the Potsdam declaration, thus gaining a legitimate (if laggardly) foothold in Korea.

The Allies hoped that there would be no need to divide Korea into occupation zones, but Japan's sudden collapse forced the "temporary" partitioning of the country so as to facilitate the surrender of Japanese troops there. The 38th Parallel was arbitrarily chosen as the dividing line for these zones. Not long afterwards, the United States noted that the Soviets were building fortifications on their side of the parallel. In an effort to work out a plan to unify Korea, officials of the United States, the Soviet Union, and Great Britain met in Moscow in December 1945. At that meeting they agreed to trusteeship for up to five years for Korea under four powers, including China. This trusteeship was intended to lead to the reestablishment of Korea as a sovereign state. At Moscow the three nations also approved the formation of a joint American-Soviet Commission to assist in the organization of a single Korean government.

This commission quickly became another example of the United States' and the Soviet Union's growing distrust of each other's motives and plans. Even during World War II, when the two powers were putative allies, this distrust simmered just below the surface. From allies, the two sides soon became enemies, each seeing the other as seeking to dominate the world. Other than in Europe, in the years immediately after World War II, it would only be in Korea that the U.S. directly faced the Communists.

---

34. Ki-Baik Lee, trans. by Edward W. Wagner and Edward J. Shultz, *A New History of Korea* (Cambridge, Mass., 1984), pp 268-275.

Primarily due to Soviet intransigence, the American-Soviet Commission became a study in futility. The Soviets continually insisted that only those Koreans who hewed to the Communist line would be allowed to represent a provisional Korean government. Unable to break this impasse, the U.S. brought the matter before the United Nations General Assembly. There the United States recommended that a UN commission oversee elections in both zones of occupation, and then supervise the formation of a single government for the entire country. Sensing that this would endanger their own plans to unify Korea under Communism, the Soviets rejected the recommendation. Despite these objections, the General Assembly voted for the proposal.

Although the Soviet Union and the North Korean leaders refused to allow the UN to hold elections north of the 38th Parallel, elections for a National Assembly were held in South Korea on May 10, 1948, under the observation of the UN Temporary Commission on Korea. An estimated 80 percent of the eligible voters took part in these elections, which saw the birth of the Republic of Korea (ROK). In July, a constitution was adopted and the National Assembly named Syngman Rhee as president. The Government of the Republic of Korea was formally inaugurated on August 15, 1948.

A Korean nationalist for many years, Rhee was born in 1875 of well-to-do parents, and had studied at a Methodist mission school where he became proficient in English. Possibly because of this schooling and his higher-class status, by 1895 he was involved in movements urging strong reforms of the Korean government. In the eyes of the Korean government officials, Rhee was a revolutionary and he was soon arrested. After seven years of sometimes brutal imprisonment, Rhee was released in 1904. Exiled, he came to the United States where he naively hoped to influence President Theodore Roosevelt to support Korean independence. If he had known Roosevelt's true feelings, Rhee would have been shocked to learn that Roosevelt believed the Koreans were incapable of managing their own affairs, and that a Japanese-controlled Korea would serve as a check against an expansionist Russia.

Rhee remained in the United States, attended several colleges and obtained various degrees, including a PhD in political science from Princeton. In 1919, while still overseas, he was named head of a Korean provisional government by former members — and exiles like Rhee — of the reform movement to which he once belonged. Except for a short-lived attempt in 1910-1911 to return and live in Korea, he spent the years until 1945 traveling about the world lobbying for Korean independence. Finally, in October 1945, he returned to Korea where he was generally greeted with enthusiasm by the populace. Despite U.S. hopes for a true democratic government in South Korea, though, Rhee's government eventually became a corrupt autocracy.[35]

A few weeks after General of the Army Douglas MacArthur spoke at Rhee's inauguration, the Democratic People's Republic of Korea, backed by the Soviet Union, held its own installation in P'yŏngyang. The leader of this Soviet-controlled regime was Kim Il-Sung. A somewhat mysterious individual, Kim (whose original name was Kim Song-chu) was born in 1912. When he was seven, he and his family moved to Manchuria. Details of his life between then and his return to

---

35. David Detzer, *Thunder of the Captains* (New York, 1975), pp 44-49; Lee, pp 381-385.

Korea in September 1945 are untrustworthy, with innumerable conflicting stories purporting to describe this period. What is known for certain is that he fought in a Chinese Communist guerrilla army against the Japanese in Manchuria. After the guerrillas were defeated, he moved to the Soviet Union where he served in the Russian Army. He returned to North Korea in September 1945 as a major in the army. Backed by the Soviets, Kim soon became the head of both the North Korean Communist Party and the government.[36]

The UN General Assembly, however, refused to recognize the North Korean government, stating in late 1948 and again in 1949 that Rhee's ROK government was the only lawful body in Korea. By this time there seemed no doubt that the Soviet Union was building up the North Korean forces with the ultimate purpose of making all of Korea a Communist fiefdom.[37] Still, on September 20, 1948, the Soviet Union announced it would remove all its occupation forces from North Korea by January 1, 1949, and invited the U.S. to do the same. The problem with this proposal was that while the Soviets had made sure the North Korean military forces were reasonably well-trained and equipped, the U.S. had not taken similar steps in the south.

North Korean forces had armed and trained under Soviet supervision since just after World War II. Selected individuals had been sent to the Soviet Union to undergo intensive training to become officers in the North Korean armed forces. Supplies of weapons had been stockpiled. On the eve of battle in June 1950, the North Korean People's Army (NKPA) had eight full-strength divisions and two more at half-strength, an armored brigade, and miscellaneous other units for a total of approximately 135,000 men. Many of these troops were veterans of fighting in World War II or against Nationalist Chinese forces during the recent Communist revolution in China.

The North Korean units were well-armed, being supplied by the Soviets with excellent small arms, artillery (of which many pieces had a longer range than those of their South Korean counterparts), and 150 of the tough T–34 tanks. Although the T–34 was first used in combat in July 1941, its excellent design was superior to the American World War II-vintage M–4 medium and M–26 light tanks and was difficult to knock out.[38]

In the air, the North Korean Air Force (NKAF) fielded approximately 162 aircraft. All were Soviet-built, propeller-driven aircraft of the World War II era. Sixty-two were Il–10 ground attack aircraft which had first seen operational service in February 1945. Seventy Yak–3s, Yak–7Bs, and Yak–9s were also available for ground attack and fighter missions. The remaining North Korean planes were twenty-two Yak–16 transports (a type similar to the USAF C–45) and eight PO–2 trainers (a biplane design dating from 1927).[39] The men flying these aircraft were relatively inexperienced, but had been carefully trained by Soviet instructors and had developed an aggressive spirit. On the night of June 24/25, 1950, the NKPA and NKAF were ready for war.

---

36. Tai Sung An, *North Korea, A Political Handbook* (Wilmington, Del., 1983), pp 30, 202-203; Sung Chul Yang, *Korea and Two Regimes* (Cambridge, Mass., 1981), p 162.
37. Yang, pp 306-308; An, pp 64-68; Lee, p 379.
38. Roy E. Appleman, *South to the Naktong, North to the Yalu* [U.S. Army in the Korean War] (Washington, 1961), pp 9-12; James F. Schnabel, *Policy and Direction: The First Year* [U.S. Army in the Korean War] (Washington, 1972), p 39.
39. Robert F. Futrell, *The United States Air Force in Korea 1950-1953* (Washington, 1983), p 19. (Hereafter cited as Futrell.)

The same cannot be said for South Korea's military forces. The sad state of the ROK military had its beginnings in late 1948. On December 12 of that year, the UN General Assembly, urged on by the Soviet Union representative, voted for the withdrawal of all U.S. troops in Korea. This was not unappealing to the United States. As early as September 1947, the Joint Chiefs of Staff (JCS), their attention firmly fixed on Europe (which they perceived as the critical area in the world) were reporting to President Truman that Korea held little strategic interest for the United States and that if war broke out, those U.S. troops in Korea (approximately 45,000 at that time) would be a military liability.[40]

One of the critical problems for the U.S. armed forces in these postwar years was that although they had been given even greater and more widespread tasks than ever before in peacetime, the means to accomplish these tasks had been drastically reduced. There were massive cuts in the military budgets following World War II with personnel strength for the Army dropping from 5,984,114 on June 30, 1945, to 591,487 at the end of June 1950. Likewise, Army expenditures for "military functions" over the same period plummeted from $27,094,110 to $4,305,834.[41] The USAF fared no better. All-inclusive expenditures dipped from $11,357,390,523 in June 1945 to $2,062,806 in June 1950. In June 1945, 2,282,259 men and women served in the Army Air Forces. By June 1950, only 411,277 remained in the USAF.[42] As these figures show, before war broke out in Korea, U.S. armed forces had been shorn of much of their strength, and money was difficult to come by for almost every project. Naturally, those areas that did not seem to be vital to U.S. interests, such as Korea, were subject to manpower or financial reductions or both.

Gen. Douglas MacArthur, the senior officer of the U.S. military in Japan and also of the occupying forces, agreed with the Joint Chiefs that Korea held little strategic interest. Responsible for the defense of Japan, he had not considered fighting in Korea, preferring instead to

General of the Army Douglas MacArthur thanks his personal pilot, Lt. Col. Anthony F. Story after returning from a trip to Korea. Behind MacArthur is Maj. Gen. Doyle O. Hickey.

40. Schnabel, pp 29; Rosemary Foot, *The Wrong War* (Ithaca, N.Y., 1985), p 57; James F. Schnabel and Robert J. Watson, "The History of the Joint Chiefs of Staff," *The Joint Chiefs of Staff and National Policy*, Vol. III, *The Korean War*, Part I (Washington, 1979), p 13. (Hereafter cited as "History of the JCS," Vol III.)
41. *World Almanac, 1951* (New York, 1951), p 508.
42. *Army Air Forces Statistical Digest, 1946* (Washington, 1946), pp 13, 215; *USAF Statistical Digest, January 1949-June 1950* (Washington, 1950), pp 28, 302.

neutralize the country through the employment of sea and air power. Following a JCS request in January 1949 for his recommendations on the possible effects of a removal of U.S. troops from Korea and on a timetable for such a withdrawal, MacArthur suggested the first anniversary of South Korea's elections, May 10, 1949, as a suitable date to complete the removal. With State Department and JCS approval, the National Security Council recommended to President Truman that all United States combat troops be withdrawn from Korea by June 30, 1949. The last U.S. tactical troops departed Korea on June 29, leaving only an advisory group of about 500 officers and men (designated the United States Korean Military Advisory Group or KMAG).[43] These 500 or so U.S. Army troops were to develop and train a South Korean force that would be able to preserve internal security, prevent border raids, and deter major aggressive acts, such as armed attacks, by the North Koreans. It was a daunting task.[44]

Even before the Americans pulled out of Korea, the North Koreans, aided by leftist groups in the south, began an extensive guerrilla campaign in South Korea. This campaign ranged from propaganda to armed violence, sometimes leading to full-scale battles with the ROK Army. Both sides suffered heavily before the guerrillas were defeated.[45] With their covert operations in shambles, the North Koreans apparently felt there was only one option left to them if they wished to continue with their plan for the unification of Korea — overt action using North Korean military forces. While Stalin probably knew of the attack plans, he did not know when the attack would take place, and even if he did, preferred that the North Koreans take the risks without Soviet influence.[46] It may have seemed to the North Koreans that an attack across the 38th Parallel might be just the thing to finally gain control of all Korea, for it appeared that the United States would not come to the ROK government's aid in such a situation.

There were sound reasons for this perception by the Communists. First, it was obvious that the United States was more interested in Europe than the Far East, the situation on Formosa (now Taiwan) being one manifestation of this. In December 1949, with its defeat by the Communists in the Chinese civil war, the Nationalist government moved to Formosa. Although the United States supported the Nationalists earlier, it now blamed this defeat on the Nationalists' own corruption and incompetence. President Truman stated that the United States would not help the Nationalists with either military aid or advice. Even when it appeared that the Communists were preparing to invade Formosa, the United States refused to interfere, much to General MacArthur's distress. Only with the North Korean invasion of South Korea did the United States' position on Formosa change.[47]

The speech of Secretary of State Dean Acheson to the National Press Club on January 12, 1950, added to the ferment. Acheson stated that the U.S. defense perimeter in the Pacific ran from the Aleutians to Japan, then south through the Ryukyus to the Philippines, and that it would be unilaterally defended by the

---

43. "History of the JCS," Vol. III, pp 23-27; Schnabel, pp 30, 34.
44. Schnabel, p 34.
45. Ibid., pp 37-38
46. Callum A. MacDonald, *Korea: The War Before Vietnam* (New York, 1987), p 28; William Stueck, "The Korean War as International History," *Diplomatic History*, Fall 1986, pp 292-293.
47. MacDonald, pp 18-20; Foot, pp 45-51; Clay Blair, *The Forgotten War* (New York, 1987), pp 23-25.

United States. Formosa and Korea were not mentioned as part of this perimeter. Predictably, Republicans swiftly criticized Acheson for giving the Communists carte blanche regarding Korea and Formosa. (It should be mentioned, though, that MacArthur in March 1949 himself made a similar statement regarding a defense perimeter which also omitted Korea and Formosa.) However, Acheson implied that, while the U.S. would not unilaterally defend South Korea, if the ROK government appealed to the United Nations for help, the U.S. (along with other UN members) would come to its aid.[48]

South Korea would need all the aid it could get, for there was precious little with which to defend itself. In early 1949, President Rhee wanted a combined army-navy-air force-police establishment of over 200,000 men. Initially, the air force portion was to be 3,000 men and 122 aircraft, including 75 fighters and 12 bombers. Given Rhee's militantly anti-Communist line and the possibility that he might use a large military force to attack North Korea, the United States offered to build only a force large enough to provide and maintain internal security and public safety. For these purposes, it was estimated that an army of about 65,000 men, a police force of 35,000 men, and a navy of 4,000, all armed primarily with hand weapons, mortars, and machine guns, would be needed. Notable by its absence was a provision for an air force.[49]

By the date of the invasion, the ROK Army had grown to a strength of about 98,000 men, of which some 65,000 were considered combat troops, the Navy to 6,145, the National Police to 48,273, and, at last, an Air Force that numbered 1,865 men. However, all of these forces were poorly equipped, with only enough supplies for 15 days of defensive operations. The Army had no tanks (Korea was thought to be poor tank country), no artillery larger than M3 105-mm short-barreled howitzers (which had a range about 5,000 yards less than the standard North Korean howitzer), and just a few armored cars and half-tracks. The Navy possessed a handful of small vessels, mainly minesweepers and patrol craft.[50]

The Air Force was no better off. Rebuffed in his earlier plans for a 122-plane air force, in mid-1949, President Rhee asked retired Maj. Gen. Claire L. Chennault, former commander of the Flying Tigers and the Fourteenth Air Force, and founder of the well-known Asian airline, Civil Air Transport (CAT), to develop a plan for a slightly scaled-down 99-plane air force. Included in this number were 25 propeller-driven F–51s. Rhee's proposal was turned down by MacArthur, who believed that South Korea did not need so large an air force because it might destabilize the already precarious peace in Korea, and also give the Communists one more propaganda weapon to use against supposed U.S. attempts to promote an arms race in Korea.[51]

Nevertheless, the U.S. did allow South Korea to obtain a few trainers and observation aircraft. According to the official ROK history of the Korean War, at the onset of hostilities the ROKAF consisted of only a small aviation component

---

48. J. Lawton Collins, *War in Peacetime* (Boston, 1969), pp 30-31; Foot, pp 47, 58; Schnabel, pp 51-52; MacDonald, p 28; David Rees, *Korea: The Limited War* (New York, 1964), pp 18-19; "History of the JCS," Vol. III, p 38.
49. Futrell, p 16.
50. William Stueck, *The Korean War, An International History* (Princeton, N.J., 1995), p 29; Appleman, pp 13-14; Schnabel, p 36.
51. Futrell, p 17.

of eight L–4s, four L–5s, and ten T–6 liaison aircraft and trainers. Of the 102 pilots undergoing training, only 30 were fully trained.[52] The ROKAF's main bases were the Kimp'o and Yŏŭi-do airfields at Seoul, with detachments at Suwŏn, Taegu, Kunsan, Cheju-do, and Kwangju. Having few aircraft and none a combat type, the ROKAF was completely outmatched by its North Korean counterpart.

In terms of equipment and capabilities, United States forces in the area were not in much better shape. General MacArthur had two command responsibilities: as Supreme Commander, Allied Powers (SCAP), he exercised command over all occupation forces and, in essence, ruled Japan; as Commander-in-Chief, Far East Command (CINCFE), he exercised unified command of all American forces allocated him by the JCS. Although he was also Commanding General, United States Army Forces, Far East (USAFFE), he never used the title or had a USAFFE staff, since these functions were also those of CINCFE. The Far East Command (FEC) included the U.S. forces in Japan, Korea, the Ryukyus, the Philippines, the Marianas, and the Bonins. A General Headquarters (GHQ) in Tokyo administered FEC.[53]

Vice Admirals Arthur D. Struble and C. Turner Joy discuss Korean operations with Secretary of the Navy Francis P. Matthews

While MacArthur's command encompassed a tremendously large geographical area, the troops to man it were spread woefully thin. The main ground force was Lt. Gen. Walton H. Walker's[54] Eighth Army with four infantry divisions in Japan: the 1st Cavalry (now walking, not riding), 7th Infantry, 24th Infantry, and 25th Infantry. These divisions were occupation, not combat, forces and were not up even to their authorized peacetime strength of 12,500 men each. Competent officers were scarce, and of the enlisted men, many were in the Army's two lowest intelligence classifications! Shortages of everything from rifles to tanks plagued the Eighth Army units. Other understrength units included seven antiaircraft artillery battalions in Japan, and one infantry regiment and two antiaircraft artillery battalions on Okinawa.[55]

52. *The History of the United Nations Forces in the Korean War*, Vol. IV (Seoul, 1975), p 650-651. Robert F. Futrell, author of the official history of the USAF in Korea, writes that the ROKAF had 16 aircraft, and only 39 fully-trained pilots, out of a total of 57. (Futrell, p 17.)

53. Schnabel, pp 47-48.

54. In World War II, "Johnnie" Walker commanded the XX Corps in General George S. Patton's Third Army. Following the war he commanded the Fifth Army, headquartered in Chicago, then took command of the Eighth Army in September 1948.

55. Schnabel, p 54; MacDonald, p 203.

The Army was not the only military arm in the Far East suffering from post-war cutbacks. Still the largest in the world, the U.S. Navy, nevertheless, had shrunk drastically from its wartime size. Of the Navy's active peacetime personnel strength (381,538 as of June 30, 1950), only about a third were in the Pacific, and just a fifth of these were in the Far East. As Commander Naval Forces Far East (COMNAVFE), V Adm. C. Turner Joy[56] had few combatant vessels on hand — one antiaircraft cruiser, four destroyers, one submarine (on loan from the

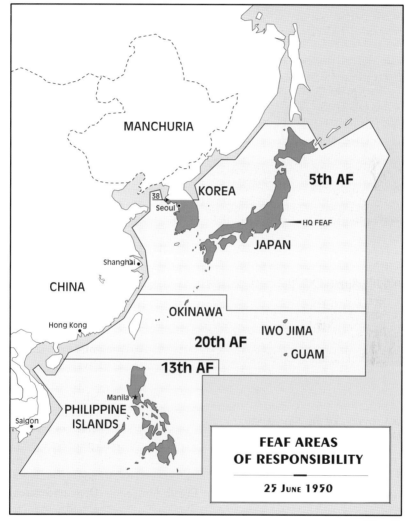

Map 2.

---

56. Admiral Joy saw action in the Pacific during World War II from almost the beginning, first as a staff officer during the early battles, then as a cruiser captain, and finally, after a tour of shore duty, as commander of Cruiser Division 6 during 1944-1945. After the war he held several positions until being promoted to vice admiral and COMNAVFE in August 1949. From July 1951 to May 1952, he was senior U.N. delegate to the armistice negotiations. Prior to his retirement in 1954, he was Superintendent of the Naval Academy. In an ironic twist, a destroyer named for Joy was covering another destroyer, the *Maddox*, in August 1964 when the latter ship reported it was being fired upon by North Vietnamese forces in the Gulf of Tonkin, an action that caused repercussions, both military and political, still reverberating today.

Seventh Fleet), a small amphibious force of five ships, and some auxiliary vessels. The Seventh Fleet, based in the Philippines, was available to Admiral Joy in an emergency. This force consisted of the carrier *Valley Forge* (carrying 86 aircraft), a cruiser, eight destroyers, three submarines, and supporting vessels. Like Walker's Eighth Army, Admiral Joy's command was really an occupation force, not one designed for combat. Its primary duties were defensive in nature, mainly concerned with air attacks on naval installations in Japan, the security of these installations, and the evacuation of U.S. citizens in an emergency.[57]

The final part of the U.S. military triumvirate in the region was the Far East Air Forces (FEAF), which controlled three widely-spaced air forces: the Thirteenth Air Force in the Philippines, the Twentieth Air Force on Okinawa and Guam, and the Fifth Air Force in Japan. FEAF's primary mission was distinctly defensive in nature — to provide an active air defense of FEC's area of operations. Definitely subordinate were such missions as the conducting of air transport operations, the maintaining of a mobile strike force, and the providing of air support of operations "as arranged with appropriate Army and Navy commanders."[58] Though FEAF was the United States Air Force's largest overseas command, with 35,122 people assigned, several factors militated against it being a truly effective force for any major contingency. There was inadequate engineering support, shortages of personnel in specific categories (*i.e.*, navigators and bombardiers), reduced training time because of budget cuts, and, while FEAF had most of its peacetime allotment of aircraft, little fat in the form of extra aircraft to replace combat losses.[59]

Maj. Gen. Howard M. Turner's[60] Thirteenth Air Force was headquartered at Clark Field near Manila. Also based at Clark were the 18th Fighter-Bomber Wing (77 on-hand/64 combat-ready F–80Cs), the 374th Troop Carrier Wing's 21st Squadron, with eight C–54s and four C–47s, and the 6204th Photo Mapping Flight (Provisional), with two RB–17s used to map the Philippines.[61]

---

57. James A. Field, Jr., *History of United States Naval Operations, Korea* (Washington, 1962), pp 45-47; Richard P. Hallion, *The Naval Air War in Korea* (Baltimore, Md., 1986), pp 30, 32; *World Almanac, 1951*, p 509.
58. *FEAF Report on the Korean War*, Vol. I, p 10.
59. Robert F. Futrell, *United States Air Force Operations in the Korean Conflict, 25 June-1 November 1950* (U) (USAF Historical Study 71, Maxwell AFB, Ala., 1952), p 3. (Hereafter cited as Futrell No. 71); *USAF Statistical Digest, January 1949-June 1950*, p 33.
60. Maj Gen Howard M. Turner commanded the 100th Bomb Group for a short time in 1943 before rising to command of the 102d and 40th Combat Bomb Wings and, then, Commanding General, 1st Bomb Division (later redesignated the 1st Air Division). Various assignments followed after the war until he became the Thirteenth Air Force's leader on June 12, 1949. He later became a delegate to the Korean armistice negotiations.
61. In World War II, combat wings were large organizations controlling several combat groups and other service units. After the war, many of these wings were redesignated air divisions. Then, beginning in 1948, the USAF adopted a new wing structure in which the wings, rather than the groups, became the basic combat element. A combat wing generally consisted of a combat group and three support groups (air base, supply and maintenance, and medical), all possessing the same numerical designation as the parent wing, *i.e.*, 18th FBW, 18th FBG, 18th ABG, etc. The combat wing, however, was primarily an administrative organization, whereas the combat group held operational control of the tactical squadrons. Eventually, squadrons were assigned directly to the wings and combat groups were eliminated from the wing structure. In the 1990s, groups saw a resurgence as the USAF was drawn down. In this volume, the terms group and wing as they pertain to the combat units are used interchangeably. (See Charles A. Ravenstein, *The Organization and Lineage of the United States Air Force* [Washington, 1986], pp 43-59, for a discussion of the various organizational changes in the USAF since its establishment in 1947.)

The Twentieth Air Force was commanded by Maj. Gen. Alvan C. Kincaid[62] from Kadena Air Base on Okinawa. At Kadena were the six RB–29s of the 31st Photo Reconnaissance Squadron, Very Long Range. The 31st was a Strategic Air Command (SAC) unit attached to FEAF for operations. The 51st Fighter-Interceptor Wing was equipped with F–80Cs (76/59), while the 4th Fighter All-Weather Squadron had propeller-driven F–82s(7/5). As its designation implies, the 4th's radar-equipped planes were to operate in all types of weather and at night. The F–80s did not have that capability. These latter two units were based at Naha, south of Kadena. Far to the east, at Andersen Air Base on Guam, were the B–29s (22/21) of the 19th Bombardment Wing. This wing was not part of SAC.

Lt. Gen. Walton H. Walker, the newly-appointed commander of the Eighth Army, confers with Maj. Gen. Earle E. Partridge, commander of the Fifth Air Force, at Taegu on July 16, 1950.

Largest of the air forces in FEAF was the Fifth Air Force headquartered in Nagoya, Japan. Maj. Gen. Earle E. Partridge commanded the Fifth. Tall, lean, gray-haired "Pat" Partridge had led the Fifth since October 1948. During World War II, he had been chief of staff of the XII Bomber Command in North Africa, then commander of the Eighth Air Force's 3d Air Division. Following a brief stint as commander of the Eighth Air Force in the Pacific, he returned to Washington in January 1946 to become Assistant Chief of Staff for Operations, Army Air Forces. Prior to assuming command of the Fifth Air Force, he was director of training and requirements in the Office of the Deputy Chief of Staff for Operations, Headquarters, USAF.[63]

Five wings comprised the Fifth's major components: the 8th Fighter-Bomber Wing (72/53 F–80Cs) was at Itazuke Air Base on Kyushu, along with the F–82s (10/6) of the 68th Fighter All-Weather Squadron; on Honshu's northeastern shore lay Misawa Air Base. where the 49th Fighter-Bomber Wing (71/52 F–80Cs) was stationed; near Tokyo was Yokota Air Base, which housed the 35th Fighter-Interceptor Wing (69/54 F–80Cs), the 339th Fighter All-Weather

---

62. Maj Gen Alvan C. Kincaid held many training assignments during World War II before becoming chief of staff, then Deputy Commanding General/Administration, IX Tactical Air Command. After the war, he returned to Air Training Command prior to becoming Commanding General, Twentieth Air Force on September 8, 1948. After leaving the Twentieth on July 31, 1950, he was the Fourth Air Force's commander and vice commander of the Continental Air Command.

63. Robert P. Fogerty, *Biographical Data on Air Force General Officers, 1917-1952* (USAF Historical Study 91, Maxwell AFB, Ala., 1953).

Squadron (15/8 F–82s), and the 8th Tactical Reconnaissance Squadron (Photo Jet) with RF–80s (25/8); just north of Tokyo was Johnson Air Base, home to the two B–26 (26/18) squadrons of the 3d Bombardment Wing (Light); rounding out the Fifth Air Force's wings was the 374th Troop Carrier Wing at Tachikawa Air Base, with two squadrons of C–54s (26/22).

As of May 31, 1950, FEAF held 1,172 aircraft, of which there were 504 F–80s, 47 F–51s, 42 F–82s, 73 B–26s, 27 B–29s, 179 transports, 48 reconnaissance planes, and 252 miscellaneous types (T–6, SB–17, T–33, L–5, etc.).[64] However, of these aircraft, only 657 (not all of these combat ready) were actually available for use in Korea.[65] The remaining aircraft were either in storage or had to be used for missions with the Thirteenth and Twentieth Air Forces and in the defense of Japan. The F–80C was by far the most numerous and most modern aircraft in FEAF's inventory, but this is not saying much because this aircraft was itself rapidly growing obsolete.

For Stratemeyer and the Air Force and, for that matter, the other services, the Korean War was a tough war. Yet, ironically, it was also a delicate war. It was tough in that resources were slim and often strained to the limit. As mentioned earlier, many of FEAF's planes were obsolete or rapidly approaching obsolescence at the start of the war. Additionally, FEAF was seriously undermanned. The budget cuts of the post-World War II years left the Air Force short of personnel in many categories. To take up the slack, many reservists and Air National Guardsmen had to be called up during the war. This was not necessarily a blessing because the training of many of these people was often substandard, again primarily because of the budget cuts.

Still, Stratemeyer kept his forces trained as well as possible considering that the cuts severely constrained both the amount and nature of training his troops could receive. For example, cross-country flights were curtailed, so navigation missions were flown generally flown between well-known landmarks or using radio aids. This was not a satisfactory situation, considering the type of terrain and lack of navigational aids in Korea and Japan. Moreover, little rocket firing could be done because stocks of the rockets were not to be depleted.[66] Nevertheless, Stratemeyer appears to have had FEAF much more ready for wartime operations than either the Army or Navy in Japan. Certainly, mistakes and personnel failures occurred, but on the whole, FEAF performed admirably during the Korean War.

Korea was tough for FEAF because of the conditions in which it had to operate: mountainous terrain; primitive living conditions (at least for those in Korea); dusty, hot summers; cold, snowy winters. Maintenance personnel were particularly affected by these most trying conditions, yet these unsung heroes of the war kept the planes flying.

But Korea was also a delicate conflict. The first of the so-called "limited" wars, it required a delicate military and diplomatic touch by the United States.

---

64. A close examination of various sources on the number of aircraft FEAF had on hand revealed numerous discrepencies. These were perhaps caused by variations in accounting techniques and are impossible to reconcile today. Total figures are taken from the FEAF Total Aircraft Inventory, page 51 of the FEAF History, January-30 June 1950, Vol. III. Aircraft on hand by squadron are taken from the 25 June 1950 Station List, page 14 of the FEAF Operations History, 25 June 1950 Through 31 October 1950, Vol. I.

65. Futrell, p 689.

66. Ibid., p 60.

The Far East was not where the United States planned to fight; it was not where it expected to fight. The eyes of Washington focused on Europe, where it was believed the Soviet Union would most likely instigate a military conflict.

When the Korean War erupted, the Joint Chiefs of Staff and most of the high-level advisors in the Truman administration believed that the war had been launched on the specific orders of the Soviet leader, Premier Joseph Stalin. Not to resist this threat would be perceived as an open invitation for Communist mischief around the world; yet, to overreact would leave Europe vulnerable to attack. Thus, the delicate balance of a limited war colored both the planning and the execution of these plans.

Related to these factors were the interests not just of those nations actively engaged in the Korean fighting, but those of the entire world, primarily through the offices of the United Nations. Other countries did not view the world political situation in the same light as did the United States. They were not necessarily anti-American nor pro-Soviet, but wished to pursue their own agenda and poli-cies. Though the United States furnished the bulk of the manpower and supplies and played the major role in formulating policy concerning Korea, other countries had a great deal of influence on this policy.

Two major decisions during the war illustrate the delicacy of such policy making. The first concerns the crossing of the 38th Parallel as the UN forces coun-terattacked northward. There was much apprehension among the United States' allies and even among the members of the Truman administration that such a move would be taken by the Soviets as a threat to their borders and could possi-bly lead to an escalation into a general war. Others, particularly Republican mem-bers of Congress, saw it as a way to split the Chinese and Soviets and to place the United States in an influential position in the Far East. These divergent views required a deft touch in reconciling both points of view into a coherent policy.

The speed of the military operations and the fact that this crossing was pre-sented as a way to unify the whole of Korea rendered the matter a *fait accompli*. When the Soviets did not react militarily to the crossing, it appeared to many that the decision to cross had been correct.[67] In reality, the delicate touch needed in this decision was ignored or misunderstood. The consequences of this lack of "touch" was painful.

This delicateness was also noticeably lacking in the decision to pursue to the Yalu. Information gathered from various sources indicated that the Chinese would intervene if the UN forces drew too close to the Yalu. However, the United States downplayed most of these sources, notably the Indian ambassador to Peking, K.M. Panikkar, as biased and untrustworthy. Also permeating the Washington and Far East scenes was, if one may borrow a Japanese World War II term, a "Victory Disease" atmosphere, the result of the glowing reports from MacArthur and a lamentable lethargy by the policy-makers in Washington to examine critically the situation as it was unfolding. Instead of a delicate feel in the handling of this matter, a ham-handed heaviness is evident. The outcome was disaster.[68]

General Stratemeyer took no part in the above policy decisions. If he had, he probably would have tried to steer these decisions in another direction. His diary

---

67. Foot, pp 67-69.
68. Ibid., pp 74-90.

entries reveal that he was in favor of carrying the war as far as needed, including its expansion into a general war. He had little regard for the politicians in Washington and was perhaps slow in realizing that the politicians (and the JCS) were formulating new "rules of engagement" in light of the new world-wide political realities.

For Stratemeyer, the Korean War evolved into three "wars." These "wars" eventually wore him down physically and contributed to the heart attack which brought his service career to a close. The most important of these, of course, was the shooting one with the Communists. Prosecuting the war created a tremendous strain on him as he was forced to fight it with meager resources. A concomitant factor were the political restrictions of a limited war, restrictions which galled him. But there were two other "wars" that engaged his attention to a great degree and also imposed heavy burdens upon him. And it should be stressed that these were not minor skirmishes to him. One was a "war" with the press; the other was a "war" with the Army and Navy.

Public relations were very important to Stratemeyer, and he usually had top-flight people working as his Public Information Officers (PIOs). He also enjoyed a good rapport with many reporters and spent a great deal of time, perhaps too much, acting as his own PIO. But the publicity was not for himself. As General Holloway stresses, Stratemeyer "was not particularly concerned with looking good unless there was good reason to look good, and if there was he was much more concerned for credit going to those most directly responsible than for getting favorable press for himself or the command as a whole."[69]

The bloody infighting by the services in 1949 over the relative merits of the Air Force's B–36 and the Navy's supercarrier left its mark on Stratemeyer. This imbroglio, which featured the B–36 and the supercarrier as the catalysts for the two services' quest for money, roles, and missions (particularly concerning the Navy's place in strategic air warfare), was reported with great relish by the U.S. press. Eventually, this very complicated matter was resolved in the B–36's favor, but not before some careers had been ruined and a residue of mistrust had settled over the two services.[70]

Stratemeyer saw how the press had handled the B–36/supercarrier matter and was not impressed with what he felt was biased and error-filled reporting. Thereafter, he wanted to make certain that the accomplishments of the Air Force received the publicity he believed the service deserved. As will be seen in a number of his diary entries, the Korean War only heightened his desire to see the Air Force's deeds recorded.

Still, in his view, the press too often either had no idea of how to report the air war, described it inaccurately, or was used by the other services to denigrate the Air Force's contributions. Stratemeyer believed the Navy, in particular, used "sharp tactics" and did not play fair with the Air Force in this regard.[71] Thus, he fought a continual battle with the press. He did not always leave the the press to his PIO, but often became directly involved in press and public relations matters. When dealing with the press he was frank, friendly, and according to General Holloway, "absolutely devoid of guile."[72] An example of a direct relationship to

---

69. Holloway letter.
70. Steven L. Rearden, *The Formative Years, 1947-1950* (Washington, 1984), pp 410-422.
71. Smart interview.
72. Holloway letter.

the press was Stratemeyer's weekly letters to the noted aviation writer Gill Robb Wilson[73] describing various aspects of the air war and FEAF's role in it. The information in these letters was intended for publication, which Wilson was happy to accommodate.

Public relations was only one of the problems Stratemeyer faced. His third "war" was with the Army and Navy. This struggle included misunderstandings (sometimes real, often feigned) by the other services of the close air support role of the Air Force in the Korean War; attempts by the Army to control FEAF and make it its own air arm; and attempts by the Navy to run its own air war without regard to other air activities, even though MacArthur had given Stratemeyer the authority for "coordination control" over all air units. Matters such as these occupied Stratemeyer's attention almost as much as the fighting in Korea.

On May 20, 1951, Stratemeyer suffered a severe heart attack, ending his part in the Korean War. After several months recovering at a hospital in Japan, he returned to the United States in November to continue his recuperation at Winter Park, Florida, a small town near Orlando. He retired from the Air Force on January 31, 1952, having served for over 36 years. In May 1953, he had a second heart attack from which he never fully regained his health.[74]

By mid-1951, Stratemeyer was gone from Japan and the Korean War. MacArthur was gone also. But as the war in Korea ground on, attempts were made to negotiate a cease-fire. By a circuitous route through the Soviet government, the United States offered to discuss with the Chinese and North Koreans the possibilities of a cease-fire. Mutual distrust, though, conspired to frustrate an immediate cease-fire.

Finally, on July 10, 1951, negotiators from both sides met at Kaesŏng to thrash out an agenda for an armistice. This was the first of many meetings that would be held at Kaesŏng and later, P'anmunjŏm. These negotiations, which lasted over two years, were marked by heated arguments, intransigence, propaganda, harangues, oppressive silences, and, occasionally, real work toward obtaining an armistice. In the two years these talks went on, thousands of men on both sides fell, not for miles of territory but for yards. The war turned into positional, trench warfare reminiscent of World War I. Some of the bloodiest battles were fought during this time. Gaining huge chunks of territory was not the purpose of these battles; the goal was to gain the upper hand on a piece of territory bordering the strip of land that, following the armistice, became the demilitarized zone (DMZ). Bloody Ridge, Heartbreak Ridge, Old Baldy, Pork Chop Hill, and many other unnamed peaks were the sites of the bloodletting. It was "King of the Hill" writ large.

In the air, the action was as nasty as on the ground. Early in the war, FEAF met little resistance from the overmatched North Korean Air Force. Flak was another story. Close support missions are always dangerous, and as the Communist antiaircraft defenses increased, aircraft losses began to climb. Nevertheless, these attacks continued, as did B–29 attacks over the whole of Communist-held Korea. By the fall of 1950, the 18 strategic targets chosen by the JCS had already been eliminated by FEAF aircraft.[75]

---

73. For years, Wilson was publisher and editor of the magazine, *Flying*. In the mid-1950s, he was president of the Air Force Association.

74. *New York Times*, May 28, 1953, p 10.

75. Rees, p 370.

Along with an increase in the number of antiaircraft weapons, the number of enemy aircraft available soared. By June 1951, FEAF intelligence estimated that the Chinese Communists had some 1,050 combat aircraft. About 690 of this total, including more than 300 MiG–15s, were based in Manchuria. By contrast, FEAF had only 89 F–86As available.[76] A little over a year later, the Communist air strength in the Far East swelled to about 7,000 aircraft (5,000 Soviet, 2,000 Chinese, 270 North Korean).[77]

The appearance of the Soviet-built (and often Soviet-flown) MiG–15 in November 1950 caused the air war to heat up considerably. Far East Air Forces aircraft went after the airfields in North Korea with great success, but the fields on the other side of the Yalu could not be attacked. With their planes usually having both a numerical and altitude superiority, and their fields enjoying a sanctuary status, the MiG–15 pilots began to show a greater aggressiveness. Surprisingly, however, the Communists never used their numbers of aircraft to overwhelm the UN air units. Still, the effectiveness of the MiGs resulted in a FEAF policy placing that area of northwest Korea known as MiG Alley off limits to all Bomber Command aircraft unless accompanied by fighters. Eventually, the B–29s were forced to carry out most of their raids in MiG Alley at night. In pure fighter against fighter combat, though, the UN planes (primarily American F–86As, F–86Es, and F–86Fs) most often had the upper hand.

During the last two years of the war, FEAF remained busy attacking a variety of targets. Two major interdiction campaigns were mounted in 1951. One was flown against the North Korean highway network, while the second targeted the enemy railway system. Both campaigns received the same name, "Operation Strangle," an unfortunate choice because neither effort was able to completely sever the enemy's lines of communication. A lack of aircraft, increased resistance by enemy fighters and flak, and an intensive repair effort by the Communists all combined to reduce the effectiveness of these two campaigns.

Seeking a way to take better advantage of FEAF resources and to apply more pressure on the Communists to negotiate, in early 1952, FEAF's new deputy for operations, Brig. Gen. Jacob E. Smart, recommended the "selective destruction" of targets in North Korea. This was a shift away from the current emphasis on the interdiction of rail lines and bridges. It represented, however, the possibility of breaking away from a growing stalemate in Korea. Smart believed that the territorial limits placed on UN air attacks created few problems for the real enemy powers, the Soviet Union and Communist China, but by applying "air pressure" on selected targets of importance to these two powers would break the stalemate and influence them to seek an armistice.[78]

Among the group of likely targets for "selective destruction" were the North Korean hydroelectric plants and their subsidiary installations. The destruction of these plants would have severe repercussions on both sides of the Yalu. Between June 24-27, 1952, these targets were attacked, knocking out an estimated 90 percent of North Korea's electric power potential. Although the plants required continuing neutralization, the raids still stunned the Communists.[79] The attacks,

---

76. Futrell, pp 401-402.

77. Ibid., p 506.

78. Ibid., pp 477-480; Memo, ND, subj: FEAF Operations Policy, Korea, Mid-1952. In 1952 Addendum to 1952 FEAF History. AFHRA No. K720.01.

79. Futrell., pp 482-488.

however, resulted in a furor throughout the world, particularly in Britain. Not for the first time was the specter of World War III raised, and not for the last time the Communists saw that the Allies would continue to limit the war to Korea.[80]

Although by this stage of the war targets were becoming scarce, FEAF fighter-bombers continued to range all over North Korea during the day, while the B–29s and B–26s attacked at night. Two of the more notable air efforts during the last year of the war were "Operation Pressure Pump" and the attacks on the enemy's irrigation dams. Pressure Pump involved two massive strikes on P'yŏngyang in June and August 1952 which effectively removed that city from FEAF's target list. The irrigation dam strikes in May 1953, which wiped out miles of rice fields, railroad tracks, and highways, also proved highly effective.[81]

While the B–29s, B–26s, F–84s, and other planes hit targets all over North Korea, the F–86s dueled daily in MiG Alley with the MiG–15s. Most of the enemy pilots appeared still to be learning the ropes of fighter combat and could be "easy meat." Occasionally, however, the F–86s met very skilled adversaries ("Honchos," who were most likely Soviet pilots) and the outcome did not always favor the Sabres. Throughout the war, the ratio of MiG–15s to F–86s was weighted heavily on the side of the MiGs. This resulted in the Sabre formations being much smaller than their opponents. By May 1953, however, two more F–86 wings were available as well as more of the new F–86F models. These additions finally enabled FEAF to more actively seek the Communists in MiG Alley. Some of the fiercest fighting of the air war, and some of the greatest victories by the Sabre pilots over their adversaries, took place in May, June, and July 1953. One day, June 30, saw the F–86s down 16 MiGs to set a new one-day record for the war.

Meanwhile, a couple of significant events occurred in the last months of the war. In the United States, President Truman decided not to run for re-election and the Democratic candidate, Adlai Stevenson, was defeated in November 1952 by Dwight D. Eisenhower, who had promised to go to Korea in an attempt to bring the Korean War to a close. Eisenhower did go to Korea the following month, but did not discuss with the field commanders whether the war would be expanded or an armistice sought quickly.

Also, the truce talks in Korea had broken off in October 1952, primarily over the repatriation of prisoners, and would not resume for six months. From October 1952 until the armistice was signed in July 1953, ground fighting was confined primarily to the grumbling and muttering of artillery duels, with occasional bursts of intense close-in fighting, as each side jockeyed to gain the upper hand over a desired piece of real estate. During this same period, FEAF pilots sharpened their skills in close support, as well as mounting various interdiction, reconnaissance, and airlift missions.

Although Eisenhower wished to end the war peacefully, he was not averse to considering a military conclusion to the conflict, including carrying the war into Communist China and/or the use of nuclear weapons. Such considerations were hinted at to certain nations, particularly India, which was believed to be keeping Communist China apprised of U.S. diplomatic actions in regard to the war. Eventually, the Communist Chinese realized that the Soviet Union (especially

---

80. Ibid., p 489; See also selected press comments on these bombings in *FEAF Report on the Korean War*, Vol. I, p 113.
81. Futrell, pp 517, 525, 667-669.

since Stalin's death on March 5, 1953) was not going to come to their aid in the event the Korean War escalated into Chinese territory, that haggling over prisoner repatriations was not worth the problems that could ensue, and that the increased tempo and power of the FEAF attacks was having a serious effect on their ability to sustain their operations in Korea. Finally, in late March 1953, the Communists agreed to repatriate sick and wounded POWs ("Little Switch"). Full armistice talks resumed at P'anmunjŏm shortly afterwards and on July 27, the armistice agreement was signed. "Operation Big Switch," the final exchange of POWs, took place over the next few days.[82]

This "limited" war had been exceedingly bloody. A full accounting of the casualties probably will never be known. Recent estimates of losses indicate that military casualties on both sides were approximately 2.4 million, while another 2 million civilians were casualties. These civilian figures may be conservative. For the United States, 54,246 men were dead and another 103,284 were wounded.[83]

It had been a bloody battle for the Far East Air Forces as well. During the war, FEAF lost 1,466 aircraft (out of a total of 1,986 UN planes destroyed). These were split almost evenly between 1,041 combat and 945 non-combat losses. The always dangerous flak claimed the greatest number of aircraft, 816 (most of these on ground attack missions), while 147 were lost in air-to-air combat. There were human losses as well. FEAF suffered a total of 1,841 casualties, including 1,180 dead.[84]

In the process of suffering these losses, FEAF units flew 720,980 sorties. Considering that FEAF was never a large organization, this was quite an accomplishment. On these sorties, FEAF planes delivered 476,000 tons of ordnance, which destroyed a tremendous amount of enemy equipment and facilities, and killed numerous enemy soldiers. Among the equipment claimed destroyed (by Air Force, Navy, Marine, and other UN aircraft) were 976 planes, including 792 MiG–15s, 1,327 tanks and 82,920 vehicles. Some 184,808 enemy troops were also reported killed.[85]

Meanwhile, General Stratemeyer returned to the United States in November 1951 to continue his recuperation at Winter Park. Now viewing the war from afar and though in relatively poor health, he continued to voice his concern with what he perceived as the failure of the United States to "win" the Korean War. One year after the armistice was signed, on August 25, 1954, he publicly stated his views on this subject. The forum was a hearing in Orlando by Senator William F. Jenner's (R-Ind) Internal Security Subcommittee of the Senate Judiciary Committee. These hearings had a dual purpose: first, to investigate the handling of the Korean War (and, in the process, to bash the Truman and Eisenhower administrations) and, second, to investigate possible subversion in the government. (This period was the height of the demogogic phenomenon known as McCarthyism, after Senator Joseph R. McCarthy [R-Wis].)

Appearing before the committee, Stratemeyer did not mince words. "We were required to lose the war," he stated. "We weren't allowed to win it."[86]

---

82. Foot, pp 232-243.
83. Blair, p 975.
84. Futrell, p 692.
85. Ibid., pp 689-692, 695-696.
86. *New York Times*, Aug 26, 1954, p 23.

He also opined that this was not the fault of the JCS but of the State Department.

"It is contrary," he said, "to everything that every military commander that I have been associated with or from all of our history — he has never been in a position where he could not win the war he started to win. That is not American. And who did it — I don't know. I know that General MacArthur's hands were tied, I am sure, not by the Joint Chiefs of Staff, but by the then State Department. I make that as my opinion, and I still believe it."[87]

During the Korean War, however, Gen. Stratemeyer did not complain publicly about the situation. Of interest is his statement to the press on March 26, 1951, concerning national policy. "We are *prepared* to carry the air war to the enemy wherever he may be," he said, "but a decision to extend the employment of our bombers or our fighters beyond the confines of Korea is not one that should be made by the field commander. This is a basic decision that quite properly must be made at governmental and/or United Nations level. It might be wise to point out that the military man *implements* foreign policy in our democratic form of government — the military do not *formulate* foreign policy."[88] [Emphasis in the original.]

General Stratemeyer was not a major figure during World War II, but he was involved in planning at the highest levels, both in Washington and in the CBI. Unconditional surrender, unlimited warfare, the seizing of all of the enemy's territory were the terms of reference with which he was most familiar. Korea brought a harsh new reality to him, that of limited warfare. In his remarks before the subcommittee and later, it is obvious that he did not understand the political realities of the Korean War. The idea that artificial, inviolable boundaries could be placed on war was foreign to him, as it was to many other military leaders of that time.

Additionally, during these hearings Stratemeyer stated that the Eighth Army's November 1950 offensive was a "masterful stroke" by MacArthur designed to prevent the Chinese from organizing against the UN force. Stratemeyer chose to believe that the offensive was solely intended to blunt a Chinese counterattack when, in fact, it was intended to end the war by a drive to the Yalu and took little account of a major Chinese intervention. The number of Chinese already in Korea took MacArthur and many of his lieutenants, including Stratemeyer, by surprise.[89]

Like many of his contemporaries in the military, Stratemeyer tended to be "conservative" in his political views. This led him to become involved, albeit indirectly, with Senator Joseph McCarthy. In 1950, the senator began a sensational hunt for Communists and other subversives in the government. His methods were irresponsible, and his charges were usually unsubstantiated, but he gained a following. His downfall was precipitated in a showdown with the United States Army in the spring and summer of 1954 over supposed Communists in the Army. On June 11, 1954, McCarthy's Senate colleagues introduced a resolution condemning him. For the next several months the Senate wrangled over the resolution.

---

87. *U.S. News and World Report*, Sep 3, 1954, p 85.
88. Futrell, pp 377-378.
89. *U.S. News and World Report*, Sep 3, 1954, p 85; Blair, pp 375-472; Goulden, pp 312, 317, 321-329.

While this debate droned on, a number of McCarthy admirers formed groups either supporting the senator or attempting to propogate his ideas. The publisher and editor of the *Chicago Tribune*, Col. Robert R. McCormick, formed one such organization, called For America, in May 1954. This group was against "super-internationalism and internationalism" and for states rights and "enlightened nationalism."[90]

On November 13, 1954, McCormick announced a policy committee consisting of 43 people for his organization. General Stratemeyer was on this committee, along with retired generals Albert C. Wedemeyer, Mark Clark, and James A. Van Fleet. A day later, a subsidiary group of For America, "Ten Million Americans Mobilizing for Justice," was announced. The purpose of this group was to amass over a ten-day period 10 million signatures on petitions urging the Senate not to censure Senator McCarthy. The group's reasoning was that the censure was Communist-inspired propaganda.

General Stratemeyer headed this group from his home in Winter Park. In a statement to the press, he said that his "nonpolitical and nonpartisan" organization showed that the great majority of Americans were against the censure because McCarthy was only "doing his sworn duty" in investigating the executive branch.[91]

As the censure hearings neared, the "Ten Million" held a rally at Madison Square Garden on November 29. Rallies in other cities had also been planned, but these were cancelled when it became apparent there was little support. Although the organizers hoped that the Garden, which could hold over 22,000 people, would be filled to overflowing, only 13,000 showed up to hear the speeches, one via radio from Stratemeyer in Winter Park.[92]

The turnout was a disappointment to the sponsors. What was even more disappointing to the group was the number of signatures obtained on the petitions. Having set 10 million signatures as the target, the approximately 1,150,000 names that were tabulated was deflating.[93]

On December 2, 1954, by a vote of 67 to 22, the Senate censured Joseph McCarthy. He never recovered politically, and died on May 2, 1957.[94] The "Ten Million" disbanded quietly shortly after the censure, its goals not reached, its inspirational leader in disgrace. The troublesome matter of subversion and Communism would not go away, though, and in this regard, General Stratemeyer's name again appeared in the newspapers.

Stratemeyer's testimony before the Internal Security Subcommittee in August 1954, as well as the testimony of other Korean War commanders (Clark, Van Fleet, Almond, and Joy, all now retired) was recycled in January 1955 in the subcommittee's final report. At this time, the United States was developing a new policy concerning Formosa. The subcommittee hoped that lessons learned from the Korean War would be considered as this new policy was being studied.

---

90. *New York Times*, Nov 14, 1954, p 42.
91. Ibid., Nov 15, 1954, pp 1, 16.
92. Ibid., Nov 29, 1954, p 12.
93. Ibid., Nov 30, 1954, pp 1, 22.
94. John M. Blum, et al, *The National Experience*, Part Two (New York, 1968), pp 782-784, 799-801.

The subcommittee also hoped that Stratemeyer and the other four officers would help identify "subversive" elements in the government. In this it was unsuccessful, although the final report stated that the former commanders had "supplied some clues to subversion in Government departments."[95]

Four months later, in the May issue of the conservative magazine *American Mercury*, Stratemeyer listed what he called the "Fourteen Commandments for America Today." Reflecting his conservative views and strong anticommunist feelings, they were:[96]

1. Don't surrender one more inch of ground to Chinese Communists.
2. Don't let one more American ground soldier die in preventing Red China from taking any of Chiang Kai-shek's territory.
3. Equip, feed, and arm President Syngman Rhee's forces and Generalissimo Chiang Kai-shek's forces, and encourage turning them loose.
4. Organize an American Foreign Legion *of all people in the Far East* [emphasis in original] who want to fight Communism, just as the Soviet does in China and Germany to fight the West.
5. Stop all appeasement to Communism.
6. Let Great Britain give Communist China Hong Kong if they are so anxious to give other people's real estate away.
7. Let's get our prisoners out of Red China dungeons even if we have to fight for them.
8. The same people who sold China and European Soviet satellites down the river should not now be advising the present American administration.
9. Let's get rid of fear — repeat fear — and practice "In God We Trust," with fight in it.
10. "In God We Trust" should be our cry from the house tops by all veterans, American Legion members, Veterans of Foreign Wars, etc., and all Americans with guts.
11. I agree with General Chennault that Communist China is a "paper tiger" of bluff and bluff. Let us stop — repeat stop — bluffing, and call Red China's bluff.
12. Withdraw recognition of the Soviet and all her satellites and kick them out of the United States of America.
13. We should reserve our real power for the real enemy, "the Soviet," and not fritter it away on Korean type actions.
14. Every American citizen should vote in local, Congressional, and Presidential elections.

For one last time in early 1957, Stratemeyer's name was coupled with that of a conservative group. In February of that year, a Citizens' Foreign Relations Committee was formed. The group consisted of a number of prominent individuals, among whom, besides Stratemeyer, were generals Wedemeyer and Willoughby, noted writer John Dos Passos, and a number of Republican congressmen. Many of this group were frequent critics of United States foreign policy. The breaking of diplomatic ties with Communist countries and the support

---

95. *New York Times*, Jan 26, 1955, pp 1, 4.
96. *American Mercury*, May 1955, p 40.

of "democratic subversion" in these same countries were among the policies urged by this right-wing group.[97]

In the late 1950s, General Smart visited Stratemeyer and was saddened when he saw his former commander. He saw "a man possessed with exaggerated, if not irrational perceptions of reality."[98] He believed that General. Stratemeyer (and his wife) had been used by demagogues and sensationalists for their own purposes and should have been protected from these unscrupulous persons. It is also possible that the two heart attacks Stratemeyer suffered affected him to a greater degree than was then apparent.

Following this last attempt to draw attention to perceived defects in U.S. foreign policy, General. Stratemeyer's name faded from the pages of the newspapers as he lived out his last decade at his Winter Park home. On August 6, 1969, as another war (in many ways remarkably similar to the one he had fought in Korea) raged in Vietnam, he passed away. He was 78. His devoted wife of almost 53 years, Annalee, survived him. A few days later, in a simple but moving ceremony, Lt. Gen. George E. Stratemeyer was laid to rest at the United States Air Force Academy.[99] The three "wars" he had fought in Korea were long since over; his last battle was now done.

---

97. *New York Times*, Feb 11, 1957, p 11.
98. Gen Smart manuscript comments, Sep. 19, 1988.
99. *New York Times*, Aug 11, 1969, p 35; *Airman*, Nov 1969, p 64.

Part One

The Black Days

June 25 – September 14, 1950

**With June 25 to June 28, 1950, entries from
Maj. Gen. Earle E. Partridge's Diary**

Situation Summary

June 25, 1950 — September 14, 1950

At 0400 on June 25, North Korean troops poured south across the 38th Parallel to launch the Korean War. Outmanned and outgunned, most of the South Korean defenders were quickly routed. Although some units, after unsuccessful counterattacks, were able to retreat in reasonably good order, many units were decimated and ceased to exist as effective forces. On the first day of the war, the South Korean Army, along with its KMAG advisors, suffered a shattering defeat.

With the enemy driving hard for Seoul, the American ambassador to South Korea, John J. Muccio, asked Gen. MacArthur to evacuate all American civilians from the capital. On the 26th and 27th, under the watchful protection of Japan-based F–82s and F–80s (no U.S. ground forces would see action until July 4), these people were evacuated via ship and C–47/C-54 airlift.

Far East Air Forces fighters shot down several NKAF Yaks and Ilyushins on the 27th, considerably dampening the enemy's enthusiasm for air combat. Still, with their airfields north of the 38th Parallel off limits (the President forbade any attacks above the Parallel in a futile attempt to limit the war), over the next few days enemy aircraft continued to attack various targets in South Korea. On June 29, one day before he received permission from the President and the JCS to conduct such operations, Gen. MacArthur authorized Gen. Stratemeyer to attack the North Korean airfields and other military targets north of the 38th Parallel. MacArthur emphasized that these attacks were to stay well clear of the Manchurian and Soviet borders. Almost immediately upon receipt of this authorization, FEAF aircraft began hitting North Korean targets. Within a few days the NKAF ceased to be an effective force, and was capable only of nuisance-type raids. With little effort, FEAF had gained air superiority.

Fighting on the ground was a different story. Seoul fell on June 28, and Suwŏn (15 miles south of Seoul and the site of a major airfield) was lost on July 4. During this time the B–29s of the 19th Bombardment Group, the B–26s of the 3d Bombardment Group, plus F–80s, F–82s, and F–51s struck a variety of tactical targets in attempts to slow the enemy and to also show MacArthur's headquarters (which was critical of FEAF's efforts) that the Air Force was doing all that it could. These attacks hurt the enemy, but they were too scattered to stop the onrushing North Korean forces.

On June 30, President Truman decided to throw U.S. ground forces into the fray and by July 4, the first units, elements of Maj. Gen. William F. Dean's 24th Division, reached the peninsula. The first clash between U.S. and NKPA forces took place on July 5 south of Suwŏn, near Osan. Like so many of the encounters during the following days, in this fight the Americans were unable to stop the North Koreans.

The ground situation would probably have been worse had it not been for the work of FEAF. Its planes, joined by those from the Navy's Task Force 77, hit targets from P'yŏngyang in the north to the front lines in the south. On July 8, FEAF Bomber Command (Provisional) was established to exercise operational control over the B–29s of the 19th Group, the 31st Strategic Reconnaissance Squadron, and two Strategic Air Command B–29 groups that would be arriving shortly. Though the B–29s were intended for deep strategic bombing, the almost daily crises caused them to be used more often as tactical bombers attacking targets in and near the front lines.

These attacks cost the enemy many men, vehicles, and much materiel, yet helped only to slow the enemy's drive south. But these missions did enable the tired and hard-pressed U.S. and ROK troops to regroup and conduct a fighting retreat. At last, on August 4, with more U.S. troops available (the 1st Cavalry Division and the 25th Infantry Division had now been thrown into the fight, and more reinforcements were on the way), and with the North Korean supply lines being pounded daily by FEAF and Navy planes, the retreat halted. United States and ROK forces now held a line running approximately 100 miles north from Korea's southern coast generally along the Naktong River, then east from the Waegwan area to Yongdŏk on the east coast. Pusan, the only major port now available to the defenders for supplies and reinforcements, lay within this defensive line, which soon became known as the Pusan Perimeter.

Intense, fierce fighting continued throughout August, with FEAF aircraft providing support through the bombing of North Korea, the interdiction of enemy supply lines, and through the close air-support of friendly forces. Though the situation often became critical during the month and there were local reverses, the perimeter line held. And while this fighting was going on, Gen. MacArthur was planning a bold stroke to regain the initiative and drive the NKPA out of South Korea — an amphibious assault at Inch'ŏn.

The Diary _____

COPY
HEADQUARTERS, FIFTH AIR FORCE
Office of the Commanding General, APO 710
8 October 1950

Dear General Stratemeyer:
I am sorry so much time has elapsed since you asked me for the inclosed notes.
The delay arose because we found a page is missing from my diary covering the early part of 27 June. My secretary has searched everywhere to no avail.
All I can recall from that date is that you arrived and that you did not desire to attend the teleconference which took place in the afternoon and which is adequately covered in the notes herewith.

s/ P.
E.E. PARTRIDGE
Major General, USAF
Commanding

_____

To – DEE
1. Let Col. Sykes[1] read.
2. Put this data on diary sheet and put in front of my diary No. 1.
   G.E.S.
In order to have a complete picture of the Korean conflict "personalized" from the beginning of hostilities I am adding General Partridge's Diary Notes for the period 25 - 28 June as he was acting in my stead during my absence from my command post.

SUNDAY
25 June
1950
_____

Nagoya. Fine except showers. Hot. Skeet shooting in morning; five rounds for 116 out of 125. Made 1.00 on Howe.[2]
Returned to learn of invasion of South Korea by North Korean Army. First news from Tucker about as follows: 1130 - trouble started (OSI [Office of Special Investigations] info) about 0400 local time.[3] By 0600, attacks had spread from west to east along 38th Parallel. Ongju under attack, Kaesŏng taken(?). Tanks used. Twenty boats employed to turn ends.[4] 374th [Troop

---

1. "Dee" has not been identified but was probably Stratemeyer's secretary. Col Ethelred L. Sykes was a special assistant to Stratemeyer and was later Chief, Korea Evaluation Group.
2. Probably Col John D. Howe, 5AF deputy for operational engineering, later deputy chief of staff for services.
3. Col Edwin L. Tucker had been 5AF assistant chief of staff since February 1948. In June 1950, he became 5AF acting vice commander and later became deputy vice commander for the 5AF Rear Echelon. FEAF Headquarters first learned of the invasion at 0945, when the OSI head in Seoul radioed the news. Although the North Koreans poured across the 38th Parallel in strength at 0400, it took the OSI and other agencies in Seoul almost five hours to verify that a full-scale invasion was taking place.
4. Only two to three miles south of the border, Kaesŏng fell quickly. "Ongju" probably refers to the Ongjin peninsula on the west coast. The North Korean "end-around" by a collection of junks and small boats took place near Samch'ŏk on the east coast.

Carrier Wing] and 8th [Fighter-Bomber Wing] were alerted to implement FAF [Fifth Air Force] Ops Plan #4.[5] Reported this to Crabb[6] and told him of my intentions to remain in Nagoya, etc. Talked to Ted T[imberlake].

Returned from golf with Kay and Katy[7] to find call from Timberlake. Talked to him 1750.

Situation at Kimp'o reported through radio from tower to our ADCC [Air Defense Control Center].[8] Field surveyed by 2 Yaks about 1100. Attacked three times by single pairs of Yaks. We (MATS) [Military Air Transport Service] had a C–54 on ground with damaged aileron and it was destroyed by enemy action. Two other aircraft (one C–54 with aileron for one on ground and one B–17 with a special passenger) enroute to Kimp'o were recalled.[9]

War officially declared by North Koreans 1100. Conference at my house about 1900. Timberlake, Lt. Col. White (FEAF A-2), Simpson, Thompson, and Sheehan.[10] Reviewed situation.

We agreed FAF ready - must await instructions.

White expressed view that U.S. would abandon South Korea to Reds. I disagree. This line of action is unthinkable and I await with interest the policy of the U.S. JCS.

Arranged 1000 conference at FEAF for FEAF, FAF, FEAMCOM [Far East Air Materiel Command] and MATS.

News came later that General Stratemeyer will arrive Tokyo on 27th.

MONDAY
26 June
1950

Nagoya. Up early, but before that, 0045, Crabb called to say his instructions from GHQ [General Headquarters] are that dependents will be evacuated by freighters from Inch'ŏn.[11] We are to provide fighter cover and are authorized to fire on enemy aircraft to protect these vessels. I told Crabb to put this in writing to FAF and to send info copy to GHQ so that they may object to the language if it is not appropriate.

Departed Nagoya in 3411 [an aircraft with that serial number] with White (A-2), Sheehan and Thompson at 0800.

---

5. This operations plan detailed the procedures and equipment to be used for the evacuation of U.S. civilians and military personnel from Korea. (5AF Operations Plan No. 4, Mar 1, 1950, Change No. 1, Mar 23, 1950.) Additionally, 5AF was directed to increase its surveillance of the Tsushima Strait. (FEAF Opns Hist, 25 Jun-31 Oct 50, Vol. I, p 19.)

6. Brig Gen Jarred V. Crabb's assigned job was FEAF deputy chief of staff for operations, a position he had held since June 1949, but at this time he was also acting as Vice Commander, FEAF. Crabb also served with 5AF in World War II.

7. Kay was Partridge's daughter and Katy, his wife.

8. An air defense control center was an air operations installation which, using radar and other early warning devices and facilities, provided aircraft control and warning, and also contributed and directed the active air defense in a given air defense sector.

9. Located several miles west-northwest of Seoul, Kimp'o was the city's main airport. The planes were identified as Yak–9s. The destroyed C–54 (from the 1503d Air Transport Wing) had been on a regular run to Seoul for the U.S. Embassy and KMAG. The plane had been damaged the day before when a Korean laborer drove a forklift into an aileron. Several of the venerable B–17s were still being used for VIP transport and search-rescue service.

10. Lt Col John M. White, Jr.; probably Lt Col O'Wighton D. Simpson, 5AF deputy for intelligence; probably Lt Col Clyde A. Thompson, 5AF assistant deputy for operations. Sheehan has not been identified, but may have been one of Partridge's aides.

11. Early on the morning of the 26th, evacuation operations began at Seoul. Evacuees (totalling 682) boarded the Norwegian merchant vessel *Reinholte*, which had just finished unloading fertilizer at Inch'ŏn. At 1630, the ship got underway and was escorted by F–82s throughout the night. U.S. Navy destroyers, along with several

Maneuver Lexi #1 (amphibious training exercise southwest of Tokyo) underway today so had to avoid area thereabouts.

A conference was held at FEAF hq [headquarters] with General Doyle, General White, Lt. Col. Thompson (FAF) and FEAF staff in attendance.[12] The intelligence situation was outlined and every possible aspect of the situation reviewed.

It is agreed that there had been an intelligence failure in the field in that the uprising in Korea occurred without prior warning.

Action to be taken by the Eighth Army in loading 8,000 tons of ammunition were discussed.

The plan to provide air cover for the dependents and non-combatant civilians, who are being evacuated from the Seoul area, was presented and General Crabb noted that General MacArthur had expressed a firm desire that no details of the evacuation be made public.

General Crabb noted that the 512th Weather Recon Sq [Reconnaissance Squadron] had been directed to provide additional flights to include our weather and reconnaissance coverage.

General Crabb said eight (8) F–82s have been brought into the Itazuke area from Okinawa and that he was anxious to return these aircraft to their home base as soon as the situation permitted.[13]

General Crabb stated that the twelve (12) C–54s of the 374th Troop Carrier Group which had been gathered at Itazuke had been released to return to their normal duties.

It was agreed that the C–47s and C–46s being held in reserve for possible flights to Korea might be dropped back from an "alert" status to one of "overall readiness."[14]

It is apparent from the conversation that there is a plan in the mill to give the Koreans ten (10) F–51s; appropriate instructions were issued to Material to prepare these aircraft for dispatch.[15]

General White mentioned that there were eight (8) C–47s in the Philippines enroute from the U.S. so that these aircraft may proceed as a group to Saigon.

B–26s, met the *Reinholte* the next morning to continue the escorting duties to Fukuoka, Japan. During the evacuation, a single enemy fighter bounced a pair of F–82s. Although authorized to fire on any enemy aircraft while performing this cover mission, the U.S. pilots did not return fire. (Hist, FEAF, 25 Jun-31 Dec 50, pp 29-31.) The enemy plane did not tarry long, quickly returning to its side of the border. Meanwhile, American dependents from Taejŏn, Taegu, and Pusan boarded another cargo vessel at Pusan. (Futrell, p 9.)

12. Brig Generals John P. Doyle, commanding officer of Far East Air Materiel Command (FEAMCOM), and Edward H. White, 1503d Air Transport Wing commander.

13. Having a greater loiter time than the F–80s, the long-legged, twin-engined F–82 night fighters were to cover the evacuation of civilians from Seoul. Not enough of this type of fighter were in Japan, so the F–82-equipped 4th FS moved to Itazuke this day. The squadron returned to Naha on July 8. (Futrell, p 8; FEAF Opns. History, 25 Jun-31 Oct 50, Vol. I, p 14.)

14. These World War II-vintage transport planes had been readied to evacuate the civilians, but over-optimistic reports that the situation was stabilizing caused the evacuation plans to be shelved and the transports stood down. However, about midnight on June 26, FEAF received word of a worsening situation north of Seoul and the air evacuation operations were restarted. Most of the C–54s were not now available because they were being used for other purposes, but 2 from the 374th Wing, plus 9 C–47s and 2 C–46s from FEAMCOM and the FEAF base flight were obtained. These planes eventually flew out 851 people before the evacuation was completed on June 29. An additional 905 people came out of Korea by ship. (Futrell, p 12; FEAF Opns. History, 25 Jun-31 Oct 50, Vol. I, p 22.)

15. A number of ROK pilots had been selected just prior to the invasion for training on the F–51. With the outbreak of the war, the need for their services became great and a detachment, named "Bout-One," was formed out of the American 36th FBS to hasten their training. The F–51s were former tow target aircraft. The half-trained Korean pilots and their instructors, led by Maj Dean Hess, moved to Taegu on June 30 and began flying combat missions almost immediately. (Hist, 5th AF, Vol. I, Jun 25-Oct 31, 1950, p 3; Futrell, p 89.)

This subject is highly classified and he mentioned it to me only because of the necessity of MATS to retrieve the forty-one (41) crew members after the airplanes had been delivered.[16]

During the conference a message was received from General Chennault offering use of ten (10) transports for evacuation purposes.[17]

General Doyle expressed his concern over the security of his AVAMMO [aviation ammunition] dumps. Colonel Rogers[18] is to look into this matter and if the situation warrants, he will request assistance from Eighth Army.

General Eubank[19] dropped in to suggest that if such action had not already been taken we should initiate an investigation into the B–29 accident which occurred off Guam on Friday, 23 June. This action had already been taken by General Crabb.

I attended a teleconference at 1400 hours in the Dai Ichi Building at which General MacArthur, Gen. Almond, Admiral Joy, General Wright, Gen. Willoughby, Gen. Eberle and Gen. Back were in attendance.[20] (General Stratemeyer should read the transcript of this and the previous teleconference).

Five major points were covered:

1. The request for approval of a survey to determine the minimum amounts and types of equipment which should be provided to Korea and an estimate of the forces which might be used in stabilizing the situation there was approved. The survey is to determine the requirements if we are to retain and control the area around Seoul, Kimp'o and Inch'ŏn. The survey party of fourteen (14) members, headed by Major General Church[21], will depart at 0400 in a C–54 from Haneda direct to Kimp'o (later changed). Fighter cover will be provided. The Navy and the Air Force each to furnish one (1) officer for this party.

2. CINCFE authorized to ship arms and equipment to Korea and to protect the shipments.

---

16. These aircraft were originally to be delivered to Metropolitan France, but because of the increasing strife between the French and the Viet Minh in Indochina, the planes were flown directly to Saigon. No formal U.S. agencies had yet been established in the area when the planes (the first to be given to the French by the U.S. in southeast Asia) arrived and were turned over to the French. (Robert F. Futrell with Martin Blumenson, "The United States Air Force in Southeast Asia," *The Advisory Years to 1965* (Washington, 1981), p 6.)

17. Whether General Partridge knew that Chennault's Civil Air Transport (CAT) was now owned by the Central Intelligence Agency (CIA) or that, because of FEAF's need for cargo lift capacity, this knowledge would have made any difference, is unknown. The first three CAT aircraft in the combat zone actually operated more in support of covert projects than in a transport role. By November, however, some 24 CAT aircraft were hauling freight, both inter- and intra-Japan. (William M. Leary, *Perilous Missions: Civil Air Transport and CIA Covert Operations in Asia* [University, AL, 1984], pp 116-120; Hist Synopsis, Dir/Ops, FEAF, Sep 16-Oct 1, 1950, Ops Req Div, p 2; Hist Synopsis, Dir/Ops, FEAF, Oct 1-Oct 15, 1950, Ops Req Div, pp 2-3.)

18. Probably Col Craven C. Rogers, FEAF deputy for intelligence.

19. Brig Gen Eugene L. Eubank, deputy inspector general at the Kelly AFB, Texas, Field Office of the Inspector General.

20. Maj Gen Edward M. Almond commanded the black (segregated) 92nd Infantry Division in World War II. From November 1946, he was Deputy Chief of Staff, GHQ (initially named Army Forces, Pacific, and later, Far East Command [FEC]). Since February 1949, he had been FEC chief of staff. Brig Gen Edwin K. "Pinky" Wright was FEC G-3; Maj Gen Charles Willoughby, FEC G-2; Maj Gen G.L. Eberle, FEC G-4; and Brig Gen G.I. Back, FEC signal officer. The Dai Ichi Insurance Company building (now FEC headquarters) was built just before World War II and was one of the few left in the area that was partially air conditioned and had been undamaged by the air raids.

21. Actually a brigadier general, John H. Church, a GHQ staff officer, was directed initially to determine the kind and amount of equipment needed by the ROK forces. The following day, the 28th, Church's survey party received a new task, that of being the GHQ Advance Command and Liaison Group (ADCOM). This was in response to instructions finally received from Washington on the afternoon of the 27th directing MacArthur to

3. CINCFE is authorized to use arms if necessary to insure the safety of the evacuation movement out of the Seoul area.[22]

4. The Seventh Fleet is to proceed to Sasebo and come under the operational control of Admiral Joy; the comment on this provision that the JCS did not feel that the situation with respect to the Russians was critical; otherwise the fleet would not have been directed to such a confined location.[23]

5. General Roberts[24] will be returned to Korea immediately. He is presently on the high seas and expected to land on the West Coast 4 July.

During the course of the conference, I had an opportunity to talk to Gen. Willoughby re Colonel Dale[25] entering Formosa as an advisor to the Chinese Air Force. Willoughby objects and suggested that we bring the Chinese air commanders up here for the Chinese Mission.

General Almond had directed that we study the situation with regard to our transports and their operation into Korean airfields. General Eberle will make known his requirements in case the logistic situation becomes critical and we may be called upon to assist. We must have a plan.

The plan to bring ten (10) Korean AF pilots out of Korea and to land them at Itazuke is under way at 1000 today.[26] These pilots are to be checked in the F–51 and are to fly their aircraft back to Korea.

When I first learned of this operation, I protested to General Almond that it was useless to attempt such a procedure not only because the Koreans are entirely incompetent as F–51 pilots, but because their logistics situation will not permit the support of this complex type operation. General Almond recognized the truth of my arguments, but said that General MacArthur had promised to give the airplanes away. I then proposed that it would be far more productive if we could provide officers and airmen who could assist with the maintenance, communications, etc. He not only concurred, but told me to make a plan by which a group of officers and airmen might be assembled and transported to Korea to arrive at the same time the F–51s reach there. This personnel will be made supplement to the KMAG organization.

General Almond also expressed the thought that the pilots assigned to the group might actually operate the F–51s to the extent necessary to carry out their advisory mission.

About 1930 hours, General Almond called to relay information which he had just received from Colonel Wright[27] in Korea. He stated that one of our Mustangs had jettisoned two tanks in the Seoul area and that one of these struck and killed six Koreans. The General was disturbed that our aircraft were avoiding

---

use air and naval forces to support the South Koreans. After establishing his command post in Suwŏn, Church assumed control of the KMAG personnel and began to seek ways to lend as much assistance as possible to the ROK Army. (Appleman, p 43.) There are reports that Church had little faith in the ROK Army and apparently did not exert himself greatly on its behalf. (Joseph C. Goulden, *Korea: The Untold Story of the War* [New York, 1982], pp 92-93.)

22. This meant Air Force and Navy units only; the Army was not mentioned. ("History of the JCS," Vol. III, pp 80-81.)

23. Sasebo was a major American naval base on Kyushu's west coast.

24. Brig Gen William L. Roberts, former chief of KMAG, then enroute home for reassignment.

25. Nothing has been found on Col Dale or his assignment.

26. A main FEAF installation, Itazuke Air Base was on the island of Kyushu and was one of the closest bases to Korea.

27. Col W.H.S. Wright, acting chief of KMAG, pending the arrival of a permanent replacement.

At the beginning of the war, Maj. Gen. Edward M. Almond was MacArthur's deputy chief of staff. He later commanded the X Corps.

combat rather than engaging and destroying the North Korean airplanes. He directed me to take the necessary action to insure that our AF patrols maintain an aggressive attitude in the accomplishment of their mission. (General Almond was especially caustic regarding the failure of one of our F–82 pilots to shoot down a Yak which flew over Inch'ŏn anchorage. The F–82 was "bounced" but not shot at. Pilot of '82 ducked into the low cloud and when he came out seconds later, Yak had disappeared. See messages to and from Washington 27 June.)

This matter was discussed with General Timberlake who promised to advise Price[28] and see that appropriate instructions were issued.

A message confirming this and directing certain specific action by the FAF was prepared but was held by me until early in the morning of the 27th. It was subsequently dispatched and its contents were concurred in by General Wright of GHQ. It directs the FAF to maintain air superiority over the Seoul, Inch'ŏn and Kimp'o areas and to provide air cover for aircraft and for shipping when specifically directed by FEAF. The message specifically directs aggressive action in the event that hostile aircraft interfere or attempt to interfere with FAF mission or acts in an unfriendly manner to South Korea forces or our own.

General Crabb, Colonel Rogers and I discussed the deteriorating situation in the Seoul area until about 2330 hours. Colonel Rogers had been in on the telecon with Mr. Nichols[29] when the announcement was made that the city was under shellfire and that the conference had to be terminated.

There were several calls between General Crabb and me during the early morning hours and also in conference with Mr. Muccio's liaison officer, Major Hammond.[30]

The latter relayed a message which he was endeavoring to relay to General Wright stating that the Ambassador was most anxious that air cover be provided Tuesday morning because the situation was slowly deteriorating. This information was relayed through Rogers to General Wright.

During the night requests began to be received covering the evacuation of additional dependents and non-combatants from Kimp'o. General Crabb set up

---

28. Col George E. Price, FEAF assistant deputy for operations.
29. Chief Warrant Officer Donald Nichols, commander of OSI's District 8 in Seoul. Warrant Officers are usually referred to as "mister." A telecon was a link between two or more teletypewriters. They could record "hard" paper copies, while simultaneously projecting the texts on viewscreens.
30. Hammond's full name is unknown.

these missions using C–46s, C–47s and C–54s. The mission is to depart in time to reach Kimp'o soon after daylight.

TUESDAY
27 November
1950

A redline from General Vandenberg[31] requested further data as to why our F–82 pilot avoided combat over Inch'ŏn yesterday. This message was answered about 0820 stating that the pilots were operating under normal instructions, but that these instructions have now been amended.

There seemed to be a lot of pressure to secure an answer to the Vandenberg redline, but it was most difficult to secure any additional data other than that which had already been submitted.

(Page as per General Partridge missing from his diary.)

F–82s undergo engine maintenance. An F–82 pilot scored the first victory of the war for the USAF.

He mentioned the fact that the British Commonwealth Overseas Forces [BCOF] were not available for employment against the North Koreans.

I had scarcely returned to my office from this conference when I was again called to the Dai Ichi Building for a teleconference with Washington. Present were Generals MacArthur, Almond, Hickey, Beiderlinden, Willoughby, Wright and Eberle, and Admiral Joy. Colonel Fortier was also there.[32]

The teleconference directed a major reversal of policy on the part of the US government. CINCFE [Commander-in-Chief, Far East] was directed to employ such naval and AF [air forces] as were at his disposal to bolster the SK [South Korean] forces and restore the territorial integrity of that nation. Seventh Fleet was given the task of establishing Formosa as a neutral island, preventing attacks

---

31. A "redline" was the designation given certain very important messages for prompt and special handling. By then-current Air Force regulations, the Secretary of the Air Force, the Under Secretary, the Chief of Staff, USAF, and certain other individuals as spelled out in the regulations were the only persons authorized to send or receive redline messages. As Chief of Staff, Gen Hoyt S. Vandenberg was authorized to send this redline. (Woodford A. Heflin—editor, *The United States Air Force Dictionary* [Maxwell AFB, Ala., 1956], p 431.) General Vandenberg held many important positions during World War II, including that of Chief of Staff, 12AF; Chief of Staff, North African Strategic Air Forces; Deputy Chief of Staff, Headquarters AAF; Deputy Commander in Chief, Allied Expeditionary Air Force; and Commander, 9AF. After the war, he was Assistant Chief of Air Staff for Operations, Commitments, and Requirements, then held several intelligence assignments. Between September 1947 and April 1948, he was Air Force vice chief of staff. On April 30, 1948, Vandenberg became Chief of Staff, USAF.

32. Maj Gen Doyle O. Hickey, Deputy Chief of Staff, FEC; Brig Gen William A. Beiderlinden, FEC G–1. Col L.J. Fortier was on the FEC intelligence staff.

from the mainland and vice versa. There were other pertinent details, particularly those regarding public relations. CINCFE was adamant that the successful operation in Korea depended largely on the restitution of the spirits of the Korean Army and the people, and, for that reason he urged that Washington immediately announce the provisions of the decision. Washington hedged and intimated that 12 hours would elapse before the announcement was made.

CINCFE turned to me and directed immediate action, but, at the same time he warned that it would be necessary for FEAF to be prepared to continue the air defense of Japan against the attacks of the Russian AF.

He directed that a message be sent to British Commonwealth Overseas Forces stating that our instructions included action by US forces only, and that no operations outside Japan are contemplated for BCOF units. CINCFE said that he had received a message from Chennault regarding the use of his transports and if we needed those transports we should ask GHQ to secure them. Concurrently, it was announced that PanAm and Northwest Airlines would be used to evacuate dependents and non-combatants (civilians) to the U.S.[33] It was announced that 682 people were aboard the *Rheinholte*. CINCFE agreed that General Church should proceed to Suwŏn under air cover. His survey group is now being changed to a command group and will provide the advanced echelon for GHQ headquarters. CINCFE has assumed operational control of KMAG and General Church is to be the directing commander on the spot.

The move of the 19th Bomb Group to Okinawa was approved by General MacArthur and he stated flatly that it sounded like a good idea.[34]

CINCFE stated his firm belief that the third night following 27 June will be the critical one here in Japan. He feels that if there is an attack in the near future, it will be made on the night of Thursday or Friday of this week.

CINCFE decided that the strategy of air defense was a matter for the air commander to decide and directed that this authority be delegated to General Stratemeyer.

CINCFE then directed that following each air mission, a communique be prepared and sent to General MacArthur's headquarters for issuance. The general was almost jubilant at the end of the conference.

He outlined the far-reaching results which will be achieved if the air effort can be made effective tonight and tomorrow. He stressed again and again the necessity of hitting the North Korean forces in the next 36 hours with every resource at our disposal, carrying the action through the night if this is possible. He expressed the firm conviction that vigorous action by the FAF would result in driving the North Korean forces back into their territory in disorder.

Upon return from the teleconference, I briefed General Stratemeyer and thereafter visited Intelligence and Operations in order to set up a better system of reporting for the operations that are to be conducted. Not long afterwards I was called again to GHQ to sit in on the final staff conference on FEC's field order. There were no new major items covered during this talk. Following the conference I again briefed General Stratemeyer on the plan.

---

33. As FEAF's, or for that matter, the entire Air Force's, airlift capability was seriously understrength at this time (the Military Air Transport Service had only 597 aircraft in 1950), it was necessary to use commercial carriers for non-essential work such as this. (Dick J. Burkard, *MAC Historical Handbook, 1941-1984* [Scott AFB, Ill.,1984], p 95.)

34. The 19th BG moved 22 four-engine B–29 medium bombers from Guam to Kadena Air Base immediately upon receipt of orders.

The evening was spent in endeavoring to ascertain what action had been taken during the past 24 hours and in the preparation of an "Air Intent" for the following period.[35]

During the course of the evening, General Almond called to give me a very rough time indeed regarding the failure of the AF to drop a single bomb in Korea yesterday. During the course of the teleconference, I had been so incautious as to predict that we would have a B–26 mission operating against the North Korean forces before dark. This mission did come off, but smaller than had [been] anticipated because most of the B–26 aircraft were engaged in escort activities. The small force of five airplanes which finally took off were aborted due to bad weather; in addition to that, the strikes that were scheduled to continue through the night were scattered because of the bad weather.

General Almond took a dim view of the entire proceeding and said so in no uncertain terms, particularly when he discovered that the forecast for this morning's weather was bad. He repeated again and again that in order to save the South Korean forces and their government from collapse, it is mandatory that we take some visible action in support. He wanted bombs put on the ground in that narrow corridor between the 38th [Parallel] and Seoul, employing any means and without any accuracy. Following my extended conversation with General Almond, I called Timberlake and Al Kincaid and did my best to convey the urgency of the situation and to spur them on to a full-out effort. Both were most cooperative and understanding.

Following the staff meeting, I briefed General Stratemeyer on the proposed operations for the day and endeavored to secure additional information on the actual progress of events.

At ten o'clock General Crabb and I were called to General Almond's office and discussed with him not only the current plan of operations, but the mechanical method by which we would brief him and he in turn was to brief General MacArthur.

We returned from this conference barely in time to improvise a new map and return for the Chief of Staff's conference at 1130; briefings by Admiral Morehouse.[36] General Crabb brought the people present up-to-date on past events and current contentions.

General Almond made a considerable point of insisting that the Joint Information Center which is being set up on the sixth floor of the Dai Ichi building must be used for the Joint Staff. It was pointed out to him by several people there it would be impossible to operate in this manner, but he insisted that we try it and we supply the necessary liaison and intelligence officers to make the system function. FEAF's room is 619 and is at present entirely bare of all except the most meagre furniture.

During the course of the conference, I made arrangements thru General Hickey to insure that the AF might use in Korea such elements of the anti-aircraft artillery units now under our operational control as may be necessary to insure some security for our advanced bases such as Suwŏn. Initially, there had been considerable opposition to this project because the directive issued by CINCFE precludes the use of Army troops in support of the SK forces.[37]

---

35. An Air Intent Notice was a summary of proposed air actions that were to take place within the next few days.
36. Rear Adm Albert K. Morehouse, chief of staff to Adm Joy.
37. Though the fighters and radars were part of the Air Force, the third part of the air defense team, the antiaircraft artillery (AAA), belonged to the Army. This separation had been a bone of contention between the two

General Willoughby announced with great pride that he had produced the war's first propaganda pamphlet and provided each man present with a sample.

During the course of the afternoon, arrangements were made with Major Story[38] to provide for a flight by the *Bataan* to Suwŏn; aboard will be CINCFE.[39] General Stratemeyer will accompany the party and they expect to be gone approximately two (2) days. In order to insure the completeness of the arrangements, I appointed Lieutenant Evans[40] as project officer for FEAF and sent him to Itazuke and thence to Suwŏn. In this way he becomes my official liaison officer and he will, incidentally, secure a reading on the "folks" at Suwŏn. This will provide me with some additional second-hand information on the field and will, at the same time, give Evans training which will later prove invaluable to him.

The flow of information has improved considerably this date. We are still hours behind on events in the FAF and almost entirely without information on those of the Thirteenth.

I also had a long conversation regarding the positive information reaching this headquarters. He (Timberlake) assured me that the details were being supplied and after perusal of our daily intelligence, I'm inclined to believe him. Of all the confusion I've observed in wartime, that produced in Ops [Operations] Intelligence wins the prize. They are operating in a temporary establishment pending the completion of their Ops Room and are completely disorganized with respect to each other and to the remainder of the hqrs. This must be corrected.

After endeavoring all night to find enough information so that Col. Van Meter[41] could issue a public relations release, I abandoned the project at one o'clock in the morning and went to bed.

WEDNESDAY
28 June
1950

Up late and barely made the 8:30 staff meeting. This was a rainy day in Tokyo in contrast to our recent excellent weather and the weather was dubious in the vicinity of Itazuke and Seoul.

The early reports indicated that even with the utmost effort on our part, our actual accomplishments in support of the Korean forces were negligible. Bad weather prevented any take-off before seven o'clock and some of the aircraft which departed returned almost immediately.

* * *

This entry concludes Gen. Partridge's portion of this diary.

---

services for many years. With the exception of those AAA units belonging to divisions, 5AF exercised operational control over all other AAA units. But at this early stage of the war, before permission was given MacArthur to use Army troops in Korea, he was understandably reluctant to authorize the use of <u>any</u> Army forces in that country. (Futrell, p 430: FEAF Mission Directive, July 12, 1950, Annex 4 of FEAF Opns Hist, 25 Jun-31 Oct 50, Vol. I.)

38. Lt Col Anthony F. Story, MacArthur's personal pilot.

39. MacArthur's personal aircraft was a C–54 named *Bataan*.

40. First Lt William J. Evans, Partridge's aide-de-camp. This type of training apparently did prove invaluable, for Evans retired from the Air Force in 1978 as a full general.

41. Lt Col Samuel N. Van Meter, acting PIO for FEAF.

The Diary of General Statemeyer.

SUNDAY

25 June

1950

Enroute back to Tokyo after two weeks' temporary duty in Washington, D. C. and landed at Hickam [AFB in Honolulu] when the news reached me that North Korea had declared war on South Korea as of 1100 hours that day. Actually, North Korean forces had crossed the 38th Parallel as early as 0400 hours, 25 June, to take not only South Korea but the rest of the world by surprise. Field intelligence had broken down somewhere and FEC had no forewarned knowledge of the massing of the estimated 200,000 troops nor their intent to cross the Parallel. Upon receipt of news of the civil war, I changed my plans to return direct to Tokyo via Wake instead of Okinawa.

MONDAY

26 June

1950

In the meantime, Major General E. E. Partridge, my Fifth Air Force commander who had been acting in my stead, set the wheels moving. General MacArthur, after several teleconferences with the Joint Chiefs, ordered evacuation with fighter cover of all American personnel in South Korea. Transports were unarmed, although fighters were armed, and orders were for use of those arms for protection of the American evacuees only. However, materiel was ordered carried in via air transport to the South Koreans and 10 of our F–51s were ordered, against FEAF's request, to be turned over to the South Korean Air Force for their use. This latter order entailed training on our part of the pilots who were to fly the craft, and the supplying of T/O&E pertaining thereto.[42] Reconnaissance developed that North Koreans were supplied with a quantity of tanks and were pushing through South Korea without too much effort. The South Koreans were further handicapped by the lack of military leadership in that General Roberts, chief of our Military Mission, had just left on rotation and was on the high seas back to the States. KMAG was being administered by a full colonel and a handful of trained staff. General MacArthur appoints Brigadier General Church and a group of 14 selected officers, including one Air Force and one Navy representative, to proceed to Korea to assist the South Koreans. I landed at Wake and took off immediately for Tokyo.

TUESDAY

27 June

1950

Arrived Haneda 1120 hours.[43] Immediately assumed command and was briefed on events to date by General Partridge. Since it was apparent that South Korea needed more than "support and supplies" from the Air Force, the President commits the United States toward assuring the political integrity of South Korea and decrees such support entails tactical methods. (At the same time the President brought Formosa into the defense orbit.)[44] Airlift progressing; evacuees taken out by airplane and sea. Reconnaissance and actual combat proving that North Koreans

---

42. T/O&E — "Table(s) of organization and equipment." An Air Force document that prescribed the personnel structure and equipment for a unit. The term is now obsolete

43. Haneda is located in the southern part of Tokyo on Tokyo Bay.

44. On this day, President Truman ordered the Seventh Fleet to take what actions and dispositions were necessary

supported by Yak–3s, Yak–5s, and some Il–10s. FEAF handicapped in this shooting war by not being permitted to cross the 38th Parallel to destroy enemy at its source of staging. Seventh Fleet, under Vice Admiral Struble[45], participating.

WEDNESDAY
28 June
1950

Unfavorable weather; B–26 sortie aborted. Government of South Korea has moved to Taejŏn.[46] Ambassador Muccio encountering difficulties in bolstering morale of Rhee and his general staff. South Koreans falling back; Kimp'o and Seoul taken. My big headache at present is to man my command and get it operating on a 7-day, 24-hour day week. USAF promises AC&W [Aircraft Control and Warning] personnel and equipment needed for the primary mission of FEAF - the

Evacuees from Korea are assisted from a C–54 after arraiving in Japan on June 27, 1950

defense of the home islands of Japan. All combat aircraft and crews of the 19th Bomb Wing moves to Okinawa. 850 people evacuated without incident.

THURSDAY
29 June
1950

0600 hours departed with General MacArthur (with Generals Willoughby, Almond, Wright and Whitney)[47] aboard the *Bataan* from Haneda for Suwŏn Air Field, South Korea. Told CINCFE that in order for me to support him full-out must have authority to attack the enemy (his aircraft and airdromes) in North Korea. Permission granted at once and we now cross the 38th Parallel! Wired Partridge re the authority.[48] (With CINCFE's authority to cross the 38th and as a result of my wire to Partridge, General Timberlake got off a B–26 strike north of the 38th

---

to prevent a Communist attack on the island of Formosa. At the same time, he strongly urged Chiang Kai-shek to discontinue his attacks on the Communist forces on the China mainland and in neighboring waters. The Seventh Fleet was also to make sure this advice was followed. (See relevant materials in *Foreign Relations of the United States, 1950*, Vol. VII [Washington, 1976], pp 179-180, 187-188, 201-203.)

45. In Washington when hostilities commenced, Vice Adm Arthur D. Struble immediately headed for the Far East. At this time, the Seventh Fleet was operating off the Philippines. Within hours, this naval force was en route to Buckner Bay on Okinawa's eastern shore. The Seventh Fleet's responsibilities would be split between Korea and Formosa.

46. Because of the chaotic and obviously dangerous situation developing north of Seoul, the South Korean government decided to move to Taejŏn, a town about 85 miles south of Seoul. Some of the members of the National Assembly decided to remain in Seoul, most being captured and executed by the Communists when the city fell.

47. Maj Gen Courtney Whitney, MacArthur's military secretary.

48. The President initially forbade air attacks on North Korean targets. It had been thought that vigorous action by ROK forces, supported by U.S. aircraft, would drive the invaders back across the 38th Parallel.

the afternoon of 29 June.)[49] Spent the day interviewing Lt. Colonel McGinn, Brigadier General Kim Chung Yul, General Church and other officers in KMAG, and, in general being "briefed" on the actual situation.[50] Our liaison officer, on CINCFE's advanced headquarters - commanded by Brigadier General Church - is a Lt. Colonel McGinn who is doing an outstanding job with the margin of equipment. His needs were many and varied - including 24 shovels with which to dig foxholes around the air strip! Also talked at length with General Kim who commands the South Korean Air Force. Promised him his supply requirements to keep his F–51s going. Timing on my escorting fighters for the *Bataan* excellent; CINCFE impressed. A Yak attempted to intercept *Bataan*, but was driven off by our escort. Returned to Tokyo and landed Haneda 2205 hours. Came straight to the office where I briefed General Partridge who is now functioning as my vice commander. Left the office after midnight.

FRIDAY
30 June
1950
_____

Unfavorable weather; what sorties we had concentrated on strafing, materiel, personnel, and marshaling yards. F–80 lost and a B–26 down.

Beginning to get our first casualties. Reds begin to cross the Han River in numbers.[51] 851 persons airlifted with no incidents from Korea. Wired CSAF [Chief of Staff, USAF] for permission to keep General Eubank and his team until 15 July. (His IG [Inspector General] team had just completed their yearly inspection of FEAF. Their services will prove invaluable.) $6,500,000 completely obligated at 2400 hours this date for construction on all airfields in Japan and the aircraft and warning sites.

SATURDAY
1 July
1950
_____

Unfavorable weather; however, took off at 0800 in B–17 for Itazuke and Ashiya - our advance bases.[52] Spent the day there; returning at 1823

Haneda. South Korean ground armies giving way; morale non-existent. CINCFE sending in U. S. infantry troops to attempt to bolster their lines and also secure security of our few bases.[53] Reported that Suwŏn Airfield taken by the enemy. CSAF grants permission for my retention of Eubank and his

---

This perception was quickly dispelled by the stunning reverses suffered by the ROK troops. Finally, permission was granted on the 30th (Korean date) to attack airfields, troop concentrations, and other military targets in North Korea. U.S. planes were to stay well clear of the Manchurian and Russian borders. As can be seen, General MacArthur anticipated the release of his air units by almost a day. It would not be the last time he would take action without consulting either the JCS or the President. ("History of the JCS," Vol. III, pp 108-110.)

49. This first strike north of the 38th Parallel, an 18-plane effort, hit the main military airfield at P'yŏngyang. One enemy plane was reported shot down and 25 others were claimed destroyed on the ground. (Futrell, p 98.)

50. Lt Col John McGinn was a member of General Church's ADCOM staff and had been quite active in organizing the base at the Suwŏn airfield. Brig Gen Kim Chung Yul was ROKAF chief of staff.

51. A major river, and major obstacle for invading forces, the Han is born in the T'aebaek Range (only about 20 miles from the Sea of Japan). It runs some distance south before turning northwest to flow through Seoul and empty into the Yellow Sea.

52. Because of their proximity to Korea, the Kyushu bases of Itazuke and Ashiya became the primary fields for jet operations against the enemy. (At this time, the few Korean fields were ill-suited for these operations.) One squadron of the 49th FBG moved from Misawa to Itazuke on the 1st to join the 8th FBW, while a second squadron went to Ashiya. The group's last squadron remained at Misawa. Moving to Ashiya on July 6 was the 35th FIG, less its 41st Squadron, which went to Johnson AB for air defense. (Futrell, pp 67-68.)

53. President Truman's first decisions on June 25 were based on recommendations from the State and Defense Departments. These decisions were: order MacArthur to send arms and ammunition to Korea; furnish ships and planes for the evacuation of American dependents; and order the Seventh Fleet to report to MacArthur.

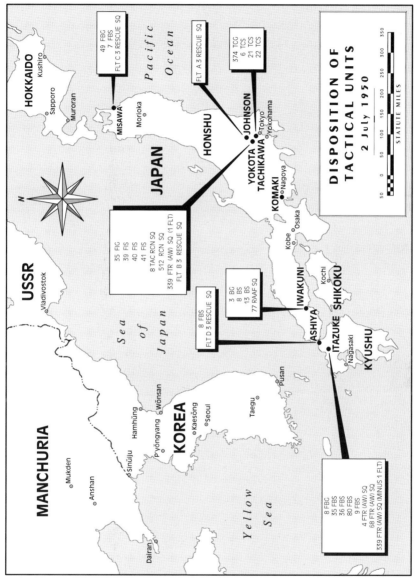

Map 3.

DISPOSITION OF
TACTICAL UNITS
2 July 1950

team's services. All requests so far approved by CSAF. Will make report of my visit to 8th Fighter Wing to GHQ staff, tomorrow morning.

SUNDAY
2 July
1950

As of this date, 12 aircraft have been lost. Koreans officially take over the F–51s given them tomorrow. The RAAF [Royal Australian Air Force] (77th Fighter Group, based at Iwakuni) joins us in combat missions in their F–51s.[54]

Made the following rather disconnected report during staff meeting in GHQ this morning. Morale of 8th Fighter Wing and 3d Bomb Wing "superior." In spite of the strenuous flying and fighting that has been done, they were all raring to go. I described the particular flight of the F–80C that took off in order to gather weather over the Seoul area. This particular pilot flew the entire distance on instruments, under severe turbulence, let down over the sea to some 600 feet, flew in over the Seoul area and returned, giving his weather report. The trip was entirely on instruments. Seven (7) C–54 loads successfully going into Pusan under the most adverse weather. General Timberlake ran this show similar to VITTLES, taking off every 20 minutes, letting down, and if they got into the airdrome, well and good; if not, they were to continue their flight and return to base.[55] I also described the miraculous return of four F–80Cs to Itazuke where they arrived with a ceiling of 100 feet and one mile visibility. I further explained that I had talked to the Koreans undergoing training and they with their fighters would proceed to Taegu which would be turned into a fighter base. I stated that Pusan Air Base would be improved to take all the airlift heavy transports.[56] I pointed out that in strike pictures of the P'yŏngyang strike, not only much materiel was destroyed and the hangars, but six airplanes were destroyed on the ground. I further pointed out that as soon as I could release General Partridge, he would return to the command of the Fifth Air Force and he would establish his advance command post along side General Dean, the U. S. Army ground commander in South Korea.[57] I pointed out that the Australian 77th Squadron had been turned over by General Robertson and that one mission of three airplanes

---

The next night he directed a lifting of restrictions on U.S. air attacks below the 38th Parallel. Additionally, the Seventh Fleet was ordered to prevent a Communist attack on Formosa. On the 29th (Washington date, the 30th in Korea), air operations against military targets in North Korea were authorized. Early the next day, the movement of one regimental combat team to Korea was also authorized. Just a few hours later MacArthur was told to employ in Korea "such Army forces as he had available" except for those needed for the defense of Japan. (Futrell, p 37.) A second directive set up a naval blockade of North Korea. ("History of the JCS," Vol. III, pp 113-123; Futrell, pp 22, 37.)

54. Actually No. 77 Squadron RAAF. MacArthur requested the squadron on the 29th in a message to Lt Gen Sir Horace Clement Hugh Robertson, Commander in Chief, British Commonwealth Occupation Force (BCOF). Correspondents with MacArthur during his Korean visit knew the text of the message and filed stories about this request when they returned to Tokyo. Release of this message irked the Australian government which, with U.S. approval, had begun withdrawing its forces from the occupation forces in Japan prior to the war. Thus, this request came as a nasty shock to the Australians. After some discussion, the Australian government approved on June 30 No. 77 Squadron's use in Korea. Robertson felt that MacArthur's release to the press of the request for the squadron had been done deliberately to force the Australian government's hand. (Robert O'Neill, *Australia in the Korean War 1950-1953*, Vol. 1: *Stategy and Diplomacy*, Canberra, 1981, pp 36-37, 51-55.)

55. "Operations Vittles" was the Berlin Airlift of June 26, 1948-September 30, 1949.

56. Luckily for the Americans, the best port in Korea and the closest one to Japan was Pusan, on Korea's southeast corner. Plans were initiated to make Pusan the main supply base in South Korea. Also, since the two best airfields in the country, Kimp'o and Suwŏn, had been (or were about to be) lost, airfields near Pusan would be needed. It appeared that the already built Pusan airstrip could be utilized, but it quickly broke up under the weight of transport aircraft. Only heroic efforts by engineers kept the field operating until other airstrips were ready.

57. Dean's tenure as commander of his own 24th Division and of U.S. Army Forces in Korea (USAFIK) was distressingly short. On July 20, during the retreat from Taejŏn, Dean became separated from his men. After 36 days of wandering alone through the hills trying to reach his own lines, Dean was captured by the North

had flown as cover this morning and that seven others were acting as cover for the B–26 strike in the Seoul area.

General MacArthur dispatched my draft signal to the Joint Chiefs of Staff requesting certain Air Force units and combat crews to the extent of 700 airplanes.[58]

Our B–29 bomb strike on Yŏnp'o, North Korea, was not successful as strike photos showed only 16 airplanes on the ground while our recon photos showed 68. The airdrome was fully covered with frags [fragmentation bombs].[59]

General Eubank returned from Kadena Air Base, Okinawa, and reported that the morale of the Twentieth Air Force, and particularly the crews of the 19th Bomb Wing, was high.

MONDAY
3 July
1950

Radioed Vandenberg for full colonel to be head of my PIO as section must be augmented and a colonel needed. Colonel Van Meter doing a superb job. Received information from SAC [Strategic Air Command] that the 22d and 92d Bomb Groups (Medium) were being alerted for service in the Far East.[60] Have queried Twentieth and Thirteenth [Air Forces] re sites. Mission reports for day meager. Those reports that are in indicate heavy traffic moving south. Lost an F–80; shot down by tank fire. The 24th Infantry under General Dean in Korea or in transit. Our ground forces and those of the North Koreans should clash within the next day or two. Suwŏn reported holding; heavy fires observed about that airfield.

TUESDAY
4 July
1950

Just received information, Vandenberg to Stratemeyer, that Major General Rosie O'Donnell[61] as bomber commander, and the 22d and 92d Bomb Groups, were proceeding to Far East Command for temporary duty. Vandenberg suggested that the 19th Bomb Group be placed under General O'Donnell. Vandenberg wishes - although he apologized - that all targets back of immediate battlefront

---

Koreans. Only in September 1953, after being released by the enemy, did he rejoin the Army. For his actions at Taejŏn, where he personally destroyed a tank, Dean was awarded the Medal of Honor.

58. This refers to a message from MacArthur to the JCS endorsing Stratemeyer's needs and requesting immediate action. General Stratemeyer sent several requests to Washington. Two, on June 30, were for 164 F–80s, 21 F–82s, 22 B–26s, 23 B–29s, 21 C–54s, 64 F–51s, and 15 C–47s, plus enough men in certain categories to bring all assigned units up to wartime strength (1&1/2 times peacetime). The additional aircraft would also provide a ten percent reserve for combat attrition. On July 1, Stratemeyer requested more units - a medium bomb wing, two F–51 wings, two F–82 all-weather squadrons, one troop carrier wing, three F–80C squadrons, a B–26 wing, another two B–26 squadrons to bring the 3d BW up to strength, an RF–51 recon-naissance squadron, an RB–26 night photo squadron, and a tactical air-control squadron. Some of these units were to be used in Korea, others for the air defense of Japan. (Futrell, pp 68-69.)

59. Another reason for the lack of success was that the B–29 crews reported many of the bombs bursting thou-sands of feet in the air. (FEAF Opns Hist, 25 Jun-31 Oct 50, Vol. I, p 32.)

60. SAC units, the 22d BG came from March AFB, and the 92d BG from Spokane AFB. When Lt Gen Curtis E. LeMay took command of SAC in October 1948, he insisted on a high standard of training. He also insisted that his units be mobile and prepared to fight anywhere in the world. Still, LeMay said later that these two units had been low-priority units that were neither fully manned nor combat-ready for the overall strategic war plan. However, the movement of these two groups proved SAC's mobility plans were sound. (It should be noted that the movement of these two groups was aided considerably by the use of seven commercial carriers to move both personnel and cargo. Air Force airlift capability was still hindered by peacetime cutbacks.) The two groups began leaving their stateside bases on July 5. On July 13, they flew their first combat missions. (Hist, SAC, Jul-Dec 50, Vol. I, pp 15-20.)

61. Maj Gen Emmett "Rosie" O'Donnell, Jr. commanded a squadron of the 19th BG in the Philippines in the early days of World War II. Later in the war he commanded the 73d BW in the Marianas. Since 1948, he had commanded SAC's 15AF, the parent organization of the 22d and 92d Groups. Being an experienced bomber leader and familiar with the two bomb groups, O'Donnell was an obvious and good choice to command them

Armorers load a 2.75-inch rocket on an F–80 for a July 4 mission.

within North Korea be taken out; of course I agree with this procedure and that was my intent. LeMay[62] personal radio received urging teleconference with me; answered that [I] would hold a teleconference only after my conference this afternoon at 1430 hours with my Air Force commanders and FEAF staff, at which time specific information would be obtained, and forwarded by radio. If after this FEAF conference and my radios LeMay had any unanswered questions, then would hold the teleconference with him. Word received that Generals Wolfe, Everest, Strother, Weyland, accompanied by a party of colonels and lt. colonels and a Brigadier General Guest, Signal Corps, USA, would land approximately 2240, Haneda.[63] General Wolfe will be my houseguest. The rest of the party to stay at the Imperial. Press reports the President is sending Marine air units and members of the U.S. Marines to Korea. Also received

in Korea. His temporary duty was for an indefinite period. Headquartered at Yokota, his command was designated the Far East Air Forces Bomber Command (Provisional). The "provisional" designation indicated that this command had been organized with personnel and equipment from other units and was just a temporary organization intended for a specific mission.

62. During World War II, Curtis E. LeMay led the 305th BG in Europe, then moved up to command the 3d Bombardment Division, followed by the XX and XXI Bomber Commands and 20AF. For several months he was Chief of Staff, U.S. Strategic Air Forces in the Pacific. Returning to the U.S., he became the first Deputy Chief of Air Staff for Research and Development in the AAF. As a lieutenant general, he next commanded the U.S. Air Forces in Europe before becoming commander of SAC in October 1948.

63. Because the gulf between what Stratemeyer wanted and the Air Force could supply was so wide, General Vandenberg dispatched an inspection team from the U.S. to explain why FEAF was not going to get certain items and what was being done to alleviate other shortages. Leading the team was Lt Gen Kenneth B. Wolfe, Deputy Chief of Staff, Materiel, Headquarters USAF. Others in the party included Maj Gen Frank F. Everest (Assistant Deputy Chief of Staff, Operations), Maj Gen Otto P. Weyland (Commander, Tactical Air Command), Maj Gen Dean C. Strother (Director of Military Personnel), and Brig Gen Wesley T. Guest (Chief, Signal Plans and Operations Division, Office of the Chief Signal Officer, U.S. Army.)

word that inadvertently, portion of the South Korean line was strafed by my planes inflicting some damage to that portion of the line.[64]

9:35 P.M., or 2135 hours, VIP party landed. Also in group is Brigadier General Agee.[65]

Project name for F–80 squadron from Clark Field joining FEAF is called the "Dallas" squadron.

Our mission over Korea report strafing with results on materiel - trains, convoys, etc. Also reported refugees still streaming south out of Seoul.

Press reports that small advance American infantry unit successfully repelled North Korean ground reconnaissance unit. However, as was emphasized in papers, clash on small scale.

Following is a list of colonels who accompanied VIP party: Colonels J. L. Hicks, C. P. Brown, E. D. Ely, J. L. Jeffers, A. G. Stone, W. M. P. Northcross, C. R. Landon and C. A. Winton.[66]

The SAC bomber group headquarters and one bomb group will be located at Yokota; the other bomb group and 19th Bomb Group will be located at Kadena in Okinawa.[67]

WEDNESDAY
5 July
1950

Briefing with the Hq USAF group headed by Lt. General Wolfe; started at 0800 hours and continued until 1020 hours at which time we went to the Ops briefing in GHQ. After the Ops briefing, I took all the visiting generals, including my commanders, to pay their respects to General MacArthur where we stayed about an hour and heard a marvelous discussion of his contemplated actions in Korea. At this meeting, General MacArthur told General Wolfe that the question of the 19th Bomb Wing staying in the Far East Command, or its return to the United States and its being replaced by a rotational medium group, was a "question that he left entirely in General Stratemeyer's hands."

At the Ops briefing the Navy sprang a surprise on their actions in Korea on 3 and 4 July; we had been told that the results of their action would be brought here by Admiral Struble; instead, unbeknownst to any of the Air Force people, the results as reported by the Navy representative [are such that] anyone that attended that briefing might be led to believe that the Navy was winning the air war in Korea.[68] It is my opinion that it was deliberately done because of the visiting group from Hq USAF and the Department of the Army. We must do a better job at these Ops meetings in presenting the air picture before such a high-ranking group.

---

64. This "blue on blue" attack was made by No. 77 Squadron F–51s at P'yŏngt'aek. It was the squadron's first combat action in Korea. An interesting account of this mission and MacArthur's subsequent claims that no such attack on friendly forces took place is found in George Odgers, *Across the Parallel* (London, 1952), pp 42-52.

65. Brig Gen Walter R. Agee, Chief, Collections Division, Headquarters USAF.

66. Col Joseph. H̲. Hicks, the Chief, Programs Monitoring Office, Directorate of Supply and Maintenance, Air Materiel Command; Col C. Pratt Brown, from the Office of the Deputy Chief of Staff, Operations, HQ USAF; probably Col E.B. Ely, in the Office of the Assistant Chief of Staff, G-3, U.S. Army; Col Alexander G. Stone, in the Office of the Assistant Chief of Staff, G-1, U.S. Army; Col W.M.P. Northcross, in the Office of the Chief of Ordnance, U.S. Army; Col Charles R. Landon, in the Office of the Deputy Chief of Staff, Comptroller, HQ USAF; Jeffers and Winton have not been identified.

67. The 92d BG was based at Yokota and the 22d BG was at Kadena.

68. The first test for U.S. Navy aircraft came on July 3 when F4U Corsairs, AD Skyraiders, and F9F Panthers from the carrier *Valley Forge* hit the airfield and marshalling yards in the North Korean capital of P'yŏngyang. Planes from the British light carrier *Triumph* also participated in this attack. (This carrier was part of a naval force of ten vessels that the British Admiralty made available to COMNAVFE on June 29.)

Members of the inspection team from USAF Headquarters pose with Stratemeyer and Partridge and other FEAF officers. Seated in the front row, left to right: Stratemeyer, Lt. Gen. Kenneth B. Wolfe, Partridge, Maj. Gen. Eugene L. Eubank, and Maj. Gen. Alvan C. Kincaid. Standing, left to right: Col. Joseph H. Hicks, Col. C.P. Brown, Maj. Gen. Otto P. Weyland, Maj. Gen. Howard M. Turner, Brig. Gen. Walter R. Agee, Maj. Gen. Frank F. Everest, and Maj. Gen. Dean C. Strother.

General Wolfe and his group intend leaving Haneda tomorrow at 0500 and will visit Iwakuni, Itazuke, and Pusan, South Korea. They will return tomorrow evening and expect to depart for the United States about midnight, 6 July.

It is my opinion that the visit of this group will be most helpful and after they have visited Itazuke and Pusan, they will be in a position to inform the Air Staff of our needs.

I cleared with General MacArthur the flying forward to Taegu and Taejŏn of the General Wolfe group.[69] I have directed Colonel Erler[70] to go with the group and while in Korea with General Partridge and General Wolfe, Colonel Erler will interview Mr. Muccio and Korean officials in order to gain authority to use a part of the $10,000,000 set up by our government for the defense of South Korea for the purpose of building airdromes in South Korea.

All the general officer group came out to my house for cocktails; during this period, General Wolfe had an appointment with Mr. Akabane at 1900 hours and Messrs. Asajiro Ikeda (Ikeda-Gumi Co., Ltd.) and M. Kambe (Hazama-Gumi

---

Although MacArthur wanted the two carriers to strike other targets on July 4, their planes returned to P'yŏngyang that day. In this two-day strike, several enemy planes were claimed destroyed and many other targets destroyed or damaged. No Allied planes were lost to enemy action. (Field, pp 55-56, 62-65.)

69. At this time Taejŏn was the site of ADCOM headquarters. Taegu, located about 55 miles north-northwest of Pusan, became U.S. Eighth Army headquarters on July 13. Taegu was also the only suitable site in central Korea for an airfield.

70. Col Leo J. Erler, Director of Installations, FEAF.

Co., Ltd.)[71] at 1930 hours and he discussed with the latter two Japanese gentlemen named the possibility of their building airdromes with Japanese and Korean laborers in South Korea.

THURSDAY
6 July
1950

Lt. General Ho Shai-Lai[72] of the Chinese Mission called at 1100 hours this morning and I brought him up to date on our situation here and in Korea. I consider this a great stroke on the part of the Generalissimo to place this honest and courageous Chinese here in Tokyo.

Admiral Struble called at 1130 and we reviewed his strikes on 3 and 4 July, after which we discussed possible future strikes, the gist of which as follows:

(1) CINCFE feels that all traffic on east coast of North Korea can be stopped by bombing rail and highway system from Tanch'ŏn south some 20 miles to Ch'aho. (FEAF to recon this area and turn pictures over to 7th fleet re this tunnel complex.)[73]

(2) Since there is this possibility that [*sic,* for] Adm. Struble to make another air strike, FEAF to designate primary and secondary target, if [air]craft on ground, of the airdromes at Wŏnsan north, including Kankō and Yŏnp'o, and secondary, transportation centers and tunnels between Tanch'ŏn and Ch'aho.

(3) Instructed my Ops and Intelligence coordinate with me before signalling Adm. Struble and also info 5th AF of signal.

Dispatched signals to General LeMay, Gilkeson[74] on Guam and Kincaid on Okinawa that General O'Donnell with his bomb command and 92d Bomb Group (M) will be stationed at Yokota; the 22d Bomb Group (M) will be stationed at Kadena with the 19th Bomb Group (M); directed Gilkeson and Kincaid to make all arrangements for proper lodging and effect transit to final destination.

Handed General Wolfe the following memorandum:

Dtd [dated] 6 Jul 50: I have learned informally that General of the Army Douglas MacArthur is most anxious to have a staff Constellation[75] assigned to the Far East Air Forces for his use for long trips, particularly if he returns to the United States and on long trips such as to Formosa, etc. I think there is great reason for one being assigned because of his advanced age (seventy years plus) and because of the position he occupies for the United Nations, the Allied Powers, and the United States of America. I consider this of such importance that it be discussed with General Vandenberg and the Secretary of Defense in order that one can be made available to me for his use, and mine, should the occasion arise. If such an assignment is made, then one of the C–54s that is set aside for use in the Far East Command could be made available to my troop carrier wing or MATS in the Far East.

---

71. These individuals have not been identified.
72. Chief of the Chinese Mission in Tokyo.
73. Though rail and road systems do narrow along the coast in that area, a study of the map shows the tunnel complexes farther south.
74. Brig Gen Adlai H. Gilkeson, commander of the 19th BW.
75. Designated C–121 by the Air Force, this was the military version of the Lockheed-built airliner of the same name. The Air Force used the type primarily as a VIP transport.

Sent the following memorandum to General MacArthur:

Dtd 6 Jul 50: It is recommended that: *(a)* All available channels of communication be used by you to notify those responsible for current operations of the North Korean armed forces that it is your intent to destroy by air bombardment all vital air, rail, highway, and port facilities in North Korea. *(b)* To avoid needless loss of life, all persons are warned to leave such areas and remain at points sufficiently far removed as to preclude personal injury, and *(c)* That the sole action on the part of North Korea which will prevent the intense pursuit of this plan is the withdrawal of all North Korean armed forces above the 38th Parallel, complete cessation of all hostile activity by North Korean Forces, and an agreement by the North Korean government to abide by any future decisions of the United Nations.[76]

Gloomy press report from ground forces; South Koreans falling back, left pockets of our ground forces units in advanced positions, cut off. Weather bad; 2 out of 7 B–29s of one mission aborted. Intelligence showing that our continued hammering at supply lines beginning to have appreciable effect upon the ground action of the North Koreans.

Afternoon's sorties - B–29s and B–26s highly successful; 6 to 10 enemy tanks destroyed and an unknown number of enemy ground personnel; one factory bombed with explosion resulting; also bombed what was believed to be 4 subs. One B–26 lost on a strafing, bombing and rocket mission.

General Wolfe and party landed at 6:15, Haneda; they did not make it to Korea. After landing they all came to the house for an informal dinner.... Generals Wolfe, Partridge, Weyland, Everest, Strother, Agee, Eubank, Banfill, and Colonel Landon, Annalee and myself.[77]

Brigadier General Charles Y. Banfill,[78] my new vice commander of the Twentieth Air Force, arrived unexpectedly and unheralded via PanAm at about 5:15.

---

76. This memorandum was most likely a reaction to pressure being exerted from Washington. From the outset of the war, the United States took into account the feelings and policies of the other United Nations members supporting the U.S. on the Korean problem. These feelings and policies did not always coincide with those of the U.S. There was general agreement that the fighting must be confined to Korea, but this, of course, placed heavy restrictions on military operations there, not the least of these affecting FEAF.

While most wars have some political orientation, in the Korean War such sensibilities played a much greater role than in previous conflicts. Political restraints laid a heavy hand on military operations, but there was another, less defined, policy that also contributed to restrictions. This concerned "humanitarian ideals." Many individuals believed that bombing was morally wrong, and they were more than eager to share their views with the press. Being sensitive to the real and imagined "power of the press," politicians tended to react to possibly negative stories in the newspapers. Every so often a newspaper raised the question of the morality of bombing, often tying in the atomic bomb. Thus, President Truman, no slouch as a politician, wanted to make sure there would be no "indiscriminate" bombing in Korea and that only military targets would be hit. (Futrell, pp 41-42.)

77. A convivial type who enjoyed good food and conversation, Stratemeyer often gave dinner parties at his home. As will be seen, there are numerous entries in his diary about various parties given by him and his wife, Annalee.

78. Banfill spent World War II in intelligence assignments. Just before coming to the Far East, he was Deputy Commandant, Armed Forces Staff College. He was with 20AF less than a month, July 16-August 4, before becoming Deputy for Intelligence, FEAF.

**FRIDAY
7 July
1950**

As of noon, released General Partridge who will return to command of Fifth Air Force. General Eubank appointed vice commander. USAF group depart for Washington 1340.

1440 Colonel Van Meter called Colonel Bunker[79] the ADC to CINCFE re: Colonel Van Meter explained to Colonel Bunker that numerous correspondents had requested a press conference with me as they believe that as air commander on CINCFE's staff, I should be able to give the American public something of the first ten days of air operations over Korea. Another request for an interview was received by me from Mr. Harry F. Kern, the foreign editor of *Newsweek*, re his doing a personalized story for his magazine. Colonel Bunker was told by Colonel Van Meter that he (Colonel Van Meter) had contacted Colonel Echols (PIO for CINCFE)[80] on several occasions requesting info whether CINCFE had any objections to my holding a press conference or holding interviews and to date he (Colonel Van Meter) had not had a reply of any kind. While Colonel Van Meter was on the telephone, Colonel Bunker said he would speak to CINCFE re same, which apparently he did, because when Colonel Bunker returned he told Colonel Van Meter that CINCFE had no objections to my either granting interviews or holding a press conference.

General O'Donnell arrives this evening (1900 hours, Haneda) and I have directed he report to me at 8:30 A.M. in time for the briefing. Colonel Nuckols[81] due to arrive, accompanied by his wife, and he will be appointed PIO.

Complimented by General Almond, Chief of Staff, GHQ, FEC, on our news release as of today which started out - "Far East Air Forces has now completed 1,100 sorties." He directed we back it up with some pictures which we are doing soonest.

I told PIO that he could release the name of the bomber commander immediately after his arrival tonite.

3:00 P.M. had interview by *Newsweek* foreign editor, Mr. Harry F. Kern. I gave him background on what we have done, what we are doing and what we contemplate doing.

Sent memo to CINCFE requesting he send following radio to Collins[82], personal from MacArthur:

Due to current situation in this theater and the recent decision of Secretary of Defense that SCARWAF [Special Category Army Personnel with Air Force] units would remain with D/A [Department of the Army], it is essential that immediate action be taken to supply SCARWAF personnel for Far East Air Forces units as they are under strength both in numbers and quality.[83] Requirement for runway rehabilitation and extension, taxiways, hardstands, and communications facilities in Korea, Japan and Okinawa is urgent and is far beyond capabilities of FEAF SCARWAF

---

79. Col Laurence L. Bunker, MacArthur's aide-de-camp.

80. Col Marion P. Echols.

81. Col W.P. Nuckols.

82. Gen J. Lawton Collins, U.S. Army chief of staff. Collins commanded the 25th Infantry Division in the Pacific in late 1942 and early 1943. In 1944, he took command of the VII Corps in Europe. Other assignments following the war included; Chief of Staff, Army Field Forces; Army chief of information; deputy chief of staff to General Eisenhower; vice chief to General Bradley; and on Oct. 1, 1949, Chief of Staff, U.S. Army.

83. These personnel were aviation engineer troops that were recruited, trained, and assigned to units by the Army but were charged against Air Force strength. Two aviation engineer group headquarters and service

units as currently manned. Stratemeyer sent personal message to Vandenberg on this subject 5 July 50 and Department of Air Force is familiar with detailed manning requirements for these units. I urge that you take immediate action to supply the required personnel as I can give him no help at this time.

Issued memo to my Deputy for Operations:

Navy-Land-Based Aircraft and Navy Carrier-Based Aircraft - Operational Control.... We must obtain the results of Navy reconnaissance and operations immediately upon completion. You will take the necessary steps to contact Admiral Joy to see that they are delivered by air courier and, in turn, rushed to the Chief of Staff, United States Air Force. We must be very careful when we give the Navy targets and a section of North Korea in which to operate that it does not interfere with and is well coordinated with the operations of our three B–29 medium bomber groups.... All land-based Navy aviation and carrier-based, except those units used for anti-submarine operations, will be under my operational control. You will take the necessary steps to see that this is done. I have written a memo to General MacArthur today recommending same. When any Navy units are based ashore, except the P2V squadron to be based at Johnson, they must have their own support ashore as we will be unable to support them operationally. Make this clear.

Sending to CINCFE (dated 8 July), subject: "Navy Unit." Text of memo follows:

It is my understanding that the Navy contemplates bringing into your theater some land-based aircraft (CVE's [escort carriers] - fighters); also, as you know, the Seventh Fleet contemplates another strike with air at your direction in North Korea. I request that all land-based naval aviation and carrier-based aviation when operating over North Korea or from Japan, except those units used for anti-submarine operations be placed under my operational control. The land-based fighters based in either Japan or Korea will in turn be placed under the operational control of the Commanding General Fifth Air Force. In the case of the carrier-based aviation in order that proper coordination can be maintained with my Bomber Command (B–29s) and with the Fifth Air Force, I must be able to direct their operations, including the targets to be hit and the area in which they must operate. I urge your immediate approval and that both Admiral Struble and Admiral Joy be so advised. Should you so desire, I am on call for any discussion on this subject.[84]

---

companies, five aviation engineer battalions, and one aviation engineer maintenance company were assigned to FEAF. Unfortunately, these units were ill-trained and ill-equipped for what they were being asked to do. When the Korean War began, these units had only 2,322 officers and men assigned as compared to a war-strength authority of 4,315. In mid-July, the first of some 870 specialists arrived in Japan, and any SCARWAF people slated to rotate home were kept in the Far East. It was not until September that FEAF was allowed to reorganize its aviation engineer units under new increased-strength TO/Es. Despite this increase, SCARWAF units remained a problem area throughout the war. (Futrell, pp 62, 72-73.)

84. Stratemeyer would not gain operational control of the Navy air units. Admirals Joy and Struble felt that giving Stratemeyer "operational control" of their air units was asking too much of them. The often acrimonious

(Sending copy of my memo to CINCFE to CSAF with an informal note forwarding same for his info and also thanking him for sending the Wolfe party.)

1750. General Dean called from Korea and gave me four targets over which he wanted air support. Apparently as has been shown by test, our bazookas can not penetrate the Soviet tank. Report received that during a penetration test, starting at 30 yards, our fire failed to penetrate and then only at a distance of 10 feet. General Dean's targets were all mostly on arteries - rail, ferry crossing and the road between P'yŏngta'ek and Osan. The latter target we had already scheduled, but the other three I have to [schedule] Ops for follow through.

Weather unfavorable; two F–80s lost; missions directed against factories in the North, bridges, convoys, and troop movements. F–82 on an "intruder mission" in the Inch'ŏn area dropped one napalm bomb; results believed by pilot to be good. Reported by returning flyers that rocket fire from planes does not appear to penetrate Soviet tanks.

SATURDAY
8 July
1950

Major General O'Donnell arrived.[85] Attended briefing at which time General Robertson reported how to disable Soviet tanks. These are the tanks that are of a 60-ton type, and about 21 feet in length. General Robertson stated they should be hit in the tread from the side.

Word received that Colonel Nuckols, the PIO I requested, would not arrive until the end of next week.

Dispatched copy of my memo to CINCFE to General Vandenberg in GHQ; after the briefing, took O'Donnell to meet CINCFE and heard another superior dissertation re his problems. After leaving MacArthur's headquarters returned to the office briefly and then O'Donnell and I went to the house for lunch.

2:30 appointment with Colonel Withers[86] (PIO for Eighth Army) and Mr. Donald Morrison, Shell Oil Company representative. My discussion with two gentlemen re the Doolittle's proposed visit to the Far East while on their round-the-world tour.[87] Colonel Withers will call my PIO upon arrival of General and Mrs. Doolittle and my PIO will call Annalee.

The first use of napalm brought about these results (I have been urging its use now for about a week): 2 F–51s on a bombing and strafing mission report using 1 x 6 napalm and destroyed: 4 small tanks, 5 trucks with 35 ft trailers. Four vehicles exploded - other equipment damaged by 50 cal. fire.

---

roles and missions hearings in the late 1940s left wounds that had not yet healed. The Navy harbored very strong feelings against the Air Force controlling their aircraft. Out of these hearings, the Air Force had been given the task of interdiction of enemy ground forces and communications. Only through a rather complicated and convoluted procedure would the Navy be allowed to participate on interdiction missions. In Korea, however, there was no time to go through these involved steps. Seeking to break the Air Force-Navy impasse, General MacArthur issued a directive on July 15 giving Stratemeyer "coordination control" of Air Force and Navy air operations. (This control will be discussed later.) (Futrell, pp 49-50; Field, pp 111-112.)

85. O'Donnell was officially designated Commanding General, Far East Bomber Command (Provisional) this day. (FEAF General Orders No. 30, 8 Jul 1950.)

86. Col William P. Withers had been Chief, Information Section, 8th Army since 1949. Later in the month he became Armor Officer at 8th Army headquarters.

87. The purpose of Doolittle's proposed visit is unknown. At this time he was a special assistant to General Vandenberg, advising on matters concerning the Air Materiel Command and the establishment of the Research and Development Command. (The latter was established on January 23, 1950, and redesignated as the Air Research and Development Command in September 1950.) Doolittle was also a member of the Air Force's Scientific Advisory Board.

Now that General Partridge has joined his command and is in close contact with General Dean in Korea and General O'Donnell has reported in and has been placed in command of the FEAF Bomber Command, my headquarters will now get out of the operations business and divide all our missions between the Fifth Air Force and the FEAF Bomber Command.

SUNDAY 9 July 1950

Sent two memoranda to COMNAVFE:

(1) Sorry but could not afford to withdraw a helicopter from my Air-Sea Rescue Units to replace the one Seventh Fleet lost inasmuch as my bombers covering distances over water, etc. *(2)* that which is quoted in full hereafter: "Your attention is invited to the attached clipping headlined 'Navy Flier Doubts Subs Near Korea,' from the Pacific Stars & Stripes of Saturday, 8 July.[88] It appears to me that this sort of thing is in bad taste. We are trying to operate a unified team out here under General of the Army Douglas MacArthur and such statements certainly don't add to the unification of such a team. There are many things in the reported results of any strike that could be questioned. Every remark I have made with reference to the Navy's strikes has been complimentary and that goes for my staff and officers. For God's sake, let's don't get into a service controversy out here where we are pulling for one cause and that is the destruction of the Communist Korean Forces in Korea.

1500 hours, Vice Admiral Sprague,[89] COMAIRPAC with Rear Admiral Hardison,[90] COMNAVMARIANAS, and accompanying Navy officers. (Also Capt. R.W. Ruble, USN, Capt. F. H. Turner, USN, Col. S.C. Dyer, USMC, Capt. A.S. Hill, USN & Capt. A.S. Heyward, USN.)[91]

1745 interview with Miss Charlotte Knight,[92] *Air Force* magazine's Far East representative and also Far East representative for *Collier's*. I cautioned her that anything she wrote she must be very careful of security. I gave her some background.

Red Forces in Korea pushing steadily; our ground forces being isolated (those advance positions) or driven back. Our infantry battalion near Ch'ŏnan cut off.

President Truman names CINCFE to command all United Nations forces fighting Communist Northern Koreans. Ground situation dismal.

---

88. This short article, an interview with Air Group 5's commanding officer, Comdr Harvey P. Lanham, was actually rather innocuous. The subject of submarines took up only a couple of paragraphs, with Lanham saying that what some B–29 fliers took for submarines were probably gunboats. (Cpl Larry Sakamoto, "Navy Flier Doubts Subs near Korea," *Stars and Stripes* [Pacific Edition], July 8, 1950, p 1.)

89. Vice Adm Thomas L. Sprague, Commander Air Force, Pacific.

90. Rear Adm O.B. Hardison, Commander Naval Forces, Marianas.

91. Capt Richard W. Ruble had been an aide to the Secretary of the Navy but had just been appointed Commander, Carrier Division 15; Capts Frank Turner and Alexander S. Heyward, Jr., were on Admiral Sprague's staff; Capt Arthur S. Hill was Navy liaison officer at FEAF headquarters; probably Col Edward C. Dyer, Operations Officer, 1st MAW, and later, Deputy Chief of Staff for Close Air Support, X Corps.

92. Two of her articles, one in *Air Force* and the other in *Collier's*, appeared in August and September. The *Collier's* article described a mission on which she flew. The *Air Force* article was a sympathetic but candid story of the problems facing FEAF. Stratemeyer hammered home to Ms. Knight that FEAF's mission had been the air defense of Japan and that lack of materiel (particularly planes and pilots) hampered any possibility of offensive warfare. Nevertheless, Stratemeyer pointed out that without the Air Force, South Korea would have been overrun. (Charlotte Knight, "Air War in Korea," *Air Force*, August 1950, pp 21-34.)

FEAF missions concentrating on bridges, etc. Tabulation report showed 23 tanks destroyed, 13 damaged, 2 large guns knocked out, 92 trucks destroyed and 43 damaged, etc. No aircraft losses.

MONDAY
10 July
1950

Received following reply from COMNAVFE with reference to their press release and my memo to him of 9 July:

If any of young Lanham's statements are generally interpreted to imply real criticism of his Air Force flying comrades, I am sure that I would speak for both of us in expressing sincere regrets. Both services, at the pilots' level, have high mutual regard for each other's professional abilities and I trust that we will avoid any tendency to become over-sensitive about the remarks attributed to relatively junior individuals who are not fully experienced in dealing with press conferences. The flying that your people have been doing the last two weeks is described by my air officers as superb. The United States Air Force officers in our carrier air groups have made an enviable reputation as outstanding "operators." We certainly will not let any small matter of unconfirmed quotes mar this high mutual regard.

Received a bit of "static" from the C of S [Chief of Staff], GHQ - particularly my deputy for operations, General Crabb, which prompted me to write and discuss following memo with CINCFE:

During the past war you had great confidence in General Kenney[93] and then in General Whitehead[94] who followed General Kenney. It is my desire to perform in the same manner and to gain the same confidence that you had in them. What the Far East Air Forces have done so far in 15 days, operating from bases in Japan and Okinawa, I consider outstanding. It is my opinion that had not we gone into action when we did in conjunction with the Ground Forces that you have been able to get into South Korea that the whole of South Korea would now be in the hands of the North Koreans. Per your instructions given to me last night by the Chief of Staff, General Almond, I have changed the B–29 targets for today to tanks, vehicles and troops on the roads and railroads north of Ch'ŏnan; this is to be done without control. If we are successful in gaining contract with General Partridge's and General Dean's tactical control group and targets are designated south of Ch'ŏnan, certain B–29s will be diverted to these targets. Yesterday, today and until further notice all effort of the Fifth Air Force is and will be in direct support of our ground troops in South Korea. It is my opinion and unless you direct otherwise, I will operate every combat airplane in the Far East Air Forces in support of ground troops against only those targets in battlefield support as suggested by the Fifth Air Force advanced CP [Command Post] in conjunction with General Dean's tactical air direction center.

---

93. During World War II, Gen George C. Kenney commanded 5AF and Allied Air Forces in the Southwest Pacific, and subsequently, the Far East Air Forces. From almost the beginning he had enjoyed a good relationship with MacArthur. From April 1946 to October 1948, he was commander of SAC. He then was Commander, Air University until his retirement in August 1951.

94. Lt Gen Ennis C. Whitehead took over command of 5AF from Kenney in June 1944. Whitehead also replaced Kenney as FEAF commander in December 1945. He, too, had a good relationship with MacArthur. Stratemeyer relieved Whitehead as FEAF commander in April 1949.

There are now in Japan and Okinawa, in the 92d Medium Bomb Group, Yokota, Japan, fifteen (15) B–29s and in the 22d Medium Bomb Group at Kadena, Okinawa, twenty-six (26) B–29s. I have been informed by General O'Donnell that we will be able to fly our first mission Friday, 14 July. Your directions to me will be conducted in the most efficient manner that we can plan and I am sure that it is not your intention to tell me how to do the job. My leaders and I are fully competent to direct and control the Far East Air Forces. I urge your support in this confidence.

Following the Ops briefing in GHQ, I talked to CINCFE and added this note to the above quoted memo:

Memorandum for the record - 10 July 1950 - I talked with General MacArthur for about twenty (20) minutes - 1135 to 1155 hours - this date and he gave me entire confidence and support in every question I raised. He stated he had the same confidence in me that he ever had in Generals Kenney and Whitehead and emphasized that I would run my show regardless of instructions as I saw fit.[95]

Dispatched the following redline message (Top Secret) to CSAF and COMGEN [Commanding General] SAC:

Redline personal to Vandenberg from Stratemeyer: reference today's B–29 bomber mission CINCFE considers and I agree ground situation in Korea so critical that every possible effort must be used to break up motorized concentrations on roads in battle areas. He fully understands that this is emergency procedure only. He is most enthusiastic about the results obtained from the Far East Air Forces since our commitment to combat.

(Redline to CSAF: originated 1345K [local time]; placed on the wires 1355K; received at Hq USAF 1406K; received by Vandenberg 1418K - total elapsed time - 33 minutes!)

Received word from staff C–54 (I had sent Hill and Melgard on 8 July to Hickam to pick up the Craigies) that it would land tomorrow, 11 July at 1100 hours at Haneda.[96] Annalee will meet them on my behalf complete with flowers and our offer of hospitality, etc. Maddocks,[97] Craigie's administrative assistant, will meet the plane and see that they are taken care of.

---

95. The FEC staff was Army-dominated, with few Air Force officers in positions of responsibility. This was a carryover from World War II when MacArthur never had, nor wanted, a joint staff. However, at that time, air matters had been left to Kenney to handle. Much of this same thinking and staff setup was utilized in the immediate post-war years. MacArthur told Stratemeyer what he wanted done, but it was up to Stratemeyer to see how it was carried out. However, when South Korea was attacked, there were many officers, of which General Almond was a particular offender, who tried to take the direction of air operations upon themselves. This, of course, was a circumvention of Stratemeyer's position as FEAF commander. Most of the Army officers had little knowledge of Air Force philosophy and/or operations and wished to run the war from Tokyo. General Almond ordered that any requests for air support had to go through GHQ before being passed on to FEAF and 5AF. This was a slow, laborious, and utterly inefficient way to run tactical air operations, and Stratemeyer quickly objected to this and other attempts to usurp his authority. Fortunately, MacArthur saw the fallacy of letting some of his Army subordinates run an Air Force show and allowed Stratemeyer to act as he saw fit on Air Force matters. If MacArthur had not had confidence in Stratemeyer, this matter might not have ended in the Air Force's favor. (Futrell, pp 45, 48.)

96. Maj Clayton C. Hill, Stratemeyer's personal pilot; 1st Lt Robert B. Melgard; Maj Gen Laurence C. Craigie, the incoming FEAF vice commander for administration and plans.

97. Maj Robert. A. Maddocks.

At 1700 hours held a meeting with the press. Following are my remarks:

Because of the many requests that have come in to my PIO, Colonel Van Meter, for an interview with me, I am holding this meeting this afternoon. I have here some very carefully prepared statistical data which I have had mimeographed - copies of which will be given to you. I will read it to you so that in case there are any questions that you desire to ask, I will attempt to clear them up. I urge upon you the importance of security and that you not publish anything that I do not cover this afternoon. I am sure you understand that during World War II there were cases where information was published which gave great comfort to the enemy and brought about the killing and wounding of many Americans. We have now been at this business of war in Korea for the past 15 days and when you consider that we have operated from bases in Japan and other bases, the great effort that has been brought to bear upon the North Korean armed forces, in my opinion, has not only been outstanding, but, in many many instances unbelievable and almost miraculous. We have brought air power in the form of United States Air Force jets, light bombers, medium bombers, night fighters and day fighters to bear on the enemy both in the air and on the ground wherever it has been necessary. The only deterrent to these operations thus far has been - WEATHER. When it is good in Korea, it is usually bad in Japan, and when it is good in Japan, it has been bad in Korea. In spite of this, though, our American officers and airmen have performed so superbly - both in daring and efficiency - that I have nothing but praise - repeat - praise for them. Every request that General of the Army Douglas MacArthur has indicated as a desire has been met in spite of the bad weather, the long flights to the battle area, and the instrument conditions under which many, many, many of our sorties have had to land. The Fifth Air Force, under the command of Major General Earle E. Partridge, has carried the brunt of the air war so far. Just last night, one of his F–80s returned to base and it took 11 passes by GCA [ground controlled approach], the last one being with flares, to get him down. This was successful. Recently, one of our flights returned to base with 4 jet airplanes; GCA was not operating; the ceiling was 100 feet with one mile visibility and light rain; and the flight commander brought his entire flight in safely. Our RAAF comrades with their 77th Fighter Squadron have performed magnificently from the date they were put under my operational control. Our transport pilots, C–54, C–46, and C–47, who carry out their mission over the battle zone from Suwŏn to Pusan, do so with daring, with skill and with bravery. As you gentlemen know, a unit under my command is the 19th Bomb Wing serving under the orders of Major General Alvan C. Kincaid. From its base in the Far East, it has daily - except for two days of bad weather - done a great job over both North and South Korea. The South Koreans, although only a handful, are doing the job with their few Mustangs. Naval aviation under Admiral Struble, on air strikes 3 and 4 July, effectively performed their mission. The Army's liaison pilots are daily flying missions over the combat zone, assisting us in Far East Air Forces as well as the Army in its command and staff job. I desire to call to your attention the great work that has been done by my entire staff, my logistics command under Brigadier General John P. Doyle, and the weather and communications people. Without this laborious and technical effort we could not function. Theirs has been a job well done too. I guarantee to you gentlemen that the Far East Air Forces is a well integrated team; furthermore, the Far East Air Forces is a part of a bigger team and that is the Far East Command made up of the Army, the Navy and the Air Force. Under the great leadership and command ability of our boss, General of the Army Douglas MacArthur and all his assistants, I am confident, that because we are in the right and have the backing of the world democracies and the United Nations, we will be successful in our operations on the ground, at sea, and in the air against the Communists of North Korea.

Following is the matter I quoted (bulletin circulated to all pressmen present) and read at the meeting:

Far East Air Forces Activity Report, 25 June to 10 July 50: Since the beginning of Korean operations, weather has been continuously deterrent to FEAF operational effort. In spite of this, FEAF combat aircraft have flown a total of 1,570 sorties. These figures do not include cargo missions by C–54s, C–46s and C–47s. FEAF combat losses since the beginning of operations total 20. These do not include 5 C–54 aircraft or the one Australian Mustang reported missing. FEAF personnel losses to 1100, 10 July, total 26, including officers and airmen. Total number of aircraft claimed by FEAF, the Navy, the South Korean Air Force and ground troops are: DESTROYED: FEAF 17, NAVY 5, S. KOREANS 1, GROUND FIRE 1; total 24. PROBABLY DESTROYED: FEAF 5, NAVY 0, S. KOREANS 0, GROUND FIRE 0, total 5. DAMAGED: FEAF 4, NAVY 8, S. KOREANS 0, GROUND FIRE 0, total 12. Breakdown of the above totals is as follows (does not include naval air): SORTIES (flown) 128 B–29; 212 B–26; 1078 F–80; 100 F–82; 52 F–51 (including RAAF) - 1570 total. COMBAT: (Losses) 0 B–29; 8 B–26; 10 F–80; 2 F–82; 0 F–51. Total 20. PERSONNEL (Losses) Dead - 7 officers, 2 airmen; Wounded 5 officers, 0 airmen; Missing 8 officers and 4 airmen. Total 20 officers and 6 airmen. Total damage inflicted by Far East Air Forces, including RAAF (does not include naval air strikes): DESTROYED: 71 tanks, 272 trucks, 14 locomotives, 0 railway cars, 16 other vehicles, 2 buses, 9 half tracks, 2 troop trains, 65 box cars. PROBABLY DESTROYED: 3 tanks, 22 trucks, 0 locomotives, 4 railway cars, 8 other vehicles, 1 bus, 0 half tracks, - troop trains, - box cars. DAMAGED 49 tanks, 183 trucks, 10 locomotives, 10 railway cars, 6 other vehicles, 1 bus, 2 half tracks, 1 troop train, 12 box cars. TOTAL: 123 tanks, 477 trucks, 24 locomotives, 14 railway cars, 30 other vehicles, 4 buses, 11 half tracks, 3 troop trains, 77 box cars. In addition to the reports shown in the above figures, Fifth Air Force fighter and ground attack aircraft have attacked ground troops with unknown but considerable losses; blasted artillery positions; strafed and burned oil storage tanks, railroad tracks, inflicted damage on marshaling yards; and at all times, when weather permitted, given ground support to our troops. B–29 bombers have blasted important port installations at Chinnamp'o and Wŏnsan; major oil, nitrogen and other important industrial targets at Wŏnsan, Hŭngnam and P'yŏngyang; and major North Korean airfields and the largest South Korean airfield at Seoul.[98] Vital rail and highway bridges, both north and south of the 38th Parallel, have been destroyed. As a result of these missions, FEAF aircraft have held air

---

98. Chinnamp'o lies on North Korea's west coast at the mouth of the Taedong River. It was the site of some important metals producing plants. Although small, its harbor could take ships of almost any draft. On the opposite coast, Wŏnsan was a well-developed port and a major railway center. Concentrated here were North Korea's oil refineries. About 50 miles north of Wŏnsan is Hŭngnam, another major port. Its importance lay in the fact that it had the most

Lt. Ralph Hall taxis his bomb and rocket-laden F–51 for another ground attack mission.

superiority from the first and enemy activity has all but disappeared. Strategic strikes on rail, bridge and highway communications already have brought numerous reports of bottlenecks in North Korean transportation and damage resulting from these is being keenly felt by North Korean Forces in the forward area. Vital supplies such as gasoline and ammunition are known to be short and becoming short in many localities. By these efforts, FEAF has played an important role in slowing the North Korean southward march against the time when our own forces can be marshalled in sufficient strength to turn the tide. Given a break in the weather, an increased FEAF air potential will shortly make itself felt in no unmistakeable terms. The Air Force contribution up to now has been effective. Its effectiveness will increase immeasurably with each passing week.

Members of the press who heard my above statements were: Russell Brines, Associated Press; Murray Moler, United Press; Howard M. Handleman, International News Service; Frank Gibney, *Time-Life*; Bob Frew, *Air Force Times*; William Costello, Columbia Broadcasting System; Lindsay Parrott, *New York Times*; Raymond F. Falk, North American Newspaper Alliance. Members of my staff who were present at the time were: General Crabb, D/O [Director of Operations], Colonel Rogers, D/I [Director of Intelligence], Colonel Van Meter, PIO, Major Maddocks, Adm. Asst to VC, Major Hower and Mr. Smith, PIO.[99]

After my meeting with press, immediately called CINCFE and thru the ADC [aide-de-camp], Colonel Bunker, at 1740 hours informed him the results of a B–29 mission which hit visually from 1355 hours to 1530 hours and which encountered

extensive basic-chemical and light-metals industry in the Far East. P'yŏngyang, as the capital of North Korea and its largest city, was a major target from the beginning. It was also the site of a large arsenal complex (second in size in the Far East only to Mukden in Manchuria), extensive railway yards, and an aircraft maintenance center.

99. Maj Henry H. Hower, a FEAF staff officer; Smith's full name is unknown.

no flak and no fighters. Results reported: 14 excellent; 2 poor. This call was at CINCFE's request. At 1745 hours called General Almond to read him the report of the mission.

Mission reports from the daily ops sheet indicate an excellent show for the Air Force over targets. However, notice recurrence of reports that our aircraft "unable to contact controller" when in controller area.

TUESDAY
11 July
1950

From radio coverage and newspaper coverage, the press meeting accomplished the desired results of getting the Air Force story across. PIO reports "very favorable" reaction. First press release on inhumane treatment of POWs [prisoners of war]. Bodies of 7 American soldiers, "hands tied behind them were found by the roadside in territory recaptured from the North Koreans Monday. Each had been killed by a bullet in the face." Bodies found by a 1st Lt. Gates.[100]

The results of the missions yesterday proved that we were in error in putting the B–29s on a close ground support target. However, since General MacArthur personally directed same, we did it yesterday and will do it again today. Because of the B–29 strike, all of our B–26s yesterday hit bridges and other targets that were B–29 targets. The B–26s should have been used on the columns, motorized vehicles, tanks, etc. They were used this way as a result of orders issued by General Partridge and General Dean in close contact with their forward CPs.

My vice commander, Major General Laurence C. Craigie, and Mrs. Craigie, arrive Haneda 0943 hours. They were met by Annalee, our offer of hospitality, and by Major R.A. Maddocks, Craigie's administrative assistant here in FEAF. Also aboard were Colonels Lee and Botts, both to be assigned to Fifth Air Force - tentatively Lee goes into the air defense slot there and Botts will go to the 374th Troop Carrier at Tachikawa.[101] Melgard reports 7 other colonels, all part of the USAF augmentation of FEAF, awaiting transportation out here from Hickam.

Generals Collins, Vandenberg, Rawlings, McKee, and Smith due to arrive tomorrow night at Haneda for a look-see and assist on our problems.[102]

1830 hours an appointment with CINCFE: following items are those I will discuss with him.

   1. On 13 July 50, initial strikes by FEAF Bomber Command (Prov)[isional] will be on the Wŏnsan Marshaling Yards and Rising Sun Petroleum Company. The 92d and 22d Bomb Groups will make up the strike force. Succeeding strikes on targets indicated on charts (Also took along several target photos.) will be assigned to facilitate a systematic collapse of a target system.

   2. The 92d and 22d Bomb Groups from SAC have a high altitude all-weather capability.

---

100. Lt Delbert C. Gates of the 24th Division. This incident took place near Chŏnŭi.

101. Col Joseph D. Lee, took command of the 6132d Tactical Air Control Group (Provisional) on July 14, and later commanded the 6151st Air Base Unit; Col Herbert A. Bott, became CO of the 374th TCG on July 22.

102. Lt Gen Edwin W. Rawlings, Deputy Chief of Staff, Comptroller, Headquarters USAF; Maj Gen Frederic H. Smith, Jr., Chief, Plans and Programs Section, Headquarters USAF; Maj Gen William F. McKee, Assistant Vice Chief of Staff, USAF. The President had directed Collins and Vandenberg to obtain first-hand information on the personnel, materiel, and monetary requirements of the U.S. forces in the Far East (specifically Japan and Korea). From this information the President and the JCS could evaluate what exactly was needed and what could be given. ("History of the JCS," Vol. III, pp 190-191.)

The shoreline of Korea is dimly visible in the center of the photo as a formation of 92d BG Superfortresses head for their North Korean target.

3. Bomber Command will be given an opportunity to select targets within the systems except as otherwise indicated by FEAF.

4. General Partridge advised General Eubank by telephone today, at the present time, he had more fighter-bomber and fighter-strafer effort than profitable targets existed in the battle area. It is our opinion that this is an example of which we are right proud - that is we gave the working people on the ground much more than their needs.

5. Discuss the B–29 effort yesterday in support of the ground troops versus the B–26 effort on the isolation of the battlefield by the destruction of bridges.

6. Our target systems have now been completed to such a point that General O'Donnell, my bomber commander, can select and destroy targets regardless of weather.

7. I have issued direct orders to him (General O'Donnell) that no urban area targets will be attacked except on direct orders from you through me.

8. Again, since our first strike targets are bound to kill and wound civilians, I recommend that an announcement be made by you urging them to vacate all urban centers that are close to military targets; namely, railroad centers, airfields, heavy industry locations, harbors and sub bases, and POL [petroleum, oil, and lubricants] storage facilities and refineries.

Ground forces take beating in tank battle; those advanced armored groups were caught by Soviet-type tanks and gunfire that penetrated our tanks. From the press reports, vicious trading of blows, with our forces having to give way.

Craigie reports on job 12 July; they are coming to dinner and lunch with us.

Nuckols arrives, unannounced, via PanAm; billeted at the Imperial.

WEDNESDAY

12 July

1950

Following memo delivered via officer courier to General Willoughby personally, Imperial Hotel, Room 248.

Memo to CINCFE subject: Announcement to the North Koreans - *(1)* Reference your approval of my recommendation of last evening it is recommended that: *(a)* All available channels of communication be used by you to notify those responsible for current operations of the North Korean armed forces that it is your intent to destroy by air bombardment all railroad centers, airfields, heavy industry locations, port facilities and sub bases, POL storage facilities, refineries and railroads and highways used by their armed forces. *(b)* All persons be warned to leave such areas and remain at points sufficiently far removed to avoid needless loss of life. *(c)* The sole action on the part of North Korea which will prevent such action on your part is the withdrawal of all North Korean armed forces above the 38th Parallel, complete cessation of all hostile activity, and an agreement by the North Korean government to abide by any future decisions of the United Nations.

1310 General Almond forwarded the following message at express wish of CINCFE:

He (CINCFE) has noticed in a radio from USAFIK to CINCFE, dtd 12 July, #ROB 312, Part 2, in which General Dean reports that the 1st Korean Army Corps, south of the river on the general line (1043 - 1534 to 1172 - 1567), pressure decreasing on the front.[103] The 1st Division lost all ammo and some trucks as a result of a B–29 raid (General MacArthur interpreted 1st Division to be the 1st North Korean Division) and expresses high appreciation for those B–29 strikes. In Part 4 of the same radio, General Dean again expresses his appreciation for the close support of FEAF planes against railways, etc. and commends FEAF on excellent help.

1500 hours in conference with General Partridge who reported to me today on his operations thus far in Korea and Japan, and received the following information from me: *(1)* I directed that while General Vandenberg was here we would not discuss the improper use of the B–29s as I agreed with General MacArthur to use them as close support because of the ground situation. *(2)* I informed him that the *Boxer* would bring to Japan 150 F–51s, 150 pilots and 400 mechanics.[104] (I have just learned that it will sail from San Diego, today, 12 July.) Sent *Boxer's* departure date to General Partridge. *(3)* I asked him if we here in Hqs were hindering his operations in any way and, if so, how and what we can do to help him do his job. He gave me his plans for the reduced air defense of

---

103. Although there had been an earlier command designated USAFIK, this message refers to a new ground command established on July 4 under Major General Dean. The main force under Dean's command was his own 24th Division plus a smattering of small units. USAFIK was short-lived, being replaced on July 12 when Lt Gen Walton H. Walker, commander of the Eighth Army, took over. Walker's command was then referred to as EUSAK (Eighth U.S. Army in Korea).

104. The Essex-class carrier *Boxer*. In reply to General Stratemyer's requests for more men and materiel, these F–51s (actually only 145 plus 6 L–5s), along with pilots and mechanics, were recalled from the Air National Guard. Shipment by carrier was the most expeditious method of moving large quantities of aircraft and men. (Field, p 89.)

Japan which I approved. He called my attention to the fact that he had heard a rumor to the effect that we were forming an engineer command. I told him that we had heard nothing of it and that if any such command would be formed, I would so advise him as it is his business, would be at his recommendation, and under him and not under FEAF. *(5)* I informed him that his plan for the use of fighter squadrons from Clark and Naha was approved and awaited only his request for the movement orders. *(6)* I informed him and directed that he pass it down along the line that there would be no inter-service criticism by any of us. *(7)* I warned him that I was sure General Vandenberg would want to come direct to his Advance CP to discuss his plans with him; however, General MacArthur had requested that I discourage any trip to Korea by General Vandenberg. There has been too much publicity re his arrival and General MacArthur bases his request to me on that publicity.

The following memorandum for the record [underlined in the original] dated 12 July 1950, subject: "Fighter Defenses for the Japanese Home Islands," was given to General Partridge:

The following arrangements will be made by the Fifth Air Force for the defense of the Japanese home islands. At Misawa, Johnson, and Itazuke Air Bases, there will be established a minimum of one squadron of F–80s and one flight of F–82 aircraft. During the hours of daylight, when good weather prevails, four F–80 aircraft will be maintained on a strip-alert status. During inclement weather and during darkness, at least two F–82 aircraft will be maintained on the alert. The remainder of the F–80 squadrons and the F–82 flights not required for the regular alerts will be retained in the local area and will be prepared to engage in combat operations in a minimum of time. By this arrangement, normal training and transition can be accomplished, but the possibility that the aircraft might be called upon for combat operations will be kept constantly in mind. As soon as the number of pilots and aircraft permit an additional squadron of F–80s will be stationed in the Tokyo area and the strength of the F–82 aircraft in that area will also be proportionately increased.

Mission reports - continued strafing, bombing of targets and support of ground units. However, member of F–80 flight reporting in from a strafing mission in Chungin [?, probably Ch'ungju] area, the target being Chungin area, that destroyed 4 trucks, 1 half-track, and a jeep-type vehicle; damaged 1 truck and saw considerable vehicles between Ansŏng and Yangsŏng all previously knocked out. Contacted by B–29 who reported being attacked by 2 Yaks and crew was bailing out. Had insufficient fuel to go to their aid. All crew of B–29 bailed out. Recommend no flights to same area because no targets of value.

Another report from a C–47 mission:

...cargo and passenger mission completed... Yaks over strip at Taejŏn; no attack; L–4 shot down two minutes west of field; crewmen evacuated to Kyushu. Guerrilla activity around strip.

General Stratemeyer greets the Air Force chief of staff, Gen. Hoyt S. Vandenberg, upon his arrival in Japan on July 13, 1950.

THURSDAY
13 July
1950

Lt. General Walker named CG [Commanding General] Eighth United States Army Korea (EUSAK).[105]

0700 Generals Vandenberg, Collins, and party (Lt. General Rawlings, Comp, USAF; Maj. Gen. F.H. Smith, Chief Plans & Programs Sec, USAF; Maj. Gen. Wm. F. McKee, Asst Vice CSUSAF; Rear Admiral Augustus J. Wellings, Deputy Dir, MSTS; Colonel Grussendorf, USAF; Colonel McHugh, USAF; Colonel Denson, G-4, USA; Lt. Col. Dickson, G-3, USA; and Lt. Col. Larsen, Aide.)[106] arrive Haneda. Greeting party: General MacArthur, Walker, Almond; Admiral Joy and myself. Party to go direct from Haneda to GHQ for conference.

1000 hours, our briefing for General Vandenberg and party.

1100 take off, in staff C–54 with Vandenberg party for Itazuke. Left approx[imately] 1500 hours, C–47 for Taegu; returned Korea 1930; (returned Haneda 0030 hours, 14 July.)

Ground forces withdrawn to Kŭm River.

First raid by FEAF Bomber Command (Prov); 56 B–29s out of 57 on target mission, bombing by radar, the Wŏnsan marshaling yards. Results unobserved because of weather. 22d and 92d Medium Bomb Groups participated.

---

105. When Walker took command of EUSAK, he controlled a force of approximately 18,000 Americans and 58,000 Koreans. (Appleman, pp 109-110.)

106. Rear Adm Wellings, Military Sea Transportation Service vice commander; Col Richard A. Grussendorf, General Vandenberg's executive; Col Godfrey D. McHugh, Vandenberg's aide-de-camp; Col L.A. Denson was in the Office of the Assistant Chief of Staff, G-4, U.S. Army; Lt Col D.D. Dickson was in the Office of the Assistant Chief of Staff, G-3, U.S. Army; Lt Col Stanley R. Larsen, General Collins aide-de-camp.

Weather generally unfavorable. One C–47 crashed after unloading cargo at Taejŏn; aircraft damaged beyond repair; crew returned to base.

One B–29 aircraft lost due to mechanical reasons; no details available at present, but six of the crew picked up by fishing boat.

Got to bed at 0300 hours, the morning of the 14th.

FRIDAY
14 July
1950

Departed Mayeda House[107] at 0830 and proceeded to General O'Donnell's FEAF Bomber Command headquarters.[108] General Vandenberg conferred with General O'Donnell, his staff and Colonel Zoller[109] (base commander) for about 1 hour 15 minutes. A very fine congratulatory letter was drafted, patting the FEAF Bomber Command, plus the 19th Medium Bomb Group, on the back. Text of letter:

Subj: Recognition of Achievement.

(1) I was delighted to find upon my arrival in the Far East yesterday morning that you had already launched ninety-eight percent of your available bomber strength on your initial strike against strategic targets in North Korea, only nine days after receiving word in the United States, 8,000 miles away, that you were to move to the Far East Command. Your accomplishment clearly indicates the mobility and striking power of the United States Air Force. It is in the highest tradition of our service and superbly demonstrates the high degree of esprit, mobility and technical competence that you have achieved. *(2.)* The 500 tons of bombs you delivered in the face of adverse weather conditions, which necessitated one hundred percent radar bombing, should give food for thought to those in the world who would violate by military aggression the peace and independence of others. *(3.)* Please pass on to all members of your command my sincere congratulations. s/ Hoyt S. Vandenberg, General, USAF.

Departed Yokota and proceeded to FEAMCOM where we were met by General Doyle and while here General Vandenberg became familiar with our putting into commission all F–51s in storage - which was completed today. He observed the B-26 reconditioning, some eleven of which were under individual crew chief build up concurrently.

At 1100 hours departed FEAMCOM for Mayeda House where we had lunch, after which we proceeded to my office and General Vandenberg, with Generals McKee, Rawlings and Smith completed and signed a number of administrative messages to be sent to Washington. *Following from CSAF to AVC/S [Assistant Vice Chief of Staff] USAF, Top Secret, Redline, quoted in full:*

Redline to Norstad[110] from Vandenberg. Immediately upon arrival had conference with General MacArthur who outlined past actions and current and anticipated situation. He expressed satisfaction with Air Force

---

107. This was a so-called "U.S. house" — a fine house taken over for use by U.S. personnel.
108. At Yokota Air Base.
109. Col Virgil L. Zoller, then Yokota AB commander and later, 3d BW commander.
110. Lt Gen Lauris Norstad had been 20AF chief of staff, deputy chief of Air Staff, and assistant chief of Air Staff

contribution to date, calling it superior. I next visited Partridge at Itazuke. The Fifth Air Force is going all out under sound leadership. I talked to the pilots of two of the fighter groups engaged in continuous support missions. These young men have the old stuff on the ball. Group and squadron commanders display courageous leadership and amazing initiative and ingenuity. I visited Taegu, the first operational fighter field in Korea, now operating together with a small Korean force, fourteen F–51s. The Fifth plans to increase force there to four squadrons as soon as steelmat, engineer troops and equipment can be forwarded via the over-worked railroad from Pusan. It is estimated that this will be completed within two weeks. A strip on the east coast above Pusan, K-3, is operational today with two squadrons of the 35th Fighter Group with F–51s.[111] Eventually they plan to put both F–51s and F–80s on this strip. The theater will have made Army commitments to the limit of its resources by mid-August. Prior to that time the ZI [Zone of Interior] must have taken up the burden for all necessary reinforcements and replacements.

NEW SUBJECT. Expect to leave here today at 1400 arriving Washington early Saturday morning. Request Weyland meet me in my office at 1000 hours Saturday with Stearley.

NEW SUBJECT. Stratemeyer assures me that if we had aviation engineer units at nearly even full strength with proper SSNs[112] as our Air Force units, the operations from Korea would have been initiated from both strips last Friday. Our insistence on operational units rather than skeleton units paid dividends in our ability to go into action immediately. Believe this should be brought to the Secretary's immediate attention.

1330 hours, General Vandenberg had his appointment with General MacArthur at which time he very explicitly and masterfully explained to General MacArthur the use of ground support aviation and the use of strike B–29s. General MacArthur agreed with everything General Vandenberg said and so announced himself. He (General MacArthur) did however point out that there would be times when we would have to use B–29s in close support. General Vandenberg then departed for Haneda, and, with General Collins, boarded the Constellation after saying goodbye to General MacArthur and myself.

I advised General Hickey of our B–29 plan and he agrees that it is OK and proper.

During General Vandenberg's drafting of his redline to Norstad, he asked me how much sooner would we have had airfields operating in South Korea if we had had aviation engineer units at nearly even full strength with the proper SSNs. I told him Friday (this in concert with my Deputy for Materiel).

---

at AAF Headquarters in World War II. In October 1947, he became Deputy Chief of Staff for Operations, USAF, and since May 1950, also acting Vice Chief of Staff, USAF. The following October, he became Commander-in-Chief, USAFE.

111. Because of the wide variety in spelling of Korean place names, it was decided to assign each airfield in Korea a "K-site" number to provide an exact identification/location. The accompanying table shows K-sites in the Spring of 1951.

112. Now obsolete, the Specification Serial Number corresponds with an Air Force Specialty Code which identifies a related grouping of duties and tasks making up a job or specialty.

K-SITES	
K-1	Pusan West
K-2	Taegu No. 1
K-3	P'ŏhang-dong (Yŏng-ilman)
K-4	Sach'ŏn
K-5	Taejŏn
K-6	Pyŏngt'aek
K-7	Kwangju
K-8	Kunsan
K-9	Pusan East
K-10	Chinhae
K-11	Ulsan
K-12	Muan
K-13	Suwŏn
K-14	Kimp'o
K-15	Mokp'o
K-16	Yongdungp'o (Seoul)
K-17	Ongin
K-18	Kangnŭng (Koryo)
K-19	Haeju (Kaishu)
K-20	Sinmak
K-21	P'yŏnggang
K-22	Onjŏng-ni
K-23	P'yŏngyang
K-24	P'yŏngyang East
K-25	Wŏnsan

K-26	Sondok
K-27	Yŏnp'o
K-28	Hamhŭng West
K-29	Sinanju
K-30	Sinŭiju
K-31	Kilchu (Kisshu)
K-32	Oesich'ŏ-dong
K-33	Hoemon (Kaibun)
K-34	Ch'ŏngjin (Seishin)
K-35	Hoeryŏng (Kainsei)
K-36	Kanggye No. 1
K-37	Taegu No. 2
K-38	Wŏnju
K-39	Cheju-do No. 1
K-40	Cheju-do No. 2
K-41	Ch'ungju
K-42	Andong No. 2
K-43	Kyŏngju
K-44	Changhowŏn-ni
K-45	Yŏju
K-46	Hoengsŏng
K-47	Ch'unch'ŏn
K-48	Iri
K-49	Yangsu-ri
K-50	Sokch'o-ri
K-51	Inje

SOURCE: Fifth Air Force Histories, 1 January - 30 June, 1 July - 31 December 1951

Following is Alkire's[113] statement for the record:

It is estimated that with combat-ready, fully-equipped engineer aviation units, assigned to command in FEAF, completely manned with the proper SSNs, two airfields (K-1 and K-3) would have been completed by 7 July 50 and a third (K-2) would have been operational today (14 July 50).

After Vandenberg's departure, sent the following memos to my staff:

To the Deputy for Intelligence: Ball the jack[114] on answering CSAF's questions re North Korean airplanes, where they are located, or dispersed, where they are being serviced - and how. In Manchuria? NEW SUBJECT: Strike target on the hydro-electric power plant on the Manchurian border which is just inside North Korea.

---

113. Col Darr H. Alkire, Deputy for Materiel, FEAF.
114. "Ball the Jack" was an old railroad term meaning "full speed ahead." In other words, Stratemeyer was telling his deputy to expedite this matter.

To the Deputy for Personnel: Ball the jack on getting latest info that was passed on by General Rawlings re the Armed Forces Mutual Benefit Association insurance company, and getting such info to our young pilots and young officers. NEW SUBJECT: FEAF getting 800 critical SSNs for our aviation engineer units - they are being airlift[ed]; be sure procedure set up to insure proper assignment and an ample number gotten to the engineer units now operating under the Fifth Air Force.

To the Director of Communications: General Ankenbrandt and General Maude enroute to FEAF;[115] have your communications and personnel needs ready (CSAF says plenty of equipment available for our use); set up an 'instant flash' communications net connecting Yokota AFB and Advance Fifth AF hqs and Twentieth AF on Okinawa. Be prepared to discuss number of TPS–1–B that we need throughout the command.[116]

To the Deputy for Materiel: Be sure that ALL OLD AMMUNITION is either dumped and destroyed by other means.

To the Deputy for Operations: Look into the possibility that all these fishing boats being reported off the shore of Korea are fishing vessels; think they are slipping oil, etc. through out blockade by that means. Even if cargo only fish, my opinion this would help the effort in Korea if we could stop even that industry.

Informed via memo the Deputy for Materiel that we are getting 100 F–80Cs and that is all we get until we holler for more or when we reconvert back to F–80Cs from F–51s.

Sent a memo to CO of 2143d Air Weather Wing that CSAF authorized me to divert airplanes and crews of the weather squadrons whenever essential for the operation of the Bomber Command or for other weather service in FEAF; however, when this is done, an info redline shall be sent for me to him so stating in order that he can keep General (MATS) Kuter[117] advised as to the diversion.

Sent a letter to O'Donnell telling him to make up a folio of blip pictures of Wŏnsan marshaling yards, blip pictures of Seoul bridge complex and bridge complex of P'yŏngyang - so can point out difficulties to CINCFE of radar bombing compared to visual bombing.[118]

Colonel and Mrs. Nuckols, my new PIO and his wife, had dinner with us.

Mission report: Weather unfavorable for part of day, lifting later on. F–80s report 2 Yaks destroyed on ground at Kimp'o; also that damage to field repaired and 7 camouflaged Yaks reported at Kimp'o.

After some absence, Yak fighters reappear; F–80s report while on a rocket and strafing mission, N and NE of Suwŏn area, Yak–9 made a run on some B–26s, knocking out the #2 engine of one of the '26s. When F–80s attacked, they ran;

---

115. Gen Francis L. Ankenbrandt, Director of Communications, Headquarters USAF; Brig Gen Raymond C. Maude, Assistant for Development of Programs, Headquarters USAF.

116. A TPS–1–B was a type of early warning radar.

117. Maj Gen Laurence S. Kuter, commander of the Military Air Transport Service (MATS) since 1948. During World War II, he commanded the 1st Bomb Wing in England and the Allied Tactical Air Forces in North Africa before returning to Washington to become Assistant Chief of Air Staff for Plans and Combat Operations.

118. "Blip" pictures were radarscope photos of targets.

however, fuel supply prevented the F–80s from following: The B–26 landed safely at Taejŏn; crew OK - back at Ashiya.

SATURDAY
15 July
1950

Directive issued and received from General MacArthur through General Almond to hit Kimp'o airport and the marshaling yards at Seoul today, using B–29s, and still maintain B–29 ground support in front of the South Koreans. My decision as follows: continued use of B–29s in ground support; the remainder of B–29s in the 92d Bomb Group to hit Kimp'o; maximum effort of the 22d and 19th Bomb Groups on Okinawa on the marshaling yards at Seoul tomorrow.

General MacArthur agreed 100 percent on my recommendation and even went so far as to beat me to the recommendation not to bomb Seoul marshaling yards unless visual bombing.

After my talk with MacArthur, I had a good heart-to-heart talk with Brigadier General Pinky Wright, G-3, and he thoroughly understands our position and at all times support it. I informed both General Almond and General Hickey as well as General Fox[119] of General MacArthur's approval of my recommendations.

Lunch with Rosie O'Donnell at the Union Club.[120] Ate the low calorie meal and you surely get filled up; I can well understand why there are no calories on it!

General O'Donnell and I will depart for Kadena from Haneda at 1000 hours tomorrow for a visit to his bomb units at Kadena and for the purpose of a conference with my Air Force commander, General Kincaid.

Commendation letter to CG Twentieth Air Force for the 19th Bomb Group and Twentieth Air Force personnel on the excellent work that they have done was approved and prepared. I will take it with me tomorrow. Also, I have approval and citation prepared for the Legion of Merit for Colonel Graff.[121] The presentation of which I will make at Kadena.

Continued strikes at North Korea; B–29s hit Kimp'o and other targets reporting excellent results. Lost an F–51 from small arms fire; pilot killed.

Brigadier General Charles Y. Banfill, my new Deputy for Intelligence arrived 1800 hours; billeted Imperial.[122]

SUNDAY
16 July
1950

Generals Ankenbrandt and Maude arrived 0930; billeted Imperial. 1000 departed for Kadena with General O'Donnell. Press reports North Koreans assaulting our positions on Kŭm River and that we are holding although meager groups of North Koreans did manage to cross in some locales. First figures of casualties announced by FEC - estimated 8 to 9 thousand North Korean casualties; American casualties in neighborhood of 500.

USAF reports that General Weyland, who will be my vice commander for

---

119. Maj Gen Alonzo P. Fox, Executive for Economics and Industrial Affairs, Office of the Deputy Chief of Staff, SCAP from 1946-1947. Since then, he had been D/CS, SCAP.

120. The Union Club, another Japanese building taken over by the occupying forces, now was the FEAF Officers Club.

121. Col Theodore Q. Graff, CO of the 19th BG. The medal was presented for the achievements of his group. By July 30, however, Graff was under fire from FEAF because his group had fallen below the FEAF combat readiness standard. (Hist, ComOpsDiv, FEAF, Jun 25-Oct 31, 1950, I, Jul 30 entry.)

122. Originally scheduled to be 20AF vice commander, Banfill hardly got his feet wet in that job before being reassigned to his new duties.

operations, due to arrive Tokyo 19 July; General Stearley, who is Kincaid's replacement, will arrive 21 July.[123]

B–29s over marshaling yards at Seoul; had high cover of F–80s; target visual for approx 2 min[utes] of bomb run, then target obscured by clouds, but results believed to be excellent; flak moderate to light. However, 2d squadron in contrast to first, reported enemy aircraft seen, but they did not attack. 3d squadron bombed visually, good results, flak moderate, inaccurate, and no fighters. The bombing mission in the Ch'ungju area reported light and meager anti-aircraft fire; results good to excellent; no enemy aircraft encountered.

United Nations have opened an office on the second floor of the building - adjacent to the Allied Council chambers.[124]

Was met at Kadena by General Kincaid, Colonel Graff, Colonel Condron,[125] and some members of the 19th and 22d Bomb Groups. Immediately proceeded to the 22d Bomb Group camp which was inspected and which represents hard work and much help from the Army on Okinawa. General O'Donnell was greatly pleased with the improvements that had taken place in one week. I remained there until the 22d returned from its strike mission on Seoul; listened to some of the debriefings and then addressed the majority of the combat crews and said generally, the following:

I told them about General Vandenberg's letter of commendation, and welcomed them to the Far East Air Forces. I specifically let them know that my headquarters and that of the Twentieth Air Force Headquarters would help them with every means possible. I cautioned them about their gunners being alert at all times over Korea; I advised them to keep their historical records daily; I also pointed out that they would be called up to perform from time to time a mission that is not known to them as members of SAC and that on these missions they would simply have to throw the book away and get in and pitch and destroy the targets that would be assigned to them. Such ground support missions would not last long, but would last until the ground situation stabilized.

I then proceeded to the 19th Bomb Wing debriefing room where I made the award of the Legion of Merit to Colonel Graff, their group commander; following that, General Kincaid read my letter of commendation to the 19th Group after which General O'Donnell addressed the group.

My remarks to the 19th were the same as those made to the 22d Group except I emphasized the need for alertness on the part of gunners while over Korea.

Made a broadcast on the local station by tape, thanking General Sheetz[126] and his staff, the anti-aircraft artillery and all ground personnel, both military and civilian, for their help to the Twentieth and the bomb groups now stationed here.

General Kincaid had a group of 12 for dinner which included General Sheetz, his chief of staff, Colonel Graff, Colonel Edmundson (22d group commander),

---

123. Kincaid was finishing his tour as commander of 20AF. Maj Gen Ralph F. Stearley relieved him on July 31.

124. The Allied Council for Japan had been constituted shortly after World War II. Comprised of representatives from the U.S., the British Commonwealth, China, and Russia (all with veto powers), it was an advisory group to the Washington-based Far Eastern Commission. This latter organization consisted of 11 nations that had fought Japan and was supposed to run Japan in a similar manner to what was done in Germany. Actually, neither the Allied Council nor the Far Eastern Commission had much effect except to muddy the political waters.

125. Col John E. Condron, 20AF PIO.

126. Maj Gen Josef R. Sheetz, commanding general of the Army's Ryukyu Command.

Colonel Ganey, General O'Donnell's top man in the Bomber Command whom he has placed there to supervise the work of the two groups, Colonel Weltman, and Colonel and Mrs. McHenry.[127]

Got to bed about 10:30 P.M.

MONDAY	0130 via PanAm, General and Mrs. Doolittle arrive at
17 July	Haneda. Billeted at the Imperial. Departed Okinawa 0655
1950	hours and arrived Haneda

1130 hours. Came direct to the office where I had a sandwich for lunch and read my personal mail. Signed a letter to General MacArthur on how we are to operate the ground support for General Walker.[128] General Eubank is taking this direct to General Hickey and General Almond along with a set of pictures showing the destructive effect of the FEAF Bomber Command strike yesterday on Seoul - 1,504 x five hundred pound bombs were dropped - or 376 tons.

92d flew all thirty of its bombers and the 19th flew seventeen.

The Doolittles and General Banfill had dinner with us.

Fighters of the Fifth Air Force shot down two Yaks.

TUESDAY	I attended the ops session, Far East Command headquarters,
18 July	this morning and at the conclusion of which I called attention
1950	to the support given the Air Force on Okinawa in the estab-

lishment of the camp for the 22d Group. I also pointed out the necessity for highest priority on the airlift of engines for our B–29s from the States, stating that if we do not get these engines our B–29 effort would gradually reduce to a "nil" operation. I was promised that the engines would receive the very highest priority.

At the conclusion of the ops session, I called on General MacArthur and asked him to read my letter to him which sets forth the coordinated effort between the Fifth Air Force and the FEAF Bomber Command. He agreed in principle with the letter, but pointed out that there was a gap in it to which I agreed -although our intentions were as he discussed; GHQ had been side-tracked. General Almond was called into his office and he covered with him what he desired FEC's reply to my letter should be, which I agreed to. During the discussion, however, while General Almond was present, I very emphatically stated that you can not operate B–29s like you operate a tactical Air Force - it must be well-planned, well-thought-out and an operation that should not be changed daily if we wanted to get the best effect out of the '29s. General MacArthur agreed with me in the presence of General Almond. It is my opinion that henceforth, as a result of this conference with General MacArthur, that our relationship with Far East Command staff will be better.

---

127. Col James V. Edmundson had seen action at Pearl Harbor, Midway, the Solomons, Europe, and with B–29s in the CBI and the Marianas in World War II; Col Wiley D. Ganey, FEAF Bomber Command deputy for operations; Col John H. Weltman, 51st FIW commanding officer; Col George A. McHenry, commander of the 6332d Air Base Wing.

128. Stratemeyer proposed that Walker make all his requests for close air support directly to General Partridge, who would honor these requests within 5AF's capabilities. Any requests in excess of these capabilities would be forwarded to General Stratemeyer for action. The following day, MacArthur agreed to this proposal but noted that any conflicts in this process would be decided by him. (Ltr, Lt Gen George E. Stratemeyer to Gen of the Army Douglas MacArthur, 17 Jul 1950, subj: Close Support for the Ground Troops in Korea, w/1st indorsement, 18 Jul 1950.)

Eubank and I had lunch at the Non-Com's Club - at his expense.

Had a nice conference with Generals Ankenbrandt and Maude re our communications setup.

Colonel Unni Nyar[129] called on me with a letter from the Ambassadress of India,Madame Vijiya Pandit.[130] He made a good impression.

Mrs. Picher had dinner with us.

WEDNESDAY
19 July
1950

Invited Sir Alvary Gascoigne[131] to attend the briefing with me. Cleared same with my intelligence people. However, after meeting General Robertson, pointed out that this might lead to precedence, the setting of which might prove embarrassing. I explained that my gesture was well-intentioned, etc., but that could see his point too.

0930 hours presented awards to MATS pilots re their combat zone flying. (Capt. Ernest C. Ford, 1st Lt. Donald W. Akers, 1st Lt. Garland G. Virden, T/Sgt Irving W. Moore, T/Sgt. Adolph J. Yescalis.)[132]

1200 hours, Major General Robert B. McClure, USA,[133] who is the new Ryukyus CG, called; we had lunch at the house.

Results of the Navy's air strikes reported. Claim 26 airplanes destroyed at P'yŏngang; since we destroyed 2 aircraft yesterday and 3 today, convinced an air build-up underway in North Korea. Sent radio Fifth AF Adv[ance headquarters] and BomCom directing intensification of reconnaissance.

Had a conference with General MacArthur at 1815 hours and talked from the following notes:

> From the results of the Navy's air strike yesterday, where they destroyed - damaged 26 airplanes at P'yŏngang and our destroying 2 yesterday and 3 more today, I am confident that there is being made an air build-up in North Korea. Our intelligence people indicate that there are airplanes on the ground at (#1) P'yŏngang, (#3) Onjŏng-ni, (#5) Mirim-ni. Bombing will be visual if possible; by radar if not. The weather over the immediate battlefront is predicted "poor" for tomorrow (20 July); however, one bomb group medium will be given targets in the area between the 37th and 38th Parallels and will attack if possible. I propose for air strikes tomorrow (20 July) to use one bomb group medium on the airfield and supply dump of bombs and fuel at (#1) P'yŏngang, (#3) Onjŏng-ni, (#5) Mirim-ni. Visual if possible; by radar if not, and one bomb group medium on the airfield and supply dump of bombs and fuel at........ [in original] Our reconnaissance pictures show that there are great supplies of fuel, bombs and other types of supplies just adjacent to these airdromes. Because of weather, we might have to do radar bombing; however, these airdromes are in North Korea and if all bombs do not hit target areas, it should be no concern. If an air build-up is made in North Korea and they should be able to hit Itazuke and Ashiya, such a loss would be greater than the

---

129. Col M.K. Unni Nyar, Indian military observer for the UN Commission. He was killed in Korea about two weeks later when his jeep hit a mine.
130. Vijaya Lakshmi Pandit, the Indian Ambassador to the United States and Mexico. She was president of the U.N. General Assembly in 1953-1954. Her brother was Shri Jawaharlal Nehru, the Indian prime minister.
131. Head of the United Kingdom Liaison Mission in Japan.
132. What unit these men are from or what awards they were given is unknown.
133. Maj General McClure had just taken over as the Ryukyus area commander. In World War II, he had seen action in the South Pacific and from 1944 to 1946 had been the U.S. chief of staff to Chiang Kai-shek.

loss of a battalion, or a regiment, or even a division in the outcome of the battle for Korea.

General MacArthur agreed with me in the presence of General Almond where we had a discussion reference the airdrome missions. During this discussion I pointed out to General MacArthur, in General Almond's presence, that I had a target section that was working hard on strips of targets south of the 38th Parallel and forward of the bomb line and strips north of the 38th Parallel which, if in our opinion, would be destroyed, would be most beneficial to the battle. I emphasized my target section and Far East Command target section should get together and come to a mutual agreement in order to avoid presentation to General MacArthur for decision. He, General Almond, and I agreed that should and could be done. I also pointed out to General MacArthur that still in the lower sections of the staff, the officers in effect believe that you (General MacArthur) had not approved my Wŏnsan strike and in General MacArthur's presence I urged the Chief of Staff to eliminate this feeling in order that we can get a ball team and eliminate the dissension between his staff and mine. General Almond agreed to do this.

After returning to General MacArthur's office, his remarks to me were: "Strat, we always have that kind of thing," to which I replied, "I know it, but we ought to eliminate it when it crops up." He agreed.

About 2300 hours I called General Picher[134] and directed that he inform all commands that for the next few days great effort should be put on the reconnoitering of hostile airdromes.

Following is a brief of the "remarks" from the mission reports: 3 Yak–9s destroyed and one Yak–9 probably destroyed in aerial combat with F–80. One F–80 shot down by a Yak–9 in vicinity of Taejŏn. Jeep dispatched to attempt to locate downed aircraft and pilot. Fourteen fighter-type and one twin engine-type a/c [aircraft] destroyed and 7 fighter type a/c were damaged all on ground at P'yŏnggang. Total: 18 aircraft destroyed; one probable; and seven damaged.

Asked my Operations for a report on napalm usage.

THURSDAY **20 July** **1950**	Major General O. P. Weyland,[135] my new vice commander for operations, with a Colonel Meyers,[136] arrived 0715.

During the Far East Command ops meeting this morning, I stressed the fact that we were devoting all recon efforts for the next two or three days to the location of North Korean aircraft on the ground besides taking pictures of both airdromes and post-strike results. After the ops meeting with General Almond, I introduced Craigie and Weyland to MacArthur and heard a wonderful discourse by him on our operations and efforts from the receipt of the President's directive to date.

General Orders issued relieving General Eubank and designating Craigie as my vice commander of administration and plans and Weyland as my vice commander for operations.

---

134. Brig Gen Oliver S. Picher, normally Inspector General, FEAF, but then acting as deputy for operations.
135. Earlier in the month, Weyland had been part of the inspection team led by General Wolfe. In World War II, he commanded the XIX Tactical Air Command and then 9AF. His assignments after the war included being the assistant commandant of the Command and General Staff School, Air Force assistant chief of staff for plans, director of plans and operations at Headquarters USAF, and deputy commander of the National War College. He had been Commander, Tactical Air Command for one week before being reassigned to FEAF.
136. Probably Col Gilbert Meyers, 5AF deputy for operations.

1400 hours I told General Crabb and Colonel Price to discuss with General Weyland and bring General Craigie into it, General MacArthur's plan of maneuver come about 15 September. I directed that they consider and have recommendations ready for my approval of a small command group in case General MacArthur's plans materialize; when he moves, I will move.

1600 hours visited FEAF Bomber Command and had a long talk with General O'Donnell in the presence of General Eubank and explained to O'Donnell in great detail why the Bomber Command, for a while, would really be a battle support command south of the 38th Parallel.

I made it plain to him that he must follow out General MacArthur's and my directives and become a member of the ballteam. He accepted this in fine spirit and he told me that I need not worry about his group or crews - that they would put out and do as directed. He did point out, however, the great confusion that had been caused by constant change of orders. I explained why this happened and apologized, and gave him to believe that we would do everything in our power to get orders to him in ample time to brief his crews and plan his mission.

We had dinner in his quarters, present: Generals O'Donnell and Eubank and myself, Colonel Bondley[137] (O'Donnell's C of S), Colonel Ganey (O'Donnell's operations chief), Colonel Putnam[138] (92d group commander), and a squadron commander and bombardier who flew one of the missions the other morning.

F–80 on armed recon mission reported at 1815 K, north of Kŭm River at Taejŏn, 2 Yak–9s made pass in the air. Both enemy a/c destroyed; one went down burning and a pilot was observed bailing out.

B–29 mission reported one Yak–3 and 1 LAGG–3 damaged in air; observed smoking. One of the B–29s was hit by fighter fire and one B–29 by flak; each sustained only minor damage.

FRIDAY

21 July

1950

General Robertson posed the question if the 77th RAAF Squadron moves to Korea, as suggested by General Partridge, how is it to be maintained - down to and including food and PX [Post Exchange] supplies for the personnel. Operations has been delegated to come up with a solution.

Robertson also requested help so that he can advise Air Marshal Jones,[139] C of S, RAAF, whether to buy jet close support-type equipment or reciprocal engine-type equipment, based on our experience. Operations to prepare the study for me.

Relieved Picher from duty with operations; he will function as IG and will report directly to me and will be my roving trouble-shooter.

Sent memorandum to CINCFE suggesting that a target selection group be set up of general officers. Suggested Hickey, Willoughby, Weyland and a Navy representative. Present target groups in each of our headquarters could continue to function and can do spade work for this final group.

Generals Ankenbrandt and Maude in. Stressed importance of communications and cited the incident where O'Donnell's sigtot[140] broke down on 19 July (1500 hours) and took until 20 July (0500 hours) to get through to 22d and 19th

---

137. Col C.J. Bondley, Jr., FEAF Bomber Command vice commander.
138. Col Claude E. Putnam, Jr.
139. Air Marshal Sir George Jones, Chief of Air Staff, RAAF.
140. Sigtot was the name given certain two-way transmission equipment often used for the transmission and reception of classified material.

on Okinawa. Stated that "flash" and "operational immediate" orders must get through as required from the Bomber Command to Okinawa.

Press reports indicate that Taejŏn has fallen; that Major General Dean reported as missing in action. Both are unconfirmed.

Put the gist of my conversation with O'Donnell in writing, in the form of an indorsement (Top Secret - Eyes Only).

Called on General MacArthur at 1815 hours and took over what we considered a good press release and the reaction by CINCFE was not good. He stated we should in no way discuss the ground situation but should stick strictly to air matter, and that the ground situation is a matter for CINCFE. I am inclined to agree and feel that our interim report on our operations was a wrong approach. I left the paper with him and he promised to read it and I will receive the results during my meeting with him tomorrow, 22 July, at 1130 hours.

Constellation being sent me for CINCFE's use.

Mission report discloses 2 F–80s lost; on one, the tip tank pulled out, causing it to crash; on the other, crash landed at Itazuke.

SATURDAY
22 July
1950

0800 hours General Stearley reported in at my office. He and Mrs. Stearley had arrived at 0630 hours at Haneda and will be our guests at Mayeda House. He is to be CG of Twentieth Air Force.

General Partridge called and requested information from us as to when Marine aviation will arrive, if they will occupy Itami, under whose control they will be, and what their job will be when not supporting Marine brigade.[141] Instructed VC for Ops to get an answer to Partridge before midnight tonite. Partridge also protested about the Navy reserving air space of 100 miles in diameter re the recent landing of the 1st Cav[alry] Div[ision]. He was not permitted to fly thru the area to support the battlefront and could not get into one of his airdromes, K-3. Told Ops we must keep out of their hair, but we are not going to let them get in our hair - and to coordinate with Navy and get situation cleaned up as all that is necessary is to inform FEAF commanders where Navy is operating - and when.

This week's *Newsweek* out with my likeness on the cover. Also contains profiles on Partridge, Timberlake and myself.

O'Donnell called; suggested placing Colonel Wiley D. Ganey, his operations [officer] in FEAF for a 7 to 10 day liaison tour. Accepted his offer with alacrity.

Sent a radio to Nugent requesting the services of a Colonel James Ferguson,[142] for indefinite TDY with this headquarters. Weyland concurred.

---

141. Marine Air Group (MAG) 33, part of the 1st Marine Air Wing, began arriving at Itami (at Osaka) on August 1. The squadrons of the group would support the ground troops of the 1st Provisional Marine Brigade, which landed at Pusan on August 2. Two of MAG-33's squadrons, VMF-214 and VMF-323, spent little time at Itami, instead going aboard the escort carriers *Sicily* and *Baedong Strait* a few days later for operations. A third squadron, VMF(N)-513, was based at Itazuke. Its night-fighter Corsairs came under 5AF control for night heckler operations over Korea. (Lynn Montross and Capt. Nicholas A. Canzona, USMC, *The Pusan Perimeter* [U.S. Marine Operations in Korea, 1950-1953] [Washington, 1954], pp 89-90.)

Surprisingly, General Stratemeyer does not mention in his diary that he met on July 20 with Marine Brig Gens Edward A. Craig and Thomas J. Cushman to discuss the role of the brigade in Korea. At this time he assured the two men that the MAG-33 aircraft would be available at all times to support the Marines on the ground. (Montross and Canzona, p 60; Futrell, pp 120-121.)

142. Col Ferguson led the 405th FG in World War II. Following the war, he was on the Air University faculty and Chief of Staff of the American Mission in Turkey. From June 1950-June 1951, he was assistant to the Vice Commander, FEAF, and later, Assistant Deputy for Operations, FEAF.

Attended 1030 ops session in GHQ.

Received General MacArthur's memorandum in reply to my "first phase interim Air Operations Release" upon which he stated that he disapproved the type of release that I had recommended but that he had no objection whatever to Air Force communiques being put out and that he read same daily and thought them informative. I turned this paper over to PIO for necessary action. CINCFE told me again that I could write to my commanders and tell them that he was pleased beyond all expectations with the operations to date and that Air Force had performed magnificently. I directed my PIO, Colonel Nuckols, to get the draft letter that I had given him and to revamp it if he so desired and get it up to me for signature.

After the ops session yesterday, General MacArthur approved my recommendation for a top target selection group consisting of Hickey, Willoughby, Weyland, and a Navy designate.[143] CINCFE still pointed out that there would be times when some front line missions would be desired and asked me if 72 hours would be ample advance notice. I told him that I didn't need that long, but I must have 48 hours notice and those were the instructions he gave to General Almond.

The Stearleys had lunch and dinner with us and remained overnite; they depart for Okinawa 0900 hours, 23 July, from Haneda.

General Dean is officially listed as "missing in action."

Weather unfavorable; results of bombings unobserved.

SUNDAY

23 July

1950

Stearleys depart 0900 for Okinawa. Eubank to depart 2300 hours today for the ZI. (Eubank departed 1000 hours, 24 July.) Sent a memo to C/S, GHQ, FEC, on our runway completion schedule; new runway surfaced with pierced-steel plank at K-2 (Taegu) to be completed 5 Aug; will be 6,000 ft in length and will be satisfactory for the operation of any of the a/c now available in FEAF. Secondary runway to be completed 4 days after the new runway, or 9 Aug. Re the K-3 runways and dispersal hardstands to be completed 25 July; the whole base will be rehabilitated so that we can operate F-51 fighters from K-3.

Sent a "Dear Van" letter re the outstanding work that Alkire has done and compared him with my other officers who are deserving of promotion to brigadier general.[144] Stated that Alkire should be considered before the rest, which should in no way detract from those others.

---

143. This group was the outcome of an attempt by MacArthur's headquarters to establish some kind of target selection and priority. Initially, a GHQ Target Group (consisting of an officer from the G-2 section, one from G-3, and an Air Force member and a Navy member from the Joint Strategic Plans and Operations Group, all working part-time on this project) recommended the targets and what needed to be done to ensure the coordinated use of the available air power. It also analyzed the target systems and the priorities assigned, and advised on how to use FEAF and Navy aircraft on a day-to-day basis. Unfortunately, the target group attempted to control target selection too closely, leaving FEAF and 5AF out of the decision making process.

The GHQ Target Group was unable to perform its duties as had been planned (numerous mistakes in target selection being one problem area), and Stratemeyer requested on July 21 that a senior officer GHQ target selection committee be established. Based on information from the GHQ Target Group and the FEAF Target Section, this high-level committee would present its target recommendations to General MacArthur.

Admiral Joy would not name a member to the committee, stating that the Seventh Fleet's primary mission was the defense of Formosa and that in light of this, any decision to employ its aircraft in Korea really rested with MacArthur. Nevertheless, he said that Navy aircraft would continue to be used in Korea for general or close support strikes under FEAF's coordination control.

This senior committee lasted litle more than six weeks. When it became obvious that most of the information on targets was coming from FEAF, a FEAF Formal Target Committee was established. This group soon became the de facto theater agency for target selection. (Futrell, pp 50-55; Hist, FEAF, 25 Jun-31 Dec 50, pp 9-10, 49.)

144. Stratemeyer sent these letters on an occasional basis to promote (outside official channels) certain programs,

Colonel Ganey, O'Donnell's liaison officer, in to see me to report for duty with FEAF. Answered CSAF redline T.S. [top secret] radio with a redline T.S. re his request for us to release an air evaluation. My answer to him was that situation still too critical from a ground viewpoint and because of that requested he wait for more opportune time. Told him we did have an evaluation prepared, but because of above, had been shelved. Suggested we wait until the tide turns.

MONDAY
24 July
1950

General Eubank departs for the ZI from Haneda. At 1145 hours Air Vice Marshal Ragg, the senior air staff officer to Air Vice Marshal Fogarty, and Air Commodore Davies, Air Officer Commanding Hong Kong, Wing Commander Barclay, the air liaison attached to the British Embassy here in Tokyo, and Squadron Leader Sach, who is attached to FEAF on an exchange basis, called.[145] Took them all to lunch at the Union Club.

Annalee and I had a few members of FEAF call at the house at 1800 hours to have cocktails with us and to honor General and Mrs. Doolittle.

Weather very favorable. B–29s report best visibility since they began their interdiction campaign.

Fifth AF Advance Hqs now set up along side Eighth Army Advance Hqs.[146]

Sent radio to Partridge asking to be kept fully informed re:

Is he able to meet Walker's requirements on threatened left flanking movement around 8th Army? Request number of sorties devoted to area between Taejŏn and 1st Cav front lines subsequent to evac[uation] of Taejŏn; and what effort devoted to enemy activities in Yongdŏk area. Also, is there sufficiency of AT–6s and/or liaison a/c for control purposes? Again he is to keep me posted. [Underlining in original.]

TUESDAY
25 July
1950

Answer received from my T.S. redline to CSAF dtd 23 July re submitting evaluation air power. My reasoning approved. Also in message was info that we are receiving better news coverage re the exploits of the AF in Korea. Keep photos coming.

Drafted a proposed memo to CINCFE for the signatures of the Target Selection Committee, laying out a program for the B–29s of the FEAF BOMCOM. The 19th will continue direct support of ground forces until defense line stabilized or acceptable; other 2 groups, 22d and 92d will devote efforts to targets on attached chart; reasoning behind this to permit Fifth to support Walker with their resources without interference or interruption and will permit the severing of North Korean communications lines, and damage will be done in North Korea - rather than in South attaining same and better results if we came entirely south of the 38th Parallel.

---

ideas, or in this case, individuals. Alkire did receive his first star in August.

145. AVM Robert L. Ragg; AVM Sir Francis J. Fogarty, Commander in Chief, British Far East Air Force; Air Commodore A.D. Davies; Wg Cdr Ronald A.C. Barclay; Sqdn Ldr John F. Sach. British Far East Air Forces (BFEAF) was headquartered in Singapore.

146. Just after midnight, 5AF Headquarters (Advanced) became operational at Taegu. Later that day it was renamed Headquarters, 5th Air Force in Korea. Located next to Walker's Eighth Army headquarters, this headquarters (commanded by General Partridge personally) directed the tactical air war in Korea. This arrangement helped shorten the time between when air support requests were received and when they were accomplished. In Japan, 5AF Headquarters (Rear) continued to function from Nagoya for air defense of the country and for logistical and administrative matters. From August 10, it was commanded by Brig Gen Delmar T. Spivey, who became a 5AF vice commander that day. (Futrell, p 104.)

The draft that was finally signed by the Target Committee is quoted en toto:

Memo to CINCFE, subj:

Targets for FEAF BOMCOM. *(1)* Your Target Selection Committee as approved by you on 22 July has, according to our understanding of your approval, laid out the following program for the B–29s of the FEAF Bomber Command. *(2)* One medium bomb group will continue operations in the close proximity of the battle area until there is a reasonable stabilization of an acceptable defense line. *(3)* The other two groups will devote their major effort to a planned interdiction program primarily north of the 38th Parallel. *(4)* We feel that by this method the isolation of the battlefield will be secured and will allow the Fifth Air Force with its fighters, fighter-bombers, and light bombers, assisted when possible by carrier aircraft, to perform their mission in support of General Walker without interference or interruption. This method should cut the enemy's lines of communication with equal or better results than if we came entirely south of the 38th Parallel, inflicting damage in North Korea rather than in South Korea. *(5)* It is requested that this plan be approved. s/ Major Generals D.O. Hickey, USA; Charles A. Willoughby, USA; Otto P. Weyland, USAF.

(These people were on original target selection committee on B–29s, Far East Command, prior to my recommendation to put Weyland, Hickey and Willoughby on the committee. Their recommendations, as I understand it, went direct to General Almond and were based to a great extent on his suggestions.)

(1) Colonel E.C. Ewart
(Member)
Present: G-2, GHQ

Dep Dir of Info & Ed Dn., ASF
Aug 44 - Mar 45
Mil Attache to Denmark,
Jul 45 - Mar 49

(2) Lt. Col. R.C. Cassibry
(Alternate?)

CO 15th FA Bn, Jan 44 - Aug 47.
Student, Command & Staff Col, 47 - 48

3) Lt. Col. W.W. Quinn
(Member)
Present: G-3, GHQ

Provost Marshal duties prior to 42;
Staff Asst G-2 for 9th Army
Jan 42 - Jun 3 44;
Chief Operations, Control Intel. Gp.,
Wash., D.C., Jan 47 - Aug 47
Asst G-3 of I Corps
Sept 49 - Mar 50

(4) Lt. Col. T.R. Hanna
(Alternate)
Present: G-3, GHQ

Operations Staff Officer, WDGS
Sept 43 - Sept 45
Plans Officer, U.S. Forces, China
Sept 45 - Mar 47

5) Commander J.D. Reilly (Navy)
(Member)
Present: Secretary JSPOG, GHQ

Navy Training Station,
Gunnery officer on carrier

6) Captain Gamet (Navy)
(Alternate)

Communications Officer
West Coast

Took Mr. Edward R. Murrow (Mr. Murrow representing Columbia Broadcasting Company.)[147] and my PIO to lunch at the Union Club; discussed many Air Force problems with him for the "behind-the-scene" record.

Colonel Nuckols brought in Mr. Joe Fromm, *U. S. News and World Report* correspondent, at 1715 and I discussed with him many subjects reference the use of the Far East Air Forces in Korea. He also was informed that many things that I told him were for background and off the record; I told him that he could quote me on anything provided he cleared the quotes with Colonel Nuckols.

1740 General Gilkeson arrives Tokyo. Billeted at the Imperial Hotel.

GHQ PIO release says that United Nations Command officially established 25 July with General MacArthur as C-in-C, as per resolution of the Security Council of the United Nations of 7 July 50.

Mission reports indicate from fair to some excellent results; one Yak reported in vicinity of B–29 target area, but it did not attack.

WEDNESDAY
26 July
1950

Craigie brought in Mr. Frank L. White, Manila representative of Associated Press. Had a brief talk with him.

Took Gilkeson, Craigie and Banfill to lunch at the Union Club. Sent a strong redline Personal to Van re his redline T.S. to me - utilization of aircraft and percentages of use as compared to World War II flying hours and tonnage dropped. Although our tonnages dropped and sorties flown are based on per aircraft available, it is higher than those logged during World War II from Tinian-Saipan.

THURSDAY
27 July
1950

0630 takeoff from Haneda with General MacArthur aboard the *Bataan*. We visited Korea - General Walker's headquarters, General Partridge's headquarters; had lunch with Partridge and Weyland and then discussed the airdrome construction program with Colonel Mount.[148] I was greatly impressed with the intelligence and ability of Colonel Mount. Our airdrome program in Korea is in good hands.

Returned from Korea approximately 1930 hours.

B–29 on recon mission reported back apparent activity around Wŏnsan air strip. GHQ Intelligence reports an enemy aircraft dropped 1 incendiary bomb on Fifth Air Force Hqrs., no damage done.

A B–29, scheduled to attack front-line precision targets, due to weather, changed its course for P'yŏngang; however, due to poor navigation and non-alertness, the pilot discovered he was right over Dairen, at which place, he was intercepted by two Russian fighters, but they did not fire. The pilot pulled away, dropped his bombs on P'yŏngang marshaling yards and beat it for home.[149]

FRIDAY
28 July
1950

General Partridge telephoned early this morning and stated that movements in the south by North Koreans was not good. He further stated that he had used F–82s last night with napalm as harassment. He is evacuating the Korean Air

---

147. Murrow was the noted CBS radio broadcaster who became famous for his radio broadcasts from England during the height of the "Blitz" in 1940. In the 1950s-1960s, his TV programs "Person to Person" and "See It Now" set a new style in news broadcasting and would ultimately be regarded as the best of their types.

148. Col Glynn O. Mount, 5AF director of installations.

149. Dairen is over 200 miles west of P'yŏngyang and is just a few miles east of Port Arthur.

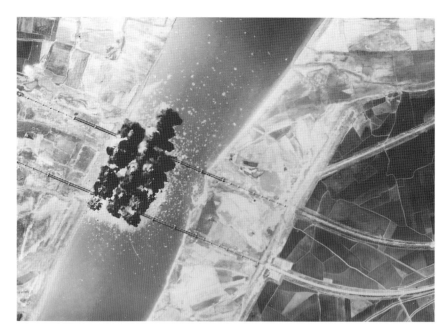

Bombs from FEAF Bomber Command B–29s smother a pair of railroad bridges north of P'yŏngyang on July 27.

Force from the airport at Sach'ŏn; he definitely stated that the bridges at Seoul were out and that he had pictures to prove it.[150]

While I was in Korea, General Partridge told me of the following two incidents: one where operations between Colonel Witty,[151] base commander at K–3, and the South Koreans operating south of Yongdŏk, were of the very closest cooperation. Two days ago, an air-controller airplane, after securing information from the South Koreans, directed an F–51 into a town and instructed the pilot to fire through a certain second-story window of a building in which there were many Communists. This was done successfully. Another incident was where the mayor of a town south of Yongdŏk had informed our flying coordinator that at a certain time all the inhabitants of the town would evacuate and that because of the large number of communists present, they wanted the town fired. This also was done successfully.

Because of this close relationship between Colonel Witty and the South Koreans, he was informed that the Government of South Korea intended to decorate him.

1530 hours with Colonel Nuckols saw Mr. John Osborne, one of the senior editors of *Time* magazine.

At 1615, with Colonel Nuckols, saw Mr. Frank Tremaine, the United Press correspondent.

General Picher gave me the following memorandum, dated 27 July 50:

Your question on the return of dependents to the U.S.: *a.* Dependents whose principal has completed his normal overseas tour may go home at

---

150. Sach'ŏn is about 60 miles west of Pusan and was the the site of a small sod strip. The village fell on July 31.
151. Col Robert W. Witty commanded the 6131st FW at P'ohang (K–3).

government expense, including crating and shipping of household goods. *b.* The same is true of officers and airmen who are actually in combat. *c.* It is not true for you or me or the PX officer at Itazuke. This should give you enough latitude to send any obnoxious wives home. I feel that system should be the one used, rather than a mass movement of all dependents, as many of them are probably dependable and a help to the fighting warrior and not a burden on the phone to the Operations Office. NEW SUBJECT (phrased carefully). I don't agree with General Eubank's suggestion that special emissaries from here be sent to the south country to harangue the wives. I fear the feeling in the hinterland would be that the "fat cats" from Tokyo are far from the war, are in no danger, and what are they doing down here giving us good advice on a subject on which they are not competent.

SATURDAY
29 July
1950

1150 hours, Mr. Tofte,[152] of Headquarters CIA delivered letter addressed to me. *Sent message to COMNAVFE, with info copies to CINCFE, Com 7th Fleet, CG BOMBCOM:*

Request you pass following message to Royal Navy: Sincerely regret instance Seafire aircraft apparently fired upon by our B–29s and one Seafire was set afire. Happy that pilot was rescued. Action under way to revise electronic recognitions procedures to preclude future unfortunate instances. Hope you will instruct Royal Navy pilots to remain outside of .50-calibre machine gun range when attempting to identify, prior to an attack, four-engine aircraft. Signed Stratemeyer.

Top Secret study completed last night; re my plan for the utilization of Far East Air Force[s] units in support of the defense of Formosa in case the Chinese Communists attack; finished at 1830 hours, and approved by me. I will submit this to General MacArthur tomorrow - or on my trip to Formosa. Total of 7 copies were made which will be distributed if and when General MacArthur approves it as follows: 1 cy [copy] General Turner, 1 cy General Stearley, 2 copies (red comeback cy and another) to Plans, 1 cy (green file copy) with AG Top Secret Control Officer, 1 cy to be left with the TS Control Officer, and the original to CINCFE.[153]

Annalee and I had dinner with Lt. Cecil,[154] FEAF Officers' Club Manager, and Mrs. Cecil at 2000 hours, University Club.

---

152. Hans V. Tofte was the CIA head in Tokyo. (For a look at Tofte's remarkable career, see Joseph C. Goulden, *Korea: The Untold Story of the War* [New York, 1982], pp 464-475.) The CIA apparently worked more closely with Stratemeyer and the Air Force than with MacArthur, who harbored a deep antipathy toward clandestine operations dating to World War II. Among the CIA's inventory at the time was the ostensibly commercial airline, CAT, which had planes operating in logistical support of U.S. forces in Japan and Korea. The CAT planes were often used on various covert missions.

153. This study was the result of intelligence reports that a Communist invasion of Formosa was imminent. Reacting to these reports, on July 27 the JCS sent MacArthur a message which, for all intents, appeared to be a "war warning." The Joint chiefs recommended (they did not order because such actions had not yet been approved by the President) that the Nationalist forces be allowed to make air strikes on the China mainland, as well as mine the coastal waters. Additionally, MacArthur was to send a survey team to Formosa to assess what military aid the Nationalist's might need. (Bevin Alexander, *Korea: The First War We Lost* [New York, 1986], p 164; Blair, p 173; Schnabel, p 368.)

154. Lt Cecil's full name is unknown.

*Superfortresses unload their 500-lb. bombs onto the Chosen Chemical Com-
pany Plant at Kōnan (Hǔngnam).*

SUNDAY
30 July
1950

B–29s struck with 23 aircraft the Chosen Nitrogen Chemical Company plant at Kōnan (Hǔngnam) which is 50 miles north of Wǒnsan.[155]

Explosions rocked planes which were above 15,000 feet. Initial strike with radar; overcast cleared away, presumably by heat generated by ground fires, remainder bombing visual. Raid highly successful.

1220 hours conferred with CINCFE. Took with me the plans for FEAF support of Formosa should that island be attacked by the Chinese Communists. He approved the plan as drawn for planning purposes. Copies of same, after approval, dispatched to Turner and Stearley, cautioning them to limit the knowledge of this plan to certain few of their staff and also to bear in mind that it was for planning purposes only.

*Partridge called; on his behalf sent the following personal redline
to Vandenberg:*

Partridge's headquarters with Timberlake now permanently in Korea. His rear echelon at Nagoya still has the job of air defense of the islands of Japan and the other necessary duties required of a rear echelon. He needs and has urged me to secure for him a good brigadier general to take on the job at Nagoya. At one time, as you remember, we had two

---

155. Actually, 47 aircraft struck the target. (Futrell, p 190.)

air divisions in Japan to run the air defense set-up. Because of shortage of both officers and enlisted personnel, I eliminated the two air divisions and set up three air defense areas with wing commanders in charge of air defense. It is noted that an air division was recently activated in Europe headed up by a general officer. I feel that since we are at war our genuine need for a general officer at Nagoya is greater than that of Europe. As you know, General Weyland did not replace General Crabb. Crabb cannot be released for Nagoya assignment. Partridge feels and I agree with him that we need a general officer to command his rear echelon. Colonel Edwin L. Tucker, who has been here two and one-half years, is the commander there now but he must be sent home for compassionate reasons. I urge the immediate dispatch of a young and up and at 'em general.

Radio received from USAF from Twining stating that Brig General Theron B. Henebry (Reserve) being recalled to active duty to command Reserve light bomb wing being activated and deployed as unit to my command.[156]

Mr. Akabane[157] was in briefly at 1530 hours. Have him settled with a yen salary acceptable to him out at FEAMCOM. Gave him a letter of introduction to Doyle.

MONDAY
31 July
1950

Took off at 0600 hours, aboard the *Bataan* with CINCFE for Formosa.[158] Those accompanying us: Joy, Struble, Ho, Almond, Whitney, Canada[159] (CINCFE's physician) and an orderly. The others left in the standby C–54 (FEAF flagship out of commission because of faulty engine): Marquat,[160] Willoughby, Wright, Eberle, Navy member, my Materiel (Alkire), 7th Fleet member, and an orderly left in GHQ C–54. Plan is to remain through Monday, returning Tuesday, 1 August.

---

156. This Air Reserve unit was the 452d BW(L), which had less than two weeks notice before being recalled on August 10. Considered to be the most ready of the Air Force Reserve wings, the Long Beach-based 452d had a great deal of talented personnel, with many of its members working for the various aircraft plants in the area. On October 25, the first B–26 of the 452d arrived in Japan, and the first wing mission was flown two days later. From recall to combat took exactly 77 days. (Gerald T. Cantwell, *The Evolution and Employment of the Air Force Reserve as a Mobilization Force, 1946-1980* [Robins AFB, Ga., 1981], pp 20-25.) Thereon B. Henebry should not be confused with Brig Gen John B. Henebry, who took command of the 315th Air Division on February 8, 1951.

157. Unable to identify this individual.

158. MacArthur had already planned to visit Formosa, but the supposed seriousness of the situation on that island gave added impetus to the trip. Although the JCS did not tell MacArthur he could not go, the Joint Chiefs did suggest he send a senior officer in his place. Thus they were not too pleased when they learned that MacArthur intended to lead the survey party. Their concern about MacArthur seemed valid when word reached them that he planned to base 3 F–80 squadrons on Formosa, a decision he had no authority to make. Neither the JCS nor the State Department knew of such a plan. As it turned out, MacArthur did not intend to transfer the aircraft to Formosa. (*Foreign Relations of the United States, 1950*, Vol. VI [Washington, 1976], pp 410-411, 412-413, 439.)
Nevertheless, public statements by MacArthur and Chiang Kai-shek after the trip seemed to indicate that a "deal" had been sealed between the U.S. and the Nationalists. President Truman and his advisors were furious over these statements and about the survey trip as a whole. The outcome was Truman's deepening distrust of MacArthur, a distrust that eventually led to MacArthur's removal from command.
And what of the invasion force that triggered the entire affair? It seemingly disappeared without a trace. (Blair, pp 173-176; Alexander, pp 164-165; Schnabel, pp 368-369.)

159. Col Charles F. Canada had been MacArthur's physician since 1949.

160. Maj Gen William F. Marquat, Chief, SCAP Economic and Scientific Section.

Radio received from USAF stating that Brigadier General Spivey[161] enroute 4 August from Fairfield-Suisun, via MATS. He will head up the Fifth Air Force Hq rear echelon.

F–51 crashed at Koch'ang, 30 July. No details.

Partridge reports first replacement Mustangs from States started to arrive at forward fields 30 July. Build up promises to be rapid. Weather caused the loss of a T–6; crew returned uninjured. He also reported strong need for Navy representative with Fifth AF. Only one Navy representative and he [is] assigned to Eighth Army.

5th Combat Team landed 1700 hours in Korea.[162]

TUESDAY
1 August
1950

First contingent of Marines to land at Pusan at 1700 hours.[163] Original plans were for them to stage in Japan and then go to Korea - however, they are going direct. This group completely equipped with airplanes, etc.

Sent radio to CSAF, attention Twining, concur in choice of General Henebry for this command.

Weyland worked out verbally through Price obtaining Navy liaison for Partridge. Three Navy men presently attached to Fifth Air Force air defense, who can be considered surplus at moment, to be directed by Morehouse to Korea for purposes of liaison.

Returned from Formosa 8:15 P.M.

One F–80 crashed near Choch'iwŏn area. No details; presumed to be from small arms fire.

WEDNESDAY
2 AUGUST
1950

A quick brief of what took place during my trip to Formosa is as follows: Arrived late at about 2:00 P.M. at Taipei; at 4'clock all, with many, many Chinese officers, attended a general briefing of the Commie Order of Battle and the Chinese Government Order of Battle on Formosa.

I thought it a very interesting and excellent briefing, although there were some misunderstandings between General MacArthur and the Chinese officers due to language difficulties. Immediately after this general briefing, General MacArthur had all his people meet him in his billet where he gave his general observations. He stated that the Chinese forces had a poor organization, that they were not deployed properly, that if they had about 75,000 to 100,000 people properly organized on paper and on the ground, the proper commanders in charge, they could hold Taiwan; that our job would be to send without delay a liaison group made up of Army, Air and Navy and that although we would not command, we would assist and direct what we as Americans considered proper in the defense of the islands. There would be no integration of forces, but that we

---

161. Brig Gen Delmar T. Spivey had been chief of the Plans Division in the office of the DCS/Ops at USAF Headquarters since August 1949. In August 1950, he was assigned to 5AF and assumed command of 5AF Rear. The following December, he became commanding general of the 314th Air Division.

162. On July 13, the JCS authorized the Commanding General, U.S. Army Pacific, to send the the 5th Regimental Combat Team (RCT), then based in Hawaii, to Korea. The RCT sailed for Korea on July 25, arrived at Pusan on the 31st, and was engaged in combat almost immediately afterwards. (Schnabel, pp 90-92.)

163. These were men of the 1st Provisional Marine Brigade and they actually landed the next day. When it took up positions in the southeast corner of what would become known as the Pusan Perimeter, the brigade was composed of the 5th Marines plus a battalion of the 11th Marines. (Montross and Canzona, pp 51, 90-91.)

would work along parallel lines, that our activities on Formosa would be concerned with defense only, that we would assist the Chinese, that we would in no way get involved with political aspects and that our activities would be purely professional. We were then dismissed and went to our billets and later that evening at 8 o'clock attended a dinner as guests of the Generalissimo and Madame Chiang.[164] We stayed up too late - not getting home until 11 o'clock.

The next morning, 1 August, General MacArthur's key people and a selected group of Chinese key military people met with General MacArthur, the Gissimo [Generalissimo] and his lady in General MacArthur's billet. Here General MacArthur reviewed his intentions, making them very definite and clear to which the Gissimo and his people agreed.

We departed for Okinawa at 12 noon Tokyo time, landing at Naha where all of us were then driven from Naha to Kadena in order to give General MacArthur and all of us a quick look-see at the island and at the improvements made by General Kincaid and General Sheetz. We were there 1 1/2 hours and General MacArthur and all members of his staff were greatly impressed with what had been done and with what was taking place. We took off for Haneda and landed about 8:15

This morning received a call from General O'Donnell, who is departing for Okinawa today, and he made a very strong request that the 31st Recon Squadron stay in the Kanto Plain area.

His second request was to rush the completion of extra hardstands at Yokota.

I made affirmative decisions on both and so instructed the staff.

Letter arrived from Gene Eubank dtd 27 July in which he stated "I am telling my friends around here not to worry about the Far Eastern situation - that it is in good hands!"

When I returned last night, sent the following (via STRATLINE)[165] to Turner with info to Struble, Stearley, and CINCFE:

...Desire you immediately fly to Taipei, Formosa, and check in with General Chow,[166] Chief of Staff Chinese Nationalist Forces. He knows you are coming and will lend all possible assistance to your plans. I will send a team of engineers to Taipei to make survey of flying fields to select under your direction one in northwest and one in southwest for F–80C use. Chinese have labor, cement, gravel, etc. to lengthen runways to 7500 feet and have guaranteed all necessary facilities for housing, maintenance and supply for Air Force people. We will ship JP [jet propulsion] fuel to Formosa immediately. Suggest you contact Stearley on Okinawa and have Col Weltman with his 51st Fighter Group commander meet you in Taipei and up and down west coast and inland over population centers landing at Shinchiku airfield for familiarization and publicity purposes before end of this week. (AVGAS [aviation gasoline] is available and can be used in F–80Cs.) Just as soon as possible, I want all three squadrons of F–80Cs to visit Formosa for morale and publicity purposes for Chinese

---

164. Madame Chiang Kai-shek (Mayling Soong Chiang) married the Generalissimo in 1927. Although very charming, she was also known to be very determined and to possess an iron will.

165. "Stratlines" were high priority messages from Stratemeyer to his major commanders, *i.e.*, to Maj Gen Howard M. Turner, the 13AF commanding general.

166. Stratemeyer is probably referring to Gen Chou Chih-jou, the Commander-in-Chief, Chinese Air Force and also Chiang's chief of staff.

Nationalists. General MacArthur is behind this procedure 100 percent. You will furnish immediately a liaison group of at least two officers to work with Chinese Air Force and FEC liaison group when established. Your officers will contact Capt. Grant,[167] U. S. Navy, on arrival. He is Admiral Struble's liaison officer in Taipei. Your people will then assist the Chinese Nationalists Air Force in every way possible. New Subject: You, your command group and your liaison are purely professional and have nothing to do with political aspects. Your activities on Formosa will be concerned with defense only. I repeat, you are there to assist the Chinese Air Force. If and when Formosa is attacked, then you operate under Admiral Struble, Commander Seventh Fleet with your fighters. All reports will be addressed and submitted to me only repeat to me only.[168]

The Chinese Nationalist's Air Force consists of 367 to 417 aircraft of all types; they have 331 combat aircraft, 199 of which are operational and ready to fight.

They estimate that the Communist's Air Force totals 167 aircraft of all types; they also estimate that Soviet Russia has in Communist China the following types and manned by Russians: 40 twin-engine bombers; 77 fighters; 38 jet - or total of 155 aircraft.

The total armed forces on Formosa consist of 680,000 men which includes 85,850 Chinese Air Force personnel.

Sent Partridge a "Stratline personal" re "because of the knowledge that you have on atomic energy and the function of SAC in any possible atomic offensive, you are directed to discontinue flights over hostile territory in Korea."

General Kincaid called to say goodbye this afternoon; he departs 1800 hours tonight.

Replied to a letter sent me by Cabell.[169] In his letter he compared Navy strikes against FEAF strikes and was in somewhat of a flap because he said Vandenberg in an embarrassing position if he can't prove (he used the word "irrefutablely") that FEAF is accomplishing its mission. He said, "this situation can be corrected by an all-out effort in reconnaissance to give us the information required." In my reply to Cabell, although a bit sharp, told him to keep his shirt on. That I thought we were doing all right, and that we would get better.

THURSDAY 3 AUGUST 1950 Timberlake in at headquarters from Korea. Sent a memorandum to COMNAVFE telling them they would have to get out of Johnson Air Base as we needed it and they couldn't go into Kisarazu. Recommended Itami which we were turning over in toto to the Navy (they could go into Sendai and Misawa).[170]

Called to General MacArthur's office at 1900 hours. Those present were: (other than CINCFE and myself) Almond, Wright, and Weyland. We discussed with him a signal which he had received from General Walker telling him that a pilot had reported several convoys going south toward Seoul and three trains

---

167. Capt Etheridge Grant, formerly Commander Fleet Air Wing One.
168. Because of JCS and State Department concerns about these actions (mentioned above), the F–80s were not sent to Formosa.
169. Maj Gen Charles P. Cabell, Director of Intelligence, Headquarters USAF.
170. More aircraft were arriving at Johnson and there wasn't any more room to accommodate them, thus the Navy was forced to vacate the base.

moving south toward Seoul. In the discussion, CINCFE reiterated that he wanted a line cut across Korea, north of Seoul, to stop all communications moving south. Of course, I was delighted to receive that direction as we had preached that doctrine since the B–29s arrived. Our intention is to pull the 19th Bomb Group, which was scheduled for close ground support, back to targets that will really isolate the battlefield.[171] We were authorized to continue the third strike against Hŭngnam Chemical and Munitions Plant. After this strike, all three groups will be placed on interdiction of the rail and road communications net north of Seoul.

I directed General Weyland to put this into effect and to get information to General Partridge to put fighters and light bombers on the reported trains and convoys.

One F–51 believed hit by small arms ground fire; crashed near Kŭmch'ŏn.

FRIDAY
4 AUGUST
1950

Headquarters' Advance evacuating Taegu for Pusan.[172] Visited FEAMCOM: departed my CP [command post] 1100 hours for FEAMCOM. Lunched with General Doyle in his new officers' club which to my mind is the best club in FEAF and which was built by General Doyle in spite of many handicaps. He has always had my support in this. Visited all his maintenance and supply buildings as well as his machine shops. Met all his Japanese foremen as well as the non-commissioned foremen. I made a special effort to meet the Japanese foremen to tell them and to have them pass on to the Japanese in FEAMCOM's employ that we in FEAF appreciate very much the effort and fine work that the Japanese employees are doing for us in our effort against the North Koreans in Korea. They all seemed very pleased to receive this statement. Returned to my CP at 1630 hours.

B–29 bombed marshaling yards at Seoul. Reported, in addition to their strikes, that 4 single-engine aircraft were observed taking off from Kimp'o during the bomb run but that no attacks were made on the B–29s.

Sent a letter to Gill Robb Wilson of the New York Herald Tribune as a result of a squib (squib referred to quoted in red in my letter to Mr. Wilson.) that appeared under his name in the Nippon Times of 3 Aug 50. My letter as follows:

I was quite amazed and disturbed at a piece by you published yesterday, 3 August, in the *Nippon Times*. I understand that it is quite an old article of yours published in the States on or about 6 July. I refer

---

171. Because the ground situation up until then was so precarious, the B–29s had been used in a ground support role with little opportunity for strategic or interdiction bombing. On July 24, General Weyland was able to persuade the other members of the Target Selection Committee to release the B–29s from their ground support missions in order to pursue an interdiction role north of the 38th Parallel. Two days later, MacArthur approved this recommendation and set a line between Suwŏn and Kangnŭng, north of which the B–29s would destroy key targets, such as rail and highway bridges, supply depots, and communications centers. An initial list of interdiction targets was issued on July 28 and expanded on August 2. The following day, Stratemeyer ordered 5AF to destroy targets along a belt between the 37th and 38th parallels while the B–29s of Bomber Command went after targets farther north. Thus, when General MacArthur told Stratemeyer on the evening of the 3d to "stop all communications moving south," Stratemeyer already had a comprehensive interdiction plan in place. (Futrell, pp 125-128.)

172. Since the invasion began, the NKPA had enjoyed a succession of victories and was compressing the U.S. and ROK troops into a steadily shrinking area anchored on Pusan. Despite tremendous losses inflicted on both armored and infantry forces by FEAF and Navy planes, the North Korean attacks continued unabated from the south coast near Hadong to the Naktong River west and north of Taegu and thence east to Yongdŏk. Yet, there was a sense of desperation about these enemy assaults, a sense not yet felt by the ground troops who had to stem these vicious attacks.

specifically to the article which contains the paragraph: "Our land-based tactical air power effectiveness has been so poor against North Korean targets that the planes of the aircraft carrier *Valley Forge* and the British carrier *Triumph* had to take over the burden of the tactical air action in North Korea." Knowing you so well and also your penchant for accuracy, I am sure that you had either *(a)* inaccurate information, *(b)* partial information, or *(c)* were deliberately misinformed. The facts in the case are something like this: Since the Korean affair started, the Far East Air Forces fighters (F–80s, F–51s and F–82s) have flown more than 6,000 sorties, firing more than 3 million rounds of ammunition, launching more than 12 thousand rockets, and about 300 tons of bombs released on enemy targets. Our light bombers (the B–26s), although only a meager force, have flown 700 sorties, firing 135 thousand rounds of 50 caliber ammunition, launching more than 650 rockets and have dropped 1,000-plus tons of bombs. Our medium bombers (the B–29s) have flown about 700 sorties and have dropped more than 5,000 tons of high explosives. By far the greater proportion of the above accumulative effort has been in a tactical air power role, for, as you of course know, even the B–29s for quite a period were used in a close interdiction program sometimes within a few miles of the front lines. Air supremacy was gained early in the conflict by the Far East Air Forces and has been maintained ever since. Tactical air power, as represented by our F–51s, F–80s, F–82s, our B–26s, and in many instances by our B–29s, have operated every day since we first went into action on June 27. Without exception, close support to our embattled ground forces has been given every day in spite of some spells of weather that normally would be classed as "unflyable." Our sorties rate has risen as additional aircraft became available from a scant 140 - 160 per day to a figure of more than 500 per day. Once again, I repeat <u>every day</u> [underlined in original] - not in sporadic efforts with large time gaps in between. Now a word about our accomplishments. Forty-nine enemy aircraft have been positively destroyed by the Far East Air Forces, either in air to air combat or by

---

The North Koreans realized that time was running out on them. More U.S. divisions were arriving in Korea, along with more equipment for the ROK forces; FEAF planes were roaming the skies at will and more aircraft were becoming available. If the North Koreans had any chance of victory, it had to be now, before the U.S. and ROK defenders grew too strong.

Now in Korea to help bolster the battered 24th Division were the 1st Cavalry and 25th Infantry Divisions. The 2d Infantry Division and the 1st Marine Brigade would also soon be in action. But like the 24th Division, the first battles of these ill-prepared and undermanned units were costly to them.

A major enemy attack from any place around the shrinking perimeter was possible, but General Walker, the Eighth Army commander, felt the main thrust would occur in front of Taegu. Taegu is 55 miles from Pusan, with a railroad and a good (by Korean standards) road between the two cities. A major water barrier, the Naktong River, runs east to west above Taegu before turning south and then southeast to empty into the Korea Strait at Pusan. Walker did not have sufficient forces (only the 1st Cavalry Division and the 1st and 6th ROK Divisions) to oppose five North Korean divisions in the Taegu area. (Appleman, pp 335-336.) Preferring to have the Naktong in front of him rather than behind, General Walker ordered his forces to retire across the river on the night of August 1. The North Koreans followed close behind the retiring troops and pressed on toward Taegu. They never reached the city, though at one point they were in artillery range of it. Both Generals Walker and Partridge began planning to move their headquarters south. Eighth Army headquarters did not actually move until September, but General Partridge decided to split his staff, sending most of them back to Pusan to open an alternate command post on August 4. He and a skeleton staff remained at Taegu with the Joint Operations Center (JOC). In late September, the Pusan detachment returned to Taegu. (Futrell, pp 120, 176.)

ground attack on enemy airdromes. An additional 7 have been claimed as destroyed and finally, 19 aircraft are in the totals as damaged. The effectiveness of our air supremacy may be indicated by the fact that there has not been a single sighting of an enemy aloft for almost two weeks. Our accomplishments in direct support of the battle are significant and are the true payoff of tactical air power. Our pilots claim to have destroyed 232 tanks and to have damaged 209 more. These claims are unevaluated and are just what the word implies - claims. However, General MacArthur's headquarters, only three days ago, announced that careful evaluation of pilot claims, augmented by factual findings by ground observers, credit the Air Force with definitely destroying 111 tanks which ground observers or others have seen to burst into flame or otherwise show evidence of total destruction. North Korean prisoners of war have stated that the most feared enemy of the tank man is the F–80 and its rockets. Of these they are in constant mortal fear. During the period of the operations of the Far East Air Forces in combat, we have materially assisted the ground forces by destroying almost 1,000 trucks, about 30 locomotives, more than 38 field guns and many box cars. While I have no exact totals on the operations by other arms of our military establishment, I can assure you that their total number of sorties is well under 1,000 and that even their accumulative and unevaluated claims of destruction to enemy materiel are only a fraction of the authenticated destruction by the Far East Air Forces. These facts I place at your disposal, Gill, not in an effort to refute your article, which I am sure was written in good faith, but rather to keep you informed and advised on progress of our air operations here in the Far East. If the information contained in this note is of value to you, I will be happy to keep you filled in from time to time on air operations as we see it here at FEAF. With kindest and warmest personal regards, I remain, etc. P.S. As a last word, may I tell you that contrary to pre-Korean prophecies by some on the complexity of the F–80 and its unsuitability for close support work, this jet fighter originally designed for high altitude interception has flown about 70% of the total fighter sorties to date and has done 85% of the damage thus far inflicted. G.E.S.[173]

Reconnaissance reports high activity in the Seoul - Inch'ŏn area.

Marines expect to have Corsair sq. operating with their controllers, but under Fifth Air Force general coordination, today.

[There was no 5 August diary entry.]

SUNDAY
6 AUGUST
1950

0923 ETA [estimated time of arrival] of Harriman party. This group composed of Mr. W. Averell Harriman, Assistant to the President; Lt. General Matthew B. Ridgway, Deputy Chief of Staff for Administration, USA; Lt. General Lauris Norstad, Acting Vice Chief of Staff, USAF; Major General Roger Ramey, Director of Plans and Operations, USAF; Major General Frank E. Lowe,

---

173. Until his heart attack, Stratemeyer corresponded almost every week with Wilson.

Reserve Officer; Lt. Colonel Frank W. Mooman, Signal Corps, USA; and Major V. A. Walters.[174] CINCFE with Joy, Almond, Sebald, Whitney, and myself form official greeting party.[175] Mr. Harriman billeted at the Embassy; the others at the Imperial, with exception of Norstad and Ramey - our guests at Mayeda House. (Also Major General C.P. Cabell arrived.)[176]

Immediately after the party landed, went direct to GHQ for their briefing. Group had lunch with General MacArthur.

Stratemeyer greets Lt. Gen. Lauris Norstad, the acting Vice Chief of Staff, USAF, upon the latter's arrival with the Harriman party on August 6, 1950.

Dispatched a radio of some length to General Vandenberg on the performance of the F–80, giving him detailed statistics, etc. re the worth of the F–80.

Two F–51s crashed behind North Korean lines; apparently lost thru small arms fire.

General Spivey reports in - to head up Fifth Air Force Rear.

SAC reports they are sending Maj. General T. S. Power[177] to Guam for a TDY period of approximately 3 days.

Had all the USAF people to Mayeda house for cocktails and dinner as well as the Craigies & Gen. Banfill.

MONDAY 7 AUGUST 1950

Harriman party departed Haneda 1/2 hour late 0630 hours and arrived Taegu (South Korea) 9:47. Was met there by General Walker and General Partridge. Proceeded immediately to Walker's Hq. We then proceeded, less Mr. Harriman and General Walker to General Partridge's hqrs. Mr. Harriman had a conference with Mr. Muccio, our Ambassador to South Korea and some of his assistants. Following that, Mr. Harriman and General Walker visited President Rhee. Then they joined us at General Partridge's Hq where a very superior briefing was given to all. All the party, including General Timberlake and General Partridge, then proceeded to General Walker's mess where we had a very fine luncheon.

---

174. Harriman had been the ambassador to Russia from 1943-1946. He was then the ambassador to Great Britain for a few months before being named Secretary of Commerce in October 1946. Since April 1948, he held the rank of Ambassador Extraordinary and Plenipotentiary. Ridgeway commanded the 82d Airborne Division and the XVIII Airborne Corps in World War II. Ramey led both the 5th Bomber Command and the 58th Bomber Wing in World War II. As a reserve officer, the 66-year-old Lowe soon received the unique assignment of presidential assistant for liaison with the United Nations Command and acted as Truman's "eyes and ears" regarding MacArthur. Mooman was on the Army General Staff. Walters is unidentified.

175. William J. Sebald, MacArthur's SCAP political advisor.

176. Harriman had been sent by the President to discuss with MacArthur the administration's and the JCS's policies on Far East matters, particularly those concerning Formosa and China. MacArthur was apparently not impressed with President Truman's thinking, a viewpoint that Harriman noted and passed on to Truman. (J. Lawton Collins, *War in Peacetime* [Boston, 1969], p 150; Alexander, pp 166-167.) Additionally, the party was there to see if Macarthur's continual requests for men and equipment were realistic or just "the sky is falling" attempts to obtain all he could get. They decided he needed what he requested. ("History of the JCS," Vol. III, pp 195-197.)

177. Maj Gen Thomas S. Power, Vice Commander, SAC. In 1957, he became Commander in Chief, SAC.

Immediately after lunch, by jeep we visited 1st Cav C.P., the Tŭksŏng-dong regimental Hq, and after that visited one of the front-line battalions. From General Gay,[178] 1st Cav Commanding, right down through the regimental CP, battalion CP - lts., capts., majors, cols., and General Gay all spontaneously praised the outstanding support that they had received from the air. Naturally, this pleased all of us airmen. We departed battalion CP about 3:30, arrived Taegu where we immediately took off for Tokyo, arriving here at 2035 hours.

My reactions - as well as those of Generals Norstad, Ramey and Partridge - was that General Walker is in great need of a staff. The presentation made to Mr. Harriman and others, to my mind, was one of the poorest - while, in direct contrast, was the outstanding presentation made by General Partridge's staff. This was noticed by all.

Two F–51s with pilots lost behind North Korean lines.

TUESDAY
8 AUGUST
1950

The Harriman party attended FEAF briefing. Set up an office for Mr. Harriman and General Norstad in Room 210. Sent a redline personal to Vandenberg telling him that "advance elements of the 2 new B–29 groups participated in FEAF Bomber Command strategic mission against communication targets in North Korea 4 days and 23 hours after their departure from the ZI."[179]

Called both Mrs. Walker and Mrs. Gay and relayed to them that I had seen their respective husbands, etc.

1000 hours, four of our combat pilots were interviewed by General Norstad in my office.

Partridge forwarded a copy of the letter Ambassador Muccio had written to the Fifth Air Force and which Partridge had circulated among Fifth Air Force:

It has been my intention, ever since the Korean airlift of June 27th, to express to you in writing my sincere and abiding appreciation for the outstanding job done by you and your command. In the face of extremely short notice and of considerable hazard, the officers and crews of the Fifth Air Force planes employed took necessary action to airlift over 500 persons to Japan and to safety. In the absence of the arduous and heroic work of your crews, it is to be feared that many of the evacuees would have fallen into enemy hands. Every commendation is due the officers and men of your Air Force who participated and I join the evacuees in expressions of gratitude for a job well done. s/ John T. Muccio, Ambassador.

---

178. A long-time associate of George Patton's, Maj Gen Hobart R. Gay had been Patton's chief of staff with the I Armored Corps, Seventh Army, and Third Army. Gay took command of the 1st Cavalry Division in September 1949.

179. Like Stratemeyer, the JCS believed that the three B–29 groups already in the Far East had not spent enough time on strategic bombing. They realized that the B–29s had been used to help keep the North Koreans from rolling up the Americans and South Koreans, but they still wanted to institute a strategic bombing program and offered two groups for this purpose on a 30-day temporary duty.
The 98th BG left the United States on August 5 and flew its first mission out of Yokota on the 7th. One day later the 307th BG flew its first mission from Kadena. Just one week before the group had been in Florida. (Futrell, pp 71, 73.)

Sent a "Stratline" to Partridge:

"It is desired that you step up night bombing sorties with all type airplanes your Air Force including B–26s, F–82s, F–51s and F–80s and when you first reach 50 sorties per night, I desire a 'Stratline' message to that effect."

Sent an R&R [routing and record sheet] to Vice Commander for Operations requesting a 100 B–29 airplane strike as soon as can get same cleared from the Target Committee. General Vandenberg will be notified by Redline on the date of the target of the strike; as soon as strike completed, I want another Redline sent to General Vandenberg giving him the results of the strike.

Gave General Norstad the following memo:

In view of the fact that we have received over here in the Far East practically all of the tactical air available within the Air Force and in view of the fact that the Army has called to active duty four (4) National Guard divisions, I feel that action should be taken as follows: Whenever the Army calls to active duty National Guard or Reserve divisions, the Air Force should call to active duty the necessary reserve units and/or National Guard units necessary to give tactical support to the ground divisions called. We do not dare in the Air Force to fail to supply the tactical support to such National Guard or Reserve divisions that are called to active duty.

Gave General Norstad the following memo:

General O'Donnell of the FEAF Bomber Command reported to me that we are encountering serious trouble with valve guides in the modified engines. The new, cast-iron guide is breaking loose from the guide boss and we have made a special check at FEAF Bomber Command and have found that 21 engines in one group with this difficulty. I recommend that you ask General Wolfe to get on this personally. Believe he knows about it because UR's [unsatisfactory reports] were submitted while these SAC organizations were based in the ZI and an emergency UR has been submitted since they have arrived here. The people at Sacramento are aware of this difficulty as are those at Oklahoma City; think it would be well for General Wolfe to have experts from Air Materiel Command or Curtiss-Wright give us some advice on this.[180] I do think this is urgent. We have representatives of the Materiel Division, FEAF, and the Materiel Officer of the FEAF Bomber Command making a detailed inspection this date in an attempt to arrive at a possible local curative action - or submit further detailed information which can be forwarded should circumstances so indicate.

Following is a copy of a letter, written by Partridge to General Walker, dtd 4 August 50:

Today for the first time I have had an opportunity to review the events of the past six weeks and to evaluate the air effort in terms of what was

---

180. McClellan AFB, near Sacramento, had processed the 145 F–51s for delivery to Korea on the *Boxer* and was processing more F–51s, F–80s, and soon, F–86s. At Oklahoma City, Tinker AFB personnel were involved with logistics support for B–29s, B–50s, and B–36s.

accomplished as contrasted with what might have been done. In retrospect, the results have been up to expectations but it would appear that there are certain fundamental deficiencies in the relationship between your staff and mine which have in some instances militated against air operations, both as to volume and as to effectiveness. Weighed down as you are with the grave responsibility of conducting ground operations under most adverse circumstances, I am loathe to raise such basic points as those set forth below; yet the urgent requirement that your units enjoy the maximum in air assistance overbalances my reluctance to present the Fifth Air Force viewpoint. Undoubtedly these considerations have not come to your attention, and the purpose of this letter is to acquaint you with the situation. In reviewing the past six weeks of operations, it is quite apparent that in anticipating requirements, the Fifth Air Force has been caught off balance repeatedly by unexpected ground force actions. For example, although we had been operating over Korea since 26 June, the movement of the 24th Division was made without any planning on the Air Force side beyond that necessary for airlift. Our coordinating parties for controlling the close-in air support eventually caught up with the division but precious time was lost. The 25th Division moved later under similar circumstances. Subsequently, important decisions affecting both the Army and Air Force were made without air participation in the planning. Some of these decisions were implemented before the Air Force was notified. The general withdrawals to the present positions fall in this category. Decisions as to headquarters locations are of especial importance and timely arrangements to install communications are essential if adequate effective air support is to be secured. Yet the Air Force planning in this respect has had to follow rather than run concurrently with yours. I mention these examples not in any sense of complaining, for I am fully aware that circumstances beyond your control or mine have intervened to prevent better coordination. The point I do want to emphasize is that the Air Force has been operating at a disadvantage, and that only the flexibility of our organization permitted us to catch up. As remedial action, it is most urgently requested that the Air Force be accorded opportunity to participate concurrently with your staff in any planning being undertaken. It is not enough that the Air Force be brought in after the project is well formed. As soon as an Army idea is presented for consideration, my staff should be advised and should immediately contact their opposite numbers at your headquarters. Similarly, Air Force projects should be discussed and worked on by your people. You have recently assigned Colonel H. S. Robertson to duty as G-3 Air in the Fifth Air Force operations center. May I suggest that he be used as contact officer, that he be kept fully informed of all projects to be taken under study, and that he be specifically directed to pass the information to Colonel Meyers, my assistant chief of staff for operations. Obviously this system will work only if Colonel Robertson enjoys the complete confidence of your planning personnel, and the same applies to Colonel Meyers who will pass project information in the opposite direction through Colonel Robertson. Both are senior responsible officers, and I have full confidence in their ability to handle this assignment. Allied to the above subject is a matter which gives me grave concern. This is the importance of Taegu to your operations in Korea. We have mentioned this point before, but I have never given you a firm appraisal of the prospects if K-2 airstrip should become untenable because of enemy action. First, the insecurity of K-2 has already caused me to withhold movement of three squadrons of F–51s to that base and one squadron to K-3. This means that even now while we still hold this strip 100 airplanes fly from Kyushu rather than from Korea and their effectiveness is roughly one-third what it would be if Korea-based. Second, it must be anticipated that should K-2 fall, K-3 in the P'ohang-dong area will soon follow. Before this occurs, the remaining two squadrons of F–51s will be returned to Japan with concurrent reduction in their rate; airlift into Korea will be almost eliminated and light aircraft for control and reconnaissance purposes will be reduced in number as well as in effectiveness. Furthermore, even after added airstrips can be built in the Pusan area, Air Force units will probably be seriously hampered in their operations from these new locations because of the unfavorable weather which usually exists in that locality.

For these reasons, I should like to suggest that in future planning you instruct your people to give a high precedence to any line of action which will afford security to K-2. In a tight situation in which air power may tip the scales in our favor, the continued utilization of Korean airfields by our fighters is a major factor. If by chance, the line of action adopted achieved marked successes in the southwest at the expense of Taegu, the net result might prove disastrous.

    E.E. Partridge.

Saw Harriman - Norstad party off at Haneda 1530 hours. Dallas Sherman[181] appealed to me re retention of their APO [Army Post Office] number. Called Hickey and got an OK for appointment.

Mission report: One enemy aircraft reported north of K-3 at 2230; type unknown, believed to be small airplane.

WEDNESDAY **9 AUGUST** **1950**	*General Orders 46 issued:*

WEDNESDAY

9 AUGUST

1950

General Orders 46 issued:

Organization of United States Fifth Air Force in Korea. *(1)* As directed by the Commander-in-Chief, Far East and confirming the VOCG [verbal orders of the commanding general] of 24 July 1950, the Fifth Air Force in Korea is established as of 24 July 1950 as a major command of the Far East Air Forces with Headquarters at APO 970 in addition to Fifth Air Force in Japan. *(2)* Announcement is made of the appointment as of 24 July 1950 of Major General EARLE E. PARTRIDGE, 33A, USAF, as Commanding General, Fifth Air Force in Korea in addition to his duties and responsibilities as Commanding General, Fifth Air Force in Japan. *(3)* As directed by the Commander-in-Chief, Far East all foreign air units (except foreign naval air units) which

---

181. Sherman was the head of Pan American Airways Far East office.

are stationed in Japan or Korea will be placed under the control of the Commanding General, Fifth Air Force. *(4)* The Commanding General, Fifth Air Force in Korea will maintain his headquarters in close proximity to Eighth Army headquarters in Korea.

General Whitney called; said he took up with CINCFE question of permitting General Frank E. Lowe (who is an advisor to the President) to fly to Korea on a FEAF Bomber Command mission. General Whitney says CINCFE says it is OK and decision rests with General Lowe as to whether he wants to go.

Bob Considine[182] (cleared into this theater as representing INS [International News Service]) with Col. Nuckols called at 1430. The following is gist of my remarks: The F–80 versus the F–51: Pilots do not want to change; quick switch from defensive Japanese mission to Korean offensive mission; F–80 has operated every day since 27 June; destruction in air - 16 kills versus one loss. F–80 flew 28 sorties per assigned aircraft; F–51s flew 26; F–80 from Japan longer than F–51 from Korea; F–80 attrition rate one per 200 sorties; F–51 nearly 2 (1.8) per 200 sorties. F–80 has driven enemy from the sky; hence ground forces freedom of action. F–51 can be used for ground support only because of above. F–80 has performed all tactical reconnaissance. F–80 can take battle damage and come home. F–80 is superb as a gun and rocket platform; no torque like F–51. F–80 defends itself against obsolescent aircraft and jet; F–51 cannot. F–80 can escort bombers 600 nautical miles. F–80 can protect Army's rear bases against high altitude bombers. F–80 can do more things and better than F–51.

Bomber Command: Interdiction north of 38th Parallel; mass destruction of targets in North Korea.

Special Orders No. 131 issued naming Brigadier General Delmar T. Spivey as Vice Commander, Fifth Air Force, Rear, as of 6 August 50.

Operations analysts reports in on BOMCOM operations of 7 Aug over P'yŏngyang marshaling yard and arsenal; almost complete destruction of entire arsenal installation; damage so complete on marshaling yard tabulation impossible to make re the damage. Stated to press that "this is the second military target that we can scratch from our current list. The first was the industrial complex at Kōnan."

THURSDAY 10 AUGUST 1950

General Turner arrives at Haneda, 1230 hours accompanied by Colonel Wimsatt.[183]

At 1510, Mr. Charles Corrdry[184] of United Press called with Colonel Nuckols.

Dispatched a "Stratline" to Partridge and O'Donnell with info to the Bomb Groups on Guam and Okinawa, and info to CSAF - necessity of prompt receipt in this hqrs. of certain info which we consolidate and forward to USAF. This info in turn is used to brief Bradley[185] who briefs the President. To insure prompt

---

182. Considine was a noted newspaperman, author and movie screenwriter. Among his books were *30 Seconds Over Tokyo* and *The Babe Ruth Story*.

183. Col Robert W.C. Wimsatt, commander of the 6208th Depot Wing.

184. Corrdry later became *The Baltimore Sun*'s military editor.

185. Gen Omar N. Bradley, a West Point classmate of Stratemeyer, was Chairman, Joint Chiefs of Staff. At this time, the chairman had no vote on JCS deliberations. He presided over the JCS meetings, provided an agenda for these meetings, helped steer the JCS toward the right decisions in the most timely fashion, and attempted to resolve disputes.

receipt, such info to be sent in clear as per my outline; only when material assembled would it be classified. Gave addresses outline to be used in my message. All received and acknowledged message within four hours - except Partridge, which denotes wire troubles somewhere along the line.

Turner and Weyland our guests to dinner at Mayeda House.

FRIDAY 11 AUGUST 1950
At briefing this morning, brought out that 42 night intruder missions were flown night of 10-11 August. I informed General Partridge by telephone that his method of reporting damage, reference the signal for Vandenberg, would continue as he had been reporting in the past -that is, divide by three.

It is reported that fighting was going on in the P'ohang-dong, 6 miles from our K-3 Fighter Strip. Am very concerned about the loss of this as signal came in about 1020 hours that all cryptographic and security materials were destroyed at K-3. This message was addressed to Fifth Air Force Advance, information to me. In talking with General Timberlake, he informed me that Generals Partridge and Walker had gone to K-3 to get first-hand information. The loss of this air strip would mean the cutting-down of fighter-bomber sorties about one-half.

Sent a redline to Cabell:

"Have received another urgent request from Partridge for a 'superior quality intelligence officer to head up intelligence program and to organize it so that he may achieve full coverage of activities.' Request earliest possible solution."

Sent a Stratline message to Partridge telling him that [I] had reiterated your [*sic*, his] need for an intelligence officer.

Sent following memo to O'Donnell:

The Bomber Command has been plugging away at the west railroad bridge at Seoul from 28 June to date, and it still stands. I am confident that motor traffic is proceeding over it. Apparently 500, 1000 and 2000 pound bombs are ineffective. There are larger bombs available for the destruction of this target at Okinawa. I do not like to tell you how to do your job, but certainly B–29s with the proper bomb can take out this bridge. I still want it taken out and urge that it be a continuing target for the FEAF Bomber Command until it is destroyed. At this writing, nothing would please me more than to have a post-strike picture of a couple of the spans of this bridge in the river at Seoul.[186]

---

186. Nicknamed the "elastic bridge" for its ability to not fall but bounce back after these attacks, the west railway bridge at Seoul underwent numerous bombings. The 19th BG went after the bridge day after day for almost a month without success. MacArthur finally offered to commend the unit that would drop the bridge into the river, and Stratemeyer offered a case of Scotch to the crew who destroyed it.
On August 19, nine B–29s of the 19th BG laid 54 tons of bombs on the bridge, reporting numerous hits, yet the bridge still stood. That afternoon, 37 Corsairs and Skyraiders from CAG–11 had a try at the bridge. The bridge was shaky but still not down following this attack. The following day, however, when the 19th returned to try again, two spans of the bridge were in the water. Bombs from the B–29s sent a third span crashing. A delighted MacArthur presented both the 19th BG and CAG–11 with trophies for their work. An equally delighted Stratemeyer managed to round up two cases of Scotch for the two groups. (Futrell, pp 130-131.)

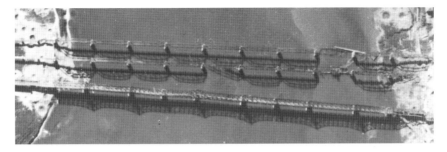

Nicknamed the "elastic" or "rubber bridge" for its ability to withstand bomb-ings, the west railroad bridge at Seoul can be seen at the far right of the photo.

FEAF BomCom General Order No. 4, as dated 8 August 50, announced that Brigadier General James E. Briggs,[187] announced as Commanding General, FEAF Bomber Command, ADVON, APO 239, Unit 1.

Rad[io] received from USAF dtd 9 Aug:

...Effective this date the Commanding General FEAF is delegated author-ity to make awards, to personnel of any foreign government which is a co-belligerent with the United States in the Korean theater and is co-par-ticipant in such operation, of the following decorations: Silver Star, Dis-tinguished Flying Cross, Bronze Star Medal, Air Medal.

(For info: Medal of Honor and DSM [Distinguished Service Medal] reserved for Hq. USAF: DSC [Distinguished Service Cross] and LM [Legion of Merit] reserved for theater commander. Reserved for CO FEAF: Silver Star [underlining in original]; DFC [Distinguished Flying Cross], Soldier's Medal, the Air Medal, Commendation Ribbon, Bronze Star Medal and Purple Heart given to our commanders of major general rank.)

Had conference with Generals Craigie and Turner reference our survey group for Formosa. I instructed General Turner, in his conversations with Gen-eral Stearley, to utilize all possible help that can be made available from the 51st Fighter Wing for this survey group as well as people from Clark Air Force Base. The people at Naha and what is left of the people at Clark are in no way involved in the Korean situation, and, therefore, most of the survey group should come from Naha and Clark - exceptions being those individuals that Deputy for Materiel, Colonel Alkire, feels should come from here.

**SATURDAY
12 AUGUST
1950**

In accordance with my instructions, General Banfill pre-sented a written request to General Willoughby to prepare psychological warfare leaflets for dropping in North Korea, for the purpose of warning the civilian population, particularly women and children, to move away from military objectives within North Korea.

---

187. General Briggs had been commander of the 307th BW at MacDill AFB, Florida. When the 307th BG was sent to the Far East, Briggs was assigned as deputy commander of FEAF BomCom. In this capacity, he was given operational control of the 19th, 22d, and 307th groups at Kadena, and his headquarters was designated as the advanced echelon for FEAF BomCom.

General Banfill also expressed to General Willoughby my concern over the latitude given the press in reporting both enemy and our own dispositions. This has reached a point where American lives are definitely being jeopardized and I recommend that consideration be given to the imposition of some form of censorship. General Willoughby's answer was to the effect that while he himself agreed in principle, the Commander-in-Chief was definitely opposed to censorship in any form.

Major General T. S. Power of SAC arrives Tokyo. Took Generals Power, Craigie, Weyland and Timberlake (in from Taegu, Korea) to lunch at the Union Club.

Major General Frank E. Lowe, USAR, sent me the letter he wrote to General O'Donnell, commending the latter on the efficiency of his command, his abilities as a leader, and extending his thanks for the "ride" over targets in the "Tiger Lil" - piloted by a Capt. Bill Campbell of the 31st Recon Sq. Forwarded the letter on to O'Donnell expressing my gratification and pleasure on General Lowe's successful flight over Korea and that said flight would produce an accurate report back to the President. General Lowe is the Presidents personal representative out here.

Dispatched the following letter to General LeMay:

Here are a few highlights on the operations of FEAF which are of particular interest to you. As you probably read in news dispatches, elements of the 98th Bombardment Group participated in an attack four days and twenty-three hours after their departure from the Z.I. Not to be out done, the 307th Bomb Group did equally well having flown an additional 3,000 miles in approximately the same relative time. The performance of the 22d and the 92d Bombardment Groups has been outstanding and far exceeded our planned operations to date. Personnel in the bomb groups have performed their duties on the ground and in the air in an exemplary manner. The combat crews have worked side by side with the maintenance crews loading bombs, arming turrets and assisting generally in the engineering maintenance of the aircraft. Inclement weather without the benefit of cover or hangar space, has made this no easy task. The 19th Bomb Group is being rapidly built up and their results have been excellent against precision targets. I believe you'll find them well qualified to participate in your overall plan when called upon. They are nearly on a par with the 22d and 92d right now. Rosie O'Donnell is doing a bang-up job and although not able at all times to use his '29s on targets to his liking, he has loyally and efficiently carried out the directives given to him. Thanks for letting him come. We are now using the five (5) medium bomb groups on targets north of the 38th Parallel. Until certain interdiction targets which require precision bombing have been taken out, the FEAF Bomber Command will be directed to employ: Two bomb groups with their main effort on interdiction targets and three bomb groups on the mass destruction of selected targets. I take this opportunity to tell you of the very superior service that your liaison officer, Lt. Colonel James E. Trask[188] has performed since joining FEAF. He knows the bomber business, he has pitched in and

---

188. Col Trask was a FEAF plans and programming officer.

worked in my plans section - at times straight through twenty-four hours. I consider him one of the finest young officers that I have come in contact with for a long time. His smartness, his knowledge of medium bomber tacts, his loyalty to you and the Air Force and his absolute loyal cooperation with me and my staff have all been outstanding. I commend him to you when he returns for any important assignment that you have - and for promotion. He will wear a decoration when he leaves which I will award to him personally. I also take this opportunity to thank you for the personal interest that you have taken in our job over here and the expeditious manner in which your units have moved to the Far East and the spirit with which they have jumped in to do the job that has been assigned to them. A visit from you, in which General MacArthur joins me, would be most welcome. Tommy Power is here with us today which has been most worthwhile to us and I am sure will be to you. Again, many many thanks for your help and the spirit in which it has been rendered.

At 1530 hours did a telecast at the request of Charles DeSorias of the *Los Angeles Times* TV Station. Mr. DeSorias did the interviewing. His questions were: what can I report to the American people as to the AF position to-date, something about the fighters - what they have done, the performance of the Mustangs, the striking force of the '29s - and a summary from me. I answered all questions at length - re the first, our position - we have been operating for 47 days straight, driven the Reds from the skies with our F–80s in particular, and giving close support to our gallant ground forces. The F–80 has proven itself; has the speed and fire power, its magnificent close support of the ground forces has brought nothing but praise - General Gay stated he nor his men have ever been harassed by enemy air action. The '51 is doing a superb job, but in fairness to both a/c, the '51 is obsolete - F–80 can do everything the '51 can do and do it better. The employment of '29s is an excellent example of mobility and capabilities of the B–29. Within 8 days after their move from the ZI - total of 8,000 miles, they were bombing the enemy's dockside installations at Wŏnsan. B–29s have 2 major missions: destroying the enemy's transportation system at key points north of the 38th; and destroying enemy's military supply production. In my summary I told him that the FEAF of the U.S. had shifted from a defensive mission to an offensive mission in the first 24-hours of the war and since then have carried the fight to the enemy. Everyone doing a magnificent job, the great pride I have in my command in that it is proving itself to be such an effective Air Force and that the resourceful American youth, in the air and on the ground, is once again doing his stuff.

Will give Major General Lowe, USAR, representative of the President, some pre- and post-strike photos as well as a report on our operational activities for the past 47 days.

SUNDAY 13 AUGUST 1950

I furnished an album to General Lowe, the President's representative, covering FEAF's operations in Korea the past 47 days since the war started. It included the operations of the fighter-bombers, the recon, the B–29s, the light bombers and the cargo aircraft. It gave our kills and losses including personnel, aircraft, tanks, etc. It also included strike pictures of the P'yŏngyang marshaling yards and arsenal, the oil refinery and marshaling yards at Wŏnsan and the chemical complex of three targets at Kōnan (Hŭngnam) and several pictures of the actual tank kills by the Fifth Air Force. General Lowe's remark to me this morning, prior to his departure, was to the effect the Air Force was "tops" out here and if the war could be ended by middle of November, the credit belonged with the Air Force.

After talking with Pat, wrote the following memo to VC for Ops (info to VC A&P):

In a telephone conversation with General Partridge at Taegu this morning, he reported the following: Captain Tracy,[189] USN, was assigned to the Eighth Army as Navy liaison. He was sent over to General Partridge for use as a Navy liaison officer with the Fifth Air Force. General Partridge felt that since his assignment was with the Eighth Army, he could not utilize his services and now has assigned to him a Lieutenant Commander Burch,[190] USN. This morning, General Walker called on General Partridge and they had a very crisp, but pleasant, difference of opinion as to the use of the Joint Operations Center and its location. Field Manual 31-35, published by the Department of the Army, clearly states the functions of the Joint Operational Center, its location and the overall control of that body as an Air Force function although it is made up of the three (3) Services –Army, Navy, and Air Force– and justly so. General Partridge reported to me that there was a great possibility that General Walker would protest the control and operation of that center to Headquarters, Far East Command and this paper is written to you to prepare you to defend the Air Force interpretation and use of the Joint Operational Center before the Far East Command staff who might raise the question. Your experience in Europe should very definitely prove beyond all shadow of a doubt the proper use of a Joint Operational Center and I desire that you represent me in any discussions that are raised on this subject.[191]

General Orders #46, dtd 9 August AS CORRECTED issued:
Subject: Organization of United States Fifth Air Force in Korea.

1. As directed by the Commander-in-Chief, Far East and confirming the VOCG of 24 July 1950, the Fifth Air Force in Korea is established as of 24 July 50 as a major operational command of the Far East Air Forces with headquarters at APO 970. The Fifth Air Force with headquarters at Nagoya, Japan remains as now established and organized.

2. Announcement is made of the appointment as of 24 Jul 50 of Major General Earle E. Partridge, 33A, USAF, as Commanding General, Fifth Air Force in Korea in addition to his duties and responsibilities as Commanding General, Fifth Air Force in Japan.

3. As directed by the Commander-in-Chief, Far East all foreign air units (except foreign naval air units) which are stationed in Japan or Korea will be placed under the control of the Commanding General, Fifth Air Force.

---

189. Capt John S. Tracy.
190. Lt Cdr John A. <u>Murch</u>.
191. The Joint Operations Center (JOC) was composed of Army and Air Force personnel and comprised two sections. One, the air-ground operations section, was Army-manned and sent to the second section Army

4. This order does not change the structure, administrative organization or functions of the Fifth Air Force, Nagoya, Japan, to which all Fifth Air Force units and personnel remain assigned.

5. The Commanding General, Fifth Air Force in Korea will maintain his operational headquarters in close proximity to Eighth Army headquarters in Korea.

Sent a buck slip to IG in answer to an R&R submitted by Weyland re the establishment of an Air Evaluation Board which would collect, record, correlate evaluate and inform me and the VCs on: past, present, and future training of FEAF units and associated Army and Navy units; shortcomings or difficulties and action taken to overcome them; coordination procedures within FEAF and with other major commands under FEC; efficiency of operating procedures; and bomb, rocket, and other loadings and their relation to different type targets. In my buck slip to the IG referred him to my memo dtd 21 July, relieving him from duty with D/Ops [deputy for operations], returning him to IG and memo of 25 July, subject: Inspection System during Korean Operations. Told him I considered the IG and his group of officers to be my Air Evaluation Board, and, in addition, to the directives that I have issued, desired that the IG perform those suggestions as listed by Weyland above.

Air base at K-3 evacuated. PIO at K-3 announced above. This should not have been done; however, reporters were present and they would have said something. Eighth Army does this all the time.

MONDAY
14 AUGUST
1950

On the 21st of July I wrote a letter to COMNAVFE expressing my appreciation as to the marked success of the carrier air strikes on 18 and 19 July against North Korean targets and also commented that it was gratifying to hear that 47 enemy aircraft had been destroyed - indication of resurgent North Korean air power and the warning furnished us by that attack will be instrumental in avoiding losses to friendly forces. Asked that this appreciation on behalf of the Air Force be extended to Admiral Struble.

Following is a memo dated 10 Aug from COMNAVFE to me:

(1) Your letter of 21 Jul 50 is acknowledged with pleasure and appreciation. I know it will be received with pride by Vice Admiral Struble and the personnel of his fleet when it is delivered to them. *(2)* Your headquarters furnished most of the target information, coordination effort, and photographic data which markedly assisted in the success of the 18-19 July strikes. *(3)* The spirit of willing and energetic cooperation exhibited

---

requests for tactical air missions. The second section, made up of Air Force personnel, then ordered available tactical air units to implement the Army requests. The JOC first began operating from Taejŏn on July 5 but had to relocate to Taegu between July 16-19 when the fall of Taejŏn became imminent.

Though not part of the JOC, a tactical air control center (TACC) worked closely with it. Through the TACC, which was really a communications center, General Partridge was able to control his aircraft. Although air defense was one of its duties, the TACC at Taegu operated primarily as fighter director control for close support missions. Target identification and control of the actual strikes were functions of two different teams. Operating in the front lines with radio-equipped jeeps were the tactical aircraft control parties (TACP). The other team used T–6 aircraft, known as "Mosquitoes," for airborne control of strike aircraft.

In actual practice, most of the functions of the JOC were taken over by 5AF personnel, the Eighth Army being unable, or unwilling, to staff its air-ground section. It would be some months before the JOC truly became a joint operation.

by your staff, and key members of the Far East Air Forces with whom they deal, has brought forth much favorable comment from officers of my command. This fine spirit continues to build a high mutual regard and firm bond of understanding between the U.S. Navy and the U.S. Air Force in this theater. signed C.T. Joy.

Rcvd [received] following letter from O'Donnell dated 12 Aug:

I certainly appreciate your comprehensive letter of the 10th on support of the B–29s. You can fully depend upon my staff to work together with your own, and that of FEAMCOM, in resolving the difficult logistic problems with which you are faced. You can, of course, readily understand my own concern over anything that might prevent us from giving you the maximum possible tonnage of bombs on North Korean targets. I have been so concerned with the many B–29 supply and further maintenance difficulties since I assumed command of the Fifteenth [Air Force] that is difficult to suddenly divorce myself from such problems and think only of operational matters. My small materiel staff here is comprised of individuals who have, through early appreciation of B–29, B–50 and B–36 deficiencies in the past, earned the respect of all in SAC and AMC. They are sometimes overzealous and I have tried to direct their enthusiasm in the proper channels - so far to good effect. You can depend upon them to keep your materiel command well-informed on anticipated troubles, and to assist in their solution in every possible way. s/ E. O'Donnell

In answer to my "Stratline" dated 8 Aug 50, to Partridge re stepping up night bombing sorties to 50 per night, received the following letter from Partridge dtd 11 Aug 50:

According to my original understanding it was a straightforward directive to use all the type of aircraft available to me for night bombing with the objective set at not less than 50 sorties per night. Accordingly, a plan was set up by which all the B–26 effort would be used at night with an expectation of 36 sorties daily. There are three F–82 aircraft not equipped with radar which have been employed as night intruders. We estimated that by a full-scale effort, we could get 5 sorties per night out of these 3 airplanes. As for F–80s, our experience has not yet been too satisfactory and in view of this and the fact that we are yet unable to carry bombs we decided not to use F–80s, on a continuing basis. The F–51 is not a satisfactory night intruder, but can be effective in good weather under optimum visibility conditions. One of the major objections to this type aircraft is its lack of radio compass. By utilizing all our B–26 effort, all the F–82 effort not reserved for the air defense of Japan and a full squadron of F–51s we might be able to achieve 50 sorties nightly when weather permits. Before discussing it with Craigie and before Timberlake talked to you, this is the plan which we adopted as the only one which would achieve the desired number of sorties. The 162d Night Reconnaissance Squadron, equipped with photographic B–26s should be in operation within the not too distant future.[192] Initially, they will have 16 aircraft. This squadron is able to bomb and can be diverted from its primary role of night photographic work if the priority to be accorded night bombing is sufficiently high. If the 162d is used, it might be possible to run 50 intruder sorties per night, using B–26s alone. In addition to the Fifth Air Force effort, we can anticipate that some sorties will be available each night from the Marine night fighter squadron which is based at Itami and staged out of Itazuke. We have not included the Marines in our estimates. Following your talk with Timberlake, we have relieved the one F–51 squadron from its requirement to put out night intruder aircraft, and as the situation now stands, we expect to fly 2 squadrons of B–26s, a few F–82 and a few Marine night fighters whenever the weather permits. No one knows better than I the pressing need for a better night bomber and intruder effort. Nevertheless, I am reluctant to continue employing all our light bombers for night work. Accordingly, I should like to make the following suggestions to secure a more effective distribution for the night effort now available to the Fifth Air Force, and to augment that effort. Continue to employ one B–26 squadron full-time for night intruder work; concentrate at Itazuke all the night fighter aircraft in this theater regardless of their condition as to operational radar. Employ these aircraft full out on a night intruder effort until such time as more suitable aircraft can be secured; continue to employ Marine night fighters over Korea as can be made available by them; employ the 162d Night Reconnaissance Squadron for both photographic and night intruder work; these airplanes can drop bombs in an emergency; initiate a firm request to the United States for them to reconstitute night light bomber squadrons in such number as the equipment now on hand will support. Action by your headquarters to this end is requested; secure from the ZI a nucleus of a night bombing section for Fifth Air Force headquarters. I am not personally acquainted with any officers whose previous experience qualifies them for this position, but I do know that there was a light bomber group which specialized in night operations, and I should like to have the benefit of their experience. Action by your headquarters is requested; if the United Nations wants to support the war effort in this theater by supplying aircraft squadrons from the RAF [Royal Air Force], RCAF [Royal Canadian Air Force], or elsewhere, I should like to suggest that night bomber squadrons would constitute the greatest contribution which they could make; even a meager number of Lancasters or Mosquitos operated from bases in Japan would be most welcome. If you think the idea has merit, please pick up the ball from here.

Lastly, I feel certain from my previous experience in England and Africa that there exist munitions and techniques which would assist us in carrying on our night bomber effort. I believe we should explore the possibility of securing, probably from the RAF, a few experts together with

---

192. The 162d had been alerted at Langley AFB, Va. on July 5. Brought up to near-wartime strength by fillers who knew nothing about RB–26s, the squadron was shipped overseas. Flash cartridge equipment had been fitted on 10 of the squadron's 16 planes (the other planes could not be modified), but it was then discovered that this equipment made the RB–26s too heavy for the overwater flight to Japan. The flash units were removed for air shipment, but this was somehow changed to water shipment. It would not be until August 26, 53 days after it was alerted, that the 162d was ready for its first mission. (Futrell No. 71, p 100.)

samples of their munitions and proposed standard operating procedures. Perhaps you would like to discuss this matter with the recently arrived Air Vice Marshal Bouchier[193] from the RAF. As a general thought, I do not believe that we are getting over-all effectiveness by trading good day sorties for questionable night missions, particularly when the number of day sorties is roughly twice that we can fly at night. For that reason, my suggestions above have run toward the objective of increasing our night potential rather than toward the diversion of day effort for night purposes. s/ E.E. Partridge.

In answer to above received ltr from Partridge, sent him following:

Upon receipt of your letter of 11 August, I reviewed my message A 392906, dated 8 August, and find that it conveys a more firm and rigid meaning than I had intended. Therefore, please consider that directive rescinded. What I had intended to convey, and what I still desire, is for you to step up night intruder operations as much as possible with units now available and to become available, while maintaining an optimum balance between day and night operations. I leave to your judgment and on-the-spot knowledge of conditions, the determination of the best way and rate of augmenting your night operations to achieve optimum overall results. With the foregoing in mind, I want to say that I concur, in general with most of your suggestions in paragraphs <u>a</u> to <u>h</u>, inclusive, of your letter. I do not, however, concur in your suggestion to employ *all* [emphasis in original] F–82s on night intruder work, and I want you to retain not less than a flight of night fighters in each air defense area. With reference to assisting you in getting qualified personnel for a night bombing section in your headquarters, I have initiated action to obtain Colonel F. R. Terrell[194] for you, and also to get an RAF officer experienced in night bombing and intruder work. Other suggestions involving action by my headquarters will be investigated and followed up as circumstances dictate. I want to tell you again that I am proud of the magnificent work being done by the Fifth Air Force, and am especially appreciative of your own personal contributions.

The United Press staff correspondent, Robert Miller, under dateline 14 August with the Marines, published one of the most reprehensible pieces of carefully contrived propaganda and untruths that I have read in my military career. It is my opinion and that of my PIO that this was not only stimulated by Navy sources, but was even prepared by them in detail. This article is filled with innuendoes and make odious comparison between the Marines on the ground and the Army units, interspersed with similarly odious comparisons between Marine aviation and the USAF. It is my opinion that this will result only in

---

193. With the British considering what role their forces might play in Korea, the government recalled Air Vice Marshal (later, Sir) Cecil Bouchier to represent the British Chiefs of Staff in Japan. Bouchier served with the BCOF from 1945-1948 and had developed a great rapport with MacArthur. He arrived on August 8.

194. Terrell commanded the 47th BG from January 1942 to June 1943. This group later became the premier USAAF night intruder unit in the Mediterranean and was, until converting to a jet bomber unsuited for the role, the only such outfit in the USAF prior to the Korean War. After Terrell was assigned to the War Department General Staff in April 1944, he was (according to his official USAF biography) "instrumental in establishing night tactical bombing operations as U.S. air doctrine."

fanning the fires of dissention between the services here under MacArthur where, to date, we have had great team play. I consider it a blatant, service-inspired series of mis-statements.[195]

Following memorandum given to General Crabb, Deputy for Operations, as a directive:

We can cover an area five (5) miles long by one (1) mile wide, dropping with seventy (70) B–29s, 2,520 x 500 pound bombs. FEAF Bomber Command will be loaded and ready to perform such a mission on Wednesday 16 August. We must have clear weather as the drop will be made from an altitude of 5,000 or 6,000 feet. There must be a definite terrain feature such as the Naktong River in order to prevent dropping on our own troops. It is believed that when the North Koreans commit themselves to any mass attack east of the Naktong River, such a bomber strike would pay dividends. (Wednesday, 16 August weather permitting; maybe postponed until 17 August if weather bad.)[196]

8:30 A.M. Air Marshal Jones (RAAF) in; attended FEAF briefing with me.

12:30 P.M. Rear Admiral Alfred Carroll Richmond,[197] of the United States Coast Guard. Interested in LORAN stations throughout the Pacific and west coast of P.I.[Philippine Islands].

2:00 P.M. Lunch (stag) with General and Mrs. MacArthur honoring the Prime Minister of Australia, Rt. Hon. Menzies.[198]

8:30 P.M. Dinner (stag) at Commonwealth House, Embassy of Australia, honoring Rt. Hon. Menzies.

---

195. Miller's article grossly misrepresented the differences between the Air Force and Marine systems of close support. While effective for short periods and with small numbers of troops, the Marine system of having aircraft either attached to or operating closely with specific ground units was very inefficient and a costly use of air power when done with a large ground force or over longer perods. Additionally, there was a point that seemed to have escaped most of the ground commanders but not Stratemeyer; that FEAF had established complete air superiority over the enemy. The Marine system relied upon other air power assets to provide the key prerequisite to effective close air support.
In an October 2, 1950, memorandum on the subject of historical reporting of the war, Stratemeyer mentioned several times that if not careful, wrong conclusions could be drawn on the matter of close support. "There was no hostile interference from hostile air...," he commented.
"If there had been an enemy air force, it is questionable — to my way of thinking — that the ground troops could ever have been supplied by long truck columns and train as they were from Pusan.
"The great proportion of our air effort would of necessity have been to knock out hostile air both on the ground and in the air." (Memo, Gen G. E. Stratemeyer to ?, subj: Final Reporting—Korean Conflict, Oct. 2, 1950.)
196. The buildup of North Korean forces in front of Taegu worried General Walker, particularly since his own troops were spread dangerously thin. The Waegwan area, where the main highway and railroad crossed the Naktong, appeared to be an especially critical sector. Though 5AF fighter-bombers and B–26s attacked an enemy bridgehead at Waegwan with some success, General MacArthur remained alarmed at this North Korean threat. He therefore desired that the entire FEAF B–29 force be used to "carpet bomb" those areas where large enemy forces appeared to be concentrated. On the 13th, General Partridge learned that the B–29s would be used on August 15 to bomb near Waegwan. (Futrell, pp 138-139.)
197. Adm Richmond was Assistant Commandant of the Coast Guard.
198. Sir Robert Menzies had been Prime Minister of Australia in 1939-1941. From 1943-1949, he was Leader of the Opposition before once again becoming Prime Minister, a post he then held for the next 17 years.

TUESDAY
15 AUGUST
1950

Sent an R&R to VC Ops, ATTN D/Ops:

Reference my memorandum to you dated 14 Aug on the mission set-up for Wednesday, 16 August or Thursday, 17 August, all ground troops down to and including the squad must be briefed on this strike prior to time of drop. I talked with General Partridge at 0740 hours this morning and cautioned him of my desires reference this matter. He guaranteed that he would take same up with General Walker and that it would be done. Even though General Partridge will do as stated above, I want a very carefully worded directive given to him with information copies to the CG, 8th Army and CINCFE, clearly defining the boundaries of the target area with time and date of the attack.

Received a letter from Gill Robb Wilson in which he explained that getting news of what is happening is like "prospecting for diamonds in a bathtub."

My reply to him was that I had thought that he wasn't getting the news - correctly and factually, and that I, besides sending him straight dope from time to time, he would find news coming in better at home because I was getting my PIO difficulties ironed out. Told him we both hope to see him in November - and re his running for Congress would make no comment; however it will be great to have another real booster for air power in Wash on the Hill.

Sent the following memo to VC for Ops attention D/Ops:

Reference my memorandum to you dated 14 August (Reference the mass B–29 [70 aircraft] attack drop from 5,000 feet on North Korean front lines.) on the mission set up for Wednesday, 16 August, or Thursday, 17 August, all ground troops down to and including the squad must be briefed on this strike prior to the time of the drop. I talked with General Partridge at 1740 hours this morning and cautioned him re my desires reference this matter. He guaranteed that he would take same up with General Walker and it would be done. Even though General Partridge will do as stated above, I want a very carefully worded directive given to him with information copies to the Commanding General, Eighth Army and CINCFE, clearly defining the boundaries of the target area with time and date of attack.

Sent the VC for A&P [administration and plans] a memo:

I want copies of the two T.S. signals that were sent to the CSAF reference our plans for the construction of a jet flying field and a transport flying field at Pusan forwarded to General Partridge. Maybe the two signals can be combined and the data set forth therein put in a letter in the form of a directive to Partridge. If the latter is done, I want to sign it.

Memo sent to VC for Ops thru VC A&P:

In a conference that I had with General MacArthur at 1810 hours last evening, the coming amphibious operation was discussed and the two points that he raised, and with which he is concerned were: *(1)* quickness with which we can rehabilitate the airfield at Kimp'o, and *(2)* have available fuel at that airfield as well as ammunition and bombs.[199] He indicated to me that the distance from the salt water to the airfield was only some 15 miles. He was confident that a tanker could be docked and fuel quickly placed as well as ammunition and bombs. It is desired that the planning people working on this operation consider and study the above two questions raised and that a prepared expeditious solution be presented to me for approval.

Memo to VC for A&P:

Some two weeks ago I asked that some thought be given to the organization of a small command group, representing FEAF, to accompany me when I accompany CINCFE on any Far East Command movement outside of Japan. To date, I have received nothing on this subject. Please give it attention and come up with a recommendation on the size and composition of such a command group.

Presented a strike album to CINCFE; book contains representative types of FEAF strikes accomplished; vehicular traffic attacked by fighters as their contribution toward interdiction and close support; strikes by light bombardment a/c in their contribution towards isolation of the battlefield; industrial targets attacked by medium bombardment a/c showing their contribution toward total destruction of the enemy's capability to wage war.

Sent a message to Norstad stating

In conference with CINCFE last evening, he directed that a signal be sent you reference your statements to him during your departing conference in his office regarding B–29 groups in theater. General MacArthur desires that the two recently arrived medium bomb groups be retained in this theater at least for an additional month which would mean 8 October and, further, that you be informed that in all probability he will request another and final delay until 8 November.

---

199. Before U.S. and North Korean troops clashed at Osan on July 5, MacArthur was already envisioning an amphibious operation against the enemy. Even at that time, MacArthur's choice for a target was Inch'ŏn, and he believed that a landing could be accomplished as early as July 22. Planning began immediately but the serious reverses the American and ROK troops were suffering doomed these plans to early deaths. Undeterred, MacArthur continued to consider an amphibious thrust behind enemy lines. When Collins and Vandenberg were in Japan in mid-July, MacArthur outlined a tentative plan regarding an amphibious operation to take place after the North Koreans were stopped. Several landing spots were considered but MacArthur believed that Inch'ŏn still was the best target.
(It appears that the Inch'ŏn landings did not spring full-blown out of MacArthur's fertile mind. Such a plan, called SL-17, had been produced by the Army and distributed on June 19, 1950. During the first week of the war, MacArthur's headquarters "urgently" requested 50 copies of SL-17.) (Clay Blair, *The Forgotten War*, New York, 1987, p 87.)
Not everyone was as sanguine as MacArthur that Inch'ŏn was a good choice for an amphibious landing. Collins and Adm Forrest P. Sherman, the Chief of Naval Operations, were among those with doubts about the landings. Tremendous tidal changes occured at Inch'ŏn, leaving amphibious craft with limited times that they could operate safely. Extensive mud flats covered the harbor, areas that could be death traps if the landings did not go well or were off schedule. The "beaches" were just strips of waterfront protected by seawalls that were too high for landing craft to be able to use their ramps. It also had to be assumed that a pair of islands between Inch'ŏn's inner and outer harbors were sites of enemy defensive positions. Inch'ŏn was a place where everything had to go smoothly, but where everything wrong could happen. (D. Clayton James, *Refighting the Last War: Command and Crisis in Korea 1950-1953*, New York, 1993, pp 162-163.)
Tidal conditions at Inch'ŏn narrowed MacArthur's options considerably. September was a month of transition between the low tides of summer and the high tides of fall. While tides in mid-October would be satisfactory,

B–29s report on their strike north of the 38th Parallel, one of the B–29s was attacked by a single-engine fighter. The fighter identified as an La–5, made two or three passes at the Superfortress, but broke off the engagement after the Super-fort tail gunner fired some 100 rounds.[200] Several other enemy fighters were observed, but they did not close in for an attack.

11:30 A.M., General Ho called.

2:30 P.M., Ed Murrow with Nuckols. Murrow came by to say goodbye and said he was going to pass on to Van and Norstad the superior job we were doing out here.

7:00 P.M., Nuckols, Weyland and the Pichers to dinner at Mayeda House.

WEDNESDAY 16 AUGUST 1950

Sent a 6-page, strong, carefully-worded redline, T.S., to Norstad, re the United Press story as written by Robert Miller. Radio in M2 parts; in first part was my own personal reaction to the type of article written; part 2 was an analysis of the major contentions and innuendoes made by Miller in his release.

Sent a redline to Vandenberg:

About 90 B–29s in heaviest concentrated bomber operation to date, today dropped more than 800 tons of 500 lbs. GP bombs, instantaneously fused, on 3 1/2 by 7 1/2 area immediate northwest of Waegwan, in close support of our forces. First element over target at 1050K, with visual bombing conditions; excellent results. Bombing completed about 1300K. Attack made on south to north axis, with Naktong River serving as eastern boundary. Flash reports from planes still airborne indicate generally excellent results.[201]

Copy of a signal sent by Joy (Comnavfe) to his command forwarded me by Joy with attached buck slip:

"Hope the attached dispatch to all naval units under my command will stop any more irresponsible comments which I deplore as much as you do." The radio reference is as follows:

To NAVFE, info - CINCPACFLT and CNO [Commander in Chief, Pacific Fleet and Chief of Naval Operations]. It has been brought to my attention that criticism is being voiced by members of the naval service

---

the probable bad weather at that time placed constraints on both air and ground operations. Thus, the only days in September when tides would be high enough for landing operations were September 15-18. MacArthur decided upon a September 15 landing. The rehabilitation of Kimp'o was a requirement because it was to be used by FEAF transport aircraft for the delivery of ammunition, rations, and other needed cargo to the front-line troops.

200. The radial-engined Lavochkin La–5 had first entered combat in the autumn of 1942. It was probably a replacement aircraft for the NKAF, which had been almost wiped out.

201. Instead of a one mile by five mile area as noted by Stratemeyer on Aug. 14, the area the Army wanted bombed was 3 1/2 miles wide by 7 1/2 miles long. Nevertheless, the 98 bombers of the five B–29 groups dropped the majority of the bombs (which had a blast effect similar to that of 30,000 rounds of artillery) with what appeared to be excellent results. Some 40,000 enemy troops had been reported to be in the target area west of the Naktong, but when General O'Donnell personally inspected the scene from the air, he could see no signs of enemy activity. This massive attack apparently had been a waste of time and materiel, because later information indicated that the enemy troops had already crossed the Naktong before the bombing and had been untouched. From a psychological standpoint, though, General Walker believed the bombing had raised the morale of the U.S. and ROK troops considerably, while depressing that of the opposing force. (Futrell, p 139; Futrell No. 71, pp 47-48; Appleman, pp 352-353.)

against other services of our country. In connection with this situation I concur completely in the following remarks from the Chief of Naval Operations, quote: "It is essential that officers refrain from comparison which derogate the efforts or effectiveness of other services. Such comparisons whether correct or incorrect are in bad taste and are prejudicial to the national interest." unquote. Take action to insure that all personnel both public relations and others are appropriately instructed.

My discussion with General MacArthur this evening resulted in his approving my recommendation not to do any area bombing with B–29s until we really get a clear-cut evaluation of what took place this morning. The reasons backing up my recommendation were: *(1)* area northeast of Naktong River selected for B–29 bombing on 18 or 19 Aug is dangerous to ground troops and completely unsuitable. Fifth AF recommends against this, and EUSAK does not want bombing in this area. *(2)* area M/B [medium bomber] bombing is suitable if ground forces intend to make a break-through, capitalizing on shock and disruption created by the bombing. In this particular case where ground forces are to make a limited attack to reduce the NK [North Korean] salient and drive the NK across the river, accurately controlled close support by fighter bombers is the air weapon most suitable. *(3)* other areas west of the Naktong River are too extensive for B–29s to bomb effectively. Would be waste of effort and would not greatly affect our ground force counter attack except to interfere with fighter bombers. *(4)* fighters and dive bombers of Navy could be utilized in this area to search out specific targets and would have less effect on close support operations of Fifth AF and Marine Air. *(5)* it is imperative that B–29s continue interdiction and destruction missions in North Korea if essential effect is to be achieved by 15 Sep 50. *(6)* JCS have assigned additional NK targets for B–29 destruction. *(7)* Stockpile of 500-pound bombs is critical at this time - available stock pending replenishment should be used in NK. (8) earliest liaison necessary in order that interdiction targets be studied and B–29s properly bombed up, therefore.

Recommend: support of U. S. counter attack be normal type Fifth AF and Marine close support, and U. S. Navy carrier effort be laid on and kept in SK where it is needed. Areas west of Naktong River be assigned to Navy aircraft as coordinated by Fifth Air Force in consultation with EUSAK, and the B–29s resume and stay on the NK interdiction and destruction program.

10:00 Air Marshal Bouchier and I had our pictures taken together for the *London Illustrated News.*

Following is quoted in toto Partridge's personal daily summary to me of 16 Aug:

Part 1. Ref part 4 of yesterday's msg on reuniting hq at Taegu, prospects of continued occupation this location swing with opinions on the ground situation and this morning's situation reverses plan to reunite here. After further consultations with Gen. Walker and his staff and reviews of rail and truck transportation which it now appears might be avail[able] for our use, decided to move aviation engr [engineer] unit from K-2 to Pusan and concentrate work on strip east of city. This stops construction K-2 but insures safety of critical engineer equip which must move by train. Pusan Hq will be made fully opnl [operational] soonest so that control of AF may be transferred to Pusan without delay. Hq being pared down to minimum and impediment either evacuated or made ready for move on 1 hour notice. Exception of signal gear for which several hours notice will be required. We are watching EUSAK and will start dismantling our signal set up when they do. K-2 will remain opnl as at present. *Part 2.* For political reasons General Walker is determined to remain Taegu long as possible. Apparently his staff feels move a military necessity. *Part 3.* B–29 strike observed by Gen Walker who expressed keenest interest and appreciation since this was his first opportunity to watch heavies from air.

THURSDAY *Sent the following letter to Partridge:*

17 AUGUST Reference the Bronze Star Medal for Colonel Witty,
1950 Nuckols did not make it clear in his conversation with you
this morning as to why I was so anxious to present this medal to him prior to his departure. Last night at the Press Club (Nuckols was present), a number of reporters discussed a rumor that was floating around that Witty was being sent home because of the evacuation of P'ohang-dong and which, if publicized, would place the blame on him. I am sure that is not the case. [Underlining in original.] From all the reports I have received from you, Picher and others who have visited K-3, I understand that Colonel Witty as base commander and wing commander 35th Fighter Wing did an outstanding job up to the time it was evacuated. I felt that since you agreed for his personal reasons that he should go home after two and one-half years over here. Further, since you had a replacement for him, a reflection of any kind that might come out on the job that he did might hurt Witty in the eyes of his comrades and would certainly not be true according to the facts. I pinned the Bronze Star Medal on him this morning and will furnish your Headquarters a copy of the citation.

1000 hours presented the Bronze Star Medal to Colonel Witty.

Sent a letter and radio to General Turner clarifying his dealings with the Chinese on Formosa - specifically stating that any instructions that we give them must have the concurrence and approval of Rear Admiral Jarrett,[202] the Attache there. This in no way effects our survey group as they are there in order to determine what is needed by the Chinese Air Force in order for them to defend Formosa. This letter was written per instructions from CINCFE from the Joint Chiefs of Staff.

General Partridge called about 1900 hours and stated that there was quite a push coming from the northwest and that General Walker had committed one of his Army Reserve RCT's [regimental combat team] to stop it. He stated that all of the heavy aviation engineering equipment would leave early tonight for Pusan and he further stated that he could pull out upon one hour's notice. He said, "Don't worry - we are all right, but I felt I should let you know."

Wing Commander P. G. Wykeham-Barnes[203] due to arrive in Tokyo 1650,

---

202. Rear Adm Harry B. Jarrett.
203. Wykeham-Barnes (later Air Marshal Sir Peter Wykeham and commander of the BFEAF) had been a night intruder pilot in Europe during World War II.

19 August. His mission is to assist in night intruder operations. Will be attached to Fifth Air Force, Advance.

8:30 P.M., dinner (stag) honoring Ambassador to the U.S. Wellington Koo.[204] General Ho host. (Ambassador Koo failed to arrive. His airplane was late.)

FRIDAY
18 AUGUST
1950

Comments on B–29 mission of 16 August were as follows: [underlined in original] *From Partridge:*

The value of the effort, in my opinion is that *(1)* Walker and other Army personnel had an opportunity to learn pattern and inflexibility of arrangements, expectancies as to overs and shorts in an area in which a squadron can normally land; *(2)* FEAF bombers gained experience in improving next strike of a similar mission; *(3)* the machinery essential for coordination received a vigorous work-out.

From Walker to CINCFE:

Observations from light aircraft after the attack revealed excellent pattern, rail and road lines between Kŭmch'ŏn and Waegwan were cut; U. S. and ROK ground forces in the area report partial withdrawal of enemy across Naktong River to west after the attack. Friendly units in the Waegwan area which had been receiving heavy artillery fire prior to the attack report none in the area since the attack. I (Walker) am of the opinion that these strikes are of definite psychological advantage, but they would be of more value were they followed up immediately by ground assault into and through the bombed areas.

From O'Donnell:

In answer to your request for my evaluation of the 16 August effort. I was in area about 2 1/2 hours and observed no activity other that our own flak. No planes. Dispersion of squadron drops entirely too large for concentration bombing. I therefore seriously doubt that any real damage other that psychological resulted. Of course, there is always the chance that some enemy concentrations may have been squarely hit. Good rule of thumb for this type effort is 300 tons per square mile. With force at my disposal an area of 3 square miles may be covered adequately. Advise against this type of mission except when small target is available and situation deemed to be truly critical. It is of course extremely costly in bombs. We are approaching bottom of barrel in 500ers [500-lb. bombs] at Yokota.

Received a call from Partridge at 0945 hours in which he stated that they were OK and did not intend to move and that they would stay put. He further reported that KMAG gave the Air Force light fighter-bombers credit yesterday for stopping the drive from the northwest and by so doing this permitted the South Koreans to counter-attack late yesterday afternoon. He reported that all the engineering equipment would leave today and per my instructions to him over the telephone said that all of the engineer effort would be put on the new troop strip at K-9 in Pusan.

---

204. Vi Kyuin Wellington Koo was a long-time official in the Chinese government. From 1946-1956, he was the Chinese Ambassador in Washington.

Following copy of ltr received this date from Partridge, written to Walker on the 15th of Aug:

Thanks for the use of the pamphlet on the "Conduct of Air-Ground Operations," returned herewith. I had not seen this document previously, but find it in accord with FM 31-35, "Air Ground Operations," dated Aug 46, and I am in complete agreement not only with the concepts but also with the details of procedure outlined. As far as I can determine, we have been following the doctrine set forth in these documents except in the matter of the name "J.O.C." The sign on the door has been changed to conform in this respect as well. In passing, I should like to explain that the title "Air Operations Center" was selected because it was felt during pre-war exercises that some people thought the Air Force was trying to set up a true joint staff agency of army, navy, and air elements to run all [emphasis in original] operations. It was believed, incorrectly as it developed later, that the introduction of the word 'Air' into the title would eliminate any intimation that the center was intended to run anything other than air operations in close support of your ground units. I regret that this change of nomenclature increased rather than eliminated the confusion. Additional copies of "Conduct of Air-Ground Operations" are being mimeographed and will be distributed to my people as soon as possible. Extra copies above Fifth Air Force needs can be printed for your use in any number you may designate. Please have someone tell Colonel Howe the number you require.

    s/ E. E. Partridge.

In ink, on bottom of letter in Pat's handwriting: "General Strat - for your information. P."

In reply to above letter to Partridge stated:

Thanks for the copy of your letter to Johnny Walker dated 15 Aug in which you refer to the pamphlet he lent you on "Conduct of Air-Ground Operations." This letter will be helpful to Weyland in any discussion he has with Far East Command staff and/or any paper that he prepares on the subject to CINCFE. At your convenience, I would appreciate receiving a copy of the pamphlet when you have a spare one mimeographed. Thanks so much for your call early this morning; it was most re-assuring because of your splendid air effort in support of the South Koreans. Earle, leave no stone unturned to get K-9 operational as well as concurrently K-1 as a jet field. You are doing a splendid job and I know of no one in the Air Force who could fill your shoes. My commendations and congratulations. With best personal regards, etc.

Copies of above furnished both Weyland and Craigie.

1115 hours saw the Chinese Ambassador to the United States, his Excellency Mr. Wellington Koo with General Ho in my office.

1130 hours had a session with Mr. John [*sic*] Alsop (of the team of John and Stewart Alsop)[205] and later took Mr. Alsop, Colonel Nuckols and General Craigie to lunch at the Union Club.

Prior to going to the Union Club and while at the Union Club, Alsop asked me many questions about the Korean show. One question being - "when do you think the Korean affair will be over?" My answer to him was that "I thought we'd be in North Korea by Christmas." This rather astounded him and I told him I based my answer on the fact that in my opinion the forces in front of our forces will fold up because of lack of supplies, tanks, other armor, munitions, gasoline and oil, that they were being punished so much from the air, and with our inter-diction program, it was my opinion they could not last. He said he couldn't agree with me and then I said you don't know all the facts and that there is something being planned that I can not tell you about. (When I said that I meant the amphibious landing that MacArthur expects to make towards the end of next month or early Octoner and I reiterated that in my opinion if we held any beachhead in South Korea the United Nations forces will be in North Korea by Christmas.)

There was also quite a discussion on the jet fighter versus the F–47 or an air-plane especially designed for close support.[206] I pointed out that we wanted to get out of the reciprocal engine business and that any close support airplane should be a jet; certainly we can design our jets, with a little more experience, to be used on short runways and with lower fuel consumption and then we will have a sup-port airplane that can defend itself. We have a jet almost comparable to the F–47 in the F–84 series; where in the last war we had the F–51 as a high altitude fighter and the F–47 as a ground support weapon as well as a high altitude fighter, today we have the F–80 that can do both jobs, as well as the F–84 which is just about as rugged as the F–47 as a ground support airplane and can also do high altitude fighting. I told him (Alsop) it was just a question of money. Of course, if funds were unlimited, it might be well to have a specially designed close-support weapon, but that if we did, we would have to furnish it with an air umbrella for its protection if we are fighting a major enemy that was equipped with jets. He would not agree with General Craigie and me, but our points were well taken and I believe that after he sleeps on it, he might come to our way of thinking.

Mr. John [*sic*] Alsop is a very smart man.

SATURDAY **19 AUGUST** **1950**	General Partridge called at 0920 and reported the following: He is consolidating his hqrs at Pusan and the opening of the JOC took place last night at 2000 hours at Pusan. He with a small command group will remain along side General

---

205. <u>Joseph</u> W. Alsop, Jr., and Stewart J.O. Alsop were well-known columnists, together writing the "Matter of Fact" column carried in many newspapers. Joseph Alsop served on Chennault's staff in World War II, while Stewart had been in the OSS. Joseph Alsop had been a vocal and active member of the so-called "China Lobby" for some time.

206. During the last part of World War II, the P–47 had become one of the best ground attack aircraft in the USAAF inventory. Though the P–47 was capable of delivering and receiving tremendous punishment, after the war it was decided that the Mustang would be the primary piston-engined fighter in the Air Force, and the Thunderbolt was rapidly taken out of service. At the outbreak of the Korean War, there were 1,167 F–47s (the new designation for the plane) on hand. Only 265 of these were active (with National Guard units) and all were considered second-line aircraft. (USAF Statistical Digest, 1949-1950.) Being less susceptible to ground fire because of its radial engine and heavy construction, the F–47 would have made a better ground attack aircraft in Korea than the F–51.

Walker with his small command group at Taegu. He has excellent communications (telephone) with the JOC.

Yesterday morning apparently the Communists spread a rumor in Taegu that any of the civilian population that remained there would be shot, and, as a consequence, nearly the complete evacuation of Taegu took place by the civilians. The military did not know why this happened, but finally got the information. As a result, the roads to the rear from Taegu were a mass of humanity. They feel though the civilian population will begin to flow back to Taegu.

General Partridge reported the ground situation far less tense and that he along with General Walker was most optimistic.

I queried him as to whether he was obtaining "flash" reports from the 31st Recon Sq.[207] He said he knew of one, but couldn't answer as to whether they were coming in daily. I asked that he investigate and let me know as I am not satisfied that the information that should get to Partridge is being sent by "flash" report from the 31st Recon airplanes. (Carbon copies of above made - given to Craigie and Weyland.)

Prepared an official letter (T.S.) to CINCFE subject: Evaluation of B–29 Area Bombing Effort 16 August 1950. Inclosed with this letter were copies of evaluation reports from Walker, Partridge, O'Donnell, and FEAF director of intelligence highlights of photo interpretation of post strike photos. Also inclosed was a map. I summarized the above inclosures and made the following recommendation: *(a)* that the B–29s not be employed on additional areas tentatively selected near the battle line. *(b)* that the B–29s be employed on the interdiction program and JCS targets in North Korea. *(c)* that aircraft of the Seventh Fleet normally be available for tactical employment.

The above letter delivered to Colonel Bunker, CINCFE's ADC at 1240 hours, today (19 Aug).

Following quoted in toto:

P'OHANG

The initial build up of P'ohang (K-3) started 10 July when an advanced Air Force party, engineer outfit, and AAA moved into the then vacant air strip which the Japanese had constructed in 1940. On 11 July Air Police security teams, OSI and advanced parties of the tactical and support squadrons arrived. 400 airmen were airlifted on 13 July and 14 July we flew our first missions. Initially it was only planned to operate the 40th squadron from K-3 until the 39th Squadron could be converted from jets to '51s on or about 1 August. The 40th with 20 aircraft was scheduled to fly between 30 and 40 sorties a day, and this average was maintained from 14 July to 1 August.

Our initial targets were generally on the east coast in support of the 23d ROK Regiment which at that time had been pushed back to Yŏnghae from some 30 miles up the coast. From the 14th of July on the east coast show became more or less a personal battle between the 40th Fighter Squadron and the 5th North Korean Division, whose drive was stopped

---

207. A "flash" report gave the first available details pertaining to a given mission, usually the number of aircraft or personnel lost on the mission. A "flash" message (see later entries), on the other hand, was a message of such importance as to have transmission priority over all other messages.

at Yongdŏk for the first time about July 23rd. Close liaison was established between K-3 and the following KMAG advisors with the 3d ROK Division and the 23d and 27th ROK Regiments: Colonel Emmerick, Major Britten, Captain Austin, Captain Putnam.[208]

These officers have all stated that it was largely through the efforts of the Air Force on the east coast that the two ROK regiments were able to finally hold the 5th Division at Yongdŏk. Up to this time they had been chopped almost in half in numbers and lost very nearly all of their weapons, other than personal arms. The resultant stiffening of their resistance forced the 5th Division to dig into slopes surrounding Yongdŏk and for better than two weeks their offenses were stalled.

After this stoppage at Yongdŏk the front quieted down, suspiciously so. It became evident through South Korean police reports and KMAG intelligence reports that the North Koreans were infiltrating down through the slopes just west of P'ohang. I requested permission from the Fifth Air Force Hqrs to mount an air strike in these hills, and though very closely controlled by spotter planes the wooded area provided very little in the way of targets.

The information that 2,000 to 3,000 troops was in that area was passed through normal intelligence channels, and since about the 25th of July has appeared in very nearly all intelligence reports. The South Korean police and the South Korean naval headquarters at P'ohang were so concerned about this force that they evacuated all of the small villages just west of P'ohang. POW's brought in from these hills revealed to the OSI that they had left their battalions at Wanson[209] in groups of 25 under a junior officer with about 10-days supplies and had infiltrated through the hills to their present position. Only the officers were in possession of information regarding the mission, and none of these were captured.

From the 20th of July on we kept constant surveillance on this force with spotter type aircraft. It wasn't until the 8th of August that the force began to move toward Kigye. Sporadic fighting that day occurred between South Korean police forces and the naval battalion and the North Koreans. On 9 August the North Koreans moved into Kigye. General Farrell[210] of KMAG flew to K-3 that day and advised us that this band was merely a small group of guerrillas operating independently. This information was directly opposed to what our own intelligence people had learned from the South Koreans. That day General Farrell started out toward Kigye in a jeep with Bill Lawrence of the *New York Times*, Bill Boyle, Associated Press, and two other correspondents. They got no farther than P'ohang where he learned that the force in Kigye, and now some three miles south of Kigye, was larger than he had anticipated. He immediately requested 8th Army for a task force to be in place that night at K-3. It was this task force, composed

---

208. Lt Col Rollins S. Emmerick, senior advisor to the 3d ROK Division; Capt Gerald D. Putnam, advisor to the ROK 23d Regiment; Maj Britten and Capt Austin are unidentified.

209. "Wanson" has not been identified. It is possible that the named area is actually Sŏnsan, located about 65 miles west of P'ohang.

210. Brig Gen Francis W. Farrell had been scheduled to command the artillery of one of the divisions. Dean's loss caused a change of plans and he assumed command of KMAG on July 25.

of tanks and infantry, which ran into the road block eight miles out of P'ohang and which suffered heavy casualties in trying to push through to the field at one o'clock in the morning. Parts of this force were ambushed in a defile southwest of P'ohang and chopped up pretty badly with small arms and machine gun fire. Through most of that night and the next day the objective of the North Koreans was P'ohang. Very little fighting occurred in their move on the town and they were in complete possession of it by noon.

From noon that day and for 24 hours P'ohang burned. All during the day of the 11th, South Korean police kept reporting bands of NK's encircling us over the ridges to the west and south of the field. Sporadic firing onto the field and at the airplanes occurred all during the 10th, 11th, and 12th.

On the 9th of August I asked for three LSTs to be spotted in the harbor on the east coast, nine miles from our base. This was done and all of our heavy equipment was put on board. A perimeter was established about the town with Air Force troops with Lt. Colonel Adams[211] commanding. This perimeter, however, was infiltrated on the 11th and the LSTs came under sniper fire and were forced to retire 2,000 yards off shore. General Bradley,[212] in command of the task force assigned to guard the field, felt he could not guard the field adequately and still guarantee the road to the port. Therefore, all vehicles going to and from the port area with equipment were under heavy Air Force guard, and the three wounded that the Air Force sustained during this operation were the result of sniper fire on this road.

It wasn't until the morning of the 13th when General Partridge found out that *(1)* encirclement was more or less complete on three sides of the air field; *(2)* that the enemy had brought down artillery from Kigye; and *(3)* it looked as though little could be done about the sporadic firing the base was sustaining, that he ordered movement of the aircraft to K-2 and airlift of the remaining personnel to Tsuike in Japan. This decision was made since it was no longer feasible to operate from K-3 on a reduced efficiency basis. With the airmen dug in and firing and undergoing firing all during the hours of darkness, it left them little energy to do their daylight jobs.

In summary, I do not know whether more infantry would have helped the situation, but I do know that K-3 became less and less valuable as the enemy was about to infiltrate and take any part of the air strip under fire. Our efficiency fell off rapidly with the first all-out perimeter defense of 300 men I established on August 9th. From there on out it was just a matter of time as to when we would have to move to another field in order to make our efforts worthwhile.

s/ Robert W. Witty, Colonel, USAF, Commanding Officer, K-3.

---

211. Lt Col Louis C. Adams, commander of the 6131st Air Base Group.
212. Brig Gen Joseph S. Bradley, 2d Infantry Division assistant division commander. During World War II he had been a regimental commander and chief of staff of the 32d Infantry Division.

(17 Aug 50 date Col. Witty departed for ZI.)[213]

The above statement was read and initialled by: Craigie, Weyland and Crabb, 18 Aug 50.

SUNDAY 20 AUGUST 1950

0930 hours, Wing Commander Wykeham-Barnes and Squadron Leader John F. Sach. Wykeham-Barnes arrived last evening; he is to be our "night-intruder" specialist.

Sent the following letter to "Jack" Slessor[214] (Marshal of the Royal Air Force):

Your night intruder specialist, Wing Commander Wykeham-Barnes arrived last evening. I had a very pleasant conference with him at 0930 hours this morning. He is leaving immediately for Korea to confer with Major General Earle E. Partridge, Commanding General, Fifth Air Force, under whom our night intruder missions will be flown. I send my thanks to you for making him available - and so expeditiously. I am sure that the Far East Air Forces will benefit greatly by the information that he will pass on to us on night intruder operations. I would like to report direct to you also, that your Squadron Leader John F. Sach, who is the RAF liaison officer with my headquarters from the Far East Air Force (RAF), Singapore, is doing an outstanding job. He is treated by me and my staff as a member of our team. He is very popular and has the brain power that is so important in the position that he occupies. I commend him to you. Major General Laurence C. Craigie, who is my Vice Commander for Administration and Plans, and Major General Otto P. Weyland, who is my Vice Commander for Operations, both send warm personal regards to you. Again, many thanks for making Wing Commander Wykeham-Barnes available to us.

Sent a redline personal to Norstad:

Reurad [regarding your radio message] cite 51762, 18 Aug. Desire immediate dispatch Colonel Ethelred L. Sykes, bringing with him a junior officer and one airman stenographer. Priority number for the party of three is NWUS-1D-0034-AF 8. This priority number must be utilized from Fairfield [-Suisun AFB, later Travis AFB] during the month of August, otherwise new priority number required.

(Colonel Sykes is Norstad's answer to my TS to him re obtaining the services of a top-flight interpretive analyst - had suggested a Brigadier General W. B. Leach,[215] USAFR, professor at Harvard. Norstad said Leach's services utilized in more of a consultive manner and suggested Sykes.)

General Partridge called mid-morning and stated that the JOC was running smoothly at Pusan.

---

213. According to the official Army history, there had been no "effective" mortar fire on the airfield and that reports of the small-arms fire were greatly exaggerated. (Appleman, p 329.) The feeling was that the field was abandoned precipitously.
214. Marshal of the Royal Air Force Sir John C. Slessor, Chief of the British Air Staff.
215. A professor of law at Harvard, Walter Barton Leach also served as a consultant to the Air Force.

Ground situation much improved; he contemplated bringing some of the engineer effort back to Taegu from Pusan without interference at Pusan to complete the layout at Taegu.

General Walker was a bit put out because I gave the Bronze Star Medal to Colonel Witty. I told Partridge that this was none of Walker's business to which he agreed, but he said he gave me the information in case it was raised by General Walker.

Partridge stated that he was not too happy with the way Witty evacuated K-3. Apparently he was influenced greatly, so Partridge said, by his family troubles back home and did not return to K-3 as he had indicated to Partridge that he would.

Sent a letter to Colonel Kight,[216] with info copies to General Kuter and Major T. P. Tatum, the CO of the 3d Air Sea Rescue Sq. at Johnson AB, commending the performance of the Third Air Sea Rescue Squadron on its handling of its mission.[217]

Among the aircraft used by the 3d Air Rescue Squadron was the venerable Flying Fortress. Still armed but also fitted with a chin-mounted radar and often carrying a lifeboat under their bellies, SB–17s performed long-range search and rescue missions.

Sent the following letter to Partridge:

The Joint Intelligence Indications Committee (Washington) has just reported that North Korean air capabilities may be increased soon, and

---

216. Col Richard T. Kight, commander of the Air Rescue Service, a subordinate command of MATS.

217. The 3d Air Rescue Squadron employed a wide variety of aircraft in its job - the SB–17, SB–29, SA–16, C–47, H–5, and L–5. An SA–16 plucked a Navy pilot out of the water on August 4. On August 15, another SA–16 picked up an F–51 pilot after he had been in the water just 15 minutes. The 3d also utilized its helicopters for air evacuation of wounded from the front lines, a job that grew in importance in the coming months.

other sources have given this same indication. The GHQ G-2 *Intelligence Summary* of 20 August lists the following known North Korean aircraft: *(a)* P'YŎNGT'AEK: 18 Aug PI [photo intelligence] shows 8 a/c [aircraft] on field; *(b)* KIMP'O: 18 Aug PI shows 35 a/c on field; *(c)* YŎNP'O : 18 Aug PI shows 17 a/c (6 damaged); *(d)* KOWŎN: 19 Aug Pireps [pilot reports] 7 or more camouflaged in revetments N and S of field. Even though we are enjoying complete domination of the air over

Lt. Gen. Idwal H. Edwards, USAF Deputy Chief of Staff for Operations, is greeted by General Stratemeyer on August 21, following Edwards' arrival with the Collins-Sherman party.

Korea, the maintenance of that air superiority always stays in top priority and we must constantly guard against the possibility of a sacrificial strike against the base logistical at Pusan, our air bases or other targets. I want you to give this your personal attention and just as soon as your situation permits, take out those North Korean airplanes. I am deeply aware of your personal efforts - keep up the good work.

We are having dinner with the Craigies tonight at 7:00 P.M.

MONDAY 21 AUGUST 1950

0800 hours met the Collins-Sherman party which included: ARMY, General Collins, Brig. Gen T. S. Timberman, Brig Gen John Weckerling, Col. H. H. Nutter, and a Col. Moomaw; NAVY: Admiral Sherman, Rear Adm. Briscoe, Capt. Dietrich and a Lt. Comdr H. H. Anderson: AIR FORCE: Lt. General I. H. Edwards and Major General F. Armstrong (Surgeon); additional arrivals Adm. A. W. Radford, Rear Adm. Denebrink, a Lt. Gen L. C. Shepherd, Maj. Gen. O. P. Smith, Brig Gen E. A. Cushman.[218]

Sent a redline personal to Vandenberg: "Three spans west railroad bridge, the only one that was standing yesterday morning, now in the drink. Edwards and Armstrong with me now."

---

218. The Army Chief of Staff, General Collins, and the Navy Chief of Naval Operations, Adm Sherman, had come to Japan to get a first-hand briefing from MacArthur on the upcoming Inch'ŏn landings. Others in the party included: Brig Gen Thomas S. Timberman, Chief, Operations Division, Office of the Assistant Chief of Staff, G-3, U.S. Army; Brigadier General Weckerling, chief of the Ryukyus Military Government Section in MacArthur's headquarters; possibly Col <u>William</u> H. Nutter, Chief, Control Office, Office of the Assistant Chief of Staff, G-4, U.S. Army; Lt Col Lorris W. Moomaw, an assistant executive in the Office of the Secretary of the Air Force; Rear Adm Robert P. Briscoe, Assistant Chief of Naval Operations (Readiness); Capt N.K. Dietrich, Sherman's executive assistant and senior aide; Lt Cdr Anderson, Sherman's personal aide; Lt Gen Idwal H. Edwards, Deputy Chief of Staff for Operations, Headquarters USAF; Maj Gen <u>Harry G.</u> Armstrong (Collier Award winner in 1939 for achievements in aviation), Surgeon General of the Air Force; Adm Arthur E. Radford, Commander in Chief, Pacific Fleet; Rear Adm Francis C. Denebrink, Commander, Service Force, Pacific Fleet; Lt Gen Lemuel C. Shepherd, Jr., Commanding General, Fleet Marine Force Pacific; Maj Gen Oliver P. Smith, 1st Marine Division commander. "E.A." Cushman may actually be Brig Gen Thomas J. Cushman, 1st Provisional Marine Brigade deputy commander and commander of the Forward Echelon of the 1st Marine Air Wing.

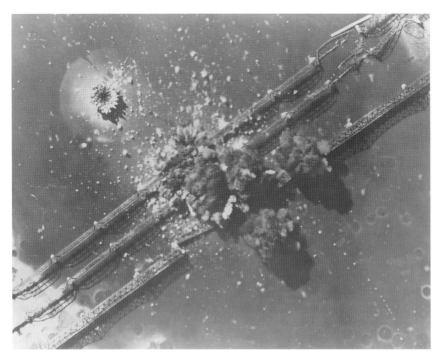

Bombs from 19th BG Superfortresses make sure that the "elastic bridge" does not bounce back. One span of the bridge (lower) can be seen in the water.

Stearley arrives from Okinawa. He joined Edwards, Craigie, Weyland and myself at lunch at the Union Club at 1230.

Partridge's morning report to me indicated that OSI info he is getting is good and timely and he is making use of it. However, General Willoughby was thru there several days [earlier] and indicated in a "vague" manner that the OSI was to be reconsolidated. Partridge stated that full impact of Willoughby's casual remark was lost on him until Nichols expressed concern over reconsolidation of some of his activities with location at another spot. Partridge stated he viewed this with alarm inasmuch as Willoughby did not enlighten him as to whole picture of reconsolidation. Partridge further stated that Harris[219] is now at Pusan and comes to Partridge's hqrs. daily.

Upon my return from meeting General Edwards I was informed that three spans of the main RR [railroad] bridge at Seoul was down; immediately sent Vandenberg a redline message to that effect.

There is now some controversy as to who caused this destruction. I talked with Colonel Graff and the lead pilot of the 19th Group and they both informed me that prior to the release of bombs, all spans were put [in place] but one was leaning out of line and they very definitely stated that none were in the water. About 1220 hours, General Briggs called from Okinawa and stated that they have

---

219. This is probably Maj Gen Field Harris, USMC, commander of the 1st Marine Air Wing. Two of his squadrons, VMF-214 and VMF-323 (as part of MAG-33) began operations from the escort carriers *Sicily* and *Badoeng Strait* in early August.

An RF–80 provides proof that the bridge is indeed down. Both the 19th BG and Carrier Air Group 11 shared credit for the bridge's destruction.

a photograph taken just prior to the 19th Group's attack and that the photograph showed spans down and in the water. I directed that a Stratline message be sent confirming the Briggs report to me.

My reaction to all the above is as follows:

The bridge has been under constant attack with 500, 1,000, 2,000 and sixteen 4,000 lb. bombs since this war started. The Navy has attacked the bridge twice and day before yesterday with 1,000 pounders. The fact that the bridge is down is the important thing and the credit should be given to the Navy and the Air Force although the majority of the bomb drops have been from B–29s.

If I am confirmed in my above reaction, such a statement will be made at the GHQ briefing tomorrow.

Sent a "morale" letter to General Gilkeson who is unhappy that he is on Guam and not in the thick of things. Explained to him that Buster Briggs is not in command of the 19th - but it is under the command of O'Donnell. Since 4 of the 5 B–29 groups were SAC units, it seemed only sensible to add Gilkeson's group too as their missions were identical. Briggs has only a few officers and airmen and acts as a link and coordinator between the 3 groups on Okinawa and O'Donnell's headquarters. He is not a commander and issues no orders to the three groups.[220]

---

220. Perhaps Briggs did not command the three groups, but he did exercise "operational control" over these units. (Hist, FEAF BomCom, Jul 4-Oct 31, 1950, Vol. I, Book I, p 62.)

TUESDAY
22 AUGUST
1950

Visited Korea taking over with me General Collins, Colonel Nutter and Colonel Everest; General Edwards and General Armstrong and Colonel Brothers.[221] We visited Taegu; attended General Walker's briefing (which was the best I've heard so far) and before the meeting broke up, asked that General Partridge give the air side. He did, and without question, the best job there for which I was very very proud. General Armstrong and Colonel Brothers pointed out to me that the Army was not using our air evacuation as it could be used. They attempted to investigate the why's, but were unable to contact the proper people. General Armstrong while here in Tokyo will look into this on a high-level with Major General Hume,[222] Far East Command Surgeon.

We landed and spent a short time at Pusan and while there General Partridge thoroughly explained our plan for the jet fields in Korea to General Edwards. We then visited Itazuke; Colonel Jack Price[223] gave a quick picture to General Edwards of his problems and while there, General Edwards and the rest of us listened to a very interesting debriefing of three (3) F–80 pilots. Theirs is a great story to be written on the air controller and the jets.

We departed Itazuke and landed Iwakuni where we were entertained by the RAAF, after which I presented the Legion of Merit to Wing Commander Louis T. Spence.[224] We dined with Colonel McWhorter,[225] wing commander of 3d Bomb Group, with 15 RAAF officers as guests.

Arrived back at Haneda about 1000 hours.

WEDNESDAY
23 AUGUST
1950

Following memorandum taken by me to CINCFE at 1135 hours in reference to a radio I received from Norstad quoting in full an article written by a Wayne Thomis aboard a carrier off the coast of Korea.[226] Of course USAF wanted my comments.

Memo to General of the Army Douglas MacArthur:

It is my personal opinion, substantiated somewhat by evidence of the Wayne Thomis' article, dateline "Aboard U. S. Support Carrier Off Korea," is another step in a planned program to discredit the Air Force and the Army and at the same time to unwarrantly enhance the prestige of the United States Marines. This situation in my opinion has become so acute that I bring it to your personal attention while Admiral Sherman is in the theater with the suggestion that you discuss this matter with the Chief of Naval Operations, and General Collins, who are both members of the Joint Chiefs of Staff. I have instructed all my commanders and my staff in strict terms against public or private criticism of a sister service even in spite of provocative statements that have been made in the press. I am so concerned about this matter that I fear it will affect the fine team play that exists between all three services under your com-

---

221. Col Clyde L. Brothers, FEAF Surgeon.
222. Maj Gen Edgar E. Hume.
223. Col John M. Price, 8th FBW commander.
224. Commander of No. 77 Squadron.
225. Lt Col William A. McWhorter commanded the 6133d BW(L) until August 1950.
226. This article appeared in the August 19, 1950, edition of the *Chicago Tribune*.

mand and I therefore urge that something be done at your level. I worry about dissension spreading to the lower ranks. G.E.S.

After my discussion with CINCFE, he gave me the outline for my answer to Norstad - some of the phraseology I used in toto; final message evolved as follows:

Personal Norstad from Stratemeyer. Re the Wayne Thomis article which distresses me greatly. It is completely unrealistic and plainly dogmatic propaganda and is probably and unfortunately part of a planned conspiracy for the accomplishment of basic changes in the Defense Department. Counter-action must be on a much broader scale than the Korean theater of operations to safeguard the interest of the Air Force and the national defense in general. Everything possible to correct such biased reports is and has been done in this theater. From CINCFE down through all ranks of the Army and the Navy, and largely in the dispatches, commendations of the Air Force have been of the most complete and generous nature. The cooperation between the services could not be improved. I regard it as near perfection as is possible. This article is not only a planned affair but is a scuttlebutt one and a certain number of scuttlebutts always exist whenever men assemble together and whenever action is undertaken. Attention has been drawn to the Marine high command here of the damage caused by this type of irresponsible and scurrilous reporting and I believe that the Marines themselves do not in general support this type of mockery. The mad scramble among pressmen for sensational headlines can only be suppressed by the publishers and editors themselves. The reporters respond to the impulse from the top and up to the present time such impulse in the Korean operations has been to encourage and foster the most highly sensational articles irrespective of the psychological damage they might cause. I recommend most urgently that the journalistic higher-ups be informally requested to discourage doubtful articles which can only tend to create dissension and disunity within our own ranks and give comfort and aid to the enemy. I have furnished a copy of this message to CINCFE who is exerting every possible effort to dry up the flow of injurious reporting.

Along the same subject, I amplified my views and sent Vandenberg the following "T.S. - Eyes Only" letter:

Dear Van, this letter supplements my two recent messages: V 0193 and VC 0212; the first in reply to 51337, and second to 51952 - both from Norstad.
There is little to be added to my two replies. In fact, the first part of my V0193 could well have been my reply to Larry's second message. The detailed similarity of the Robert Miller article dated 14 August and the Wayne Thomis article dated 18 August is not mere coincidence and since both of them appear to have originated on carriers, it is evident that both were inspired from the same or similar sources.
Upon receipt of Larry's message on the Wayne Thomis article I discussed the entire matter with General MacArthur who, although unaware of the

Thomis piece, had already discussed with Admiral Sherman the absolute necessity for a cessation of such derogatory and dissension-sowing reports as the Miller article. After reading the Thomis piece, General MacArthur was even more wrought up and in fact suggested the tenor, and in many cases, the phraseology of my VC 0212 message.

As background, you may be interested to know that Thomis arrived in the theater about the second week of August and was immediately taken aboard a CVE. During the twenty-four hours he was in town prior to departure, one of his newspaper colleagues discussed air power in general with Thomis. My understanding is that Thomis, during the conversation, outlined the type of article he was planning to write, thus indicating that he had been thoroughly briefed by service sources prior to his departure from the ZI.

When the text of the Thomis article was shown to his colleague here in Tokyo, this colleague said (again my understanding) substantially as follows: "He had the article written in his mind before ever leaving Tokyo and apparently went out on the carrier merely to get an authentic date line."

Short of censorship, which as you know General MacArthur is loth to impose, I can see no possible solution to this service inspired propaganda, and even censorship would merely defer the articles rather than halt them. I am completely convinced, as I have said in both of my messages quoted above, that the carefully planned campaign is designed to do two things: (a) discredit the Air Force, and (b) unjustifiably enhance the prestige of the United States Marines at the expense of both the Army and the Air Force. Ops [sic] 23 may have been dissolved following the B–36 undercover campaign but there now appears to be every indication that its successor not only has been formed but is in action.[227]

Our defense against these and perhaps other attacks has and will continue to be the telling of the complete facts on the accomplishments of tactical air power as represented by Earle Partridge's Fifth Air Force and any and all United Nations Forces that operate under Earle. They not only have flown fifty-eight consecutive days in direct and intimate support of the ground forces, but they also have been credited with being the decisive factor that prevented the ground forces from being driven from the Korean peninsula. Next week, we plan to take a group of correspondents on a special tour throughout the Fifth Air Force from the JOC (Joint Operational Center) right up to the front lines and the ground and airborne controllers. Marine aviation claims to maintain a CAP [combat air patrol] over Marine ground forces throughout the day. Their two carriers are required to cap three thousand men operating on a front frequently mea-

---

227. OP-23 was a research and policy unit under the Deputy Chief of Naval Operations (Administration). Its head in 1949 was Capt Arleigh A. "31-Knot" Burke. In April of 1949, Secretary of Defense Louis Johnson cancelled the construction of the "supercarrier" *United States*. In what became known as the "Revolt of the Admirals," the Navy then attempted to discredit the Air Force's current premier weapon, the B–36. At the forefront of this attempt was OP-23, which compiled information to use against the B–36 program. Apparently, OP-23 was involved in more than information gathering, but in the "dirty tricks" department also. Thus, Stratemeyer was quick to see OP-23's hand in the various articles praising the Navy in Korea. (Rearden, pp 385-422.)

sured in yards. The Fifth Air Force is providing a close support cap on the entire 140 -160 miles of battlefront and are doing it so effectively and so continuously that frequently the ground forces or our airborne controllers are unable to produce targets as rapidly as our fighters knock them out - or appear over front lines requesting targets.

Van I sincerely feel, after considerable deliberation, that I can be of much greater service to the Air Force in directing its activities both present and planned rather than butting my head against the stone wall of service-inspired propaganda which, although appearing to emanate from here, actually had its conception back in Washington.

"The Jeep Carrier," "With the Marines" or even "Tokyo" are merely date lines used for the final dissemination of material that had its stimulation many thousands of miles away. General MacArthur is very concerned, I am very concerned, but until and unless the Navy can and desires to control its personnel, there is little that can be done here.

You may be interested to know that two Navy "masterminds" – Captain Walter Karig and Captain Charles Duffy both arrived in the theater about three weeks ago.[228] Both are public relations experts. Neither has any apparent duty assignment. Bill Nuckols is of the opinion that they are merely the Tokyo link between the successor to Ops [*sic*] 23 and the fleet itself.

Please, Van, understand that my opinions to you as expressed above are given from here as they would be if I were sitting in your office there in Washington. I can prove nothing.

"I do the very best I know how - the very best I can; and I mean to keep doing so until the end - if the end brings me out, all right. What is said against me won't amount to anything; if the end brings me out wrong, ten angels swearing I was right would make no difference." (From a Rail-Splitter's Philosophy, by Abraham Lincoln).

Abe and I are in the same boat.

   G.E.S.

Issued a memo to PIO telling him to get a sharp newshawk on the story of the air controller. It is a natural.

Issued a memo to Banfill, Craigie, Weyland and Nuckols telling them that they were authorized to initiate their own, but which must be cleared thru me for signature and approval, any info that might be of interest and assistance to CSAF that he does not receive from any other source. Type of material desired that would be of help to CSAF in his contacts with the President or other high governmental officials.

On 16 Aug I sent General Walker the following ltr:

The enclosed article by Robert Miller, indicating that close air support is a new type of operation employed by the USMC, has created considerable concern here and in the Air Force. Since the ground action referred to in this article was under your command and direction, and

---

228. Karig later wrote a semi-official history of the Navy in the Korean War as part of the "Battle Report" series. Capt C.G. Duffy was head of the Media Division, Office of Public Relations, U.S. Navy.

the associated air action was well known to you, I would greatly appreciate your comments on the article as a whole. I would particularly like to get your specific reaction to those paragraphs which are marked. I entertain the highest regard for the air and ground Marines, and feel that the harmonious and close relations which have existed between the Army, the Air Force, and the Marines should not be disrupted. I also feel that the facts in this instance should be established, and I am, therefore, hoping for an early reply from you.

On 18 August this letter received from General Walker in answer to mine above quoted:

Your letter arrived today concerning the article by Robert Miller on the comparative merits of Marine and Air Force capabilities in the role of close air support. The article, written in typical journalistic style of the sensational variety, undoubtedly has inaccuracies such as the statement that planes worked over enemy positions 50 yards ahead of Marine troops, when 300 yards is probably nearer the truth. I feel, however, it is never worthwhile to comment on newspaper articles in defense of myself, my decisions, or of units or individuals under my command or with which I am cooperating. I have never done so, and do not intend to start now. As for the support rendered my troops by the Fifth Air Force, I have every praise for the cooperation and assistance of Partridge and his people and have gone on record in this regard. Without the slightest intent of disparaging the support of the Air Forces, I must say that I, in common with the vast majority of officers of the Army, feel strongly that the Marine system of close air support has much to commend it. Marine aviation is designed, equipped and trained for the sole purpose of supporting Marine ground forces. It operates equally well from land bases or carriers, often permitting support from short distances not possible if there is sole dependence upon land air bases. During training and maneuvers, Marine aviation works constantly with ground units to perfect the communications and coordination so essential in the application of any type of supporting fires, whether delivered by aircraft, artillery, or supporting infantry weapons. Tactical air support parties are available to units down to and including the infantry battalion. In short, although there are probably strong reasons such as governmental economy to the contrary, I feel strongly that the Army would be well advised to emulate the Marine Corps and have its own tactical support aviation.

In my opinion this is the result of General Clark's attempt to secure tactical aviation as a part of the Army. I am greatly disappointed in Walker's reply.[229]

---

229. In a December 1950 *Air Force* magazine interview, Gen Mark W. Clark, Chief of Army Field Forces, claimed that he did not want the Army to have its own separate air force. He did, however, feel that the Air Force clung to "arbitrary and unyielding" priorities regarding its role in the ground support mission. It seemed to Clark that the Air Force's first priority was to stay alive in the air regardless of the situation on the ground. He went on to say that the Army should have a larger voice in the design of those aircraft to be utilized in the support of the ground forces. Finally, he believed that the commander of a "ground" campaign

THURSDAY
24 AUGUST
1950

19th Bomb Gp, employing 3 aircraft with 8 each 1,000 lb bombs from an altitude of 16,000 to 17,400 ft struck the RR bridge west of P'yŏngyang.

Bombing results: one direct hit on bridge and one near miss. One bomb hit a building near south edge of bridge causing building to explode on impact and burn viciously. Functioning of bombs: functioning of control: - due to Razon equip malfunction, control over all bombs not accomplished.[230] Only one bomb which scored a direct hit reacted properly to control equipment. Control of other bombs ranged from fair to poor. Weather factor: Weather was clear and was not a factor in poor results. Anticipated improvement: - Next scheduled combat mission is 26 Aug. Practice mission to be flown locally on 25 Aug to air check all item of equip[ment]. Upon elimination of technical difficulties, subsequent Razon bombing should be highly successful.

Upon receiving above report, sent following Redline to Vandenberg:

"Razon bombing initiated 23 August on trial basis without previous practice or tests. Results poor due to malfunction Razon control. Combat mission 26 August after equipment checks."

General Turner and Partridge in headquarters.

The United States Navy hqrs in Tokyo announced in the *Nippon Times* this date its participation in a campaign to destroy industrial facilities with possible links to the Russian atomic program. This article was released through International News Service.

It is my impression that this type of information was of the very highest classification; further it was announced that the Navy with destroyers had bombarded Ch'ŏngjin as well as the Mitsubishi Iron Works. The harbor installations and warehouses were also hit. All of these targets had been previously struck by the FEAF Bomber Command.

Here again the Navy with destroyers as they have done with carrier based aviation have hit targets that the FEAF Bomber Command have practically destroyed. Mark my words, when the history is written, the Navy will claim the destruction of targets throughout North Korea that FEAF Bomber Command had destroyed. This entry in my diary is made for the record that might be made of the history of Air Force participation in the Korean War.

When I arrived at my desk found the following radio from CINCFE to FEAF and COMNAVFE which stated:

(1) in view of current planning CINCFE is concerned with the increased evidence of a build-up in enemy air potential. Reference is made to the recent sporadic enemy air attacks, including the attack yesterday on a British destroyer off the west coast. Reference is also made to the reports of revetments being constructed on airfields at Kimp'o, Suwŏn and Taejŏn and the possibility of an air operations hqrs near Kunsan. *(2)* it is desired that all FEAF and Navy air operations provide for frequent interdiction of known or

---

(Korea was intimated, but not mentioned) should be able to employ air and naval forces as he saw fit.
(Intvw, Gen Mark W. Clark, *Air Force*, Dec. 1950, pp 24-25, 52.)

230. A World War II development, Razon was a regular bomb to which movable control surfaces had been added to its tail. These surfaces were radio controlled in range and azimuth.

suspected enemy air facilities, with particular regard to those facilities, other than the runways, at Kimp'o, Suwŏn and Taejŏn. It is considered desirable that these targets also be frequently utilized as secondary targets. The use by the enemy of these or other airfields south of 39 degrees north must be refused from this date forward.

Sent a buck slip to Plans thru Weyland to prepare a FEAF plan to support the contemplated amphibious landing. This is to be a plan, separate and apart from anything that is done by GHQ staff; further, the plan is to encompass the use of all FEAF combat aircraft except the minimum essential to the close support of the ground troops in Korea. Suggested they call in representatives of Fifth, FEAF BomCom, and Twentieth. I feel that it is incumbent upon me to present to CINCFE our conception of a FEAF Plan to support this operation.

The Collins-Sherman-Edwards party to take-off tonight from Haneda at 2100 hours.

Annalee and I have invited to have dinner with us tonight at Mayeda House: Colonel and Mrs. Brothers, Colonel and Mrs. Nuckols, General Edwards, General Armstrong, and General O'Donnell.

Sent a redline message to Vandenberg telling him that 441 night intruder missions have been flown between the dates of 24 July and 23 August inclusive; break-down: B–26s - 335; F–82s - 36; F–51s - 25; F–80s - 2; Marine F4Us - 43. 385 of the above flown after 4 August; highest number in one night was night of 9 - 10 August - 42 flown and since that date we have averaged about 35.

In answer to TS 3746 (re Turner's mission - scope of same etc and in which USAF voiced the subject of possible evidence of NK Air Force build-up and activities) *sent the following redline to Vandenberg; courier to Partridge and O'Donnell:*

...Fifth AF and 31st Strat[egic] Rcn [Reconnaissance] Sq are maintaining constant surveillance of all NK airfields. 5th AF fighter bombers have made and are continuing strikes on these airfields. All sources available are being used to determine any movements of aircraft along Manchurian border. SOP [standing operating procedures] set up whereby strat rcn aircraft covering most of the NK daily must stay in constant radio contact with 5th AF control center near Pusan and with Bomber Command near Tokyo. They have standing instructions to report in the clear to 5th AF control center and Bomber Command any targets of opportunity or aircraft sightings. In addition, one aircraft in each B–29 formation has now been directed to come up on this recon broadcast frequency and to augment sightings reported by strat rcn ships. I have directed 5th AF to increase daily air reconnaissance fighter sweeps in NK to assure a force on the spot and to destroy rail and road traffic now being disrupted by progress of interdiction program. The tactical rcn RF–80s have the same SOP of reporting to control any target of opportunity. All flights entering Korea area check in with 5th AF control, thus providing means of diverting effort to any target reported by recon as profitable. The system has been slow in getting into action, but we are getting some results now with continued attention from my staff.

Also in answer to TS 3784, sent a redline to Norstad stating that Tunner[231] will get picture while here and depart for U.S. on 26 August. Desire that he return for 60 to 90 days, departing U.S. not later than 3 Sept with small staff, also TDY. Tunner has selected those he wishes - 5 colonels, 2 lt. colonels, 3 majors and 1 captain.

FRIDAY
25 AUGUST
1950

Sent following redline to Vandenberg:

A/C from 31st Strat Recon Sq while engaged in recon mission on 24 August reports receiving 40 bursts of flak near Manchurian border at approximately 40° 4' N - 124° 20' E. This a/c had reconnoitered rail line leading NE from Sinanju to Yalu River and then proceeded SW on Korean side of Yalu River to vicinity of Sinŭiju. Crew estimates 6 of these bursts came from across Yalu River in Antung area. Estimate caliber 88 or 90 mm. All bursts missed a/c but firing was definitely more accurate than most flak encountered to date. Comment: Firing encountered from characteristics described indicates predicted concentrations. This is first indication of this type of fire in Korean conflict. This is also second report within three-day period of flak suspected as originating from Manchurian territory. Due to difficulty of aircrew accurately pin-pointing flak positions, this report should not be considered as completely reliable.

At 1100 hours a Mr. Maxwell Kleiman who was preceded by a letter of introduction from Cy Marriner dropped by the office.[232] Mr. Kleiman's forte "matters which will assist to restore some degree of Japanese industrial economy and assist U.S. industrialists in re-establishing their interests in Japan."

Sent Courtney Hodges[233] a letter assuring him the C–47 assigned to him was undergoing check at Clark and for him to let me know when he receives it, and if received in satisfactory condition. Also told him to call on me any time with reference to airplane for assistance.

Redline message sent to Vandenberg as follows:

Study of strike photos taken during mission on Kōnan yesterday reveals that the one building thorium plant indicated to us by the Joint Chiefs of Staff as critical target has been 35 percent destroyed and has suffered an estimated additional 40 percent heavy damage. Plant area immediately adjacent to this building is heavily and accurately hit. Post strike photos still not available because weather forced reconnaissance aircraft to land at Misawa. It is thought that buildings in this area were used to process monazite which is a primary source of thorium and other elements in the atomic energy program. Mission conducted by 92d Group. Final evaluation from post-strike photos will be forthcoming soonest.

231. Maj Gen William H. Tunner commanded the India-China "Hump" airlift operation in World War II, and had been in charge of the Berlin Airlift. At this time deputy commander of MATS, Tunner later returned to Japan to organize the FEAF Combat Cargo Command (Provisional), which functioned in both the air transport and troop carrier roles. As Combat Cargo commander, Tunner reported directly to Stratemeyer. (Futrell, p 155.)
232. These two gentlemen have not been identified.
233. Gen Courtney H. Hodges commanded the U.S. First Army in World War II and retired from the Army in 1949. He now was serving as the military advisor to the U.N. mediator in the India-Pakistan dispute over Kashmir.

Following "cipher message" from Australian Military Forces received 31 July (Col. Marson from Charlesworth)[234] and for my information:

Australia agrees that the procedure for accounting for transfers of supplies and equipment between FEAF and BCOF in Japan and Korea is the recording of all such transfers the reconciliation to be effected later on an inter-governmental level. Major aircraft maintenance is to be done at Iwakuni and replacement aircraft and spares are to be from Australian sources where readily available supplies such as rations, fuel, bombs, etc. to from American sources.

British furnished me a copy of their message to Air Ministry re my request to them for a night-intruder specialist, dated 10 August:

Foreign Office please pass to Air Ministry for Pearson from Barclay. The Commanding General of the United States Far East Air Forces has an immediate requirement for an RAF officer experienced in latest night bombing and light bomber night intruder techniques to advise the United States Fifth Air Force in planning a night tactical bombing plan employing B–26 aircraft. Paragraph two. This officer would be required for 14 days upwards. I suggest that in the RAF and Allied interests an officer should be supplied as requested and that as soon as possible he should proceed to Tokyo by air. I suggest that the most suitable ranking would be wing commander. Gascoigne.

Ltr rcvd today, dtd 24 August from General Cushman in reply to my letter of 16 August which refers to the Miller story of 14 August. Cushman reports:

(1) It is most unfortunate and regrettable that such a press release had been published when all services are doing their utmost to bring the present conflict to a speedy and successful conclusion. *(2)* The subject correspondent originated the article while visiting a carrier at Sasebo on which one of our squadrons was based. He is not accredited to this headquarters and the views expressed are entirely his own. The basis of this article is unknown to this office. *(3)* The portion of paragraph three (3) of the subject release, Enclosure 1 to reference a, which has been underlined, "first constant air coverage," is obviously incorrect. *(4)* In regard to statements attributed to certain individuals, measures have been taken from the Chief of Naval Operations on down to prevent statements of a controversial nature on the part of naval and marine personnel. *(5)* The cooperation and assistance rendered this command by both the U.S. Air Force and Army in becoming established in Japan has been splendid. Without this whole-hearted support, our units could not have been deployed into action as rapidly as they were. *(6)* I have the highest regard and admiration for the work the U. S. Air Force and Army are doing and have done in the past. To insure speedy and successful termination of hostilities it is mandatory that the armed services continue to maintain close and harmonious relations. s/ T. J. Cushman.

---

234. Air Commodore A.M. Charlesworth, the BCOF chief of staff; Marson is unidentified.

I turned the entire Marine-Army-Air Force controversy file over to Colonel Tidwell,[235] FEAF JA [Judge Advocate], to prepare a letter for my signature to General Norstad reference the reply to the Cushman letter which came in today and the reply to the Walker letter which has been on hand for some time.

Group Captain Barclay came to see me this morning and stated that he was on the spot with the British Foreign Office because he had used their "emergency immediate" communications set up in order to get word to the Air Ministry and wondered if I would give him some support in his reply. I told him he could use my name and very firmly state that it was an emergency and that I had urged the quickest action possible to get an RAF night-intruder specialist out here to the Far East to assist the Commanding General, Fifth Air Force, in his night-intruder work. Group Captain Barclay was very grateful and said he would use my name.

SATURDAY 26 AUGUST 1950

Two humorous bits of info redlined to Vandenberg - *(1)* the catchword these days by the 19th Group is - "who has the bomb-bay door?" Seems doors are transferred from a/c undergoing maintenance to those coming out. One bomb-bay door is missing. Item *(2)* Marines were without air cover and under fire from heights near Masan; called for air support and some of our Mustangs returning without ammunition from a raid, "strafed" the North Koreans for 20 minutes without firing a shot - which enabled the Marines to regroup and organize their position.

Informed Vandenberg via redline that next Razon mission scheduled Monday, 28 August with 3 a/c. Technical difficulties today. Razon radio receivers scheduled for airlift and necessary for next mission did not arrive necessitating postponement. 2/3s of all these receivers must be rejected because of deterioration while in storage.

General Partridge called at 1000 hours and stated the following: He is moving more a/c into Taegu and he felt that the Army would reconsider their evacuation of the wounded, possibly utilizing more air evacuation. He further stated that he was having difficulties with the "boys in blue" [Navy] and that they had indicated to the JOC that they didn't intend to participate in close support.

I told General Partridge of the signals sent to CINCFE and dispatched by CINCFE where CINCFE didn't really know what they had said, that Weyland had straightened this out with Wright and it was my opinion that the Navy would be back in close cooperation with the Fifth Air Force and operating under my control.

Sent Norstad a letter inclosing my letters to Walker and Cushman requesting their comments on the Robert Miller article and their replies to me. Forwarded them with my comments, pointing out that Cushman's desire for harmony in line with CNO's directive and that I was disappointed in Walker's reply - he refused to comment, and although did praise the support we have given him, stated that he thought like, as he stated, so many Army personnel, that the Army should have its own tactical support as the Marines. Pointed out in my conversations with Collins that Collins would not ask for Army tactical air force, happy with us in our efforts and cooperation. As a talking point for Van on JCS level, suggested he throw out the idea that perhaps there should be an increase of Marine divisions and a cut in the divisions of the Army.

---

235. Col Moody R. Tidwell, Jr.

Sent a redline to Vandenberg:

Daily sorties are approaching the 600 mark; with 553 sorties by FEAF a/c and 26 by Australian Mustangs reported up to 0600 this morning. 33 night intruder sorties flown by FEAF a/c and 8 by Marines. 112 C–47s lifted 292 tons of cargo and 314 passengers to Korea.

Still a mainstay with the USAF, the C–47 performed yeoman service throughout the Korean War.

Following redline sent to Vandenberg:

Statement being released to press here for Sunday morning publication stateside sums up FEAF operation for first 60 days. Says, 20,559 sorties flown, 13,000 of them by fighters, 1300 by '26s, 1500 by B–29s, and 2,800 by transports and 1,700 recce, more than half the latter figure being flown by T-6 air controllers. Also states, more than 600 attacks have been made on tanks, armored cars or half-tracks by FEAF. 72 enemy a/c destroyed compared to 58 AF airplanes lost in 20,500 sorties. Our losses for period 26 dead, 23 wounded and 25 missing.

Informed Turner via signal that since the Navy does not understand the terms "operational control" and in order to be uniform with their understanding, wherever the words appear in my directive to you in your plans of action on Formosa, change the wording to "coodinational control" as defined and used by the Navy.

With Tunner called on CINCFE.

Annalee and I had dinner with the Pichers, their home - 7:00 P.M.

SUNDAY
27 AUGUST
1950

Sent a personal redline to Vandenberg:

An interesting report on POW reaction has come from SK Navy. Among 25 NK POW's, captured at T'ongyŏng (34° 50' N/ 128° 26' E) by SK Marines, was an infantry company commander who reported that his unit departed Haeju (38° 02' N - 125° 46' E) 28 July, in high spirits, confident of success of North Korean Army but as they traveled southward and observed blown bridges and the deep fear of air attacks noted among other North Korean troops met on the way, they lost their confidence and, by time they reached point of capture, they were sure that they would lose and only expected to be killed upon capture as they had been informed ROK troops took no prisoners.

Prepared memo to Plans thru VC A&P with info copies to CINCFE and General Tunner, reminding them that Lt. Col. J. L. McGinn, now at Tsuiki, in the 6131st Wing, knows more about Suwŏn Airport, its surrounding terrain than anyone in FEAF and urging that General Tunner and his operational and plans people should discuss same with McGinn.

Sent Gill Robb Wilson another weekly letter - which I intend to have dispatched to him by each Monday. (Also inclosed my 60-day FEAF Summary of Air Activities - the PIO official release.)

Reference the article that was received late today from Sory Smith,[236] appearing in the *Baltimore Sun*, written by Phillip Potter, I have directed that the following action be taken. That Colonel Nuckols answer Sory Smith's radio and give him the best reply available from our records - including a statement that I referred the article to Admiral Joy and to General Partridge.[237]

In my letter to Admiral Joy I directed that General Craigie include the following: that if I have at any time since the Korean war indicated an inhospitable attitude reference any matter, it was certainly unintentional and I apologize; that it was my impression from the records and from memory and from Admiral Joy's letter to me dated 10 August that the relationship between naval air, Admiral Joy's office, and my headquarters has been most amicable and that we tried in every instance to meet their many requests for assistance. Our records show that as a result of our meeting with the 7th Fleet aviators and my staff, it was agreed that the Navy would furnish some three (3) control teams and a mutual agreement, which met everyone's satisfaction, was resolved; I did not know there was a shortage of maps or charts and if there are, will meet every possible request that they have; that I constantly requested the 7th Fleet air to participate with the Fifth Air Force in air support to the ground forces, and that if there are any deficiencies existing as of this writing on our part, that I can remedy, it is requested that he make them known and that I will do everything possible to correct those deficiencies; that I do desire his comments on the

---

236. Brig Gen Sory Smith, Director of Public Relations, Headquarters USAF.

237. The Potter article and a *Baltimore Sun* editorial, which Stratemeyer quoted in their entirety, are printed below. In his article, Potter ignored the fact that the Navy had a different communications philosophy and limited, and often different, communications equipment. He also conveniently ignored the fact that it was the Navy that had been reluctant to become involved in the operation of the JOC, an important cog in the air support role; that two separate TACPs was a duplication of effort; or that the kind of support the Marines were then getting would be an extreme waste of air power over the long run. (Futrell, pp 49n, 115-118, 342-343.)

article since the article indicates that admirals of the 7th Fleet are unhappy with cooperation of FEAF.

My instructions to General Craigie that the article be referred to General Partridge for his comments with the statement in my letter of transmittal that I do not want him to worry nor to personally answer the letter, but to have one of his staff people investigate the whole operations with the Seventh Fleet for my information and to remedy any deficiencies that exist on our part.

General Mundy[238] checked in at headquarters and Colonel Sykes arrives to take over the spot that I requested a Brig. General Leach for - to document the history of our activities out here that will be available and valuable as source material for Hq USAF.

Received a "thank you" letter from Bozo McKee for the flags and which also included the following paragraphs:

We are very proud here of the fine job the Air Force is doing in Korea. It is a great tribute to you and your staff. As a purely personal suggestion from me - why don't you write the Chief a letter occasionally, telling him the picture as you see it, and in which you could put a lot of things that you probably do not wish to put in a cable. My idea is that it would be purely an informative matter between you and the Chief and not an action letter to the Staff.

In answer to the above letter from McKee, sent him the following "Top Secret - Eyes Only" [underlining in original] (This letter, AG# 112-OL-50 burned 27 Sept as per my instructions (answered by McKee's ltr dtd 13 Sept.) See full quote of letter contained in diary under date of 27 Sept.) letter:

Your letter of 22 Aug just received and I have already beaten you to the punch on your suggestion of a letter to the Chief - having mailed quite a lengthy one 23 August 1950. Thanks for the suggestion and I will continue a letter every now and then giving him the unfavorable as well as the favorable. During the visit of Collins and Sherman, Sherman was very cool towards me which was quite a contrast to his trip out here with Van several months ago. Collins, of course, was just the opposite and during one of my conversations with Collins reference Robert Miller's critical news item on the Air Force versus Marine close-support for the Army, Collins indicated that Van had shown to Sherman my personal redline to Norstad, dated 16 August 1950, number V 0193 (Top Secret). I am in great hopes that the only part of that radio that he showed to Sherman was Part Two. Of course, if Part One was shown to Sherman, I can readily understand Sherman's coolness towards me. For my own defense and knowledge could you diplomatically find out if Sherman saw the whole message which included Part One or did he only see Part Two? It is very important that I know because of my close relationship with the Navy (Admirals Joy and Struble) out here. Please

---

238. Brig Gen George W. Mundy, Deputy Director of Supply and Maintenance, Air Materiel Command.

treat the latter part of this letter with the very highest of classification and for your eyes alone. Am glad that you like the flags, etc.

Sent a letter to Partridge asking why I have been receiving no reports on the use of napalm and why it has not been used more both in your close support missions as well as against trucks, tanks, convoys, and concentrations of troops. I had success in India and Burma with it; Chennault with it in China, and George Kenney had success with its use in his campaign here in the Far East. With all the enthusiasm for its use and the lack of reports from you on your using same is a bit disturbing. Requested his comments reference napalm.

PHILLIP POTTER STORY WHICH APPEARED
IN BALTIMORE SUN

NEWSRELEASE - Story, Tokyo, August 23.

Navy airmen hesitate to speak out openly on the subject for fear reopening old wounds in the unification struggle, but they believe the Korean conflict has shown up the glaring deficiencies in American ground support aviation. Admirals responsible for aviation of the United Nations Task Force 77 which is primarily an American show - complain that failure of the Far Eastern Air Force[s] to provide adequate tactical air control has kept the effectiveness of carrier based planes at about 30 percent of their potential at a time when doughboys in Korea need all the help they can get.

Their complaints and suggestions for remedying the situation, including a proposal for use of the Navy's own tactical control parties, have been thoroughly gone into at recent conferences in Japan between Douglas MacArthur's Far Eastern Command and such distinguished visitors as General J. Lawton Collins, Army Chief of Staff; Admiral Forest P. Sherman, Chief of Naval Operations; and Vice Admiral Arthur W. Radford, Commander-in-Chief of the United States Pacific Fleet. Those who have been directing operations from the two American carriers already operating in Korean waters are known to have told superiors the Fleet is experiencing difficulties which must be remedied if effective support of Army Ground Forces is to be achieved.

Specifically, they have complained that there is no adequate direct means of communication between the JOC, the Far Eastern Air Forces have set up in Korea, and naval forces; that no properly gridded air-support charts have yet been made available; that there has been trouble in establishing communications with the Air Forces' mosquito planes whose job it is to direct fighters and bombers to their targets; and there have not been enough mosquitoes to adequately carry out their mission. Charts are gridded on a scale too large to allow speed and accuracy of control, but they claim they have been inadequately supplied even with such charts.

Navy flyers have frequently reached Korea, where they were to be assigned targets by the Air Forces' mosquito planes, only to find that they were already busy with the Air Forces' F–80 jets and Mustangs, or they had to leave a target area due to gasoline exhaustion without making arrangements for proper relief. Navy men have suggested use of the Navy's own tactical air control parties, some of which are aboard a communications ship which is now in Japanese waters, but is operating with Rear Admiral J. H. Doyle's Amphibious task Force instead of with the carriers.

Lt. Gen. George E. Stratemeyer, Commander of the Far East Air Force[s], however, is reported to have been inhospitable to this proposal although the Army is crying for air support equivalent to that Marine flyers provide for Marine ground forces.

A feeling that their potential striking power is being aborted is universal among fleet airmen, from ensigns to admirals, and this is reflected in reports of virtually all carrier pilots returning from combat missions. The following are typical examples Lt. j.g. E.L. Carpenter - "Couldn't get mosquito controller so dropped ordnance on target of opportunity" (meaning anything he could find). Lt. Comdr. R. W. Fleck "Contacted controller but he was too busy so went to targets of opportunity." Lt. F. Dalzell - "Reported to JOC which tried to give instructions but was cut out (radio contact was lost) continually. Circled for 45 minutes but finally had to give up and proceed to bomb line to strafe sampan." Lt. j.g. N. R. Quill - "Flew to city where JOC was located and got contact but was told to wait 10 minutes, then was directed to mosquito controller but could not get effective contact so expended ammunition on town in same area where Air Force F–80 jets were working." Lt. Cmdr. T. Deacon - "No directions from either JOC or mosquito controller. Radio channel overcrowded. Attack bomber finally got controller but were told to wait. Waited an hour, then hit target other (Air Force) planes were leaving. Nothing constructive accomplished."

Many naval aviators are as well trained as are Marine Corps flyers in close support work but there has been no system in Korea such as the Marine Corps employs to put their talents to use. Special mobile tactical control units accompany all the Marine ground forces into action, communicating by radio with squadron leaders who know with what ordnance each of their planes is loaded. If the ground party wants a machine gun next taken out with a general purpose bomb, the squadron leader goes down and marks the target with a smoke rocket, then he calls down the plane he wants to make the strike. If the target is a NK tank, a plane loaded with rockets does the job.

There is "nothing mysterious about close air support," Rear Adm. Edward C. Ewen said. "There are a few simple principles. It is mainly a matter of proper communication between AF and GF." He said that due to chaotic Air Force communications in Korea, the carriers contribution as far as close support is concerned is almost negligible." The kids just wander around, the racks loaded with bombs and rockets, and [no] place to put them," he said.

Ensign Sam Clauzel, Avista, California, one of the carrier pilots put it even more pungently: "This carrier has almost 3,000 men aboard," he said, "and there is a tremendous effort put forth by every one of them to get out planes in the air, then we are useless." We have and are capable of putting in the field tactical control parties with whom we trained in maneuvers, but they won't let us use them.

EDITORIAL

Mr. Phillip Potter, *Sun* paper's war correspondent, reports that in Korea the effectiveness of carrier-based airplanes is being held to about 30 percent of its potential because of inadequate tactical air control. The Navy lays the blame on the Far Eastern Air Force[s].

According to Navy men there is no adequate means of communication between the Air Forces JOC and Navy Air Force: Support charts, they say are not properly gridded and sometimes are not even available. The Navy flyers all report trouble establishing communication with the Air Forces' mosquito planes whose job it is to direct fighters and bombers to their targets. The result of this, they say, is that they often receive no instructions. In consequence they have to look for a target themselves or else fly home with a bomb-load unused. Mr. Potter states that these complaints are now receiving the attention from the Big Brass. Well they might, for they are serious and should be fully investigated. It is conceivable that the trouble is due to some oversight in planning that could be readily adjusted. The emergency in Korea came so suddenly that there had to be a good deal of improvisation. The use of carrier-based planes to support Army ground forces was a novel combination, and it would be surprising indeed if 100 percent efficiency were had immediately. Such a failure as the Navy complain of, if only temporary, might be excused. What can not be excused is that condition should be permitted to continue. In particular, it should not be allowed to go on if the failure is in any way attributable to Service prejudice which so often has bedeviled unification. The American public is being called upon to throw into this Korean operation both its blood and its treasure. It has the right to demand that both be used with the strictest economy but they will not be used economically if responsible officers of the respective services carry into the war any of the silly, childish notions of Service loyalty that have prevailed during the peace.

This is the problem for the President of the United States, the Joint Chiefs of Staff, and General MacArthur to handle. If those on the top level let it be known that service jealousies will not be tolerated, such mis-placed loyalty will soon disappear. The American public is very much a party to this matter. In the specific case of air control, it will insist that the attention the subject is getting from the High Command will not be diverted until the conditions of which the Navy flyers complain have been corrected or the complaints have been shown to be unjustified.

MONDAY **28 AUGUST** **1950**	Had a fine conference (1530) with Mr. Ben Wright[239] this afternoon and will lend him every possible assistance. Sent a redline to Vandenberg so stating.

————— I was impressed with the PIO (alert) abilities of Colonel Wright. I agreed with him that he should do his job out here as a representative of American Airlines rather than as a consultant for General Vandenberg. I feel

---

239. Ben George Wright, director of public relations for American Airlines, was now serving as a civilian consultant to Gen Vandenberg. Wright later became publisher of *Field and Stream* magazine.

confident that his stay here, after he thoroughly sees our set up and operations and with his contact with the Army, the Marines and the Navy at his service back home, General Vandenberg will be benefited. Just prior to his departure from FEAF, he will pay me another visit.

Sent the following cryptic message to Cabell (in answer to his T.S., "Eyes Only" handwritten letter):

Reference the conversation I had with you just prior to your departure and at which time I brought Banfill into the picture, and in view of receipt of your letter written in longhand dated 21 August, I assume you are not interested in further reports of the nature that we discussed at the airport. The initiative is now in your hands as your letter referred to above absolutely stymies me. I have issued instructions accordingly.

As per my instructions to Nuckols, quoted in full, is his interim reply to Sory Smith re the Phillip Potter newstory released in the Baltimore Sun, and the Sun's editorial comments re the release:

Sory Smith from Nuckols - This is radnote #41, 28 Aug 50, reur USAF-49 dated 25 Aug. I have discussed the matter in great detail with General Stratemeyer and suggest you advise General Norstad that the following action is being taken: *(1)* General Stratemeyer is writing a letter to Admiral Joy, transmitting both the story and the editorial and asking for specific comments on the allegations contained in said story. Specifically he is asking, do the quotations attributed to senior naval commanders in fact represent the views of these commanders? He is also specifically requesting Admiral Joy to provide additional Navy controllers and controller teams both at JOC and at combat troop level if, in Admiral Joy's opinion, such a requirement continues to exist. *(2)* General Stratemeyer is asking General Partridge, CG Fifth AF, for detailed information as to allegations contained in story and on Fifth AF acceptance or request for additional Navy controllers and controller teams. He is impressing on Partridge that he is not repeat not to let the above request interfere with his operational responsibilities. These comments, both from Admiral Joy and General Partridge, will be forwarded by General Stratemeyer to General Norstad as soon as available with his comments. It is interesting to note the following extracts from a memo dated 10 Aug from COMNAVFE (Admiral Joy) to General Stratemeyer: the letter is in reply to a letter of congratulation to COMNAVFE from General Stratemeyer expressing his gratification of 47 enemy aircraft destroyed by naval aviation. Following are extracts from Admiral Joy's reply: "Your hq furnished most of the target information, coordination effort and photographic data which materially assisted in the success of the 18-19 July strike. The spirit of willing and energetic cooperation exhibited by your staff and the members of the Far East Air Forces, with whom they deal, has brought forth much favorable comment from officers of my command. This fine spirit continues to build a higher mutual regard and warm bond of understanding between the U. S. Navy and U. S. Air Force in this theater." It is difficult to reconcile the above statement with the allegations contained in the *BALTIMORE SUN* article, none of which have been brought to FEAF's attention through official channels. General Edwards, Deputy Chief of Staff Operations, during his recent visit to this theater, discussed the general subject of Air Force-Navy cooperation in great detail with General Stratemeyer. Believe General Edwards understands the problem, both as it exists here and also as it exists Stateside. Stratemeyer recommends Norstad discuss whole problem with Edwards. The following item from Combat Ops Center diary, dated 11 August, is quoted for your information: "The AF combat ops officer, in discussing difficulties in coordinating Navy strikes, pointed out three deficiencies: *(1)* Navy was sending too great a number of aircraft into the areas at one time. *(2)* JOC did not have info as to their time of arrival. *(3)* No naval liaison officers were present." Diary item continues to say that items 1 and 3 have been eliminated. Navy has reduced number of aircraft coming into the area at one time and 4 naval officers and one Marine officer have been assigned as liaison officers. Diary item continues, "JOC expresses no complaint against coordination with Navy and commends their excellent job." Diary item then contains the following paragraph: which deals with conversation between Major Lynch, 5th AF officer in JOC and Commander Murch, USN[240] - "When asked if a briefed secondary target should be assigned each Navy flight, Maj Lynch queried Commander Murch, USN, who answered 'No' as he was satisfied with their present procedures, and if forward controllers were filled up at the time, armed recn areas are and can be assigned." The above is completely at variance with the Potter article. For your info, it is interesting to note that CG FEAF has constantly requested Navy air to operate in battle area and that 7th Fleet has consistently asked for area assignments outside of enemy battle area due to "scarcity of targets in battle area." Further interesting to note that an agreed upon Navy plan, arrived at after joint AF-naval planner conference, states that for close support work Navy would supply three controllers from the close support carrier. One controller would be relieved about 1700 each day to return to carrier to provide day to day exchange of information. Copy of memo of record is on file in this HQ. Personal comment from Nuckols to Smith: The pattern of the planned attack on tactical aviation is similar if not identical to the recent abortive attack of strategic air power. Cast of characters remains the same. Plan of maneuver essentially the same. The only difference being change in target.

General Craigie presented the following letter to Partridge for my signature re the Potter article:

I am referring to you the attached article and editorial which were published in the 23 August issue of the *Baltimore Sun* and which were referred to this Hq for comment by Headquarters, USAF. This is the third example of this type of malicious attack against our operations in support of the ground forces which has come to my attention. I realize that inquiring

---

240. Maj J.A. Lynch and Lt Cdr John A. Murch.

into this sort of thing can very seriously detract from the time and effort which you are able to devote to your primary operational responsibilities. It is my desire that you turn this over to a staff officer for preparation of comment in order that it may interfere as little as possible. It is my desire that your comments include statements relative to the utilization you have made of Seventh Fleet controllers or control teams. Please inform me also relative to direct offers of such teams which you may have received from the Seventh Fleet. One of the serious allegations concerns deficiencies in the communications between 7th Fleet and your headquarters. I would appreciate your comments relative to that matter also. I am enclosing copy of letter written this date to Admiral Joy.

My letter to Admiral Joy:

Dear Turner, I have had brought to my attention an article and editorial which have appeared in the *Baltimore Sun* in which the writer, Mr. Phillip Potter, after having interviewed various high-ranking members of the United States Navy in the Pacific, including Rear Admiral Ewen, has made very derogatory statements relative to: *(1)* the operation of FEAF in Korea; *(2)* the cooperation which exists between FEAF and Unites States Navy carrier aviation; *(3)* my inhospitality toward the Navy's proffered assistance, and *(4)* the failure on the part of FEAF to supply the Navy with information and/or equipment which the Navy required. As I indicated to you previously, during our discussion on the Miller article on "Marine close support aviation," this sort of thing upsets me very greatly. I am concerned because the picture which is created in the mind of the reader of such an article is vastly different from the picture which I carry in my mind of the cooperative spirit which has characterized the actions of my staff in dealing with the Navy. Contrary, to the impression created in this article, I have urged maximum participation of the Navy in close support of the battle line. I have, in fact, been quite disturbed over repeated (occasional) indications that the Seventh Fleet was more anxious to operate in North Korea than in the close support zone. Admittedly, good battle area targets are, and have been from the beginning, rather scarce and hard to locate during daylight hours. The importance to the ground effort has, at times, however, dictated the use of practically all available Naval air strength, as well as all FEAF tactical air strength, in this less lucrative area. Thus, we have endeavored to insure our ability to attack a worthwhile target when and if it did appear. This has, at times, resulted in what might appear as an over-saturation of the battle area which after all is a cap. As the ground situation improves, the necessity for this will become much less. The statement is made that I have been inhospitable and non-receptive to offers of the Navy to supply controller teams. This is not the case. On the contrary, following a joint meeting on 3 August, there was delivered to my headquarters on the following day an agreed upon Navy plan which stated that, for close support work, the Navy would supply three controllers from the close support carrier. One controller would be relieved about 1700 each day, returning to the carrier in order to provide day-to-day exchange of information. A copy of this memorandum is on file in this headquarters. If, at any time in your opinion, the requirement exists in Korea for additional Navy controllers or controller teams, please be assured they will be very welcome. General Partridge has informed me that he shares this view. With reference to our failure to supply proper grids, maps and target material to Fleet personnel, I am informed that the Navy has been supplied the same material which has been made available to our own personnel and in at least as generous quantities.

Regardless of the nature of the articles which certain misguided writers or publishers are printing in the United States, my single idea in connection with the Korean effort has been and is to do _my_ utmost, and encourage all under me to do their [both words emphasised in original] utmost, to bring about a United Nations victory. If I have at any time appeared inhospitable to offers from you or your people, I apologize and if I have appeared non-receptive to suggestions submitted by the Navy, I would appreciate it if you would bring such incidents to my attention in order that I may take appropriate corrective action. I consider it of vital importance that you and I and our staffs work together smoothly and with a minimum of public recrimination and criticism. Anything less than this can only result in a loss of confidence in the military establishment on the part of the American people. I, therefore, am asking you to inform me if and when in your opinion, misunderstandings have developed or are developing between us or between our respective staffs. It is possible that the time has come for a meeting of appropriate individuals on our respective staffs for the purpose of ironing out such differences as may be developing. After all, there have been many new arrivals (both Navy and Air Force) to the theater during the past few weeks and it may well be possible that some of these individuals have brought with them ideas which are not in consonance with agreements which you and I reached relative to the coordination of the operation of our respective combat air units. It is possible that it is necessary at this time to again reiterate the terms of the CINCFE directive (GHQ, FEC, file AG 370.2 (8 July 50) CG) which delegated to me coordination control of United Nations air over Korea "when both Navy Forces, Far East, and FEAF are assigned missions in Korea." If you believe that we are not seeing eye to eye on such subjects as the utilization of Navy tactical control teams or, as I said before, on any matter of mutual interest, I would consider it a favor if you would bring such matters to my attention with the view of having appropriate individuals on our respective staffs get together and iron out the difficulties. It appears to me that such a get together between your operations people and mine would be appropriate in the immediate future in order to preclude the recurrence of that which occurred on 26 Aug. On that date, the CG 5th AF expected and counted on approximately 80 sorties from the Seventhth Fleet in direct support of the ground forces in the battle line; only 4 flights of 4 a/c each reported in to the JOC although I note that 19 additional close support sorties were reported in your flash summary, Air Ops, 26 August. I am sure that you will agree with me it could be extremely serious for misunderstandings of such a nature to occur at that level. Lastly, I would appreciate receiving your personal views as follows: in your opinion do the deficiencies alleged in the article, in fact, exist? Does the picture painted by this article accurately portray the views held by senior commanders in the 7th Fleet? If the deficiencies do exist, it is indeed unfortunate that they have to be brought to my attention through the press rather than through a meeting between the two of us.

Issued following Stratline to Partridge:

re 15-mile column enemy troops sighted vicinity of Kyŏmip'o (38°35'; 125°45'): CINCFE desires hourly reports starting 1500 hours today on location, progress, results our air attacks, and any other pertinent information to include negative reports throughout the hours of daylight and such reports as you can obtain during hours of darkness.

Radio - to Ramey from Stratemeyer:

Officers of this and my AF hqs have had earlier "M" atomic energy clearances continued here. Disregarding duty assignment of officer, request statement of AF policy on allowing officers holding M or Q clearances to go on combat missions over Korea. Because of rapid changes and improvements in atomic weapons, and because of great amount of information previously classified which has appeared in press and periodicals believe any restrictions that may exist should be tied to date officer when to school at Kirtland or was briefed by General LeMay at his hqrs. Any policy applying to staff officers of this and my AF hq should be in consonance with any restrictions that have been placed on SAC units operating in this theater.

TUEDSAY 29 AUGUST 1950

Sent following two redlines to Vandenberg in line with my policy of keeping him informed of happenings that might not otherwise get to his immediate attention and which he can pass on to Bradley for the President:

(1) Following just received from Chinese sources and evaluated B–3 by FEAF: "54th, 55th, 56th, and 74th Chinese Communist armies all crossed Yalu River and are now in North Korea." This report, if true, assumes additional significance in the light of earlier intelligence indicating *(a)* hurried large-scale construction and repair of revetments in Korea, some capable of sheltering twin-engine bombers or transports, *(b)* continuing frantic efforts, despite heavy air attacks, to reconstruct bridges across the Han River, and *(c)* Monday's charge by the Chinese Communists that American airplanes have violated Manchuria 5 different times which is without foundation. We did scare hell out of the Ruskies though when we bombed Rashin and patrolled in Korea across Manchurian border opposite Antung.[241]

---

241. Intelligence sources were rated with letters from A (the most reliable) to D (least reliable). In addition, the

(2) As experimental mission FEAF BomCom to furnish 1 B–29 to drop flares over bridge complex at Seoul during period 0001 through 0300, 30 Aug, while 5th AF strafes and bombs the Seoul bridge complex.

Late this afternoon received the following from Admiral Joy:

Your confidential letter of 28 Aug is acknowledged with misgiving. The *Baltimore Sun* editorial has given a misleading picture of Navy-FEAF cooperation which has been excellent from my observation; the article in question has been the subject of previous strong dispatch from the CNO. An investigation is being conducted. I will reply to your letter in detail at an early date when facts bearing on the case are made known to me. Be assured that your personal interest in the success of our joint efforts is well known and appreciated at this headquarters.

At 7:00 P.M. we had dinner at the Craigies; Craigie was most thoughtful and had the Supply and Maintenance people; namely, Col. and Mrs. Alkire, Col. and Mrs. Ausman;[242] also General Banfill and his daughter.

WEDNESDAY   *Sent the following to Vandenberg redline for his info:*

30 AUGUST   Suggest USAF initiate immediate project to develop news-
1950   reel shorts plus a feature color picture depicting USAF tac-
tical air operations Korea. MAAF picture *Thunderbolt* and late starting Ninth AF Europe are examples. Assume Navy doing something along lines *Fighting Lady*. Most desirable USAF be first.

Following is my redline to Partridge:

I want immediate investigation instituted at TOP SECRET level to ascertain fullest details of incident reported your ADV-INT-D-563. Submit partial reports as investigation progresses in order that this headquarters will be kept informed. Matters of special interest which should be reported ASAP are: *a.* Weather conditions in areas involved during periods; *b.* Details of surrounding territory with special reference to location of river and nearest town, with respect to airfield. *c.* Type of construction of runway. *d.* Details as to aircraft observed. *e.* Flak encountered. *f.* Number of aircraft in flight dispatched on 27, 28, 29 August; *g.* Corroborating reports from other personnel on flight, if any.

Re my signal to Partridge reference the action that I have taken and my proposed action redline to Vandenberg, General MacArthur at 1143 hours this morning approved wholeheartedly my procedure; he indicated he did not want a copy sent to his hqs, but to handle it strictly with the Air Force. He commented that the '51 pilot must have been a pretty damn poor navigator and that if he were guilty, disciplinary action should be taken, but insofar as he was concerned, that action should simply be to send the offender to the ZI.

---

information these sources supplied were given numerals from 1 to 4, with 1 being accurate or highly probable, and 4 being inaccurate or improbable. Thus, B-3 information was from a reasonably reliable source but was deemed to be only a possibility and not necessarily accurate. (Goulden, p 280.)

Two F–51s did strafe an airstrip near Antung on August 27.

242. Col Neal E. Ausman.

After seeing CINCFE, dispatched the following redline to Vandenberg:

Preliminary report from Partridge in Korea indicates strong probability that F–51 aircraft of the 67th Fighter Bomber Squadron had strafed workers on an airstrip in Manchuria, near the NK border, on 27 Aug 50. Attack resulted in possibly killing or wounding 10 to 15 workers. Pilot reported the location of airstrip attacked as being near Anju (39°36'N: 125°40'E) however two subsequent flights failed to locate the airfield attacked in this vicinity. This suggested possibility that the airstrip attacked was located at Antung (40°10'N; 124°25'E) some 5 miles inside Manchurian border. Partridge has been directed to make a detailed investigation at TOP SECRET level with partial reports as investigation progresses. Further details will be forwarded as received. Directive received redline Stratemeyer from Norstad, 021955/Z, was promptly issued 3 July to my responsible AF commander. Further on 14 Aug, following directive was issued to my responsible AF commanders: "it is dir[ected] that no repeat no attacks against targets w/i [within] 50 mile of Manchurian and USSR border be undertaken without prior specific approval of this hq." If an error has occurred, it will be admitted as soon as facts can be determined. There is doubt in our minds that an attack was made in Manchuria.[243]

1400 hours - the meeting in conference room outside General MacArthur's office on the coming amphibious operation was a very good one. Following were present: Admirals Joy and Struble; Generals Almond, Hickey, Wright, Ruffner, Weyland, Crabb, Fox; Colonels Chiles, Ganey, Ferguson, Warren, Zimmerman, a Navy Commander, and Captain Hill, and myself.[244] The point that I want to make in my diary is that I raised the question of coordination control, I being General MacArthur's air commander. I looked at Admirals Joy and Struble and asked if they were satisfied with the agreement that we were operating under and which was issued by General MacArthur. They both indicated that they were and General Almond commented that it was working satisfactorily.

Dispatched the two information redlines to Vandenberg which had to do with our experimental flare mission, and the superb training evidenced by SAC in their GCA landings from a 9-hour mission. These radios as follows:

(1) Re my redline 290551/Z, cite A 4936 CG, mission successful. Seoul bridge complex lighted from 0059 to 0130/K. Eight B–26 a/c attacked in

---

243. That such an attack would occur had been a worry to Stratemeyer for some time. As noted in his redline, as early as July and reiterated on August 14, he had warned his fliers about the grave consequences of border violations. Following the August 27 incident, he again cautioned his commanders and their subordinates about knowing the proper locations when operating near the borders. He ended this message with the admonition, "There must repeat must be no slip up in this matter." (Msg, HQ FEAF to CG 5AF Japan, et al, 2 Sep 50.)

Nevertheless, border violations (including reconnaissance and "hot pursuit") continued throughout the war. At least one source believes these violations, if not officially sanctioned, were tolerated by higher authorities. (Jon Halliday, "Air Operations in Korea: The Soviet Side of the Story," in *A Revolutionary War: Korea and the Transformation of the Postwar World* [Chicago, 1993], pp 154-156. See also Robert F. Dorr and Warren Thompson, *The Korean Air War* [Osceola, Wis., 1994], p 118.)

244. Probably Col John H. Chiles, the G-3 for X Corps; Col Don Z. Zimmerman, Director, Plans and Policy, FEAF; Capt Hill may be Arthur S. Hill, the Navy liaison officer at FEAF headquarters.

flare light but full moon interfered. Will utilize again on dark nights when needed. All bridges are out.

(2) All 24 B–29s of 92d Bomb Group at Yokota, after 9-hour mission to Ch'ŏngjin on 29 Aug, made GCA landings in 300-foot ceiling at 4 repeat 4 minute intervals, all without incident. LeMay advised on efficient results SAC training.

Sent the following to LeMay with info to O'Donnell:

I am happy to report that all 24 B–29s of 92d Bomb Group at Yokota, after 9-hour mission to Ch'ŏngjin on 29 August, made GCA landings in 300-foot ceiling at 4 repeat 4 minute intervals, all without incident. The results of SAC training was most evident on the efficiency with which the 92d landed yesterday. All your units as members of FEAF Bomber Command are performing superbly on their destruction of Joint Chiefs of Staff targets and also on their now excellent precision bombing against bridges in our important interdiction program.

THURSDAY 31 AUGUST 1950	Wrote another letter to Vandenberg urging temporary promotion for Darr H. Alkire to Brigadier General. Sent a carbon of this letter to Nate Twining[245] to see if he can't push it a little. Feel very strongly about Alkire's promotion -

which is deserved, and some tangible recognition for his efforts is due him.

Craigie came up with his "first nickle"[246] with respect to the informational redline I send to Vandenberg which is as follows:

Of 31 RR bridges and 12 highway bridges designated primary targets for BOMCOM, 19 RR bridges and 8 highway bridges were reported intact as of 22 August. As of this date, only 3 RR bridges and 2 highway bridges remain usable. One of these RR bridges was damaged but was again placed in operation by the enemy. We are really getting precision results from our B–29s.

(Info'd Curt LeMay on this redline)

Also sent a commendatory letter re "Increased Effectiveness of Bombardment Attacks Against Bridges" to Col. James V. Edmundson, CO, 22d Bomb Group, thru O'Donnell, with copy to LeMay. I commended them for their enthusiasm, determination, and outstanding professional ability - and told them, I didn't and do not, forget the ground crews who make such bombing possible.

Group Captain Barclay left the following transcripts of cypher signals:

Following signal is for the Air Adviser from Air Ministry London: AX 4329 30 August. The following is for Barclay from Pearson. Begins. With

---

245. At this time, Lt Gen Nathan F. Twining was head of personnel at Headquarters, USAF. In October, he became Vice Chief of Staff, USAF. Later he became the Air Force chief of staff and, finally, Chairman of the Joint Chiefs of Staff.

246. In the context of Stratemeyer's comments, the term "nickle" is unclear. However, during World War II the term was used to indicate a propaganda leaflet and it is possible Stratemeyer is using it to mean a propaganda or public relations effort.

reference to your signal AAJAP 122 of 28 August we are dispatching on 30 August 24 low level bomb sights Mark 3 with mounting brackets, flexible drive, computer lighting control panels, and pocket handbook. Par 2. Consignment consists of crates 28 which are going via America by U.S. military a/c. Par 3. It is presumed the Americans know how to fit and that they are aware that suction drive is needed. Will you please state whether or not a technician is wanted. I shall be grateful if you will notify me when these items are safely received in Tokyo.

Also follows is a copy of the confidential letter written Sir A. N. Noble Bart, C.M.G., Foreign Office by Sir Alvary Gascoigne:

I showed your ltr of 11 Aug (YT 223/6) to my air advisor who drafted the telegram of which you complain. He tells me that General Stratemeyer, the CG of FEAF, has himself asked to be quoted as asking for the highest possible priority to be given to the telegram requesting provision of a night intruder expert from the R.A.F. for duty with the 5th AF. The General wishes me to stress that the appointment was of such urgency that even the saving of a few hours in lodging his request was of the utmost importance. The General has written personally to the Chief of the United Kingdom Air Staff, Sir John Slessor, to thank him for the very prompt action which was taken in the matter. I think that you will agree that, in view of the above, we were in fact justified in using the priority "emergency" in this case, strange though it may have looked at your end.

Redline, TS received from Vandenberg:

I must have not later than 2400Z, 31 August as complete a report as possible of your investigation of possible F–51 attack on airfield on Manchurian border, 27 Aug 50. Report should be in two parts: A. Statement of facts as determined by that time; B. Based on facts available, statement of your judgment as to whether the attack was made. Par. 2. Assume you are keeping MacArthur informed. The necessity for closest security on this subject at this time should be apparent to you.

After receipt of above, immediately sent following reply to Vandenberg - TS - redline:

Have arranged to conduct investigation today my headquarters Tokyo. Parties concerned have been ordered here. Report will be made to you prior to 2400/Z, 31 August. MacArthur has been and will be kept fully informed.

The personnel concerned in above redline to Vandenberg arrived at Haneda at 1855 hours and were immediately brought into headquarters where the investigation was conducted. Draft of redline reply to Vandenberg brought to Mayeda House at about 2100 hours, was re-drafted by me and dispatched last night. *Following is the signal that I dispatched:*

Par. 1. An investigation of circumstances surrounding incident reported to you in my redline AO 229 is in progress. Part A. Facts, as disclosed, indicate that an attack of an airfield in Manchurian territory, southwest of city of Antung, was made on 27 Aug 50, in late afternoon. One (1) F–51 aircraft, of 67th Fighter Bomber Squadron, 18th Fighter Bomber Group, made attack. Facts further substantiated by pilot of second F–51 aircraft, of same unit, who was following attacking aircraft at higher altitude but did not participate in attack. Pilot in second aircraft witnessed attack. Part B. In my judgment, an attack was made. Par. 2. MacArthur will be informed this message. Investigation is continuing and detailed report will be courier mailed soonest.

In the meantime my PIO has been in the line of fire from newsmen. *He sent following radnote to Sory Smith:*

Press queries here ask for comment on charge presented to United Nations that four American fighters flew across Yalu River on August 29. Following is our response to these queries: "All of our pilots and air crews have been meticulously briefed to scrupulously avoid any action that might be construed as a border incident. Specifically they have been cautioned to refrain from crossing any North Korean border. We do not plan to comment on each detailed individual report." Request comment and/or guidance.

FRIDAY
1 SEPTEMBER
1950

Nuckols received from Sory Smith in answer to his radnote the following:

Your quoted response to queries concerning border incidents checked with Chief of Staff, Secretary of Air Force, and Under Secretary Early.[247] Your handling exactly correct. Mr. Early suggests particular emphasis on final sentence, "we do not plan to comment on each detailed individual report." signed Smith

Partridge arrives. Gave him my copy for action of the Norstad redline to me which reads:

The fol[lowing] statement was introduced at UN Security Council today, quoted in part: "At 1745 hours on Aug 29, 4 U.S. fighters flew over from Korea and invaded and reconnoitered from the air above La-koo-shao of the Kuan-Tien district of China on the right bank of the Yalu River. After that they flew along the right bank of the Yalu River to Chang-tien-ho-kou, about one kilometer from La-Kao-sho, where they fired shots at Chinese civilian boats, killing one Chinese fisherman and wounding 2 others. At 1750 hours the same fighters came to the air above Koo-Lau-Tsu to the northeast of Antung where they again fired shots at civilian boats, killing three Chinese fishermen, severely wounding two and slightly wounding three others." Investigate and report as to possible basis for this statement.

---

247. Stephen Early had been Under Secretary of Defense since April 1949. Earlier he had been President Roosevelt's press secretary.

My immediate redline reply to Norstad is:

Partridge in my office and signal has been turned over to him for investigation. Report will be made as soon as received. My comments are: On 29 Aug, F–51 flights were made over northwest Korean territory in order to investigate incident of 27 August; the pilots were particularly thoroughly briefed not to violate the border and it is my opinion that they did not repeat not.

Quoted in toto is the redline Vandenberg sent me in reference to this whole border incident as it emanates from the floor of the Security Council:

The US delegate[248] to the Security Council of the United Nations today made this statement: "On August 28 there was submitted to the Security Council a communication from Chou-en-Lai complaining that military aircraft operating under the Unified Command in Korea had overflown and strafed Chinese territory in Manchuria. On Aug 29 on behalf of my Government I submitted to the Council a reply to that complaint which stated that the instructions under which aircraft are operating under the Unified Command in Korea strictly prohibit them from crossing the Korean frontier into adjacent territory and that my government had received no evidence that these instructions had been violated. In that communication, I also expressed the view that my government would welcome an investigation on the spot by a Commission appointed by the Security Council. As soon as we received the complaint from Mr. Chou-en-Lai, the United States military authorities operating under the Unified Commander of the United Nations Forces in Korea were instructed to make an immediate investigation to determine whether there was any evidence to indicate that the charges were well-founded. Reports have now been received which indicate that one F–51 aircraft of the 67th Fighter Bomber Squadron may have violated Chinese territory in Manchuria and strafed an airstrip in the late afternoon of Aug 27, 1950. This evidence has not been confirmed, but indicates the possibility that the F–51 aircraft attacked an airstrip at Antung in Manchuria approximately 5 miles from the Korean border. If this evidence is confirmed my government is prepared to make appropriate response in compensation for the damages which have occurred. As I stated in my communication of Aug 29 strict instructions have been issued by the military authorities in Korea to confine their operations to the territory of Korea. For example, on June 29, 1950, in an order to the military forces it was stated that 'special care should be taken to insure that operations in North Korea were well clear of the frontiers.' Again on July 2, 1950, the Secretary of Air Force of the United States directed the CG of Air Force operations to emphasize the necessity of full briefing to air crews so that there will be no possibility of attacking targets beyond the territory of North Korea. These same instructions were emphasized again to the military commanders in the beginning and middle of August. The evidence which has so far been developed, indicating as it does the possibility that an aircraft of the

---

248. Warren R. Austin.

United Nations Forces in Korea may have violated territory in Manchuria and attacked an air field there, only serves to emphasize the desirability of sending a United Nations commission to the area which can make an objective investigation of these charges. My government believes that the Security Council should establish such a commission without delay. The authorities of North Korea and Manchuria should provide it with the necessary freedom of movement and safe conduct so that it may make a thorough investigation of the facts. For their part, the United States military authorities would extend to the Commission full cooperation including access to pertinent records. The Commission when established can make an immediate investigation of the incident complained about an Aug 27 and if it finds that an attack did in fact occur, my government is prepared to make payment to the SYG [Secretary-General] for appropriate transmission to the injured parties such damages as the Commission shall find to be fair and equitable. (In such case, my government will see that appropriate disciplinary action being carried out by the Unified Command in Korea.) I am requesting that the SYG O[ffice] transmit a copy of my statement in the Council this afternoon to Mr. Chou-en Lai." If queried on this subject you will restrict your comments to the facts as stated in this statement.

Received the following letter from General Spivey, the VC for Fifth AF in Nagoya:

Just before leaving Washington, I participated in actions leading to greater protection of our strategic Air Force. General Vandenberg and General Fairchild,[249] before his death, as well as the Air Staff, put very great emphasis on protecting SAC aircraft and SAC and MATS bases essential to the implementation of our war plans. I believe I am correct when I state that the reason they placed such great emphasis on our strategic capability is that they felt that our atomic capability is the greatest single deterrent to Russian aggression, and that if war ensues it will be our greatest capability for winning the war. As a consequence, the Joint Chiefs of Staff, as well as the North Atlantic Treaty Organization, have given first priority to our atomic capability in all their planning. It is the Air Force's position that in case of war, the targets most likely to be attacked by the enemy will be our atomic carriers. The logic behind this is obvious when one considers that if our atomic carrier capability is destroyed, the enemy need not fear destruction by our bombs but may take his time in delivering his own stockpile. General Vandenberg ordered the following actions be taken to protect SAC's atomic capability: *(1)* All SAC and MATS bases to be utilized by SAC in carrying our agreed war plans have been fenced with a perimeter fence enclosing the flying field and inhabited areas; an inner fence with guard towers and search lights surrounding the parking areas, maintenance areas, operation areas and gasoline dispersion points. This fencing program cost approximately $3,000,000. *(2)* Restriction

---

249. Gen Muir S. Fairchild was Vice Chief of Staff, United States Air Force when he died on Mar. 17, 1950.

of the bases to all personnel not essential to the operation of the base. Those entering must have passes and are checked in and out of restricted areas. *(3)* The Air Police squadron of each base has been augmented by 200 additional guard personnel. *(4)* FBI, OSI and CIC activities have been greatly increased in the vicinity of each base. *(5)* Notified the Joint Chiefs of Staff that the Air Force must have at least one fighter squadron and one AAA battalion on or near each critical base. During my recent inspection of Fifth Air Force bases, I found at Yokota a most lucrative target for the enemy. Two groups of B–29s were parked two to a hardstand and wing tip to wing tip along the parking ramp. They were loaded with bombs and gasoline and were so closely jammed together that it appeared to me that detonation of the bombs on any one of the aircraft would start a chain reaction destroying the other, or that if one caught fire, the others might also burn. The proximity of this base to North Korean bases makes it possible for Yak type aircraft to make flights from North Korea to Yokota. Even if the North Koreans lacked the navigational and pilot ability to fly to Yokota, it is not inconceivable to me that well-trained Manchurian or Chinese pilots might be used for this purpose without implicating China, Manchuria or Russia. I am sure, and my air defense people agree with me, that if only one or two such aircraft arrived at Yokota, damage to the B–29s would be exceedingly great, possibly disastrous to both groups. Inspection of the radar installations in the vicinity, ADCC and the TCC [tactical control center] at Johnson, convinces me that it is possible for low flying aircraft, or aircraft taking advantage of background clutter caused by the mountains near Tokyo, to reach Yokota without being detected before they are within two or three minutes of the field. There are three gun battalions and one AW [automatic weapons] battalions located in the vicinity of Yokota. It is problematic whether they would keep a flight of two or three aircraft from strafing or bombing the aircraft at Yokota. On the ground I found that there was a distinct lack of defense against overt or covert action. I believe it is possible for an armed group of Reds to do material damage to aircraft at Yokota or at any other base in the Fifth Air Force if they were clever and disguised themselves as American officers. In a staff car or truck they could drive onto the base and down the line without so much as being challenged. The strategic Air Force believes that the danger from sabotage and overt action poses a threat greater than that of air attack. I believe this is especially true in Japan. In order to lessen the possibility of damage to the aircraft based at Yokota, I have taken the following actions: *(1)* Directed the base commander to confer with General O'Donnell concerning protection of his aircraft at Yokota. *a.* To increase the guard personnel at Yokota to the extent necessary to secure the base properly. *b.* To restrict access to the base to the extent necessary to keep unauthorized persons off the base. *c.* To inaugurate a pass system which will positively identify authorized personnel. *d.* To set up strong points on the base, this to be accomplished in conjunction with the AAA. *(2)* Directed the air defense commander at Johnson Air Base to increase to the greatest possible extent the air protection for Yokota Air Base. I recommend that the following actions be taken to insure greater security for the B–29 groups now located at Yokota: *(1)* That dispersal areas be rushed to completion at the earliest possible date. *(2)* That the aircraft now at Yokota be dispersed to hardstands which have already been completed. *(3)* That the possibility of deploying one group to another base be explored. In this connection Komaki should be considered. *(4)* That the recommendations of the anti-aircraft commander concerning the replacement of the AW battalion, which was recently removed from the Tokyo area, be expedited. *(5)* That the heavy anti-aircraft artillery now on Johnson Air Base be deployed to recommended off-base positions. *(6)* That manproof fencing be installed at Yokota to the same extent being erected on SAC bases in the U.S. I feel so strongly about preserving our atomic capability that I am constrained to write you this letter. I believe that we should not accept any risk which we can anticipate and eliminate when our long-range striking force is involved. I shall keep you posted as to our air defense and ground defense capabilities.

Sent above letter with this R&R to Craigie:

Attention is invited to the attached letter from General Spivey, etc., which has the concurrence and approval of Major General Partridge, CG Fifth AF. I approve every recommendation made by General Spivey and direct that every possible action be taken by FEAF Hqrs to bring about the action recommended. It is realized that some of these actions will require additional funds and must receive the approval of CINCFE. You will utilize the attached letter and this memorandum to secure such funds and approval as is necessary from higher authority.

This morning, in conference with CINCFE, I secured his approval to deploy and make available to Fifth Air Force for operations in Korea the following units: The wing hqrs and two squadrons from Okinawa - F–80Cs; leaving there one squadron with its essential supporting units. One squadron from Johnson AFB, leaving there one squadron. All the F–80s from Misawa except one flight of F–80Cs; to utilize the squadron that I have required for air defense at Itazuke, to be utilized for operations in Korea. The all-weather fighters to remain as now deployed.[250]

I presented to General MacArthur the complete file on the F–51 incident around Antung, Manchuria, including the last signal from Norstad, and the long signal from Vandenberg in which he quoted Mr. Austin before the UN. General MacArthur's instructions to me were to put out no publicity except that as shown in Vandenberg's signal reference Mr. Austin.

The letter (which is quoted in full above) from General Spivey, approved by General Partridge, received by me this date, makes strong recommendations for the security of our air bases in Japan - particularly those in the Tokyo area. I approved every one of those recommendations and directed the VC for A&P to

---

250. General Partridge requested these changes on August 30. (Ltr, Maj Gen E.E. Partridge to Lt Gen George E. Stratemeyer, 30 Aug 1950.)

take the necessary action to implement them. I further directed my VC A&P to make requisition on the AF in Washington to replace for air defense purposes all units with supporting organizations that I have turned over to Partridge for operations in Korea.

While in conference with General MacArthur, at which General Partridge was present, I told him that I was very concerned about the ground situation. For the first time, he impressed me that he was concerned also and that he indicated that he turned over to Walker the Marine Brigade, the 17th ROK Rgt., and all ammunition that he contemplated using on the planned amphibious operation. He then stated as follows: "Strat, I'm not ordering you to do this, but if I were you, as the overall Air Force commander and because of the seriousness of the ground situation in Korea, I would utilize every airplane that I had, including the B–29s to assist in the latest all-out effort that the North Koreans are mounting against General Walker's ground forces." I indicated to him that that was exactly what I intended to do.

Upon my return to my office, Generals Weyland, Craigie, Partridge and I went into a conference; the same time got in touch with General O'Donnell and directed that he report to me without delay. We discussed the use of the '29s; the use of what Navy and Marine airplanes we could secure, and I was just informed at 1435 that the Navy would be able to make available this afternoon 40 sorties for close support and that the Marines at Itami would be flown to Ashiya and also will get into the fight in close support this afternoon. Generals Weyland, O'Donnell and Partridge are now in conference to come up with the recommended use of the B–29s tomorrow.

In my conference with General Partridge this morning, the following subjects were discussed: General Lowe's visit to Korea tonight or tomorrow; the use of the night recce squadron at Itazuke; the use of napalm on the ferry slips and facilities near Seoul; the operations of the 3d Bombardment Group (light); the possible desire of Marines to utilize Tsuiki when they are required to vacate Miho (I gave an emphatic "No") and temporary assignment to me of a bachelor F–80 pilot, who had flown some 50 missions in order to let Capt Melgard to get into the battle. On this latter subject, he stated that Timberlake was securing the individual and that I would be informed.

It is my opinion that the American ground forces are not taking the initiative and fighting. It is further my opinion that they are not aggressive unless they have total, all-out air support. Yet, the North Koreans without any air support and in spite of tremendous casualties that they are receiving from our air, they are aggressive at all times. When one considers the tremendous havoc and casualties that we (air) have inflicted on personnel, armor, and on trucks, and they still keep coming, one can not but admire them as an enemy. Again, in my opinion, General Walker needs a staff - and an aggressive one. I wonder what would happen within our lines if there was enemy air and it had killed 1,200 of our people on a division front as we did yesterday in front of the 3d South Korean Division.[251]

---

251. This F–51 attack near P'ohang apparently killed 700 enemy troops. (Futrell, p 140.)

Dispatched the following memorandum to CINCFE by courier:

The normal effort of three B–29 bomb groups will participate in support on designated targets at safe distances beyond bomb line tomorrow, 2 September. Two groups with normal effort which are already loaded with 1,000 lb. demolition bombs will continue the priority interdiction program. Plans are being made to utilize B–29s in support of ground forces on Sunday, 3 September. I have had General Partridge and General O'Donnell together with my Operations people this afternoon and we will continue efforts utilizing the B–29s wherever in our opinion they will favorably affect the ground situation.

After conferring with O'Donnell, I sent the following priority message to LeMay and Twining, with info to the Bomb Command:

This radio in 2 parts: Part I For LEMAY: I am in great need of a commander to command 19th Bombardment Group (Medium). I have in mind Lt Colonel Payne Jennings, now Assistant Operations Officer, FEAF Bomber Command, but who should be promoted immediately to the grade of Colonel. General O'Donnell in my office and concurs in this transfer. If promotion recommended cannot be approved, can you furnish me a qualified group commander? Part II for TWINING: If LeMay agrees to this transfer, urgently recommend promotion to temporary Colonel, Lt Colonel Payne Jennings. Will appreciate you advise on action taken. I have known Jennings since 1943 as he was with me in India-Burma-China as first pilot on B-24 and performed superbly. After serving two years overseas he was returned to ZI and assigned to SAC. He was one of the few lieutenant colonels in SAC who commanded outstandingly for one year a B–29 group, namely the 301st Bombardment Group (Medium) at Salina, Kansas. Although 19th Group has been in the war since 27 June and has performed creditably, it now needs an energetic, highly technically qualified group commander. The present group commander, Colonel Theodore Q. Graff has commanded the group for approximately a year and in combat over two months. It is my opinion that he now should be rotated, as I contemplate recommending in the case of other group commanders, to the ZI, and a new group commander appointed.

Colonel Heflin,[252] SAC, called on me in my office.

SATURDAY 2 SEPTEMBER 1950

T.S. redline, EYES ALONE, Vandenberg to Stratemeyer, received and read 0745 hours:

The operations in Korea are the responsibility of General MacArthur, operating under the directives of the Joint Chiefs of Staff. I cannot therefore prescribe any limitations or special rules governing your operations in any particular area or in any special situation. However, the directives from the Joint Chiefs of Staff and from

---

252. Probably Col Clifford J. Heflin, commander of the 9th BG(H).

me are clear and complete as to the necessity of avoiding any violations of the Manchurian or Soviet borders. The probable attack of an F–51 on Manchurian territory as reported by you has had, as you know, the gravest political implications. There must repeat must not be any repetition or appearance of repetition of this incident.[253]

My comment is: The signal does not sound like Van. To me, it is a passing the buck signal and indicates that the crossing of the border by an F–51 was condoned - and that we had not attempted to carry out the directives from the Joint Chiefs of Staff. Again, I say this does not sound like Vandenberg. It is one of those signals sent purely for the record. Such signals do not help morale. Again, I quote Lincoln: "I do the very best I know how - the very best I can; and I mean to keep doing so until the end - if the end brings me out all right, what is said against me won't amount to anything; if the end brings me out wrong, ten angels swearing I was right would make no difference."

First Lieutenant Thomas C. Langstaff[254] reported on permanent change of station from the 49th Fighter Bomber Group; he will make it possible for Bob Melgard to go on detached service and join the 8th Fighter Bomber Group at Itazuke where I have instructed him to be given the opportunity to fly some 50 or 60 missions. Lt Langstaff has flown 53 F–80C combat missions; he is the nephew of Elise Boyd.[255]

Dispatched to Admiral Joy (info copies to CINCFE and Partridge) the following letter:

I would like to express my appreciation and admiration for the way Task Group 77.4 was put into battle line support on 1 September 1950. All of us realize the difficulty of making emergency changes in plans and my staff and I am unanimous in our respect for your efficient handling of yesterday's operations. Please convey to your staff and the officers and men of Task Group 77.4 my thanks (and I am sure, General Walker's) for the prompt and aggressive support they gave. Best regards.

In answer to LeMay's letter of 21 Aug in which he raised several questions, following extract is my answer to his letter:

Ref Par. 2. In reply to your first question, I am of the opinion that your training program is very sound and is producing crews capable of doing excellent bombing, both visually and by radar. The crews of your units in this theater have demonstrated outstanding professional skill in bombing operations against industrial targets. Although not trained for bombing attacks against bridges, the crews are gradually mastering the techniques peculiar to such bombing. The results achieved recently have been most gratifying. Low altitude, visual bombing, when it is necessary to perform missions when the cloud deck is low, in my opinion, needs attention. When I say this I realize this is not a normal technique

---

253. See "History of the JCS," Vol. III, pp 249-263, for a discussion of the border issue from the viewpoint of the JCS.
254. Langstaff flew with the 8th FBS, 49th FBG, before becoming Stratemeyer's junior aide-de-camp.
255. Elise Boyd is unknown.

for SAC, but there will always be occasions in war where low altitude, visual bombing will be a requirement should the targets be fruitful. This is not a criticism, Curt, it is merely a suggestion. Ref Par. 3: Concerning your 2nd question, I think your mobility plan is adequate for the mission for which it was designed, that is, conducting only atomic bombing operations for a period of approx. 1 month. Operations employing conventional bombs as Rosie is now doing require a large amount of base support. Both at Kadena and at Yokota, we are furnishing the equivalent of the wing support provided by your bases in the ZI. In this connection, I might add that we are in a position to furnish better support than you can hope to find in any other part of the world. This fortunate situation is largely attributable to the fact *(1)* we have the largest AF organization outside the ZI, and *(2)* we enjoy a highly advantageous priority because of the war and we are not competing with other areas for resources. Ref Par. 4: Depending upon the world location of bases, various augmentations of your mobility plan in personnel and equipment will very probably be necessary. Because the problem is rather complex, I heartily welcome your proposal to send over a couple of your organizational experts. Ref Par. 5: Rosie O'Donnell has just returned from a visit to Guam. Heflin returned with him and briefed me and some members of my staff, including Trask. Nevertheless, I am planning to send Trask, as soon as possible, for a visit with Heflin and his organization.

Redline to Vandenberg with info to CINCFE, 5th AF, 20th AF, 13th AF, FEAMCOM, 5th AF in Korea:

Part I. Because of critical conditions in Korea and contemplated offensive operations demanding additional fighter-bomber support, I am decreasing the air defenses of FEC by 4 F–80 sqdrs [squadrons] and supporting elements, and augmenting the offensive effort of the 5th AF in Korea by the same amount. This action places 4 day fighter groups in offensive tactical air operations, and leaves one day and one all-weather fighter group for air defense of Japan, Okinawa, and the Philippines. Part II. Request that a 4 squadron fighter wing be transferred to FEAF to rebuild our air defense capability as expeditiously as possible.

The above radio, re additional squadrons and utilization for air defense of Japan put in form of directive in a letter to Partridge and Stearley this date.

Drafted a letter to O'Donnell re plans and methods of new techniques in the utilization of B–29s; asked him to come up with some ideas. Sent my draft over to Operations for them to mull over letter before I send it out.

Called General Marquat and pointed out to him that the complete approval, that he concurred in on the employment of Japanese National engineers at FEAMCOM, has been complied with insofar as we are concerned; but it is held up there in his office, by his people, and has been since 23 August. He said he would immediately get on it.

I telephoned Colonel Bunker and asked him to tell the boss that the three B–29 sorties against targets in rear of the battle line had been excellent, and, further, that we would operate 48 B–29s, 3 September, against targets, data for which is being flown to BOMCOM direct from Fifth Air Force.

SUNDAY 3 SEPTEMBER 1950

Following is redline personal to Vandenberg sent out in line with my policy of keeping CSAF advised of pertinent info:

AP report from front quotes Major General Wm. B. Kean,[256] commander of the 25th Div, saying: "The AF saved this division." AP report then continues, saying: "Kean issued a statement saying 'the close air support rendered by 5th AF again saved this division as they have many times before. I am not just talking. I have made this a matter of official record.'" AP report. UP report quotes Kean as saying: "Close air support rendered by 5th AF has been magnificent." UP report. I am querying Fifth Air Force for complete text of "official record." Perhaps above statements will be of significance in connection with the current Washington interest in tactical aviation.

Major General Wm. E. Hall with a Colonel Welchner arrived in Tokyo.[257] General Tunner, who reported in this morning, informed me (which I have passed on to Weyland) that General Vandenberg was sending to FEAF one group of C–46s (30 airplanes) which were due to arrive 1 October. (Queried Weyland to find out if we are getting with that group the supply and maintenance people - that I feel it should be a wing and not a group.) General Tunner also stated that General [Edward H.] White's (MATS) transport squadron could be made available upon our request for airlift as this squadron was being furnished 3 crews per airplane, but if we use it, we must notify General Edwards, D C/S, Ops, USAF, in advance, giving him the time with inclusive dates that its use is desired. Advised Weyland to keep me posted re above 2 subjects.

Sent the following official letter to O'Donnell, with copies to Craigie, Weyland and Crabb (and LeMay with the note: Dear Curt - just to keep you informed):

(1) This is to confirm my suggestions to you as given in General Weyland's office 1 Sept 50, that you figure out with your people some methods and new techniques on the use of your B–29s for emergency purposes in order to affect the outcome of the ground battle now taking place in Korea. You know the ground situation, plans of maneuver and the locations of their corps and division CPs. *(2)* I want these plans perfected in order to utilize the 500-pound and 250-pound frag clusters and the 500-pound napalm bomb of which we have a great supply. Also, consideration must be given to utilizing B–29s at low altitudes, perhaps in flights of three, squadrons, or even groups, in order to bomb visually below cloud decks. *(3)* Certainly with imagination and study as we can use this SAC weapon now more advantageously than in the past. Practically all

---

256. Commander of the 25th Infantry Division since 1948, Kean had been Gen Omar Bradley's chief of staff, then chief of staff of the First Army in World War II.

257. General Hall had worked closely with Stratemeyer during World War II as Secretary of the Air Staff and then Deputy Chief, Air Staff. Presently, he was Director, Legislation and Liaison in the Office of the Secretary of the Air Force. Lt Col Carl A. Welchner also worked in the L and L office.

the Joint Chiefs of Staff targets have been destroyed. *(4)* I desire that you give this immediate study and submit to me by indorsement hereon your ideas on how best to employ the '29s in this emergency, using non-SAC tactical methods.

In answer to my redline of yesterday asking for additional air defense and telling Vandenberg that I'm stripping my forces to put all the power I can in Korea, the following was received: "re redline request this hq four F–80 squadrons for air defense requirement FEAF. This matter under study. You will be advised."

My immediate reply to above redline: "reurad TS 4070 AFOPD: my request was for a four squadron fighter wing. I did not specify F–80 squadrons."

Sent the following Memo to CINCFE: "I thought you would be interested in the attached chart which depicts graphically the weight, in terms of sorties, and the continuity of the joint air effort over Korea."

To Major General William B. Kean, CG of the 25th Infantry Division, sent the following:

The courageous action of your 25th Division in containing the heavy North Korean thrust during the past two days has been magnificent. Although your men have been in action almost continuously since first committed early in July and in spite of the numerical superiority enjoyed by your opponents, the 25th has not only absorbed everything that could be thrown at them, but also have bounded back in remarkable fashion. The deep admiration of the airmen of the Far East Air Forces goes to the men of the fighting 25th.

I have just read the investigation conducted by General Banfill, assisted by Colonel Tidwell, Staff Judge Advocate, and Major Ranlett,[258] an officer from the Inspector General's office, and as far as I can determine, the investigation is complete and I like the recommendation made; however, I am having it looked over by my Vice Commander, Administration and Plans, in order to seek his advice. The directive for the investigation was dated 31 August, subject: "Alleged Attack on Neutral Airfield Near Antung, Manchuria by United States Air Force F–51 Aircraft," to: Brigadier General Charles Y. Banfill, and signed by me.

On the 13th of Aug I sent a ltr to CINCFE, subj: "Air-Ground Operations," and stated that although 5th AF procedures in coordination with 8th Army operations are based on FM 31-35, dtd Aug 46, which is based on WW II experiences and certain refinements derived from subsequent field exercises and maneuvers, I feel that more effective use could be made if an air-ground operations system were established within the Army. Amplified my reasoning for above and gave an estimate of personnel and equipment required: 1 senior officer with G-3 air experience to supervise the operation of the air-ground system; at the JOC in Hq 5th AF, there should be 9 G-3 air duty officers, 6 G-2 air duty officers, and required clerical help; one ground liaison officer team to brief pilots who are assigned missions which are closely integrated with ground action and to interrogate these air crews subsequent to each mission; suggest an Army photo interpretation center be established; and a communications of a mobile type to

---

258. Maj Charles A. Ranlett, Jr., executive officer of the FEAF Inspector General Office.

connect the components of the air-ground operations system mentioned above.

The following reply to my letter that is briefed above has been sent to 5th AF in Korea & Nagoya, read by Colonel Sykes, and copies made for the AG [adjutant general] File; the reply is quoted in part:

The CG, 8th Army has established an air-ground operations system in Korea based upon the principles of organization and procedure outlined in FM 31-35 and the pamphlet "Conduct of Air-Group Operations." The latter pamphlet was prepared jointly by the Office, Chief of Army Field Forces, and the Headquarters, Tactical Air Command, and represents the latest guide for the conduct of air-ground operations. This pamphlet has been reproduced by GHQ, FEC, and 40 copies were furnished by hq by referenced letter. The CG, 8th Army, is cognizant of the discrepancies in the present air-ground organization, as outlined by your letter, and every effort is being made to overcome these as soon as possible. The arrival of additional personnel, presently assigned or expected, will permit the complete staffing of the JOC with qualified personnel ... and will permit the dispatch of the necessary ground liaison officers to each 5th AF combat group to brief pilots and to interrogate crews subsequent to each mission. The personnel and equipment required to establish the Photo Interpretation and Reproduction Center and the necessary air-ground communication system are not presently available in the FEC but have been requisitioned from the ZI with request that movement of personnel and equipment be expedited....

MONDAY
4 SEPTEMBER
1950

Dispatched my weekly letter to Gill Robb Wilson. Banfill brought in this "nickel" in line with my policy to keep Vandenberg abreast of items of interest, but decided to hold it for 24 hours. Banfill stated:

Observation of 162d TAC Rcn Sq aircraft from 3,000 feet at 040030/K Sept 50: Scattered lights of estimated 200 vehicles going generally south from Yangsi (39°59'N - 124°28'E). Numerous vehicles coming across Manchurian border above Yangsi into Korea. Other vehicular convoys observed on adjacent roads in general area between Yangsi and P'yŏngyang. Fifth AF reports missions have been laid on to attack these targets.

COORDINATION OF AIR EFFORT OF FAR EAST
AIR FORCES AND UNITED STATES NAVAL FORCES, FAR EAST.

AG Ltr, 370.2 (8 July) CG, signed by General Almond reads as follows:

In order to obtain the maximum effectiveness in the employment of all air resources in the Far East Command and to insure coordination of air efforts, the following conclusions agreed to by the Commander, United States Naval Forces, Far East, and Commanding General, Far East Air Forces, are approved and adopted as policy:

(a) CG, FEAF, will have command or operational control of all aircraft operating in the execution of Far East Air Forces mission as assigned by Commander-in-Chief, Far East. This includes operational control of naval land based air when not in execution of naval missions which include naval reconnaissance, anti-submarine warfare, and support of naval tasks such as an amphibious assault.

(b) Commander, U.S. Naval Forces, Far East, will have command or operational control of all aircraft in execution of missions assigned by Commander-in-Chief, Far East, to Naval Forces, Far East.

(c) Coordination: *(1)* Basic selection and priority of target areas will be accomplished by the GHQ target analysis group with all services participating.*(2)* Tasks assigned by CINCFE, such as amphibious assault, will prescribe the coordination by designation of specific areas of operation. *(3)* When both Navy Forces, Far East, and Far East Air Forces are assigned missions in Korea, coordination control, a Commander-in-Chief, Far East, prerogative, is delegated to Commanding General, Far East Air Forces.[259]

(The above ltr sent to both COMNAVFE and myself)

On 4 September, I sent to CINCFE, subject: Coordination of Air Operations, as follows:

1. References: *(a)* Annex 'F' to Operations Order No. 1, "Coordination of Air Operations, Headquarters United Nations Command," 2 September 1950 (TS).

(b) Letter, CINCFE, AG 370.2, (8 July 1950) CG, subject: "Coordination of Air Effort of Far East Air Forces and United States Naval Forces, Far East." (Secret)

2. During the joint meeting of Army, Navy and Air Force commanders held in the office of Chief of Staff, GHQ, 30 August 1950, I presented the air coordination directive of 8 July 1950 (reference b), and it was agreed by the commanders present that this agreement would remain applicable to future operations. Annex 'F' to Operations Order No. 1 (reference a) contains some elements which are not in accordance with this agreed to directive. In order to avoid misunderstanding, I deem it imperative that Annex 'F' be in complete consonance with this directive.

---

259. The term "coordination control" was almost an oxymoron in the Korean War. Throughout the war, both General Stratemeyer and his successors had trouble establishing either "coordination" or "control" of the various Air Force, Navy, Marine, and foreign air units fighting in Korea. One reason for this problem was that the term was a newly-coined one and had not been officially defined. Almost as an afterthought, the following unofficial definition was prepared by a GHQ staff officer later in the war:

"Coordination control is the authority to prescribe methods and procedures to effect coordination in the operations of air elements of two or more forces operating in the same area. It comprises basically the authority to disapprove operations of one force which might interfere with the operations of another force and to coordinate air efforts of the major FEC commands by such means as prescribing boundaries between operating areas, time of operations in areas and measures of identification between air elements." (Futrell No. 71, p 12.) Despite the fact there was no official definition of the term, General MacArthur never clarified its meaning and apparently never intended to. MacArthur evidently attached little importance to this matter, his July 8 directive on this subject being written in such a way as to indicate that his headquarters would retain the final say on "coordination control."

With the term unclarified by MacArthur and only an unofficial definition written much later, it is no wonder "coordination control" would remain ambiguous and subject to diverse interpretations by the various services. It remained a problem area for Stratemeyer for months, causing him to expend much energy and time on the subject that could have been better spent in other areas. (Futrell, pp 49-51, 54-55; Futrell No. 71, p 12.)

3. *a*. Par. 3 of reference a states in substance that aircraft operating outside of the objective area on missions assigned by CINCUNC [Commander in Chief, United Nations Command] to COMNAVFE are subject to coordination as arranged between COMNAVFE and CG FEAF.

b. It is recognized that COMNAVFE must have control of air operations within the objective area during the amphibious phase. Air operations outside of the objective area are part of the overall air campaign, and during the amphibious phase contribute to the success of the amphibious operation. Air operations before and after D-Day, outside of the objective area, must be coordinated in accordance with paragraph c (3), reference b, which states: "When both Navy Forces, Far East, and Far East Air Forces are assigned missions in Korea, coordination control, a Commander-in-Chief perogative, is delegated to Commanding General, Far East Air Forces."

4. *a*. Par. 4 of reference a states in substance that the sweeping of airfields within a radius of 150 miles from a point located at latitude 37 degrees and longitude 125 degrees is a mission assigned COMNAVFE, effective on receipt of the order.

b. The mission of maintaining air supremacy over all of Korea is the continuing responsibility of the Commanding General, Far East Air Forces. With the exception of Kimp'o and Suwŏn airfields, the remaining airfields are outside of the objective area. The mission of sweeping airfields at all times, with the exception of the two fields in the objective area during the amphibious assault, is a responsibility of the Commanding General, Far East Air Forces, and coordination control must be exercised by him in accordance with paragraph c (3), reference a.

5. Par. 8, reference a, states in substance that COMNAVFE will designate approach and retirement routes for aircraft such as troop carrier and cargo aircraft in the objective area. The operations of troop carrier aircraft are of special nature and require thorough knowledge for the successful accomplishment of their mission. Before designating retirement routes in the objective area, COMNAVFE must coordinate with CG FEAF.

6. The principle established in par. a of reference b that CG FEAF will have "control of naval land-based air when not in execution of naval missions which include naval reconnaissance, anti-submarine warfare, and support of naval tasks, such as amphibious assault" has been omitted in reference *a*. To avoid any possible misunderstanding, this principle should be applied and stated in ANNEX 'F' to OPERATIONS ORDER NO. 1.

7. I therefore recommend that:

a. The last line of paragraph 3, reference a, be changed to read: "These latter missions are subject to coordination control of CG FEAF."

b. The 3d sentence of par 4, reference a, be changed to read: "The sweeping of these and other located fields in the area indicated, to insure air supremacy within the objective area, is a mission assigned jointly to COMNAVFE and to CG FEAF with coordination control exercised by CG FEAF." Delete the 4th sentence of par. 4, reference a.

c. The 1st line of Par 8, reference a, be changed to read "COMNAVFE, through appropriate commanders, and after coordination with and approval by CG FEAF, will designate approach and retirement routes for a/c such as troop carrier and cargo a/c and other transient a/c in the objective area."

d. Add par. 9 to reference a to read as follows: "Control of air operations including those of land-based naval and marine units in the objective area will pass from COMNAVFE to CG FEAF when directed by CINCUNC after completion of the amphibious phase."

8. The foregoing recommendations are indicated in Inc. C, recommended "Revised Copy - Annex 'F' to OPERATIONS Order No. 1." Signed G. E. S., etc.

(Recommended Revision - Annex 'F' - Coordination of Air Operations to OPERATIONS ORDER NO. 1.)

1. Appendix 1 delineates the Initial Objective Area. Within this area, COMNAVFE, thru appropriate commanders and agencies, control all air operations, including air defense and close support of troops from 0600 D-3 until relieved by orders of CINCUNC.

2. Appendix I further indicates:

a. A number of areas, designated as areas MIKE, NAN, OBOE, PETER, and QUEEN, which will be employed both in the pre-assault and post-assault phases to assist in the coordination between Far East Air Forces and Naval Forces Far East in the area outside the objective area.

b. A zone in which COMNAVFE is responsible for tactical interdiction affecting the objective area from 0600 D-3 until relieved by CINCUNC. This zone is the area between the outer limits of the objective area and the line R-R as shown on Appendix I.

3. Far East Air Forces controls the operation of all a/c outside the objective area with the exception of a/c operating in the execution of missions assigned by CINCUNC to COMNAVFE. These latter missions are subject to coordination <u>control by CG FEAF</u>. [emphasis in original.]

4. Various airfield lying within a radius of 150 miles from a point located at Latitude 37 degrees and Longitude 125 degrees constitute a definite threat to the conduct of the operation. Such fields have been located at or in the vicinity of P'yŏngyang, Sinmak, P'yŏnggang, Ongjin, Haeju, Kimp'o, Suwŏn, Taejŏn and Kunsan. The sweeping of these and other located fields in the area indicated, to insure air supremacy within the objective area, is a mission assigned <u>jointly to CG FEAF and</u> [emphasis in original] COMNAVFE effective on receipt of this order, with coordination control exercised by CG FEAF. (See paragraph 3, above). In correlation with such sweeps, Navy air elements will conduct strikes against military targets of opportunity and will, at the request of FEAF, undertake such interdiction missions as are consistent with the primary mission.

5. Requirements for air operations in the objective area, during the period 0600 D-3 to disestablishment of the objective area, which exceed the capabilities of COMNAVFE, will be requested from CG FEAF by

COMNAVFE. In the event CG FEAF is unable to provide such support without undue interference with other missions assigned, he will so report to CINCUNC and inform COMNAVFE.

6. Except under emergency conditions, requests on CG FEAF for medium bomber strikes will be requested at least 72 hours prior to the TOT [time over target] desired. Where a question arises as to priority of missions, the decision will be made by CINCUNC.

7. In emergency, the tactical air commander in the objective area may request air support direct from CG 5th AF. If such support is not consistent with 5th AF commitments and capabilities, priority for such support will be designated by CINCUNC.

8. COMNAVFE, thru appropriate commanders, <u>and after coordination with and approval by CG FEAF</u> [emphasis in original], will designate approach and retirement routes for a/c, such as troop carrier and cargo a/c, and other transient a/c in the objective area. Such a/c will be subject to the control of established control agencies in the objective area.

9. <u>Control of air operations, including those of land-based naval and Marine units in the objective area, will pass from COMNAVFE to CG FEAF when directed by CINCUNC after completion of the amphibious phase</u> [emphasis in original]. (By Command of General MacArthur.)

TUESDAY 5 SEPTEMBER 1950

Wrote Jack Slessor a letter, telling him because of a telephone conversation I had had with Bouchier, apparently he (Bouchier) was a bit unhappy about the channels we used to Slessor. Bouchier too had apparently dressed down both Squadron Leader Sach and Group Captain Barclay inasmuch as he thought they had been presumptuous. Told Slessor that Bouchier had never indicated to me that he was out here to help us - my understanding was that his level was too high to approach, as in the case of obtaining flares - which is the case in point - and that Sach and Barclay had both done a superior job for us and that Gascoigne, too, had been most helpful. "I write this letter to you in order to protect Squadron Leader J. F. Sach (he is a real member of my team) who is doing a superior job for me as an exchange officer from Air Marshal Sir F. J. Fogarty's show in Singapore and Group Captain Barclay. They have both gone out of their way to assist me in my dealings with the RAF - both in Singapore and in London."

Decided not to send the Banfill "nickel" as suggested info to Vandenberg as it had not been confirmed. (See reference under date of 4 September.)

After the briefing, had a nice talk this morning with Air Vice Marshal C. A. Bouchier, RAF, and he was sorry that he had not made it clear that he was in a position to act direct between myself and Slessor on any of our needs. He indicated that he had made all arrangements for flares for Partridge's night intruders and Squadron Leader Sach is preparing a signal, Norstad from Stratemeyer, requesting that the flares be lifted from the British Isles to Japan.

I instructed Squadron Leader Sach to confer with Wing Commander Wykeham-Barnes when the latter returns to Tokyo and secure from him two or three names of RAF officers that he considers capable of being assigned out here to assist Partridge in his night operations and then utilizing these names, prepare a memorandum from me to Air Vice Marshal Bouchier, requesting that a signal be sent to Jack Slessor for their assignment here.

Received a call from Partridge at 0955 hours and he stated that things were all right and that he was hopeful. He pointed out though that the weather over there was not good and that the T-6s reported the weather in the P'ohang - Kigye area was so bad that fighter bombers could not operate. He related to me the following incident which was witnessed by General Lowe in a T-6.

A Lt Wayne,[260] who was recently on the cover of *Life* as having shot down the first two Yaks in the war (Lt Wayne was flying an F–80), was forced to bail out in a rice paddy, after the F–51 he was in was hit, behind enemy lines. A helicopter was dispatched immediately, it went back of the lines and rescued Wayne - all of which was taking place under enemy fire. When Wayne arrived back at Itazuke, he discovered that his wife had had a baby.

General Lowe stated to General Partridge, relating the incident to him, that all participants should receive not less than the Medal of Honor. Partridge said recommendations for awards would be forthcoming.

After talking with Bouchier, I added the following P.S. to Slessor in my letter which is quoted above: "Had a nice talk with Bouchier this morning and everything is properly channeled and all my dealings with you from here on out will be through Air Vice Marshal C. A. Bouchier. I am still sending the letter, though, Jack - just for the record."

Redline to Vandenberg:

Razon operations successful 3 September from research point of view. We experienced several malfunctions but all can be evaluated and corrective action taken. Two direct hits accomplished resulting in span out of bridge, with other near misses. Reason known for misses and corrective action can be taken. Will keep you advised.

With respect to "affair Manchuria," I sent this date the following letter to Partridge:

(1) Enclosed for appropriate action is copy of the report of investigation of violation of the Manchurian border by two F–51 a/c of the 5th AF on 27 Aug 50. The investigation reveals that the border was violated and that the leading airplane of the flight fired on an airstrip southwest of Antung, Manchuria. The investigation was confined to establishing the truth or falsity of the allegation. There are many questions left unanswered as to the contributing causes of this incident which I am sure you will want to check and eliminate in present and future operations. *(2)* I do not wish to dictate the corrective action that should be taken as a result of this case. You are well aware of the seriousness of the violation. I consider that the lack of judgment on the part of the flight leader, 1st Lt Ray I. Carter, warrants careful consideration by a Flying Evaluation Board. *(3)* In reading the report, I find several serious deficiencies in operational procedures.

---

260. 1st Lt Robert E. Wayne was the first pilot to be rescued from behind enemy lines, being saved by Lt Paul W. Van Boven in an H–5 helicopter on September 4. (Futrell, p 577.) Wayne shot down two Il–10s on June 27.

As examples, when new targets in unfamiliar territory are assigned, greater study of maps and terrain features should be made by the pilots; positive steps to insure that the latest weather reports brought in by earlier flights is considered in the dispatch of later flights. The fact that there was no specific briefing on the importance of staying clear of the Manchurian border is not only a reflection on the briefing at squadron level, but suggests that my instructions to you are not reaching the operating levels. *(4)* Corrective action will be taken by you to remedy all deficiencies brought out by this case. G.E.S.

On same subject as above, the following was dispatched to Vandenberg:

(1) Per statement made in my radio AO 233 CG, I am inclosing, herewith, a report of the investigation of the Manchurian incident. (See Inclosure No. 1). The investigation definitely shows that two of our F–51s of the 67th Fighter Bomber Squadron, 18th Fighter Bomber Group, 6002d Fighter Bomber Wing, now designated as the 6002d Fighter Bomber Wing, did, in the late afternoon of 27 August 1950, violate Manchurian territory by flying over the Manchurian border and the lead airplane fired on an airstrip just southwest of Antung, Manchuria. *(2)* The investigation discloses that both pilots involved had had combat experience in ETO and had flown combat missions in Korea prior to this incident. They knew that they were not to fly over Manchurian territory. *(3)* The mission involved was to destroy six barges near the mouth of the Chŏngeh'on-gang[261] River in North Korea. The weather was not good, as had been forecast, and the flight had to fly at 14,000 feet, and came out of the clouds at a place the pilots thought was south of their target. Instead, they were north of it and mistook the Yalu River for the Chŏngeh'on-gang River. Being fired upon, they turned and circled to their left to avoid the flak, turned south and passed over the airstrip involved. Not until the 29th of August, when they made another flight to determine where they had been, was it definitely ascertained that they had been in Manchurian territory. *(4)* Specific instructions from this Headquarters have been given to the various Air Forces to avoid Manchurian and Soviet territory and to brief their crews accordingly. Note our radios enclosed. (See inclosures Nos. 2, 3, and 4.) *(5)* The investigation disclosed several deficiencies in the operational procedure of Fifth Air Force in Korea. These have been called to General Partridge's attention and he has been instructed to remedy them. (See Inclosure No. 5). *(6)* The report of the officers investigating the incident has recommended that Lt Carter, the flight leader and pilot of the airplane that fired on the airstrip, be ordered to appear before a Flying Evaluation Board, special attention being called to Lt Carter's lack of judgment, which I approved. The report of investigation has been forwarded to General Partridge for necessary action. G.E.S.

1130 hours, Major General Harris, U.S. Marines, called with Brigadier General Cushman.

---

261. Also known as the Ch'ŏngch'ŏn River.

1500 hours, Mrs. Nora Waln,[262] novelist, visited me with Colonel Nuckols for about 30 minutes, during which time she discussed her coming article for the *Saturday Evening Post*, in which she writes about the Air Force cadet training in Korea, with particular emphasis on character building of the Korean cadets, our treating them as equals - all of which will be presented most favorably to the Air Force. She asked if I had any comments or quotes for her story and I stated that I felt the main part of the instruction which she should convey to her readers was that the democratic way of life was being instilled in these cadets and that all of our instructions to them emphasized equality for all and that the most competent should lead - all of which is the basis for our way of doing things.

General Partridge called about 6:00 P.M. and stated that all was well in Korea - that he was not worried about the North [Koreans] or the battlefront. He stated that there would probably be a change in the location of General Walker's set up tomorrow, but that his present location would remain the same.

WEDNESDAY 6 SEPTEMBER 1950 General Partridge called; reported that the weather was good; he considered the ground situation the same as yesterday and maybe a little better. There is no rain and that General Walker, with a command group slightly larger than his, was remaining in Taegu.

At about 1015 hours, went over to the AEP school and talked to Mrs. Overacker's group of volunteer teachers. (These women assist in the established Japanese schools by giving of their time in leading class discussions in English. All is on a volunteer basis.)

I congratulated these women on their initiative and suggested that they emphasize DEMOCRACY [emphasis in original] - giving all the why's; cover our Constitution, equality of person, institution, etc. Suggested that their teaching not stop in the classroom, but continue their efforts in their own homes. Personalized it by stating from my own experience of one and one-half years, that it tends to build up happiness and efficiency when you endeavor to train your servants.

Also told the ladies that they have a job here in the occupation just as real as General MacArthur's; through their efforts - and all our efforts - the imprint that we leave behind will stay for many years to come.

I ended up with Abe Lincoln and his Rail-Splitter's philosophy in dealing with these people - and it was good to keep in mind no matter what job that they attempted to do.

My above efforts seemed appreciated and well received.

In answer to my letter to Rosie of 3 Sept on the emergency use of B–29s, I received the following from which I quote in toto:

1. The proper utilization of B–29 a/c on tactical targets has been of continuous concern to myself and my staff since arrival in this theater. From the outset it has been evident that destruction of vital strategic targets in North Korea could be accomplished with my available effort in very

---

262. In addition to several novels, Waln had also written numerous articles for various magazines. It was in this latter capacity that she was visiting Japan and Korea.

short time. It has been equally apparent that the continued gravity of the ground situation would dictate diversion of medium bombardment aircraft to tactical usage from time to time.

2. In general, the only limitations in the tactical use of the B–29 are those imposed by the unwieldiness or clumsiness of the weapon itself and the avoidance of self-inflicted damage. Subject to these restrictions, I believe the B–29s can be EFFECTIVELY [emphasis in original] employed against tactical targets under the following conditions: a. Assignment of targets before take off with designated aiming points. b. Attacking by visual methods only. c. Attacking at an altitude such that: *(1)* Self-inflicted damage from bombs dropped will not occur. *(2)* Cluster-type bombs, when used, will open in time for dispersion of the components. *(3)* Synchronous bombing using the bombsight will be permitted. (We must resort to fixed angle bombing below 6000 feet). d. Receipt of the directive in time to properly plan the missions, bomb-up, brief the crews, and preflight the aircraft.

3. I suggest that I be given a list of targets, with designated aiming points, by Lt General Walker, in coordination with Major General Partridge. We will strike using the available bombs by type in accordance with the effects desired, and employing the aircraft either individually or in formation, depending upon the assigned target. I think you will agree that aimless flying in the general battle area in search of targets of opportunity or in wait for flash directives from the ground, is not an efficient way to utilize the weapon. If some special, important unorthodox task seems feasible to you, I know you will pass it on to us. I need not tell you that we will promptly take a crack at it.

Twin fireballs of napalm dropped by a 452d BW Invader sprout from a North Korean rail yard.

Passed Rosie's comments on to D/Ops and for them to keep me aware of any unusual operations in which B–29s are to be used.

Partridge answered my query to him of 28 August re the use of napalm. Since difficulties now ironed out in accumulating stocks of tanks, mixers and igniters, and when F–80s can utilize by virtue of their basing in Korea (up to now they have had to carry their own external fuel), employment of napalm is to be stepped up.

In answer to Fogarty's radio re Woodruff, and particularly to his statement "I shall welcome a combat veteran of the Korean war as he will no doubt be able to teach us a lot - if agreed, I would like to put him into a combat squadron for 3 or 4 months before I employ him on any staff duty" - I sent him the following:

Part 1. Glad to have your complimentary remarks concerning Woodruff. Concur in your plan to place the officer I send to you with a combat sqdn. Will forward pertinent details regarding this officer very shortly. *Part 2.* Ref your proposed visit, about 26 Oct, I shall be most happy to have you come to Tokyo. This will be an excellent time to discuss mutual problems. Incident to your flight here, we need a roster of personnel, a/c type and number, grade of fuel required and proposed itinerary to Japan. This may be sent at any convenient time, say 10 days before your departure from Singapore. Billeting and messing while in Japan will be arranged for your party by my hq. Billeting and messing while enroute will be aranged by this hq upon receipt of your itinerary. Part 3. I shall look forward to seeing you again and am sure the visit will be interesting and profitable.

Colonel Brothers just reported 1405 hours that he felt I should be informed on the possibility of a blow-up reference air evacuation. Col Ohman[263] just returned from a trip where he visited Itazuke and was informed by the Army doctor of the hospital there that some 16 fatalities due to gunshot wounds had occurred where and if they had been evacuated by air from Korea there was a great possibility that many of the lives could have been saved.

When Colonel Ohman arrived at Taegu, he ran into a reporter who was securing data reference this matter. Further, Colonel Brothers reported that Charlotte Knight had interested herself in this subject and intended riding an air evacuation ship from Korea to Japan and then she intended to ride a surface vessel evacuation ship.

I queried Colonel Brothers as to the cleanliness of our skirts and he indicated that he and Colonel Kelly,[264] the Fifth Air Force surgeon, had both talked with Colonel Dovell,[265] 8th Army surgeon and Colonel Kelly had talked with Lt Colonel Willis[266] at the hospital in Pusan, urging air evacuation. They pooh-poohed the idea and have continued to evacuate by surface ship to Itazuke hospital, and thence to Yokohama and Tokyo by train.

As of today, though, through General Hume, or because of finally realizing the error of their ways, they are now evacuating from Korea to Itazuke and on to Tokyo by air. Over 200 evacuees came out of Korea yesterday and over 300 from Itazuke area to Tokyo.

From all the information I could gain, the Air Force has gone out of its way to set up this air evacuation but have been stymied by 8th Army surgeon and by, as Colonel Brother's put it, a nincompoop lieutenant Colonel in Pusan.[267]

---

263. Lt Col Nils O. Ohman commanded the 97th BG in World War II. At this time he was a FEAF operations staff officer. In June 1951, he became the 3d BW commander.

264. Col Frederick C. Kelly.

265. Col Chauncey E. Dovell.

266. Lt Col William D. Willis was an Army medical officer.

267. The medical evacuation problem was not quite as simple as General Stratemeyer makes it out to be. A short-age of ambulances restricted the Army's choices. With the Taegu airfield eight miles over rough roads from the hospital, the Army thought it better to place patients on the train from Taegu to Pusan, thence by ship to Japan. Also, those patients awaiting evacuation by air from Pusan often were kept for inordinate lengths of time, a problem not of the Army's making. (Futrell No. 71, p 108.) Eventually, a smooth-running operation was achieved by Combat Cargo Command using C–46s, C–47s, and C–54s.

THURSDAY

7 SEPTEMBER

1950

Sent the following informational redline to Vandenberg:

Construction at K-9 (east field at Pusan) progressing rapidly. Completion of second taxiway delayed awaiting removal of AMMO. Total completion by 15 September. Anticipate 6002d Fighter Wing (F–51s) to be in place tomorrow.

Received the following msg from Edwards quoted in toto:
Present decision, here, reurad AO 259B to send 437th Troop Carrier Wg to FEAF for assignment and date departure from ZI has been stepped up to October 1st.[268] Decision on retention of C–119 sqdns in FEAF will have to be made in accordance with future situation. Present plans based on conference with Tunner and consideration of engine supply and other maintenance difficulty is to return C–119s to ZI unless your requirements at the time are paramount.

At their base at Pusan, 12th FBS Mustangs await another mission.

General Partridge called at 0930 hours and stated that in his opinion they would make it. The situation in the north is stabilizing and that the status of the break-thru in the east P'ohang area was not too bad.

He stated that the weather was bad but that airplanes were flying. Further stated that he had had a particularly good day yesterday and that he had actually destroyed 19 tanks and damaged 22 for an overall 41 tanks. These tanks were not in the front lines but were in rear areas and that in his opinion, the result of air action, they would not make the front lines. He further stated that they knew where there were 30 more and they would be on them this morning.

Sent the following redline to Vandenberg: "Fifth AF destroyed 19 and damaged 22 tanks yesterday. These figures confirmed by Partridge to me this morning."

---

268. The 437th TCW was a Reserve organization based at Chicago's O'Hare Field. Mobilized the same day, August 10, as the 452d BW, the 437th's training period was very chaotic. One reason for this was the fact that the wing was one of the five lowest-manned wings in the Air Force Reserve. Administrative records were in a shambles and there were a number of men attempting to obtain deferments for this recall. Nonetheless, training began at Shaw AFB, South Carolina, on August 22. The 437th's first C–46 reached Japan on November 8, with the first mission flown on the 10th. (Cantwell, pp 25-34.)

FRIDAY
8 SEPTEMBER
1950

Per our directive to FEAF Bomber Command, they are experimenting today with four (4) B–29s loaded with 500 pound GP [general purpose] bombs, attempting to cut rail lines between Seoul and P'yŏngyang. It is my opinion that this is going to be a worthwhile operation.

In reference to the personal signal sent to Vandenberg dated 2 September 50 in which I told him I was stripping my air defensive set up in order to meet the all-out effort required because of the ground situation, and my request to him for replacements for these squadrons, received the following decision from him:

This hq recognizes your problems in air defense. However, critical deficiencies elsewhere make it impossible to provide requested augmentation to your command within the time period which concerns you now. Principal reasons follow: All F–80s are required to meet contemplated expansion of the AF and to support your operating unity. Trouble with F–84s, particularly their engines, precludes further overseas commitments at this time. The few fighter units equipped with F–86 aircraft cannot be commited to overseas theaters at this time because of logistics problems as well as the ZI requirement for air defense. There are no conventional fighter units available in the ZI. NATIONAL GUARD FIGHTER UNITS NOW BEING FEDERALIZED MIGHT BE MADE AVAILABLE AT A LATER DATE BUT DECISION ON THEIR DEPLOYMENT SHOULD AWAIT THE OUTCOME OF PLANNED OPERATIONS. (Emphasis mine).

Following is quote of my "personal - confidential" letter to Van:

Col Ben Wright who was sent out here by you to take a look-see is due to depart today. We have lent him every possible assistance and I am sure that he will bring you a picture of our present public information set-up and our needs - particularly here for Nuckols and for Scott[269] in Korea.

I agree with him 100 percent on the recommendations that he will make to you with reference to beefing up with suitable people the PIO set up here (in Tokyo) and Partridge's set up at Pusan, Korea. I have asked him in what way I could assist and he has given me some suggestions - all of which I intend to follow. He will relate them to you.

There are two things that I recommend that he discussed with you; one is the campaign that is being carried on headed by General Clark, CG of the Army Field Forces, to secure for the Army their own tactical air. I consider this of such importance that you discuss it with Joe Collins who, from all the conversations that I have had with him, is diametrically opposed to any such proposal. The other subject is "beating the Navy to a movie of our operations here in the Far East."

I am wondering if the redlines that I have been sending you meet your requirements for those items that are a bit unusual and which no one else receives but you? If there are too many - or not enough, I would appreciate your desires.

I want to take this opportunity, Van, to thank you and all the headquarters staff for the support and the fulfillment of nearly every request that I have

---

269. Col Cecil H. Scott, Jr., the 5AF Public Information Officer.

submitted which includes personnel, equipment, units and materiel. Through your help, I now consider that we have an all-around first team here in the Far East Air Forces and I am confident that all of us will live up to the responsibilities and actions that you place on us.

Bestest to you and Glad from Annalee and me. P.S. Again, I'm making a strong plea for Alkire's promotion.

I quote in toto the awaited letter from Admiral Joy in reply to my letter to him of 25 August:

Commander, U.S. Naval Forces, Far East, Navy No. 1165, Fleet Post Office, San Francisco, Cal., dtd 7 September 1950,

Dear Strat,

This will answer your letter of 25 August in more detail than time permitted for my brief note of 29 August.

Before answering your specific questions in detail, I should like very much to reiterate my appreciation for your cooperation and the cooperation of your staff. I have felt that our two staffs work together with commendable harmony and in the spirit of getting a difficult job done effectively and expeditiously. I, personally, as well as the naval forces under my command, are appreciative of your frequent tributes to naval air and of your desire to increase the mutual assistance so necessary among our fighting forces. You can be assured that I and my staff will continue to do everything that we can do to promote friendly relationships among our armed forces.

You have asked whether the deficiencies alleged in the Potter article do, in fact, exist. To a degree they do. The experience of the pilots in Task Force 77.4 assigned to close support missions at the time this article was written would justify the opinion that neither the organization nor the communications available for the tactical control of aircraft in close support missions in Korea were prepared for that assignment. I am informed recently that those factors have been improved. At no time, however, have I ever been given the impression that any of the echelons of FEAF command were non-receptive to constructive criticism or suggestions for improvement.

You further asked whether the picture painted by the article accurately portray the views held by senior commander, 7th Fleet. I am of the opinion that such views are held, except that there is no basis for the statement that you have been unhospitable to any proposals for improvements. I know of no senior officers who hold this view.

Nevertheless, it is extremely regrettable that these deficiencies reached the press. They have been, however, the subject of considerable discussion by the various echelons of our commands. Specifically:

a. LCDR Capp,[270] from PhibGruONE [Amphibious Group One] staff, the Navy's best authority on TacAirControl in this command, visited 5th Air Force JOC in Korea after the P'ohang landing and made specific

---

270. Stratemeyer apparently means Cdr Arlie G. Capps, who became the gunfire support officer of TF 90, the Inch'ŏn naval attack force.

recommendations as to how it might be organized and equipped to meet Navy standard operating procedures. This visit was made, according to my information, with full knowledge of Commander 5th Air Force and staff who were reported to have been most receptive to the ideas he presented.

b. Commander 7th Fleet SECRET dispatch 090422Z of August, with information copy to FEAF states in part:

"REPORTS RECEIVED DURING PAST FEW DAYS HAVE INDICATED ONLY PARTIAL EMPLOYMENT OF USN AIRCRAFT WHEN SENT TO TAEGU FOR CLOSE AIR SUPPORT MISSIONS X PARA X FIRST DIFFICULTY APPEARS TO BE THAT THE JOC CONTROLLER TO WHOM ALL INCOMING FLIGHTS ARE REQUIRED TO REPORT COULD NOT BE CONTACTED OR DID NOT ASSIGN SUCH FLIGHTS AFTER REPORTING TO HIM WITH THE RESULTSTHAT FLIGHTS CONCERNED HAD TO FORAGE FOR AIR CONTROLLERS ON THEIR OWN INITIATIVE X PARA X SECOND DIFFICULTY AIR CONTROLLERS THAT WERE SUCCESSFULLY CONTACTED APPEARED TO HAVE MORE AIRCRAFT THAN THEY WERE ABLE TO CONTROL WITH THE RESULTTHAT CERTAIN FLIGHTS WERE UNABLE TO OBTAIN ASSIGNMENT TO TARGETS BY CONTROLLERS"

Other similar information was made known to me as a part of a recommendation by Commander, 7th Fleet, for a changed operating policy for the 7th Fleet. The subject of TacAirControl was part of an overall presentation made to CINCFE's chief of staff, who, at this time, advised that changes were being made in the procedures governing control of close support, air.

If during the busy moments of the last few weeks this matter has not been the subject for personal discussions between us, no significance should be attached to that fact. My feelings about the Far East Air Force, and its leadership, are expressed in a recent memorandum to my command.

I will be very glad to meet with you and the members of your staff, at such time as you suggest, to discuss the whole question of TacAirControl. We may have a lot to learn from each other. I feel certain that we can overcome any difficulties and arrive at a solution to our mutual problems. s/Sincerely "Turner" (C. T. Joy).

The above letter was received at 1000 hours, 8 September from Admiral Joy.

Forwarded Joy's letter to Nuckols with this R&R:

(1) Your attention is invited to the attached letter from Admiral Joy. *(2)* It is desired that you now assemble as enclosures to a draft letter that you are herewith directed to prepare for my signature to General Vandenberg a copy of the attached letter (Adm Joy's letter dated 7 Sept), a copy of my letter to Admiral Joy (dated 25 Aug), a copy of my letter to General Walker (dated 16 August), a copy of General Walker's reply to that letter (dated 18 Aug), a copy of Admiral Joy's acknowledgement of receipt of my

letter of 25 Aug (dated 29 Aug), and a copy of Admiral Joy's memorandum to me which contains the quote of his statement to all his commanders (dated 30 Aug). *(3)* Particular attention is called to the last paragraph of the attached letter from Admiral Joy. *(4)* You will pass on to General Weyland (after both Generals Weyland and Craigie have read the letter) my desire that members of my staff meet with members of Admiral Joy's staff to discuss the whole question of tactical air control and my desire that they make specific requests that when the Navy participates in close support that the Navy supply the required number of tactical air control teams, augmenting Fifth Air Force teams, to the point where all possible Naval close air support can be proficiently handled.

Sach and Wykeham-Barnes were both in the office. Wykeham-Barnes is due to depart this theater reference this quoted British Cypher Message - Immediate & Secret:

The following is for the Air Adviser, Tokyo, from Air Ministry London (A.3995): Reference your telegram No. 908, Wing Commander Wykeham-Barnes is to leave by air on Tuesday, the 15th of August. His date of arrival in Japan will be notified to you later. Will you please request the Commanding General of United States Far East Air Forces to allow Wykeham-Barnes to return to England by mid-September as he is engaged on important work.

In discussing with Sach and Wykeham-Barnes the overall picture of our night-intruder missions, I gave to Sach a letter to Air Vice Marshal Bouchier, Senior British liaison officer, here in Tokyo, the following letter for him to handcarry to Bouchier:

Dear Air Vice Marshal Bouchier:
After consultations with my staff, Wing Commander Wykeham-Barnes, and Squadron Leader J. F. Sach, we have come up with the following signal which I urgently request you send by quickest possible means to Marshal of the Royal Air Force Sir John C. Slessor: "For Slessor from Stratemeyer: Your night interdiction expert Wing Commander Wykeham-Barnes will be leaving here for the United Kingdom on 11 September as requested. He has accomplished an outstanding job, and General Partridge, my Fifth Air Force commander in Korea, has asked that Wykeham-Barnes be allowed to remain for a further period. This, I realize is not possible, but perhaps you could make availabe to me an officer of similar operational experience who would be required to work and fly with my squadrons on the vital night campaign against the North Korean forces. The aircraft at present being used for this task is the B–26 Douglas Invader. Subject to your decision in this matter, I would be grateful if the officer selected could be made available by the quickest possible means."

Had Sach and Wykeham-Barnes to Mayeda House for drinks and dinner. It was one of the best meals ever turned out at our home.

SATURDAY
9 SEPTEMBER
1950

After a conference with General Weyland about 1815 hours, I decided not to bother General MacArthur reference the subject of "coordination control" reference which directives are now coming our from CINCFE interferring with this control. I do intend as soon as the opportunity affords to take this matter up with General MacArthur and have it cleared once and for all.

Sent the following T.S. EYES ONLY letter, individually, to the following: Partridge, O'Donnell, Turner, Stearley, and Doyle:

I am sure it is not necessary for me to tell you that the Air Force is again being harrassed by our sister services and although we have a war on in Korea, we have another one on to defense our position reference tactical air from sniping attacks from both the other services.

The Navy, having been whipped on B–36 skullduggery, has its very best PIO people here in the Tokyo area and throughout the Far East Command following the pre-designed, laid-out plan of advancing carrier based aviation as against land based tactical air.

At the same time, General Mark Clark, Commanding General of the Army Field Forces, is putting on an undercover campaign to lay the groundwork to secure tactical aviation as a part of the Army, and, from my observations, has influenced a number of the Army's senior generals.

I personally ask that you give inpetus and continued guidance to your entire PIO set up and that on every opportunity the story of our proven methods of handling tactical aviation be discussed with news media representatives or with influential private citizens. For your information, some slight additional help in the way of qualified PIO personnel will arrive in the theater soon. You will get a share of these people to further aid in the problem.

Upon reading the above, destroy this letter and report to me personally by radio signal that you have done so. s/G.E.S., etc.

I learned about 1500 hours that Wing Commander Spence, RAAF, was killed this morning in the vicinity of A'gong-ni in close support of the ROK forces. It was a terrible blow to the 77th RAAF Fighter Sq as well as to FEAF.

Sent letters of sympathy to both Mrs. Spence and to General Robertson.

The first B–29 was lost because of flak, over North Korea, in the vicinity of P'yŏngyang. The '29 was from the 92d Bomb Group. Six (6) parachutes were seen to open shortly after which the B–29 blew up in the air.

The B–29 rail-cut operations were considered excellent. This was the first time that this type of operation was flown and it was done at my suggestion and urging. Nine (9) cuts took place between P'yŏngyang and Sariwŏn; three (3) cuts between Sariwŏn and Kaesŏng, and four (4) cuts between Kaesŏng and Haeju.

SUNDAY
10 SEPTEMBER
1950

At 0930 hours, I made the award of the Air Medal to Wing Commander Wykeham-Barnes.

Following were my "talking notes" when I saw CINCFE this noon.

(1) Area outside objective area should have some one individual controlling air - should be I.

(2) Par 4 states effective upon receipt of order COMNAVFE is responsible. When order is issued, naval air was at Sasebo refueling.

(3) Land-based naval and marine air units should pass to my coordinational control after amphibious phase.

(4) Troop carrier and cargo lift routes must be coordinated with me although COMNAVFE has been directed to designate routes, types of aircraft involved - C–47s, C–119, and C–54s.

After my conference with CINCFE [regarding the upcoming Inch'ŏn operation], sent the following directive to General Weyland, with info copies to Craigie, Crabb, and my Director of Plans, Col Zimmerman:

1. I took up with General MacArthur at 1230 hours today the question of air control. I pointed out to him that I had found errors in ANNEX F to Operations Order No. 1 and that on 4 September, I made certain recommendations which admittedly were minor in character, but which violate the principles as laid down in the approved CINCFE directive; subject: "Coordination Air Effort of Far East Air Forces and United States Naval Forces, Far East, 8 July, AG 370.2."

2. The main topics discussed with reference to ANNEX F were as follows:
    a. Someone must control all air effort in Korea and that individual is I. General MacArthur agreed.
        (1) In the order as published in ANNEX F, there was no control of the areas outside of objective area.
    b. Paragraph 4, referenced ANNEX, stated that effective upon receipt of this order, COMNAVFE is responsible. COMNAVFE could not be responsible from date of receipt forward as they were in port refueling part of the time at Sasebo. My recommendations for coordination were the only correct solution. In this case, General MacArthur also agreed. "I am responsible for coordination control."
    c. ANNEX F Order stated that COMNAVFE will designate approach and retirement routes for aircraft such as troop carrier and cargo aircraft. I pointed out to General MacArthur that this could not be done without my coordination as COMNAVFE nor his appropriate commanders did not know the characteristics of our aircraft and that it must be a mutual understanding and coordinated effort. To this, General MacArthur gave his nod.
    d. Reference land-based naval and marine air units, I pointed out that when they were no longer performing a mission for the Navy, that they must pass to my coordination control, and his (General MacArthur's) comment was, "Why, of course, Strat, there is no other way to do it."

3. During my conference with General MacArthur today, it was my desire to obtain his approval and consent to dispatch VC 0260 CG which is in reference to CX 62085. He gave it. Here again I pointed out the necessity for one individual to coordinate control of air effort. General Partridge, CG Fifth AF, due to his responsibility for tactical air operations, including

close air support of the Eighth Army, must be the coordinating individual. General MacArthur read this signal and he indicated that it was O.K. and to send it.

4. In reference to the last sentence, Paragraph 1, First Indorsement to my original letter, 4 September, subject: "Coordination of Air Operations," I can see no reason to review the basic principles as laid down in the 8 July 1950 Directive on "Coordination of Air Effort" as it meets all contingencies that might arise. There have been directives issued by CINCFE staff, though, that are contrary to the policies as laid down in this 8 July letter. I, therefore, want the necessary action taken, as soon as the current operation is over, to assure that subsequent directives clearly establish the coordination of air efforts of FEAF and COMNAVFE in accordance with the policies agreed to and stated in the 8 July letter.

5. You are authorized to use all statements made above in connection with accomplishing this purpose. s/ G.E.S.

Reference above, sent the following message "courier" to all addressees: TO CINCFE, INFO CG 8th Army, COMNAVFE, CG Fifth AF:

Cite VC 0260CG
Reference is made to CX 62086.
My understanding is that CG 5th AF is responsible for tactical air operations including close air support 8th Army. Request for augmentation of 5th AF effort in support of 8th Army should therefore normally come from 5th AF with EUSAK believes their need for air support not adequately considered by 5th AF. However, responsible agency should not be bypassed if proper coordination of air effort is to be achieved with minimum wastage and danger to ground forces.
I have therefore directed CG 5th AF Korea to submit direct to this headquarters requests for air effort which exceed his capabilities including medium bombers, strategic reconnaissance, cargo or troop carrier or support from TF 77. Such requests involving naval air will be referred by my headquarters to CINCFE for approval or disapproval after coordination with COMNAVFE. (Note: This message was cleared personally by me with General MacArthur shortly after 1300 hours, this date - 10 September 50.)

1430 hours, Dr. Bowles' Weapon System Evaluation Group [WSEG], from the Department of Defense, called. (Weapons Evaluation Group: Major General J.M. Gavin, Dr. E.R. Smith, Dr. E.L. Bowles, and Dr. C.C. Lauritsen.)[271] Besides the group had present Generals Weyland and Craigie and Colonel Zimmerman.

---

271. Maj Gen James M. Gavin, commander of the 82nd Airborne Division in World War II, was named Army member of WSEG in 1949. He was also chief of the group's Military Studies and Liaison Division; Dr. E.R. Smith's field is unknown; Dr. Edward R. Bowles was a noted scientist in the field of electrical engineering and communications and a professor at MIT. Since 1947, he had been a scientific consultant to the Air Force; Dr. Charles C. Lauritsen was a physics professor at the California Institute of Technology. The WSEG group was studying problems of tactical air support.

MONDAY
11 SEPTEMBER
1950

Partridge called at 1515 hours and stated that he had received my letter on the PIO business and would get his requirements in.

I told him that Ben Wright had discussed the whole situation with Scott and that we knew his requirements, but for him to go ahead and send them in anyway.

He stated that he had my signal which was delivered by courier on "Coordination Control" and was very grateful for its receipt. He stated that this would solve many of his problems.

He stated that reference a certain individual that was investigated by Banfill (meaning Lt. Carter) on the Manchurian boundary violation, that he felt that my approved recommendation was not the answer. I told him that since Lt. Carter was a member of his command that he had my authority to administer such discipline and to take such action as he deemed advisable.

He stated that he had a very unfortunate incident take place at Taegu at 0600 hours this morning; an F–82 made four (4) passes over Taegu and that twelve (12) people (Koreans) were hit - four (4) killed and eight (8) wounded. He stated that the pilot had missed his target by some twenty (20) miles and he (Partridge) could not understand how such an error could be made. His intentions are to try the pilot for the gross carelessness displayed.

He stated that the ground situation was such that he fully expected that they would make it. All he asked was that the supply of rockets, fuel, bombs, and ammo be kept coming his way. He indicated now that when they found a tank they let go with all eight (8) rockets - and that they are getting them! (Copy above diary entry sent to: Generals Craigie, Wekyland and Banfill.)

Sent General Vandenberg following informational redline:

Our method of tank kills is firing all 8 rockets at target and we are really getting them as confirmed by following kills: 6 September, 19 destroyed; 7 September, 4 destroyed; 8 September, 6 destroyed; yesterday, 11 destroyed. In addition, 40 tanks damaged during those dates.

Received reply to my letter to Partridge reference the Potter incident. I forwarded it with a letter of transmittal, copy of my letter to Partridge and copy of his reply to Vandenberg with the statement that no further comments from me were deemed necessary.

TUESDAY
12 SEPTEMBER
1950

General Toohey Spaatz[272] due in today; ETD Tokyo 25 September.

Sent the following informational redline to Vandenberg:

634 sorties yesterday was all-time high for FEAF aircraft. In addition, RAAF Mustangs flew 38 sorties and F4U Marine aircraft 11 sorties. Grand total of 683 sorties. Two new words coined

---

272. General Carl A. Spaatz was the Commander, U.S. Strategic Air Forces in Europe and subsequently, U.S. Strategic Air Forces in the Pacific during World War II. He became commanding general of the Army Air Forces in February 1946 and the first Chief of Staff of the Air Force in September 1947. He retired from the USAF in June 1948. Following his retirement, he wrote numerous columns on aviation matters for newspapers and magazines.

Korean war: Army stating that naval gun fire was "wonderful and General Keiser,[273] 2d Division Commander, described air support as "delightful."

Sent the following commendatory letter to Joy:

I have just learned this morning that the First Marine Air Wing with 48 assigned a/c flew a total of 208 sorties in a 3-day period (1, 2, 3 Sept). I consider this sortie rate of nearly one and one-half sorties per assigned a/c exceptionally fine and records well the maintenance and operational readiness of the First Marine Air Wing. I would appreciate very much your extending my congratulations to the Navy personnel concerned and the Commanding General, First Marine Air Wing.

Major Woodruff (Sach's counterpart) reported in briefly from Singapore. He brought with him a personal letter from Todd Melersh who said that he was planning a trek to Japan and of course wanted to see me here in Toyko. Wrote him (which Woodruff will carry back with him) that inasmuch as Spaatz arrives tomorrow and intends to leave 25 Sept and Kenney arrives 23 September and intends to leave 3 Oct, and since they will be guests of mine - which will entail taking them to Korea and the bases here in FEAF, would appreciate his putting off his trip if at all possible; if not, and my schedule does not permit my greeting him personally when he arrives, he is to get in touch with my ADC who will see that he gets to the house and is taken care of and that Annalee will be delighted to have him.

Bouchier (Air Vice Marshal - Senior British Liaison Officer, GHQ, FEC) passed along to me the following extract of a telegram he received from Slessor in re Wykeham-Barnes:

Please pass following to General Stratemeyer from Chief of Air Staff: Your message through Bouchier and your letter of 20 August. Am very glad to learn Wykeham-Barnes has done a good job of work as I expected he would. Sorry we must have him back but will certainly arrange for a relief to be sent our earliest possible. Am also glad to learn that Squadron Leader Sach fills your bill. Air Ministry has been asked to select an officer to meet requirements given in Gen Stratemyer's message and Paragraph 2 of your CAB 35 and you will be informed of details and time of arrival as soon as possible.

Quoted above in a message to Partridge plus bucking the statement amongst my staff.

General MacArthur at 1500 hours left to join the 7th Fleet in order to be present for the coming amphibious landing. I have been informed that there will be an advanced GHQ CP set up in Korea which will contain an advanced FEAF hq. My foresight in planning such a hq makes our job an easy one. We were able to give our answer without delay.

---

273. Maj Gen Lawrence B. Keiser saw combat in World War I and was VI Corps chief of staff in World War II. After serving as the division's assistant division commander, he became the 2nd Division's commander in February 1950.

At 1430 hours Weyland, Craigie, Crabb and I attended COMNAVFE's amphibious landing briefing.

WEDNESDAY 13 SEPTEMBER 1950

Information received that Spaatz will arrive at 2300 hours tonight. Annalee and Colonel Van Meter will meet him. Bill Hall left, after dining with us last night, at 0400 hours this morning, via Northwest Airlines and Alaska.

Sent the following information redline to Vandenberg: "

Tank destruction 1 September through 12 September, both dates inclusive, 71 kills and 73 damaged. Our 8-rocket tactics are paying dividends." Report of investigation received from Gen Partridge on violation of Manchurian border near Sinŭiju on 29 Aug states that no violation of the border occurred when four F–51s on armed reconnaissance attacked Sinŭiju airport and destroyed buildings and hangars. This flight was most carefully briefed prior to take off, was cautioned by the flight commander prior to the attack on the airport to stay south of the Yalu River, and all members of the flight were in sight at all times and did remain south of the river. This report forwarded to the Vice Chief of Staff, USAF, 13 September, stating "I consider the case closed."

In addition, the following message was dispatched, personal Norstad from Stratemeyer:

Included in protect on violation of Manchurian border on 27 Aug 50 was vague reference to another violation on 29 Aug. On that date carefully briefed flight of four F–51s made armed recon of P'yŏngyang-Sinŭiju area, exploded hangar on Sinŭiju Airfield with one rocket and strafed other airport buildings. All members of flight stayed south of Yalu River at all times. Report of investigation by Fifth AF coming to you by courier. I consider case closed.

Sent the fol informational redline to Vandenberg:

New tactics successfully developed cutting railroad lines exclusive of tunnels, bridges, and marshaling yards, by FEAF with B–29s. Rail cuts have been made along unpopulated lines of track. Since 9 Sept to 12 Sept inclusive: 18 cuts between Sŏngjin and Wŏnsan; 4 between Kuwon [?] and P'yŏngyang; 4 between Wŏnsan and Ch'ŏrwŏn; 2 between Ch'ŏrwŏn and Seoul; 1 between Ch'ŏrwŏn and Kosŏng [Kaesŏng?]; 1 between Seoul and Kaesŏng; 4 between Kaesŏng and Haeju; 3 between Kaesŏng and Sariwŏn; 9 between Sariwŏn and P'yŏngyang. Total 46 rail line cuts. Will continue on other rail lines.

With reference the personal radio from Norstad suggesting that because of the possibilities for such a posthumous award for Wing Commander Spence, that perhaps I should approach CINCFE to see if he, as Commander of UN Forces, would give the award. I sent Norstad a radio telling him that action has been initiated with FEC.

THURSDAY
14 SEPTEMBER
1950
_____

Annalee left at 0615 this morning to pick up General Spaatz as we were notified that he would arrive at 0655. However, since arriving at the office have learned that he arrived at 0640.

Approved Sykes' letter - gave him the go ahead signal to send same to Mr. Finletter.[274] Mr. Finletter had written Sykes thanking him for his assistance in USAF and stating that he would be looking forward to his findings.

Following is quote of Sykes' reply:

Your thoughtful note of 25 August 50 is much appreciated. You will recall the Joint Secretaries proposal, made sometime ago, that a Joint Evaluation Board be sent to this theater; I heard that this proposal was disapproved by the Secretary of Defense on the grounds that the activities of the board might burden the hardpressed operating staffs out here. Upon arrival here I found that General Stratemeyer was preparing a formal request that an "Air Evaluation Board" be sent out here as promptly as possible, and I am now informed that this formal request went forward on 10 September 1950. File reference: AG 10719 (Secret) subj: Air Evaluation Board.

From what I have picked up so far, there are many valuable lessons to be learned from this operation, as well as many opportunities for drawing false conclusions. I am still of the opinion that an Evaluation Board could operate out here without imposing on the operating staffs, and that such a board could perform a avery valuable service both in connection with discussions of current operations and in connections with the possible future establishment of a "Bombing Survey." s/ Sykes

C–119 lost last night due to weather.

Sent informational redline to Vandenberg: "Spaatz arrived today 0640/I. Will be my guest. Have you any message for him?"

Sent Vandenberg this informational redline:

According to NK propaganda radio, FEAF has been experiencing some tough opposition lately. An extract from one report: "Our brave eagles... attacked two vicious rocket planes... one plane plummeted to the ground, leaving a trail of black smoke; the other started to flee but it was pursued and shot down also. Later, while returning to base, this same airman spotted 17 enemy aircraft. He charged into the formation at surprising speed, frightening them and forcing them to flee. By pouring accurate fire into them, he downed two more planes." This report of course has no, repeat no, basis in fact.

Bucked the gist of my telephone conversation with Robertson to D/O, VC A&P, VCO, and D/P:

Received a telephone call from Lt General Sir H. C. H. Robertson, Commander-In-Chief, British Commonwealth Overseas Forces, this morning he indicated that 2 officers were being sent soonest from Australia to the

_____
274. Thomas K. Finletter, Secretary of the Air Force since April 25, 1950.

77th RAAF Fighter Squadron. A Wing Commander Ford[275] will replace Wing Commander Spence, deceased, and Squadron Leader Cresswell[276] to command the squadron. He stated that he had a signal from Air Marshal Jones indicating that he (Jones) had received no information from South Africa reference the forming of a wing of British Commonwealth Forces at Iwakuni. General Robertson indicated that he was sending the following signal to Air Marshal Jones: "CG FEAF desired that a wing be formed of the South African Fighter Squadron and the 77th RAAF Fighter Squadron and that it was within FEAF commander's authority to do so and he therefore urged that a wing hqrs be dispatched to the Far East to form this wing." He asked me if that was what I desired. I said, "yes" and thanked him.

In reference to the Manchurian Incident, Partridge wrote me:

Yesterday we talked on the telephone about the case of 1st Lt Ray I. Carter and I promised to write you regarding the action which I consider appropriate in his case. The proceedings in his case have been reviewed by my JA [judge advocate] and he is of the opinion that a lack of judgment in a single instance is not deemed adequate cause under the applicable regulation for grounding the individual concerned. There is no other evidence which will support the allegation that the pilot is below standard and therefore I am reluctant to proceed with a Flying Evaluation Board. An incidental difficulty in proceedings before a Flying Evaluation Board is that the incident under consideration is still classified TS. There would be considerable difficulty retaining that classification of the facts in the case if the matter comes up before the Flying Evaluation Board. My JA also considers that disciplinary action should not be predicated upon error in judgment. Gross carelessness and the failure to obey orders may be taken cognizance of under the Articles of War but it is doubtful that any court would find the officer guilty on these counts. Accordingly, it is recommended that 1st Lt Carter be censured and that the censure be imposed by his wing commander. I agree with your thought that the man should not be relieved from combat duty but should be retained in his organization for the duration of his tour.

Replied to above and stated...

at the time I studied the investigation report, I thought of the things which you pointed out and realized there were several problems involved....the officer is in your command and such disciplinary or other action to be taken is one for you to decide. I have complete confidence in your judgment on such matters.

Via telecon note informed Partridge and I would be arriving, C–54, at Pusan, with Spaatz, 1030 hours (I time) Saturday, 16 September.

Went on record with a letter to Colonel Simons, complimenting Sergeant Billy Dixon for the restraint he showed in handling the incident that took place

---

275. Ford is unidentified.
276. Squadron Leader R.C. Cresswell commanded No. 77 RAAF Squadron from September 1950 to August 1951.

in front of the Meiji Building when some Russians insisted on parking in the "restricted" parking zone.

Sent a redline to Edwards pointing out to him that my two previous queries to him have yet to be answered re Najin (Rashin). Three good targets remain and that I desire to bomb them visually. Asked him if it were possible for him to give me the green light on those targets - or should I drop the subject.

Part Two

The Intoxicating Days

September 15 – November 25, 1950

Situation Summary

September 15, 1950 — November 25, 1950

By 0630 on the morning of September 15, the opening moves in MacArthur's bold counterstroke to regain the initiative in Korea were underway. These initial moves involved the 1st Marine Division of Lt. Gen. Edward M. Almond's (formerly MacArthur's chief of staff) recently-activated X Corps. A battalion of Marines landed on Wolmi-do, the small island guarding Inch'ŏn's harbor, but because of falling tides and the shallowness of the harbor, these men would be the only U.S. troops landed until late in the afternoon when the rising tide permitted the rest of the 1st Marine Division to land.

Fortunately, surprise was complete. Air strikes and naval bombardment isolated the target area and Inch'ŏn fell swiftly. By the 18th, Kimp'o airfield had been captured and the 1st Marine Division, 7th Infantry Division, and ROK troops were on the outskirts of Seoul. At this point, North Korean resistance stiffened but the outcome was never in doubt. MacArthur declared Seoul recaptured on the 26th, though heavy fighting continued for the next two days. Because of unloading problems in Inch'ŏn's shallow harbor, much of the assault force's supplies were furnished by FEAF's Combat Cargo Command through airdrops or a round-the-clock airlift into Kimp'o. On September 29, General MacArthur and President Rhee returned to Seoul for ceremonies to reestablish the government of South Korea in its capital.

Meanwhile, General Walker's Eighth Army began its push out of the Pusan Perimeter, driving north to join the X Corps. B–29s helped to blast a path through the enemy lines with a carpet-bombing attack at Waegwan. At first, the North Koreans resisted vigorously (having launched their own offensive across the Naktong River on August 31-September 1), and the fighting was savage and bloody. But the enemy was in serious straits. Although U.S. intelligence had estimated the NKPA forces around the perimeter to number about 101,000 men, there were only about 70,000 troops, most of them suffering from serious shortages of equipment and supplies caused by the almost daily attacks on their supply routes by FEAF aircraft. Suddenly, the enemy's front collapsed. What began as an organized retreat turned into a disorganized rout as the NKPA, fearful of being cut off by the thrust from Inch'ŏn and greatly outmanned and outgunned in the south, fled north.

By the end of September, what was left of the NKPA (estimated to be not more than 30,000 men) was hurrying back across the 38th Parallel. Naval forces, primarily on the east coast, encouraged the North Koreans on their way with many bombardment missions. Whether or not the U.N. forces should follow the

NKPA across the parallel was a difficult question that took long hours of discussion by many individuals and organizations before being settled. Not only did U.S. and South Korean interests have to be considered, but also those of the various U.N. members whose troops were in Korea. Additionally, MacArthur's own desires played a very large part in the final decision to allow the U.N. force to cross the parallel. There was an important caveat to the directive on the crossing of the 38th Parallel; the U.N. forces were to stay "well clear" of the Manchurian and U.S.S.R. borders.

South Korean forces crossed the 38th Parallel on October 1, followed by troops of the Eighth Army on the 7th. Flushed with the success of the Inch'ŏn landings, MacArthur planned a second amphibious assault by the X Corps at Wŏnsan on Korea's east coast. This "assault" proved anti-climactic because ROK troops captured Wŏnsan before the landings took place. Mines in the harbor, which cost the U.S. Navy three minesweepers and the ROK Navy one more, forced the ships carrying the 1st Marine Division to remain at sea for several extra days. The landings finally took place on October 26.

Though Wŏnsan was useful as a port, the logistical logjam caused by the switching of the Eighth Army from the east to the west and X Corps from the west to the east side of Korea created supply problems that were not completely solved before the Chinese struck in late November. A major reason, generally unspoken at the time, for this switch of army and corps was that of personalities. By this time, General Walker had fallen out of MacArthur's favor, while General Almond enjoyed MacArthur's confidence. Buoyed by the success of the Inch'ŏn landings, MacArthur saw Wŏnsan as a chance both to trap the enemy and to enjoy yet more publicity. So, instead of Walker, he chose Almond and his X Corps for this job. For the time being, however, the supply problems were not considered important because it seemed the war would be over shortly anyway.

By mid-October, General O'Donnell was complaining that FEAF Bomber Command was running out of targets. Tactical air strikes by Air Force and Navy planes continued apace, but even these were scaled down as the target area constricted. North Korea's capital, P'yŏngyang, fell on October 19. An airdrop north of P'yŏngyang of the 187th Airborne Regimental Combat Team on the 20th by Combat Cargo Command C–119s resulted in a sharp engagement which caused little delay in the movement north.

With the collapse of North Korean resistance, it appeared that the Korean War was almost over. There were reports of Chinese Communist Forces (CCF) moving into Korea, but these were thought to be either unreliable, indications that a few "volunteers" were aiding the NKPA, or were just saber-rattling by the Communists in an attempt to "blackmail" the U.N. forces into retiring from North Korea.

By the 24th of October, the Eighth Army was crossing the Ch'ŏngch'ŏn River. Two days later, a regiment of the ROK 6th Division reached the Yalu River near Ch'osan. To the east, in the X Corps area, the 1st Marine Division finally landed at Wŏnsan, while the ROK Capital Division kept pushing closer to the Russian border. But the heady days of pursuit against a fleeing enemy were coming to an end.

On the 25th, the CCF hit the ROK II Corps near Onjong and over the next five days, sent it reeling back south of the Ch'ŏngch'ŏn. The unlucky regiment that reached the Yalu was wiped out. Other CCF attacks halted the Eighth Army's advance northward. In the zone of the X Corps, however, smaller CCF attacks beginning on October 25 only blunted the advance. The 1st Marine Division continued toward the Changjin (or Chosin) Reservoir, while the 7th Infantry Division (which had landed at Iwŏn, north of Wŏnsan, on the 29th) and the ROK Capital Division continued to press to the north. The 7th Division's 17th Regiment reached the Yalu at Hyesanjin on November 21.

These initial Chinese attacks were only harbingers of things to come. Within a few days, the assaults ceased and the Chinese seemingly vanished. Most of the intelligence reports considered these actions to have been little more than spoiling attacks by a few Chinese "volunteers," and that major CCF involvment in Korea was unlikely. MacArthur, too, believed that the Chinese would not enter Korea in force, but to ensure that they would not, MacArthur ordered on November 5 a series of strikes by Air Force and Navy planes on the Yalu River bridges. However, he also ordered that the Manchurian border was to remain inviolate. Naturally, this order limited the effectiveness of the air attacks on the bridges. Also, the Communists supplemented the permanent bridges with a number of easily repairable pontoon bridges. Finally, the Yalu was beginning to freeze over and it wasn't long before supplies and men were coming directly over on the ice.

Even before the bridge attacks began, the Chinese were moving into North Korea, and they continued to move south despite the efforts of the airmen. The U.N. Command continued to believe that most of the activity on the bridges involved the movement of supplies and that the number of Chinese troops in North Korea was small. That the CCF was already in Korea in large numbers was dramatically underscored on the evening of November 25 when the CCF launched a massive surprise offensive against the U.N. forces. Ironically, the day before, General Walker had renewed his own offensive toward the Yalu only to be brought up short by the Chinese counter-offensive.

For the U.N. troops, the heady wine of the pursuit days in late summer-early fall had been drained dry. Now a new enemy would force them to drink again the bitter dregs of retreat.

The Diary.

**FRIDAY
15 SEPTEMBER
1950**
Received a letter from Partridge in which he stated the Navy had an "in" with the Ambassador in that they were furnishing him air transportation complete with naval attache. Partridge suggested a C–47 be put at Muccio's disposal for his use and for the use of ranking South Korean dignitaries, and that this Air Force airplane be used entirely at Muccio's discretion. Partridge also suggested the appointment of an AF attache to the Ambassador.

Sent the letter to my Vice Commander for Adm and Plans, concurring in the suggestion.

Informed the Vice Commander for Operations that because of the enemy's nite movement of war materiel, personnel, etc., he should draw up a suitably worded directive for my signature instructing the FEAF Bomber Command to do a little experimenting on night interdictions with the '29s. FEAF Bomber Command should carry in their B–29s a mixture of fragmentation clusters and G.P. bombs.

Twining confirmed my request to USAF for the promotion of Lt. Col. Payne Jennings to colonel. Jennings will relieve Ted Graff who is due for rotation to the States.

Received from Vandenberg a detailed letter, with study attached, re "Night Tactical Air Operations." Bucked the letter to Vice Commander for Operations with instructions that he comply with Vandenberg's desire, that is, to designate the 3d Bomb Group (L), including the one squadron of the 452d Group at Victorville [California] (to be redesignated) as a night attack group and to operate only on night missions. As soon as action has been completed, he is to let me know in order that an outline of our action taken might be sent CSAF.

Received signal from Norstad stating that the JOC [*sic*] had directed MacArthur not to bomb targets at Rashin.[1]

At the briefing this morning, I introduced General Spaatz to all present and indicated that since he was a retired Chief of Staff, United States Air Force, and an aviation news writer, he would be assisted in every way possible by every member of my staff to determine the facts REPEAT facts.

Mr. Bascom Timmons[2] called and indicated that it was his intention to write an article on Air Force operations in Korea. I gave him about thirty minutes and recommended that he go into the details with Colonel Nuckols re our operations. He also indicated that he intended making a trip to Korea the early part of next week.

---

1. Not the "JOC," but the JCS. Rashin is only 60 miles from Vladivostok and was the location of railway yards and naval oil storage facilities, these useful to both North Korea and the Soviet Union. The State Department, particularly, was worried that the Soviets might react violently to attacks so close to their borders. This concern had been heightened by the Antung incident and an incident on September 4, when Navy fighters shot down over the Yellow Sea an aircraft that had flown into a U.S. formation and began firing at the Navy planes. A body recovered from this plane was that of a Soviet officer. ("History of the JCS," pp 249-255.)
2. Timmons, a long-time reporter and columnist for numerous newspapers, was reporting for *Colliers*.

I have invited Mr. Hugh Baillie, president of United Press, to go with me to Korea along with General Spaatz tomorrow morning. General Spaatz had made the request that while he toured installations in Korea where he thought Mr. Baillie might also cover, that Mr. Baillie be permitted to accompany him. To this I agreed.

0630 hours Marines debark Inch'ŏn.

0900 hours general offensive, EUSAK.

SATURDAY 16 SEPTEMBER 1950 With Spaatz and Mr. Hugh Baillie, United Press, flew to Pusan where we were met by General Partridge. Immediately went in and called on General Walker who appeared to be more optimistic than I had ever seen him. We then visited General Partridge's headquarters where we got the latest information on the morning attack. The B–29s were not able to operate because of the weather. We had lunch with General Timberlake and then proceeded to Taegu; while enroute from the field to General Partridge's quarters, we visited General Milburn's[3] First Corps headquarters. General Partridge had Milburn and his chief of staff as guests to dinner with Mr. Baillie, Spaatz and myself. After dinner, Spaatz retired to the guest house to work on his article and I then had about an hour's visit, and a good one, with General Partridge. Went to bed about 2300 hours.

An F–80 leads a formation of B–26s against targets near Iri on September 16. White spots just to the left of the fighter and under its wing mark rockets just fired at some enemy tanks.

SUNDAY 17 SEPTEMBER 1950 I got General Partridge's ADC to get General Spaatz's article typed; as soon as that was done, after breakfast, I departed the airport for Tokyo and landed Haneda 1215. Came immediately to the office where I cleaned up papers that had accumulated, and approved by signing a directive to O'Donnell to do night intruder work with B–29s.[4] Signed a letter to Partridge directing that he

3. Maj Gen Frank W. "Shrimp" Milburn commanded the XXI Corps in Europe during World War II. He brought the IX Corps to Korea in Sept. 1950, but in a trade switched corps command with Gen John Coulter's I Corps.

4. This use of the B–29 as a night intruder was a short-lived idea that took place primarily during the last half of

3d BG Invaders wheel around to attack flak installations near Iri.

A parabomb floats toward a bridge near Iri. The North Koreans have spanned a destroyed portion of the bridge with a crude but effective earth and timber structure.

create a night intruder group and a day group with the six squadrons of B–26s that he will eventually have. Also promoted 1st Lt Donald NMI [no middle initial] Nichols[5] to grade of captain. This fellow is a one-man army in Korea. He has been there some 4 1/2 years and on several occasions with a GI or two and a group of Koreans he has performed the impossible. A couple of days ago he stopped a suicide squad of some 12 Koreans who had infiltrated through the lines with the intention of sabotaging the aircraft at Taegu. He captured four, killed seven, and one got away. I turned the Spaatz article over to Mr. Pakenham[6] at 1335 hours.

Received the following letter from Major General L. B. Keiser, 2d Infantry Div:

Dear George: I wish to express my appreciation to you and to members of the Far East Air Force[s] under General Partridge who flew some highly successful missions in front of my division yesterday. These missions were performed in a highly effective manner and in many instances given voluntarily in localities where I did not have sufficient enemy information nor where we could effectively control the operation of aircraft. These flyers took on enemy groups on both controlled and uncontrolled missions and effectively reduced threats against the division which were making our position rather precarious. I consider that the effectiveness of these air strikes definitely damaged the morale of the enemy to such a degree that his capabilities against us materially decreased. Moreover, the improvement in the morale and combat efficiency of my command has been enhanced by this valiant effort. My appreciation to all of you.

Bucked copies of above letter, with appropriate remarks, to both Generals Vandenberg and Partridge (18 Sept 50).

Sent out commendatory letters (dated 15 September) to: Partridge, O'Donnell, Stearley, and Doyle. Each letter contained a summation of their efforts during phase one of the Korean campaign - since the beginning of hostilities to 15 September, or beginning of the offensive.

Replied with thanks to Joy's letter to me of 16 September which reads as follows:

The exceptionally fine performance of the Far East Air Force[s] on 10 and 11 September is a source of pride to all forces in combat in this area. It is noted that on the 10th of September alone the AF had the phenomenal success in destroying 11 tanks and damaging 12 more.

September. The 98th BG flew a number of sorties over enemy-held territory and North Korea, trying to bomb vehicular traffic moving on the roads. For the most part, these attacks were unsuccessful. Attempts to bomb targets with the use of flares also gave unspectacular results. While these attacks may have had some psychological effect, the B–29 was just not suited for night intruder work against moving targets. Operations were halted on October 3. (Joe Gray Taylor, *Development of Night Air Operations* [USAF Historical Study 92, Maxwell AFB, Ala.], pp 221-224; Futrell, p 165.)

5. Nichols' remarkable career is described in his privately-printed autobiography *How Many Times Can I Die?* (Brooksville, Fla., 1981). The introduction to the book was written by an obviously impressed General Partridge.

6. Compton Pakenham was *Newsweek*'s Tokyo bureau chief.

In addition to this record of tank busting, it is noted with great satisfaction that your excellent pilots destroyed a large number of trucks,
vehicles, box cars and other enemy transportation. On 11 Sept your
force again demonstrated its outstanding capabilities by flying a total of
683 sorties, on this date, destroying 8 tanks and damaging 5 and wreak-
ing havoc on the enemy's transportation facilities. This fine performance of duty and exhibition of aggressive spirit is in accordance with
the high standards of the AF. The Naval Forces Far East are grateful to
the AF for the destruction inflicted on the enemy and share your pride
in the exploits of our comrades-in-arms. Please extend my congratulations to those pilots who have contributed so much to the success of our
forces in the Far East.

Called Darr Alkire in and presented him with the radio which stated that
his brigadier generalship had been approved by CSAF and was awaiting
congressional O.K.

MONDAY
18 SEPTEMBER
1950

*Sent following informational redline (Banfill's marble)
to Vandenberg:*

In support of attempted breakout effort of 8th Army, Partridge reports on 17 September that fighters killed at least
1200 enemy troops while they were attempting to retreat across the Naktong River in 2d Division area. 260 110-gallon napalm tanks dropped
throughout area. This despite adverse weather.

Got my weekly letter off to Gill Robb Wilson.
Admiral Tomlinson[7] called at 8:30 A.M.; the Thai Minister called (Mr.
Sanga Nilkamhaeng) at 3:00 P.M.; and Pete Jennings called at 2:30 P.M.

TUESDAY
19 SEPTEMBER
1950

Departed for Korea 0700 hours; arrived at Taegu at 1040
hours where I made the award of the Distinguished Flying
Cross to General Partridge at the airdrome at Taegu; returned
with General Spaatz and Mr. Hugh Baillie, United Press,
landing at Haneda at 1406 hours.

Sent Nuckol's marble via redline to Vandenberg:

Add the word "beautiful" to the several words already coined by ground
force in Korea to describe FEAF air efforts. Latest word -"beautiful" was
used by Major General Hobart Gay, First Cav. commander, in describing
B–29 tactical strike on Communist positions west of Waegwan on Monday, September 18, when 1600 bombs were dropped on a 2 square mile
area just in front of U.N. positions.[8]

---

7. Rear Adm William G. Tomlinson, Commander, Pacific Division, MATS. (At this time, MATS was a combined
USAF/USN operation with four Navy squadrons assigned.)

8. A carpet-bombing attack by the B–29s had been scheduled for September 16 in front of Waegwan. This was
intended to punch a hole in the North Korean lines that would enable the Eighth Army to break out of the
Pusan Perimeter. Foul weather caused by a typhoon delayed the mission, although F–51s and F–80s did strike
various positions on the perimeter on the 16th and 17th. In the early light of September 18, 42 B–29s of the
92d and 98th groups finally bombed two areas just behind the front lines. (Futrell, pp 161-162.)

Informed Vandenberg via redline that first C–54 of FEAF Combat Cargo Command landed at Kimp'o Airdrome at 1426I [local] this date. It will be followed by approximately 31 other C–54s today. Night lighting equipment included in initial lift. In all probability, Kimp'o will be operational on 24-hour basis by tomorrow, 20 Sept.

Mr. Hugh Baillie, United Press, had dinner with Spaatz and me at Mayeda House, 1900 hours.

WEDNESDAY 20 SEPTEMBER 1950

South African contingent, represented by Commandant J. D. Pretorius, A.F.C. and Major Swanepoel[9] called at 8:15 this morning.

General Partridge called this morning and stated that he went into Kimp'o yesterday afternoon at 1500 hours, that there was no confusion and that Tunner's transports were landing regularly about every ten minutes.

Colonel Lee, the Kimp'o Air Force Base commander, was there but that it would be several days before his base personnel and equipment arrived.[10]

Partridge met Brigadier General Cushman who stated that today (20 September) there would be 24 Marine aircraft that would come in and be based at Kimp'o.[11] The 10th Corps has its headquarters in Kimp'o and General Lowe with his jeep and sergeant were present.

He had information that 3,800 dead were found by the ground forces in the walled city and that it is our opinion that our 60-tank napalm attack on 17 September did that job.[12]

Partridge reported that all in all, the entire ground situation was good and that the ground commanders were reporting that the Air Force had killed many, many more North Koreans than we had estimated.

Partridge also stated that he was concerned about air evacuation and that information had come to him that some reporters were looking into the matter. He stated he had brought this to General Walker's attention and he was issuing orders to Fifth Air Force that they would not discuss the matter and they would in no way criticize the Eighth Army. He asked me if I would do likewise with FEAF and I told him that I not only would but that it had been my policy; however, certain doctors in the hospitals here in Japan had stated that lives could have been saved and amputations been prevented had certain wounded been air evacuated. This morning I talked with Colonel Brothers and re-stated my policy of not criticizing a sister service and he indicated to me that he had not nor did he intend to and that he would instruct his people along those lines. He did submit a report to General Parks[13] showing clearly that the Air Force's skirts were clean reference air evacuation of wounded.

9. Commandant Jan D. Pretorious and Maj Daniel Swanepoel. Pretorious was the senior SAAF liaison officer. Initially equipped with F–51s and later with F–86s, No. 2 Squadron, SAAF, began operations on Nov. 19.

10. Col Joseph D. Lee's command, the 6151st Air Base Unit, was activated at Kimp'o on Sept. 23. Less than a month later, the outfit moved to Wŏnsan to administer the airfield there.

11. The first Marine aircraft to be based at Kimp'o were the helicopters and liaison planes of VMO-6, which set up operations on the 19th, followed shortly by five F7F–3N Tigercats of VMF(N)-542. (Montross and Canzona, *The Inchon-Seoul Operation* [U.S. Marine Operations in Korea, 1950-1953] [Washington, 1955], p 169.)

12. The "Walled City of Ka-san" was actually a mountaintop (Hill 902) where ruins of an ancient fortress were located. A 30-foot-high stone wall encircled the crest of the mountain. The North Koreans turned this area into a formidable defensive position which had held up the advance of the 1st Cavalry Division. (Appelman, pp 421-432.)

13. Brig Gen Harlan C. Parks, Deputy Director for Personnel Planning, Headquarters USAF. He was in Japan to confer about FEAF manning requirements.

Mr. Don King, Vice President of Northwest Airlines, was in and wanted me to start the proper wheels turning to get Northwest back into operation into Korea. Turned the information over to my Vice Commander for Adm and Plans and asked him to coordinate with Far East Command.[14]

1115 hours, Squadron Leader Bodien,[15] who is taking Wykeham-Barnes' job reported in to me with Squadron Leader Sach.

Sent personal, in the clear radio to McKee: "No answer received my query in Par[agraph] 4, personal T.S. letter to you dated 28 Aug. Would appreciate answer."

Left the office earlier than usual in order to be out at the Bomber Command in time for Rosie's dinner for Spaatz at 1730.

THURSDAY
21 SEPTEMBER
1950

Sent the following Stratline to Partridge:

Dr. Bowles, General Gavin and one other will arrive Taegu approximately 1700 hours today. They are representatives of the Department of Defense and desire to see General Walker and you and then visit frontline ground organizations as well as Air Force operations. Suggest you advise Walker their arrival.

Bucked the following to Weyland and Craigie:

Colonel Heflebower,[16] our senior air officer in JSPOG, brought in attached message to me this morning, which I have read and which I desire you read. It is not to be shown to anyone else and will be kept secure and will be handcarried by General Weyland to General Craigie and by General Craigie back to me.

(The paper contained certain pertinent conclusions reference current operations in Korea and the actions that should be taken if Russia or Communist China should enter the conflict in North Korea, in South Korea, or would implement the North Korean forces by replacements from Russia or Communist China. It also contained data on the actions that CINCFE must take reference the crossing of the 38th Parallel with his ground forces and his instructions in case of a general global war.)

Redlined the following information to Vandenberg:

Further reference my secret letter of 10 September 1950, AG 10719, subject: "Air Evaluation Board." For you information three (3) separate parties of analysts are now in this theater looking especially into general subjects of tactical air support of ground forces: one party headed by Dr. Ellis Johnson[17] from Department of Army's Office of Operations Research; this party presently consists of four (4) people with more to come later. Another party from WSEG headed by Dr. Bowles and including General Gavin. And still another party of seven (7) from Headquarters Army Field Forces headed by Colonel Onslow Rolfe.[18]

---

14. Despite an ongoing war, Northwest officials were quite anxious to resume operations into Kimp'o. On Oct. 19, Stratemeyer recommended, and MacArthur approved, the resumption of two flights a day into Kimp'o starting Oct. 29. (FEAF Opns Hist, 25 Jun-31 Oct 50, Vol. 1, pp 231, 246.)
15. Squadron Leader Henry E. Bodien was an experienced night intruder veteran of World War II.
16. Col Roy C. Heflebower later became FEAF director of plans.
17. Dr. Ellis A. Johnson, a physicist, had been Director, ORO since 1948. Previously, he had worked for the Air Force as a special weapons technical director.
18. Col Onslow S. Rolfe, Chief, Development Section, Army Field Forces, at Ft. Monroe, Virginia.

This last party includes a Major Smith[19] from the Tactical Air Command who is the only Air Force representative in any of the three parties.

Redlined Nuckols marble to Vandenberg:

Aircraft under operational control of FEAF set several new records yesterday, 20 September. All-time high of 702 sorties flown, 44 of them by RAAF Mustangs which is also new high for them and 18 by Marines. With capture of Kimp'o Airfield, FEAF Combat Cargo Command airlifted 635 tons cargo and 1055 passengers into Korea in 139 flights, latter three figures representing new records.

Sent Partridge a personal letter asking him for the notes he talked from in briefing me of the happenings 25, 26, and 27 June. Told him I needed same not only for my diary but for the documented history.

Dr. Bowles dropped by the office and gave me the two log books that were found in the two Russian aircraft at Kimp'o. Sent them up to D/I [Deputy for Intelligence] and asked them for the complete translation and to send same on, over my signature, to the CSAF. Dr. Bowles also presented to me in memo form the info to several questions they had asked regarding these two planes and their log books:

(1) What are these two books? (Answer) Both are plane performance records. *(2)* Do they pertain to the same plane? (Answer) No. [No.]1. Engine - AM - 42; Series -3; No. - 471951; Type - ?; Last record of flight 9 Sept 50. [No.] 2. Engine - AM - 42; Series - ?; Factory No. 8011; Type Il 10 (ground attack); Last record of flight 1 Sept 50. *(3)* When was plane or planes transferred from Russian to Korean hands? (Answer) Both planes transferred from Soviets to Koreans on 28 June 1950 and receipted for by CHO, Tae Sik, Tech, 867 (Squadron?).

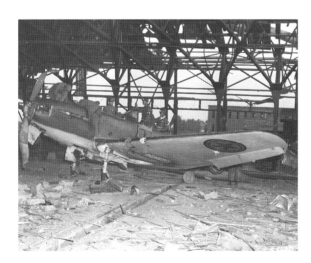

An abandoned Il–10 similar to those found at Kimp'o. This plane was recovered at Wŏnsan.

19. Maj Earl L. Smith, Jr.

General Kenney due in tomorrow.

Bouchier passed the following info to me from Slessor: Sq. Ldr. Bodien, from Hong Kong joining me in place of Wykeham-Barnes and hopes that Bodien will meet our requirements inasmuch as he has worked with Wykeham-Barnes who recommends him strongly.

After reading Tunner's Operations Plan, sent him a "well done" letter.

Sent via Sory Smith my greetings to the Air Reservists Convention conclave in Fort Worth.

Reassured Vandenberg by radio, answering his 53782, that we are pushing hard to take better care of the correspondents who are streaming into Korea - teletype circuit for release of their stories, messing, etc. ..."everything possible is being done and situation will improve as soon as additional public relations personnel, soon to depart from the States arrive here. Korea, as Ben Wright well recognizes, is entirely different than Europe."

The Navy sent over a courier message thanking us for the air coverage given them in their rescue of the SKs that had been aboard a grounded LST near Yongdŏk. Returned to the Navy via courier my statement "that we were more than happy to oblige."

On the 18th, Del Spivey sent me a letter which pointed out that the decision to employ all our fighters, with the exception of one F–82 and one F–80 squadron in the Korean conflict had left nothing more than a token force available for air defense of FEC.[20] He and Partridge had gotten together and agreed that 3 groups is their minimum requirement for an acceptable peacetime air defense deployment. Urged that I request CSAF to deploy 3 National Guard fighter groups to this theater. In my reply to Spivey told him that I had already placed my cards before CSAF and asked him to transfer a four-squadron fighter wing to bolster our air defense capabilities to its previous level of three groups, totaling ten squadrons. Although this force alone would not be sufficient for defense should an all-out war develop, nevertheless I consider my request for the additional four-squadron fighter wing meets 5th AF requirements - for which you had suggested I request three groups

FRIDAY
22 SEPTEMBER
1950

I had Major VanderPyl[21] report to me prior to his assignment to Misawa Air Force Base. This reassignment within FEAF was occasioned by stupid actions on his part. The actions, though, were not of such a nature as to cause his relief and return to the ZI. He is a competent, hardworking and intelligent individual, although, at times, he fails to use his head. I pointed out the errors of his ways prior to his reassignment.

SATURDAY
23 SEPTEMBER
1950

CINCFE ordered yesterday, 22 September, the 187th ABN [Airborne] Regimental Combat team airlifted from its present station to Kimp'o and upon its arrival at Kimp'o to be assigned to the X Corps.

We have recommended that the ROK AF consisting of 300 officers and men with four F–51s be moved to Kimp'o soonest. Reason - international political

---

20. The 339th FS was assigned approximately 12 F–82s, while the 41st FS had about 25 F–80s.
21. Maj Ellis VanderPyl was a 5AF Directorate of Intelligence briefing officer.

value. This has been referred to CG X Corps for comments or concurrence. CINCFE has indicated in a signal to X Corps that the plans to establish a GHQ UNC (Tac) in the Seoul area has been suspended indefinitely; in view of this decision, the establishment of the Advanced Hq by FEAF will be indefinitely suspended.

Stratemeyer and Maj. Gen. Laurence C. Craigie greet General Kenney upon his arrival at Haneda. Kenney was then commander of the Air University at Maxwell AFB, Alabama.

Went down to meet General Kenney who arrived at 1430 hours. After his arrival, the two of us went direct to General MacArthur's residence where we waited until he came downstairs about 1730 hours. We accompanied him to his office and visited with him for about an hour.

Kenney has joined us at the Mayeda boarding house and will remain with us until he departs.

SUNDAY 24 SEPTEMBER 1950

Learned last night of the accidental bombing by napalm of a sector held by the British ground units.

Rosie O'Donnell in a covering letter forwarded to me four reports written by his airplane commanders on their night intruder missions. Bucked the letter and reports to Crabb, thru Craigie and Weyland, with the comment that "it appears to me that if flares are carried on all those missions, a better job can be done."

Sent Partridge a Stratline telling him that Spaatz, Kenney, Hugh Baillie and I would be taking off tomorrow at 0700 hours for Kimp'o and that we would return via Taegu, Ashiya and Itazuke. We would RON [remain overnight] Taegu 25 September.

While Kenney, Spaatz and I were having lunch with CINCFE, Partridge called the following info to Weyland and immediately upon my return to the office, sent it to General MacArthur. *The gist is as follows:*

(1) An accidental attack by friendly fighters was made on the British Brigade. The extent of casualties is not known at this time.

(2) Fifth Air Force and Eighth Army inspectors will carefully investigate the incident.

(3) The conditions under which the accident occurred are substantially as follows:

The British Brigade were trying to cross the river at a ferry site. They had no bridges. The troops of the brigade were astride the stream. North Koreans were shooting at the British troops in the vicinity of the ferry site. Fifth Air Force fighters attempted to help the British troops in their predicament. The request for fighter assistance was made by the tactical air controller who was on the east side of the river. A Mosquito control airplane was in the area directing fighter aircraft according to instructions given by the tactical air controller on the ground. The North Korean troops, who were supposed to be the target of attack, were to one side, but in the rear, of the most advanced elements of the British Brigade. Through some tie-up in recognition or instructions, the British Brigade were hit by friendly fighters.

(4) Will keep you informed re further developments.[22]

Quoted in toto is my redline to Vandenberg on the same subject - accidental strafing of British Brigade:

Reur 54161 from Norstad, Partridge this date states: Accidental attack by friendly fighters was made on British Brigade. Extent of casualties not known. Fifth Air Force and Eighth Army inspectors will carefully investigate incident. Accident occurred while British were trying to cross river and their forces were astride stream at time. Enemy were opposing crossing and fighters were requested by jeep tactical air controller on east side of river. A T–6 airborne controller was in area directing fighters according to instruction from tactical controller on ground. Enemy troops were to one side but in rear of most advanced elements of British Brigade. Through some tie-up in recognition or detailed instructions, British were hit by friendly fighters. Detailed investigation being conducted. I will keep you advised on any developments.

Annalee and I gave a small dinner party, with my general officer staff present, in honor of Generals Spaatz and Kenney. We also invited a Mr. Al Jolson[23] who was in the Tokyo area with his accompanist, Mr. Harry Akst. In consideration of General Spaatz, we invited the *Newsweek* representative, Mr. Pakenham, as well as Mr. Hugh Baillie of United Press and Mr. B. Timmons, *Collier's*.

MONDAY 25 SEPTEMBER 1950 Departed Haneda this morning with the following guests: Generals Spaatz and Kenney, Mr. Hugh Baillie and Mr. Bascom Timmons. We flew via the east coast of Korea to Kimp'o where we landed and discussed the situation with Colonel Lee, the base commander; inspected the two IL–10s and the Yak–12 in the hangar; paid our respects to Brigadier General Cushman, the Marine aviation commander.

I called General Almond, CG X Corps, but both he and General Ruffner[24] were up at the front and would not be back until 1600 hours. Gave up all intentions of visiting X Corps, but did emphatically tell the Colonel that I talked to (he was General Ruffner's executive) that for their own good and the maintenance of Kimp'o Airport, our aviation engineer battalion and our air base troops for Kimp'o should be debarked without delay. Everyone agreed, but they indicated that it had been held up on General Almond's order as he needed fighting doughboys and ammunition.

---

22. After a T-6 "Mosquito" was fired upon, four F–51s strafed and napalmed the vicinity on the 23d. These attacks struck troops of the Argyll Highlanders of the British 27th Brigade. First of the British contingent to arrive in Korea, they moved into the front lines west of Taegu on Sept. 7.
23. The famed entertainer was on a USO tour of the Far East.
24. Maj. Gen. Clark L. Ruffner, X Corps chief of staff.

I found that the airport at Kimp'o was in first-class condition except for one large hole about 1/3 of the length of the runway from one end. They have temporarily placed a mat over the hole, but if it isn't repaired shortly, they are going to have trouble. Found great need for air base personnel, as the only security for the whole base was some 300 South Koreans that had been obtained by that very superior officer, Captain Nichols. Of course, the Marines have their own guards, but it detracts from their efficiency as the guards should be put to other use. Col. Lee reported that he needed some 4,200 pounds of rice in order to feed the South Koreans who were actually his only security, and, later in the day with General Partridge, I directed that this rice be flown in and have since learned through General Tunner that it was done.

We departed and flew to Taegu where we were met by General Partridge at which time he explained to me the catastrophic error made in our strafing of the British troops. He said it was terrible and showed it by his eyes filling with tears when talking to me; however, he informed me that both General Robertson and Air Vice Marshal Bouchier had absolutely cleared the Air Force, stating that it was one of those errors that takes place in war and although everyone felt bad, they do not hold it against the USAF. Twenty (20) were killed and twenty-one (21) injured. The strafing included napalm. I also found out that at the same time we strafed the battalion, the 19th Infantry artillery had fired an artillery barrage in front of the other battalion which stopped their attack.

I discussed the stopping of building K-1 into a jet field and will take the necessary steps when I get back to Tokyo. It is desirable to use Vinnell people and all our aviation effort personnel on Taegu, Suwŏn and Kimp'o as we have a good field at K-9, in Pusan.[25]

General Partridge also discussed with me the absolute necessity of returning to him his C–47s. They were taken from him for the air drop and now that there is to be no air drop, he needs his staff C–47 in order to operate and perform his duties as Air Force commander. I agreed and took the necessary steps to return at least one-half of his requirement - and all as soon as possible.

General Partridge told me that Colonel Robert Burns, Army artillery officer and G-3 Air, Eighth Army member of the JOC, had indicated time and time again that our estimates of North Koreans killed have been way below the actual number that we have killed. He gave as an example that once we estimated that 500 were killed when 2,500 had been actually killed. Recently, General Walker, during a briefing, stated to General Partridge: "Partridge, you certainly are modest with your estimates of killed and damage done." I directed that Partridge make a note of these statements and record them in some manner. He had not been doing this.

General Kenney and Mr. Bascom Timmons remained at Taegu as General Partridge's guests and joined me the next day at Ashiya.

---

25. Because of a severe shortage of engineer personnel, civilian contractors had to be hired to assist in airfield construction. A brief experiment using crews of the Vinnell Corporation as a single unit to turn the K-1 strip into a full base was a failure, primarily because of airfield conditions, not because of the performance of the contractor's crews.

It was decided, though, to parcel out the construction crews of Vinnell Corporation to the various aviation engineer battalions. This was a more practical use of the civilians, plus it enabled all of the engineer units to gain badly-needed experienced construction people. (5th AF Hist Data, Phase I—Korean War, Jun 25-Oct 31, 1950, Vol. I, pp 113-14.)

Mr. Baillie, General Spaatz and I pushed on to Itazuke where we were met by Colonel Jack Price. He took us to the guest house where we had a delicious dinner and comfortable night.

I paid for dinner and breakfast which cost $7.74.

After dinner, Colonel Cellini[26] and three other jet pilots came to the house and discussed F–80C operations with General Spaatz. All four officers were certainly in love with the F–80C and had nothing but praise for it in all types of operations - including close ground support.

TUESDAY 26 SEPTEMBER 1950 The next morning we departed at 0900 hours for Ashiya where we were met by General Tunner who took us to his headquarters where we were given one of the finest briefings I have ever attended. Major Hoag,[27] the briefer, did a superior and outstanding job. All the charts he used were excellent and I complimented the captain who was instrumental in their preparation.

After the briefing we drove around the field and visited the airborne RCT and its deputy commander and had a very thorough briefing by him on the ground. We inspected one of the C–119s that was loaded with three pontoons and other bridge material. Believe it or not, the Air Force is moving one pontoon bridge <u>complete</u> [emphasis in original] from the Tokyo area to Kimp'o via Ashiya!

We inspected other C–119s that were loaded and being loaded. The entire operation at Ashiya is one of efficiency and orderly operation. We then proceeded to General Tunner's quarters where we had a delicious luncheon with him and his staff.

We had expected General Kenney and Mr. Timmons to arrive by 1400 hours and when they didn't, we proceeded to clear and take off. While warming up our engines, Kenney and Timmons arrived by B–17 so we waited their boarding FEAF's C–54 and then proceeded back to Haneda arriving here about 1800 hours.

We were all tired and went home and went to bed although General Kenney wanted to stay up and talk, but we all turned him down.

WEDNESDAY 27 SEPTEMBER 1950 *Arrived early at the office to get caught up and send out the following signal to O'Donnell with info to Partridge:*

The handling of the recent attack north of the Manchurian border by a B–29 has been embarrassing to me and to the Air Force as a whole. The fact that the attack had been made north of the border was known to the crew prior to landing and to members of the group staff soon thereafter. However, no apparent effort was made to pass this vitally important information to those in authority. This matter first came to the attention of my staff thru press reports from Moscow and London over two days after the mistake was known. If this incident had been properly and specifically reported, the US would have been able to assume the blame for its mistake in the United Nations and thus would have been able to forestall the Communist blast. I appreciate that it is

---

26. Col Oliver G. Cellini commanded the 51st FIG. The group began moving from Okinawa to Itazuke on Sept. 22.
27. Probably Maj Robert <u>Hogg</u>, Executive, Combat Cargo Command.

hard for an individual to understand that his acts may have national significance regardless of his station or grade, but that awareness must be
pushed down from your level to combat crews. I desire that within the
restrictions required by the classification of this message you pass it to
your people immediately.[28]

*McKee in answer to my TS, EYES ONLY ltr of 27 August, and my
radio to him dated 20 September sent the following:*

Concerning your letter of 28 August and your question with regard to
who saw the message, am unable to find out for sure but it is my best
judgment that he did see the entire message. Am sorry I cannot give you
more positive information, but am unable to with restrictions which you
placed upon me. Am sure proud of the Far East Air Force[s] and the job
they are doing. When the final score is tabulated, I am confident that the
contribution made by your command will become abundantly clear. With
highest regards, signed: Bozo (McKee).

*Sent the following memo to General MacArthur, subject: "Return of
Medium Bomb Groups to the Zone of the Interior."*

Just prior to the successful amphibious landing at Inch'ŏn, I concurred in
retaining the last two (2) medium bomb groups to arrive in this theater
until 8 November 1950.
I consider the present status of the destruction of the enemy in Korea to be
so much in our favor that I now consider it no longer necessary to retain
all four (4) additional medium bomb groups in your command.
The Joint Chiefs of Staff directive received your headquarters directs cessation of attacks on all strategic targets and three (3) medium bomb groups
are an ample medium bomb force to destroy remaining tactical targets.
I'm sure you realize as well as I that the United States Air Force plans are
to re-equip medium bomb groups with either the B–50 or B–36 and that
the sooner they are returned to the Zone of the Interior the quicker that
re-equipment can take place. Thereby, the Strategic Air Command will be
in a better position to perform its mission.
I, therefore, strongly urge that a signal be dispatched to the Joint Chiefs
of Staff recommending the return without delay of two (2) medium bomb
groups to the Zone of the Interior.[29]

*Received the following letter, dated 25 Sept from Admiral Joy,
COMNAVFE:*

25 Sept was another day in which the AF broke its previous excellent record.
I note that your planes flew over 700 sorties in addition to destroying a large
number of tanks, enemy transportation, and enemy gun emplacements. I
want to again congratulate your force upon this excellent record. Although
the bombers and close supporting a/c frequently receive the greatest praise,

---

28. On Sept. 22, a 98th BG B–29 bombed Antung's marshaling yard.
29. On Oct. 22, General MacArthur authorized the release of the 22d and 92d groups back to the U.S. The two
    units began their return on the 27th. (Futrell, p 207.)

I would especially like to commend your reconnaissance a/c. These a/c have performed a most valuable service in locating enemy concentrations and in timely reporting of enemy movements. Their cooperation with the naval forces operating in this area has been exceptionally noteworthy and has resulted in the prompt destruction of enemy forces which threatened our forces ashore. The valiant crews who man these planes on their long, difficult, and lonely missions have contributed a great deal to the successful accomplishment of our joint endeavors.

In answer to above, I said:

We all appreciate letters such as you wrote complimenting the AF in breaking its previous record when 700 sorties were made with gratifying results. Thanks for your congratulations but I think the USN forces, Far East, is to be congratulated for, as we have both so many times stated privately and publicly, it is the close support the services give each other that make the team really work. I agree with you that the reconnaissance aircraft have done a splendid job, as has yours, for they play such an important part in preparing the way for both the air, the service ships, and the ground to follow them. Many thanks again for your very kind letter.

Received two letters of appreciation from members of the Press (1) Walter Simmons, *Chicago Tribune,* and a Member of Parliament, the Hon Thomas Driberg, who is out here representing Reynolds News.[30] Sent copies of both to General Vandenberg and General Partridge. To General Tunner sent a copy of Mr. Simmons' letter.

Sent a Stratline to Partridge:

"All aviation engineers and effort in Korea are placed at your disposal to utilize as you see fit. You are authorized to discontinue all engineer effort at K-1."

Craigie sent me the following memo:

(1) At the GHQ briefing on 26 Sept, General Hickey stated that, in his opinion, there was a distinct possibility that the UN might move north of 38° N. Lat. and, after hostilities have ceased, assume the responsibility for rebuilding many of the NK facilities destroyed by our medium bombers. Specifically, he referred to hydro-electric power plants, one of which was a target for 26 Sept. He requested that FEAF give serious consideration to refraining from hitting targets of this type. I told him we would give consideration to the matter, but that there was one aspect, covered in JCS correspondence, which I wished to discuss with him after the briefing.

(2) In the discussion which took place in his office, I informed General Hickey that the destruction of power plants and other similar targets which supported the NK economy was consistent with the spirit of the JCS directive under which the medium bombers were sent to the

---

30. Simmons was the *Tribune*'s Far Eastern Bureau chief and had been in Tokyo since 1946. A Labor Party M.P. from the Maldon Division of Essex, Driberg was also a correspondent in World War II.

theater. He stated that he, nevertheless, felt it extremely important that we not 'take out' the particular group of hydro-electric plants in the Wŏnsan-Hamhŭng area. I agreed to get word out to FEAF Bomber Command to defer the program until he had obtained the CINC's reaction. I did so immediately after the briefing. Approximately 30 minutes later, General Hickey called and stated that the CINC did not wish to interfere with FEAF plans with reference to these targets and that we should continue with our program as planned. This information was passed to Deputy for Operations.

Prepared the following memo to CINCFE which I am to handcarry to him tonight: "Subject: P'yŏngyang Bombing Mission."

I proposed to direct a major B–29 strike against several of the most important remaining military targets in the P'yŏngyang area. Selected targets include several military barracks and training areas, warehouse storage areas, and marshaling yards. Plans call for using over 100 B–29s on this mission in order to saturate the anti-aircraft defenses and insure elimination of these important targets in one strike.

The execution of this plan will require standdown the day prior to the mission. Fifth Air Force fighters and bombers will be made available for tactical support on that day in lieu of the B–29s. From a tactical standpoint this type of mission is desirable since it will minimize flak damage. We have suffered increased battle damage over P'yŏngyang recently.

I consider this operation fully authorized by my current directives from you; however, it is submitted for approval to insure that a mass strike of this nature is consistent with your most recent target directive from the Joint Chiefs of Staff and with your wishes.

Attached is city plan of P'yŏngyang, showing selected targets. Also attached is a self-explanatory draft of a signal proposed to the Joint Chiefs of Staff in the event you desire to obtain approval for this operation.

Following is my suggested radio to be sent by CINCFE to Joint Chiefs of Staff:

This message in three parts.

PART I. Among the more important remaining military targets in North Korea are several military barracks and training areas, warehouse storage areas and marshaling yards in the P'yŏngyang area. In order to saturate P'yŏngyang anti-aircraft defenses and insure elimination of these remaining targets in one strike, I proposed to undertake an attack with over 100 B–29s. All selected targets are considered to have a direct bearing on the tactical situation and are not of strategic nature. Strike will be visual and precision bombing.

PART II. This plan is submitted for your approval to insure that there is no objection on part of Joint Chiefs or other agencies to the execution of such a mass bombardment attack.

PART III. In the event you do not approve of this proposed mass operation, it is assumed that there is no objection to destroying these selected targets one at a time, but anti-aircraft losses may occur.

Met with General MacArthur at 1800 hours.

With reference the dispatch of two medium groups back to the ZI, General MacArthur directed that until a decision was made as to whether he would go beyond the 38th Parallel he did not dare return the two medium groups, but did state that if he was not authorized to go beyond the 38th Parallel that he would immediately return the two groups, but that if he did go forward beyond the 38th, he would retain all four.

Reference the <u>one bang</u> [underlined in original] attack on military targets in the P'yŏngyang area, he approved my paper of this date (27 Sept) at 1815 hours and he very emphatically stated that there was no reason for him to send my draft signal to the Joint Chiefs of Staff! Hooray! God bless his soul![31]

During my conversation with CINCFE he specifically invited Partridge and O'Donnell to the coming ceremonies at Seoul.

Immediately upon my return to the office from General MacArthur's, I dispatched the following signal: STRATLINE to Partridge and O'Donnell.

There will be a ceremony in Seoul 1100 hours, Friday, 29 Sept. General MacArthur invites you to be present, but you must get there under your own airplane power. I desire your presence if it does not interfere with your military duties.

Coordinated a radio earlier in the day to Partridge and O'Donnell stressing again the necessity of not repeat not violating the Manchurian border. Directed that all crews operating north of a line from P'yŏngyang to Wŏnsan be specifically briefed prior to each mission on these points and further that any airplane north of this line that cannot definitely determine its position make no attack.

**THURSDAY
28 SEPTEMBER
1950**

At 0935 hours, General MacArthur called me on the telephone and stated that he had had a directive from Washington to offer surrender terms to the Korean Reds and that in view of his directive, he desired to hold in abeyance the "one bang" attack on P'yŏngyang. He indicated that if he had no offer from the North Koreans to his surrender that he would give me the green light to go ahead with the attack. Again, God Bless his soul!

I instructed General Weyland to notify General O'Donnell that his attack was off for 1 October and he would put it up for 3 October but would make the attack only on my specific word. This is being confirmed by "Stratline."

Sent formal condolence messages to Bouchier and Robertson re the accidental attack by FEAF on elements of the advance units of 27th British Brigade. Also asked Bouchier to forward by signal my message Marshal of the Air Force Sir John C. Slessor:

Personal Slessor from Stratemeyer. Receipt of the knowledge that elements of the Far East Air Forces accidentally strafed advance units of the 27th British Brigade came with deep shock to me. The contribution of the

---

31. The "one bang" attack was to be a massed bombing by 100 B–29s of military targets in P'yŏngyang. Stratemeyer believed that this strike could, at least, impress the North Koreans and possibly hasten the collapse of North Korean resistance. (Futrell, p 205.)

Commonwealth to United Nations efforts is a source of constant admiration to members of this command and each keenly feels the tragedy of this unfortunate incident.

FRIDAY　　　　Departed 0600 hours from Haneda, direct for Seoul aboard
29 SEPTEMBER　the SCAP[32] with General MacArthur and a group of his staff
1950　　　　　to attend the ceremonies wherein CINCFE turned over the
　　　　　　　　 Korean capital, Seoul, to President Rhee. The ceremonies
were in great dignity and simplicity. MacArthur, near the end of his message, broke down completely and he had to stop and collect himself prior to the saying of the Lord's Prayer.

President Rhee, in his statement, was impressive and I admired his stamina and courage. Mrs. Rhee was also present; she is a sweet, little old lady.

Stratemeyer talks with Brig. Gen. Edward A. Craig, assistant division commander of the 1st Marine Division, and a naval officer prior to the ceremonies in Seoul.

We departed immediately after the ceremony and arrived back at Haneda 1600 hours.

Prior to the ceremonies, General MacArthur met with his commanders and discussed the coming operations and conditions under which we would cross the 38th Parallel.

He indicated to Walker that he should not stop the momentum of his pursuit and if the ROK Army wants to go forward, not to stop them, but encourage them.

The Distinguished Service Cross award was made to General Walker at the conclusion of which I told General MacArthur that I felt that General Partridge was entitled to the same award. He agreed and authorized me to submit a recommendation for the award which he will approve.

General Weyland informed me that he had sent a redline message, dated 28 Sept, to Vandenberg stating that the 49th Jet Fighter Group was based and operational that date from K-2, Taegu, Korea.

In opening my mail, found a note from Partridge re the "favorable" comparison between AF and ground force "kills" which I bucked to members of my staff. We consistently have underestimated our kills.

---

32. "SCAP" was the name given MacArthur's new Lockheed Constellation.

Also the following letter was received from Jack Slessor who reported that Wykeham-Barnes had returned, thanked me for his receiving the Air Medal, and added:

> ... We shall have to be careful that the land forces don't come to think they can never do anything unless they have overwhelming air support. We have seen something of the dangers of that six years ago, and I gather from Wykeham-Barnes that they are inclined to suffer a bit from that complex in Korea. That's all very well where there is no air opposition, but it won't be the form if there is a show-down in Europe...

Following is the exchange of messages on the movement of the fighter wing to Suwŏn Airfield:

25 Sept Partridge sent to X Corps:

Req permission to deploy the 6131 Tac Sup Wing to Suwŏn airdrome in Korea. This organization is a fighter wing and is to be employed from Suwŏn Airfield. Present plans of the Fifth AF contemplate airlifting in an adv[ance] detachment of the 6131 Tac Sup Wing consisting of 50 people and equipment. This is to be followed by the 1st, 2d and 3d echelons at a later date. Req that your hq expedite reply and info to adees [addressees] listed above.

28 Sept X Corps signalled 5th AF:

No objection to deployment 6131 Tac Support Wg to Suwŏn Airdrome in Korea.

Immediately following receipt of their above message they sent this signal:

It should be pointed out that the concurrence given in above reference radio is with the clear understanding that the establishment of ATDC support wing on Suwŏn Airdrome at this time will in no way reduce the allocation of air cargo to X Corps. Further, that all tactical aircraft operating in this area will be under the control of the X Corps Tactical Air Command.

Partridge immediately wired me on 29th:

The condition cited in Ref Msg for movement of a tactical support wing to Suwŏn is not acceptable to this headquarters. The 6131st Wing will not be moved to Suwŏn unless it is clearly understood by all concerned that command and control of this unit remains with CG 5th AF. Inasmuch as action has already been initiated to have supporting equipment and supplies into Suwŏn, it is requested that this matter be cleared with CINCFE and this hqs advised earliest.

My message to CINCFE with info to all adees:

Essential to support of EUSAK and contemplated future opns that 5th AF ftr bmr gps be estbd as soon as possible at K-13, Suwŏn, and at K-14, Kimp'o. These units must remain under centralized control Fifth AF in execution of Fifth AF overall missions. Forward displacement of FEAF air units w/require some support fr FEAF Combat Cargo Cmd. As Inch'ŏn opn has progressed well beyond amphibious phase, req that upon arrival of 5th AF units in the Seoul area, control of all land based acft, including Marines remaining at Kimp'o, pass to CG FEAF as set forth in CINCFE policy ltr of 8 Jul 50, file AG 370.2.

SATURDAY 30 SEPTEMBER 1950

Sent Toohey Spaatz (who departed yesterday aboard PanAm for the ZI) the following airmail special delivery letter:

I think you would be interested to know that while en route to Seoul yesterday, when General MacArthur turned over the capitol to President Rhee, in a conversation I had with Brigadier General Courtney Whitney, Chief of SCAP Government Section, General Whitney informed me that up to that time, 29 September, General MacArthur had not received a single commendation or congratulation note on the successes that he has had in Korea from anyone connected with the administration — including the President. General Whitney stated "none of the Secretaries of the Service, nor members of the Joint Chiefs of Staff (including General Bradley), nor any member of the Department of Defense, nor any member of the State Department had sent one word of praise to the Boss."

I thought you might be interested and might slip in a line or two on this subject in one of your articles.

When I heard this news, I just plain couldn't understand it.

Hope your trip back was pleasant, etc.

In my letter to Spaatz added a PS to the effect that CINCFE did receive congratulatory messages from Chiang Kai Shek and PI [Philippine Islands] President Quirino.[33]

Admiral Struble under date of 27 Sept informed me:

The *New York Times* of Sept 8 carried an article headlined, "Russians Stirred by Plane Incident - Resentment Against U.S. Rises Over Bomber Loss Off Korea - Press Features Protest." *The last two paragraphs of this article, headed "Moscow," read as follows:*

"Meanwhile, the Literary Gazette added three American generals to a list of Westerners it calls 'War Criminals,' and cartooned them in uniforms dripping blood.

"They were Lt. Gen. George E. Stratemeyer, Far East Commander of the United States Air Force; Maj. Gen. Earle E. Partridge, Commander of the United States Fifth Air Force in Japan; and Brig. Gen. Edward J. Timberlake, Jr., Vice Commander of the Fifth Air Force."

It was a great shock to me to read your name as one of the "war criminals." Trusting that all goes well, etc.

---

33. This message was not sent, perhaps because Stratemeyer learned that, in fact, there had been many congratulatory messages from members of the administration, including the President, and the JCS. (James, p 484; Collins, pp 140-141.)

In reply I told Struble:

Your succinct letter of 27 Sept was read with a great deal of interest.
However, I feel that when the Commies get around to giving "war criminal" Stratemeyer a cell-mate, it will be none other than that old "buccaneer" Arthur D. Struble, USN! etc.

Also bucked copies of Struble's letter to Earle Partridge and Ted Timberlake - "as further indication of their effective leadership of the Fifth Air Force."

Directed Deputy for Personnel to get started on the citation for Partridge for the Distinguished Service Cross.

Sent a short note to the Honorable Robert A. Lovett,[34] Deputy Secretary of Defense - telling him I didn't know whether to congratulate or condole with him re his new appointment.

Drafted up another letter to Vandenberg urging tangible recognition of Jack Doyle's efforts - either permanent brigadier general, a temporary major generalship, or preferably - both.

Sent Vandenberg an informational redline as of today we had passed the 40,000 sortie mark - 40,190 to be exact.

Received from USAF (Sory Smith) the following signal:

Your message of 21 Sept,..., to President Air Reserve Association, National Convention, Hotel Texas, Fort Worth, Texas, was passed to Brigadier General Lafeton Whitney[35] as you requested. I feel sincerely that your well-timed and masterfully worded message to ARA members and guests could not help but both impress and inspire the delegates. The text of Secretary Finletter's address to this same group at 0930, local this date, has been airmailed to you FYI.

Sent the following redline to Vandenberg - personal:

Further reference requirement for Air Evaluation Board. Recognizing necessity for securing corroborative evidence results of air effort, Partridge is initiating limited survey of areas now uncovered. We shall continue to do our best within limits of resources. In view of rapid enemy roll-back earnestly recommend movement of Evaluation Board or Bombing Survey personnel be expedited.

"FLASH" message from Joint Chiefs to General MacArthur received this morning as follows:

At the time the situation in Korea was going against the UN forces, some consideration was given to an all out bombing attack on the enemy capital at P'yŏngyang. We do not know what your views or plans are in this connection under the existing circumstances. Because of the serious political implications involved it is desired that you advise the Joint Chiefs of Staff, for clearance with higher authority, of any plans you

---

34. During World War II, Lovett was Assistant Secretary of War for Air. When George C. Marshall became Secretary of Defense, he recruited Lovett as his deputy. Lovett became Secretary of Defense when Marshall retired in the fall of 1951.
35. Whitney is unknown.

may have before you order or authorize such an attack or attacks of a similar nature.

MacArthur to DA replied as follows to above quoted signal:

For JCS. I have no present plans or purpose to bomb the enemy capital at P'yŏngyang and at no time has consideration been given to attempt any operation designed to do more than destroy its military installations. I am trying to end the campaign with as little added loss of life and destruction of property as is possible. In the case of P'yŏngyang, if it becomes a citadel of defense against our attacking ground forces, I would plan to use such air concentrations as might become necessary to minimize our own losses. At present, however, I have no intention of launching an all-out bombing attack of the nature to which you refer. Signed MacArthur.

General MacArthur forwarded copies of the following statements.

1. Message from the White House.
The President - "I know that I speak for the entire American people when I send you my warmest congratulations on the victory which has been achieved under your leadership in Korea. Few operations in mil[itary] history can match either the delaying action where you traded space for time in which to build up your forces, or the brilliant maneuver which has now resulted in the liberation of Seoul. I am particularly impressed by the splendid cooperation of our Army, Navy and Air Force, and I wish you would extend my thanks and congratulations to the commanders of those services - Lt Gen Walton H. Walker, Vice Adm Charles T. Joy and Lt Gen George E. Stratemeyer. The unification of our arms established by you and by them has set a shining example. My thanks and the thanks of the people of all the free nations go out to your gallant forces - soldiers, sailors, marines and airmen from the United States and the other countries fighting for freedom under the United Nations banner. I salute you all, and say to all of you from all of us at home - 'Well and nobly done'."
2. From the Joint Chiefs of Staff.
The Joint Chiefs of Staff are proud of the great successes you have achieved. We realize that they would have been impossible without brilliant and audacious leadership and without the full coordination and the fighting spirit of all forces and all arms. From the sudden initiation of hostilities you have exploited to the utmost all capabilities and opportunities. Your transition from defensive to offensive operations was magnificently planned, timed and executed. You have given new inspiration to the freedom-loving peoples of the world. We remain completely confident that the great task entrusted to you by the United Nations will be carried to a successful conclusion.

SUNDAY
1 OCTOBER
1950

General MacArthur has ordered the following statement dropped 1 October 1950. Leaflet written in both English and Korean and is addressed to: The Commander-in-Chief North Korean Forces. It states:

The early and total defeat and complete destruction of your armed forces and war making potential is now inevitable. In order that the decisions of the United Nations may be carried out with a minimum of further loss of life and destruction of property, I, as the United Nations Commander-in-Chief, call upon you and the forces under your command, in whatever part of Korea situated, forthwith to lay down your arms and cease hostilities under such military supervision as I may direct - and I call upon you at once to liberate all United Nations prisoners of war and civilian internees under your control and to make adequate provision for their protection, care, maintenance, and immediate transportation to such places as I indicate. North Korean Forces, including prisoners of war in the hands of the United Nations Command, will continue to be given the care dictated by civilized custom and practice and permitted to return to their homes as soon as practicable. I shall anticipate your early decision upon this opportunity to avoid the further useless shedding of blood and destruction of property.

Hugh Baillie lunched with us at Mayeda House.
General Kenney returned about 1500 hours from his trek to Korea.
ROK forces reach and cross 38th Parallel.[36]

MONDAY
2 OCTOBER
1950

Received Stratline from O'Donnell in which he stated, listing his reasons, that the American-made flares of 1943 vintage were dangerous and hazardous and his statistics were showing their use not worthwhile. British flares, which were of 1950 manufacture, were available in theater and he was requisitioning a supply.[37]

The following memo was given to Vice Commander A&P, Vice Commander Ops with an additional copy for Deputy for Operations - and Plans - in order

---

36. As early as mid-July, MacArthur had considered crossing the 38th Parallel into North Korea, believing that it might be necessary to occupy the entire country in order to bring the war to a successful conclusion. He was perhaps responding to the rather vague and imprecise U.N. Security Council's June 27 resolution to "repel the armed attack and to restore international peace and security in the area."
   Also in July, both the JCS and the National Security Council (NSC) began studying the possibility of crossing the parallel. After the JCS reviewed an initial study, the NSC issued a revised paper, NSC 81/1. This paper, a somewhat waffling and obtuse document, among other things stated: (1) U.N. forces could advance north of the 38th Parallel so as to either force the NKPA to withdraw from the south or defeat it; (2) if Russian or Chinese forces entered North Korea before U.N. troops crossed the 38th Parallel, there would be no advance farther north, though bombing operations in North Korea would still be allowed; (3) operations "close to" the Manchurian and U.S.S.R. borders would be forbidden, as would operations across these borders; (4) only ROK troops would be used in the "northeast province or along the Manchurian border;" and (5) occupation plans for North Korea would be drawn up by MacArthur, but only executed with the "explicit" approval of the President.
   Curiously, NSC 81/1 also said that if the Russians intervened <u>anywhere</u> in Korea, MacArthur was to go on the defensive, whereas, if the Chinese Communist Forces (CCF) intervened in the south (North Korea not being mentioned), he was to continue operations as long as he deemed them to be successful. The JCS finally noticed that NSC 81/1 did not mention Chinese intervention in North Korea and in early October, amended its directive by substituting the word "anywhere" for "south of the 38th Parallel." (FRUS, 1950, Korea, Vol. VII, pp 685-93; "History of the JCS," Vol. III, pp 224-228.)
   The main provisions of NSC 81/1 were sent by the JCS to MacArthur on Sept. 15, followed on the 27th by a JCS directive authorizing movement north across the parallel. The first U.S. patrols crossed the 38th Parallel on Oct. 7, the main force following two days later. ("History of the JCS," Vol. III, pp 228-230.)
37. O'Donnell also recommended that the use of B-29s on night target of opportunity missions be discontinued, to which Stratemeyer agreed. (Ltr, Maj Gen Emmett O'Donnell to Lt Gen George E. Stratemeyer, 2 Oct 1950, subj: Emergency Use of B-29 Aircraft; Memo, Lt Gen George E. Stratemeyer to Vice Commander, Operations, 3 Oct 1950, subj: O'Donnell Ltr of 2 Oct 1950, "Emergency Use of B-29 Aircraft."

to guide them in their preparation of any indorsement that I sign, sending forward reports from my four major commands regarding the Korean conflict:

MEMORANDUM - Subject - Final Reporting - Korean Conflict.

When the final reports of the Korean campaign are submitted from FEAF Bomber Command, FEAF Combat Cargo Command, Fifth Air Force, and FEAMCOM, we must be very careful in preparing my forwarding indorsements to indicate besides the lessons learned, the lessons not learned. For examples:

(1) In the FEAF Bomber Command, there have been only four (4) losses, two (2) of which were due to enemy action and only one (1) of those - air action. The great tonnages they dropped and the number of aircraft they kept in commission could not have been accomplished had there been an aggressive air opponent.

(2) The tonnages carried by the FEAF Combat Cargo Command could not have been a semblance of what they carried had there been aggressive hostile jet aircraft to interfere. The straight pattern of course they flew from Ashiya, around the tip of South Korea, up to a point opposite Inch'ŏn, and then straight into Kimp'o - a half dozen jet aircraft could have picked them off like clay pigeons. If the statement were made that air cover could have protected those aircraft, this would be a fallacy if there is aggressive enemy air present inasmuch as friendly fighters would be needed to attempt to gain air superiority. In this case, we would have to go into some form of group formation and fly in the cargo or the troops just as we would move out with a bomber formation. We must keep in mind that our home bases here in Japan, and even in South Korea, have not been interfered with by hostile air.

(3) The Fifth Air Force, after the initial two or three days was able to concentrate practically its entire effort on the support of United Nations ground troops. There was no hostile interference from hostile air and the great support that we were able to give might lead to a wrong conclusion.

If there had been an enemy air force, it is questionable - to my way of thinking - that the ground troops could ever have been supplied by long truck columns and train as they were from Pusan.

The great proportion of our air effort would of necessity have been to knock out hostile air both on the ground and in the air.

There never has been any real hostile aircraft with which to contend.

General Walker, General Gay, and other senior ground people realize the fact that there was not hostile air and thereby their rear echelons operated freely due to this fact.

One hears frequently of the "package Marine (ground-air) units." For certain types of operations, such as amphibious landings, this type organization is good, but the United States government simply cannot afford to have all ground divisions equipped with their own tactical air in packages. The senior commanders would be unable to divert from one side of the line, as was done by General Partridge during the period 1-5 Sept, had they had the packaged form of close support.

The type of support rendered by the Corsair and the F–51 could not have been had they been opposed by an aggressive air opponent equipped with jets.

The F–80 not only is capable of as great a wallop as the '51 or Corsair, but it can protect itself, and, further, the combat losses have been in the ratio of about 4 to 1, favoring the F–80. If the F–80 had only one-third the effectiveness it had, it would still be a better air supporting airplane than the '51 because of the minimum losses that would be sustained from ground fire.

The chief of staff of a North Korean division who surrendered, in an interview with Dr. Bowles, indicated that the most feared piece of equipment utilized by the United Nations in the Korean conflict was the American jet.[38]

(4) FEAMCOM has been able to operate here in Japan and in forward bases without any interruptions from hostile air, and we must not assume that in a war with a major power could FEAMCOM's activities been carried on as they have been. One hostile raid at Tachikawa would have made a great difference in the supply and maintenance rendered to the Far East Air Forces.

Furthermore, we will never have available in other theaters of operations the technical and industrial help that we have been able to secure here in Japan from the Japanese civilians employed by FEAMCOM.

Our lines of communications here in Japan and in Korea have not been interfered with by hostile air. Again, I'm wondering what would have happened to our supplies and maintenance problems.

(5) Now, a word about my own headquarters which operated here in the Meiji Building under the most advantageous conditions that one could imagine - even including air conditioning. There were no bomb raids, no black-outs, no harrassment of any sort that would always be present in a war with a major power.

At times, our communications did not function too efficiently, but overall, to my mind, it was superior as compared to conditions that would be present were we in the field and dependent upon communications we would have to set up.

The point I want to make is: the war has been fought with a minor power against a very aggressive ground opponent and if we are not careful, people back home in the Pentagon will draw conclusions from this war which will not be true.

Our ground people, in their defensive situation, on many occasions were absolutely dependent upon the air support to maintain the security of the great gaps in their lines.

Again, we have the Navy, offshore with their carriers, making a great show with their sweeps and their light tonnage attacks against hostile targets with no enemy air to interfere in the air - or against their carriers - which would be sitting ducks for an aggressive hostile bomber force.

All of us must be very careful not to draw inept conclusions from this small, "police action" war. GES

P.S. Here are several other thoughts that must be considered: (1) We have

---

38. This North Korean officer was Senior Lt Col Lee Hak Ku, Chief of Staff, N.K. 13th Division. In 1952, he became notorious as the leader of the Communist prisoners in their Koje Island riots. (Appleman, pp 589-590.)

had no communications jamming. Our security in messages - both by telephone and radio - has been very lax as compared with what it would be when engaged in a war with a major power, particularly where the enemy had an aggressive Air Force. Practically all of our routings and reportings of aircraft, especially those having to do with FEAF Combat Cargo Command, have been in the clear, whereas if we were really pitted against a first-class enemy, they would have had to have been in code.
(2) We have not considered in all of our night operations the fact that the enemy could well employ night intruders against our light and medium bomber activities. GES

General Turner arrives Haneda 1030 hours.

Generals Turner and Kenney dinner guests at Mayeda House (General Kenney is a house-guest).

At 1700 hours a Colonel John L. Holcombe, with a letter of introduction from Rawlings, and who is employed in a civilian capacity in the Comptroller Office, Department of Defense, called at the office. He is over here to look into Army budget and finance problems. Colonel Holcombe is also anxious to look into AF materiel utilization and loss factors. Colonel Corr[39] has him in tow. I authorized him to make a flight with the FEAF Bomber Command.

1815 hours had a long conference with CINCFE, and, although he was one hundred percent for having me be in controlling head of all air operations, he indicated that the defense forces were not organized that way and that such a decision could not be made by him, but must be made by higher authority.

After pointing out that the Annex Order to the coming Wŏnsan operation put the coordination of air effort outside the objective area, after the assault, in his headquarters, he agreed with me that that should be changed - that I should be the controlling controller of all air operations after the assault phase.

At his direction, I discussed this with General Doyle Hickey, the acting chief of staff, and, after explaining General MacArthur's desires, we came to a quick decision and a change in the order was made to my satisfaction by changing the word "post-assault" to "assault" and by striking out the words "in his headquarters."

My interpretation of this is that I am the coordinating headquarters for air operations throughout the Wŏnsan operation.[40]

TUESDAY **3 OCTOBER** **1950**	Press conference at 1030 hours was received with enthusiasm and many complimentary remarks were made by the correspondents. About 25 members of the press were present plus members of my staff. Took about 30 minutes for the

---

39. Col Francis J. Corr, FEAF comptroller.
40. On Korea's east coast, Wŏnsan is a major port and industrial city. MacArthur planned to make a landing there on Oct. 20 using the troops of the X Corps. This was not received with great enthusiasm by many commanders who believed removing troops from action to embark them for the landings would slow pursuit of the enemy. A more proper strategy, they thought, was an overland attack to Wŏnsan.
There were other problems with this operation. It was feared that major logistical headaches would be created by the plan, both at Inch'ŏn where the 1st Marine Division would load, and on the road between Inch'ŏn and Pusan, where the 7th Division would embark. Indeed, this is what happened. In addition, the diversion of shipping from hauling supplies to carrying the two divisions caused serious problems later as stockpiles dwindled in the face of increased enemy activity.
The amphibious "assault" at Wŏnsan was anti-climactic. On the day the X Corps began to stage for the landings, Oct. 7, the ROK I Corps was only ten miles south of Wŏnsan, and the city fell to the ROK troops three days

statement and then about 30 minutes was used for questions and answers. The telegraphic dispatches to Stateside papers sent out by reporters were well worded and covered the subject although the information sent was based more on the answers to the questions than on the statement made.

Captain Hoagland,[41] General Kenney's son-in-law, joined us - and General Kenney - at dinner at Mayeda House.

WEDNESDAY 4 OCTOBER 1950

Mr. Joseph Alsop called at the office. Saw him with Colonel Nuckols at 1515 hours. (Believe I won the jet support controversy.)

Bouchier sent over the following memo which I sent to Earle Partridge for his records and to return to me to become a part of the official FEAF files:

I have just received the following telegram from Sir John Slessor in reply to the one you sent him as contained in your letter to me dated 28 Sep 50.

Quote: "Personal for STRATEMEYER from SLESSOR. Reference telegram CAB 63 most grateful your personal message through Bouchier. Assure you both Slim and I realize that this sort of tragic accident is bound to happen occasionally in war. Anyway, it was clearly not the fault of pilots in the air." Unquote.

(Slim referred to above is General Sir William Slim, Chief of Imperial General Staff).

May I take this opportunity also of thanking you for your most kind letter to me dated 28 Sept. The sincerity and deep regret and concern that both you and all officers and airmen of the Far East Air Forces have shown with regard to this well understood and pure accident of war is greatly appreciated by us all. For myself, may I ask that in any investigation you may possibly have made into this accident that you or General Partridge will deal compassionately and as lightly as possible with anyone you may consider to blame in any way.

No one makes a mistake of this sort purposely and if you should find that some blame attaches to anyone in particular I earnestly hope that you will see it, as I do, that any mistake made is, in itself, full punishment enough and that no further action is necessary.

THURSDAY 5 OCTOBER 1950

I addressed the WAF Detachment, Captain Temple[42] commanding, this morning in the FEAF Auditorium at which time I welcomed them to FEAF, explained my experience with 300 WACs in India and China and then personally told them what a great job the WACs had done for me in the war. I wished them well and told them I was glad they were here.

---

later. Air Force base units and 1st MAW air units were actually operating from the Wŏnsan airfield before the landings took place. The 1st Marine Division arrived off Wŏnsan on Oct. 20, but extensive minefields in the harbor kept the ships offshore until the 26th, when an "administrative" landing was made. On the 29th, the 7th Division landed at Iwŏn, 105 miles northeast of Wŏnsan. (Futrell, pp 202; Schnabel, pp 190, 205-210, 219.)

41. Capt Edward C. Hoagland, Jr., was married to Kenney's daughter, Julia.

42. Capt Charlotte E. Temple.

I saw Squadron Leader Soen,[43] Royal Thai Air Force, who is here with the Thailand Mission.[44] He brought me a beautiful cigarette case from Air Marshal Fuen Ronnapakat- Ritthakani.[45] Soen was in great hopes that we could arrange to have MATS return their wounded to Bangkok from Korea and bring back replacements. I indicated I had no authority to do this and it was something that would have to be taken up by his Mission with CINCFE. He also asked for some instructional photographs and maps which Major Paradis[46] arranged for and secured for him from Intelligence.

At 1530 hours had a conference with Hanson Baldwin,[47] *New York Times* military expert (bushwa). Present were General Weyland and Colonel Nuckols.

Rather proud of the way I conducted myself and was nice and gave him some of the lessons learned - as for example the proving of the F–80; the fact that we had an Air Force in Korea where you could swing the weight of its attacks from one front to the other; and the great job that our air evacuation people have done, wherein I noted that we have saved many American boys' lives; and that I was opposed to having for the Army "packaged" type air support which I believe is correct for the Marines, but not correct for the Army. Mr. Baldwin left around 1615 apparently well pleased.

1730 hours made the award of the 4th cluster to General O'Donnell's Distinguished Flying Cross. Present were Generals Craigie and Weyland; Colonel Toro (AG)[48] read the Order and Colonel Tidwell (JA) read the citation.

**FRIDAY
6 OCTOBER
1950**

Colonel William P. Nuckols, my PIO, received his star - appointed Brigadier General (temporary). Pinned his stars on him and also gave him the *copy of my signal to Vandenberg which I had sent out earlier this morning:*

> Personal Vandenberg from Stratemeyer: I was in process of recommending Nuckols for his temporary star and therefore good news of his promotion received this morning most gratifying and most deserved. His work has been outstanding.

At 1200 hours today I checked with General Hickey by telephone to find out if General MacArthur had sent out his ultimatum to the commander of the North Korean Forces, and if he knew General MacArthur's plans for the strike at P'yŏngyang in order to destroy the seven military targets in that area if the North Korean commander did not answer his ultimatum.

General Hickey indicated that in view of the present political situation he was confident that General MacArthur intended to hold the attack in abeyance for some time and that he had not sent out the ultimatum to the commander of the North Korean forces.

I have directed General Weyland, Vice Commander for Operations, to

---

43. This is probably Wg Cdr <u>Suan</u> Jitaiboon.
44. This was the diplomatic mission to Japan. On June 24, 1951, a Royal Thai Air Force detachment of three C–47s arrived at Tachikawa. Attached to the 374th TCW's 21st Squadron, the detachment began operations in July. (*The History of the United Nations Forces in the Korean War*, Vol. I [Seoul, 1972], pp 584-588.)
45. The Thai Air Force commander in chief.
46. Maj Joseph C.E. Paradis, Stratemeyer's aide-de-camp.
47. Baldwin was the military editor for the *New York Times*. Author of numerous articles and books on military topics, he won the Pulitzer Prize in 1942.
48. Col E.E. Toro, FEAF's adjutant general.

inform General O'Donnell of the above and that if the attack is directed, we will receive at least 48 hours notice - or most likely, 72 hours notice.

General Courtney Whitney, Chief of SCAP's Government Section, sent me a copy of Drew Pearson's[49] column in the *Washington Post* of 30 Sept which delineated with accuracy my exchange of notes with the Navy, my feelings, etc. re the "air controller" situation and the JOC in Hq Fifth AF in Korea. *Sent him a thank you note for the article and also a copy of my letter to Admiral Joy which is quoted in toto:*

> Dear Turner: The recent and completely unwarranted article by Drew Pearson in the *Washington Post* distresses me greatly and I hasten to reassure you of my continuing and complete confidence in the naval forces under your command.
>
> It is indeed unfortunate that minor divergencies, which you and I are always able to reconcile, have to be aired in public print. How this information came into the hands of the author is unknown to me, but one thing is certain - it was not from this headquarters, its files or any member of my staff who are operating under rigid and unmistakable orders. I sincerely trust that the unrealistic and exaggerated Pearson article will not hamper the intimate and effective coordination that has existed in the past between your headquarters and mine - and between you and me personally.

I sent Joy the clipping from the paper with my letter.

1650 hours, Dr. Bowles called at the office to say goodbye.

SATURDAY 7 OCTOBER 1950   Left the office about 0930 hours for Haneda. Flew to Taegu in the T–33, Lt Langstaff piloting and made the award of the DSC to General Partridge. Pictures were taken and brought same back with me and turned them over to the PIO. Had lunch with Colonel Smith[50] in his pre-fab lunch hall. General Partridge lunched with us.

I explained to Partridge that he better have a second plan whereby he could still support General Walker with all possible sorties and turn over the necessary storage space at Kimp'o for the Cargo Command if they are required to pick up the 187th Airborne Brigade there and drop them some place in North Korea.

Partridge pointed out, and I agree with him, that this is contrary to all methods of dropping an airborne brigade. The forward flying fields should be made available for fighter- bombers and the brigade should be picked up from fields in the rear area.

I told him that I would do everything I could to allow him to occupy Kimp'o with the 51st Fighter Wing.

(Passed the above on to General Weyland).

Walker's C–47 has been returned to FEAMCOM where it was found they had to pull a motor and while this is being done, it was decided that both motors should be changed. Told Alkire to put the bee on FEAMCOM to get this job completed and the C–47 returned for General Walker's use as early as possible.

---

49. The famed and notorious columnist ("The Washington Merry-Go-Round") noted for his investigative work.
50. Col Stanton T. Smith, commander of the 49th FBG.

General Partridge informed me that Mr. Muccio's airplane was now assigned and available for his use along with Captain W. J. Brown who used to be stationed at Misawa and who has had service in Korea and who knew Mr. Muccio personally. The Ambassador is very happy with this assignment.

General Partridge informed General Walker that B–29s (strikes) will be made available to him on call. I confirmed this. (Passed same to Weyland).

To Craigie I sent the following memo:

General Walker and General Partridge are concerned about the fact that American troops are not to pass the MacArthur Line, after they cross the 38th Parallel, which extends from Sinanju to Kunu-ri, Yŏngwŏn to Hamhŭng.[51] The reason for their concern is that there are control parties with ROK divisions as well as KMAG officers. If the ROK divisions are permitted to go forward, they desire that they be informed as to whether KMAG officers and our ground control parties are to proceed beyond the MacArthur Line along with the ROK divisions. It is desired that you (Craigie) secure this information and pass it to General Partridge from me and request CINCFE to inform Walker. If you feel that this cannot be done at your level, I will take it up personally with General MacArthur.

General Partridge has informed me that Major Smith who is a member of the Army Field Evaluation Group told him that General Almond had written letters to Army Field Forces, General Clark, and others that he does not believe in the Air Force - Army type of air support by cooperation and he feels and has recommended that the Marine type of air support, where the Marine aviation operates under the ground commander, is the type of air support he desires. Major Smith pointed out, as did General Partridge to me, that he makes this recommendation when he has never been supported by the USAF in any of his ground actions. It is, therefore, difficult to understand his attitude.

Colonel Sykes (my Special Assistant) sent me the following buck slip which I approved:

Inasmuch as the expression "coordination control" does not appear in the joint dictionary of military and naval terms, I suggest for the record that we footnote the GHQ 8 Jul 50 directive with a local definition of "coordination control." Attached is a memo from Col Heflebower in response to my request for the JSPOG understanding of what "coordination control" means. It might be desirable to ask GHQ for an official definition of this expression; however, such a request might appear academic, arouse suspicion, do more harm than good. Therefore, I do not recommend that we ask GHQ for an official definition unless future controversy should develop. Meanwhile, request your approval or changes in Col Heflebower's suggested definition.[52]

---

51. This line actually started at Chŏngju, which is west-northwest of Sinanju, and ran just above the narrowest part of Korea. On Oct. 17, MacArthur removed the restriction against using American troops north of this line. However, he established another line restricting an American advance farther north extending generally from Sunch'ŏn north to Ch'ŏngsŏngjin and thence across country to Sŏngjin on the east coast. (Schnabel, p 216.)

52. As noted earlier, there was never an official definition of this term.

Follows a verbatim quote of Colonel R. C. Heflebower's memo re "Definition of Coordination Control, dtd 26 Sep 50." Reference: Ltr, GHQ, FEC, File 370.2 (8 Jul 50) CG, subject: Coordination of Air Effort of Far East Air Forces and United States Naval Forces, Far East, dated 12 July 1950.

> *(1)* There apparently is not recorded a definition of "coordination control" as employed in reference letter, nor is it known whether the principals party to the agreement outlined therein discussed "coordination control" in specific terms. The GHQ officer who prepared the background papers for the C/S, GHQ defines the phrase as follows:

"Coordination control is the authority to prescribe methods and procedures to effect coordination in the operations of air elements of two or more forces operating in the same area. It comprises basically the authority to disapprove operations of one force might interfere with the operations of another force and to coordinate air efforts of the major FEC commands by such means as prescribing boundaries between operating areas, time of operations in areas and measures of identification between air elements."

> *(2)* The specific definition above is reconstructed by the staff officer referred to above and has NOT been officially approved by GHQ, FEC.

Sent a Stratline to Partridge telling him that Walker's C–47 being tested Sunday, 8 Oct, and in all probability would be delivered to Walker Monday morning, 9 Oct, and for him to inform Walker re same.

SUNDAY
8 OCTOBER
1950

Sent Toohey Spaatz the following letter:

Enclosed herewith are the general purpose maps and the handbook on Inch'ŏn (under separate cover) which Willoughby had given you as part of the fittings for the map case which you so kindly left for Annalee.

I feel, and hope that you agree, that one of your future articles should be on the tactical air support that the United States Air Force furnishes to the Army in conjunction with the AF's job of isolating the battlefield by operating light bombers and fighter-bombers well to the rear, as well as in direct support, of the ground forces.

I have been told that there is quite a drive on in the Army, headed by Mark Clark, to attempt to secure for the Army its own tactical support air force, and one of the proponents of this out here is (as I was told by the Air Force member of the Army Field Forces Evaluation Board that recently visited this theater) Major General E. M. Almond. General Almond has boldly stated that he does not like the "cooperation type support" that has been agreed upon by the Army and the Air Force, but wants the Army to secure its own similar to the Marine "packaged type of support."

If you will remember, we discussed this while you were here and both agreed that it would certainly be a backward step - besides being uneconomical - at a time when our government is spending all it can for defense - to set up for all divisions in the Army packaged type close support. General Almond has made such statements even though he has never operated as a commander with the United States Air Force giving him close air support. The other commanders out here, as you know, who have received our close air support, have nothing but praise for the effort we give them. As I see your job, you need not mention names, but can surely point out the fallacy of the Army attempting to further divide the air effort of this country. (Frankly, I think we even made a mistake when we gave them their liaison planes and artillery spotting planes.)

I had the great pleasure yesterday of pinning the Distinguished Service Cross on Earle Partridge. I flew over to Taegu in a two-place F–80 [T–33], made the presentation, and returned to my headquarters - flying time over and back about three hours and five minutes!

Annalee and I send love to you and Ruth and hope your fishing trip to the Northwest and your trip home were pleasant ones.

Bucked the following letter received from Admiral Joy to my PIO who in turn was instructed to file it with my "special" file in Toro's office:

Ltr from Joy, dtd 7 Oct:

Your letter of 6 Oct 50, expressing distress concerning an enclosed clipping of Drew Pearson's article is acknowledged. Your thoughtfulness in bringing this article to my attention and your reassurance that your forces have continuing and complete confidence in naval forces is appreciated.

In turn, I should like to state that we do not attach much importance to such articles. We recognize that malicious and exaggerated articles will, at times, appear regardless of the steps taken to prevent them and regardless of the actual conditions.

The Navy has had and will continue to have great respect for the integrity of the AF. We have a high regard for the ability and the effectiveness of AF units. Newspaper articles will not shake confidence built on the experience of our two services working together. The foundation of mutual respect and mutual confidence between our services is not susceptible to deterioration by outside comments.

Among sincere people who are attempting to solve complex and intricate problems, there will always be differences in viewpoints and differences of opinions. Without such differences among qualified personnel, there is no progress. An alert, virile organization has a wide range of opinions within itself. This is a normal healthy condition. It is regrettable that these sincere differences are sometimes exaggerated and distorted. As time goes on, and the people who do distort views realize that that distortion has no effect on the cordial relationships between our services, we expect the distortions to be gradually reduced and finally disappear.

I am positive that the excellent relationships existing between ourselves, our staff and our services will continue to get even better.

Sent a letter to Chennault, in reply to his, re the ability of his CATS people to "deliver the goods." Told him that their help has been of assistance in seeing us through the tough spots, but that they had over-estimated their abilities such as promising a number of aircraft and being able to produce a fewer number than they had committed themselves to.

> *Sent a T.S. message to Partridge which contained 2 subjects:*

(1) My alarm about inadvertently bombing with the '29s UN POW camps that might be in barracks areas or training areas and have directed that no more such targets be bombed.[53] I am wondering if Capt. Nichols through his sources could secure any info on UN POW locations.

(2) Informed Partridge that he was authorized to continue with ROK divisions north MacArthur line (Sinanju - Yŏngwŏn - Hamhŭng) your ground control parties. Walker has been informed by CINCFE that KMAG officers can also continue with ROK divisions. (Bucked this signal with its two subjects to Weyland, Crabb, and Banfill - and to TS Office for file - for their info.)

MONDAY
9 OCTOBER
1950

Got my weekly letter off to Gill Robb Wilson. Enclosed with the letter was the clipping from the S&S [*Stars and Stripes*], 8 October, re Partridge's DSC award (also sent this clipping to Hugh Baillie, Toohey Spaatz and Vandenberg), the complete FEAF news release on this award, and also the FEAF story on the air evacuation of wounded.

Immediately when I got into the office this AM received the "flash" radio from Partridge which states that pilot reports indicate flight F–80s this afternoon strafed airfield northeast Korea containing about 20 P–39 or P–63 type aircraft. Mission directed to sweep Ch'ŏngjin 4146, 12948. Interrogation of pilots will be carried out this headquarters and further details supplied soon as possible.

Mr. Tsufa Lee, accompanied by his friend Mrs. K. K. Chai, called and we reminisced for quite a period.[54] He indicated that on his next trip to Tokyo, he would bring his wife, Eta. He has just returned from one month's activities in the United States, working with his company.

TUESDAY
10 OCTOBER
1950

Sent Vandenberg following redline after receiving several Stratlines from Partridge re the sweep of the F–80 pilots of an airfield upon discovering about 20 P–39 or P–63 type aircraft thereon:

Possibility two F–80 violated USSR border afternoon of 8 Oct 50 on mission to sweep Ch'ŏngjin airfield. On letting down through low overcast discovered sod field with about 20 P–39 type aircraft and destroyed one, damaged one or more. From pilot's description of landmarks and terrain possible airfield is in Rashin area. B–26 reconnaissance mission 9 October not successful and will be repeated today with F–80 pilots aboard. Will forward you further details as received.

---

53. By now, General O'Donnell's Bomber Command was having difficulty in finding profitable targets for the B–29 groups. In searching for likely targets, several North Korean replacement training centers (which had been identified during POW interrogations) were considered to offer possibilities for the B–29s. After attacks on four of these centers, FEAF received information that some of these training camps were also holding U.N. prisoners of war. To be on the safe side, Stratemeyer ordered no more attacks on these targets. (Futrell, pp 205-206.)

54. These individuals are unidentified.

My radio (stratline) to Partridge:

Soviet Government according to Moscow radio has protested to the U.S. violation of Soviet frontier by U.S. airplanes. The note charges that two American F–80s attacked and fired upon a Soviet airdrome one hundred kilometers within Korean-Soviet border located on seacoast in Sukhaya Rechka area. Incident is said to have taken place 4:17 P.M., 8 October local Soviet time.

This to my mind confirms the violation of the Soviet border by your F–80 fighters as recently reported by you on 8 Oct as having possibly taken place.

General MacArthur and I are most unhappy about this violation. It shows a disregard for orders issued by you and me as well as from your organization commanders. At such a time near the end of the Korean war, you and your people must repeat must be sure of your targets and not permit such exhibition of haphazard navigation and disregard for instructions issued. To be over 100 miles off in navigation is inexcusable.

A thorough and complete investigation of this incident will be made without delay and submitted direct to me.

(Had copy made of the signal to Vandenberg and sent it to General MacArthur.)

Attended the "double ten" party at the Chinese Mission with Annalee and then we went on to dinner with Sir Alvary and Lady Gascoigne, their residence, British Embassy, at which they were honoring Under Secretary for Air, A. M. Crawley and General Harding, Commander Ground Troops, Far East (British).[55]

WEDNESDAY 11 OCTOBER 1950

Reached the office this AM and waiting for me were the following redlines from Vandenberg:

(1) from Norstad, TS 4840; "reference reported violation of USSR border. Report of your investigation, including your judgment as to whether the attack was actually made, is required here not later than 1400/Z (0900 local), 11 October."

(2) The redline from Vandenberg, strongly worded (which I fully expected) asked that I ascertain and name of the responsible commander of the pilots who violated the USSR border and relieve him from duty within 48 hours.

The first radio I turned over to Picher for reply.

Sent a redline to Vandenberg telling him that Major General Glenn O. Barcus[56] and his group arrived (last evening, 10 October) and "reported to me this morning. They will be given all-out assistance. Col Sykes has been assigned to the Barcus group for duty while they are here."[57]

---

55. Journalist, film producer and flier, Alden Merivale Crawley (in addition to being the Parliamentary Under Secretary of State for Air) was a Member of Parliament for the Buckingham Division of Buckinghamshire. Lieutenant General Sir John Harding was the commander-in-chief of the British Far East Land Forces. Later, he became Chief of the Imperial General Staff.

56. Barcus, after earlier fighter and air defense commands during World War II, became the commander of the XII Tactical Air Command in February 1945. He became Commanding General, Tactical Air Command in July 1950.

57. Although Colonel Sykes had come to the Far East in August to analyze the Korean air war, General Vandenberg

Issued instructions assigning Col Sykes to Barcus group - copies to General Barcus, General Nuckols, and Col MacNaughton[58] (Historical), and of course to Col Sykes.

Finally received a newsy letter from Weikert[59] and among other items he wrote about was the fact that the Navy was getting the preponderance of publicity in the Washington papers and passed along the info (which I've been aware of for months) that Admiral Sherman on his trip out here was dissatisfied with the publicity the Navy was getting, assigned three top-notch Navy colonels [captains] to step it up. Sent P.D. the mimeographed gist of my press briefing, complete with charts to help in backing up his arguments.

The RAF Under Secretary of State for Air A. M. Crawley was my guest at our briefing.

Barcus reported in at 0930; assigned him the office next to mine - Room 210.

1030 hours, Lou Pick[60] called on me.

Left the office for lunch at the American Embassy. MacArthurs honored General Sir John Harding and Under Secretary of State for Air Crawley.

A pair of 49th FBG F–80s await takeoff on another mission while a C–119 lands.

Immediately after the luncheon, the Under Secretary of State for Air Crawley and I departed for Haneda where we boarded the C–54 and flew to Iwakuni. Mr. Crawley was most appreciative of my trip to Iwakuni with him. While there I made an award of the Air Medal to a young RAAF flyer - Flight Lieutenant Pritty.[61] This award was made for his volunteering to fly as navigator with the 3d Bomb Group. He flew seven (7) missions to Korea, nearly all of which were night intruder missions and on the last mission the aircraft was forced down on

---

desired a broader and larger evaluation of this topic for use in future planning. He sent General Barcus and a team of senior officers to Tokyo to undertake this project. The Barcus group remained in the theater until the end of the year. Their report, titled "An Evaluation of the Effectiveness of United States Air Force in Korea," became more popularly known as the Barcus Report. The final report, in seven volumes with numerous appendices, was issued on March 12, 1951.

58. Probably Lt Col F.H. MacNaughton from the FEAF History Office.

59. Brig Gen John M. Weikert had been FEAF vice commander until June 8 and was now Deputy Commandant, Administration, National War College. His nickname was "P.D." for Pennsylvania Dutch.

60. It is unknown if Stratemeyer is referring to General "Lew" Pick, the Army's Chief of Engineers or some other individual.

61. Flt Lt W. I. Pritty.

the beach about 70 miles behind enemy lines; however, he was rescued by Air-Sea Rescue along with the entire crew.

I like Under Secretary of State for Air A. M. Crawley.

**THURSDAY
12 OCTOBER
1950**

Sent a redline TS to Vandenberg as per his deadline instructions:

Reurad TS 4837 Colonel Stanton T. Smith, Jr., has today been relieved of command of 49th Fighter Bomber Group based at Taegu, Korea, and the two pilots who made the attack will be tried by court martial. My investigation report will follow soonest by T.S. radio.

My stratline to CG Fifth or VC Fifth:

You are directed to try by court martial 1st Lt. Alton H. Quanbeck and 1st Lt. Allen J. Diefendorf for the violation of the Soviet border on 8 October 50.

I called attention of the Barcus group to my radnote to COMNAVFE pointing out that the ten (10) Marine C–54s should be made a part of the Combat Cargo Command.

Took over to CINCFE my formal report on the Violation of Soviet Border incident. Report is as follows:

I. FACTS:
(1) On 3 Jul, 14 Aug, 2 Sept, and 26 Sept radios were sent to my major commanders emphasizing the importance of not violating the Manchurian or Soviet borders. In the radio of 26 Sept 50, I repeated that crews operating near the North Korean border be specifically briefed on this point and set a line from P'yŏngyang to Wŏnsan north of which no airplane would attack if it could not positively determine its position. *(2)* Fifth Air Force Operations Order 100-50 directed the 6149th Tactical Support Wing located at K-2 airfield at Taegu, Korea, to dispatch a four-ship flight to sweep Ch'ŏngjin airfield on 8 October 50 with take-off time 1500 Item. *(3)* The flight was composed of: 1st Lt. Norvin Evans, Jr., Flight Leader; 1st Lt. Alton H. Quanbeck, 1st Lt. Allen J. Diefendorf, 2d Lt. Billy B. Watson. These officers are all assigned to the 49th Fighter Bomber Group, flying F–80C aircraft, located at Taegu. *(4)* The flight was specifically briefed at 1300 I, 8 October 50, to stay clear of Manchurian and Soviet borders. The target folder included the location of the airfield with respect to the city of Ch'ŏngjin and reports of previous strikes. No target photographs were available. *(5)* Based on available data on winds aloft, the flight commander computed time to the target as one hour and five minutes. This flight plan was followed. *(6)* Lt. Watson aborted prior to take-off due to engine trouble. The flight leader, Lt. Evans, aborted 40 minutes after take-off because of engine trouble and turned command of the flight over to Lt. Quanbeck. Lt. Quanbeck and Lt. Diefendorf continued climbing on a magnetic heading of 05 degrees through broken clouds to 35,000 feet and continued above an overcast. After one hour and

five minutes, they let down into a valley, under broken clouds one to two thousand feet above sea level, then followed a dry stream bed two or three minutes to the coast. The flight leader identified his position to his own satisfaction as being northwest of Ch'ŏngjin, turned southeast between the coast, road and railroad to a 3500-foot sod field occupied by about twenty (20) P–39 type aircraft marked with red stars with white edges. These were attacked in three strafing passes each, destroying one and damaging one or more. After strafing, the flight commander noted terrain features did not agree with the landmarks on his map. On the return to base, time in climb and cruise consumed 50 minutes, at which time the Taegu radio homer was picked up far to the west. After turning to the homer course of 265 degrees, Taegu was reached after 45 minutes flying. This position far to the east of Taegu was also an indication to the pilots that they had attacked the wrong target.

II. CONCLUSIONS:

(1) That an attack was made by two F–80C aircraft at about 1520 Item 8 October 1950, on Soviet aircraft on an airfield in the vicinity of Sukhaya Rechka, USSR. *(2)* That the pilots had been briefed on the importance of not violating the Manchurian or Soviet border. *(3)* That the winds at altitude were not as forecast. *(4)* That the attack was the result of pilot error and poor judgment, in that it was made without positive identification of the target.

III. ACTION TAKEN:

Above information has been radioed "personal for General Vandenberg" per his radio direction.

Sent the above in toto to General Vandenberg with exception of Par. 3, Part III, which read: Above information has been furnished CINCFE this date.

General MacArthur's reaction to my memo, reference the violation of the Soviet border was good. He asked what would happen to Colonel Smith and I told him that I intended to leave that up to General Partridge; however, he was one of the best and most outstanding commanders that we had. CINCFE then asked if the info had been sent to CSAF and I said that it was in the process of being sent at that time. His first reaction was only to punish the pilots by disciplinary action under the 104th Article of War.[62] I told him, "General, you just can't do that in this case." He finally agreed and then asked what did I think the court will do to them. I told him that I thought they'd fine the flight leader and the number two man would probably get off with an admonition. His remark then was, "Very good, Strat, and thanks."[63]

---

62. The Article 104 that MacArthur refers to concerns the powers of commanding officers to impose disciplinary punishment upon members of their commands for minor offenses without having to hold a court martial as prescribed in the 1949 edition of the *Manual for Courts-Martial*, also known as the Articles of War. These articles were revised and reissued in May 1951 as the Uniform Code of Military Justice (UCMJ). Under this revised Code, Article 104 became Article 15.

63. In 1990, both Quanbeck and Diefendorf recounted this incident, Quanbeck in an article in the *Washington Post* ("My Brief War With Russia," *Washington Post*, Mar 4, 1990) and Diefendorf in a magazine article (Daniel Bauer, "The Pilots That Nearly Started World War Three," *Air Classics*, April 1990, pp 28-41).

Weyland this date sent General Hickey, the acting chief of staff, GHQ, UNC, the following memorandum:

Annex F to OPERATIONS ORDER NO. 2, GHQ, UNC, dated 2 October 1950, [concerning the Wŏnsan operation] reads in part as follows: "2. Appendix 1, herewith, delineates the Initial Objective Area. Within this area COMNAVFE, through appropriate commanders and agencies, control all air operations, including air defense and close support of troops from 0600 D-5 until relieved by orders of CINCUNC, at which time CG FEAF assumes operational control of all land-based aircraft in accordance with CINCFE Letter Directive of 8 July 1950, subject: 'Coordination of Air Effort of FEAF and NAVFE'." II CINCFE outgoing message, CX 66169, dated 111135 October 1950, reads in part as follows: "Part 1. (2) Wŏnsan Airfield will be utilized for land-based aircraft under control of Tactical Air Commander, X Corps, effective on arrival elements of X Corps in the Objective Area.' III. The quoted reference in paragraph 2 above appears to be in conflict with the quoted reference in paragraph 1. IV. For clarification and for planning purposes, information is requested as to whether it is intended: *a.* That control of land-based Marine air units at K-25, Wŏnsan, pass from COMNAVFE to CG FEAF, or *b.* That two separate land-based tactical air elements are to operate in the constricted area of North Korea under separate air control and different command arrangements.

FRIDAY 13 OCTOBER 1950

Copy of CINCFE's signal to the Joint Chiefs of Staff re the Soviet border incident reached my desk this morning. I note that he paraphrased my memo to him and included the statement that he approved my conclusions and actions.

Got off a courier personal (TS) message to Rosie O'Donnell:

The recent violation of the Soviet border by our fighters has resulted in my having to direct the relief of one of the best fighter group commanders I have from command of his group, and the court martial of the officers who made the attack. When the report of investigation is released to the United Nations, which will reduce the information from its present Top Secret classification, I desire that you apprise all your group commanders of the action taken and warn them again that any further violations will result in action equally as drastic.

Sent the following letter to Earle Partridge calling his attention to:

the two instances that Fifth Air Force aircraft have violated the Manchurian and Soviet borders have one thing in common - in each case both the flight leader and deputy leader aborted, and command of the flight was turned over to a wing man in the air. This suggests that the more lowly members of the flight are merely attending the briefing and

---

Following this incident, Quanbeck became Brig Gen Delmar T. Spivey's aide-de-camp. After 22 years in the USAF, he worked for the Brookings Institution, the Senate Intelligence Committee, and the CIA. Although through flying in Korea, Diefendorf went on to fly 142 missions in an F–4 during the Vietnam War, and eventually retired as a colonel.

not being impressed with their responsibility in case the flight leader aborts. I suggest that the briefing officers focus the attention of the wing men on this responsibility in that the flight leader job could fall on them with startling suddenness.

Received information copy of radnote from Marine Air Wing 1, to Marine Air Transport Sqdn, VMR 152:

Advance echelon VMR-152 with 10 R5D aircraft assigned now TAD 1st MARAIRWING from Pearl. Colonel Dean C. Roberts command. Report to CG FEAF Combat Cargo Command for operational control.

Sent the following note to Follett Bradley[64] complete with editorials clipping from the N.Y. Times:

Dear Follett - The *New York Times* <u>B. S.</u> [emphasis in original] This paper to my mind is just plain anti-Air Force. Not a word except where underlined about the great part air power played in the turning of the tide in Korea. I took the *N. Y. Times* for years, but I am through now. Damn their souls and hides - and if you see Sulzberger[65] you can pass this on for me. G.E.S.

Right after the briefing, General Robertson made presentation of the Australian flag to me; the reason, the 77th Royal Australian Air Force Fighter Squadron operates under FEAF control; therefore, I am authorized to fly the Australian flag. It is my understanding that this is my personal property.

Weyland came out to the house for Mexican food with us. I ate too much.

**SATURDAY
14 OCTOBER
1950**
Besides the principal lesson learned not to draw wrong conclusions from Korean War because of absence of aggressive hostile air, main two lessons relating to the tactical war learned thus far to my mind are: *(1)* We must develop equipment and tactics to seek out, see, and attack hostile ground equipment and troops at night; *(2)* necessity for development of good night photography.

Received the following signal for Admiral Joy which I had bucked to FEAF Combat Cargo Command:

Joy to Stratemeyer. The op control of the Marine transports was resolved to the satisfaction of your deputy Major General Craigie and my chief of staff prior to receipt your Cite A 21868. CG 1st MAW disp[atch] DTG [date-time group] 120620A which you have an info copy of refers: the Marine transports have been loaned to NAVFE for a brief period at the expense of TRANSPAC airlift and I expect to release at least five of them to return Pearl by D plus 10. I am confident that present arrangement will insure the best interests of the Marines and Cargo Command. Be assured that the airlift provided by the Cargo Command for the Marines at Kimp'o has been the subject for much praise from those who know.

---

64. Bradley, a retired USAAF major general, had been the assistant to the president of the Sperry Gyroscope Co. since 1944.
65. Arthur Hays Sulzberger, president and publisher of the *New York Times*.

Sent the following to O'Donnell:

See by summary of 13 October missions that B–29s bombed at 16 different bridges with possible damage to 2 bridges and missing the others. This appears to be below standards you had set earlier. I realize that there is a lack of interesting targets, however, the war is not over and I hope that interest in BOMCOM does not lag to the extent that the outstanding precision and capabilities of your individual crews retrogresses.

SUNDAY 15 OCTOBER 1950

Hugh Baillie sent me a formal "thank you" to which I replied, as well as sending me an "informal" thank you letter. Had copies made of his formal letter and bucked it to Vandenberg, Partridge and Tunner, as well as sending copies to Toohey Spaatz, with appropriate remarks to each.

Left the office early in order to be at hand when CINCFE lands at Haneda upon his return from a conference with the President.[66] He landed at 1600 hours.

MONDAY 16 OCTOBER 1950

1100 hours - Bell representatives Charles Barr and Charles H. Schmidt called at the office.

Colonel Harold R. Maddux,[67] officer-in-charge of the Bob Hope troupe, came in and discussed with me the Howard Hughes movie that is being made on the Korean war indicating the part played by USAF.[68] I told Colonel Maddux I would be delighted to have Mr. Hope to dinner and would also arrange a golf game for him if he so desired.

General Nuckols and Colonel Sykes read the Howard Hughes movie script in order to offer practical suggestions.

At 1600 hours, made the presentation of the Commendation Ribbon to: 1st Lt. William T. Wilkinson, 1st Lt. Claude D. Lamb, T/Sgt. Vincent W. Hesler, and Staff Sergeant Jimmie J. Stanley.

At 1630 Wing Commander Johnny Johnson[69] reported in as Marshal of the Royal Air Force, Sir John Slessor's representative to look us over, etc.

---

66. The highly-publicized first-ever meeting of Truman and MacArthur took place on tiny Wake Island this day, MacArthur having left Japan the day before. What this meeting was actually supposed to accomplish is still subject to interpretation. Some historians, including the iconoclastic I.F. Stone and John W. Spanier, believe the meeting was in response to the October 8 attack on the Vladivostok airfield. (See their reasoning in I.F. Stone, *The Hidden History of the Korean War*, [New York, 1952], p 150, and John W. Spanier, *The Truman-MacArthur Controversy and the Korean War*, [New York, 1965 ed.], pp 111-112.) Truman later claimed that it was held to discuss policy and improve his somewhat shaky relations with MacArthur; others said it was just a public relations ploy, mainly on the President's part, though MacArthur was never one to turn down an opportunity in the public relations field.
   What this meeting was not was a serious, organized review of Korean and Far Eastern policy. The discussions, which lasted less than two hours on the 15th, were generally shallow and often digressed into matters far afield of Korea. Though MacArthur, for once, did not orate at length, his various statements at the meeting still added up to more conversation than the other eight people at the conference combined! One of his comments, that there was little chance that the Soviets or Chinese would interfere in Korea, gave his detractors much ammunition later as MacArthur's star began to wane. It should be noted, however, that virtually all of the U.S. intelligence agencies made the same assumption. (See James, pp 500-517, for a good short summary of this meeting; also see "History of the JCS," Vol. III, pp 263-270, 285-286.)
67. Maddux was Secretary of the Air Staff. Bob Hope was touring the Far East at the time for the USO.
68. This movie became the terrible John Wayne/Janet Leigh potboiler, "Jet Pilot." Although made in 1951, it was not released until 1957.
69. A 38-victory "ace" in World War II, Johnson was in Korea observing FEAF operations for the RAF.

General Hickey, this date, sent Weyland the below quoted memo which is answering Weyland's memo to him of 12 October. Hickey also enclosed a copy of a signal which is included in the below quoted material:

1. Reference is made to your memorandum of 12 October 1950 [about the border violation], copy attached. (Incl 1). *2.* It is believed that CINCFE message dispatched this date, copy attached (Incl 2), clarifies the matter concerned and is sufficient for planning purposes. *3.* No conflict exists if phases are considered in proper sequence.

Inclosure #1 see my diary item under date of 12 October).

Inclosure #2: "From CINCFE; To FEAF & COMNAVFE; Info CG 8th Army, Korea; CG X Corps, Korea; CG 5th AF Korea; Com 7th Fleet at Sea; CG BOMCOM Yokota; COMPHIBGRUF 1 at Sea. Msg dated 16 October; No. CX 66578.

"Message in 3 parts.

"Reference *a.* Annex F. Operations Order No. 2, UNC, 2 October 1950.

"*b.* CINCFE Letter Directive, 8 July 1950, subject: Coordination of Air Effort of FEAF and NAVFE.

"*c.* CINCFE Message CX 66169, 11 October 1950.

"*Part 1.* The objective area delineated in Appendix 1, Annex F to Operations Order No. 2, UNC, 2 October 1950 is disestablished effective with the passage of leading elements X Corps beyond the outer limit so prescribed. CG X Corps will report such passsage immediately when executed to CINCUNC, info to CG FEAF and COMNAVFE.

"*Part 2.* Effective with the disestablishment of the objective area, the operational control of all land based aircraft will be effected by CG FEAF through appropriate commanders and agencies. Concurrently CG FEAF will exercise coordination control of carrier based aircraft operating in Korea.

"*Part 3.* In the exercise of his control and coordinating functions, CG FEAF will assure that elements of the Fleet Marine Air Wing remain in support of X Corps units."

TUESDAY 17 OCTOBER 1950

General Kuter reported in this morning. Got off my weekly letter to Gill Robb Wilson - enclosed a press release as well as five photographs showing graphically the damage done by FEAF in North Korea on targets.

Presented Wing Commander J. E. Johnson with the following letter of introduction and sent copies of introduction to Partridge, O'Donnell, Tunner, and Doyle for their advance info.

This will introduce Wing Commander J. E. Johnson who will be in the Far East until the first week in December and who is out here at my invitation per request from Marshal of the Royal Air Force Sir John C. Slessor (Chief of Staff of the Royal Air Force).

Sir John indicated, with my permission, that he desired to send a representative out here to look us over in order that they might profit by any of the lessons we have learned and naturally I agreed.

It is desired that you extend all possible courtesies to Wing Commander Johnson, including classified material and the introduction to members of your staffs.

Dispatched a "confidential" letter to Vandenberg (copy sent to Toohey Spaatz - also bucked a copy to Sykes for his info and return to me) as follows:

Wing Commander J. E. Johnson has just reported in to Far East Air Forces Headquarters to look into the activities of the United States Air Force in the Korean war. As you know, he is on duty with Tactical Air Command Headquarters at Langley Air Force Base, Virginia.

In a conversation I had with Wing Commander Johnson yesterday afternoon, he indicated that General Mark Clark, head of the Army Field Forces, came right out in black and white, in a paper that Johnson has seen, advocating that the Army take over control of tactical air. The Royal Air Force went through something quite similar to this after the First World War and had it not been for the magnificent work of Marshal of the Royal Air Force Viscount Trenchard (Ret), the Royal Air Force would not have become the strong bulwark force which it proved itself to be in 1940-41. Again, following World War II, the Royal Air Force, by virtue of the efforts of Marshal of the Royal Air Force, The Lord Tedder, was able to retain its tactical air in spite of Montgomery's efforts to the contrary.

I have just learned that The Lord Tedder is now on duty with the British Mission in Washington, D. C. It occurs to me that it might be possible to arrange to have him testify before Carl Vinson's House Armed Services Committee. If he could be persuaded to do so, I believe it might help our cause.

I am worried, as I'm sure you are, Van, by the efforts of the Army, headed by Mark Clark, to secure tactical air. It is my impression that this is contrary to the opinions and ideas held by Generals Eisenhower and Collins, and I'm surprised that Collins has not come out strongly and opposed Mark Clark's behind-the-scene activities.

Colonel Harold R. Maddux, who is escorting the Bob Hope troupe, reported to me this morning, and he has very thoroughly covered with us the contemplated movie by Howard Hughes and the reason therefor. I can assure you that we will lend Maddux and everyone concerned with this film all possible aid. Nuckols and Sykes at this writing are carefully going over the script and any other individual who can be of assistance in this preliminary work will be made available.

As I've said many times to you, and every top Army man over here will back me up, if it hadn't been for your Far East Air Forces out here, there wouldn't be a white man in Korea today.

Best regards.

O.K'd Fogarty's itinerary and sent copies of same to both Partridge and O'Donnell requesting that each prepare a briefing in their war rooms at Fogarty's visit to their Hqs.

Sent a radnote [radio note] to LeMay strongly urging that O'Donnell remain in this theater until the show is over to complete important reports and "also to receive what glory due him for a job well done."

Following is my TS redline to Vandenberg:

General Barcus and members of his air evaluation board have arrived and with assistance from FEAF agencies is organizing to carry out General Norstad's letter directive. Individual orders of General Barcus and board members from ZI call for TDY not to exceed 60 days. In my view this board should carry on its work to final conclusions and it is very questionable whether this can be accomplished within a 60-day period. Recommend that orders for General Barcus and his board members be amended to direct this TDY with Hq FEAF until completion of project. See Par 4F of Barcus' letter directive dated 5 Oct 50. Barcus or individual board members could return your hq temporarily to render interim reports if so instructed by you.

Stearley arrived Haneda about 1300 hours.

1530 hours, Mr. Charles Corddry, United Press, attached to Fifth Air Force, came in with Bill Nuckols. I thanked Corddry again for the beautiful release he had written on Earle Partridge's receiving the Distinguished Service Medal.

Before leaving the office signed and dispatched the following memorandum to CINCFE, subject: Destruction of Sinŭiju:

1. It is requested that I be authorized to conduct an air attack on the city of Sinŭiju with all available air means at the earliest practicable date on which the attack can be launched under visual flying conditions. The types of attack recommended are listed in order of priority, as follows: *(a)* An attack over the widest area of the city, without warning, by burning and high explosive. *(b)* An attack over the entire city, after warning, by burning and high explosive. *(c)* An attack against military targets within the city limits, with high explosive, without warning. *(d)* An attack against military targets in the city, with high explosive, with warning.
2. Specific reasons favoring an attack on this city are: *(a)* This city will provide a foothold on Korean soil from which the North Koreans can maintain a government in existence, and would provide a certain validity to claims of legitimacy. This would lend stature in international discussion and provide a sounder position than if it were a refugee government on foreign soil. *(b)* This city, with considerable industrial activity and an estimate population of over 60,000 is a provincial capital and has the capability of becoming the capital of North Korea when P'yŏngyang is evacuated. Usually reliable sources have already indicated that this transfer is under way. *(c)* It is a rail exchange point between Korea and Manchuria and rolling stock can be passed back and forth since the gauge of the rails are the same on both sides of the river. *(d)* It is believed that the psychological effect of a mass attack will be salutary to Chinese Communist observers across the river in Antung.

(e) The city has a considerable industrial capacity which will provide some means of supporting a North Korean government unless destroyed.

3. I have no mental reservations as to the ability of the Far East Air Forces to carry out this attack without violating Manchurian territory. I propose, if the recommendation for an attack is approved, that it be carried out under the on-the-spot supervision of a general officer and the actual attack made only upon his order.   G.E.S.

WEDNESDAY
18 OCTOBER
1950

1100 hours Drs. Futrell and Simpson,[70] historians, checked in at the office with Colonel Corr.

At my request, General Craigie discussed with General Hickey and recommended to him that the recent comments on FEOP-1-50 made by CSAF, CSUSA, and CNO be transmitted officially to my hq for comment. General Hickey agreed to this request and thereby proved himself to be a real Chief of Staff.

I directed Craigie to take this action because I had learned unofficially from my plans section that the Chief of JSPOG contemplated obtaining the Air Force point of view by unofficial contact only and did not contemplate giving us access to the comments of CSUSA and CNO.

GHQ returned my memorandum of yesterday, subject: Destruction of Sinŭiju as follows in 1st Indorsement, dtd 17 Oct, AG 373 (17 Oct 50)-CS: "The general policy enunciated from Washington negates such an attack unless the military situation clearly requires it. Under present circumstances this is not the case."

Quoted in toto is my radnote to COMNAVFE & CG FAF, with info copies to all concerned:

VC 0387: *Part 1.* Upon disestablishment of Wŏnsan objective area, con[trol] of all land based air in Korea again reverts to CG FEAF. In addition, under provisions of CINCFE ltr dir, 8 Jul 50, subj: "Coordination of Air Effort of FEAF & COMNAVFE," and *Part 2* to CINCFE msg CX 66578, FEAF is charged w[with] coordination con[trol] of carrier based air activities in Korea. To provide basis for FEAF and COMNAVFE coordination and planning, the folg [following] measure for combined air effort are proposed eff[ective] upon disestablishment of objective area: *A.* 5th AF w/opnl con of all land based air in Korea supports UN ground forces. *B.* Close air support of EUSAK primary responsibility of assigned 5th AF units. *C.* Close air support of X Corps primary mission of elements of 1st Marine Air Wing based at Wŏnsan. *D.* Carrier based Marine aircraft, when available, to support 5th AF opns in Korea, normally in close air support X Corps elements under im[mediate] tac[tical] direction MAW TACG. *E.* 5th AF provide or arrange for such additional air support as is required by X Corps.

F. Navy acft provide close support as requested by CG 5th AF in Korea. *G.* Navy aircraft assume primary responsibility for airfield sweeps and rail and highway interdiction to the north of bomb line in area east of 127 degrees. FEAF interdiction opns, chiefly by med bombers in this area,

---

70. Robert F. Futrell was then a USAF historian working in the Pacific, and Albert F. Simpson was the Air Force Historian. Futrell later wrote the definitive history of the Air Force in Korea.

General Stratemeyer presents the United Nations flag to Brig. Gen. Delmar T. Spivey, Vice Commander, Fifth Air Force.

will cont. *H.* FEAF assume primary responsibilities for airfield sweeps and rail and highway interdiction north of bomb line and in area west of 127 degrees. *I.* No area restrictions imposed on opns north of the bomb line on the part of either land based or carrier based aircraft. However, primary responsibility for interdiction and airfield sweeps be as directed in pars G and H above . *Part II.* Rapid and eff comms [communications] should be established between elements of 5th AF and the Navy to provide continuous coordination of each day's opns. Overall coordination of air activities will be effected by daily exchange of plans at COMNAVFE and Hq FEAF level.

At 1630, presented the UN Flag to General Spivey.

At 1700, presented at the hospital the Distinguished Flying Cross to Flight Nurse Lt Jenita Bonham[71] who had been seriously injured a few weeks back in a C–54 crash.

Conferred with General MacArthur at 1345, re proposed airdrop that has not been decided upon for 20 October. Story returned to the office with me.

Prepared the following memo for him:

The information desired regarding your time of take off is as given in following quoted telecon note: "CG 180641/Z, File Time 180642/Z, from CG FEAF COMCAR COMD, Kyushu, Japan to CG FEAF (Gen Stratemeyer): TOP SECRET, Ref Gen Crabb telephone. First take off 0610/I; first jump

---

71. 1st Lt Bonham was awarded the DFC for helping, although injured herself, rescue passengers from a plane that went down at sea.

0800/I; last jump at 0900/I; weather permitting. Altitude 800 to 1,000 feet." It is desired that you give this information to General MacArthur.

Brigadier General Courtney Whitney, Chief of SCAP Government Section, called at the office. We discussed my awarding to General MacArthur the Distinguished Flying Cross. Sent Craigie instructions to draft for me, for my OK - or my corrections, the citation, that is to be in my hands by 1200 hours, 19 Oct, so that it may be in final form and that I can take it with me when I depart the office tomorrow at 1800 hours. The citation will be based on the following flights made by CINCFE into Korea to the following places on the following dates:

SUWŎN- 29 June - at which time his airplane was subject to interception by hostile aircraft, a C–54 having been destroyed by enemy aircraft just prior to his landing, and, while at Suwŏn, at least four dog fights between North Korean airplanes and USAF airplanes took place. *TAEGU* - 27 July - at which time the ground situation was in a most precarious situation - in fact, the enemy was only some fifteen miles away from Taegu; his airplane was subject to hostile air interception throughout the time he left the Japanese islands to Taegu and return. *KIMP'O* - 29 September - at which time he landed at this airstrip while it was still subject to hostile ground fire and possible air interception. *SUKCH'ŎN-SUNCH'ŎN* - 20 October - where he personally witnessed the para-drop of the 187th Airborne Brigade at which time he was again subject to air interception as enemy airplanes were known to be based at the airdrome at Sinŭiju. For a General of the Army, who occupies such extremely important positions as the Commander of all United Nations Forces, the Supreme Commander of the Allied Powers, the Commander-in-Chief, Far East, and Commanding General of the United States Army Forces to display the type of leadership and courage he has shown, and his understanding of all three of the Services is of such an outstanding character - that the Far East Air Forces takes great pride in making this award.

Received the following radnote from Norstad: (This is in reply to my message to CSAF, 17 Oct, re extending the Barcus' group TDY.)

The C/S is away but I am sure that it is his intention to keep Barcus and his party on the job until it is concluded. In setting up this group originally we felt it was desirable for a number of reasons to have it headed by a civilian of considerable stature. Mr. Finletter has been successful in obtaining Mr. Charles E. Wilson[72] of General Electric for this assignment. I do not know how soon he plans to leave, but I will learn tomorrow or Thursday and I will see that you are informed. A proposal that will be put up to him will be along the general lines of Barcus and his party being the operating agency under his general policy guidance and that he and Barcus would work out the broad conclusions. The Secretary presented it to Mr. Wilson on the basis of spending 6 weeks or 2 months in the theater now to get the program laid out and the work under way and then return

---

72. Wilson, the president of the General Electric Co., became Director, Office of Defense Mobilization in December 1950. He was known as "Electric Charlie" to differentiate him from Charles E. Wilson ("Engine Charlie") of General Motors, who became Secretary of Defense in 1953.

to the United States if necessary. The work of the evaluation board could either be presented to him by Barcus on his return here or Mr. Wilson might rather return to the theater some time after the first of the year when the work is nearing completion. This is general information for your guidance only at this time. You will be notified officially as soon as the project if firmed up.

Annalee and I had General Kuter and General Hall and General and Mrs. (MATS) White to dinner at the house. Also Colonel and Mrs. Clyde L. Brothers.

THURSDAY
19 OCTOBER
1950

Received the following radnote from Twining:

In view of concern repeatedly expressed on the highest level over potential effect of a repetition of accidental bombing or strafing north of Korean border, you should make every effort to insure against such a possibility as I am sure you are aware. I have noted your directive to Fifth Air Force, AX 5372 V, 17 Oct, on this matter and it occurs to me similar instructions might be issued to Bomber Command. Furthermore, since the rapid advance of UN forces increases danger of accidental bombing and strafing own forces, I suggest you consider elimination of radar bombing except in emergency and then only under most stringent controls.

In reply, sent Twining following answer:

Standing instructions to BOMCOM are to make no attacks against targets within 50 miles of the Manchurian and USSR borders without specific approval my headquarters. Only objectives remaining for BOMCOM are a very few bridges, and rail and highway cuts which are specified to be bombed visually. No radar targets remain, however, Sonjin [probably Sŏngjin] is last resort target for radar bombing if primary and secondaries are not visual. Greatest care continually exercised to avoid border violations or attacks on friendly troops.

Richard J. Holzworth, the International Field Secretary of the Gideon Society, presents a Bible to General Stratemeyer. Observing the presentation are Col. John C. W. Linsley, the FEAF Chaplain, and Raymond Provost, Jr., a missionary in Korea.

Bucked the following memo to Picher:

It is desired that you and your division, with the assistance of the Deputy for Intelligence, have in mind a packaged form report for my signature to the Chief of Staff, United States Air Force, of all violations of the Manchurian border, the accusations made - and by whom, the actions taken by me to stop such violations, and the reports submitted to me as well as those reports made by me to higher headquarters. I think you should include those newspaper reports made by Red China where we have been accused of flying over the border with the simple statement that "reference these reports, I took no action" - if such was the case. In the above, I am referring to just Far East Air Forces and not to any possible Navy or Marine aviation violations.

At about 1520, a Mr. Holzworth, representative of the Gideon Society dropped by the office to present me with a bible.

The citation for CINCFE approved and corrected by me (let General Whitney read it as well as Col Story - in order to give them a pre-view of same) as follows. Six extra copies were made in order that I can give them to the press members who accompany us on the trip.

GENERAL ORDERS NO. 93, dtd 20 October 1950, AWARD OF THE DISTINGUISHED FLYING CROSS. By direction of the President, under the provisions of the Act of Congress approved 2 July 1926 (WD Bulletin 8, 1926), National Security Act of 1947, Air Force Regulation 30-14, 22 August 1950 and Section VII, GO No. 63, Dept of the Air Force, 1950, the Distinguished Flying Cross for heroism while partici-pating in aerial flight during the period indicated is awarded to General of the Army DOUGLAS MACARTHUR, 057, United States Army.
General MacArthur serving as Commander-in-Chief, Far East, and Com-mander-in-Chief, United Nations Command, distinguished himself by outstanding heroism and extraordinary achievement while participating in aerial flights during the period 29 June to 20 October 1950.
On 29 June General MacArthur made a flight to Suwŏn, Korea, during which his aircraft was subject to effective interception by hostile air action. Another friendly aircraft in the area was attacked and destroyed by enemy air immediately prior to General MacArthur's landing, and the Suwŏn airstrip itself was bombed and strafed during the course of his visit. On 27 July he made a flight to Taegu, Korea, during which his air-craft was again subject to hostile air interception and at which time the ground situation in the immediate area was most precarious. On 29 Sep-tember, General MacArthur made a flight to Kimp'o, Korea, again under conditions presenting the threat of hostile air interception and while the Kimpo airport itself was subject to hostile ground fire. On 20 October he made a flight to the Sukch'ŏn-Sunch'ŏn area of Korea in order to observe and supervise the para-drop of the 187th Airborne Regimental Combat Team. During this entire operation his aircraft was subject to attack by enemy aircraft known to be based at Sinŭiju.
These aerial flights in an unarmed aircraft were made by General

MacArthur in furtherance of his mission as Commander of the United Nations forces in Korea. Each flight involved the risk of death or capture by the enemy. In General MacArthur's case this risk was multiplied a hundred-fold in view of his personal stature and his position as Commander-in-Chief. That General MacArthur unhesitatingly took part in these extraordinarily important and dangerous missions is a further demonstration of the unfaltering devotion to duty which characterizes his every action as a leader. His conduct in these instances has been an outstanding source of inspiration to the men he commands.

Throughout the Korean campaign the strategic concepts underlying General MacArthur's command decisions have reflected a superb understanding of the most advantageous employment of air power and made possible the victory which is being achieved with minimum losses and unprecedented speed. By his heroism and extraordinary achievement, General Douglas MacArthur reflects the highest honor upon himself, the United Nations, and the Armed Forces of the United States.

FRIDAY 20 OCTOBER 1950

Departed Haneda aboard the SCAP with General MacArthur at 3:35 A.M. We proceeded on course and after arriving well into the interior of Korea, received word that Kimp'o airport was closed and that the para-drop had been postponed three hours. We turned around and made a landing at Pusan (K-9). While there I talked with both Generals Partridge and Tunner and found out that because of the weather, the scheduled time of take off for the drop had been postponed six hours. This made the drop at 1400 hours instead of 0800 hours.

We departed K-9 (Pusan) about 1120 hours, flew direct to Kimp'o, where we circled and watched the take-off of many of the '119s, witnessed their assembly and squadron formation and then proceeded direct to the drop zone - Sukch'ŏn-Sunch'ŏn.[73]

We missed the first drop at Sukch'ŏn and then proceeded to Sunch'ŏn and there, in a regular ring-side seat, we witnessed the second drop, saw artillery and mortar shells falling in the area, witnessed both F–80 and F–51 strafing gun positions, destroying enemy troops in the villages and witnessed one F–80 burn and crash in the village due to hostile ground fire.

We then proceeded to Sukch'ŏn and witnessed another drop - this being equipment, again watching the fighters, witnessing the T–6s direct fighter fire as well as observing General Partridge (in a T–6) and General Tunner (in a C–54) witness the drop.

Directly after this we proceeded back to P'yŏngyang, the captured capital of North Korea, and checking with the ground where General Partridge had arrived, landed on the airstrip which had been secured by the 1st Cavalry Division.

---

73. The villages of Sukch'ŏn and Sunch'ŏn were about 30 miles north of P'yŏngyang. MacArthur hoped to trap as many Communist troops as possible and ordered an airborne drop on Oct. 21 for this purpose. The rapid advance to P'yŏngyang and its capture on the 19th forced a change in date to the 20th for the airborne operation. Kimp'o was the staging area for the 187th Airborne RCT and the planes of Combat Cargo Command.
After a delay on the morning of the 20th because of heavy rain at Kimp'o, 71 C–119s (making their first combat paratroop drop appearance) and 40 C–47s delivered 2,860 paratroopers and 301.2 tons of equipment in an afternoon drop. Follow-up drops over the next two days provided another 1,093 troopers and 290.8 tons of supplies. Light to moderate resistance was soon overcome in the two drop zones, and the troopers at Sunch'ŏn were joined a few hours later by men of the ROK 6th Division driving northwest toward the village. Elements of the

Paratroopers of the 187th Airborne RCT pile out of C–119s over the Sunch'ŏn drop zone.

There General MacArthur, General Hickey, General Whitney and myself were greeted by Generals Walker, Partridge, Gay, Gay's chief of staff, General Milburn, and a great many officers and soldiers of the 1st Cavalry Division.

It was a sight that I'll never forget - the drops, witnessing the fighters in action, their direction by the T–6s, and the landing on an airport that had been secured only five hours before.

The daring and bravery of General MacArthur and the timing of his operations, and his organization's abilities, and the things that he does, to me, again display his great leadership, courage and the "doing of the right things at the right time."

After a walk up the strip, following Generals MacArthur and Walker, we came back to the airplane where I introduced General Tunner to General MacArthur (Tunner having just landed). General MacArthur greeted General Tunner and stated that he had directed the award of the DSC for his participation in the drop, as well as the award of the DSC to Colonel Bowen,[74] who commands the 187th RCT. This again, to my mind, demonstrates leadership and command ability. All a professional man gets out of the service is a few pieces of ribbon and I have never known a man to know better how and to whom to make awards than General MacArthur; he is generous; and, like Napoleon, he gains loyalty and has won battles with ribbons like Napoleon did with ostrich feathers.

We then boarded SCAP; as soon as we got aboard, I made a short statement to General MacArthur and told him that in my humble way I wanted to do him

---

27th British Commonwealth Brigade reached the men of the 187th at Sukch'ŏn on the morning of the 22nd. Though MacArthur had believed that at least 30,000 enemy troops would be trapped in the airborne operation, this did not happen. Most of the North Korean troops had already moved north of Sukch'ŏn-Sunch'ŏn prior to the drop. At a cost of 46 jump casualties and 65 battle casualties, the 187th killed some 2,764 North Koreans and captured another 3,818. (Appleman, pp 654-661; Futrell, pp 208-209, 211.)

74. Col Frank S. Bowen, Jr

honor by making the award of the DFC to him on behalf of FEAF. I stated there was great affection for him and that we in FEAF appreciated his brain power, his leadership, and his strategy. I told him that I hadn't prepared that speech, but the situation was such that I just had to attempt to explain to him what we in the Air Force felt toward him. I requested him to read the citation.

He was deeply affected and became very serious; he took me by the shoulders and looked me square in the eyes and stated: "Strat, this is a great honor that I, of course, have not qualified for, but I accept this award in the spirit in which it is given - I appreciate it beyond words." Later, after he had read the citation, he looked across the aisle at me and threw me a kiss and said, "Strat, I shall wear it on top of all my ribbons." Naturally, I was affected; I thanked him, and that was that.

(For citation, quoted in full, see date 19 October 50.)

We flew direct from P'yŏngyang to Tokyo and arrived at 1830 hours.

As soon as I arrived at Mayeda House, I called Mrs. Gay, Mrs. Partridge and Mrs. Walker and told them about meeting their husbands at the airport in P'yŏngyang, the captured capital of North Korea, and that they all looked wonderful and all were doing outstanding jobs.

Earlier, I cleared with General MacArthur the return to the ZI of two medium bomb groups. They will be the 22d and the 92d Groups. General O'Donnell and General Craigie will be advised tomorrow morning.

SATURDAY 21 OCTOBER 1950

Directed the VC for Adm and Plans to write up and have prepared for me to present to General Partridge the Silver Star - based on his flight with General Walker in a T–6 over the drop zone and his landing at the P'yŏngyang airport in order to report to Supreme Commander, United Nations, that the airport was secure.

Also directed Craigie to get off a signal for my signature re the clearance I received to release the two medium bomb groups to the ZI.

General O'Donnell called later on in the day and I discussed this with him briefly.

Asked Crabb, setting a deadline for the info at 1400 hours, for the casualty figures on the drop - not to include those casualties due to enemy action. Told him that CINCFE desires this info.

At my request, Alkire got a winter flying suit for "Shrimp" Milburn - Milburn had requested of me such a suit. I sent it by courier this P.M.

Craigie is drawing up in rough draft a letter to be signed by CINCFE, citing the meritorious service of the two bomb groups that I'm releasing for return to the States.

Sent both Toohey Spaatz and Gill Robb Wilson the news release for Sunday (tomorrow) wherein is contained POW statements re the effectiveness of AF activities as well as a copy of my DFC award order to CINCFE. Both papers were sent for their general information.

When I reached my desk, found a congratulatory cable from Hugh Baillie thanking me for giving Corddry the interview. Bucked this cable to Vandenberg - "for his information."

Made a tape broadcast to the Armed Services Committee for the San Antonio Centennial celebration - Committee includes Generals Krueger, Courtney

Hodges, and Wainwright [75] At the end I gave a personal message to General Jerry Brant and Elmer Adler, AF generals retired.[76]

SUNDAY
22 OCTOBER
1950

Sent Vandenberg a redline:

"Total patient air evacuation by FEAF as of 2400 hours, 21 October: 20,534. From Korea: 11,227; and intra-Japan: 9,307." A very quiet day.[77]

MONDAY
23 OCTOBER
1950

Got off my weekly letter to Gill Robb Wilson, copies of which I sent to Follett Bradley and to Toohey Spaatz.

Attended a conference in General Hickey's office at CINCFE's direction. Those present were Generals Hickey, Craigie and Banfill and myself.

CINCFE is greatly disturbed about the unilateral action taken by the Air Force direct with my headquarters reference a matter that is too hot to even put in this diary. General Hickey informed me after our explanation of our actions that CINCFE wanted me to submit a complete report with all inclosures stating what had been done, the reasons therefor. I issued instructions to General Banfill to make copies of all inclosures and to prepare a memo to General MacArthur for my signature which I will deliver in person either to General Hickey or CINCFE, dependent upon just how I feel about it at the time.

TUESDAY
24 OCTOBER
1950

Earle Partridge due in tomorrow. I have in mind the following items to discuss with him: *(1)* For political reasons - Sweetser must command the light bomb wing and Henebry the C–46 wing.[78] *(2)* I feel that we have reached the time now when spot promotions should stop. *(3)* Leniency in awards - particularly the Bronze Star, Legion of Merit and the Silver Star. *(4)* Airfields that we should return to Korea. *(5)* The size of the Korean Air Force - two groups of fighter bombers or one group of fighter bombers and one light transport squadron. Suitable back-up for maintenance and supplies and spares. *(6)* Recommendations from you (Partridge) for promotion to Brigadier General; I have not received a one. I consider both Hall and Jack Price qualified.[79] *(7)* Timberlake's second star and his permanent B. G.

1500 hours, Mr. Moore,[80] *Indian News,* who was a PIO in India during the last war, paid me a visit, not to gain information from me, but as the British say, to make his number known.

---

75. Gen Walter Krueger led the Sixth Army in the Southwest Pacific in World War II. He retired in 1946. Gen Jonathon M. Wainwright assumed command of the troops on Bataan and Corregidor when MacArthur left for Australia in 1942. Captured, he was a POW for the rest of the war. In 1945, he received the Medal of Honor.

76. Maj Gen Gerald C. Brant commanded several training centers and the Newfoundland Base Command before being disability retired in 1944. Maj Gen Elmer E. Adler, among other assignments, commanded the 10AF's Air Service Command, and had been Chief of Management Control, Air Transport Command. He retired in 1946.

77. Stratemeyer was being modest, for on this date, by order of General MacArthur, he was awarded the Distinguished Service Cross.

78. Both Brig Gens Luther W. Sweetser, Jr., and John P. Henebry were reserve officers who commanded the 452d BW and 437th TCW, respectively. Both of these units arrived in Japan in late October-early November.

79. Col Thomas B. Hall commanded the 35th FIW, while Col John M. Price led the 8th FBW.

80. Moore's full name is unknown.

We discussed Indian politics which included Nehru, Lord Louie's[81] work there, the Kashmir difficulties etc., etc. He has a tremendous bristling, bushy and unsightly mustache.

**WEDNESDAY
25 OCTOBER
1950**

0945 hours, I made the award of the Silver Star, with presentation in my office, to General Partridge.

As characteristic of him, his statement was that "Many people in the Fifth Air Force were more deserving than he." My reply: "I don't agree, but get all those recommendations in." He stated that they were in the mill.

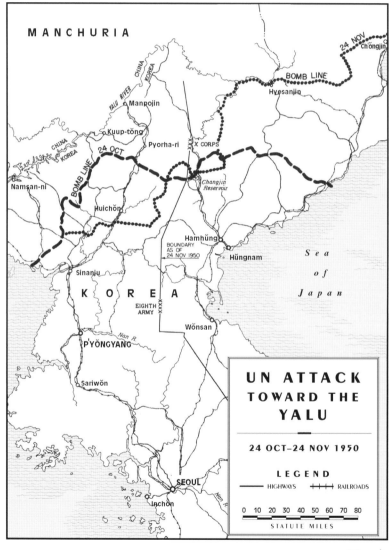

Map 4.

I then held a conference with General Partridge and covered the subjects as outlined under Diary date of 24 October.

In addition: - General Partridge asked for the policy on occupation and the movement to the border. I told him that our policy would have to be a very compact one - consisting of an American wing commander, with an integrated staff consisting of three fighter squadrons: one F–80 American squadron; one F–51 South African squadron; one F–51 RAAF squadron - all to be stationed at Kimp'o.

General Partridge discussed at length X Corps and General Almond's persistent attempts to control Marine aviation which has been turned over to General Partridge for operational control.

He (General Partridge) stated that he had talked with Major General Harris, Marine Corps, and that because of the personalities involved, he intended to give General Harris some rather detailed instructions regarding operational control to which General Harris appreciatively agreed.[82]

General Partridge called on General Almond on the 21st and made it very clear to General Almond that he intends to operate all land-based air in support of his (Almond's) X Corps operations.

Partridge pointed out that the X Corps was unable to furnish the communications that are essential on the part of the Army and that he, General Partridge, was at this time furnishing the necessary AF air support communication which the X Corps should furnish; furthermore, he was furnishing FAF Mosquito airplanes (T–6s) to direct Marine aviation to the targets in support of the ROK forces now in the X Corps and who are making their drive north.

Also, the Fifth Air Force is furnishing the ground control parties who are with the ROK Army. General Partridge invited General Almond to send representatives to his JOC and he (Partridge) did not know whether he (Almond) had sent them.

My comment again, as I have made other places in this diary, is that General Almond is not a team player and is attempting to control, contrary to all written documents, the Air Force that supports him. His attitude ever since he has been appointed a commander has surprised me greatly. I should think that he would be grateful and would express his thanks for the communications and assistance which we have given the troops that have been placed under his control, but according to General Partridge, he has not done so.

General Partridge will lunch with us at Mayeda House.

Instructed Toro (my Adjutant General) to draw up a strong recommendation for the promotion of Earle Partridge to Lieutenant General, and to go into detail as to Earle's personal gallantry, his command ability, stressing that "I believe he has the qualities for higher command and is certainly in the running before his career is over to be either the Chief of Staff or the Vice Chief of Staff of the USAF."

Instructed Merchant[83] (my Deputy for Personnel) to come up with a complete, yet dignified, draft for the award of the Medal of Honor to General MacArthur "which I intend to use through a certain source provided the occasion arises."

---

82. The operational control mentioned actually refers to the "coordination control" of the 1st MAW by 5AF during the Wŏnsan operation. The X Corps commander, General Almond, was attempting to gain control of the MAW and use it as his own little tactical air force at Wŏnsan. This attempt was defeated, although Stratemeyer did order that the 1st MAW be used primarily to support the X Corps. (Futrell, pp 212-213.)

83. Col Brintnell H. Merchant.

The award is to be based on the hazards he faced, in spite of his high position, in flying to Suwŏn, 29 June, and his personal supervision of the para-drop later, some 20 - 30 miles behind enemy lines, from altitudes of 2,000 to 2,500 feet, in the areas around Sunch'ŏn - Sukch'ŏn.

Got off a letter to Mike Scanlon[84] asking for his "late dope on new engines or airframe designs. In this Korean war I have found out to a large extent what the present capabilities of the Air Force are; now I am interested in figuring out what our future capabilities will be."

**THURSDAY
26 OCTOBER
1950**

Word received that a Dr. Alexander due to arrive at three o'clock tomorrow morning. An EYES ONLY message had been sent to me from Norstad indicating that we were to assist this man in getting to Saigon on a special mission for General Vandenberg. I turned the action over to General Craigie, but since he (Craigie) was absent on a flight to Korea as well as General Crabb, who also knew about it, it left me in a bit of a quandary this evening. I instructed General Weyland to inform General Hickey, the Chief of Staff, of Alexander's arrival and for him then to take the necessary action to comply with General Norstad's signal to me.

A Dr. Davidson is also due to arrive on the same flight, and it is my understanding that he is to be a member of General Barcus' evaluation group.

**FRIDAY
27 OCTOBER
1950**

Major General Wolfinbarger[85] checked in at my office at 0800 hours. He had arrived this morning at 0300 hours. Sent Stratline to Col Zoller that he is to represent me at Iwakuni when Air Marshal Fogarty arrives at that base tomorrow.

Sent a Stratline to Partridge and Tunner telling them that in addition to Fogarty accompanying me to Korea, Robertson is going along in order to present Brigadier Brodie[86] to General Walker. Also asked Tunner to have a short briefing prepared for Fogarty.

Received a letter from Hugh Baillie - which I showed to Nuckols:

United Press Associations, Incorporated in New York, General Offices, News Building, New York City. Hugh Baillie, President - October 9, 1950.

Dear Strat: Harry Bruno[87] just came back to town and I had a talk with him, in the course of which I conveyed your regards and those of Annalee to Harry and Nydia.

Harry was very much interested in hearing all about you and your doings. He mentioned that he was going to spend several days with General Vandenberg, so I took occasion to advise him that if it were not for

---

84. Brig Gen Martin F. Scanlon (USAF, Ret.) was at this time a vice president for Republic Aviation, the company building the F–84.

85. Maj Gen Willard R. Wolfinbarger commanded 9AF.

86. Brigadier, later Major General, Thomas Brodie commanded the British 29th Independent Infantry Brigade Group. Although he reported to MacArthur's headquarters on the 26th, his unit did not begin arriving until November 5.

87. Bruno was a public relations counsel and author and had been involved in aviation matters for many years. At this time, he was chairman of the Public Relations Advisory Committee to the USAF.

the Air Force, the Army would have been thrown out of Korea; and that it was the Air Force which made possible the rapid coverage of the Navy's show at Inch'ŏn.

I told him about the relay which FEAF had established at Ashiya.

Harry heard all this with glee, and I have no doubt that General Vandenberg will hear it, too.

With every good wish, believe me, Sincerely yours, s/ Hugh.

Sent both Gay and Shrimp Milburn "pat-on-the-back" letters.

Also sent a similar letter to Gen Walker.

SATURDAY 28 OCTOBER 1950

A Dr. David Alexander[88] reported in at ten o'clock and stated that he had come out here particularly to see the French commanding general in North Africa who had been sent out by the French government to Saigon; however, since his (Alexander's) arrival, the French general had returned to Paris and consequently there was nothing for Alexander to do but turn around and go back to Paris. This man (Alexander) is a count, apparently not a military man in the service, and who is well to do, and is a non-Communist whose sole purpose is to fight the Communists. His father was General Pershing's French aide, and his mother is an American who met his father while he was acting as General Pershing's French aide.

I arranged for him to talk to Colonel Rogers in Intelligence and see CINCFE in case MacArthur would see him. He will depart tomorrow for Washington and thence to Paris.

He will come in for a short talk tomorrow morning.

I left the office at 1115 and, believe it or not, had a swell game of golf with General Robertson, Admiral Joy and Commander Muse, one of Joy's staff officers. I'm stiff all over.

SUNDAY 29 OCTOBER 1950

Air Marshal Sir F. J. Fogarty, my RAF counterpart whose headquarters is in Singapore, with Lady Fogarty, is due to arrive at Haneda at noon today.

0900 hours, Dr. Alexander conferred with me in the office.

0730 P.M. [*sic*], with my key staff, the Gascoignes, Bouchier, and Robertson, Annalee and I gave a dinner honoring the Fogarty's at Mayeda House.

MONDAY 30 OCTOBER 1950

Departed with Air Marshal Fogarty for Seoul (Kimp'o) from Haneda at 0700 hours; arrived about 1100 hours. We were met by General Partridge, members of his staff and went directly to his headquarters.

General Robertson went direct to General Walker's headquarters across the street.

The FAF put on a very fine briefing covering the Korean conflict from the very beginning - 25 June up to the present date.

We had lunch with General Partridge in his quarters. Present besides Partridge were Air Marshal Fogarty, General Robertson, Brigadier Brodie,

---

88. The purpose of Dr. Alexander's trip is unknown. He did work for the OSS in World War II and it may be his trip was intelligence oriented.

General Timberlake and myself. We had a good luncheon - fortunate in having some pheasant which General Partridge had shot the day before at P'ohang.

Immediately after lunch departed for Kimp'o. Took off from there about 1600 hours for Ashiya where we were met by General Tunner and immediately proceeded to his headquarters where we were thoroughly briefed on his activities - the FEAF Combat Cargo Command. This also was an excellent briefing. We met all of Tunner's staff, were served cocktails and immediately thereafter boarded FEAF C–54 and proceeded direct to Haneda, arriving at about 2325 hours. Was in bed by about 2420 hours.

TUESDAY 31 OCTOBER 1950

In the office briefly to look over my papers and get off two memoranda *(1)* to VC A&P and D/P re the morale factor in extending tours arbitrarily from 15 to 24 months on Okinawa. Want a radnote re same sent out to CSAF. *(2)* to VC A&P to get our people started studying the "Post Far East Air Forces Organization" as based on Partridge's paper on same subject, which is to be submitted, and on attached paper from General Tunner, same subject.

Air Marshal Fogarty attended early morning briefing in FEAF. We then departed my headquarters for Yokota at 0945 hours and were met by General O'Donnell and his key staff. I made the award of the DSC to General O'Donnell and we were then very thoroughly and excellently briefed by General O'Donnell on FEAF Bomber Command activities. We then proceeded to General O'Donnell's quarters where we had lunch with him, his key staff and group commanders. Immediately after lunch we departed for FEAMCOM where we were met by General Doyle who also thoroughly and excellently briefed us on the activities of FEAMCOM. We made a rather complete inspection of the plant, both by car and on foot. We then proceeded to General Doyle's home where Mrs. Doyle served us hors d'oeuvres and cocktails. Arrived back at Mayeda House at about 1800 hours. Had dinner with Sir Alvary and Lady Gascoigne.

WEDNESDAY 1 NOVEMBER 1950

Left the office early (1100) hours with Fogarty for some golf with him, Robertson and Davison. Good exercise - lousy score - another 94.

Weyland in my stead sent following redline to Vandenberg:

Redline to Vandenberg from Weyland for Stratemeyer. One T–6 and one B–26 attacked this morning by three Yaks. T–6 hit but returned to base safely. B–26 not hit.[89] F–51s called in and shot down two Yaks. B–26 shot down third Yak. Confirmed by Mosquito T–6. F–80 recce pilot flash reports fifteen Yaks on Sinŭiju Airfield previously empty. Twelve F–80s being dispatched to attack same. Pilots cautioned concerning border.

Weyland sent out following redlines to CSAF:

(1) PART I. Remy A 2939B, 12 F–80s attacked Sinŭiju Afld [airfield], destroyed one, damaged six Yaks. Open ends revetments face river,

---

89. The B–26 was from the newly-arrived 730th BS of the 452d BW.

Map 5.

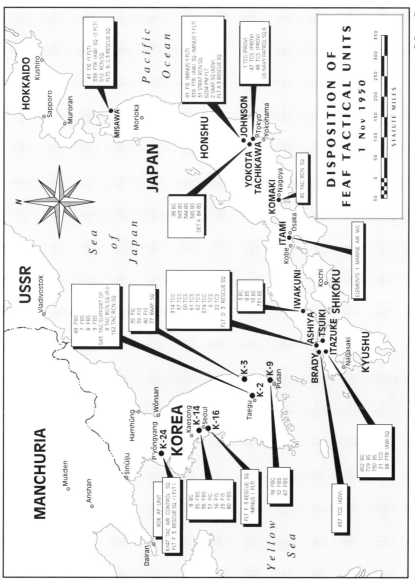

DISPOSITION OF
FEAF TACTICAL UNITS
1 Nov 1950

hence difficult to strafe. Flak most intense and accurate yet encountered. One F-80 lost. Sixteen additional F-80s being dispatched. *PART II.* F-51s in I Corps area jumped by six jet fighters believed MiG-15 type. No F-51s lost. MiGs in turn jumped by F-80s. No report of results yet. *PART III.* Unconfirmed report considerable guns and armor crossing Yalu near Namsan-ni. Armed recce strikes cleared to border in this area.

AND

(2) *PART I.* Reference my A 2952 B CG second strike on Sinŭiju Afld disclosed enemy aircraft had departed leaving only aircraft damaged by first strike. *PART II.* Hostile jet type believed to be MiG–14 not MiG–15. F–80 tangle with MiG's unconfirmed and probably mistaken report. F–51 pilot reports raking one jet. Damaged hostile jet flew across Yalu River into Manchuria. F–51 combat film to be processed soonest for identification hostile plane.[90]

The Fogartys had sukiyaki dinner with us.

THURSDAY 2 NOVEMBER 1950

Dispatched following redline to Vandenberg:

Reference three redline messages 1 November. Sightings and intelligence highlights are as follows:

PART I. Six to nine MiG–15s were seen by Mosquito pilot at XE 3515 between 1345 and 1415. Acft [aircraft] had 30/35 span, swept wings, short, thick fuselage. One acft displayed red star on top of right wing. Appeared to be burned green silver color. Made pass firing three squirts at 2000. Pass made was pursuit curve. Formation was in trail when first seen. Acft can apparently turn very sharply and have very steep angle of climb. Also very, very fast. Mosquito pilot believes one, closely observed, to be MiG–15. *PART II.* A flight of four F–51s engaged six to nine swept wing jets in dog fight and are believed to have hit two. Enemy broke engagement and damaged acft returned to northwest over Yalu River. Comment: Believe these are same jets reported above by Mosquito pilot. *PART III.* Mosquito plane, reported one conventional enemy fighter appeared about 20 minutes prior to jet attack. *PART IV.* The tentative identification of above jets as MiG–15 answers your query which caused your AFOIN 56456 to be dispatched to FEAF.

Weyland will handcarry the following memo to GHQ which is a reply in fact to a flash note just received by me from Almond's headquarters.

Memo to CINCFE - reference signal from X Corps to CINCUNC, cite X 11894, dated 2 November, I am confident Fifth Air Force will furnish

---

90. The Soviets had stationed a fighter air regiment (FAR) in China in February 1950 and followed this unit with the dispatch of the 29th FAR to China in August and September 1950. Further MiG–15-equipped units arrived later. It was an aircraft of the 29th FAR that the F–51s encountered. The MiG–15 pilots involved in these early meetings were always Soviet; Chinese and North Korean pilots only became qualified later in the war. (Yefim Gordon and Vladimir Rigmant, *MiG–15: Design, Development, and Korean War Combat History*, [Osceola, WI, 1993], p 111.)

every possible assistance to X Corps consistent with availability of TACP personnel and equipment. I do want to point out that the CG X Corps has the responsibility of furnishing personnel to the Joint Operations Center located at Fifth Air Force headquarters and therefore urge that the CG X Corps be directed to furnish G-3 Air and if possible G-2 Air to the Joint Operations Center at Fifth Air Force hdq. By so doing, these representatives can personally represent the X Corps in the assignment of missions and equipment. Either General Partridge or General Timberlake will contact in person General Almond or his Chief of Staff, General Ruffner, reference the above cited message.

Reference the above, Weyland's comment was: "General Almond has no intention of endeavoring to cooperate with the Fifth Air Force," to which I agreed.

My vice commanders, Craigie and Weyland, were hosts at a stag dinner for Fogarty at the University Club.

FRIDAY 3 NOVEMBER 1950

On my desk when I got in this morning were two radios from Partridge: *(1)* because of heavy antiaircraft fire from city of Sinŭiju and across river from Antung, requested clearance to burn Sinŭiju and *(2)* because of enemy aircraft crossing NK border into Manchuria and because their staging areas in Manchuria, requested authority to pursue the enemy into Manchuria.

I immediately got off a letter to CINCFE, subject:

Pursuit and Destruction of Hostile Aircraft - *(1)* Hostile aircraft have been sighted flying from Korean territory across the border into Manchuria. Current directives prohibit UN aircraft from continuing pursuit of such enemy aircraft beyond the border. *(2)* It is requested that clearance be obtained for UN aircraft to pursue enemy aircraft across the NK border to destroy them in the air or on the ground and to determine the location of their bases.

Met with General MacArthur at 1120 hours and discussed my letter to him reference the pursuit of hostile aircraft into Manchuria and destroying them in the air and on the ground. He indicated that due to the entire situation the UN and Washington must act and it was not his intention to refer this matter to higher authority until more information was received that the Chinese Communists were actually engaged in strength against our forces in Korea. His words were: "I want to muddle over this a bit longer."[91]

---

91. The first indication that the CCF was taking an active role in Korea came on Oct. 25 when Chinese troops decimated a ROK battalion near Onjŏng. For several days, the CCF attacks continued against the Eighth Army's South Korean units, wiping out the only South Korean unit (the 7th Regiment) to reach the Yalu and routing the ROK II Corps. Also on Oct. 25, in the X Corps zone, Chinese troops blunted the advance of the ROK 26th Regiment toward the Changjin (Chosin) Reservoir.
    The South Koreans were not the only U.N. troops to run into the Chinese. In the Eighth Army zone, the 1st Cavalry Division's 8th Regiment was roughly handled by the CCF on Nov. 1-2 and driven south. The Chinese troops who stopped the ROK 26th Regiment were themselves destroyed by the 1st Marine Division as it moved toward the reservoir.
    Within a few days of these attacks, however, the CCF melted back into the mountains and little traces of their activity could be found. A cautious Gen. Walker regrouped his forces along the Ch'ŏngch'ŏn River, while Gen. Almond kept extending his units farther north. The appearance of Chinese troops surprised MacArthur and

Reference Partridge's Stratline to me that because of heavy, intense and accurate anti-aircraft fire from the city of Sinŭiju, and requesting clearance to burn the town, General MacArthur indicated that because of his contemplated use of that town he did not want to burn it at this time. His intentions are to push the 24th Division to the Yalu River, taking Sinŭiju, and then proceed northeast and cut off the NK forces with his left flank protected by the Yalu River. As a matter of fact, he directed Admiral Struble yesterday to make a study of the use of naval forces into the harbor south of Sinŭiju. At the present time, Walker's retreat order for the 24th Division has eliminated that as a possibility.

I then queried him as to the military targets that were in Sinŭiju and his answer to me was "Strat, I have no objection to the destruction of military targets anywhere in North Korea, but I do not want barracks buildings or any other facility in Sinŭiju destroyed at this time."

I pointed out the seriousness of the anti-aircraft both from Sinŭiju and Antung and requested authority to go in low over Sinŭiju with fighters using napalm or any other weapon and try to take out the anti-aircraft. He and I both realize the difficulty of such action.

I then discussed with him the marshaling yards that are just east of the viaduct which joins onto the bridge that connects Sinŭiju and Antung and he said, "Hit that" - if I consider that a military target.

I also told him that as a lesson we could burn some other towns in North Korea and I indicated the town of Kanggye which I believe is occupied by enemy troops and is a communications center - both rail and road.[92] He said, "Burn it if you so desire," and then said, "Not only that, Strat, but burn and destroy as a lesson any other of those towns that you consider of military value to the enemy."

He stated that he realized that there were not many targets left for the '29s but he wanted to get them back in the business. I told him we could put in the air daily 24 B–29s and, with a couple of days of stand-down, we could probably mount 75, but I knew of no targets for such a formation.

He then stated that he wanted from me the very best study that I could make to prove that the Chinese Communists, in force, both on the ground and in the air, were operating in and over North Korea.

I told him of the signal that I had received from Vandenberg wherein he (Vandenberg) was a bit worried about the Russian jets that had appeared over North Korea and that I had been called on by Vandenberg to submit our best estimate of the situation as he (Vandenberg) wanted that data in order to reinforce me with F–84Es (jets) if the need arose.

I told General MacArthur that I would send him a copy of the Vandenberg signal to me and a copy of my reply.

Dispatched a Stratline to Partridge in three parts:

PART I. In discussion with General MacArthur this morning, he indicated that he would not burn Sinŭiju at this time because of contemplated

---

many of his commanders, but most of them brushed off the encounters as little more than isolated instances of intervention by a few "volunteers." The quick disappearance of the Chinese seemed to indicate that there was little to worry about and that the proposed final offensive to the Yalu should go off as scheduled on Nov. 24. Little did MacArthur and his subordinates realize that the Chinese were readying an offensive of their own to begin on the 25th.

92. Kanggye was the new home of the retreating North Korean government.

occupation by United Nations troops. *PART II.* You are authorized to use fighters with any armament you so desire to take out the anti-aircraft batteries in and around the city of Sinŭiju, at the same time not repeat not violate the border. *PART III.* Ref radnote KH-OPS 2324 [regarding hot pursuit across the border]. I have brought this matter to CINCFE's attention and at the present time he is studying your request.

A copy of the above was sent to CINCFE.

Air Marshal Fogarty attended the FEAF briefing this AM, and then I accompanied him out to Haneda, where he departed for Singapore via Okinawa and Clark AFB. Sent a radnote to both Turner and Stearley, with a copy going to Deputy Comptroller, that they were authorized to draw on FEAF entertainment funds for their modest entertainment of the Air Marshal.

Following message received from CG X Corps to FEAF, with info to CINCUNC, CG FAF (rear) and CG FAF (adv):

5th AF msg 280501Z. The TACP rqmts [requirements] of 1st ROK Corps prior to passing to operations control of X Corps are not known here. Our msg X 11645 is quoted: "Attn Maj Gen Weyland. To meet close air support rqmts for 1st ROK contemplated opn urgently require 4 AN/VRC-1 jeeps and 4 radio technicians to be airlanded Yŏnp'o airdrome soonest. Additional crew members avail to his hq. Please advise your action." The request contained in X 11645 was carefully considered in all aspects before submission. The nature of opns planned and in progress requires the personnel and equip requested.

My reply to above was:

For Almond from Stratemeyer referring to your X 11742. This rad in two parts. *PART I.* Four additional complete TACPs, equipment and personnel, will be furnished by Fifth AF to work with units of I ROK Corps as quickly as they can be assembled from limited resources. Gen Partridge will confer with you tomorrow or as soon as possible on this and other support matters. *PART II.* Urgently request you fulfill your responsibility for G-2 and G-3 air representation at JOC and appropriate communications as contemplated in FM 31-35 and current Army doctrine.

CINCFE and CG FAF were info addressees on this radio.

Received following OPERATIONAL IMMEDIATE from Vandenberg, a copy of which I sent to CINCFE:

Our estimate air situation in North Korea based on rather sketchy evidence concludes that enemy aircraft in operation 1 and 2 Nov were Yak–7 or –9 and MiG–15s, that Yaks used airfields at Sinŭiju and probably Antung, that MiGs employed from fields in Manchuria, that most likely pilots were NK or Chinese Communist or both. Thus far, only token air forces employed conforming in general with pattern in ground forces. No evidence as yet of major air threat to UN forces in Far East. Would appreciate any comment you might wish to make on above estimate. Meanwhile, inform me immediately of details of any additional indications of the employment of Chinese Communist forces, air or ground, or any change in situation which indicates significant development in present trends. Particularly essential here that we have as much forewarning as possible of any jet buildup, so that appropriate action required, such as the reinforcement of your command with F–84s can be taken in time.

Dispatched via personal redline to Vandenberg my answer to his radnote above:

Your estimate of air situation in NK is essentially in accordance with mine. Fairly reliable sources indicate that the CCAF may have up to 300 airplanes in China with possibility of an undetermined number of jet aircraft as reported sightings have been made at Canton, Nanking, Shanghai, and Antung-Korea area. Eighth Tac Rec Sq pilot in RF–80 reported having sighted at 020705/I fifty fighter-type aircraft on Antung Airfield; Recce aircraft altitude 16,000 feet, three miles east of Sinŭiju. Small numbers of enemy aircraft, not necessarily CCAF, have been observed in operation over NK, largest in flight to date has been six aircraft. First enemy jet operation in NK on 1 Nov included 6 airplanes, and our pilots reported possible damage to one of these (four F–51s against six jets). Second report of enemy jet operation on 2 Nov indicated only five jet airplanes utilized. This may indicate that our claims of damage to one jet were correct and that only six were committed. Enemy jet pilots have not been aggressive. Possibility exists that the six MiG–15s are Russian-owned and operated and are being service-tested on exactly the same basis as we contemplate service-testing six F–84Es. Reference Chinese Communists ground build-up, G-2, Far East Command, this morning estimated 12,000 Communist troops in North Korea. CINCFE informed of your message and this reply.[93]

A copy of the above radnote handcarried to CINCFE.

General Hickey called at about 1900 hours and stated that General MacArthur had approved the Partridge wire to burn Sinŭiju by the Fifth Air Force. Hickey asked that I drop in tomorrow morning and discuss other targets with him as the Boss had asked that this be done. Will go to see him at 1000 hours, 4 November 1950.

SATURDAY 4 NOVEMBER 1950

Got off my "Estimate of the Situation" to CINCFE as per his request and included my belief that if Russia entered the conflict openly it would mean World War III which in my estimation was not in the cards.

I was a bit concerned this morning when I learned that ten (10) correspondents were accompanying the B–29s on their attack (burn) on Kanggye. After

---

93. By this date, there were approximately 300,000 Chinese troops in North Korea. (Schnabel, p 259.) Because they generally moved at night and had excellent camouflage discipline, the CCF troops were never spotted. Two reasons for their not being seen was that FEAF had a very limited number of RF–80As for photo reconnaissance, with the result that some areas (such as the Yalu crossings) were considered of greater importance and received much greater attention than others. Also, neither FEAF nor Eighth Army had enough photo interpreters to screen what photos were taken. (Futrell, pp 229, 547-548) But there was another reason for

discussing with General Weyland, Craigie and Nuckols the picture, my statement will be generally, as follows: That wherever we find hostile troops and equipment that are being utilized to kill UN troops, we intend to use every means and weapon at our disposal to destroy them, that facility, or town. This will be the answer to the use of the incendiary-cluster type of bomb.

My conference with Hickey was most satisfactory. While there he confirmed the instructions that he had given me the night before that General MacArthur wanted an all-out air effort against communications and facilities with every weapon available to stop and destroy the enemy in North Korea. He reiterated the burning of towns and emphasized the importance of taking out Sinŭiju.

Warning orders were sent to Fifth Air Force and FEAF Bomber Command directing the destruction of Sinŭiju on 7 November. This authorized Bomber Command to stand down on the 6th. It also authorized direct communications to work out between FEAF Bomber Command and Fifth Air Force their cooperation on this attack.

I made the award of Legion of Merit to Colonel Ganey at 1500 hours.

**SUNDAY
5 NOVEMBER
1950**

In accordance with the exchange of radios between X Corps (General Almond) and my headquarters, and my reply signal to Almond (see 3 November 50), Partridge radioed me as follows:

Conferred today with Almond at Wŏnsan. He understands shortage of tactical air control parties and accepts delay of few days in receipt of four additional ones. When these four are delivered he will have seventeen (17) of a total of forty-six (46) supplied by FAF and this proportion is over twice his share. Recommitment of EUSAK forces, operational losses and fair wear have caused unforeseen shortages which will be liquidated as rapidly as our resources will permit. Almond agreed to send liaison officer to this hqs but demurred in establishing here G-2 and 3 air because he feels lack of contact and communications with X Corps will prevent these officers from operating effectively. I pointed out to him that communications with us was an Army function. At present Navy msgs sent by CW [continuous wave] radio are undelivered or are delayed beyond time when profitable action can be taken on them. Will review communications problem and will report later what progress we can make in solving this problem within our resources.

Received a signal (Radnote) from Cabell in which he stated that he wanted to send a small group of highly specialized target analysts to Hq to have them proceed to Korea to make detailed inspection and measurements of physical damage caused by specific weapons of various types, and also in certain cases to trace and assess the economic, industrial and military effects of such physical damage. It is contemplated that these analysts will collect certain types of

---

their not being seen — they were not really being looked for! MacArthur, the JCS, and the various intelligence organizations could not believe that the Chinese Communists would involve themselves in the war in Korea, but, instead, would use their presence on the Korean border only as a form of "political blackmail." Indeed, though MacArthur and his intelligence people kept revising upward their estimates of CCF strength, on the eve of the first major Chinese offensive, they were still grossly underestimating the enemy's strength by three-quarters.

detailed data that were not availably reported by the US Strategic Bombing Surveys following WWII and that are urgently required by the Air Targets Division as basis for its analyses of the vulnerability of both strategic and tactical targets in other parts of the world. The proposed group will include approx 10 AF and Navy analysts, and it may include a few Army analysts. It is anticipated that the group will need approximately 4 draftsmen, 4 photographers, 7 interpreters, 2 auto mechanics, 7 jeeps, and 7 trailers in order to enable them to carry out their mission. Your concurrence and support of this project are sought and your advice is requested as to whether you can obtain the necessary theater clearances and make other necessary arrangements mentioned in the preceding paragraph. If you concur and clearances are obtained, efforts will be made to have the group depart this hq by 10 Nov. Estimated duration of project is 60 days.

My reply to above, Personal radnote for Major General C. P. Cabell, Director of Intelligence, information General Twining, V/CofS:

Reference your radnote 041810/Z, subject to provisions hereafter stated, I concur in sending Target Analysis Group, will support it in the theater, and am confident that MacArthur will approve. I must remind you that we have the Chief of Staff's Evaluation Group here headed by General Barcus to which Mr. Charles E. Wilson is to be assigned as Director. There is also a Human Relations Evaluation Group coming out from the Air University. Various analyses are being done by Fifth Air Force and Hq FEAF personnel. It is therefore desired that any evaluation that is attempted augment General Barcus' Group in order to maintain objectivity, avoid duplication, and achieve maximum benefits.

Met with General MacArthur at 1105 hours. Present were General Hickey, Chief of Staff, and General Wright, G-3. The gist of General MacArthur's instructions are as follows: Every installation, facility, and village in North Korea now becomes a military and tactical target. THE ONLY EXCEPTIONS ARE: the big hydro-electric power plant on the Manchurian border at Changsi [?][94] and the hydro-electric power plants in Korea. General MacArthur reiterated his scorched earth policy to burn and destroy.[95] The other exception to his directive is the city of Rashin. Every bridge across the Yalu River, from the Russian - Korean-Manchurian border, southwest across the Yalu, is a target and will be destroyed. We must not and cannot violate the border; consequently, no part of the bridges, from the Manchurian side from the center over, will be hit. The bridge targets will be the Korean side of the river and the abutments thereto. This includes any pontoon bridge that the Chinese Communists might throw across the river.

Starting from the Yalu River into Korea, every method of surface communication will be destroyed. The towns on the Korean side, bordering the Yalu River - except between Korea and Russia - will be destroyed.

---

94. Stratemeyer apparently is referring to the Suiho power plant located in the Ch'ŏngsŏngjin area.
95. MacArthur's "scorched earth" policy was considered a very sound military decision. Much of North Korea is stark and barren, particularly in the winter, with few resources immediately available to sustain an invading force. Thus, the towns would be the focal points where troops would naturally gather for shelter and food. Burning the North Koreans and Chinese out of these towns and villages would force them to live off the land (Chinese supply efforts, especially, being relatively rudimentary at this time) as temperatures began to drop below zero. There is some evidence that many NKPA and CCF troops were lost through death or incapacitation brought on by being forced out of the towns into the brutal weather. (Futrell, p 228.)

A maximum effort for the next two (2) weeks by all of FEAF's air will be produced - flying our combat crews to exhaustion if necessary.

All the targets that are on the Yalu River and close thereto must be hit only by visual means; there will be always an alternate and that can be by radar anywhere in North Korea with the exceptions above noted.

A study of all river crossings and approaches to the Yalu River within Korea is being made by Far East Command - the directive for same being given to General Wright.

I have issued instructions to my staff directing that the above be put into effect without delay, starting the destruction of bridges and villages and communications from the Korean side of the Yalu River south and southeast.

General Craigie, Colonel Price and Colonel Rogers were present at time above dictated. I told Craigie that I think this is important enough for either Rosie or his C/S to come in here (Hq FEAF) to discuss this. Craigie agreed and indicated he was thinking along those lines and would give FEAF Bomb Command a call. Also to Craigie and Price I indicated that they must prepare a signal from me to Partridge with the information copy going to Rosie, covering generally what I said so that Partridge will thoroughly understand this and I will send this message via officer courier rather than trust it to the regular top secret courier service.

In discussing with Rogers recon of the Yalu River, and my desires to have a map (he is to check with G-3 upon completion of their directive from MacArthur and also Willoughby's outfit) which shows every crossing of the Yalu River, rail or highway and the names of the towns that they are near. Rogers indicated that because of previous recon restrictions, this was the first day we've had recon planes covering that dividing line and he indicated that because of the speed of the jets, quite possible the border would be violated. Reiterated that the border is not to be crossed and if need be we shall send the 31st up there. They can sit up there top-side and get a picture. Emphasized that we are to get these target pictures to Rosie.

In discussing bridge crossings, one example that was shown to me indicated that POW camp sites (reported), hospitals and prisons would be vulnerable to incendiary attack. Whether vulnerable or not, our target was to take out lines of communication and towns.

Copies, made direct from this diary entry, were sent to VC A&P (Craigie), D/O (Price for Weyland and Crabb), and D/I (Rogers - who is acting in Banfill's stead, the latter is on TDY to USAF).

General O'Donnell came in to the office at 1430; I let him read the above and then we discussed the whole problem of air attacks.

Cleared Nuckols' marble to Vandenberg:

Redline Vandenberg from Stratemeyer. FEAF Bomber Command this afternoon bombed the military supply center of Kanggye with about 170 tons of incendiary bombs with flash report indicating all bombing done is usually with excellent results. Entire city of Kanggye was virtual arsenal and tremendously important communications center, hence decision to employ incendiary for first time in Korea.

Brigadier General Courtney Whitney, Chief of SCAP Government Section, and advisor to General MacArthur telephoned me at 1325 hours today and stated that he had discussed the article in the 6 November issue of the Pacific Edition of *Time Magazine*, upper right hand corner, page 7, with General MacArthur. General MacArthur's remarks were as follows: "Tell Strat that nothing could be further from the truth than the statements made in that article."

I incorporated the above in an EYES ONLY letter to Vandenberg and dispatched same to him this date. (See article, [this] page).

[The following article was pasted in the diary at this spot.]

ARMED FORCES - Change of Heart
Oh, we asked for the Army
To come to Tulagi,
But Douglas MacArthur said "no!"
He gave as his reason,
"This isn't the season,
Besides, there is no U.S.O."

Such boondock minstrelsy (and other more ill-humored doggerel) summed up the feeling of many World War II marines for the U.S. Army's ranking officer in the Pacific. But by last week it was different. The word out of Korea and out of Washington was that MacArthur and [This line is unreadable in the article pasted in the diary. It probably read to the effect... "the Marines made up."] MacArthur had been heard to say that there are no finer troops on earth than the marines, and was giving all his support to the Marines' air arm, which a year ago, in the integration fight, was battling for its life. At his insistence, high Army brass had even begun a fight to take tactical aviation away from the Air Force and put it back in the Army, so that it would be coordinated with ground forces as it is in the Marines. And the ranking Marine Corps officer in the Pacific, Lieut. General Lemuel C. Shepherd, was reported to be disappointed because Harry Truman had given MacArthur "only" a Distinguished Service Medal (his fifth) instead of the Medal Honor, to add to the M.H. he won in the Philippines.

Following is my signal with reference General MacArthur's instructions to me re the destruction of North Korea:

To: CG FAF (Stratline)
CG FEAF BomCom (Courier)

Info: CINCFE (Courier)
COMNAVFE (Courier)
CG TWENTIETH AF (Stratline)

Personal Partridge and O'Donnell from Stratemeyer.
This message in five parts.

PART I. On 5 November 50, General MacArthur directed the following action: *A.* "Destroy the Korean end of all international bridges on the

Korean-Manchurian border." I interpret this as meaning the first over-water span out from the Korean shore. *B.* "Except for Rashin, the Suiho Dam and other electric power plants in North Korea to destroy every means of communications and every installation, factory, city and vil-lage. Under present circumstances all such have marked military poten-tial and can only be regarded as military installations. [Emphasis in original.] This destruction is to start at the Korean-Manchurian border and progress south." *C.* "All targets on or close to the border will be hit under VFR conditions only. There must be no violation of the border. The border cannot and must not be violated." *D.* "A maximum effort will be made by FEAF for the next two (2) weeks. Combat crews are to be flown to exhaustion if necessary." *PART II.* Effective immediately the above policy directives will be put into effect. Specific directives will be forth-coming. Direct communications between Fifth Air Force and FEAF Bomber Command is authorized. FEAF Bomber Command will station a liaison section with Fifth Air Force. *PART III.* In general, FEAF oper-ations orders will assign to FEAF Bomber Command the mission of destroying Korean end of the permanent international bridges with Fifth Air Force destroying pontoon bridges which may be built. FEAF Bomber Command will destroy the cities and large towns. Aircraft under Fifth Air Force control will destroy all other targets including all build-ings capable of affording shelter. *PART IV.* Note carefully that the above policy is effective up to the Manchurian border but not to the Soviet bor-der. In the latter area, these operations will not be conducted north of a line running from Ch'ŏngjin to Musan. *PART V.* It is essential that we obtain immediately photo reconnaissance of the Manchurian border area of North Korea, particularly of the international bridges. Your RF–80s should be put on this job at once. They must not violate the border in obtaining this reconnaissance. Advise me of any reconnaissance targets your RF–80s cannot photograph in accordance with this policy and I will assign those targets to the 31st Squadron.

General Hickey called and stated that General MacArthur liked my signal but desired that I include in Part I "B" the following: Under present circum-stances all such have marked military potential and can only be regarded as mil-itary installations. (See underscored quote in radio.)

Immediately prepared a signal to all the original addressees informing them to add the above statement to my signal to them re the "Destruction of North Korea."

Peking officially acknowledges a Chinese Communist force of "volunteers" in North Korea.

**MONDAY
6 NOVEMBER
1950**

FEAF Bomber Command liaison officer dispatched via staff T–33 to Hq Fifth Air Force.

At 0915 hours, I held a conference with General Craigie, Weyland, Alkire and Crabb reference a call I had had this morning from General Partridge. I explained that Partridge had a good day yes-terday and that he is confident that he inflicted severe damage on the enemy. Par-tridge indicated that there was hostile air action in both the east and west of North

Korea and that as a result he felt it necessary that he move his fighter-bomber units from South Korea forward. Partridge stated that he was confident that he had the situation in hand but that it would require both air and water lift. I informed Partridge that if he needed any help from me, to scream and he said he would if the occasion arose. I instructed Alkire to personally contact General Eberle, G-4, FEC, and to indicate to him that for a short period now, Partridge must be given practically all of Tunner's airlift and I indicated that to my mind this was the most important use of the airlift during the next few days. I also indicated that if there was any indication that this would not be done to let me know and that I would take care of it with Generals Hickey and MacArthur.

Partridge raised the question of spot promotions and indicated it looked to him that it was going to be a long, cold winter and asked that spot promotions be again authorized and I agreed and directed General Craigie to send out such a signal re-authorizing spot promotions.

Got off my weekly letter to Gill Robb Wilson.

**TUESDAY
7 NOVEMBER
1950**

At 0330 this morning, General Crabb called and stated there was a message in Vandenberg to Stratemeyer, redline, that we are not to bomb Sinŭiju and the Yalu River bridges. As a result, I directed that a redline be sent to Vandenberg to this effect - mission ordered by CINCFE. Any change in mission must come from CINCFE.[96]

Later, General Crabb in conversation with Colonel Warren[97] and the duty officer at FEC, found that there was a concurrent message received from the JCS. The big boner was made by Warren and Crabb in not telling me that in Vandenberg's message to me were these words: "issuing now MacArthur." Had I known this, my entire actions throughout the rest of the night would have been different. As a result of the JCS signal to MacArthur, we stood down the attack and it will be cancelled until tomorrow if a green light is not given at 0830 hours this morning.

General Hickey called me about 0545 hours and read me the MacArthur reply to the JCS and asked for my comments per instructions from MacArthur. My comment was: "Doyle, it is one hundred percent."

In view of the above, I did not sleep the rest of the night and came to the office about 0710 hours.

At about 0740 hours, I held a conference with Crabb, Craigie, and Warren and very emphatically pointed out to them that the crux of Vandenberg's message was "issuing now MacArthur," and they should have told me this immediately.

---

96. When Vandenberg learned of the proposed attacks, he quickly notified Secretary of the Air Force Finletter, who then contacted the Deputy Secretary of Defense, Robert A. Lovett. An urgent meeting with the Secretary of State was arranged to discuss this matter. At this meeting, which took place only about 3 hours before the bombers were to take off, it was revealed that the British government had been promised by the United States that it would be consulted before any action was taken that might affect Manchuria. Also, that same day the U.S. delegation to the U.N. was attempting to get the Security Council to consider the problem of Chinese intervention in Korea. All in all, the proposed attack was not happening at the most propitious moment. Additionally, Lovett, Secretary of State Acheson, and Secretary of Defense Marshall were not convinced that the bombing would be effective. President Truman, who was in Missouri to vote in congressional elections, was contacted and he directed that MacArthur justify the attacks before they took place. ("History of the JCS," Vol. III, pp 290-292.)

97. Col R.H. Warren, Director of Operations, FEAF.

I directed General Craigie to call General Hickey, General O'Donnell and General Partridge stating that if the green light for the mission was not received by 0830 hours this morning, it would be called off until tomorrow as we cannot take a chance on bombing the Yalu River bridges at Sinŭiju in darkness or even early twilight.

In answer to Vandenberg's redline re:

high officials here desire to know at once if instructions in JCS 59878 and CS TS 5364, reference postponement of bombing within five miles of Manchurian border were received and implemented. Important you reply redline immediately.

My redline answer to him was:

Instructions in JCS 59878 and your redline TS 5364 received. CINCFE has directed postponement of bombing until further orders.

Followed up my above redline with the following:

REDLINE PERSONAL VANDENBERG FROM STRATEMEYER WITH INFO PERSONAL COURIER CINCFE AND INFO PERSONAL STRATLINE PARTRIDGE AND O'DONNELL. Further to my V 0420 CG. In addition to postponing FEAF BOMCOM missions against specific targets cited JCS 59878 and your TS 5364, I have directed Partridge to refrain from bombing any targets within five (5) miles of border. He has been and still is authorized to perform armed recce flights up to border utilizing napalm, rockets, and machine gun fire against appropriate targets both in the air and on the ground.

At about 1000 hours, called on Hickey. Discussed hamstrung restrictions imposed by JCS. *At CINCFE's direction prepared the following draft of a radio for him to send to the JCS:*

PERSONAL FOR THE JOINT CHIEFS OF STAFF FROM MACARTHUR: Rate of enemy air operations on new high level yesterday with both conventional and jet aircraft employed. One (1) of these aircraft came directly across border and was sighted proceeding both east and west over Sinŭiju. Joint Chiefs of Staff's restrictions against crossing border convey to enemy full initiative in action against our aircraft near Yalu River. I view with grave alarm your instructions to me which give sanctuary to enemy equipped with modern jet fighters. He is gaining confidence and aggressiveness with experience. Further, his numbers are increasing and if this trend continues unchecked, his air operations will soon constitute a most serious threat to overall operations of United Nations forces. I must be authorized to release my aircraft to strike on and above Manchurian soil. I cannot over emphasize the gravity and seriousness of the prospects in the light of the directives under which I an now forced to operate. I therefore strongly urge that I be given authority to dispatch my aircraft across the Manchurian border in pursuit and attack both in the air and on the ground. I consider this authority mandatory if I am to protect United Nations troops which are now engaged against Chinese Communist troops.

On 06 1647/Z, CINCFE received from WAR [Department of the Army], WD GR85 the following FLASH message:

(JCS 95878) from JCS Personal for MacArthur. *1.* Consideration being urgently given to Korean situation at Government level. One factor is present commitment not to take action affecting Manchuria without consultation with the British.[98] *2.* Until further orders postpone all bombing of targets within five miles of Manchurian border. 3. Urgently need your estimate of situation and reason for ordering bombing Yalu River bridges as indicated in telecon this date.

(To JCS:) - In reply, CINCFE DISPATCHED HIS ANSWER:

C-68396 Men and material in large force are pouring across all bridges over the Yalu from Manchuria. This mvmt [movement] not only jeopardizes but threatens the ultimate destruction of the forces under my command. The actual mvmt across the river can be accomplished under cover of darkness and the distance between the river and our lines is so short that the forces can be deployed against our trps [troops] without being seriously subjected to air interdiction. The only way to stop this reinf[orcement] of the enemy is the destruction of these bridges and the subjection of all installations in the north area supporting the enemy adv to the max of our air destruction. Every hour that this is postponed will be paid for dearly in American and other United Nations blood. The main crossing at Sinŭiju was to be hit within the next few hours and the mission is actually already being mounted. Under the gravest protect that I can make, I am suspending this strike and carrying our your instructions. What I had ordered is entirely within the scope of the rules of war and the resolutions and directions which I have recd from the United Nations and constitute no slightest act of belligerency against Chinese territory, in spite of the outrageous international lawlessness emanating therefrom. I cannot over-emphasize the disastrous effect, both physical and psychological, that will result from the restrictions which you are imposing. I rqst [request] that this matter be immediately brought to the attention of the President as I believe your instructions may well result in a calamity of major proportion for which I cannot accept the responsibility without his personal and dir understanding of the sit[uation]. Time is so essential that I rqst immediate reconsideration of your decision pending which complete compliance will of course be given to your order. Signed MACARTHUR.[99]

---

98. British, or for that matter, all the U.N. allies, sensibilities were carefully considered by the U.S. government regarding various aspects of the Korean War. Not the least of these concerned the inviolability of Manchuria. The allies and the U.S. were disturbed that incursions into Manchuria might escalate the war from a local conflict into a world war.

99. This message shows a remarkable turnabout in MacArthur's estimate of the situation in Korea. Just a few days earlier he was telling the JCS not to jump to conclusions regarding the appearance of the Chinese in Korea. He apparently still refused to believe they could be there in force.
A message on the 5th from him to the U.N. Security Council was also restrained in his estimate of the situation. Yet this Nov. 7 dispatch is alarmist and suddenly full of urgency. In addition, his language is surprisingly intemperate, considering that this message is directed at his superiors on the JCS. What is perhaps more surprising is the deference the JCS showed MacArthur when replying to this message. Though the JCS deferred to MacArthur in this matter, again they were not happy with his manner. The clock was now

Because it was on a radio (excellent one) received from Earle Partridge on which I based the rough draft of answer for General MacArthur to send to the JCS (reference FEAF crossing the Manchurian border), I wrote Earle a letter, telling him so and underscoring again my confidence in, and appreciation for, his abilities as a commander.

Quoted in toto is his (Partridge's) radio:

Stratline to Stratemeyer from Partridge: Enemy air operations on new high level today with both conventional and jet aircraft employ[ed]. At least one of these came directly across border and was sighted proceeding both east and west over Sinŭiju. Our inability to cross border conveys to enemy full initiative in action against friendly aircraft near Yalu River. Although I fully appreciate delicacy of international situation, I view with grave alarm present instructions which give sanctuary to enemy equipped with modern jet fighters. He gains confidence and aggressiveness with experience. Further, his numbers are increasing and if this trend continues unchecked he will soon constitute threat to overall operations of United Nations forces. Correction of this situation will require release of our aircraft to strike on or above Manchurian soil, a clearance which I am aware lies beyond your authority. My purpose in dispatching this msg is to present on one time basis my view of gravity of prospects under existing directives. Unless developments depart from those expected, I shall refrain from mentioning this subject again.

Sq Leader Suan, Royal Thai AF, called; directed him to see Craigie. Suan presented me with two letters addressed to me from Air Chief Marshal Ritthakani. Turned these letters over to D/O for preparation of reply. Subject in question is the evacuation of Thai wounded by MATS to Thailand.

Dispatched fol rad Stratline to FEAF COMBAT CARGO COMMAND, Tunner from Stratemeyer, with info to CINCFE and FIFTH AIR FORCE:

Because of shortage of suitable airfields in central and north Korea, it is inevitable that there will be competition for the use of those which do exist. The fol factors apply to this situation: *(a)* The sudden increase in both quantity and quality of enemy air activity. *(b)* Resultant necessity for moving 5th AF combat units forward. *(c)* Initiation of rail traffic to P'yŏngyang together with opening of port facilities at Haeju and impending opening of port at Chinnamp'o. *(d)* Opening of port and availability of cargo handling facilities at Wŏnsan and Iwŏn. In view of above, it is my desire that priority be given to requirements of Fifth Air Force for use of airfields in central and north Korea and that occupancy and use of these fields by aircraft of COCARCOM be limited only to that which is nec[essary] to airlift emergency supplies and equipment. COCARCOM is directed to lend all possible assistance to the forward move of combat units of FIFTH AIR FORCE.

---

running on MacArthur and it was only a matter of time before the clock stopped. (Goulden, pp 297-302; James, pp 519-523; "History of the JCS," pp 293-294.)

The draft I sent over to CINCFE, although utilized insofar as the thought was concerned, did not reflect the air picture - but more or less reflected the ground picture - in its final form as rewritten by GHQ, FEC. *For that reason, I dispatched the following redline to Vandenberg:*

Rate of enemy air operations on new high level yesterday with both conventional and jet aircraft employed. Enemy is gaining confidence and aggressiveness with this air experience. The enemy, equipped with modern jet fighters, has a sanctuary in Manchuria into which I am not permitted to penetrate. His numbers are increasing and if this trend continues unchecked, his air operations will soon constitute, in my opinion, a most serious threat to overall operations of the United Nations forces.

Here following is CINCFE's rad to JCS, CX 68436:

1. The introduction of Chinese Communist forces in strength into the Korean campaign has completely changed the overall situation and leads me to the conclusion that all previous plans for the provision of essential U.S. ground, sea and air forces must as a minimum requirement now be immediately and fully implemented. *2.* My grave concern as to the unsatisfactory status of Army replacements was reported in CINCFE msg CX 68300 dtd 050531. As reported in that msg the FEC has been and is still seriously understrength in Army personnel. It is essential that the replacement flow be immediately resumed. As a complementary measure action should be taken without delay to forward to this command those Army units, both combat and service which were previously requested or scheduled but which as yet have not arrived in this area. *3.* To properly support the ground effort, as a minimum the currently available naval and AF must be retained and maintained in the FEC at their authorized strengths and preparatory steps be taken to augment these forces promptly on call if necessity arises. *4.* Whether units, Army, Navy and Air, in addition to those previously requested will be required cannot accurately be determined at this time. There is no doubt, however, that the full requirement for balanced forces as stated during the earlier phases of the campaign must now be met with possible appreciable augmentation thereof. The alternatives are either a stalemate or the prospect of losing all that has thus far been gained. Signed MacArthur

Also, CINCFE sent the following to JCS, CX 68411:

Hostile planes are operating from bases west of the Yalu River against our forces in North Korea. These planes are appearing in increasing numbers. The distance from the Yalu to the main line of contact is so short that it is almost impossible to deal effectively with the hit-and-run tactics now being employed. The present restrictions imposed on my area of operation provide a complete sanctuary for hostile air immediately upon their crossing the Manchuria-North Korean border. The effect of this abnormal condition upon the morale and combat efficiency of both air and ground troops is major. Unless corrective measures are promptly taken this factor can assume decisive proportions. Request instructions for dealing with this new and threatening development. Signed MacArthur.

The JCS reply: (JCS 95949)[100]

The situation depicted in your C 68396 [of Nov. 7] is considerably changed from that reported in last sentence your C 68285 [of Nov. 4] which was our last report from you. We agree that the destruction of the Yalu bridges would contribute materially to the security of the forces under your command unless this action resulted in increased Chinese Communist effort and even Soviet contribution in response to what they might well construe as an attack on Manchuria. Such a result would not only endanger your forces but would enlarge the area of conflict and U. S. involvement to a most dangerous degree. However, in view of first sentence your 68396 you are authorized to go ahead with your planned bombing in Korea near the frontier including targets at Sinŭiju and Korean end of Yalu bridges provided that at time of receipt of this message you still find such action essential to safety of your forces. The above does not authorize the bombing of any dams or power plants on the Yalu River. Because of necessity for maintaining optimum position with the United Nations policy and directive and because it is vital in the national interest of the U. S. to localize the fighting in Korea. *IT IS IMPORTANT THAT EXTREME CARE BE TAKEN TO AVOID VIOLATION MANCHURIAN TERRITORY AND AIRSPACE AND TO REPORT PROMPTLY HOSTILE ACTION FROM MANCHURIA.* [emphasis in original.] It is essential that we be kept informed of important changes in situation as they occur and that your estimate as requested in our 95878 [of Nov. 6] be submitted as soon as possible.
(Italics in message mine.)

**WEDNESDAY
8 NOVEMBER
1950**

At my direction, Crabb sent out the following rad-note late 7 November 50.

Personal Partridge and O'Donnell from Stratemeyer. *PART I.* The max effort strike against Sinŭiju originally scheduled for 7 Nov will be executed on 8 Nov. Tgt [target] times and tasks asgd [assigned] to BOMCOM and 5th AF remain unchanged. *PART II.* I reiterate that you must insure all reasonable actions and precautions are taken to avoid violation of Manchuria territory and air space.

On my desk this morning was the following AFCVC TS 5400 from Vandenberg, a copy of which I had made to take over to MacArthur when I see him this AM:

In view of the changed military situation, particularly the resurgency of hostile air and appearance of jets, I propose to deploy to FEAF on temporary duty one each F–84E and F–86A wings. Believe it particularly advantageous to test the performance of these types under combat conditions.

---

100. This was the JCS's reply to MacArthur's outburst of Nov. 7. It was a restrained rebuke and also included a clear reminder that the JCS was to be kept "informed of important changes in [the] situation as they occur."

An essential condition to this deployment is your capability of operating these units from Korean fields. Can you meet this condition and does General MacArthur desire these reinforcements? Aircraft crews and as much supporting personnel and supplies as possible would be moved by Navy carrier and MATS. Movements could begin within ten (10) days after decision has been made. Let me have your views.

Dispatched a Stratline to Partridge, giving him the above info in Vandenberg's radio, statistics on capabilities of F–84E and F–86A, telling him PSP available in Yokohama and Seoul, and asking for info from him, by 1500/I, as to how he reacts to the basing of these wings in Korea - can he handle.[101] Dispatched Erler and Alkire for a conference with him re same.[102]

My AX 5454 to COMNAVFE, with info to CINCFE, BOMCOM and FAF in KOREA:

Part I. All out commitment of FEAF bombers today atk Sinŭiju and international bridges there makes it impossible to atk [attack] bridges south of Suiho Dam where heavy eny [enemy] traffic is rptd [reported]. Our pilots rpt hundreds of vehicles moving to south fr[om] Manchuria on hwy [highway] thru Sakchu. *PART II.* Req naval forces atk and destroy international bridges at 4028/12453 [map coordinates] and 4024 /12449 to block further eny mov. Priority to be given to hwy bridge at 4024/12449.[103] CINCFE has indicated approval to destroy first overwater span on Korean side of all international bridges between Manchuria and Korea provided Manchurian territory and air space not violated repeat not violated. *PART III.* CINCFE concurs in this req. CINCFE orders are that hydro-electric plant and associated fac[ilities] at Suiho must not repeat must not be atkd.

Starting at 1230 hours the following reports on the bomb raid on the bridges and town of Sinŭiju were made to me by General O'Donnell which I transmitted to General Hickey for General MacArthur.

1st Flight: three (3) B–29s, with one thousand-pound bombs on the first over-water span at Sinŭiju-Antung bridge; result - excellent; meager and accurate flak.

2nd Flight: four (4) B–29s on the other bridge, first over-water span; result - good, intense and inaccurate flak.

The seventy (70) B–29s in squadron formations loaded with thirty-two (32) incendiary cluster bombs; all results - excellent, with first squadron receiving intense and inaccurate flak and all the remaining squadrons receiving meager and inaccurate flak.

---

101. An oblong metal strip with numerous lightening holes in it, PSP (pierced steel plank) was used for surfacing a temporary runway.

102. The first F–84 mission, by the 27th Fighter Escort Wing (a SAC unit) was flown on Dec. 6. The first F–86 mission, an orientation flight, was flown by the 4th FIW on Dec. 15. (Futrell, p 248.) The slower and less maneuverable F–84 would be most used in Korea as a ground support aircraft, while the F–86, a close match for the MiG–15, would be used in the air superiority role.

103. These bridges were about 30 miles upstream of Sinŭiju at the town of Ch'ŏngsŏngjin which lay below the Suiho Reservoir. The restrictions on overflight and on which bridge spans could be destroyed naturally hampered effective strikes on all of the Yalu bridges.

At this time, the B–29s could bomb safely during daylight. The appearance of the MiG–15 changed that completely.

Each incendiary cluster is made up of 38 individual fire bombs; consequently, there were (32 x 38 x 70) 85,120 fire bombs on Sinŭiju. General O'Donnell indicates that the town was gone.[104]
There were no hostile fighter interception of our bombers. A FEAF Bomber Command recon airplane did report that an F–80 jet shot down a MiG–15.[105]

I reported to General Hickey that the missions for tomorrow would be with incendiary bombs, maximum effort of sixteen (16) B–29s would be over the towns of Sakchu and Puckchin; that the Navy would be requested to destroy the first over-water span of bridges and that our B–29 Razon equipped flight would take out any over-water spans of any bridges that were left standing.

FLASH REPORT from Fifth Air Force: First contact between F–80 and MiG–15s this morning - results no damage to F–80s, one MiG kill, and one probable.

In reference to developing facilities in Korea to handle the two new wings - one an F–84 and one an F–86, notified USAF with information to FEAMCOM and AMC

Reurmsg AFMSS.SP. 756645, dtd 4 Nov 50 and our msg AX 3103B dtd 6 Nov 50, Im opnl necessity exists for two airfields with possible rqmt for add[itional] two airfields in North Korea. Present sup[ply] of mat [PSP, etc.] in FEAF depots is considered min[imum] tac[tical] res[erve] for this

---

104. Approximately 60 percent of Sinŭiju's built-up area was burned out but though the approaches to the bridges had been damaged, the bridges were still standing and usable. (Futrell, p 223.)

105. In the first all-jet air battle in history, six Soviet-flown MiG–15s jumped a group of 51st FIW F–80s. It was readily apparent that the MiGs outclassed the F–80s. Nonetheless, Lt. Russell J. Brown was able to down one of the enemy planes, the first in a long line of Communist jets to fall in Korea.

theater. Req im action to release five million sq ft mat now on FEAMC rqn [requisition] to AMC. Further req that first two millionsq ft mat be loaded on one vessel to expedite trans-shipment fr Yokohama to Korea. Imperative that comp[lete] ship[ment] arr this theater prior to 1 Dec 50.

TS redline came in from Vandenberg re the release by 1 Dec of Weyland and Van's placement of him in Europe.

My reply, redline to Vandenberg, is as follows:

A few days ago Korean situation seemed in hand with operational aspects FEAF functioning smoothly and stabilized to point where Weyland could be released almost any time. In the light of the present critical turn of events, however, I am constrained to ask that he stay on at least until the situation is clarified somewhat. Will try to release him by 1 December as requested. Aside from his understandable preference for a command job, Weyland wants to serve where he can do you and Air Force the most good. In the event of any change in plans you indicated, I would be glad to have Weyland in any capacity and if I should lose Partridge for return to the ZI, I would give him the Fifth Air Force.

After talking with our communications people, I sent the fol redline to Twining personally:

We have not received the communications equipment in the quantities promised as a result of Ankenbrandt's visit to Far East Air Forces early July. The main weakness in our operation today is the lack of communications facilities to provide dependable circuits within Korea to our operational bases. We are now in the process of revising our present minimum requirements and anticipated future needs. Emphasis is being placed on HF [high frequency], both RTT [radio telephone and telegraphy] and voice, in lieu of wire or FM [frequency modulation], as a primary means of communication in view of mountainous terrain and guerrilla action repeat guerrilla action. I strongly urge that when our requirements are received, that every effort be made to expedite procurement and to airlift or ship by MARINEX [Marine Express] as we so indicate.

Before I left the office I sent a memo to General MacArthur giving him a resume of the flash reports I had received all afternoon:

MEMO in four parts. *PART I.* Eighty-three (83) B–29s were mounted for the Sinŭiju /attack which was made starting at 1210 and ending at 1225/8 November. Three were known to abort, and one is unaccounted for at this time. Seventy-nine (79) B–29s made the attack. No hostile fighter interception of our bombers. The mission was 'excellent;' the border was not violated. Information being gathered from the de-briefings indicates that some of the anti-aircraft encountered came from the vicinity of Antung, the area near the airport. *PART II.* From Fifth Air Force pilots' ops reports on Sinŭiju, they indicate that the town was burning fiercely and was covered 90 percent by bombers. Flak was estimated at moderate and reasonably accurate. One B–29 appeared to be hit. No enemy fighters were sighted. In the prebombing attack on Sinŭiju, no F–80s were lost. One report indicates that one bridge span on the North Korean side was knocked out, but this cannot be verified because of the dense smoke which had reached an altitude of 15,000 feet. *PART III.* The mission for tomorrow will be a Navy-FEAF Bomber Command coordinated attack on the towns of Sakchu and Puckchin and Yalu River bridges. FEAF Bomber Command's maximum effort of 16 B–29s, carrying incendiaries, will take out the two towns. The Navy has been requested to destroy the first over-water spans of specified bridges over the Yalu River. In addition, FEAF Bomber Command will mount a flight of B–29 Razon-equipped aircraft to operate against bridges should any spans be left standing. *PART IV.* Fifth Air Force flash report of 1500 hours indicates that the first meeting of F–80s and MiG–15s took place this morning. Results: one MiG kill, one MiG probable; no damage to F–80s. S/G.E.S.

Received a reply from Cabell re my radnote to him that the team of analysts he was sending out should be fitted into the Barcus group. Cabell stated:

It is believed highly desirable that 3 target analysts (Mayer, Loftus, and Staats)[106] concerned with broad economic vulnerability and other target analysis problems work very closely with other evaluation groups in order to avoid duplication and insure that data collected are of maximum utility in future target analyses. Your support in providing or procuring for them necessary interpreters, clerical assistance, transportation, etc., will be appreciated. The other 7 target analysts headed by Walker and Allen[107] to be sent out from this headquarters constitute a team of highly specialized physical vulnerability analysts who will be seeking detailed data concerning the effectiveness of specific weapons against particular targets and in particular certain types of data not adequately reported by the bombing surveys following World War II. While this team should be regarded as augmentation of General Barcus' group, it is urged insofar as feasible they be permitted to operate as an integrated field team and to inspect particular targets preselected in a carefully worked out plan. Five of the interpreters and all the other personnel and equipment requested in Radnote 041810/Z are desired for this team. Estimated date of departure of both groups is 10 November.

Because of shortage of "indians" caused by so many "chiefs" arriving, but not wishing to appear "negative" phrased my reply to Cabell with care, in the hope of indicating to him that this above group should bring with it as many or as much of their clerical help as possible.

Part I. CINCFE has granted theater clearance to party of ten, but we need names and grades before arrival. No objection to analysis personnel working as an integrated field team. However, I strongly recommend that they work under Barcus in order to avoid any possible duplication of effort.

---

106. E.A. Mayer and J.E. Loftus worked in the Office of the Director of Intelligence, HQ USAF. It is unknown where W.T. Staats worked.
107. C.B. Walker and Henry V. Allen both worked in the Office of the Chief of Naval Operations.

PART II. Re personnel to be provided locally. *(a)* Clerical personnel: Enlisted typist only can be made available. *(b)* Draftsmen: Japanese draftsmen only are available without seriously interfering with the high priority target program now being carried on in FEAF Hq. *(c)* Interpreters: Without curtailing present interrogation program, cannot furnish interpreters who are qualified to work on material classified higher than Confidential. In the light of above, recommend that group bring with it as much as possible of supporting personnel.

Had a Mexican dinner at Mayeda House - guests were the MacNaughtons, Rogerses, Davisons, and the Adamses. The girls having had a golf tournament in the afternoon, I awarded prizes to the winner and runners up.

Presented Annalee with her birthday present - a pearl and diamond clip, to match her ring. She was really surprised, and delighted.

THURSDAY 9 NOVEMBER 1950

Weyland prepared following redline to be dispatched at 2200 hours.

Reference your redline 5400. TDY of F–84E and F–86 wings with this command highly desirable and Gen. MacArthur fully concurs in earliest deployment. Operating bases can be provided in Korea. When decision on deployment is made will furnish some detailed recommendations on supplies, spares, personnel etc. by reason of introduction of new type units into theater.

Departed Haneda for Itazuke 1000 hours to meet and welcome Brigadier General Sweetser and his 452d Bomb Wing (L). On arrival at Itazuke at 1245 hours, was met by General Sweetser, Colonel Stratton,[108] base commander, and Lt. Col. Charles W. Howe, the group commander .

Immediately proceeded to mess where we had lunch and a nice visit, and I met young Richard Leebrick.[109]

We then went out to the line and inspected several of his aircraft - which by the way are in excellent mechanical condition, some being taken direct from mothballs and having only about nine hours time.

Young Leebrick accompanied us. I had several pictures taken, copies of which I have directed Nuckols to send to the *Los Angeles Times*, to Long Beach papers, the *Peru Republican*, and to Washington papers. My secretary will send copies of these pictures, with letter of transmittal to Mr. Charles Leebrick.

General Sweetser had assembled all possible men and officers and I made a short address to them of welcome.

Departed Itazuke at 1430 hours. While in the air near Itazuke, picked up on the radio General Henebry's arrival at Brady.[110] Talked to Henebry over the radio, welcomed him. (Will try to get away tomorrow - 11 Nov 50 to go down and see him.)

Landed at Haneda at 1701 and proceeded directly home.

Talked to Col. Warren in Ops and got the results of today's missions.

---

108. Prior to this assignment, Col Wilbur H. Stratton was the 8th FBW's executive officer.
109. Unable to identify Leebrick or his father, Charles.
110. The first aircraft of Henebry's 437th TCW arrived at Brady on the 8th.

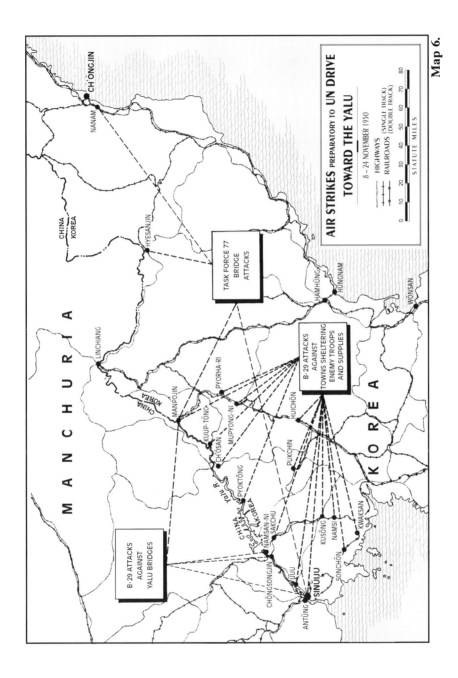

Map 6.

AIR STRIKES PREPARATORY TO UN DRIVE
TOWARD THE YALU

8 – 24 NOVEMBER 1950

HIGHWAYS
RAILROADS (SINGLE TRACK)
         (DOUBLE TRACK)

STATUTE MILES

0   10   20   30   40   50   60   70   80

TASK FORCE 77
BRIDGE
ATTACKS

B-29 ATTACKS
AGAINST
TOWNS SHELTERING
ENEMY TROOPS
AND SUPPLIES

B-29 ATTACKS
AGAINST
YALU BRIDGES

MANCHURIA

KOREA

CHINA
KOREA

CHINA
KOREA

CH'ŎNGJIN

NANAM

HYESANJIN

HAMHŬNG

HŬNGNAM

WŎNSAN

LINCHIANG

MANPOJIN

PYORHA-RI

KUUP-TONG

CH'ŎSAN

MUPYONG-NI

HUICHŎN

PUKCHIN

PYOKTONG

Yalu R.

NAMSAN-NI

SAKCHU

CHŎNGSONGJIN

UIJU

SINŬIJU

ANTUNG

SONCHŎN

NAMSI

KUSŎNG

KWAKSAN

273

FRIDAY   *Dispatched the following letter to Vandenberg:*

10 NOVEMBER Following Johnnie Walker's magnificent drive from
1950   Pusan to P'yŏngyng and beyond, I wrote him the attached
                 letter on 28 October. (See diary note under that date.) A
deep feeling of comradeship and mutual respect has developed between
FEAF, the Fifth Air Force, and Eighth Army since the arduous days of
the early part of the campaign. Johnnie Walker and his Eighth Army
have battled the enemy and at the same time have battled inadequate
supplies, lack of trained combat troops and all the other impediments
that a man could face. His warm and obviously sincere reply of
7 November also is attached. I hope you will get as much of a lift
from his letter as did I. This letter might be helpful with the Vincent [*sic*]
Committee.[111] Best Regards. s/G.E.S.

General Walker's letter reads as follows:

Headquarters, Eighth United States Army (EUSAK), APO 301, c/o PM,
San Francisco, California. Dtd 7 Nov 50.

Dear Strat: Your fine letter of 28 October is deeply appreciated. Throughout the trying days in Korea my confidence and the confidence of my
troops has been greatly sustained by the knowledge that the Air Forces in
Korea and those elsewhere in the Far East Command were giving us
unstinted and skillful support. The magnificent spirit of your commanders, your pilots and your ground crews has always been in evidence and
has been a source of inspiration to all. Your officers and airmen have won
and shall retain the affection and gratitude of all ranks in the Eighth
Army. They have shared our trials and tribulations. They have shared our
successes. They shall share the final victory. With warm personal regards,
I am, Faithfully yours: s/Johnnie Walker (Walton H. Walker, Lt. General,
United States Army.)

Dispatched a Stratline to Partridge and Sweetser:

I flew to Itazuke yesterday and called on General Sweetser, CG 452d
Bomb Wing (L) and addressed his officers and men. Was impressed with
condition of his equipment, with morale of his officers and men, and his
individual leadership and knowledge of the capabilities of his personnel
and equipment. I directed that he report expeditiously to you. It is my
opinion that the Fifth Air Force is fortunate in having this unit assigned
and I am confident that they will give a good account of themselves. Their
tails are in the air.

Crabb flashed me the news that at about 1245 today, 6 MiGs hopped on and
shot down a B–29 as it was withdrawing from the target at Ŭiju. Eleven men
were seen to parachute from the plane. Plane went down near the coast and air-
sea rescue now in process.

---

111. Actually the Vinson Committee, after the Chairman of the House Armed Services Committee, Rep. Carl
Vinson. His committee was preparing to hold hearings on tactical aviation.

Sir Esler Dening[112] (British Ambassador at Large - like U.S. Ambassador Jessup) and Sir Alvary Gascoigne called at 1030 hours. Sir Esler was a member of Lord Louis Mountbatten's staff - being his political adviser.

1530, Colonel Cleeves[113] completed my physical examination at the Tokyo General.

1800 hours, we had dinner with the Hills.

SATURDAY 11 NOVEMBER 1950

In reply to my radio of congratulations to the Navy - Personal Joy and Struble from Stratemeyer - re their bridge strikes when BomCom hit Puckchin and Sakchu - received in answer the following two radnotes:

FROM STRUBLE: Your congratulations are much appreciated and we are glad to be able to contribute to the campaign.

FROM JOY: Joy to Stratemeyer information Struble. Referring to your cite AX 3251B VCO X, your congratulations to Task Force 77 airmen of the 7th Fleet for their aggressive attacks on the Yalu Bridges are read with pleasure. Navy airmen are proud to receive praise from you and members of a command whose effective bombing and sky clearing fighter tactics over northern Korea are observed with admiration.

Left Haneda at 1000 hours and flew to Brady Air Base where I was met by Brigadier General John P. Henebry and his staff. Immediately went to his mess hall, had lunch, and a good visit, after which he assembled all of his officers, men, and I made a speech of welcome to his wing. (They all seemed to have appreciated what I said because they applauded enthusiastically at the end of my few words.)

I made it very plain to Henebry that he took his operational orders from Tunner but that he was assigned to FAF and his administrative and logistical support would come from them.

General Stratemeyer addresses members of the newly-arrived 437th TCW from the bed of a weapons carrier. Note Stratemeyer's non-standard wearing of the CBI patch on his blue uniform. A number of the 437th's officers can be seen wearing the old olive drab USAAF uniforms.

---

112. Dening had been Chief Political Adviser to the Supreme Allied Commander, SE Asia from 1943-1946, and later became Assistant Under-Secretary at the Foreign Office. At this time, he was on a special mission to Asia with the rank of ambassador. Later, he was the British ambassador to Japan.

113. Cleeves was a FEAF surgeon.

General Henebry impressed me greatly; he is 32 years old, has had a world of combat experience and I am confident he will lead his combat wing most efficiently.

SUNDAY
12 NOVEMBER
1950

Received a letter from Gilkeson which I told Craigie to show to General Hickey, C/S, FEC:

General Bolté[114] and party dropped in here the day before yesterday (ltr written 9 Nov). General Beightler[115] took care of them overnite. Last evening Beightler informed me that Bolté had tipped him off to the fact that the Navy is taking steps to have Guam declared a unified command under the Navy. I do not know any other facts in the matter. The new admiral who replaced Eddie Ewan has attempted to be very dictatorial since his arrival - in small matters so far.[116] The Sec of Navy is due in here next week (Secret). Thought you would want to know of the rumor concerning Navy plans. Best regards. s/Gilkey.

My letter to Nate Twining, this date, reads as follows:

Your attention is invited to the attached letter from Gilkeson. It has been shown to MacArthur's Chief of Staff, Major General Doyle O. Hickey, by Craigie. Thought that it would be of interest to you and some of your planning boys. As you know, the home station of the 19th Bomb Group is at Andersen Air Force Base on Guam, the 19th Wing being a part of FEAF command which operates under General MacArthur. We are spending money to improve Andersen and I am of the opinion that General MacArthur would take exception to a unified command set-up on Guam. Certainly, I could not have what little striking force exists in the Far East Air Forces stationed on Guam under the Navy. Would appreciate your comments and the return to me of Gilkey's personal letter to me (attached). Best regards.

Dispatched the fol informational redline to Vandenberg:

Enemy a/c losses 1 Nov thru 11 Nov inclusive: destroyed: two MiG–15s and sixteen Yaks. Probably destroyed: five MiG–15s. Damaged: fourteen MiG–15s and nine Yaks. Above does not include two MiG–15s claimed destroyed by U. S. Navy aircraft. Total destroyed by FEAF: forty-six enemy aircraft. Total destroyed by Navy: two. Grand Total: forty-eight enemy aircraft destroyed period 1 November thru 11 November.

Called on Turner Joy (Admiral Joy, COMNAVFE) and discussed with him (1500) hours - his office) some highly classified intelligence matters and asked for his assistance; he indicated that he would do everything he could.

---

114. Maj Gen Charles L. Bolté was the Army's deputy chief of staff, G-3 (training and operations). He arrived in Japan on Oct. 31 to discuss planned reductions in Army forces in Korea. The reductions were shelved when the Chinese offensive rendered them moot.

115. Maj Gen Robert S. Beightler headed the Army's Marianas-Bonins Command.

116. Rear Adm Edward C. Ewan took command of TF 77 in late August, commanding it until Dec. 25, 1950. The "new admiral" was Rear Adm O.B. Hardison, Commander Naval Forces Marianas.

We also discussed the coming visit of the Secretary of the Navy, the Honorable Francis P. Matthews.[117]

Immediately upon return to the office I got off a radnote to the CO Itazuke AB, with info to General Sweetser, that Adm Joy will precede the Honorable Francis P. Matthews to Itazuke on 19 November and that the Secretary will land Itazuke 1700 hours (local). Instructed that billeting and Air Force honors be given the Secretary and six officers and two enlisted Navy men the night of 19-20 November. They will depart 0700 hours, 20 Nov, for Kimp'o.

Also by radnote informed Stearley that the Secretary is due Naha 1230 hours, 19 Nov, and will depart that same day for Itazuke . Asked that he advise General McClure, also he provide AF honors and that the Secretary be afforded every opportunity to inspect Naval installations and then be driven to Kadena from where he will depart. No lunch required.

USAF sent the fol radnote (TS 5432):

Re movement of F–84E and F–86 wings to FEAF, air echelon of the 27th Fighter Wing (F–84E) and one squadron of the 4th Fighter Wing (F–86) will load on carriers *Bairoko, Bataan* and *[Cape] Esperance* on Nov 14, 16 and 17, with 110 a/c and approximately 150 officers, 1200 men, and 400 tons of supplies and equipment. Remainder of the 4th Fighter Wing will be shipped as early as possible, exact date undetermined, by either carrier or tankers. Additional materiel and personnel will move by MATS and water transportation. Request earliest information as to the availability of heavy equipment in the theater for these organizations in order to avoid unnecessary movement from the ZI and any further recommendations you may have in connection with supply and personnel as suggested in your redline.[118]

Upon receipt of the above, immediately queried FAF as follows:

Fol info received from Hq USAF: Air echelon of the 27th Fighter Wg (F–84E) and one squadron of the 4th Fighter Wg (F–86) will load on carriers *Bairoko, Bataan* and *[Cape] Esperance* on November 14, 16, and 17, with 110 acft and approx 150 off, 1200 men, and 400 tons of supplies and equipment. Remainder of the 4th Fighter Wing will be shipped as early as possible, exact date undetermined, by either carrier or tankers. Additional materiel and personnel will move by MATS and water transportation. Request any recommendations you may have on bases, equipment, supply or personnel.

Informed Partridge the Navy Secretary will spend nite of 19 Nov at Itazuke, and will arrive Kimp'o 0900 hours, local, on 20 Nov. "This for your info in order that you or Timberlake can meet them if operations will permit."

---

117. Matthews had been Secretary of the Navy since May 1949.

118. The 4th FIW had been based at New Castle Airport, Wilmington, Delaware, and the 27th FEW had been at Bergstrom AFB, Austin, Texas. Alerted on Nov. 9, planes from the two wings were loaded on carriers at San Diego between Nov. 14 and 27. The last carrier reached Japan on Dec. 13. (Futrell No. 72, p 17.)

MONDAY

13 NOVEMBER

1950

Intend to send the fol ltr to Vandenberg.

I am sending direct to you the attached recommendation for the award of the first Oak Leaf Cluster to the Medal of Honor for General MacArthur in great hopes that you and the Secretary of the AF, the Hon Thomas K. Finletter, will support me in this award. I know of no figure of important national and international status today - or in the past -that more prominently occupies his position than General of the Army Douglas MacArthur. His courage, gallantry, and valor in the Korean War have been displayed time and time again way beyond the call of duty. The United States Air Force today, in my opinion, does not have a better friend than General MacArthur. He believes in air power, he knows how to use it, and he has backed me one hundred percent in my position as Commanding General, Far East Air Forces. I feel that to have this recommendation for the first Oak Leaf Cluster to his Medal of Honor come from the Air Force would be most appropriate and of historical significance. I therefore urge from the bottom of my heart that you do everything possible to secure this very deserving award for Douglas MacArthur.

Attached to above letter was this "official" ltr with appropriate attachments:

Subject - Award of the first Oak Leaf Cluster to the Medal of Honor, to: CSAF, etc. *1.* I recommend unhesitantly, with humility, that the first Oak Leaf Cluster to his Medal of Honor be awarded General of the Army Douglas MacArthur. *2.* I base this recommendation upon his distinguished and conspicuous leadership, gallantry and intrepidity at risk of his life above and beyond the call of duty in valorous action against invading North Korean forces during the period 29 June through 20 October 1950, and on his heroically conducted defensive and offensive operations based upon brilliantly conceived concepts of modern war which turned the tide of campaign in Korea favorably to the United Nations forces. *3. a.* The specific periods in which he risked death or capture by the enemy, in furtherance of his conception of duty and mission, were: 29 June, 27 July, 15 through 21 September, 29 September and 20 October, during which periods he personally reconnoitered the area down to the Han river; surveyed the perimeter defense plans and dispositions at Taegu; directed the Inch'ŏn amphibious operations; personally turned the city of Seoul back to the Republic of Korea; and observed the landing of airborne troops north of the enemy front lines, thereby closing the trap on enemy elements in the P'yŏngyng area. *b.* The performance of all these missions involving air, sea and land travel and reconnaissance embodied great inherent risks. In General MacArthur's case these risks were multiplied many times by his position as Commander-in-Chief of the United Nations Command and foremost target of Communism in the Far East. In addition he was Supreme Commander Allied Powers; Commander-in-Chief, Far East; and Commanding General of all United States Army forces in the Far East. *c.* By making these front line contacts and forward reconnaissances he gained complete understanding of the military situation. They enabled him to formulate strategic decisions which traded space for time in defense while preparing the brilliantly conceived and executed offense which brought world acclaim to United Nations forces. d. His was absolute fearlessness and conspicuous valor in utter disregard of personal danger under fire and aerial attack; his was calm judgment in each crisis backed by the reassurance of his unshaken, confident predictions of victory. His was a leadership that galvanized, inspired and encouraged the forces under this command to desperate effort, at times against overwhelming odds, and set for them the standard of selfless performance of duty he exacted from himself. *4.* I have personal knowledge of the acts and services for which this award is recommended, and in addition am enclosing the certificates of Major General Courtney Whitney, Military Secretary to General MacArthur, and Brigadier General Edwin K. Wright, G-3, of the United Nations and Far East Command, who witnessed these operations as members of General MacArthur's staff. *5.* A recommended citation also is enclosed.

CITATION: For distinguished and conspicuous leadership, gallantry and intrepidity at risk of his life above and beyond the call of duty in action against invading North Korean forces, and for his valor in the heroic conduct of defensive and offensive operations resulting in victory for the United Nations in Korea. In constant danger of his life from enemy ground and aerial attacks, General MacArthur made repeated trips in unarmed aircraft over and near enemy-held territory. After his landings in or near the battle area he made extensive front-line inspection trips and personally directed defensive measures, delaying actions and attacks. This leadership ended the disorganized rout of South Korean forces and changed it into dogged, firm resistance and regrouping in the face of tremendous odds. At all times he risked death or capture by the enemy. His strategic concepts and superb understanding of the use of ground, naval and air forces brought about firm holding lines which an enemy greatly superior in men and equipment was unable to break. His organization and personal direction of amphibious landings at Inch'ŏn turned the tide of battle and brought about entrapment of North Korean forces south of that area. His entrapment and rout of enemy forces by airborne personal direction of parachute drops of thousands of men with their equipment behind North Korean lines greatly reduced enemy resistance. His leadership of the allied forces brought them world acclaim for their gallant defense and victorious offense. His utter disregard of personal danger under heavy fire and aerial bombardment, his calm judgment in each crisis, and his unshaken, confident predictions of victory in the face of seeming disaster galvanized the spirit of resistance and confirmed the faith of the South Korean, the United States and the other nations of the United Nations in the power of their armed might against imperialist aggression. The successful conclusion of this first great test of United Nations effort was inspired by his spirit and actions. His contribution may lead the way toward eventual unity and peace for the nations of the world.[119]

---

119. MacArthur did not receive his medal.

Had a good visit with Colonel Dennison[120] who is here from General Bertran-dias'[121] office. We discussed preventive accidents. Both he and the civilian with him stated that they had received wonderful cooperation from all my stations.

Crabb got off a redline for me to Vandenberg reporting the incident of the hung bomb which fell on Antung.[122] (Rosie O'Donnell called me earlier on this.) O'Donnell reported that the bombing of the Sinŭiju bridges were "excellent."

Annalee and I had dinner with Ambassador Sebald and Mrs. Sebald who were honoring Sir Esler Dening, British Ambassador-at-Large.

Got off my weekly SOP letter to Gill Robb Wilson.

TUESDAY 14 NOVEMBER 1950 Instructed my people to send copies of O'Donnell's radio to me with reference the strike on the Sinŭiju bridges and the "hung" bomb that fell on Antung, to CINCFE along with information of my redline to Vandenberg informing him of the incident.

Sent Vandenberg pages 1-k, 1-j, and 1-1 from Willoughby's Intelligence Summary of today. It was a resume, giving concrete figures, of the effects of our air efforts - in all phases - in Korea. In written words it acknowledges and underscores everything I've said about our activities. It will be good ammunition for Vandenberg to utilize during the coming Vinson hearings to which he (Vandenberg) tipped me off that Partridge or Weyland - or both - might be called to Washington to appear.

Reported to General MacArthur about 1145 hours to discuss with him the possibility that one of our bombs yesterday dropped on the city of Antung. I indicated that I was not too much concerned myself, that this was a pure accident, and that I in no way censored the Bomber Command. General MacArthur after looking at the photographs asked to read the Carmichael report and General O'Donnell's preliminary report of last night. After reading both he said to me "Strat, I do not admit anything. We'll make no report of this and as Bomber Command's lawyer, I propose to fight it if we are called on for a report." He said, "Carmichael does not admit it - nor does O'Donnell." I indicated that I would not admit it too much myself; however I did make it plain that the chances were that this was a damaged fin on one of the bombs that caused this bomb to deflect and hit Antung in view of the excellent pattern shown in the photographs.

I told him I had forwarded by redline to Vandenberg General O'Donnell's report. General MacArthur's remark was - "that's too bad, Strat." I told him that because of the border violations why it had to be done and MacArthur indicated that was all right. I told him that I had ended Rosie's quote with a statement that he (Vandenberg) would be kept advised. His instructions to me then were to send the Carmichael report by radio and then add this: "The facts of this case are too indefinite to reach any authoritative conclusions."

---

120. Col Junius W. Dennison, Jr.
121. Maj Gen Victor E. Bertrandias, Deputy Inspector General for Flight Safety Research and Technical Inspection, USAF.
122. As the B–29s of Col Richard H. Carmichael's 98th BG attacked Sinŭiju on the 13th, one bomb out of the 102 thousand-pounders dropped hit 1,983 feet from the average range of the bombing patterns and 3,500 feet to the side of the patterns. The area where the bomb landed was in Antung, across the Yalu from Sinŭiju. Tactics used by the B–29s could not explain why this one bomb deviated, but it was thought that defective tail fins on the bomb created the bombing error.

Since General MacArthur indicated he was not going to report this, I did not list CINCFE - or O'Donnell - as an info addressee on the following redline to Vandenberg, but did send both copies of the dispatch, which is quoted below:

Redline Personal Vandenberg from Stratemeyer. Remy A 3425 OP-op. I quote Colonel Richard H. Carmichael's report to FEAF Bomber Command: "1. On 13 November 1950, the 98th Bombardment Group (M) was ordered to destroy the railroad bridges spanning the Yalu River, connecting the cities of Sinŭiju and Antung. Three flights, composed of four, two and three aircraft respectively, attacked the bridges at 1205 local time. *2.* The first flight, composed of four aircraft, made their final bomb run on an axis of 230 degrees. The second flight, composed of two air-craft, turned slightly short of the initial point and made the final bomb run on an axis of 237 degrees. The last flight, composed of three aircraft, made their attack on an axis of 232 degrees. The altitude separation was 500 feet between each flight, with the average altitude at 25,000 feet pres-sure. A total of one-hundred two 1,000 pound demolition bombs were released from the 9 aircraft in the formation in less than 10 seconds. The remaining six bombs were not released due to a bomb door malfunction, and were salvoed at sea after departing from Korea. The intervelometer setting was 50 feet, allowing a walk of 500 feet from the first to last release. Bomb releases were made on the three squadron leads, and the three flights turned from the axis of attack immediately after bombs away to avoid any possible violation of the Manchurian border. The general bombing pattern was confined to an area of 1,400 feet in radius; however, an explosion was observed and scored 4,123 feet from the mean point of impact. The explosion was 2,800 feet from the farthest bomb in the immediate target area. The aiming point for the formation was the most eastern end of the 2 railroad bridges spanning the Yalu River. The bombs on the western perimeter of the main distribution were less than half way across the Yalu River separating North Korea from Manchuria. The explosion observed was approximately 1,800 feet southwest of the west-ern end of the railroad bridge. The divorced explosion was 1,983 feet from the average range of the flights and the deflection was 3,500 feet from the average pattern of the composite group. *3.* It is remotely possi-ble that the explosion observed was a bomb dropped by the formation of nine aircraft attacking the bridges, if the following conditions were resolved. To account for the range, distance fore and aft, the bomb would have to have been carried another nine or ten seconds along the same axis of attack. To proffer an explanation for the deflection, lateral error, an air-craft would have to assume a sharp bank of 1/4 needle width or greater. *4.* All three flights turned off the axis of attack immediately after bombs away to avoid tracking flak and the proximity of the border. No one a/c in any of the three flights broke formation, which lent no opportunity to continue on the same course to drop a single bomb. The three turns exe-cuted by the trailing flights were normal formation turns providing little or not opportunity for a 1,000 pound bomb to be centrifugally thrown almost 3,000 feet. After reaching terminal velocity the 1,000 pound demolition bomb becomes extremely stable, and it is difficult to find a suitable or logical explanation for the one explosion which occurred 4,123 feet from the aiming point assigned to the 98th Bombardment Group (M)." The facts of this case are too indefinite to reach any authoritative conclusions.

Went again to see MacArthur about 1800 hours and pointed out that due to the some 15 MiG's attacking our '29s, we had 5 that were forced down - but no known fatalities. I told him that I was against attacking these bridges without giving our bombers the fighter cover they are entitled to even though it violated the border. He agreed with me except that he could not give the green light on this procedure at this time. He said he expected the UN to act reference this subject this coming Wednesday and that if he did not hear favorably then, he proposed to make a request for me to protect my bombers and violate the air space if it becomes necessary. I told him that I would continue to wash out all cities and that 15 Nov we were concentrating our entire bomber effort on Hoeryŏng [near the west coast]. He pointed out that those bridges that we felt we could not hit without violating the border then to absolutely obliterate the communications along both rail and railroad leading to those bridges from Korea. I came back to the office and informed both Craigie and Weyland of my conference and directed orders be issued as General MacArthur directed. While here in the office I learned that only 2 B–29s were forced down due to enemy action and that the other three were due to run away props caused by engine failures due to the high altitude (25,000 feet) for the attack on the Sinŭiju bridges. This information I telephoned to General Hickey.

The two that landed due to enemy action landed at Kimp'o. One had its brakes shot out and finally got in on the ground; it washed out four F4Us (Marine fighters). The co-pilot had his leg broken due to 20 mm fire and the engineer was very seriously injured due to the enemy action.

The other B–29 made its landing satisfactorily.

WEDNESDAY 15 NOVEMBER 1950 *In response to Vandenberg's redline to me, got the following stratline off to Partridge:*

Rad in 2 parts. *PART I.* Fol redline received from Vandenberg: "From a study of your daily operations summaries for the past 12 days it is concluded that the majority of night intruder sorties now being flown in Korea are by USMC F7F aircraft under 5th AF control. I recognize that the primary objective is to increase the tempo of night operations regardless of who does it. In view, however, of our previous exchange of messages on the subject of night operations and the efforts on the part of this hqs to increase your night intruder capabilities, the AF showing in the past 2 weeks is somewhat disappointing to me. The AF must become as proficient in night air support operations as they are in the day time. This is the opportunity to begin the development of the tactics and techniques to accomplish this objective. I want you to push this program vigorously." *PART II.* I realize that operating areas have been restricted and there are probably other good reasons why more USAF night intruder operations have not been conducted recently. However, with arrival of the 452d LB Wg, I expect the 3d LB Wg, with the newly attached night intruder squadron, to specialize in night operations.[123] Until such time as the new bomb units become fully operational, step up your night operations with the squadron of the 3d Gp which has specialized in night work, and also utilize in a similar manner available operational aircraft of the new night intruder squadron.

In answer to the redline Vandenberg sent me (which is quoted in my radnote to Patridge), I told him

I appreciate your concern over night intruder operations which for a time have been curtailed. Severely restricted operating areas, extremely mountainous terrain, fog and haze at night all have affected night operations of 3d Bomb Gp which does not have radar in acft. Only four aircraft of 731st Bomb Sq Nite are operational with APQ-13 "B" components reinstalled. This equipment for other acft daily expected but hasn't arrived. Partridge instructed to employ 13th Sq 3d Gp and opnl acft 731st Sq to best advantage in nite operations and to further specialize 3d Gp in this work as availability light bombers increases.

Left the office early and got in a golf game with Adm Joy, Comdr Muse and Mr. Garey of *Time-Life*. Had a good game - and played good golf. Score was 92, but it was with a 12 on one hole.

Rosie O'Donnell called the office and left word that mission was "Excellent" - they encountered no flak, no enemy fighters - and that he was "using my name" in a radnote to his commanders.

Rad received "From Vandenberg to Barcus info Stratemeyer" in answer to my radnote to General Twining.

...sending team of target analysts to support your effort. <u>Believe these should work under your guidance to avoid duplication of effort.</u> [Underlining in original.] Seven of this gp [group] are interested in the field of physical vulnerability of targets to particular weapons and should work as an integrated team; three are analysts with general analytical experience. Names and grades as follows: TEAM COMMANDER Lt Col P.H. Taylor, Army officer assigned to Director of Intelligence, Maj J.O. Ronningen from ID. GENERAL ANALYTICAL TEAM: E. A. Mayer (GS-14); J. E. Loftus (GS-14); W. T. Staats (GS-13). PHYSICAL VULNERABILITY TEAM: C. B. Walker (GS-14), H. V. Allen (GS-13), E. S. DeLeon (GS-12); R. F. Ritchel (GS-11); L Chernus (GS-9); L. E. Dolan (GS-7); R. V. Kaiazek (GS-5).[124] Theater clearance for the 2 Army officers was requested yesterday but Col. Taylor's name was not available at that time. Group scheduled to leave here 17 Nov 1400/Z time.

---

123. Formerly part of the 452d Wing, the 731st BS (L-NA) had been especially trained for low-level operations. It had been decided to convert the 3d BG (under the 3d BW) completely to night attack. Because the 3d was also understrength, the 731st BS was attached to it. The 731st flew its first squadron mission on Nov. 24. (Futrell, p 128; Cantwell, pp 42-43.)

124. Taylor and Ronningen worked in the Office of the Assistant Chief of Staff, G-2, U.S. Army; Mayer, Loftus, Staats, and Chernus worked in the Office of the Director of Intelligence, HQ USAF; Walker, DeLeon, and Dolan worked in the Office of the Chief of Naval Operations; Allen, Ritchel, and Kaiazek are unidentified.

General Kenney's Human Resources Team under Col. Croker[125] will include a small team of psychological intelligence specialists under Dr. Fred Williams.[126] This team's operations should be coordinated by your group and their work supported in all respects so far as practicable. [Underlining in original.][127]

THURSDAY 16 NOVEMBER 1950

Reached the office this morning and was informed that General Almond, X Corps commander had sent a radnote to us asking for 34 control parties. That radio has about as much sense to it as if I had sent him a signal and told him I would like to have 10 nicely upholstered sedans, painted Air Force blue, to meet me at the airfield at Yongp'o-dong when I landed. Partridge and Meyers intend to call on General Almond and get him straightened out.

Received the radnote which Rosie had mentioned in his telephone conversation yesterday. It is a good one and I quote it in full for diary record:

Personal from O'Donnell to Briggs, Jennings, Carmichael and Hilger. *PARA I*. The sudden change in the tac sit due to act[ive] intervention of the Chinese Communists has placed a heavy load upon our combat and maint[enance] crews, our a/c, and our staffs during the past 11 days. The performance of Bomb Cmd during this max effort period has inflicted heavy damage on the enemy and, in my opinion, has been largely responsible for his rapid transition from a cocky and confident offensive to a sullen and stunned defensive. *PARA II*. During the past few years, while the Chinese Communist armies were conquering most of China against sponge defenses and little air opposition, their egos had ample opportunity for growth. The rapidity and completeness of their successes undoubtedly rendered them drunk with power and high self esteem. The insolence of their Prime Minister's recent threat against the U.S. is a good example of their arrogance and imagined prowess. *PARA III*. They have now found what it is to run up against the U.S. AF and, while I cannot say what the future holds for us, I am certain that a re-evaluation of the sit is unquestionably being made at Peiping. *PARA IV*. Our effort has not been made without cost. Enemy ftrs [fighters] attacking fr sanctuary north of the border had inflicted damage, including the loss of one a/c and crew. Engines have suffered due to formation flying at higher alts [altitudes]. Crews have become fatigued, and, to make the course more sporty for the units at Okinawa, the wea[ther] man arranged a typhoon hit right in the middle of this critical period. *PARA V*. We are today returning to normal combat effort and it is my desire that max maint effort be applied in the docks and on the hardstands until we regain the healthy airplane and engine condition we enjoyed before this phase of the campaign. *PARA VI*. Gen Stratemeyer has

---

125. Col George W. Croker.
126. Dr. Frederick Williams was assistant director of the Air University Far East Research Group in Human Resources and also head of the Psychological Warfare Research Team.
127. The purpose of the Human Resources Team visit was to study the combat situation as it affected morale and interpersonal relations. Two groups, the Personal Research Team and the Psychological Warfare Research Team, made up the larger organization.

asked me to add his congratulations to my own upon the precise and accurate bombing accomplished in the face of serious restrictive border conditions and unk[nown] ftr and anti-aircraft defense strengths.

USAF (Twining personal for Stratemeyer) sent a radio

request clearance of theater for following in lieu of Generals Curtis and Leach, whose clearances should be cancelled: Dr. Robert L. Stearns, civilian consultant to C/S, President University of Colorado; Major General Thomas D. White, Col. Cecil E. Combs, Col. John A. Brooks, III, Lt. Col. Archie J. Knight, T/Sgt. Dean D. Trots.[128] The above plan to depart Wash, Sun, 19 Nov.

My comment to Craigie was "Looks like Tommie White will take over Barcus job. Barcus 87A - White 22A [seniority ranking]. What do you think?"

1045 hours: Just received a call from General Walker and he was very anxious to have the VB-17 that I have set up for him to come to Korea for his almost daily use - rather than leaving it here at Haneda. I agreed to this and directed General Crabb to send it over to Korea and bring back the VC-47. While talking with General Walker, I asked him how he and Pat were getting along. He said, "Strat, if Pat were my brother I couldn't like him more - in fact my entire association with him has been perfect and never once have I asked him for help or assistance which was not immediately given to me." I then said, "Can I do anything for you?" He said, "No, that whenever I need anything from the air, I make my request on Pat and always get it." I further told him that I thought I'd helped him the other day when I had stopped sending supplies to the east coast of Korea which could have gone by ship rather than by airlift. He said that he had seen the message to that effect and thanked me. He then said, "Strat, I'm kind of a stepchild." My remark was, "I am most sympathetic."

Called General Walker that his plane had been tested and was enroute to him, having departed here 1625 hours, today.

FRIDAY	*The draft redline Alkire drew up for me was a good one,*
17 NOVEMBER	*and so let him know that I thought so:*
1950	I want to compliment and commend you and the individual -

or individuals - who prepared my redline to General Vandenberg setting forth so clearly the reasons why our night intruder missions with B–26s have not been successful to date. This redline indicates "education" - and, with the proper use of words paints the exact picture that I desired to give to the Chief of Staff.

Following is a quote of the redline:

---

128. Stearns was President of the University of Colorado. During World War II, he had been educational advisor at the USAAF's School of Applied Tactics. The purpose of Stearns's mission was to examine the conduct of the Korean air war in order to provide information that would help Secretary of the Air Force Finletter in the making of policy decisions.

General White, a noted linguist, had been an attache in several countries prior to World War II. Among his assignments during the war were those of deputy CO of 13AF and Commanding General, 7AF. At this time, he was a member of the JCS's Joint Strategic Survey Committee. Prior to his retirement in 1961, he was Vice Chief of Staff and Chief of Staff, USAF; Colonel Combs was deputy commanding officer of the 2d BW; Knight worked in the Office of the Director of Plans, DCS/Ops, HQ USAF; Brooks' and Trots' positions are unknown.

The redline quoted below was sent to General Chidlaw also, personal from Stratemeyer, and a copy, made from this diary entry, was dispatched (18 Nov 50) to General Partridge.

REDLINE, CG FEAF to CSAF, Cite A 3567B D/M, for Vandenberg from Stratemeyer. Reur redline 57262 and my redline A 3504-B. *PART I.* I wish to reiterate our desire to commence effective night intruder opns on a large scale at earliest possible date. I have the folg resources on hand and avail for this task: A. 1st Shoran Beacon Unit presently being estbd [established] in the P'yŏngyng area. B. 4 ea B–26C acft of the 731st Bomb Sq (L) fully equipped for night intruder missions. Remaining 12 ea B–26C acft of 731st still awaiting arrival of Group B parts for AN/APQ-13 sets from Ogden Air Depot. C. 32 ea B–26C acft from FEAF inventory awaiting arrival of APN-3 airborne Shoran sets. The folg action is reqd to fully equip the night intruder force: A. AMC expedite shipmt of Group B parts for APQ-13 sets installed in 12 ea acft of 731st Bomb Sq. B. AMC expedite shipmt of 32 ea APN-3 sets for installation in FEAF acft. These installations will be accomplished at FEAMCOM. *PART II.* Marine F7F and F4U-N acft are operating from Kimp'o with primary mission as night recon, and targets of opportunity are bombed and strafed visually. Info on any targets is passed to JOC for early morning daylight attack. *PART III.* As you know, effective night opns over the contracted area in North Korea requires specialized equip. I depended on the 731st Bomb Sq (L) to arrive with equip for this job. The first acft arrived on 25 Sept and the last acft landed here 29 Oct. To date only four complete sets of Group B parts for APQ-13 sets have arrived. Vigorous follow-up action from this has failed to date to produce the missing parts. A special case report was submitted on 10 Nov 50 to the Inspector General, USAF, Kelly AFB, Texas, outlining discrepancies incident to the movement of the 731st Sq. On 12 Oct FEAF rad AX 2201-B to Hq USAF specified firm reqmts for 53 ea B–26C acft equipped with APN-3 and SCR 718 sets, plus an additional 28 ea B–26C acft equipped with APN-3, SCR 718 and APQ-23 sets. Projs [projects] estbd to fill these reqmts were cancelled by USAF rad AFMSS-SP-1B 56598 dtd 3 Nov 50. USAF rad AFMSS-SP-18 55379 dtd 21 Oct 50 directed CG AMC to dispatch necessary parts and tech [technical] pers[sonnel] to FEAF as reqd for modification of B–26 acft in FEAF. To date no parts or papers have arrived for this proj. *PART IV.* The above resume presented not as alibi for our limited night intrusion effort but to indicate that on this specific proj there was a lack of aggressive action on the part of ZI agencies in delivering the equip I need to accomplish this task. My opnl crews are ready and eager to perform this specialized mission. We must have the equip.

Sent the fol message to COMNAVFE info CINCFE:

Reference ourad AX 4722 OP-PL and urad CINCFE CX 61420, COM-NAVFE message 150630Z and CINCFE ltr AG 370.2 (8 Jul 50) GC. This message in two parts. *PART I.* CG FEAF concurs in establishment of Naval Air Station at Atsugi Airfield. PART II. CF FEAF does not concur in its entirety with Part 1 COMNAVFE message dated 150630Z. CINCFE ltr AG 370.2 (8 Jul 50) GC delegates operational control of marine land based a/c to CG FEAF. CG FEAF insists on retention of this operational control because he deems it essential to the accomplishment of his mission under CINCFE's directives. The continuing situation in the Far East makes it necessary for CG FEAF to have authority in an actual emergency to employ available land based aircraft without delay regardless of current activities of this aircraft. There is no desire to disrupt the teamwork of Marine units. CG FEAF agrees that COMNAVFE shall retain such control over the Marine air units in question as is required for training and operations in the performance of naval missions and in the support of naval tasks. This includes training for the amphibious phase of an operation.

At 1000 hours, presented my ex-driver, Sgt. Rogers[129] with a Commendation Medal. He had been with me for a long time, leaving my service because of marriage.

At 1500 hours the Distinguished Flying Cross was presented to Corporal Harry J. LaVene.[130] I made this award to Cpl. LaVene, in the presence of his CO, Lt. Colonel Edward D. Edward,[131] of the 31st Strat Rec Sq. Cpl. LaVene was awarded the DFC because on 9 Nov 50, he was a tail gunner and on that date shot down the first MiG from a B–29 type aircraft.

Major General Junius Jones[132] arrives in the theater.

1500 hours, Ambassador Muccio of [*sic*, to] Korea paid me a visit.

1530 hours, Bill Dunn of National Broadcasting Company dropped by the office to thank me for assistance rendered.

1530 Senator Pepper,[133] of Florida, called; he asked me lots of questions about the Chinese and China, whether I thought the Chinese would make good soldiers. I very emphatically told him that I was confident that they would and all they needed was leadership and that I was one of the few, along with General Wedemeyer,[134] that believed in Generaliassimo Chiang Kai Shek. Throughout the hour's visit, at every opportunity, I praised General MacArthur. At one time during the discussion on Communism, Senator Pepper stated that he imagined that the Communists would take over Japan if they could and get us out of the Far East. My reply to him was that one man had stopped that - and he would continue to do so - and that man was General of the Army Douglas MacArthur. Pepper would get off the subject of MacArthur and I would bring the conversation back to General MacArthur again. Senator Pepper has changed his attitude, I would say, one hundred percent from what it was a year ago. However, our interview was pleasant and about the time he was leaving, I am of the opinion he

---

129. Rogers' full name is unknown.

130. As Stratemeyer mentions, Cpl LaVene received his DFC for being the first B–29 crewman to down a MiG. His plane, however, was so badly damaged in the encounter that it crashed on landing, killing 5 of the crew. (Futrell, pp 228-229.)

131. When the 31st SRS was redesignated the 91st SRS on Nov. 16, Edward continued as its commander.

132. Jones was the AAF/USAF inspector general from 1943 to 1948. Since 1948, he had been the Sacramento Air Materiel Area commander based at McClellan AFB.

133. Claude Pepper was first elected to the U.S. Senate in 1936 and, although defeated in the 1950 elections, returned to Congress in 1962 as a member of the House of Representatives. He served until his death in 1989. At this time, he was a member of the Foreign Relations Committee.

134. Lt Gen Albert C. Wedemeyer commanded U.S. forces in China from 1944 to 1946. In 1948-1949, he was Army deputy chief of staff for plans and combat operations. Before his retirement in 1951, Wedemeyer was Commanding General, Sixth Army.

wanted to finagle me out of an airplane to take him to Korea and the air bases within Korea. I was very evasive in my answers and learned that he was going on the courier. However, I did tell him that General Partridge, with his many flights in and around Korea, could take him where he wanted to go.

**SATURDAY
18 NOVEMBER
1950**
_____

Sent a letter to Bill Kepner[135] (CINCAL) asking him to send me any dope on the performance thru their tests and operations of the F–94s.[136] They have a squadron in Alaska operating, and since FEAF is to eventually receive F–94 all-weather airplanes to replace our F–82s, would appreciate any such information.

Bucked a note to General Whitney, General MacArthur's military secretary, to which I clipped an article that appears in Time Magazine for this week.

Dear Whitney, I would say this is certainly another misquote of our Boss by *Time Magazine* in its 20 November issue. Such misquotes by *Time* to the American people are not good for the morale of General Partridge and all of his airmen - both officers and enlisted men - nor does it boost my morale. I know Mr. Roy Alexander, Managing Editor of *Time Magazine*, very well. He is a scrupulously honest and accurate journalist. He would be shocked to learn that his reporting staff has been misinformed, and he would hasten to correct any mistatement of fact. Can you suggest a way of getting the truth to Mr. Alexander without involving our Boss personally?

In reply to my radio of yesterday, Twining shot back the following answer re our B–26 night intruder missions:

Personal for Stratemeyer from Twining. Reurtel A-3576 B D/M each Group 'B' parts for AN/APQ-13 and 32 each AN/APN-3 are being packed for airlift to your theater. AMC is contacting your hqs for air priority. Req you inform CG, AMC, directly of the tech pers you require to assist in this project. Project to supply you with replacement B–26 a/c equipped for night intruder opns has been reinstated. Vigorous follow-up will be made here to insure earliest possible delivery equip. <u>In the future, bring directly to the attn of this office matters such as this which play such an important part in your combat opns.</u> [Emphasis in original.]

Received copy of fol radio from CINCUNC to DEPTAR WASH DC, info FEAF, cite: C-69211.

For JCS. Tentative date for main attack of 8 Army is now 24 November. Delay has been due entirely to logistical difficulties. Partial pressure being maintained until main attack against enemy concentrations disposed along the general axis Hŭich'ŏn-Kŏin-dong-Kanggye. The air attack of the

---

135. Lt Gen William E. Kepner, Commanding General, Alaskan Command. In World War II, he had commanded the Eighth Fighter Command of the Eighth Air Force and the 2d Bomb Division.

136. An outgrowth of the F–80, with common wings, landing gear, and tail surfaces, the F–94 featured a new nose to hold radar for all-weather interception and an afterburner (the first use of this device on an operational Air Force plane). Initial deliveries of the F–94A began in June 1950, but the aircraft did not reach the

last 10 days has been largely successful in isolating the battle area from added reinforcement and has greatly diminished the enemy flow of supply. Signed MacArthur.[137]

General Partridge called at 1550 and reported that he had just returned from a visit to X Corps and their outlying commands. He indicated to me that he felt he had done some good with General Almond and his staff. When they asked for numerous things, he pointed out that he couldn't do what they asked for until they furnished the communications and other requirements of a JOC which was their responsibility. He simply told them that at the present he could not furnish the 34 control parties to which he received the reply that they knew that but sent signal for the record and because they could use that many. General Partridge pointed out that they now had more in proportion to divisions they had than the Eighth Army. General Partridge further stated that at long last he convinced General Almond and his chief of staff, General Ruffner, that they should at least read the manual on close support which very clearly covers their responsibilities as well as those of the Air Force.

Unfortunately, General Almond's only method of communications with his commanders is through Mosquito and ground tactical control parties. Here again, the Air Force is doing the Army's job. Partridge told Almond that he would turn out those control parties as fast as it was physically possible to do so. He feels that his trip was worthwhile and that General Almond and his staff appreciated his visit and learned a little bit more about the problems of the Air Force. General Partridge indicated that Almond had to have some method of air transportation. I told Partridge that I was assigning to the Fifth Air Force for Almond's use a VC–47, Partridge agreeing to the crewing and maintaining it.

Immediately after my conversation with Partridge dispatched the following radio to General Almond with info to General Partridge:

Personal Almond from Stratemeyer. Have just learned today of your requirement for better air transportation and am therefore assigning a VC–47 to Fifth Air Force who will crew and maintain it and will station it at Yŏnp'o for use by you and your staff. Best regards.

At 1100 hours, The Hon. Sihn, Sung Mo[138] (Defense Minister for the Republic of Korea) called on me accompanied by the Chief of the Korean Mission in Japan, The Hon Kim, Yong Joo.

General Junius Jones with Colonel Schmidt had lunch with us.

O'Donnell dropped by the office - just returned from his trip. Weyland reported back to hqrs after being away briefly for about 3 days.

Far East until mid-1951. (Marcelle Size Knaack, *Encyclopedia of U.S. Air Force Aircraft and Missile Systems*, Vol. I, *Post-World War II Fighters, 1945-1973* [Washington, 1978], pp 100-111.)

137. Actually, most of the Chinese troops that would launch the surprise offensive against the U.N. forces on Nov. 25 were already in place and had not been spotted by reconnaissance aircraft. Though FEAF planes had knocked out many bridges across the Yalu, the Chinese assiduously repaired them if possible, replaced them with easily-built pontoon bridges, or just forded the Yalu where it was shallow. The battlefield was not isolated.

138. Sihn also served as acting Prime Minister on several occasions during 1950.

SUNDAY
19 NOVEMBER
1950

In answer to my radnote of 17 Nov to Navy re "operational control of aircraft (land-based Marine a/c in this instance)" they replied 180546/Z as follows:

Cannot agree with the implications or demands made in Par II of your Cite AX 3594 - B CG for the following reasons. *A.* CG FEAF does not hold op control now and therefore cannot retain it. Existing agreement only gives op control to FEAF of "all aircraft operating in execution of FEAF missions as assigned by CINCFE." MAG is an integral component of an amphibious team scheduled for post Korea retention in Japan. Mission of Marine air is primarily to support operation of US Marine forces in exactly the same manner as any other component of a combat team such as artillery or tanks. Marine combat team liable to be moved to any trouble point in the Far East and should not be considered as an integral part of Japan's air defense. *B.* COMNAVFE sees no objection to op control of Marine air being delegated to FEAF by COMNAVFE for those exercises directed to by CINCFE that call for air defense operations and obviously has no objection to FEAF assuming op control in emergencies as directed by CINCFE. These periods however would normally be very small portion of the total time and such control by USAF, which is common practice in other areas, offers no probl⌄m or difficulty. Operational control as interpreted by COMNAVFE is essential in this case to the service concerned for the person holding it has the authority to change operating schedules, operating procedures, and operating techniques. Since all components of the team must work as a team all operational factors must be under the control of a single service, that is, the Navy service. *C.* Additional factors which bear on this subject are, training in carrier operations, amphibious landing operations. *D.* COMNAVFE does not understand CG FEAF's insistence on this operational control or the benefits to the FEC that will accrue if it were given nor dangers if it were withheld.

Partridge sent me a copy of a basic letter received from Major General Hobart R. Gay, dtd 21 October 50, addressed to him (Partridge) which reads:

Headquarters, 1st Cavalry Division, Office of the Commanding General, APO 201, 21 October 1950:

Dear General Partridge - The breakthrough at Hŭkkyo-ri and the subsequent capture of the enemy capital city, P'yŏngyang, on October 19, 1950, by this division was made possible only by the magnificent close air support given by the Fifth Air Force. The 1st Cavalry Division is, and always will be, grateful. Sincerely s/Hobart R. Gay, Major General, USA.

By first indorsement, General Partridge on 5 November 50 sent the above letter to all FAF commanders in Korea and Japan. "I take great pride in forwarding the above letter to all personnel of my command. s/E. E. Partridge, Major General, USAF."

Received two radios related to Dr. Stearns' visit to FEAF. Dr. Stearns is accompanied by General White (Thomas D.) and staff, underlining again Sec of AF and CSAF desires we give every possible assistance to Stearns group, including the making available either Col. Ferguson or Colonel Gilbert L. Meyers dependent upon interview with Dr. Stearns. Stated that one of these officers would work with Stearns while he was out here and the other be returned to ZI, reporting to Dr. Leach, Office of the Secretary of the AF, for temporary duty of approximately 30 days for consultation on Combat Tac Operations in Korea.

My reply to CSAF (with info cy to Partridge) reads as follows:

Redline personal Twining from Stratemeyer. Reference your 57627 FEAF will render every possible assistance to Dr Stearns and his group. Colonel James Ferguson has been Special Assistant to Weyland, has broad picture of all FEAF operations, including relations with Army and Navy, and has worked closely with Barcus group. He is well qualified and can be made available to work with Professor W. B. Leach in Washington approximately 30 days TDY. Colonel Gilbert L. Meyers is Fifth AF D/O in immediate charge of Partridge's complex operations and should remain on that job as primary responsibility. He and any other officers, of course, available for consultations, briefings, or advice on tactical air operations. If absolutely essential, Meyers or another qualified officer can be made available to work with Dr Stearns full time. Both officers, of course, will be available for interview upon Dr Stearn's arrival.

MONDAY
20 NOVEMBER
1950
Lt. General Peter Mow[139] (presently delegate to UN and an old friend) guest at Mayeda House. He attended my 8:30 briefing.

We entertained for General Mow at Mayeda House at dinner, among the guests were Mrs. Ho and certain of my key general officers and their wives.

TUESDAY
21 NOVEMBER
1950
On my desk this morning was the following radio from USAF:

Reur ad AX 3359B VCAP dtd 12 Nov 1950. Your request for additional C–54 and C–46 crews and maintenance personnel to meet future contingencies not favorably considered due to serious effects withdrawal of personnel at this time will have on other commands.

The following signal in its entirety is one of the best received during the war so far. Had we started out in this manner, many trials and tribulations would have been avoided:

---

139. Mow had been Commisioner of Aeronautical Affairs in the Chinese government during World War II. He was head of the procurement office of the Chinese AF in 1948-1949 before becoming the CAF representative to Washington. In August 1951, he became involved in a messy affair involving charges and countercharges of misuse of official funds. (Ross Y. Koen, *The China Lobby in American Politics*, [New York], pp 35, 42-45.)

From: CG Army Eight dtd 20 Nov 50
To : CINCFE Tokyo, Japan
Info: CG 5thAF, COMNAVFE Tokyo Japan
Nr : GX 28010 KAR
This msg in 2 parts.

PART I. Rqst max aval air support from 5th AF, BOMCOM, Navy, British for Army Eight offensive operations period 230700-281800 and normal sustained effort 281800 Nov - 021800 Dec 50. Recm all support be under control 5th AF in coordination with Army Eight.
PART II. Request effective immediately, in the destruction of bridges Army Eight zone that all air commands concentrate on important and critical bridges in zone south of Yalu River and within 15 miles of the border and that no further effort be placed upon preventing the enemy from restoring bridges south of above 15 mile zone.[140]
Action: G-3
Information: Commander in Chief, Chief of Staff, G-1, G-2, G-4, AG, JSPOG, Signal, FEAF, COMNAVFE, LJLCOM LNO, Air Marshal Bouchier.

In answer to above, Partridge sent to me, info EUSAK, the following:

The fol request has been received from CG EUSAK and is quoted for your info. "It is requested that effective imm, in the destruction of bridges, that all air commands concentrate on important and critical bridges south of the Yalu River and within about 15 miles of the border, and that no further effort be placed upon preventing the enemy from repairing or rebuilding bridges south of the above 15 mile zone." This command will comply with the above request. Request your Hqs notify FEAF Bomb Comd to also comply with this EUSAK request.

General Lowe, Presidential adviser, in the office this AM. Attended the FEAF briefing.

General Partridge called 0935 and stated that for the first time the Eighth Army was in fine shape for supplies. Yesterday, they moved forward 6,500 tons; further, they found the clog in the pipeline and got forward POL to the amount of 2,300 tons. Now that the railroad is operating from Seoul to P'yŏngyang and that the port at Chinnamp'o is open and that railroad and road operating forward, General Partridge reported the Eighth Army was in good shape.

He also reported that he had received my letter of 14 November reference movement of wing headquarters to Korea, designation of an air defense division, etc., and that my solution was a workable one and that he was issuing a mission directive to General Spivey today.

He indicated that the people from the 27th Fighter Bomber Wing and the 4th Fighter Interceptor Wing were there in his headquarters and that every possible action would be taken to get them into combat by increments.

---

140. Probably the reason Stratemeyer believed this message to be "one of the best" was that it recommends that all support (5AF, BomCom, Navy, and British) be under the control of 5AF in coordination with the Eighth Army. On the other hand, General Partridge in his diary entry for the same date was not that impressed, seeing it just as a request for full support for the Eighth Army. (Maj Gen Earle E. Partridge Diary, 21 Nov 1950 entry.)

He indicated that General Nuckols had put the heat on Colonel Scott to get more public relations out on tactical air support. General Partridge pointed out that by so doing, the airlift, Bomber Command, and logistics support would necessarily have to be sacrificed. Only so much could be put out. I agreed that this was proper and that General Partridge knew as well as I did the reasons why: bigger and better publicity must, repeat, must be put out on tactical air support. We must forget competitive public information servicing within the Air Force at this time.

He called my attention to the signal from Collins to CINCFE on the stand that the Army proposes to take reference tactical air support. This is a TOP SECRET message and I have it in my billfold.

Dispatched a "marble" to Vandenberg:

SAAF sq operational 19 Nov from K-24 (P'yŏngyang East) with eight (8) sorties. Remainder aircraft and personnel will arrive P'yŏngyang 27 Nov with full operations by 1 December. Commander: Commandant Thereon; T/O&E: 25 F–51s, 38 pilots, and 210 personnel.[141]

Sent a "needle" with info to BomCom to Edwards:

I have been anxiously awaiting arrival of 2 RB–29 a/c with K-30 camera installations. I anticipated being able to use them on special projects during fall period of good weather. However, arrival dates have been postponed for one reason or another from the last of September to our estimated date of 1 December. These aircraft are in work at OCAMA [Oklahoma City Air Materiel Area] on project SACISB-30. I would appreciate all possible action to expedite movement of these aircraft to my control.

Wrote a letter of thanks to Larry Bell, President of Bell Aircraft, re the Tarzon wind-tunnel model he sent me and also telling him that I was asking for specialized technical help from USAF. (See below quoted radio)

Dispatched a personal Edwards from Stratemeyer with personal information to Chidlaw:

Messrs. Charlie Barr and Charlie Schmidt, engineering representatives from Bell Aircraft have arrived back in theater on Vivian Project.[142] Since this will be the first employment of Vivian, Mr. Barr recommends and I strongly concur that Captain Lyle Bishop[143] and his crew of three be immediately sent to Kadena Air Base in Okinawa on temporary duty for thirty days, arriving 1 December. This in order to be sure that best experience possible be available when Vivian utilized.

---

141. This unit, the 2d South African Air Force (SAAF) Squadron, was attached to the 18th FBW. The squadron transitioned to F–86Fs in January 1953. (Futrell, pp 232, 638.)

142. Vivian involved the development of the Tarzon bomb, a much larger 12,000-lb. version of the Razon bomb. With the advent of the Tarzon, Razon bombing was suspended in December 1950 after a 67 percent controllability success rate. The last 150 Razons dropped destroyed 15 bridges and had a control reliability of 96 percent. Unfortunately, the larger Tarzons suffered several failures before a fix was thought to be at hand. Then, it was discovered that a Tarzon could not safely be jettisoned. Bombing with this weapon was suspended in early May 1951. (Robert F. Futrell, *United States Air Force Operations in the Korean Conflict, 1 Nov 1950- 30 June 1952*, [U] [USAF Historical Study 72, Maxwell AFB, 1955], pp 141-142. Hereafter cited as Futrell No. 72.)

143. Bishop's job is unknown, although as intimated in the message, he was probably involved in Tarzon testing.

Mr. Charlie Barr of Bell Aircraft came in to see me. We discussed substantially that which was quoted in my radio to Edwards. (see preceding page)

Weyland and I drove to Haneda to greet Dr. Stearns, President of Colorado University, who is out here on a special project for USAF, and his party which includes Major General Thomas D. White, USAF, who is acting as Dr. Stearns adviser.

Dispatched a TS Operational Immediate to CSAF with info CINCFE, CG COCARCOM, CG FAF IN KOREA:

Top Secret Personal for Twining from Stratemeyer: Radio in five parts - *PART I.* Ref ur TS 5634, 20 Nov 50, FEAF is continually faced with airlift demands of critically needed material and personnel: this over and above what has necessarily come to be considered the normal demands of forces now in Korea. Examples are: *(a)* Airlift of 375 tons of 115/145 avgas over a three-day period from Japan to Wŏnsan to keep the Marine air operating at Wŏnsan. *(b)* Lift of more than 3,400 men and 600 tons of the 4th and 27th Ftr Wings from Japan to Korea. Only by this airlift can I get these wings into action in a reasonable length of time. *(c)* Thirty-six C–46 loads of comm equipment just in from ZI and urgently needed in FAF in Korea. *(d)* An urgent request today from X Corps to give them three more C–47s to quote have a max number of a/c readily available to airdrop or airlift emergency supplies to isolated units during breaks in weather. Constantly extending supply lines require immed responses to request by front line units for airlift or airdrop of supplies unquote. *PART II.* In view of the demands placed on us and unavoidable decrease in C–119 potential which offsets gains made by arrival of 437th TCW, there is no recourse but to again request a C–54 sq capable of eight hrs a day utilization. *PART III.* In addition to rqmt for another sq of C–54s, General Tunner has advised me that nine C–54s now possessed by 374th TCW are in dire need of depot overhaul. Four have over 5,000 hrs since last DIR [depot inspection and repair], four have over 4,000 hrs and one has over 3,000 hrs, much of these hrs being accomplished into rough fields in Korea. Also, due to operational losses, the two C–54 sqs of 374th are short one a/c to the theater to fill their T/O&E. *PART IV.* I assure you that I am fully aware that by global war criteria I have more than my fair share of air transport and am asking for still more. Obviously some of this would have to be withdrawn in event of an all out emergency. As we see the overall situation, we are trying to accomplish two things: *(a)* To overcome an inconceivably difficult supply situation. As General MacArthur pointed out to the JCS in his C-69211 dated 11 Nov 50, delay in the Eighth Army offensive quote has been due entirely to logistical difficulties unquote. These difficulties are not the result of poor planning, but are a combination of many factors. Among them: *(1)* The havoc wrought by our interdiction program; *(2)* Very heavily mined harbors and beaches; *(3)* Continuous guerilla activity in rear areas, including tearing up of rail lines and ambushing trains and truck convoys; *(4)* Ice and snow covered one-way roads thru wide and tortuous mountain ranges. *(b)* While meeting the rqmt for air supply to simultaneously reduce to an absolute minimum our use of C–119s, saving them for emergencies. *PART V.* We are not panicky, but we are desperate, and are utilizing every cargo acft we own or can hire and we are still in bad shape. We need the spare air transport crews we have been requesting; we need the replacement C–54s and we need the C–54 sq.

A Sherman tank rumbles past a 15th TCS C–54 unloading supplies at a Korean airfield.

WEDNESDAY 22 NOVEMBER 1950

When I arrived at my desk this AM, found fol radnote from COCARCOM:

Personal to Stratemeyer from Pringle.[144] Reur Stratline to Tunner cite A 3753B D/O. I have discussed this with Tunner and this is his position. We concur completely with your Part 2. Because of theater-wide shortage of transport a/c we are unable to meet all emerg rqmts of using agencies. Withdrawal of three C–47s as Reqd by X Corps would reduce airlift in other areas. We are ready to furnish either C–47s or C–119s as required for X Corps emerg drops or other lift on call, but we must not further reduce the FEAF air transport fleet. We will give highest possible priority to X Corps requests, but we do not feel that it should be furnished at expense of higher priority lift for FAF and Eighth Army.

In reply to my message of yesterday to General Twining in which the cargo aircraft situation was described graphically, Twining sent in answer the following:

One squadron C–54s of 12 airplanes augmented for 6 hour utilization is being alerted for movement to FEAF this date for 90 day TDY. It must be

---

144. Col Hoyt Pringle, the 314th TCG commander.

realized that the assignment of this squadron to FEAF is at the expense of trans-Pacific lift to CINCFE and must be cleared with CINCFE. Overhaul of your C–54s must be accomplished when you see fit to schedule them to depot. Two C–54s are on a previously established project for FEAF. One is now ready for delivery. No additional replacement C–54s are available.

With Dr. Stearns and General White called on CINCFE at 1230 hours. After the call, they accompanied me to Mayeda House where we had lunch. (For notes on conference see following pages.)

Received an additional radio from USAF:

One squadron C–54s of 12 airplanes augmented for 6 hour utilization ordered FEAF this date for 90 days TDY. This squadron will be operational 1 Dec. REURAD VC-0449. Two C–54s on established project for FEAF, one of which now ready for delivery. Replacement C–54s would have to be taken from MATS. MATS presently having difficulty supplying FEAF airlift plus drastically reduced lift to other areas. A reduction of MATS lift to FEAF must be balanced against FEAF's internal lift. It is not considered advisable at this time to further weaken MATS.

In reply to the assignment of a C–54 sq, I wired Twining with info to CINCFE as follows:

Reur TS 5653, 22 Nov 50. This rad in two parts: PART I. CINCFE concurs in assignment of sq of C–54s. CINCFE further concurs in reduction of trans-Pacific lift if required as result of this assignment. Neither CINCFE nor I can understand the nec[essity] for this reduction in view of past performances on Pacific lift. Records here indicate that contract lift to the extent of 301 rnd trips from the ZI was util[ized] at the peak of the lift; falling off to a low of 89 trips and temporarily peaking again this month at 139 trips. From the foregoing, it appears that about 40 C–54s are avail in commercial organizations over and above present and planned commercial utilization. PART II. Appreciate you are constantly harassed with budgetary troubles, but must recommend strongly that you contract for commercial lift to fill void created by assignment of sq to FEAF.

Called on General MacArthur accompanied by Dr. Robert Stearns and Major General Tommy White. We went into his office about 1232 and were there until 1345 hours, and all of us, particularly Dr. Stearns, were impressed beyond words with MacArthur's comments.

* * * *

MacArthur stated, "Well, Dr., I understand you are out here to evaluate the Air Force bombing effort."

Dr. Stearns replied, "Not exactly. I am here to evaluate the tactical air support given to the Army by the United States Air Force."

MacArthur's reply was, "Well, I guess I should be your first witness," and he then, to the best of memory, commented as follows:

That the USAF efforts from the very beginning up to this moment in support of the ground forces, as well as O'Donnell's bombing and Tunner's transport activities, have been magnificent and one hundred percent. He simply praised all the activities of FEAF.

He then stated that with all that, looking towards the future, the ground forces and the Air Forces, in the close support buiness, must work and strive for a closer coordination of their respective activities.

He commented on Marine air support given to the Marine divisions and stated that their sole job was support of amphibious landings and that very, very close support was given in these operations. He stated that in any operation, at the beginning of a war, all the air forces should be under air command in order to rid the skies of hostile air and that as soon as that was done, the ground forces were then entitled to that close team work and support that is required in these days of great fire power. He indicated that if the ground had artillery back of their lines, hub to hub, there would not be sufficient fire power for the ground elements to advance and that this artillery fire power must be backed up with air power. He specifically stated that he was not discussing the command problem, but he did emphasize that there must be that close cooperation between the ground commander and the Air Force commander which would make it possible to give the ground elements in contact with the enemy the required and essential air support that they must have if they intend to advance.

He stated that at the Inch'ŏn landing, he was struck by the magnificent air support that Marine air gave to their ground people and the ease with which air, with their Corsairs, was called from the front lines to support the Marine ground troops.

He then went on to say that the Fifth Air Force with their '51s and '80s gave the same destructive fire effect in support of the Eighth Army.

With reference to reciprocal engine type versus jet type aircraft, he indicated that that was a question for the Air Force to decide, that the jet had proved itself in close support and that in his opinion the jet, because of its speed, should be utilized.

He indicated that this whole question of enough air support was a question of money. The Air Force decided that they must have the Strategic Bomber Command and by that decision maybe the tactical support of the ground troops was given too low a priority. However, again it is a question of money.

He feels that in any war - and they are all different - that the decision will be made to use soldiers and that if that is correct, then these soldiers must have air support. He indicated that there was no greater and more ferocious fighting man in the world than the American soldier, that he had been reared from boyhood with a standard of living of the very highest, and that the American soldier in the field had every right to expect - and did receive a higher standard of living than all other soldiers; therefore, he had a right to expect a fire power of both artillery and air to support him in battle.

He stated that the Marine was an excellent amphibious landing soldier, but when it came to remaining in battle, under all hazards with mud and weather, that the man on the ground must take, the Marine did not compare with the American soldier. The Marine is a specialist; he is willing to take great losses to do a quick job, but then his desires are to pull out, accept the plaudits of the American people, and let the doughboy carry on.

Upon our departure, General MacArthur asked Dr. Stearns when he had completed his evaluation to please come back to see him.

* * * * *

Bucked a carbon copy extract of meeting with MacArthur to General White:

Attached is an extract from my diary, 22 Nov 50, re our visit with Gen. MacArthur. You and Dr. Stearns may remember what took place better than I. Hope attached will be helpful in preparing a statement for signature.

Cy Marriner's friend, Mr. Kleiman, came in at 1100 hours. Turned him over to General Alkire.

Dispatched fol rad:

Personal for Twining from Dr. R. L. Stearns signed Stratemeyer. Ref your AFCVC 57791. PART I. No material required with White unless you have additional info you desire to send. PART II. Col. James Ferguson will be available for return TDY Wash on or about 29 Nov.

THURSDAY 23 NOVEMBER 1950

USAF sent the fol radio with info to AMC and FEAF BOMCOM:

1. Reurtwx AX 3743B CG dtd 21 Nov 50, the fol action has been taken to insure that the 1st operational employment of Vivian will be successful: *A.* 3 B–29 a/c were specially modified and checked out to San Antonio for Project Vivian. This was followed by proof tests at Holloman. These a/c should arrive your cmd this week. *B.* Latest Tarzon test equipment, data and nec spares were packaged in _____a/c [left blank in diary] to ensure prompt delivery. *C.* All Tarzon tails for delivery to FEAF have been completely rehabilitated at San Antonio. 20 Tarzon Bombs together with fuzes, handling equipment, and spares departed SF [San Francisco] 18 Nov 50 on *Brainard Victory*. *D.* Further, action has been taken to send 1st Lt. Arthur F. Adams on TDY along with modified B–29 a/c. Lt. Adams has been on the Tarzon program at Holloman during the last year and is thoroughly familiar with latest developments. *E.* Lt. Adams also supervised the B–29 and Tarzon modification program at San Antonio. *2.* In view of the above and considering that Capt. Bishop is essential at Holloman and Eglin on the accelerated electrical tail Tarzon program, no action will be taken to send Capt. Bishop at this time. It is considered that subsequent to 15 Jan 51, the services of Capt. Bishop can be made available to your comd if still desired at that time.

Attended the Thanksgiving game (football) between the FEAF Tornadoes and the GHQ Athletics. Score was FEAF 26 and GHQ 17. Between halves, the bands played "Happy Birthday" in honor of my natal day!

Annalee and I had Thanksgiving dinner at Mayeda House.

FRIDAY 24 NOVEMBER 1950

Departed Haneda with General MacArthur aboard the SCAP at 0610 hours. Also accompanying him were Generals Hickey and Whitney and Wright, Colonel Canada (MacArthur's surgeon), his aides Colonels Bunker and Huff, and several new[s] reporters. Our destination was Sinanju or K-29.

Landed at Sinanju at 1030 hours. General MacArthur was met there by Generals Walker, Partridge and Milburn. We immediately got into jeeps and drove to General Milburn's 1st Corps hq where we were briefed on the ground situation. From there we drove to IX Corps hq where General Coulter[145] briefed us. From there we drove to General Church's headquarters, the 24th Division hqs, and were briefed on his front and we learned that the attack was progressing favorably. General Milburn made the statement that he could go right on to the Yalu River but did not dare do so unless his right flank were secure. He made the statement there was not much resistance before him. From General Church's headquarters we went back to Sinanju and flew the battle lines and then took a course to a point about 15 miles south and west of Sinanju, and, at 15,000 feet, flew the border parallel with the Yalu River circling Kanggye, thence to Chosin and Fusan reservoirs, and thence to Hyesanjin on the Manchurian border, the town which the 17th Infantry of the 7th Division now occupies. From there we flew directly south to the coastline of the Sea of Japan, and thence direct to Haneda.

General MacArthur was thrilled with the entire operation as was everyone in his party. Prior to the departure for the Sea of Japan, General MacArthur radioed back to the escorting F–80s: "Thanks for a grand ride, MacArthur."

Shortly after leaving Hyesanjin and setting our course for return to Haneda, Colonel Story came back to the General's compartment where Generals Hickey, Wright, Whitney and I were seated, bringing five glasses and a bottle of champagne. He poured the champagne and then MacArthur, Hickey, Wright, Whitney, and Story sang HAPPY BIRTHDAY to me.

Following that, a large birthday cake was brought to me which had been baked at the American Embassy, and which was presented by General MacArthur. A table then was set for two and at General MacArthur's invitation, I sat on his left and we had a most delicious luncheon served to us.

To me, this was the highlight of my military career.

I have mentioned that being with MacArthur on the paradrop and the landing at P'yŏngyang as being the highlight, but this trip, and this salute of my sixtieth birthday by the greatest American alive, participated wholeheartedly in by him, is something I'll never forget.

Particularly was this true because he had just completed flying a course which to my mind was a most dangerous mission for a man in the position he occupies, and, there is no question in my own mind that had a determined attack by MiGs taken place - had they seen us - they could have made that attack in spite of the cover that I had provided above and at both sides of his plane. I'll never forget his remark as we started parallel to the Yalu River: "Gentlemen, there are plenty of parachutes up forward for anyone who cares to wear one. I do not propose to put one on."

For the record, I make this statement: - General of the Army Douglas MacArthur is the most courageous, brilliant, valiant of men, and the greatest leader I have ever seen or known. In all my career, I have never come in contact with a mind and manner equivalent to his, and, with it all, he is human and constantly thinks of those who work for him. As I've said before, "God bless him."

---

145. Maj Gen John B. Coulter came to Korea in August as commander of the I Corps. He commanded the 85th Infantry Division in World War II.

SATURDAY
25 NOVEMBER
1950

Reached my desk where I found the two following quoted radios:

Fm CINCFE to X Corps, info: JLCOM, EUSAK, FEAF, COCARCOM, cite: CX 69703 - dtd 24 Nov 50: Reurmsg X 12867, 21 Nov 50, CINCFE Msg CX 69502, dtd 210953Z, FEAF MSG AX 3799 B Op-Op, 22 Nov 50, notal or needed. (1) Opns control of all cargo a/c must, as far as possible, remain with CG FEAF COCAR-COM to insure max utilization of airlift to meet rqmts of all organizations in Korea. (2) Your request for emergency airdrop/airlift of supplies well recognized by CINCFE and CG FEAF. FEAF has directed COCARCOM to make every effort to meet your rqmt fully and expeditiously. The decision as to method used to meet your rqmts rests with CG FEAF COCAR-COM, who has in ref to this matter stated "we will give highest possible priority to requests of X Corps."

Fm COMNAVFE, to FEAF, cite: NIL dtd 24 Nov 50: Re your MF 17141 OP-PL. Folg comment. COMNAVFE will pass opnl control of Marine shore based a/c to CG FEAF w/o delay in any actual emerg as declared by CINCFE and for the accomplishment of such FEAF missions as CINCFE designates. This affords CG FEAF the op control needed to meet the conditions outlined in reference dispatch and reiterates views expressed in my 180546Z.

Departed for lunch late inasmuch as I had lunch with the MacArthur's at the American Embassy. They were entertaining in honor of Secretary of the Navy Francis Mathews.

At 1600 hours, Colonel Croker and his group called. They are from the Air University.

Annalee and I couldn't make it to the Navy reception for the Secretary, 1800 - 1930 hours, GHQ Officers Club.

Dispatched the following memorandum to General MacArthur after a visit from Rosie O'Donnell:

Subject: Possible violation of the Manchurian border. 1. This report and General O'Donnell's first indorsement on violation of the Manchurian border are submitted for your information. 2. Under adverse wind conditions, I consider this operation perfect, and, had we not been fired upon by anti-aircraft artillery from the Manchurian side of the border, no violation of Manchurian territory would have occurred. 3. A photographic record of the attack is enclosed in photographs numbered one to four inclusive. 4. I have personally commended General O'Donnell for a job well done and propose to take no action reference this excellent attack by FEAF Bomber Command. 5. I would appreciate the return of this report with the attached photographs for Far East Air Forces' files.[146]

Above memorandum returned to me, and in his own handwriting, General MacArthur had written: "Action par. 4 approved. Mack."

---

146. When the 98th BG bombed the Manp'ojin railway bridge on Nov. 24, because of the maneuvering to evade the flak and also a strong drift, eight bombs fell in the mud flats on the Manchurian side of the Yalu. (Futrell No. 72, p 23.

Part Three

The Bitter Days

November 26, 1950 – May 20, 1951

Situation Summary

November 26, 1950 — May 20, 1951

Everything went well at first for the U.N. offensive, but on the evening of the second day (November 25), Chinese troops struck with overpowering force against the Eighth Army. The assault turned the Eighth's eastern flank and threatened the entire army with entrapment. General Almond's X Corps did not escape the attention of the Chinese, either.

The shock of the immense Chinese assaults sent the U.N. troops reeling backward, some units in panic, others in well-organized retrograde movements. But no matter in what manner the U.N. forces pulled back, the fact remained that they had suffered a stunning and, perhaps, irrecoverable defeat. FEAF tried its best to stem the tide, sometimes with spectacular success, but was hampered by the fact that the Chinese observed outstanding camouflage discipline during the day and that it was their common practice to attack at night.

On November 24, the Eighth Army had launched its attack from the Ch'ŏngch'ŏn River north toward the Yalu. One week later, it found itself 50 miles <u>south</u> of the Ch'ŏngch'ŏn and falling farther south toward the 38th Parallel. During this period the Eighth had suffered heavy casualties. Particularly hard hit had been the 2d Division, especially during a nasty action near Kunu-ri, and it had to be pulled out of combat after losing about 5,000 men.

Though the battles in the western part of Korea were very important and bitterly fought, it was the fight of the X Corps' 1st Marine Division at the Changjin (or Chosin) Reservoir that caught the attention of the press. The Marines were stopped at Yudam-ni (on the reservoir's western shore) on the 27th. At the same time, on the other side of the reservoir, a three-battalion force from the 7th Division was trapped by the Chinese and shattered. Eventually, 1,050 men (including just 385 able-bodied survivors) of the original 2,500-man force were saved.

Pushed back from Yudam-ni, the Marines began their "advance to the sea" along what was basically a single narrow road. On December 4, the rear guard entered Hagaru-ri to join the rest of the 1st Marine Division, along with a mixture of men from the 7th Division, the Royal Marines, and various ROK units. Hagaru-ri was just a way station on the narrow road to the sea, and the U.N. troops (primarily Marines) again moved on to the final perimeter line around Hamhŭng-Hŭngnam. By December 11, after an epic running battle, the Marines had reached the perimeter.

The battles around the Changjin Reservoir and during the "breakout" cost the U.N. troops (again mainly Marines) some 6,000 casualties of the 25,000 men involved. Heavy as they were, these casualties probably would have been much greater had it not been for the yeoman work of FEAF, Navy, and Marine aircraft. Planes from Task Force 77 and the 1st Marine Air Wing handled most of the close support, while FEAF aircraft struck further afield. It was in the supply and evacuation efforts that the Air Force really shone. Combat Cargo Command's entire airdrop system had been geared to handle only 70 tons a day. Through herculean efforts this was bumped up to <u>250</u> tons a day. In addition to the many airdrop and cargo missions flown, the Cargo Command planes evacuated almost 5,000 ill or wounded troops. For their part in this undertaking, the 314th Troop Carrier Group, the 21st Troop Carrier Squadron, and the 801st Medical Evacuation Squadron received the first Distinguished Unit Citations awarded Air Force units in the war.

Crowded into the Hamhŭng-Hŭngnam perimeter were troops of the 1st Marine Division, the 7th and 3d Infantry Divisions, and the ROK 3d and Capital Divisions (the latter four divisions having quickly pulled back from their exposed positions in northeast Korea in order not to be trapped). Between December 11 and 24, 105,000 troops and 98,000 North Korean civilians, along with 350,000 tons of supplies and over 17,000 vehicles were evacuated from Hŭngnam. Fortunately, the Chinese (who were in serious straits themselves) did not interfere in the evacuation.

So quickly had the Eighth Army pulled back that the ground-bound Chinese forces were unable to keep up with the motorized U.N. troops. Instead, most of the pressure on the retreating army was exerted by revitalized North Korean units. By the middle of December, the Eighth Army held a vague line running from the Imjin River on the west generally along the 38th Parallel to the east coast. When the X Corps completed its evacuation, it was placed initially into positions backing up the Eighth Army.

Meanwhile, in early December, U.N. members began efforts to arrange a cease-fire in Korea. These attempts foundered when the Chinese, flushed with the success of their offensive, rejected the proposals. Though rebuffed for the time being, the U.N. continued its efforts to obtain a cease-fire.

On December 23, the Eighth Army's commander, Lt. Gen. Walton Walker, was killed in a jeep accident. The possibility of his death in combat had been considered earlier, and MacArthur had already decided on who would replace Walker. That man was Lt. Gen. Matthew B. Ridgway, then Deputy Chief of Staff for Operations and Administration, Department of the Army. By Christmas Day, Ridgway was in Tokyo for briefings.

Ridgway's initial encounter with the fighting in Korea was not auspicious. On New Year's Eve, the CCF, along with North Korean troops, launched another major offensive against the Eighth Army. The U.N. troops took a heavy toll of the attackers but the sheer weight and ferocity of the attack pushed the army back across the 38th Parallel, back past Seoul, back to roughly the 37th Parallel. But this would be as far south as the Eighth Army would retreat.

Because of the opposition by the Eighth Army and also because their supply and transportation system could not sustain it, the Chinese offensive faltered, then stopped. The Communist's usual practice was to advance, attack, withdraw for supply, and then repeat this procedure. And so it was now. Ridgway had already made it plain to his troops that he wanted a more aggressive attitude, and he now decided to take advantage of the withdrawal by launching a reconnaissance in force. A limited offensive began on January 25 and it did not take long for the revitalized U.N. forces to show gains. Despite a strong Chinese counterattack in the Chip'yŏng-ni area, by February 16 the U.N. forces had moved back up to the Han River, on the outskirts of Seoul, and now held a line midway between the 37th and 38th parallels.

To keep the pressure on the enemy, Ridgway initiated a series of offensives. Operation Ripper, which began March 7, retook Seoul (which would at last remain in friendly hands) and resulted in the Eighth Army closing in once more on the 38th Parallel. A continuation of the attack, code-named Rugged, by April 9 brought the U.N. forces to positions running generally southwest to northeast above the 38th Parallel.

MacArthur and Ridgway were well aware that the Chinese had no intention of retreating much farther, particularly from their staging area bounded by the towns of Ch'ŏrwon, P'yŏnggang, and Kŭmhwa, an area which became notorious as the "Iron Triangle." Consequently, Ridgway made contingency plans to repel another Chinese offensive.

As the U.N. forces moved north, the United States government planned further cease-fire overtures to the Chinese. Suddenly, and without telling his superiors in Washington beforehand, General MacArthur on March 24 issued a statement that was stunning in its blatantness and presumptuousness. In essence, he was attempting to make national policy himself and was giving the Chinese an ultimatum that the war would be extended to their mainland unless they negotiated a peace settlement. MacArthur's pronouncement succeeded in scuttling any further attempts to effect a cease-fire, a result he cannot have been so naive not to expect.

MacArthur had finally overstepped his bounds and on April 9, President Truman relieved him. The resulting uproar almost overshadowed the fact that the war was still going on. Ridgway replaced MacArthur as FEC commander and commander of U.N. forces in Korea, while Lt. Gen. James A. Van Fleet took over Eighth Army.

On April 22, resupplied and refreshed, the Chinese launched the offensive Ridgway had expected. Bitter fighting ensued and thousands fell on both sides, but this time there was no headlong retreat by the U.N. forces. A realignment of the front lines, particularly just north of Seoul, took place, but for all intents the Chinese offensive had little effect. There was a lull for a couple of weeks and then the Chinese and North Koreans tried again.

Five Chinese armies, totalling 137,000 Chinese and 38,000 North Korean troops, flowed south on May 16 to batter against the Eighth Army's line. They broke through only to find themselves caught in a terrible trap. When the Eighth Army counterattacked, the Chinese armies were decimated, close to half their men being killed or wounded. For one last time the Eighth Army struck north, recovering the ground that had been lost, and in the east even extending its gains farther north before the attack came to a close in mid-June 1951.

By this time, the first breezes of a real armistice were wafting their way upon the scene, and the front stabilized on a line winding from below Kaesŏng on the west to above Kansŏng on the shore of the Sea of Japan. But before an armistice was finally hammered out, fierce, grinding positional fighting would take place along this front for almost two more years as the cease-fire talks sputtered along.

The Diary.

SUNDAY
26 NOVEMBER
1950

Dispatched multi letters of thanks to those friends who honored me in some way on my birthday.

Dispatched the fol REDLINE PERSONAL (marble) to Vandenberg:

3d Bomb Group now with 3 sqds flew 67 night intruder missions between Yalu River and bomb line last night. JOC worked them for five hours. Practically everything ahead of front line 8th Army was aflame when they finished. Marines, under my control, flew 11 in addition to those by 3d. Total by both 78. Forty-eight B–26 night intruder and 8 RB–26 missions, plus Marines, are scheduled for tonight.

Got off a long letter to Chidlaw in which I delineated a lot of thoughts I've had on F–80Cs.

Also sent a letter to Partridge, urging him to get behind the project that I'm setting up for General Vandenberg in order that FAF, its fighters and its light bombers, be adequately recorded photographically in order that the effectiveness of tactical air can be documented before Congress when it convenes early in 1951. Told him that he was as aware as I of the impact of a complete and dramatic photographic record has on skeptics who do not understand both the capabilities and accomplishments of air power employed tactically.

Departed the office about 1130 hours. Annalee and I played golf with the Davisons - had a lot of fun - and good exercise, but my game wasn't so hot.

Todd Mellersh[1] wired me that he was to visit his Flying Boat Wing at Iwakuni early next month and expected to arrive Tokyo PM, Sunday, 3 December. He is to stay 2 nights in Tokyo, departing AM December 5.

Directed Sach to send via British telecommunications the following message, info to Bouchier, Sir Alvary Gascoigne, and General Robertson:

Delighted to have you stay as my guest for your visit to Tokyo. Please let me have details of your arrival and departure time, and airfield you propose to use. Have arranged accommodations for your staff at the BCOF Maronouchi Hotel.

MONDAY
27 NOVEMBER
1950

Dispatch fol redline to Vandenberg:

45 B–26 night intruder, 11 Marine night intruder, and 5 RB–26 night recon missions were flown last night. Total 61.

---

1. Air Vice Marshal Sir Francis John Williamson Mellersh had been Air Commanding Officer, Strategic Air Force (EAC) in 1944-1945. He was presently Air Officer Commanding, Malaya.

Sent the fol R&R to Crabb:

I have just had a long talk with General Partridge reference his communications set up and he gave me the reasons for sending the long signal that came in this morning. He states that Colonel Wagner,[2] his communications officer, was an air defense officer and not a signal officer. He further stated that Colonel Ira Stinson, who was his signal officer, could not take Korea and was sent back to the ZI for physical reasons. General Partridge stated that Colonel Wagner is a fine officer but that he is just not up to getting proper communications established in Korea. It is desired that you in consultation with Colonel Sirmyer[3] and General Weyland, prepare a redline signal to Twining from Stratemeyer urging the immediate airlift and assignment of a qualified communications officer for assignment to General Partridge, Fifth Air Force in Korea. Somebody of the caliber of Colonel Garland is required. s/G.E.S.

Had a call from Partridge at 1700 hours and he reported that the ground situation on the right flank of the Eighth Army was bad. He personally flew out over the lines at 1240 hours and arrived at this estimate of the situation from the radio chatter that he listened to. Calls were coming in for fighter support from all over the front. At my request he stated he would send me a Stratline giving his estimate late this evening. It was received at my quarters about 2330 hours. I immediately called my Ops people and inquired if the Ground Ops office was present and I was informed that he was not. I asked if they had received my Stratline and they said they had and then they stated they had sent a copy of same to Colonel Sims,[4] our liaison officer in Far East Command. When I heard this, I hit the ceiling. I asked them by what authority they had sent a personal message from Partridge to me over there and they had indicated that they had done so on instructions from General Crabb. I then called General Crabb at his quarters and he confirmed his instructions to Ops and in very plain language I told General Crabb that I didn't like it - that [it] was a violation of a confidence between me and my commanders and that in the future any personal message to me would not be passed out of this headquarters without my personal approval. Of course, Crabb said he was sorry, but that doesn't help matters. I then called the Acting Chief of Staff, FEC, and got General Keyser and told him that when he saw the message to treat it as strictly a personal message from Partridge to me and not in any sense as an official message as far as Far East Command is concerned. He had the message on his desk and stated that he would do as I requested for which I thanked him. I quote Partridge's Stratline verbatim herewith:

1. EUSAK Forces are executing a general withdrawal over entire front. In II ROK Corps Sector, retrograde mvmt [movement] net loss of over 30 airline miles. Reserve of IX Corps and 8 Army committed with latter consisting of 1st Cav Div, moving E thru Sunch'ŏn to block II ROK Corps line of retreat. *2.* Based solely on pilots' radio conversations, I am of opinion enemy is present in str[ength]. Ground reports indicate exc[ellent] use of

---

2. Col Victor H. Wagner.
3. Col Edgar A. Sirmyer, Jr.
4. Col Jack A. Sims.

night infiltration tactics similar to those employed by NK trps during period July to mid-Sept. 8 Army evaluates enemy action as an offensive rather than counterattack and I concur. 3. In order to be prepared for eventualities, plans being laid here for possible evacuation of P'yŏngyang facilities including field at Sinanju.

TUESDAY 28 NOVEMBER 1950

Went to Tokyo General Hospital and took some funny phys- ical test where they look at all my innards through a pair of goggles after I have drunk some vile white liquid, standing me in front of an X-Ray machine.

I made the briefing at about 0840 hours. Immediately after the briefing, I told Weyland of my unhappiness about passing around personal messages outside of this headquarters. I called Colonel Toro that at the next staff meeting to make plain that any personal message from one of my commanders to me would under no conditions leave FEAF Hq without my personal approval, and if I should be absent, then General Craigie must give approval.

Dispatched the fol REDLINE TS personal to Vandenberg:

PARA I. Reference my 0426. Ground situation on right flank of Eighth Army bad. Partridge will concentrate great effort there today. O'Donnell besides burning T'aech'on will burn and interdict respectively other vil- lages and communication lines today. Weather is good. PARA II. In view of critical turn again of events, I request that Weyland stay on until situa- tion becomes reasonably clarified. Am sure you appreciate that his release by one December would be to the detriment of FEAF and USAF.

Annalee and I had the Barcus group and the Stearns group to dinner at Mayeda House. Dr. Stearns honored guest

WEDNESDAY 29 NOVEMBER 1950

Stratline received from Partridge:

1. Impressions contained in my Stratline of last night are confirmed by the day's events, Chinese forces continue general offensive in EUSAK sector and according to reports received at K-27 this afternoon attacks against X Corps have started. *2.* At 1600 hours word was received at K-27 that 1st Mar Div was in need of all air support that could be dispatched and 35 Group was released for remainder of afternoon for full scale effort in close support of ground forces around Chosin Res.[5] *3.* Gasoline for both Marine Air Wing and AF in Hamhŭng area has been critical but it now appears that sufficient supply is assured. K-27 was down to last 75 rockets late today but Marine expect 4000 tomorrow and will replace those borrowed from USAF. 4. Am directing removal of all heavy equipment from Sinanju area starting tomor- row, leaving there only so much as can be moved with organizational vehi- cles and air transport. This precaution is mainly to safeguard vital communications and radar equipment that could not be replaced. 5. Craigie and party here tonight. They will depart for K-27 and Seoul tomorrow.

---

5. Two F–51 squadrons of the 35th FIG had been based at Yŏnp'o (K-27), south of Hŭngnam, since Nov. 19.

Dispatched a "pat-on-the back" to Rosie, via Stratline, with info going to CG 19th Bomb Gp, Okinawa:

Stratline personal O'Donnell from Stratemeyer. I have just examined the BDA [bomb damage assessment] photography of your bombing of a Manp'ojin RR bridge. The interpreters' report indicates that on the South end, the first span is slightly damaged, the second and third spans are damaged and out of alignment. The bridge is considered unserviceable. This shows evidence of good bombing. The results are excellent. My congratulations to you and the 19th Bomb Group. Keep up the good work.

Received the fol redline from Vandenberg: TS 108:

The addition of the 2 gps of fighter a/c now arriving in ur [your] theater makes the problem of congestion on your airdromes increasingly serious. I note here the concentration of several hundred odd a/c in Manchuria. The possibility of this having been done in conjunction with the Chinese attack is quote apparent. I believe it is possible the attack was launched by the Chinese ahead of schedule and that the possibility of their first intention was to accompany the attack with a Pearl Harbor type on your operational fields. This causes me great concern. For the future, I feel that it is imperative that no stone is left unturned to provide dispersal areas and even possible revetments since the destruction of your AF combined with an all-out attack might cause the loss of Korea and even possibly set up the Japanese Islands for invasion. Our ground troops, unaccustomed to hostile air attack might well be unable to become acclimated before a disaster could occur. Will you advise me as to your ideas and what preparations you have and are intending to accomplish in order that this threat be avoided.

Upon receipt of the above radio I bucked and R&R to VC A&P (today, General Weyland, 30 Nov on, General Craigie):

It is desired that without delay you prepare a reply to the attached TS 108, Vandenberg to Stratemeyer, covering what we have done in Korea and Japan and what our contemplated plans are for both areas.

To General MacArthur, I sent a copy of Vandenberg's above quoted radio with the following memorandum:

Your attention is invited to the attached copy of TS redline, TS-108, from General Vandenberg to me. I am in the process of preparing the reply and will secure concurrence from Far East Command prior to its dispatch. s/G.E.S., etc.

Dispatched my personal crew and FEAF C–54 to Korea in order to return General Almond to his CP. Instructed them to return tonight.

Partridge radioed in via Stratline, ref the Vandenberg radio received today,

Will require 68 Ftr AW Sq station[ed] at Itazuke to maintain a flight of four F–82 a/c at K-14 [Kimp'o] for air defense of Seoul area during hrs of darkness. Desire flight of four F–82 be order from Okinawa to augment 68 Ftr AW Sq. Plan to provide for night defense of P'yŏngyang area by utilizing Marine night fighters based at K-27. Will provide best air defense possible within limitations imposed by equipment, comm facilities, terrain and enemy ground activity.

Dispatched vis redline the following TS radio to Vandenberg in answer to his of this AM. Sent Partridge a Stratline info copy and sent a courier copy to CINCFE:

PART I. Reference your redline TS 108 fully concur in your analysis and share your concern over capabilities of Manchuria based aircraft. Dispositions FEAF units presently predicated on offensive war against NK with no appreciable opposing air power, and some of our airfields are badly congested. We are now confronted with new and grave situations. PART II. Partridge is reviewing his air defense requirements in Korea, especially for Kimp'o and P'yŏngyang, and disposing warning and GCI [ground-controlled intercept] radar accordingly. GCI equipment now operational P'yŏngyang, Kimp'o, and Yŏnp'o areas. Have already moved F–82s from Japan to Kimp'o and four F–82s from Okinawa will be moved to combat area. Plan to provide for night air defense P'yŏngyang area by utilizing Marine night fighters based at Yŏnp'o K-27. PART III. Propose to take all possible action to achieve maximum dispersal of aircraft on operational fields in Korea. Korean labor must be used to large extent as avn [aviation] engineers fully employed now to meet minimum requirements for accommodation new wings. Eighth Army will be requested to lend all possible Army service assistance to provide dispersal. We do have space at P'yŏngyang for dispersal, although it is not revetted. Terrain is such that we cannot utilize old revetments there for our aircraft and these revetments are being used for AVAMMO storage. Kimp'o presents our greatest problem. It is our best operational field in Korea but local terrain precludes effective dispersion. On east coast Wŏnsan and Yŏnp'o have satisfactory terrain for dispersal. PART IV. In Japan and Okinawa our B–29s now have ample dispersals and have good AAA protection. With the exception of Ashiya, other Japanese fields are not too congested, and with continuing progress on the airfield program the situation will improve as dispersal is provided.

Wing Commander Johnson, RAF tactical specialist who is out here, presented several papers including his conclusions.[6] Before forwarding them to Marshal of the RAF, Sir John C. Slessor, I included the fol letter with these papers to Jack Slessor:

I forward herewith report #2 - TACTICAL AVIATION IN KOREA, subject <u>Tactical Reconnaissance</u> with inclosures, and report #3 - TACTICAL AVIATION IN KOREA - <u>Air Ground Operations</u>. I have not seen nor read the first

---

6. Johnson's three reports were succinct and well thought out. As an observer for the RAF, Johnson was not criticizing FEAF's interdiction program, just pointing out that it missed a great opportunity to isolate the battlefield early on when MacArthur insisted on the B–29s being used for close support. (Wg. Cdr. J.E. Johnson, RAF, "Tactical Aviation in Korea," No. 3, *Air-Ground Operations*, Oct. 30, 1950, pp 5, 9.)

report entitled TACTICAL AVIATION IN KOREA dated 19 October 1950. I consider that Wing Commander J. E. Johnson has prepared very comprehensive and thorough reports. I do not concur in some of the statements made by Wing Commander Johnson although I am sure he arrived at them after thorough and complete observations and study. Our interdiction program had to be curtailed in order to save our greatly outnumbered ground forces from annihilation. The reason I say this is because I do not in any way want to detract from the excellence of his papers. You must realize, Jack, that when we started this show, everything in the way of air-ground support was a hurried makeshift movement to the offensive as my occupational Air Forces were primarily defensive. Had we any indication that we would be fighting in Korea or an offensive mission, we would have been better prepared for that type of show. Our mission was the defense against air attack of our occupational forces. Your Wing Commander Johnson, I would say, is top notch. s/G.E.S.

Underscored again, in an R&R to the Director of Communications, my desire for immediate assistance from USAF of the best communications officers available:

Reference USAF redline radio to me dtd 28 Nov 50, cite: RL-107, when you hold your telecon with the Director of Communications, Office of the Chief of Staff, USAF, you are directed to first present our critical personnel shortage and urge with all your power of expression the immediate airlift of the very best communications officer available as a replacement for Colonel Ira Stinson as the communications officer for Fifth Air Force, Korea. There should be a limited number of staff officers, with whom he is familiar and whom he can place in positions of high responsibility accompany him. Our whole system of communications in Korea, and from Korea to my headquarters, is dependent upon communications officers who have the know-how and can make our communications function as it should. Such personnel are not available to me at this time. After you have discussed the above, then take up the question of communications equipment and supply requirements. s/G.E.S.

THURSDAY   *Received the fol Stratline from Partridge:*

30 NOVEMBER   *Part 1.* I have instructed my wg commanders to effect
1950   maximum dispersal of a/c on their fields, within their present capabilities. Plans are being formulated for the construction of revetments and adequate dispersal areas for ea field, utilizing local labor primarily under the supervision of atchd Engr Units and Air Install pers. I will endeavor to obtain maximum assistance fr 8th Army in order to expedite completion of this program. *Part 2.* Commanders have been directed to establish passive air defense measures for all pers, to include construction of split trenches and other emergency shelters, and the use of smoke candles. A limited number of a/c are being maintained on 10 minute strip alert. *Part 3.* This will be a special subj for my Inspector Gen, and I will keep you advised of the progress being made in each area.

Part 4. Completion of the present airfield construction program will preclude the congestion caused by 2 Wgs being based on 1 fld.

Called on CINCFE just before noon, carrying with me the two following redlines to Vandenberg, with info to him (CINCFE), for his concurrence in dispatch:

Further reference your redline TS 108. In addition to all passive and active defense measures possible in Korea, plans are being made for offensive action if authorized. Further, if we are attacked in force by Communist Chinese Air Force we must be ready to deliver effective counter air effort. If this is to be effective, I feel it imperative that we be authorized to utilize our RB–45s for reconnaissance of airfields in Manchuria. I feel that the RB–45 reconnaissance of airfields can be accomplished at high altitude, 40,000 feet, without positive identification and probably without detection. Desire reply soonest.

The other radio I desired his concurrence for dispatch, is as follows:

In view of current situation in Korea, the build up of Communist Air Force units in Manchuria, and the possibility that UN forces will become involved in a war with Communist China, it is recommended that the Strategic Air Command be given a warning order to be prepared to dispatch without delay medium bomb groups to the Far East for the purpose of reinforcing FEAF Bomber Command (Prov.). Further believe this augmentation should include atomic capabilities.

The above quoted message reference the RB–45s was not dispatched as General MacArthur could not see his way at this time to concur in it. The message reference augmentation of FEAF Bomber Force was dispatched.[7]

After discussions reference the two signals, I asked General MacArthur if anything took place during his conference with Walker and Almond that I should know. He said, "No, Strat." He said that he simply had them come back to give him first-hand information on the status of the ground situation and their contemplated actions. Walker indicated that he felt confident that he could straighten our his lines, but would necessarily have to have retrograde movements. Almond stated that he wasn't in too much difficulty but that he indicated he would contract his X Corps and form a perimeter defense around Hamhŭng and Wŏnsan.

The General appeared to me pretty much depressed.

Awarded the Legion of Merit to Colonel Keach[8] - his wife, Margaret, was present.

1630 hours, Ted Tezlatt and Lowell Farrell[9] of RKO with a letter from General Eaker called at the office. Discussed Howard Hughes' proposed movie. They were accompanied by USAF Lt. Colonel Paul Latislais.[10]

---

7. A pair of RB–45s were brought to Japan on Sept. 28 for tests with Reconnaissance Detachment A, 84th BS. In January, BomCom took operational control of the detachment, attaching it to the RB–29–equipped 91st SRS at Yokota. Although only three RB–45Cs usually operated with the 91st, at least one more aircraft was added to the force for a short period.

8. Lt Col Thomas C. Keach, FEAF director of personnel.

9. Further information on these men has not been found.

10. Latislais was a member of the 5AF JOC in Korea.

Received fol radio from Twining:

1. I concur in your proposal to undertake the responsibility for the opn of aerial ports for the spt [support] of the Korean opn, specifically the weighing, manifesting, loading and unloading functions. As you propose, this responsibility should terminate at the air freight docks. *2.* Your request for 116 off and 1006 airmen spaces is not fully understood. It is assumed that you can fill the requested spaces fr resources avail to you except for the 200 airmen which you require fr ZI resources. These 200 wppl [?] airmen will be furnd [furnished] POE [port of embarkation] as soon as SSN's are known. *3.* You are authd to approach CINCFE ref this commitment.

GHQ, United Nations Command, on 29 November, General Orders No. 23 states as follows:

Attachment of Forces: *1.* Pursuant to request of the Security Council, United Nations, the Governments of the following nations have furnished Air Forces as indicated to the United Nations Command:

NATION	FORCES	REPORTING DATE
Australia	77th RAAF Fighter Squadron	7 July 1950
Union of South Africa	2d SAAF Fighter Squadron	4 October 1950
Greece	Royal Hellenic Air Force Detachment	25 November 1950

2. Having reported on the dates indicated, the above forces are attached to Far East Air Forces effective those dates. AG 300.4 (25 Nov 50) GC. BY COMMAND OF GENERAL MACARTHUR: s/DOYLE O. HICKEY, Major General, General Staff Corps, Acting Chief of Staff. OFFICIAL: s/K.B. Bush, Brigadier General, USA, Adjutant General.

Received the fol rad from USAF - personal from Twining:

Reurad A 39728 GOP-COM dtd 28 Nov 50. Ref Part 2. Colonel Henry Riera,[11] being recalled to EAD [extended active duty] will depart Travis AFB, Calif via MATS 11 Dec 50 on PCA [permanent change of assignment] to your hqs. Ref Part 3. Colonel Glenn C. Coleman and Lt. Col. Orville V. Rose, and Lt. Col. Frederick W. Shipe,[12] will depart Travis via MATS on or about 1 Dec 50 for Hq FAF, Nagoya on 90 days TDY your comd. Details of balance ur radio will be discussed in telecon now scheduled for 30 Nov 50.

---

11. Riera became Assistant Deputy for Communications and Electronics, Fifth Air Force on Dec. 18, 1950.
12. Coleman became Deputy for Communications, Fifth Air Force, on Dec. 10, 1950; Rose became Executive Officer, 934th Signal Battalion on Dec. 21, 1950; Shipe's job is unknown.

Fifth AF PIO forwarded a copy of the fol ltr that had been received by General Partridge, dtd 25 Nov 50:

Headquarters 7th Infantry Division, Office of the Commanding General, APO 7, subject: Letter of Appreciation, To: Commanding General, Fifth Air Force in Korea, APO 970, Thru: Commanding General X Corps, APO 909: I wish to express my appreciation for the very effective support rendered by the Fifth AF to the 7th Infantry Division in its advance from the beaches at Iwŏn to the Manchurian border. The performance of the tactical air control parties [TACP] and Mosquito planes left little to be desired and proved the effectiveness of air support for ground troops. The Mosquito planes not only furnished the necessary and sometimes difficult coordination between ground troops and fighter planes but, in effect, served as an additional link in our communications system by reporting enemy locations and the positions of our front lines. The tactical air control parties are especially commended for their close coordination and cooperation with the bn commanders as well as for the cheerful and enthusiastic manner in which they accomplished their task and adapted themselves to the local conditions. Their friendly spirit combined with their efficient performance was noticed and appreciated by the troops as well as the commanders. I am indeed happy to state that as a result of the close coordination and the excellent work on the part of the Fifth Air Force, many enemy were destroyed in close proximity to our front lines and yet not a single man was injured by our support aircraft during the entire advance. The cheerful and efficient performance of duty of all Fifth AF units which participated has been in keeping with the highest traditions of the Armed Services. s/David C. Barr, DAVID C. BARR,[13] Maj Gen, USA, Commanding.

AG (25 Nov 50), 1st Ind, Headquarters, X Corps, APO 909, 30 November 1950. To: Commanding General, Fifth Air Force in Korea, APO 970. I am pleased to transmit this letter indicating the appreciation from Commanding General 7th Infantry Division for the efforts on the part of Fifth Air Force to provide close tactical air support to his Division. s/Edward M. Almond, EDWARD M. ALMOND, Major General, USA, Commanding.

FRIDAY 1 DECEMBER 1950

Earle Partridge sent me the following handwritten memorandum with "eyes only" enclosure:

Headquarters Fifth Air Force, Office of the Commanding General, APO 710, dtd 26 Nov. General Strat - This is one of two copies. The other is in my personal files - P. E.E. Partridge, Major General, USAF, Commanding.

EYES Only - Headquarters Fifth Air Force in Korea, Office of the Commanding General, APO 970, 19 November 1950.

---

13. Barr had commanded the 7th Infantry Division since late 1949. A staff officer in World War II, he headed an Army mission to China in 1948 and 1949.

MEMORANDUM FOR RECORD, SUBJECT: Visit to X Corps.

1. During the past three days, Col Meyers and I have been visiting in the X Corps area in an effort to indoctrinate General Almond and his staff, to determine what procedures were being followed and to gain a better understanding of operating conditions in the X Corps area. My observations follow: *a.* General Almond has no major complaints regarding the air support being furnished him. The Marines and the Fifth Air Force, plus the Navy, are furnishing him much more support than the ground situation warrants. Within recent days, in the front of the First ROK Corps around Kilchu, there has been some fighting. In general, however, the operations are limited to patrol and guerrilla action and air is being used lavishly without commensurate returns. *b.* The photographs requested for the X Corps have not been provided promptly and in some cases, not at all. This has been due to a combination of circumstances involving communications, the movement of the Marine photographic establishment from Kimp'o to Wŏnsan, and the failure of the Army to provide either photo interpreters, ground liaison officers, or reproduction facilities. The Fifth Air Force will do its best to overcome these many deficiencies, and I believe that a workable solution is now in effect so that a minimum number of photographic prints needed by the ground forces can be supplied through Air Force and Marine sources. *c.* The conversation developed that neither Gen Almond nor his chief of staff was familiar with the doctrine set forth in Field Manual 31-35 or in the supplementary pamphlets issued jointly by the Army Field Forces and the Tactical Air Command in June and September of this year. The manuals already had been delivered to the X Corps headquarters personally by Col Meyers and by me. I again left copies with Gen. Almond and extracted promises from him and Gen. Ruffner as well, that they would read these documents carefully.

d. Conversation also developed that the X Corps had no conception of its obligations with regard to the provision of an air-ground operations system as contemplated in Field Manual 31-35. Insofar as I could determine, no provision has been made to secure the necessary personnel and equipment to implement this air-ground operations system. Furthermore, the resources of the X Corps are entirely inadequate to improvise the essential items from what is now on hand. For example, I pointed out that some weeks ago I had visited X Corps headquarters at Wŏnsan and had pointed out the requirement for a reliable communications system between Headquarters X Corps and Headquarters Fifth Air Force. At that time, the Corps' signal equipment was still afloat and as an interim measure I provided a complete 399 radio set with operating personnel, as well as a TACP, with vehicles and equipment so that the Corps headquarters could not only communicate with Fifth Air Force in Seoul, but also talk to passing mosquito and courier aircraft by VHF. Although a considerable time has elapsed since that time, the X Corps has made no move to establish the radio link or any other link with this headquarters so that the Air Force's 399 radio set could be released for its proper duty. I might add that the tactical air control party provided for Corps headquarters has also been diverted to another location within the X Corps for use as a true TACP. *e.* The X Corps is having major difficulties with its internal as well as its external signal communications. The tactical air control parties and the mosquito aircraft are being used in conjunction with the Marine tactical air control center and other ground facilities as a substitute for the point-to-point ground communications which should have already been firmly established by the X Corps. *f.* Procedure being followed in the X Corps is a hodge-podge of Army-Air Force, Marine, and improvised methods. Having no adequate communications and having no interest in establishing them, the X Corps prefers to work directly with the Marine TACC, and in many cases, direct with the Marine air unit at Wŏnsan. Actually, instead of using the TO&E equipment and the supporting arms of the ground forces, their commanders prefer to call for air strikes on the assumption that the air support costs nothing and that the use of air may cut down casualties. I was told by Gen Mead,[14] assist division commander, for example, that the 3d Division has been instructed to call directly on the Marine air unit at Wŏnsan for strikes whenever needed. *(1)* Actually my instructions to Gen Harris were that he will furnish air support within the X Corps area and elsewhere as directed by the Fifth AF daily operations order. In emergency, and when I wrote this directive, I meant emergency, the ground units were authorized to call direct on the First Marine Air Wing at Hamhŭng for such support as might be needed. Actually, there has been no emergency, insofar as I could determine. Yet, the X Corps continues to call on the First Marine Air Wing for immediate assistance. *(2)* There was a sly attitude in X Corps headquarters. They thought they were getting away with something and circumventing the instructions which are in existence. I intend to let this matter continue in its present status for the time being. Eventually, it must be brought under control. As I view the matter, it will require careful indoctrination of the ground army and this, rather than an open break, is the first step. *g.* During the course of our visits to the X Corps area Col Meyers visited two TACP's and I visited two others. All of these were in operation, but their margin of reserve was entirely too small. This will be corrected by action to be taken by Maj. Calahan[15] through his division air liaison officers and by Col. Meyers through the operations people here.

If these tactical air control parties are to remain on the air successfully, each VRC-1 jeep must be backed up by another of the same type at each location.[16] This is the objective and a great deal of organization work remains to be done in the Fifth Air Force if the desired number of TACP's is to be put in the field. See also memo for Col. Meyers of this date. *h.* Gen. Almond pointed out many times that he is now operating his force in detachments of battalion size or smaller. He is spread over a wide

---

14. Brig Gen Armistead D. Mead, 3rd Infantry Division assistant division commander (ADC).

15. Calahan, first name unknown, was the X Corps Air Liaison Officer.

16. A VRC-1 jeep carried the AN/VRC-1 radio. This radio had four channels, of which only three were normally available, the fourth supposedly being reserved for emergencies. An improved TACP jeep with more radios made its appearance in April 1951. (Futrell No. 72, p 193.)

area and he frequently runs into trouble at out-of-the-way places. Under the circumstances which now exist, he is often unable to bring in air strikes promptly because the air-ground communications do not exist due to lack of tactical air control parties. I tried to point out to him that he had none of the ground communications essential to carry out the Army's responsibility for providing information as to the targets to be attacked. If the Army were able to do this, we could provide mosquito aircraft and carry out strikes in that manner based on information sent back through the air-ground operations system. He insists that this is quite out of question and that he <u>must</u> have one TACP per battalion. Under the system in which the Army has no adequate communications with its forward ground units and its detached patrols or task groups, I am inclined to agree.

2. Before concurring in the arrangement by which the Air Force undertakes to provide a TACP and a Mosquito aircraft to accompany each forward ground unit, no matter how small, it should be remembered that there will be generated concurrently, a requirement that for each of these small ground organizations we be prepared to provide a continuous combat air patrol during flyable daylight hours. This method of furnishing air support would be prohibitably costly. 3. In reviewing the above, I note that I have made no mention of the fact that the Navy has operated quite consistently in close support of the X Corps. This headquarters is aware that the 7th Fleet has been given as a third priority task the close support of the X Corps in emergency. This mission follows in importance those of destroying the Yalu River bridges and of making interdiction strikes between the bomb line and the Manchurian border. The exact manner in which the strikes are requested and the way in which they are handled either by X Corps or by the First Marine Air Wing, is not known officially to me. Since aircraft working in close support must operate either under the control of a Mosquito or a tactical air control party, I am sure that the Navy's aircraft are reporting in to one agency or the other prior to attacking targets inside the bomb line. Thus far, I have taken no official cognizance of their actions, but I am looking into the matter.
s/P - E.E.P. copy furnished: General Stratemeyer.

Received the fol operational immediate radio from Partridge, TS, which I relayed on to Spivey as per request:

1. EUSAK continues withdrawal as planned, with only major difficulty being extraction of 2d Division from position southwest of Kunu-ri, repeat Kunu-ri. K-29[17] abandoned this date without loss of property but advanced radar site was evacuated by our personnel on advice of infantry without removing all of equipment. This incident now under investigation. 2. At conference here today following was decided. 8th Fighter moves K-23 to K-16. 18th Fighter moves K-24 to K-13. Mosquito and ROK Air Force move to K-24 to K-16. 35th Fighter moves K-27 to K-9. Marines move 1 sq from K-25 to shipboard and 2 sqs to K-27, abandoning

---

17. "K-sites" mentioned in this paragraph are: K-29, Sinanju; K-23, P'yŏngyang; K-16, Seoul; K-24, P'yŏngyang East; K-13, Suwŏn; K-27, Yŏnp'o; K-9, Pusan East; K-25, Wŏnsan; K-14, Kimp'o; K-2, Taegu.

K-25. 4th Fighter moves K-14. 27th Fighter moves K-2. Erler was in attendance and can present details. General Harris, local commanders, and Gray[18] from K-27 also participated. *3.* Plans for ground Army include continuation of independent command status of EUSAK and 10th Corps. Walker plans execute withdrawal and delaying action. Almond plans as last resort withdrawal into perimeter defense of Hamhŭng area. Removal of 35th Wing from K-27 simplifies command within 5th AF and assures fullest cooperation with 8th Army which appears destined to bear brunt on fighting. At same time move provides space for Marine a/c wing to use after abandoning K-25. *4.* Plan to give added mission directive to Harris assigning him close support mission with 10th Corps with request to go direct from 10th Corps to first Marine a/c wing. 5th AF will retain operational control but will exercise it only when necessary to balance available sorties against requirements of two ground forces. *5.* Estimate full evacuation K-23 and 24 may consume week. I remain P'yŏngyang with few people until Walker leaves but all heavy gear is moving at once. Anticipate all moves will be accomplished without any notice. Able reduction in operational effectiveness and foresee no repeat no unusual difficulties.

Immediately upon receipt of above radnote, sent the fol Stratline to Partridge:

Reurad 301140Z. Relocation of FAF units approved. I am assuming that 77th RAAF Sq will move with 35th Wing and that SAAF Sq will move with 18th Wing. Do not reply if my assumption correct. (Assumption correct.)

At 1000 hours this morning had a conference with Colonel Erler who attended the meeting held yesterday in P'yŏngyang. Main people present were Generals Walker, Partridge, Harris (commander First Marine Air Wing). Colonel Erler stated that the fields that would be retained by FAF in their retrograde movement would be as follows: K-14, K-16, K-13, K-2, K-9 as operative fields with units stationed thereon. K-3 [P'ohang] would be kept open for emergency. K-27 would be retained and all landbased Marines would operate from there. The Air Force units would be pulled out in order that the air support for the X Corps when they finally pull back to a perimeter defense around Hamhŭng would be by the Marines. The steel mat at both K-24 and K-23 is being loaded or that which is still on cars will be returned to Seoul. Steel mat extension of K-27 will be put down. Our AF engineers then will function at K-16, K-13, K-2, and K-27.

A personal EYES ONLY from Vandenberg received this morning and following people have read this signal: Generals MacArthur, Craigie, Weyland, Crabb and Hickey - and myself.

I quote a news release from Washington:

WASHINGTON (0755) President Truman Thursday hurled the threat of the atomic bomb at the Chinese Communists hordes in Korea and called a crisis conference of congressional and defense leaders to

---

18. Col Frederic C. Gray took command of the 35th FIW on this day.

decide whether total mobilization must be ordered. Mr. Truman told a news conference he is considering use of the A-bomb to end the onslaught of Chinese Reds because "we are fighting for our own survival" and he pledged that UN forces under MacArthur "will not abandon their mission" in Korea. The President said that if he authorizes use of the atomic weapon, MacArthur will decide where and when it will be employed.

Reference the above release, General MacArthur at 1400 hours today, in his office, stated that in a war with Communist China and if he was given the use of the atomic weapon, his targets in order of priority would be: ANTUNG, MUKDEN, PEIPING, TIENTSIN, SHANGHAI and NANKING. [Capitalizaton in original] That if we get in the big one, his targets would be VLADIVOSTOK, KHABAROVSK, KIRIN, and a fourth one which I believe was KUYVYSHIEVKA. (Extract of this diary item which included news release and listing of targets made for: VC Ops, VC A&P, and Director, Plans.)[19]

At 1030 hours presented a letter of appreciation to Mrs. A. Waterman, long-time FEAF civil service employee (Personnel) on eve of her return to ZI.

Sent the following "marble" redline to Vandenberg:

Seven Greek C–47 aircraft landed at Itazuke at 1458I, 1 December. One additional aircraft departed Kadena, but returned. Greeks are now a part of Far East Air Forces and attached to Com Cargo Command.[20]

Had Wing Commander Johnson's Tactical Aviation in Korea series of reports distributed as follows: 1 ea to CAS (thru Bouchier), 1 ea to Bouchier, 1 ea to Air Marshall Fogarty, 1 ea to General Barcus, 1 ea to Staff thru General Weyland, 1 ea to Wing Commander Johnson, and 1 ea to File (Sach).

Before leaving office sent the fol stratline to Partridge:

As you are undoubtedly aware, the First Marine Division and First Marine Air Wing are now undergoing an experience from which may be drawn many examples to substantiate the AF concept of air power organized and controlled so as to exploit its flexibility in support of operations on wide fronts involving either deep penetrations or retrograde movements, as contrasted to air power organized and controlled to

---

19. How MacArthur's target selection compares to the Air Force's cannot be explained here as USAF targeting during the period is still classified. It is now obvious that, despite President Truman's ill-considered remarks concerning use of the atomic bomb in Korea, the U.S. had little desire to use the weapon there except in an extreme emergency, a position MacArthur's troops were never in.
There were several reasons that the U.S. did not wish to use the atomic bomb in Korea: U.S. policy makers, both civilian and military, believed the Korean situation to be a Soviet ploy to waste the weapons in Korea so that a Russian attack in Europe (the prime theater to the planners) would not have to face a nuclear counterattack; there was a strong fear that the Russians would retaliate with their own atomic weapons; the American allies, notably the British, were strongly against the use of these weapons in the war; some military commanders felt there were no suitable targets for atomic bombs in Korea. It should be noted that the Chinese apparently were quite afraid that the U.S. would use atomic weapons against them when they moved into Korea. This fear lessened when it became obvious to the Chinese that American planes were not going to cross the Yalu into China. (Morton H. Halperin, *Limited War in the Nuclear Age* [Westport, Conn., 1978], pp 47-49; William Steuck, *The Korean War: An International History* [Princeton, N.J., 1995], pp 131-134, 145-146.)
20. Initially consisting of seven C–47s, with two more added later, the Royal Hellenic Air Force's Flight 13 arrived in Japan on Nov. 26. The unit was assigned to the 374th TCW's 21st Squadron for operations and flew its first mission on Dec. 4.

support relatively small-scale assault operations involving shallow penetration on a narrow front. In order to derive maximum value from the lessons now unfolding, I desire that you and key members of your staff keep careful, detailed, daily memoranda of record of the principal events since the beginning of the current Chinese Communist offensive, and that upon its conclusion you submit to me your personal summary analysis of air employment in support of both the Eighth Army and the X Corps, with particular attention to air support of the First Marine Division, both the support provided by the First Marine Air Wing and the support provided by other air under your control. I fully appreciate the difficulty of your position as the air commander who may be called upon to make hard decisions relative to allocation of your sortie capability and I am unreservedly confident that your decisions will be one hundred percent sound and just. This signal should be kept within Air Force family.

Dispatched the fol TS rad to CSAF:

V 0463 This rad in 4 parts:
PART I. Dr. Ellis A. Johnson, Director ORO, DA [Operations Research Office, Department of the Army], has proposed to provide GHQ within next week a critical evaluation of the pos use and effectiveness of atomic bombs in close spt of ground forces in Korea. Study is to determine whether such use is capable of providing decisive effect on the enemy, whether tactically feasible, and numbers of bombs required, logistic preparation nec, and nature of detailed planning rqmts. It is intended that the study along with info they may accrue from Washington will enable GHQ to make a factual decision with respect to recommendations concerning the use or non-use of atomic bombs. *PART II.* Dr. Johnson and associates have been in the theater in connection with a number of projects of opnl research nature. One of these projects has been tactical use of atomic bombs in close spt. It is understood that ORO analysts have been working on this project since September. *PART III.* Above proposal has been approved by CINCFE and Army, Navy, and AF reps fr G-3, Joint Strategic Plans and Opns Gp, GHQ, are being made available to assist in the proposed study. In addition this hq has been requested to furnish an officer qualified to provide advice concerning the opnl aspects of the problem fr the AF point of view. Lt. Col. James E. Trask has been selected. *PART IV.* In a memorandum to CINCFE this Hq points out that inasmuch as USAF as primary responsibility for delivery, CSAF has specialized agencies under his direction to study matters of this nature and that it is recommended that CSAF be called upon to provide assistance.[21]

---

21. This report, ORO-R-3 (FEC), Preliminary Evaluation of Close Air Support Operations in Korea, was issued on Feb. 1, 1951. It intimated that if tactical nuclear weapons had been used at certain places and times, the Chinese forces would have suffered terribly high casualties, but friendly forces close to the explosion areas could also have suffered substantial casualties. (Futrell, pp 701-702.)

SATURDAY
2 DECEMBER
1950

Reached the office this AM and was handed Twining's reply to my radio of late yesterday re Dr. Ellis A. Johnson's proposed evaluation etc.:

Personal Stratemeyer from Twining - the matter raised in your V 0463 OP-PL will be discussed with you by Gen. Cabell who will arrive your hqs in the next 2 or 3 days for a visit.

USAF (Personal Farthing[22] to Stratemeyer) to me with info to CINCFE Area Petroleum Officer received (radio):

Continued success air operations directly dependent adequate fuel supply. Suggest closest coordination operations planning with fuel supply agencies. Imperative CINCFE area petroleum office known in detail all plans affecting fuel requirements at earliest moment.

Bucked radio to my D/M and told them to get on it.

Sent the fol personal rad to Twining (redline) A-4167B.

Until this time I have not insisted upon a rotation plan for combat crew personnel based entirely upon attainment of a certain number of missions, because I felt that it would not be necessary. Twice it looked like war would end. However, in view of latest developments I feel that such a rotation plan must be established immediately. A number of my crew personnel, including some fairly recent arrivals, have been in combat most of the duration of the Korean war and have now flown as many as 140 missions. These personnel are not eligible for return to ZI under the very restricted authority contained in your radio AFPMP-1-T 57343 because they have not completed normal overseas tour. These individuals have no promise of return to ZI because of extended hazardous and difficult combat duty. Naturally they can see only one end, namely that of eventually being killed. Crew morale is already affected and if this situation is allowed to continue, will go lower. Crews lose their eagerness for combat after 30 or 40 missions unless some eventual relief is held out. Inter-theater rotation is already in effect but is of little value in solving overall problem because practically all tactical units are in combat. Replacements will have to arrive before individuals could rotate. Recommend criteria for return be established at 100 fighter missions, 75 light bomber missions, and 60 medium bomber missions. Data is now being gathered as to number who would be eligible for this rotation immediately and monthly thereafter. Urgently request concurrence in this plan in order that our request for replacements may be submitted. This matter was thoroughly discussed with General Parks during his visit in September.

SUNDAY
3 DECEMBER
1950

My radio received in USAF re crew rotations and Edwards in a personal redline stated "Your A 4167 CG received and understudy. Reply may be expected by 6 Dec.

---

22. Maj Gen William E. Farthing, Director of Maintenance, Supply and Services, Headquarters USAF.

Dispatched Stratline to General Partridge in which I stated:

General Vandenberg will want to know immediately when first F–84s and first F–86s are utilized in combat. It appears now that Colonel Packard[23] with his first F–84s will proceed to Taegu 4 December. Be sure to advise me immediately of their first mission so that I may inform Vandenberg and LeMay.

Snow and below freezing temperatures did not stop FEAF's C–47s from evacuating casualties and delivering supplies to the embattled troops at the Changjin (Chosin) Reservoir.

Redline to Vandenberg as follows:

COMBAT CARGO COMMAND C–47s evacuated 978 wounded personnel from 1st Marine Division and Seventh Division on 2 Dec and approx 1100 on 3 Dec from quickly prepared field at Hagaru-Ri CV 5272.

Got off my weekly letter to Gill Robb Wilson.

1507 hours Air Vice Marshal Sir F. J. W. Mellersh, B. E., A.F.C., Air Officer Commanding, RAF at Singapore arrived for a two-day visit with us. Met him at the airport at Haneda.

At about 1630 hours, Major General Junius Jones came in and reviewed the general topics of the report he proposes to submit to AMC as a result of his visit to FEAF. He left with us many very good suggestions. He promised to send me a copy of his report. He further promised that he would call Major General Bertrandias and secure the name for me of a top-notch flying safety officer in the grade of lieutenant colonel or major. I will request this officer's services - by name.

Received the fol TS Stratline from Partridge:

This rad in 3 parts. Subject is Escape and Evasion.

PART I. Timberlake informs me you are holding meeting 3 Dec on above subject. By chance one of my people working on this matter came to my

---

23. Col Ashley B. Packard commanded the 27th FEW. Originally intended to be based at Kimp'o, the changing military situation resulted in the wing being based at Taegu. The 27th flew its first mission on Dec. 6. (Futrell, p 248.)

office tonight and he is greatly disturbed over the lack of progress in releasing aircrew personnel who fall in enemy territory. As you may recall I visited your hq some months ago in an effort to crystalize the issue and induce action from some agency. *Part II.* My agent informs me that practical progress on evasion and escape is negative. No one has been rescued nor has any firm program been established. *PART III.* My observations confirm above. I cannot repeat not answer following in any way except negative. *(a)* Is there an evasion and escape program? *(b)* Is some one in charge? *(c)* Is any suitable information given our crews? (d) Have any evasions been accomplished thru planned program? *PART IV.* We still need 40 radios with operators for observation posts. Opportunity to place these agents on ground will soon be lost and I request assistance in this program. *PART V.* Would appreciate any efforts you could exert to bring to fruition plan for establishing sound scheme to help our crews out of hostile territory.

In reply my answer to Partridge follows:

Every person back here is doing everything possible to assist you getting this escape and evasion operation going. This includes Willoughby and Banfill who are in close association and working on project. Meeting for operational planning purposes now in progress. You will be advised results soonest and both Willoughby and I promise action.[24]

I made copies of the two foregoing "escape and evasion" radios and bucked them to General Willoughby with the fol plea:

Dear Charles, attached hereto are copies of Partridge's stratline to me and my stratline to him of this date. For your information and all possible help on this project. Charles, all I'm trying to do is to save my airmen's lives. Please help. G.E.S.

MONDAY 4 DECEMBER 1950

General Cabell with General Collins and Admiral F. S. Low[25] arrived this AM at 0830 at Haneda. They were met by General MacArthur and staff.

Was called to General MacArthur's office with Cabell to hear a discussion between Generals MacArthur and Collins on the current Korean situation and General MacArthur's contemplated plans. Additional people present: General Hickey, General Whitney, General Wright, Admiral Joy and Admiral Low. General MacArthur announced his contemplated plans which included not only retrograde movements, but, as a last resort, the holding of two beach-head areas - the Eighth Army area in the Inch'ŏn-Seoul area and the X Corps, in the Hŭngnam area, and the later entire evacuation of UN forces if the situation so demands.

---

24. A joint Air Force-Navy-CIA effort to train indigenous agents to assist downed airmen in escape and evasion was begun shortly after the start of the war but this organization was disbanded within a few months. Another organization, Combined Command Research and Activities in Korea (CCRAK), was formed by FEC in 1951 to direct all aspects of covert and clandestine activities in Korea but it was unable to fill FEAF's E&E requirements. It appears that few airmen, if any, made it back to friendly lines using preplanned covert E&E facilities. However, a number of downed fliers were rescued from behind enemy lines by the Air Rescue Service. (FEAF Report on the Korean War, Vol. III, Mar. 26, 1954, pp 5-6; Futrell,, pp 576-584.)

25. Low was the Deputy CNO for Logistics.

General Collins then reviewed the thinking of the JCS and indicated that that thinking coincided with General MacArthur's plans. General Collins then discussed at great length his opinions of the political situation both in America and the Far East and further gave his opinions as to the probable actions of the UN. There were other subject matters discussed that were of such a high classification that I dare not even put them in this document.

Again, I want to point out for the record of the unequaled and superior statesmanlike discussion that emanated from General MacArthur.

General Collins gave a very general statement as to the contemplated build up of the Army, the Navy and the Air Force, and stated that in his opinion the necessary money would be forthcoming for that build up.

It was then decided that General Collins would leave at 1230 hours to fly direct to Seoul accompanied by General Cabell where he would remain overnight and have discussions with General Walker. Tomorrow he planned to go to the P'yŏngyang area and see Milburn and Coulter, the 1st and IXth Corps commanders, leaving there Wednesday morning and proceeding to the Hŭngnam area where he would meet with General Almond and return to Japan late Wednesday night, 6 December.

See my Stratline to Partridge reference Cabell's movements quoted hereinafter:

General Cabell will arrive with General Collins in Constellation at Kimp'o, departing Haneda ETD 1230I. It is desired that you and Cabell be present with Collins when he talks to General Walker. Cabell will remain overnight with you to return to Japan tomorrow. Furnish him air transportation.

Sent a Stratline to Tunner:

In view of the very outstanding performance of your C–47 squadron, operating in and out of Hagaru-ri, evacuating the wounded, commanded by Lt. Colonel Royal S. Thompson,[26] I desire that he and such people of his organization who you deem have qualified, be recommended for the award of the Silver Star, or that you make other appropriate awards.

Dispatched the fol Stratline to Tunner:

Radio in 2 parts: PART I. Following message from COMNAVFE to CG FEAF is relayed: "The airlift of wounded from Hagaru-ri is magnificent. We are grateful." PART II. To the foregoing, I add my own sincere appreciation and commendation for yet another difficult and dangerous job promptly and efficiently accomplished.

During the conference with General MacArthur and General Collins this morning I made the following statement re evacuation from Korea as a result of information furnished me by my planning group– per 24 hours from Korea to Japan, our capability is 17,000 per day. From K-27 Hŭngnam to Pusan K-9– or Japan, 8,000 per day. The limit here being the use of only one airstrip. From the Inch'ŏn-Seoul area to the south or to Japan– or both– 16,000 per day.

---

26. Thompson commanded the 21st TCS.

The above does not mean that we can evacuate from both the Hŭngnam area and the Seoul area at the same time. The figures apply to our capability from one or the other area at a time.

At 1500 hours had a long interview with Colonel Sykes and reviewed principally some signals in my headquarters and correspondence sent to COMNAVFE reference the use of Navy controllers at Fifth Air Force.

At 1930 hours, had a bachelor party for Air Vice Marshal Mellersh at Mayeda House. Annalee was terribly ill with a cold and fever and could not be present.

(Footnote - Air [Vice] Marshal Sir F. J. W. Mellersh departs 1115 hours, 5 December, for Singapore.)

TUESDAY 5 DECEMBER 1950

Received a telephone call from Partridge at 0755 hours. Cabell being present in his office there in Korea. He asked permission to come to see me tomorrow morning at ten o'clock to discuss a plan of action in Korea to which he does not concur as he feels the Air Force which is playing the most important part is being ignored. Of course, he could not talk with me freely on the telephone, but I gathered he was concerned with the logistical side of the Air Force problem in reference to the maneuvers and actions by the ground forces. I told him to come on in.

Sent the following redline to Vandenberg:

Total number of evacuees airlifted from Hagaru-ri area to include 4 December 2,654; of this number, 1,983 have been airlifted to Japan.

Went over to the Chief of Staff's office at 1410 hours today and had a good friendly, heart-to-heart talk with Doyle Hickey, the Chief of Staff, Far East Command. I told him of my concern over the discussion that took place in his conference room yesterday between Generals MacArthur and Collins on the contemplated withdrawals and beach-head establishments in Korea with no concern being given to the security of my air bases at Taegu (K-2) and Pusan (K-9). I pointed out that the air will and must play a most important part in any withdrawal or any defense of beachheads, but that if security is not given to the bases in Korea then the air support to which the Army is entitled might not be given. I pointed out that since we were able to move out of the Pusan beach-head forward to the Seoul area, I could see no reason why we couldn't make, if it was required, an orderly withdrawal from the Seoul area to the Pusan area. I requested of General Hickey that any discussions that he has or is to have with General MacArthur that he point out this dangerous condition that might exist for the security of his air force bases in Korea. General Hickey was most receptive to all my statements and indicated that he would do as I requested.

Fol redline from Vandenberg received:

It appears here that your requirements for evacuation and resupply have been greatly stepped up due to the recent operation. I therefore propose that I send you two additional 12 plane sqds of C–54s provided you can accommodate them. They will come off the Pacific MATS run and be replaced with an equal commercial lift which is available. These units have been alerted if you indicate approval but will probably not become operational your theater prior to 7 days after you give the go ahead. I feel sure that in your planning for every contingency you have not overlooked the possibility of being required to mass evacuate personnel from Korea and in such possibility these might be invaluable. I would like any details of such a plan and any other possible emergency action which might thereby be required by this headquarters, including diversion of MATS aircraft on the Pacific run. I am sure you agree that even the planning for mass evacuation must of course be held extremely confidential at this time. S/Hoyt S. Vandenberg, CSAF.

In answer to above, Stratemeyer to Vandenberg, I stated:

Reference your TS RL 113. This rad in 2 parts. *PART I.* We have completed outline plan for mass air evacuation of personnel in conjunction with surface lift either to southern Korea or to Japan. Detailed planning continuing in Combat Cargo Command. Our plans contemplated employment of C–54s on MATS Pacific runs. In the light of rapidly changing situation request the two additional twelve plane C–54 squadrons be dispatched immediately. Specific destination will be furnished later. Request double crews, additional maintenance personnel and flyaway spare parts kits accompany these airplanes if possible. *PART II.* With present airlift, augmented by two C–54 squadrons and some assistance from Navy, estimate we can air evacuate from two areas approximately 16,000 personnel per day under good weather conditions and 12,000 per day under bad weather conditions. COMNAVFE informally advises approximately thirty additional R5Ds [Navy C–54s] could be made available starting approximately 48 hours after notification. Plan also includes utilization C–54s in 1503 ATW, MATS at Haneda. In extreme emergency we might request diversion additional Pacific MATS acft depending upon availability of airdromes at the time. Plan is being closely coordinated with Navy and Army evacuation plans. We contemplate continued combat close support and interdiction.

WEDNESDAY 6 DECEMBER 1950

Partridge in at 1000 hours. Gave me the following radio he had received from General Harris (Marine) dtd 042220Z:

Fm Gen Harris to Gen Partridge - I was upon the hill today and saw the 5th and 7th Marines return. Thank god for air. I don't think they could have made it as units without air support. Saw your B–26 boys do a superb job in clearing a position near the airfield. The next job is to get the Marine Division off the hill. I want to be able to cover their flanks and rear 100% and to blast any major resistance to their front, can use all the help you can give us until they get down. Tell your pilots they are doing a magnificent job.[27]

---

27. The "hill" that Harris refers to is apparently the Hagaru-ri area and not a specific hill. Several miles north of there, at Tok-tong Pass, a Marine company had held a hill overlooking the pass for six days, repulsing every attack thrown its way and keeping the pass open for the rest of the 1st Marine Division to break through back to Hagaru-ri.

B–26s deliver their bomb loads on a North Korean target.

Bucked the above radio to Sykes and the Barcus group, and then to my AG for file in the permanent files.

Following are notes from conference I held in my office, 1030 hours. Copies of these notes have been sent to Generals Weyland, Craigie, and Alkire.

MEETING:

6 December, General Stratemeyer's Office; Present - General Partridge, CG Fifth AF, General Cabell, Dir of Intelligence, USAF; General Craigie, FEAF VC A&P; General Weyland, FEAF VC Ops; General Alkire, FEAF D/M; General Stratemeyer, COMGEN FEAF.

Partridge: "...When I decided to pull out of Sinanju, I decided to pull out right away. Instructions were issued to evacuate the radar site on the river, unfortunately, the man in charge of the station started to demolish it and didn't work rapidly enough,and a day and one half later, he was informed by an Army demolition team coming down the road, that he should be ready to evacuate. They blew up some of the equipment, and left the rest and we had to burn it up with napalm. We did take out some of the equipment - we didn't lose it all. I started to investigate the incident, but the poor guy has gone off his head - he is completely nuts."

Stratemeyer: "That's OK, Pat. Forget it."

Partridge: "On Sinanju, we got everything off the field. The Army lost some L–5s; we had to burn some deadline vehicles and airplanes at P'yŏngyang. Made one F–80 out of two and flew it out. Evacuated everything usable from K–24. There were some rockets, some ammunition left there. My A-4 checked the items to be left and had those critical items brought out such as napalm igniters. All the items were supposed to have been completely taken care of by Army engineers, but apparently the hasty withdrawal of the Army caught them short. There was some question whether we could get our air installations equipment out and I have been told that 7 carloads came out."

Alkire: (Gives figures on those withdrawals. General Stratemeyer confirms.)

Partridge: "We didn't lose anything of any importance in the three evacuations. We did lose some napalm tanks - 2 to 3 hundred - I don't know."

Alkire: (breaks in re Army transportation servicing.)

Partridge: "The Army transportation had trouble for two reasons with their train movement. First, saboteurs took the wheels off the engines, and, strangely enough, they couldn't get water for the engines. The water point was gone.

"I understand there was a hell of an explosion at East P'yŏngyang - ammunition - but they didn't get it all and we will have to destroy it."

Stratemeyer: "Are all the bridges down - were they all blown up?"

Partridge: "Yes, but not a very good job.

"There is only one usable bridge there; they took only 1/2 a pontoon bridge. The wooden bridge across the river was burned in two places, unless they have demolished a lot more than yesterday, I would say still in pretty good shape. It can easily be repaired. The Army is doing little in the way of demolition in the wake of withdrawal."

Weyland: "We are giving GHQ another scream on this thing - asking that in all their withdrawals they pay particular attention to demolishing the bridges which we would have to destroy anyway."

Stratemeyer: "I want to get out of the bridge busting business."

Partridge: "We are now about established according to the plan which I sent to you and we are building this runway, 24 hours a day, at K-14 - that is at Seoul.

"It is the only way we have to stay in operations; we are using pierced steel planks.

"You understand Walker has not been attacked; you understand Walker is not being pushed out of these positions, but is being outflanked. He does not know how many of them are there on his flanks. We strafe and kill 500 or 600 here and there all the time." (General Partridge goes to the map, explains that Walker is pulling his troops back to the 38th Parallel - apparently shows movements on map.)

(General Partridge - still at map) "... finally along down here on the Imjin River here. He is trying to get people over on the east bank. I estimate that they will be back here (Imjin line) a week or more - 7 days, and they will be back here unless somebody stops the troops coming down there. We will be out of Seoul in two weeks."

Stratemeyer: "His plan is to execute successful withdrawals to the Pusan area?"

Partridge: "Right."

Discussion of Walker's plans.

Partridge: "He has in being, in the rear areas, organized units which are 3 weeks, 1 - 2 months old, and he is going to move these forward to the east coast and mountain areas, they are ROK troops, and leave the policing of the rear areas to the police. These units are ill equipped, partially equipped, they have no artillery whatever, but they are as well equipped as the Chinese will be when the Chinese get there, and there is no reason why they shouldn't be over here in a state of readiness. It will take two weeks to get them over there."

Discussion of ROK shock action.

General Stratemeyer asked General Partridge about conference there in Seoul with Collins. Didn't Walker say something?

Partridge: "Yes, he told General Collins he could not guarantee to hold

Seoul. He would, if ordered and will expend the Eighth Army in doing so, but it would have to be a stiff and direct order in writing, and, further, he said, I'm going to save the Eighth Army and I can do that by orderly withdrawals to Pusan.

"I told Collins that the only counter-balance force over here, the one that tips the balance is the Air Force in close support of the ground forces. We are killing Communists by the thousands and will continue - but we can't do anything unless the Army finds someplace to stop and fight and push them (Chinese Communists) in the open. We'll have to find a place where the Army can make a stand, and then we can work. We cannot agree and we should not agree to the Seoul area because we can't provide them with air support in that area."

Stratemeyer: "Pat, we are in complete agreement. This is what I'm going to tell Hickey; make an orderly withdrawal and get all the air support possible."

Partridge: "I hope that the good counsel will take effect, but in any event I have to get out of the Seoul area - and quickly. We will carefully consider the F–84 business."

Discussion of F–84 dispersals and General Stratemeyer placing 12 at Taegu - K-2.

Alkire: "Are you going to open K-1?"

Partridge: "I believe we should; we have a plan, work was started and supplies are adequate."

Stratemeyer: "That is the jet field we were building which I told Van about and which was not completed."

Partridge: "Let's not take any action at K-1 until I find out where Walker is putting his final defense line. If he will even suggest, the critical item - that the X Corps is going to put in - then we can hold until the cows come home, but if the X Corps is withdrawn back to Japan or fights independently, General Walker will withdraw to a 30-mile perimeter only, which includes K-9 and K-1, but does not include Chinhae and does not include K-3."

Stratemeyer: "With the X Corps, he can draw back to the old Taegu, Naktong River and Masan line; we can hold it. Going to be good weather now - cold, but weather will be OK for air support."

Partridge: "I will send you a message if we want to go ahead with construction on K-1."

Craigie injects his opinion that because of morale, etc., should put all of the F–84s over in K-2.

General Stratemeyer talks him down. To Partridge, he says, "We will start now with no more than 12 of them the minute you say, and that's the way we will leave it. There is a reason for that as I want to know whether their nose wheels will stand up on pierced steel planks. I also want to know what they can do. Understand not as good as '80s on plank."

Discussion by all - Evacuation must be by orderly withdrawals; no future in holding beachheads, but there is a a future in Pusan.

Partridge: "They should bring the troops from the eastern beachhead, and put the two forces under a single head, and then we can defeat the Chinese Communist armies. I don't care how many they throw at us, and it is better that we face the issue now, and defeat the Communist armies - and we can do it. Walker did say it was going to cost us - about 25,000 more casualties - but we'll kill 10 to 20 for every one we lose, and you know that no Army can stand those casualties."

Discussion re Russian Air Force by Stratemeyer.

Partridge: "We have enough Air Force to fight the Soviet Air Force unless they commit their entire force. We can defeat them if they come down and fight in our own back yards."

Discussion of deployment of the '84s and '86s. Twelve each to K-2 and K-14.

Partridge: "Matter of fact, my people worked on a plan to get them back to Pusan area as per a Nagoya Plan.[28] The 4th Fighter Wing of 2 squadrons to Johnson that would leave 1 squadron to Kimp'o, etc. I'll leave a copy of this to show you how we are thinking.

Stratemeyer: "I'm not going to put more than 12 '86s at Kimp'o at this time." (General Stratemeyer gives reasons, citing radio messages, own thinking) "...and with 150 aircraft at Taegu with no dispersal, I don't want a target sitting up there within range of Il–10s."

General Craigie reads the tonnage figures re aircraft coming in, supplies, etc. and their staging areas: Yokota, 450 thousand pounds, Haneda, 12 tons, K-14, 35 tons, K-2, 100 tons, move 13 tons yesterday from Haneda to Korea, and they are moving 15 tons - 17 tons today from Yokota to Korea. The present airplane deployment of F–84s - 26 at Kisarazu, 31 Yokota, 4 at K-2, 1 at K-3 - on barges 13 at Kisarazu.

Stratemeyer: "Pat, how many do you want to put in K-2? Remember you have no dispersal, etc."

Partridge: "Well, the thing of it is, if I don't put that unit in there, I'll have to move a unit in there any way. Intend to move the 543d Tac Recon Group from Taegu."

Stratemeyer: "Where are you going to put it?"

Discussion from Partridge. "Someplace where there is water. Pusan - like to have it at Pusan. They are operating out of K-2 now, they can operate out of K-9."

Weyland - Discussion re split of technical staff for reconnaissance. "Put RF–80s only at K-9 and put RB–26s back in Japan. The RB–26s clutter up an airdrome and are not as essential as the F–80s. You want to leave room for your fighters."

Stratemeyer: "Bring your equipment back and do your work here."

Partridge: "Let me go back and with what I've learned this morning, is all I need to know as to the finer developments. We just have to avoid getting caught at Seoul."

General Partridge is assured by General Stratemeyer that he (Partridge) has his assurance that he is not going to get caught in Seoul, discusses what he has done - talks with Hickey, conferences, etc.

Partridge: "I have a bunch of things written down here which represent my

---

28. Timberlake's planners had developed a plan to retire either toward Seoul or Pusan, and this may be what Partridge is referring to. However, nothing has been discovered that refers specifically to a Nagoya Plan. It is possible that General Partridge was talking about a setup similar to the 5AF's command structure that was divided between an advance headquarters and a rear headquarters at Nagoya. (See Futrell, p 265, for problems associated with this type of divided command.)

points of view from the other side: *(1)* the Air Force action is decisive in this campaign. If the Air Force bases - facilities - are reduced, then they are out of business. If we withdraw to Pusan, we will get the following benefits: *(1)* Inspire the ROKs to fight. But, if we withdraw to Seoul, all the rest of Korea will fall without a fight. *(2)* Withdrawal to Pusan permits us to resume offensive, *(3)* lengthens the Chinese lines of supply, *(4)* shortens ours, *(5)* gives us a good point, *(6)* eliminates any property loss on the part of the Air Force, and, for that matter, the Army - every single piece of equipment is either expended or lost. *(7)* Seoul and Inch'ŏn has a capacity of 5,000 tons maximum; Pusan can put out 30,000 tons a day and can unload more there from LST's off of the beach - right at K-9. *(8)* If you stay in the Seoul area, all our landlines and all FM relays and VHF are lost as they are all in enemy territory and communications are plaguing us now. All in all, all we would have left is radio. *(9)* If we stay in Seoul, all other airfields would be left uncovered. *(10)* You haven't mentioned prisoners - we've got about 135,000 down there. If the Commies take over, we can't evacuate those folks."

Stratemeyer: "They plan to evacuate the ROKs."

Partridge: "If we keep withdrawing to Taegu, we keep concentrated all the CP resources, all the Army forces, and all the materials pushed down in that area, and, if we don't do that, we will lose them all. All will be expended. If we could go back to Pusan area, we can support the operation from Japan alone."

Stratemeyer: "Have you gone over this with Walker? Did he indicate what he wanted to do to Collins?"

Partridge: "Yes. It is clear to me that General Walker is greatly depressed about being compressed in Seoul. Going into Seoul gave me the cold shivers."

Cabell: "Fact remains though that when we left General MacArthur's conference, no objection was raised at that time. I didn't raise any objections until I again thought back about it."

Stratemeyer: "I gave them just a couple of figures, but I was depressed as hell at MacArthur's conference. I think MacArthur was too."

Partridge: "One of the figures which General Collins had was the figure of evacuation of personnel from Seoul as 17,000 a day."

Stratemeyer: "No, overall from Korea." (General Stratemeyer emphasizes and explains to Partridge that figures given were just our capability.)

Partridge: "Can't do that when fighting a defense."

Stratemeyer: "With the transports we have available and expect to get and which Van has offered, we have a capability of 16,000 from the Seoul area or 8,000 from the Yŏnp'o area. Only a capability. Now, if you have to use that airport to fight from, of course, the figure must be lower - reduced by virtue of fighter action. So, when you go back be sure to tell Walker this. I don't want him to get wrong impression."

Partridge: "It is essential that I take steps now to withdraw in one direction or the other unless you tell me otherwise and start evacuation of my headquarters to Pusan. I want to get heavier parts of the headquarters on the way because I'll have only two weeks at the most to get out of Seoul - it might be one week -

depends how fast the enemy troops are pushed down the middle, and General Walker feels that he can break off in Taegu area. Withdrawals are going to be successful because of his mobility and the enemy can only move at night and on their own two feet. Walker moves day and night - mostly on wheels."

Stratemeyer: "Destroy every damn bridge and that means I want every bridge destroyed. This bridge busting business for me is a waste of our effort, better let our bombs stop people when the Army can just as soon do it with their demolitions."

Partridge: "With that much guidance, I can go back."

Stratemeyer: "OK, I will present that tomorrow morning that I have authorized you to move with Walker and to start a retrograde movement as you see fit."

Partridge discusses only alternative — "If I am directed to get into Seoul, then the people you would ordinarily evacuate, would be sent to Japan. I don't want to send them into Nagoya, think they will be evacuated to Itazuke or some place where a Fifth Air Force headquarters would be closest to Korea. I personally think we will be able to stop the Communists somewhere short of Taegu."

Weyland: "Any part of X Corps moving into K-18 [Kangnŭng] - that's right here."

Partridge: "No, make them go down to Pusan or P'ohang and fight north and then they can join up - preferably Pusan - and then they can go anywhere."

Alkire: "K-2 field is in better shape."

Partridge: "We are building a new field on rice straw matting at K-16."

Stratemeyer (to Partridge): "Do you estimate - of the situation - that the Chinese Communists will come down past the 38th?"

Partridge: "I think they will."

Stratemeyer: "I think they plan to destroy UN forces if they can."

Partridge: "They will fail. They <u>will</u> if we withdraw into two pockets."

Cabell: "I think our attitude has assured us that they are going to come down past the 38th."

Stratemeyer: "There is only one point - does Russia want China in Korea? I don't think Russia will permit them to go south to Pusan. China would be up near Vladivostok, etc., I think eventually China and Russia are going to have a scrape - maybe not in our lifetime."

Cabell: "I'm afraid that is wishful thinking. I think the Russians have sufficient control to turn the war off or on at will."[29]

Partridge: "My impression is that Russia did not fulfill her obligations to

---

29. Russia's ability to "turn the war on and off" was tenuous at best, for the Soviets had lost much of their clout in North Korea. Robert R. Simmons, in his book, *The Strained Alliance*, suggests that it was probably at North Korean, not Russian, instigation that South Korea was attacked. He also believed that both the Chinese and the North Koreans came to realize that the only role the Russians were going to play in Korea was that of a supplier of military hardware and of few advisors and as a sidelines rooter. Seeing this, and thinking that the U.S. was physically threatening their own territory, the Chinese intervened in Korea. This intervention would bring the Chinese and North Koreans (historically closely aligned anyway) closer together and would tend to shunt the Soviet Union toward a more peripheral foreign policy and military role regarding the war. (Robert R. Simmons, *The Strained Alliance* [New York, 1975], pp 120-124, 137-168.)

North Korea and when they finally got going, they intended to secure enough of North Korea to at least re-establish the Republic of North Korea, but when high dignitaries, like yourself, launched the Walker jump off, it was decided to go in to defend itself. Once she advances down this peninsula and accomplishes the objective of driving United Nations forces out, Chinese forces will be withdrawn and Korea turned over to North Korea."

Stratemeyer: "Another thing, they are pointing the finger at us - why we didn't see this build up, etc., and why with the tools we had, we didn't produce it. There are many reasons, short distances, Yalu River, came over in driblets, crossed the ice, etc. The finger is on us. I asked for a study be made - not an alibi - and sent it to Craigie this morning.[30]

Partridge: "That is a perfect example of the Army's not producing enough photography interpreters. Thousands of pictures were taken and no one to sit down and evaluate them." (General Partridge cites the example of a sharp PI man who picked up an enemy concentration, etc.)

Cabell: "Is that clearly in the SOP for the Army?"

Stratemeyer: "Yes, sir." (Shows him the manual)

Cabell: "They are to examine the photographs and count the men under any given tree?"

Continuation of discussion of lack of photographic analysts on part of Army.

END OF NOTES
* * * *

Dispatched the fol signal to FAF, with info to 1st MAW, CG X Corps, CG BOMCOM, and CINCFE:

To assist 1st Mar Div break out from Hagaru-ri offer is made of B–29 bombing of enemy occupied exit route upon initiation of Mar Div withdrawal. 48 hrs notice highly desirable so BOMCOM liaison officer can coordinate details directly with 1st MAW and X Corps. Normal effort approx 24 B–29s can be laid on without detailed planning preparation with 24-hour notice. Attn invited to possibility of damage to exit road and to creation of landslides. Proximity fuses could be used. Request earliest advice as many other urgent rqmts for B–29s. New subject: Request for B–29s on three towns tomorrow will be honored.

Handcarried the fol Memorandum to General MacArthur which I addressed personally to him:

I am greatly concerned about the possibility of the Eighth Army being directed to withdraw into the Inch'ŏn-Seoul area.

This course of action would, in my opinion, greatly reduce the effectiveness of the Fifth Air Force.

It is my considered opinion that the AF has been and will be a decisive force in the Korean campaign. If our air bases and air base facilities, as they of necessity would be, are reduced, the Far East Air Forces gets out of the business of close support of the ground forces. The Taegu Air Base,

---

30. This study has not been found.

where we operate 75 F–80s and our tactical recon group, the Suwŏn Air Base to which I am withdrawing an F–51 group, will not be secure and would in all probability be over run by guerrillas and Communist sympathizers. In addition, the inspiration for the ROKs in southern Korea to fight would no longer exist. The Chinese Communist lines of communications would not be extensively elongated, and, as a result, the power of the air which I have available could not destroy the Chinese Communists by the thousands as we are now doing. The farther they become extended, the more we can kill.

I, therefore, recommend that the Eighth Army make orderly withdrawals from its present position and, if need be, to a perimeter defense of the line P'ohang-dong, Taegu, Naktong River, Masan; that the X Corps fight north and join up with the Eighth Army's right as they withdraw. These recommendations are made for the following reasons:

We can evacuate our Air Force bases where need be in an orderly manner and save our heavy equipment, personnel, and base facilities; we can continue the essential air-ground support that we would then have available; Eighth Army and Fifth Air Force, if it becomes necessary to evacuate Seoul, can move their main headquarters to Pusan and keep advance headquarters first at Taejŏn and then at Taegu. These command post facilities are already in existence.

The AF would operate from the two airdromes at Seoul and one at Suwŏn as long as possible, then fall back to Taejŏn, Taegu, P'ohang-dong and the two fields at Pusan.

Those units and aircraft, when there are no longer sufficient base facilities in the old perimeter defense area, could evacuate to Japan and continue the air support needed by the UN forces in that perimeter as we did in June and July.

This maneuver would extend the Chinese Communist lines of communications to such a point that, in my opinion, thousands would freeze or die besides the thousands that we could kill by air attack.

The ROK forces would be inspired to fight and the UN forces would still remain in Korea. My opinion is that we could defeat the Chinese Communist forces in the long run. By pulling into the beachhead at Seoul, all the rest of Korea would fall without a fight.

By withdrawing to Pusan, we are permitted to resume the offensive if we desire; the Chinese lines of communication are lengthened; ours are shortened. It eliminates the great property loss on the part of the AF and the Army which would result from a forced evacuation from the beachhead. I am told by Admiral Joy that it will take six days to evacuate a division from Inch'ŏn and that the maximum capacity of that port is 5,000 tons. Pusan, on the other hand, has a capacity of 30,000 tons and can handle even more by utilizing direct loading or unloading of LSTs right next to K-9 our main airbase.

By staying in the Seoul area, all our land lines, all our FM relays, and many VHF stations would be lost. Communications are bad now and would practically stop by going into the beachhead.

As a result of a discussion on 6 December with General Partridge, I have been informed that General Walker wholeheartedly supports the concept of an orderly withdrawal to successive lines of defense clear to the Pusan area if need be and that he made this idea plain to General Collins during his conference of 5 December.

In view of the above, I strongly recommend that the Eighth Army not take up a beachhead defense in the Seoul-Inch'ŏn area and that as soon as possible X Corps be evacuated by water to the Pusan area and that General Walker be directed to withdraw by successive orderly withdrawals on the axis toward Pusan as the situation dictates. s/G.E.S.

My above memo to General MacArthur was circulated to Generals Crabb, Weyland, Craigie, Alkire and Colonel Zimmerman. This copy was handcarried and for their eyes alone.

Made the award of the Legion of Merit to one of my intelligence officers, Lt Colonel J. N. Donohew.[31]

An F–84E of the 27th FEW takes off on a mission shortly after the wing arrived in Korea.

Dispatched the fol redline to Vandenberg:

Flight of 4 F–84s from K-2, Taegu, participated in first combat mission today; results unknown.

THURSDAY
7 DECEMBER
1950

Dispatched fol redline to Vandenberg from Stratemeyer:

COCARCOM by airlift evacuated from Hagaru-ri from period 1 December - 6 December 4,369 wounded 1st Marine Division and Seventh Division personnel.

---

31. Lt Col Jack N. Donohew, Director of Air Targets, FEAF, until December 1950, when he became Deputy Comptroller, 13AF.

Attended conference in General MacArthur's conference room; present beside himself were Generals Collins, Hickey, Wright, Whitney, Willoughby, Cabell and myself; Admirals Joy and Lowe.

General Collins related his trip to Walker's and Almond's hqrs and his aerial survey of the battlefield.

Before we got into the big discussion, General MacArthur asked General Collins what in the way of replacements could he expect.

General Collins stated that the only U.S. Army forces that would be available to him would be four National Guard divisions which could be made available, departing the U. S. next March, which means that they would not be here until May or June. Complete replacements would follow to bring him up to full strength in January, that he could expect no substantial help from any of the UN forces except as stated above from the United States.

General MacArthur then pointed out the great reservoir of Chinese Nationalists on Formosa and urged that he be permitted to use them in Korea under the UN banner. He indicated that the Generalissimo would give him 60,000 or 100,000 - or all of his troops if he needed them.[32]

General Collins then asked the question that if none of the following were made available, should we seek an armistice, that is, cease fire and stop where both forces are presently located - these are the conditions: No violation against Chinese territory by air: no use of the A bomb; the Navy not be permitted to blockade the Chinese coast or fire against the Chinese coastline; that we would be barred from using the Chinese Nationalists; that no additional foreign troops would be given us such as British, French, or other reinforcements; that we cannot expect to receive replacements in ample numbers until January and then no divisional units would be available for dispatch prior to April 1951.

Each person present was asked to answer the above question with the conditions attached and we all sounded off.

General MacArthur then summed up the consensus of opinion in these words:

The Joint Chiefs of Staff should protest forcefully the above related conditions and that the only answer to the proposed question is: "this is surrender."

General Collins then posed this question - with the use of your present force, and the potential that might be made available, and a possible recommended use of the A bomb - what would you do?

The answer General MacArthur made to this in which we all agreed was that we should wait at least a month as this proposed an entirely new estimate and we would be in a better position to determine our action.

Then General Collins proposed this question: if Communist China announced that they would not go below the 38th Parallel, what would be your action?

General MacArthur answered we would accept this even to the extent of putting the X Corps, from its present location, into Pusan.

---

32. In July, both MacArthur and the JCS had advised against using Nationalist Chinese troops, believing that their use would give the Chinese Communists an excuse to intervene in Korea and would also weaken the Nationalist defense of Formosa. Now it appeared to MacArthur that these reasons were no longer valid and that the Nationalist troops were the only trained forces immediately available to him.

Washington demurred, pointing out that use of these troops would probably be unacceptable to most of the other U.N. members in Korea, these perhaps even refusing to fight alongside the Nationalist troops. It was also felt that these forces could be used more effectively on the mainland in case of a general war with China. Finally, it was considered that supplying the Nationalist troops would be unacceptable from both the political and logistical standpoint. (Schnabel, pp 295-296; also see "History of the JCS," Vol. III, pp 367, 391, 405-409.)

I am convinced that the memorandum that I sent to General MacArthur last night caused a complete reversal of the decisions made on 4 December - to the one which is in entire agreement with my memorandum. If we continue to fight and withdraw and bring the X Corps to the south where it can join forces with the Eighth Army, and be placed under the Eighth Army, I am convinced, as were all present, that we could hold the Pusan perimeter almost indefinitely, and that by General Walker's retrograde movement by successive lines, we would not only save his Army, but practically all of its equipment as well as all the Fifth Air Force equipment.

Again, it is my opinion that my memorandum played an important part in the now approved plan for Korea.

Immediately upon my return from this conference, I dispatched the fol stratline to Partridge: "Don't worry. Eighth Army will receive an order shortly."

Dispatched the fol personal Spivey from Stratemeyer with info to Partridge:

Without going into red alert or creating alarm, I want you by every method at your command to have all air defense agencies in Japan particularly readied for next fifteen (15) days. The 4th Fighter Wing less a few aircraft will remain Johnson temporarily.

Re the communications help for Partridge, sent him the fol:

Personal for Partridge from Stratemeyer: This rad in 3 parts. *PART I*. Reference my A 4068B, Lt. Col. Rose and Lt. Col. Shipe arrived this hq 5 Dec and are now enroute your hq via MATS courier to Kimp'o. Col. Coleman arrived this date and will be sent to you on MATS courier about 9 Dec. *PART II*. USAF has just informed my hq that shipment of 642 communications personnel recently requested by you has been deferred. This includes 127 for a T/D [table of distribution] radio relay Squadron plus 515 required to augment your communications squadrons.[33] Query: to what extent have recent developments altered your personnel requirements? Can we let this deferment ride or should we request that all or a portion of the personnel requested be shipped? If you still feel that you need additional personnel, please indicate numbers by SSN desired by airlift, and brief plan covering disposition upon arrival. *PART III*. Radnote from Gen Ankenbrandt this date states that further supply action on your communications requirements being suspended for ten days. This includes all equipment requisitioned on the ZI per request of Colonel Wagner.

Received a call this morning that my nephew, Sergeant Clarence Donnell, Marine Corps, had been evacuated from the Hagaru-ri area and was now in the Yokosuka Naval Hospital with frost-bitten feet.

Took off from the office at 1530 and drove to Yokosuka, arriving there a little after 1700 hours. Donney looks fine, his morale is OK, and said that if it hadn't been for the airlift, he wouldn't have made it. Both he and the doctor indicated that he will be evacuated home as they do not send frost bite cases into cold climates again without being sure of complete recovery.

---

33. The term Table of Distribution is now obsolete, being replaced by Unit Manning Document (UMD).

FRIDAY
8 DECEMBER
1950

Dispatched the fol redline to Vandenberg with info to Whitehead:

C–119s of 314th CCW, dropped entire bridge yesterday to embattled Marines and 7th U. S. Infantry elements near Chosin Reservoir. Eight spans, totalling 16 tons, and supported by 100 foot parachutes, were kicked out of flying boxcars. Drop was made after airplanes broke through overcast over drop area. Drop was highly successful and was made to aid Marine and soldier crossing of icy waters of river flowing into Chosin Reservoir. It is believed this is first operation of this type in history of warfare.[34]

Wing Commander Green,[35] RAAF, in operations in RAAF stationed in Australia, dropped by the office. Brought me greetings from Air Vice Marshal Scherger.[36]

U. S. airmen keep themselves warm by burning supplies they cannot take with them as they prepare to evacuate P'yŏngyang on December 8.

SATURDAY
9 DECEMBER
1950

Sent the fol redline to Vandenberg:

Because of restricted airfields remaining Korea and increasing threat to Jap bases, bulk of 4th Ftr Wg being retained Johnson AFB in air defense Tokyo area. Eight to twelve F–86s will operate from Kimp'o in Korea as long as field is held. 27th Ftr Wg will base at Itazuke but with minimum equipment and personnel will operate from K-2 Taegu regularly with 48 aircraft.

---

34. One span fell into enemy territory and one was damaged, but the remaining six spans enabled the Marines to cross a 1,500-foot deep gorge with all their vehicles. (Futrell, p 259.)
35. Wing Commander R.F.M. Green, Director of Operations, RAAF.
36. AVM Frederick R.W. Scherger, Deputy Chief of Air Staff, RAAF, from 1947-1951. He later became Chief of Air Staff.

To Stearley, Turner and Doyle I sent the fol personal Stratline:

The JCS have indicated that the current situation in Korea has greatly increased the possibility of general war. Such a possibility might be initiated by air attacks on our air bases and key installations. Commanders addressed take such action as is feasible to increase readiness without creating atmosphere of alarm.

The fol memorandum was bucked to me by my D/Ops:

Headquarters, Far East Air Forces, APO 925, dtd 8 December 1950. Memorandum for: Commanding General. Subject: Average Length of Fighter Missions. The following information relative average length of fighter sorties was received from Fifth Air Force this date and is submitted as a matter of possible interest to you.

AVERAGE LENGTH OF SORTIES - HRS/MIN

Base	Type A/C	Close Support or Armed Reconn		Combat Air Patrol	
		Time in Tgt Area	Total Time	Time in Tgt Area	Total Time
Seoul (K-14)	F–80	0:20	1:20	1:00	2:00
Taegu (K-2)	F–80	0:30	*2:30	1:00	*3:00
Suwŏn(K-13)	F–51	:45	2:30	2:45	4:00
Seoul (K-16)	F–51	:45	2:30	2:45	4:00
Pusan (K-9)	F–51	:30	3:30	1:30	4:30

*All F–80s based at Taegu equipped with 260 gallon tip tanks. About 75% of F–80s at K-14 equipped with standard 165 gallon tip tanks. s/JVC t/JARRED V. CRABB, Brigadier General, USAF, Deputy for Operations.

General O'Donnell called yesterday (8 Dec) and was concerned about the possible reinforcement of medium bombers to his command and the scheduled missions for his command in case of an all-out war. I invited him to come in and have lunch with Generals Craigie, Weyland and myself. He did come in at 1100 hours, we had lunch and had a very good discussion. I think he is now satisfied with the conditions under which we requested reinforcements even though FEC failed to request reinforcements as we had recommended.

I am taking care of this latest problem by a redline to Vandenberg. O'Donnell's people are to meet with my Plans people Monday, 11 December, and to satisfy themselves as well as us that our plans for the use of the mediums in case of an all-out war is the best one.

1530 hours, Air Vice Marshal Bouchier gave me the following information which he received from the British Chiefs of Staff as guidance and background for him. My understanding is that he, besides furnishing me this information, gave it to General Willoughby and General Courtney Whitney.

General MacArthur was reported in Press in England last week as referring to "the enormous handicap without precedent in military history arising from British opposition to his being allowed to operate his Air Forces across the frontier." He was probably misquoted but this is how he was reported at home.

2. British objections to violation of Manchurian border are on following purely military consideration:

(a) British have had a plain warning that to bomb across the frontier would bring Soviet Air Force into action. (Same source early in October warned that if UN forces crossed 38th Parallel the Chinese would come in.) British Chiefs of Staff have little doubt that if we carry war into Manchuria it would mean intervention of Soviet Air Force.

(b) Handicap of USAF not being allowed to attack Chinese forces L. of C. [lines of communication] in Manchuria - "cuts both ways." Our bases and L. of C. are more vulnerable than Chinese - particularly our shipping and base ports which enjoy virtual immunity. Our difficulties would be greatly increased if they were subject to scale of attack Soviet Air Force could bring against them. If it should be that our Forces have to do a "Dunkirk" from Korea it would make it infinitely more difficult and costly if subjected to intensive air attack as at the real "Dunkirk." Apart from which all hope of avoiding a general war for which we are not ready would probably disappear.

(c) British Chiefs of Staff view is that if the atom bomb was used in Korea it would not be effective in holding up Chinese advance - but make the situation more desperate by inevitably bringing the Soviet Air Force into the war. The "A" bomb is our ultimate weapon and we should surely keep it in reserve as a deterrent, or for use in event of Russia launching a third world war.

3. British Chiefs of Staff appear to be somewhat concerned about General MacArthur's alleged press statements against the British (if true) in view of our consistently cooperative attitude throughout Korean campaign.[37]

This was a tough day.

SUNDAY	Called on CINCFE taking along two radios for his concur-
10 DECEMBER	rence, both of which he "bought."
1950	*The first radnote which CINCFE O.K.'d was my*
	redline to Vandenberg:

This radio in three parts - *PART I.* Reference T.S. 0459, 30 Nov, USAF OP 301745/Z, DEPTAR 97791, 2 Dec, CINCFE 69953, CINCFE 50496, 5 Dec, FEAF TS V 0480, 9 Dec. *PART II.* I request you read carefully my redline T. S. 0459 of 30 Nov, the dispatch of which was concurred in by General MacArthur. Your reply OP 301745/Z was most welcome and was a satisfactory answer. JCS #97791 of 2 December to CINCFE from DEPTAR asked the question "can you profitably employ more air units" which, in my opinion, resulted from a misinterpretation of CINCFE's

---

37. Between Nov. 30 and Dec. 5, MacArthur issued a number of statements regarding his conduct of the war. Among these statements was his criticism of the ban on air attacks on Manchuria, calling this "an enormous handicap, without precedent in military history." He was also especially piqued over what he considered "scandalous propaganda efforts to pervert the truth" by the British. Needless to say, his pronouncements were not received enthusiastically by either the British or U.S. governments. (*Facts on File, 1950*, pp 390-391.)

message C-69953. At no time was it intended to give the impression that two additional medium bomb groups are needed except in the event of open war with Communist China. Of course, additional medium bomb groups as well as heavy bomb groups or any other type of air fighting units could be utilized. We have not sufficient air force units to support a war in Korea and, at the same time, defend Japan against air or an airborne paradrop attack. That is reason, as covered in CINCFE's C-50496, 5 Dec 50 "the all-weather part" was added. It should have read "three interceptor wings." My signal V 0480 explains deployment of 4th and 27th Fighter Wings. *PART III*. This signal is sent for background and your eyes only. CINCFE advised.

The second radio which I placed before CINCFE was a draft of a radio which I proposed that he send to the JCS - and which he bought in its entirety:

From CINCFE to JCS: - Re my C-50496, 5 Dec 50, requesting that two additional medium bomb groups be deployed to FEAF, and your JCS 97791, dtd 2 Dec 50 from DEPTAR. CG FEAF and I have continued evaluating request for these medium groups and have come to these conclusions: *A.* These bomb groups can be employed profitably in Korea for interdiction and destruction of all towns and villages capable of sheltering or otherwise supporting enemy troops. *B.* That in event of war with Communist China and/or the USSR these groups would be urgently required here. *C.* That in this latter situation, it is quite probable that the enemy would initiate the action with a surprise attack against our airfields. This could well prove disastrous to our bomber forces. Yokota and Kadena would be heavily congested with the five medium groups and would offer most tempting targets to the enemy, particularly the Chinese Communists. *D.* That in view of the present precarious balance between so-called peace and a general war, the gains to be realized in Korea from two more bomb groups do not at this time warrant the risks inherent in bringing these groups into this theater. I ask instead, that if JCS plans permit, they be kept on alert in the ZI, ready for deployment to Guam in FEC for use against China and/or Russia, at such time as the situation dictates.

At my direction VC A&P (Craigie) issued the following instructions to IG (Picher):

1. It is desired that you initiate vigorous staff action aimed at:
    (a) Increasing the general awareness of the importance of security on the part of all FEAF personnel, with particular emphasis on those in staff positions who are dealing with highly classified information.
    (b) Increasing the effectiveness of our security procedures as practiced.
2. During the last year of WWII, Allied forces held such overwhelming superiority in many departments, especially the air, that careless and loose security habits became the rule. During the present conflict in Korea, we have enjoyed air superiority from the beginning. This has undoubtedly contributed to the development of some of the lax security habits which have developed in this headquarters.

3. One of the most noticeable insecure practices has to do with the use of telephones and inter-phone boxes for the accomplishment of classified business. Although these instruments are not secure, conversations concerning classified subjects frequently take place over both telephone and squawk boxes. A most insecure practice which has become too commonplace is that of discussing classified business in semi-public places, the classic example being the dining room at the Imperial Hotel.

4. I have discussed this subject with General Doyle Hickey, C/S, FEC, who strongly concurs. It is his belief that the international situation is such at this time as to make it highly desirable, even essential, to tighten up on security.

5. It would be foolish to expect this to be accomplished overnight. It is desired that a program be drawn up which will include:

> *(a)* The education of all personnel relative to the necessity of achieving greatly improved security.
>
> *(b)* Specific action which should be taken by those concerned.
>
> *(c)* A system of policing which will uncover violations and permit those in responsible positions to take appropriate action.

Our base unit will remain at K-27 [Yŏnp'o] until completion of the X Corps evacuation at which time it will be waterlifted and airlifted to a place designated by General Partridge.

General Partridge asked me this question - are we committed to furnish the support for the Marines when they are land-based? I told him that we were certainly not; therefore, he (Partridge) will work on the premise that, when they move into K-1, they must furnish their own base support.

I further told General Partridge that normally Combat Cargo would not stage out of Itazuke as that place is going to be just too crowded when you consider that there will be based there 125 jets, plus the jet recce squadron (possibly), plus the 21st Troop Carrier Squadron. I told General Partridge that this staging base was only in case of an all-out evacuation and that the same applied to Tsuiki - would be used only in an emergency by Turner.

General Partridge was most anxious that the base at Komaki be used rather than Itami as the Marines will be in Itami. I can see no reason why this should not be done.

General Tunner has made certain requests that construction on certain fields in Korea be completed in order for him to do his job which is all well and good, but, as Partridge stated, he simply cannot do this at the expense of the engineering effort at K-1, K-2, and K-9 - which includes dispersal areas.

General Partridge again made a plea to have the '47s in the 21st Troop Carrier Sq returned to his wings for administration and routine wing lift. I told him that I would not make a decision on this at this time because of the great job that the 21st had done at Hagaru-ri and what they might be required to do out of small fields in the future.

General Partridge asked me why the shipment of our communications personnel was held up. This I did not know and told him that I would look into it. My last report was that sufficient numbers of communications personnel were being airlifted and shipped by boat.

General Partridge told me that we lost all of the 822d Engineering Bn [battalion] equipment at Chinnamp'o. It was not loaded on the LST's. He further stated that the train load of AIO [?] equipment at P'yŏngyang was lost. The premature ammunition explosion cut the tracks and this train could not be gotten out. Great quantities also of steel plank were lost. (The above resume of my conversation with Partridge given - via carbon copy - to Craigie.)

Gave Almond the fol info: Combat Cargo Command can lift under a sustained every day effort 9,000 personnel per 24 hours. This figures each man with his equipment, duffle bag, rifle, etc. to weigh 250 lbs.

MONDAY 11 DECEMBER 1950

Departed 0800 hours for K-27 (Hamhŭng) [actually Yŏnp'o] accompanying Generals MacArthur, Hickey, Wright, Whitney. Upon arrival met by General Almond and General Partridge and proceeded to Almond's briefing room and was thoroughly briefed on the actions of X Corps and their contemplated plans. Present besides Almond's staff - Generals MacArthur, Partridge, Hickey, Whitney, Wright and myself and Colonel Canada. Was there about one hour.

General Partridge greets General MacArthur upon his arrival at Yŏnp'o, December 11, 1950.

Departed K-27 direct for Kimp'o; General Partridge accompanied us. General Walker met us at Kimp'o and we immediately proceeded to Colonel Weltman's[38] (the wing commander) office where we waited while General MacArthur had a long personal conference with General Walker. At the completion of this, we departed for Haneda, arriving about 1730 hours.

Told General Partridge that Ashiya would remain in the hands of the Combat Cargo Command.

---

38. Col John W. Weltman commanded the 51st FIW.

I then discussed bases with him and his plan now is to put the Marines in K-1 as they have a jet squadron at K-27 at present. Three squadrons will return to the three C.V.E.'s and support the X Corps withdrawal from the carriers. All Marines will then go to Itami after withdrawal where they will base until K-1 is completed - that is the airlift to Itami, but the water lift to Pusan. The Marines' night fighters will stage out of Itazuke, but they will be based at Itami. There is one extra squadron that also will be based at Itami, making a total of five squadrons including the jet squadron. General Harris, Commander of the First Marine Air Wing has agreed and is satisfied. He, General Harris, did not want to occupy K-3.

TUESDAY 12 DECEMBER 1950

DEPTAR (JCS) Wash, D. C., dispatched to CINCFE, Nb98608 (Director Joint Staff sends):

For immediate consideration in connection with US position regarding cease fire resolution which may be offered UN Assembly by 13 Asiatic nations, urgently request your views as to terms, conditions, and arrangements which should be agreed to prior to US acceptance of such a resolution. JCS must formulate their position on this subject at meeting to be held 0900, Washington time, tomorrow, 12 Dec.[39]

CINCFE replied to DEPTAR Wash DC (C-51052), for JCS:

Re JCS 98608 the minimum terms for a cease fire agreement should include the following: *1.* All ground forces remain in their present positions or may be withdrawn to positions in rear. *2.* No augmentation of combat strength by build up of military personnel, units, facilities, supplies or equipment in Korea with exception of food, medical supplies and items required for health and comfort of troops. *3.* No flights by a/c of either belligerent permitted to cross the front lines of their own ground forces, except as required to service the neutral commission observing the armistice. These latter flights to be conducted in non-combat a/c. *4.* Refugees not allowed to migrate in either direction across the present front lines. *5.* The foregoing provisions require supervision by a neutral commission to insure their execution in good faith. Such a commission should be composed of representatives of nations not represented by forces in the Korean conflict. The commission should be accorded unlimited freedom of movement in Korea, should be afforded full use of the transport, communications, and logistical facilities of both forces and should be accommodated and provided all necessary assistance at the main field headquarters of the belligerents in Korea. Signed MacArthur.

I was called to General MacArthur's office at 1325 and read above message in which I concurred; however, *I sent to General Vandenberg the following redline:*

Recommend you carefully read every statement of MacArthur press release of last night. I accompanied him to Korea and back him in every word said.

---

39. The 13 Asian and Arab nations presented a resolution to the U.N. General Assembly asking Red China to negotiate a cease-fire with the U.N. On Dec. 14, the resolution passed by a vote of 52-5 (the Soviet Union being one of the countries opposed) and a three-man truce team was established. China, however, at this time being victorious, was not interested in a cease-fire.

I was a bit doubtful prior to going over there as just what the minimum would be and the four points that I intended to raise were:

1. We are not so bad off that we must seek an armistice.
2. We should never agree to move south of the 38th Parallel.
3. Under no conditions can we give up the fields near Seoul - K-14 and K-16.
4. If we go south of the 38th, the Chinese Red Communist Army must leave Korea.

The only point that I suggested was number 1; it was not included however because of General MacArthur's press release upon his return from Korea.

Got off the Gill Robb Wilson letter - sent copies of same to Toohey Spaatz and Follett Bradley.

Sent a long personal letter to Twining (copy going to Cabell) re my thinking on long-range planning and developing of intelligence officers.

Sent my senior ADC to Yokosuka to pick up my nephew to bring him into Tokyo in order that he could spend the night and day with us. He is due to be medically evacuated to the States shortly.

WEDNESDAY
13 DECEMBER
1950

Got off a personal Twining from Stratemeyer:

Dr. Stearns, General White, and party plan to depart 20 Dec via MATS a/c to Travis AFB. Request special mission plane be made available at Travis AFB about noon Pacific Coast Time on 21 Dec to take Dr Stearns to Denver and rest of party to east coast. Please inform me of arrangements made.

Through General Whitney I received the following which is a quote of a letter that the President wrote to a Mr. Hume, music critic, who had stated in a review that Margaret Truman "was extremely attractive on the stage, but her tones were flat and she cannot sing very well."

...I have just read your lousy review buried in the back pages. You sound like a frustrated old man who never made a success, an eight-ulcer man on a four-ulcer job, and all four ulcers working. I never met you, but if I do you'll need a new nose and plenty of beef steak and perhaps a supporter below. Westbrook Pegler, a guttersnipe, is a gentleman compared to you. You can take that as more of an insult than as a reflection of your ancestry. s/H.S.T.

For the record and to confirm instructions that I have given as the Senior Air Force officer in the Far East to General White, MATS commander in the Far East, that whenever there is a question of saving lives of I servicemen, he will utilize every facility available to evacuate these people where proper hospitalization can be given. In the case that took place yesterday, where pressurization was necessary to protect lives of our service people, he acted fully within his right as a general officer of the Air Force and with full approval of his actions by me and the theater commander.[40] (carbon copy of above paragraph given to General White.)

---

40. Nothing has been found on this incident.

**THURSDAY
14 DECEMBER
1950**

Banfill submitted a paper to me in which I concurred. Inasmuch as it concerned "ground business," *passed it on to Craigie with the following memo:*

The attached paper from General Banfill to me is sound insofar as the construction of obstacles, the erection of barbed wire and the digging of trenches utilizing indigenous labor somewhere in South Korea in case it becomes necessary for General Walker to pull his forces south of Seoul. Surely the old beachhead line, Taegu, Naktong River, P'o-hang-dong, could well be worked on as well as some line across South Korea to which by successive withdrawals the UN forces could occupy and defend prior to moving into the final beachhead. It might be well to let General Hickey read this paper, explaining to him that although it is a ground man's business, we submit it for what it is worth.

Dispatched the fol official ltr to CG FEAF BOMCOM; subject: Additional Medium Bombardment Groups.

(1) Reference CINCUNC message to the Department of Army for the Joint Chiefs of Staff re the implementation of two additional medium bomb groups to the Far East Air Forces which you read in my office on 9 December, the following reply has been received: "From JCS to CINCFE, 14 Dec 50: JCS concur with your conclusions. Accordingly, two medium bombardment groups are being placed on alert in the ZI ready for deployment to Guam, in FEC, at such time as situation dictates." *(2)* It is desired that you acknowledge receipt of this letter by indorsement hereon. s/G.E.S., etc.

**FRIDAY
15 DECEMBER
1950**

Departed Haneda at 1105, after a delay due to an oil leak in #1 engine in the '54; proceeded in the staff B–17 and arrived at Ashiya at about 1400 hours. Met by General Tunner, immediately proceeded to his war room where he had three of the four officers to be decorated with the staff lined up in back of them. General Tunner made a few remarks, citations were read, and the officers decorated by myself. I then congratulated the three officers and the Combat Cargo Command for their very outstanding and superior work since they have been in the theater. Luncheon was served in General Tunner's quarters for all present, after which I immediately departed. I think the trip was well worthwhile and will do good.

I landed at Miho on my return to see how the 452d was getting on. Had about a 15 min chat with the acting commander (General Sweetser sick with flu in hospital at Itazuke). They have fine morale and their tails are in the air. They are getting settled quickly and had no gripes. They did say they could use some 260 frag bombs and some windshields - particularly the left side which they are short. I am taking care of that through Alkire. Arrived back at Haneda at 1900 hours.

**SATURDAY
16 DECEMBER
1950**

Just received information this morning from Colonel Lockridge,[41] Engineer, Fifth Air Force that at Chinnamp'o we only lost 22 percent of the 822d's engineer equipment.

Was kept busy all day reading the data prepared by Sykes in order that same could be given to Dr. Stearns prior to his departure 20 December.

**SUNDAY
17 DECEMBER
1950**

Talked with General Tunner at 0925 to find out if it would be possible for the Boss to go to Yŏnp'o tomorrow. He said absolutely not as the last plane out of K-27 was due to leave this morning at 0800 hours. All radio equipment and other Air Force equipment was lifted out last night. There has been a C-47 dirt strip put in along the beach where two '47s will go in daily and move between that strip, K-9 and Ashiya.

General Tunner further stated that he had his greatest day yesterday and his greatest night last night.

I will recommend to General MacArthur that he not attempt to go to Hŭngnam area.

0950 called on General Whitney re above.

General Weyland and I had lunch with Colonel Pat Mahoney[42] who was honoring Major General Keiser. His guest list was six and when he saw us, he invited us to join him. I have a raincheck from Weyland as I stuck him for lunch.

4th FIW Sabres on patrol over North Korea.

Dispatched fol redline:

Four F–86 a/c on CAP vicinity Sinŭiju (XE 1840) [map coordinates] at 25,000' attacked 4 MiG–15 a/c at 18,000', time 170605A. Ensuing combat

---

41. Lt Col Robert W. Lockridge, 5AF deputy for installations.
42. This individual is unidentified.

resulted in claim of one MiG–15 destroyed, no friendly losses. When attacked enemy flight turned into F–86s, split up, and dived for the Yalu River border at high speed. Friendly flight leader successfully engaged enemy #2 man when enemy flight split up. Pilots claim F–86 can out turn MiG–15 and at maximum speed can close slowly.[43]

On the 12th of Dec I had written an R&R to D/O, thru VC, A&P as follows:

Now that we are redeploying some of our units to the Itazuke area, which will include Marine night fighters, I feel that steps should be taken to reinforce the Kanto Plain area with more F–82s. I discussed this yesterday with General Partridge and he is in agreement. As soon as the Marine night fighters arrive at Itami and stage thru Itazuke with airplanes and crews, it is desired that you take the necessary action to reinforce the air defense capabilities in the Kanto Plain area with F–82s.

17 December 1950: To all my CGs - 5th, 13th, 20th, 314th, 19th, BOMCOM, COCARCOM, FEAMCOM sent the fol rad:

Personal to Commanding Generals from Stratemeyer - The Communists have established a pattern of launching offensives on holidays. Insure there is no decrease in our combat alert from dawn on 24 Dec thru dark on 25 Dec.

In answer thereto, Ops dispatched today to CG FAF, CG 20th AF and CG 314th Air Div, AX 4690B, the following:

PART I. Issue nec[essary] instr[uctions] to assure that 4 all wea ftrs of the 1st Marine Air Wing are aval for air defense at Itazuke. This may be accomplished by scheduling staging opns of Marine fighters in such a way that lay overs at Itazuke provide for 4 F7Fs to be present there at all times. *PART II.* In view of above air defense support for the Itazuke area by Marine ftrs and expected early avail of 13 add F–82 a/c fr the ZI and FEAMCOM, the folg program for the deployment of F–82 acft is established. It is desired this be used as a basis for action to insure proper balance of air defense capabilities within strategic areas. Figures below show numbers of F–82 acft by location now and as desired with change of status as indicated in left hand column.

	Naha	Itazuke	Johnson	Misawa	Korea
Now	5	8	8	4	4
Upn Aval of 4 Marine Ftrs at Itazuke	5	4	12	4	4
Upon del of all F–82s by FEAMCOM	12	4	16	6	4

---

43. Lt Col Bruce H. Hinton, commander of the 336th FIS, was the victor in this action, thus becoming the first F–86 pilot to down a MiG–15 in air-to-air combat. (Futrell, pp 250-251.)

PART III. As the add[itional] 13 F–82 acft become aval fr FEAMCOM they will be asgd as fols: First 8 to FAF, next 3 to 20th AF, next 2 to FAF. It is desired that upon receipt of the 1st 4 of these F–82s, 5th AF release the flt of the 4th FW Sq now at Itazuke for ret to Naha.

MONDAY 18 DECEMBER 1950

Got off my weekly letter to Gill Robb Wilson. *Dispatched the fol Stratline to O'Donnell with info priority personal to Twining and Chidlaw.*[44]

We have now dropped four Tarzon bombs, one of which was a dud and three poorly controlled. I realize that the first team on this type of bomb was not dispatched to FEAF, but the second team, who is supposed to be qualified, is here and now assigned to the 19th Bomb Wing. Also two experts from Bell Aircraft Corp are present. It is desired that you give this operation your personal attention and let me know what's wrong. If there is anything that FEAF can do or can request from Hq USAF, AMC, or Bell Aircraft Corp in order to make the Tarzon bombing operation successful, I want to do it.

The following statement compiled by Dr. Stearns as a result of our meeting with General MacArthur on 22 November was agreed to yesterday by General MacArthur who authorized Dr. Stearns to use it in his report to Secretary Finletter:

Conversation between General of the Army Douglas MacArthur, Commander-in-Chief, United Nations Command and United States Forces, Far East, and Dr. Robert Stearns (Lt. General George E. Stratemeyer, Commanding General, Far East Air Forces, and Major General Thomas D. White, Head-quarters United States Air Force, present) on 22 November 1950 from 1230 hours to 1345 hours.

MacA: Dr. Stearns, I understand you are out here to evaluate the Air Force bombing effort.

*Dr. Stearns:*Yes, Sir, but with particular emphasis on air support of the ground forces.

MacA: Well, I should be your first witness. Let me say, I cannot speak too highly of the air participation in this campaign. It has been magnificent. I cannot praise too highly General Stratemeyer and General Partridge and their subordinates. No air commanders in history have been more superb. The United States Air Force efforts, from the very beginning up to this moment, in the support of the ground forces as well as O'Donnell's bombing and Tunner's transport activity, have been one hundred percent. No commander could have asked for better air. I cannot go beyond one hundred percent, as the mathematicians say - but it has been one hundred percent. None of this, on the other hand, is to say that we cannot make improvements. The first function of air power is to get command of the air. In modern war-fare, air supremacy is the first absolute essential. The amount of enemy air opposition in this campaign was negligible. The essential targets were elim-inated early and the air units were then able to devote their major emphasis

---

44. Lt Gen Benjamin W. Chidlaw commanded the Air Materiel Command.

on ground support. In the beginning of a war, all the air forces should be under air command in order to rid the skies of hostile air and when this is done the ground forces are entitled to ground support that is required in these days of intense firepower. Modern infantry cannot advance without close air support. It must have more of it. Modern firepower which the enemy bring to bear with the burp guns is so heavy that even with artillery back of our lines hub-to-hub there would not be sufficient power for the ground elements to advance and this artillery power must be backed up with air power. It is not a question of the courage of the ground soldier, it is only a question of survival. Air support is the only effective answer. This necessitates the closest cooperation between air and ground command. In the first stage of the war and until air supremacy has been attained there must be the closest coordination between the air and the ground command. The ground commander must be in a position to call for air support as he needs it. The question of enough air support may be a question of economics. The Air Force decided that they must have the strategic bomber command and the air defense command and by that decision maybe the tactical support of the ground troops was given too low a priority. However, it is no doubt a question of money. I think the Air Force should have more money. I feel there should be on the order of seventy to one hundred aircraft available per division. I think the Air Force should have seven thousand to ten thousand more airplanes for this work. They should be given the money [for] it. The Air Force has to perform a great variety of tasks and it costs money to provide the means.

The American soldier has been reared from boyhood with the standard of living of the very highest and therefore, that American soldier on the field of battle has every right to expect, and does expect, a higher standard of living than all other soldiers. Therefore, he has a right to expect firepower of both artillery and air force in battle.

Reference is sometimes made to Marine air. This is superb.

Their air-ground coordination is wonderful. I was particularly impressed with the magnificent air support the Marine air gave to their ground people at the Inch'ŏn landing and noted the ease with which air was called to the front lines to support the Marine ground troops. Their air people and ground people lived and trained together over a period of years. They are on a first-name basis. I know this from first-hand observation. I listened to air communications between air and ground officers and they talked together by their first names.

We differentiate between the science of war and the art of war. The principles are immutable. The art changes with each campaign and there is no such thing as a normal war. World War I was not normal. World War II was not normal. We will probably not see positioned warfare again, particularly since men may be moved one thousand miles over night. They may be transported and supplied by air, thus the coordination of joint ground-air is more than ever important. As Napolean said, "the tactics of warfare should be rewritten every ten years." Considering the coordination of air and ground forces we must be ever looking to the future no matter how good it may have been in the present Korean campaign.

* * * *

(1) Upon departure General MacArthur asked Dr. Stearns to come back to see him when he had completed his evaluation.

(2) General MacArthur stated that the views expressed above could be freely quoted in Dr. Stearns' report.

In conference with Dr. Stearns and General White this morning, Dr. Stearns reviewed for me his conference with General MacArthur yesterday at 1230 hours. Besides agreeing to the above quoted statement, General MacArthur discussed at great length his great disappointment at the way the war in Korea was being fought due entirely to the squeamish political attitude on the part of our government and that of other United Nations. "The business of having to fight a war where you cannot hit the enemy at his source is the most ridiculous thing that I have ever seen," he stated. Further, he said that he was "absolutely confident that the Chinese Communists intended to use the full weight of their armies against us in Korea and for us not to be able to hit back was not understandable." He indicated that Chiang Kai Shek's Nationalist troops should be used.

Dr. Stearns asked him his reactions to the air not being able to determine where the Chinese Communists were, and, he immediately spoke up and stated that there were certain things that the air just couldn't do by reconnaissance. He defended air's position and stated that those Chinese by three night marches, with ammunition on their backs and 8 lbs of rice in their pockets could move across Korea without being detected. He stated that when they ran out of rice and ammunition there was another Chinese corps immediately back of them to take their places and another corps back of that corps. He stated that had we been able to cross the Yalu where air could see their concentrations of troops and supplies, we could have followed them through to Korea and known what we were up against.

He stated that the situation of Almond commanding the Marine air and controlling Navy air in the northeast part of Korea was a special amphibious operation and he indicated that when the X Corps by movement was placed under Walker's command in the new location in South Korea, there would still be some controversy in the control of all the services' air but he felt sure it could be worked out.

I indicated to Dr. Stearns that I felt that there would be less difficulty when the X Corps was under Walker than there ever had been before and that I was sure that between Partridge and the ground command and the Marines, and that between myself and Admiral Joy, we would arrive at a workable solution wherein the full weight of air would be controlled and operated properly.

I let Dr. Stearns and General White read my letter of 18 December to Gill Robb Wilson and told them why I had been writing to him. They both indicated that I was smart in so doing. I also let them read my secret signal to O'Donnell, information to Twining and Chidlaw - the Tarzon bomb signal which is quoted under this date of diary entries.

Read the Colonel Sykes report (25 June thru 31 October inclusive) pages 1 to 247 (inclusive). Also read his Command Relationship study that he prepared and gave to Dr. Stearns.[45] In both papers I made a few changes.

---

45. The Sykes report was, in essence, General Stratemeyer's diary entries for those dates with amplifying material, including extracts from General Weyland's diary..

Dispatched the fol redline personal to Twining:

From investigation so far, press release on F–86s in Korean War is violation of security by press representatives in spite of our warning that this was a classified subject. *New York Times* reporter Grutzner in Korea sent story direct with the phrase "not releasable until further notification." All representatives except *New York Times* reporter have played ball. In fairness to other reporters, was story as received by *New York Times* released by Hq, USAF?[46]

Annalee and I hosted a small dinner party in honor of Dr. Stearns, General White.

Weyland was also present.

0800 hours, Colonel Reeves, USAF, reported in at the office.

TUESDAY and WEDNESDAY 19-20 DECEMBER 1950

Received the fol reply redline from Twining:

This hq did not confirm *New York Times* F–86 story. However, we are confirming at 1000 hours EST this date that F–86s are in operation in Korea since Associated Press also now carrying story out of your theater.

Departed 1000 hours for Kimp'o, Korea, where I arrived at 1515 hours. I had neglected to officially notify Partridge and Timberlake, and, consequently, neither was there. Colonel Weltman met me and I had a nice visit with him, Colonel Cellini, Colonel Meyers (who is running the F–86 outfit at Kimp'o), and Colonel Hinton who shot down the first MiG–15 from an F–86.[47] Got in touch with Partridge and he immediately came out and picked me up.

In the meantime, General Timberlake arrived from an inspection tour of the perimeter defense of Kimp'o which is being handled by the Turkish Brigade.[48]

Spend the night with Partridge and served a most delicious dinner and breakfast.

Departed the next morning from Kimp'o at 1830 hours, arrived at Taegu at 0930 where I visited with Colonel Packard of the 27th F–84 Wing, and Colonel Tyer's[49] representative. Partridge accompanied me. We spent about two hours there.

Departed Taegu (K-2) and landed at K-9 (Pusan) where we were met by Colonel Gray and the group commander, Lt Colonel Jack Dale.[50] We were there about one hour.

Departed and landed at Iwakuni about 1500 hours and were met here by

---

46. Charles Grutzner's story, which appeared in the Dec. 18 edition of the *New York Times*, described Col Hinton's victory for the first "kill" of the war by F–86s. Because of this story, MacArthur replaced the "voluntary censorship" that had been in effect with a full censorship program.

47. Col Oliver G. Cellini became the 51st FIW's commander in April 1951; Lt Col John C. Meyer, a 37.5-victory World War II air and ground ace, led the 4th FIG. (Meyer, who would also shoot down two MiGs, later became Vice Chief of Staff, USAF, and Commander in Chief, SAC.)

48. The 4,602-man First Turkish Brigade arrived in Korea in mid-October and first saw action in late November. The Turks were considered by many to be fierce fighting men. (*The History of the United Nations Forces in the Korean War*, Vol. VI [Seoul, 1977], pp 381-390.) On the other hand, Clay Blair, in his book *The Forgotten War*, believes they were very overrated. (Blair, pp 451-452.)

49. Col Aaron W. Tyer commanded the 49th FBW.

50. Dale led the 35th FIG.

Colonel Zoller's deputy, Lt Colonel Brady,[51] the 3d Bomb Group commander. Saw C. C. Hill.[52] He had flown four night missions and was raring to go.

Partridge left me here and went on to Nagoya to spend the night and discuss problems with Spivey.

I proceeded to Haneda, landing about 1700 hours.

The following subjects were discussed with General Partridge and other commanders and where action is deemed advisable, the FEAF staff designated will take the necessary action:

I directed General Partridge to discontinue the use of four RF–80s and four RB–26s on a PIO project to photographically portray ground support by the Fifth Air Force. Every available recon airplane must work to determine where the Red Chinese armies are.

The JOC, Fifth Air Force, opens at Taegu at 0010 hours, 22 December. I discussed with General Partridge the problem of photo interpreters by G-2 FEC, and G-2 Eighth Army. I learned that they were getting started, but in the interim, the Far East Air Forces will do everything within its power to perform this photo interpretation for the Army as well as the Air Force.

I discussed with Partridge the burning of certain towns in North Korea and we both came to the conclusion that P'yŏngyang, Wŏnsan, Hamhŭng and Hŭngnam should be burned without delay. FEAF staff will get clearance on the burning of these towns and the necessary orders can then be issued to FEAF Bomber Command.

Partridge urged that all units in the Far East Air Forces be brought to full war strength. I agreed one hundred percent and I want FEAF staff to take the necessary action to have this done.

The 3d Bomb Group is in immediate need of 260 lb frag bombs. They like to use them on practically every mission. Action will be taken and a letter prepared for my signature to Colonel Zoller, 3d Bomb Wing commander, giving him all necessary information on their arrival.

I discussed with General Partridge the return of the 51st Fighter Wing, less one squadron, to Okinawa in view of the critical situation in the Far East. I want the staff to study this and come up with recommendations.

I discussed with General Partridge my directive to General Banfill that we go all-out with every possible effort, both day and night, on recon in order to determine where the Chinese Communist armies are.

As a result of a conference with Colonel Meyer, at Kimp'o, I authorized his bringing the airplanes and men left at Johnson AFB from the 336th Sq to Kimp'o. The reason being that the 80th Fighter Sq departed yesterday for Itazuke. Colonel Weltman and Colonel Meyer both assured me that it could be housed, fed and maintained. This means the movement of about 75 men and 13 F–86 airplanes.

To my great amazement I found that Combat Cargo Command was flying rations into Taegu. I interviewed the base air transport officer from General Tunner's command and found that there had been some 50 plane loads (C–47, C–46,

---

51. Lt Col Henry C. Brady came from the 6133rd Air Base Group in October 1950 to become the 3d BG commander.
52. Hill had been Stratemeyer's personal pilot

C–54 or '119s) delivered to Taegu, K-2, with rations. With water transportation and rail transportation from Japan to Pusan and on up to Taegu, I cannot understand this misuse of air transportation and I want it investigated by FEAF staff.

I still want the F–86 - MiG–15 aerial encounter violation by the *New York Times* reporter Charles Grutzner investigated and a formal report prepared by PIO for my signature to CINCFE recommending that Mr. Grutzner be notified that he is persona non grata as far as the Air Force is concerned.

I found serious fuel trouble at K-9 - either due to sabotage, poor construction, or negligence. This resulted in the loss of two pilots and airplanes and a third airplane with pilot slightly injured. Both Colonel Gray and Lt. Col. Dale assured both General Partridge and myself that they now had it well in hand, but I want our D/M to follow through on the investigation and the cause of same when the report arrives in FEAF Hqs. I can give D/M any information he desires if he will come to see me.

I discussed with General Partridge Presidential Unit Citations for Fifth Air Force units. I am sure he will resubmit one for the 3d Bomb Group for the time it did such a fine job during the first month of the war - and possibly for the RF-80 sq.

(The above discusion items are extracts from CG Diary - five copies of which were made for circulation amongst FEAF Staff.)

THURSDAY 21 DECEMBER 1950

After dictating the activities of the past two days while in Korea, dispatched the fol redline to Vandenberg:

Reference my letter under date 26 Oct 50 re Partridge's promotion to lieutenant general. Now that a national emergency has been declared, I again urgently recommend Partridge promotion to lieutenant general. If this can be done now while he is actually in combat and performing so superbly, it is my opinion that great benefit will accrue to FEAF, the FEC, and the USAF.

Discussed with G-2, General Willoughby, the responsibility that the Army has in both Far East Command hqs and Eighth Army for a photographic interpretation unit and that they carried that responsibility in addition to what we did in the Air Force. I urged that he take the necessary action to establish such a unit and request that high-powered photographic interpreters be gotten out here for a unit in FEC as well as Eighth Army. He was a bit surprised that he had that responsibility and was under the impression that he had already requested same and possibly that it was turned down by the Army. I told him he would have to go after high-powered civilians, just like we were doing.

Fol is quote from ltr received dtd 18 December 1950,

Headquarters Second Infantry Division, Office of the Commanding General -Subject: Tactical Air Support, THRU: Commanding General Far East Air Forces, APO 925, TO: Major General E. E. Partridge, Commanding General, Fifth Air Force, APO 970. *(1)* It is with deep appreciation that I wish to express to you and members of your command my thanks for the close air support rendered the 2d Infantry Division upon its withdrawal from the Kunu-ri sector of 30th November 1950. The actions of the Fifth Air Force on that date enabled the major elements of the division to withdraw with minimum losses; which, if close coordinated air attacks had not been made, would have resulted in terrific losses for the division. *(2)* Throughout the actions of the 2d Infantry Division in Korea the Fifth Air Force has steadily stood by with its air support and its increasing effectiveness has been clearly demonstrated. This was particularly so in this recent operation against a numerically superior and aggressive enemy. *(3)* All members of the command express their gratitude to the Fifth Air Force for a grand job. s/L. B. Keiser; t/L. B. KEISER, Major General, USA.

My indorsement of above ltr to General Partridge read as follows:

1st Ind, Headquarters, Far East Air Force, APO 925, TO: Major General Earle E. Partridge, Commanding General, Fifth Air Force, APO 970. *(1)* It is with considerable pride that I note and pass on to you this splendid letter of appreciation from General Keiser. General Keiser's sincerity is evident. *(2)* Please add my appreciation to that of General Keiser and pass on to those units of the Fifth Air Force which were involved in the close air support of Kunu-ri of General Keiser's Second Infantry Division.

Dispatched the fol redline before departed from the office:

(A 4855 B CG) Redline Vandenberg from Stratemeyer. Recent successive rapid withdrawals of UN ground forces has resulted in almost complete lack of contact with Chinese Commies in Army Eight sectors. Field commanders have been directed by GHQ to conduct aggressive patrolling forward from defensive positions to locate enemy but best information in our opinion of pattern of enemy movement coming from air sighting and covert sources. Main supply routes in enemy rear areas are fairly well established by air reports and we are taking all possible action to interdict. Chinese advance combat elements displace forward by small elements over secondary roads and trails; are well dispersed over wide areas; apparently well trained in camouflage and concealment; and utilize very little motor transport or heavy equipment. Consequently photography furnished partial confirmation of visual sightings and is not conclusive in determining strength, dispositions, and movements. I consider situation most critical and have directed all out air reconnaissance, visual and photo, day and night, supplemented by combat crew reports to fill in picture of enemy ground dispositions. In the absence of adequate Army photo interpretation I have directed Air Force interpreters to put full effort on helping to solve problem and have requested additional interpreters from you.

Annalee and I had Major General Keiser to dinner.

FRIDAY 22 DECEMBER 1950

Tarzon bomb dropped yesterday; missed target; this makes total of five Tarzon bombs dropped to date - one of which was a dud, and the other four missed. This is most disappointing.

A Tarzon bomb being dropped during tests in the United States.

Dispatched a Stratline (T.S.) to Partridge with info to AC/S, G-2, Willoughby:

Reference any covert activities on the part of personnel operating under you, it is desired that you clear same with Colonel Dickey[53] who in turn, it is desired, will keep me advised thru G-2, General Willoughby. It is my desire that we go all out in cooperation with G-2, USAK, G-2, FEC, and CIA.

Banfill handcarried cy of above to Willoughby. On Willoughby's copy I wrote:

Dear Charles, this is in consonance with your telephone conversation with me yesterday and General Banfill's visit to your office. It is my hope that you will keep me advised as I have stated in the above signal.

Annalee and I had dinner with the Nuckols'.

I visited General MacArthur at about 1815 hours and stayed for one-half hour. He appeared rested and in fine health. This visit was one of the best I have ever had with him and he reviewed for me the peculiar position in which he and his forces find themselves. He pointed out here we were fighting in Korea, but

---

53. Dickey is unidentified.

really had been given no mission. He stated that this situation was the most unrealistic and fantastic situation that he had ever experienced and that for the life of him he could not understand the WHY.

I discussed with him the Partridge letter and his reaction was as I expected - that is, he couldn't give me the green light on violating the air space over Manchuria any more than I could give it to Partridge and Partridge could give it to his wing commanders. He did give me some excellent advice though on a way to handle the matter and that is to take it up informally by officer courier with Vandenberg. This I am doing and I quote herewith my informal letter to Vandenberg (under date 23 Dec 50).

SATURDAY
23 DECEMBER
1950

TOP SECRET EYES ONLY. Dear Van, I know how delicate this problem is, but out here it is becoming acute. Men who have to fight for their lives are becoming restless, indeed, at the unparalleled handicaps under which they now labor. They are loyal, devoted, and efficient, but are becoming rebellious against being used as sacrificial expendables. [underlined in original.]

I send you Partridge's letter which I picked up informally while at Seoul last Tuesday, 19 December. To stop the steady growth of the enemy's air power, Partridge recommends and I agree that we give our fighters a more even break by adopting this policy:
"Any hostile aircraft which are encountered over the territory of North Korea will be attacked and destroyed. If they withdraw across the border into Manchuria, they will be pursued and attacked as long as they remain in flight. No attacks against ground installations on the Manchurian side of the border will be permitted." When can we expect basic decisions which will orient us out here as to just what our mission is now that China is our enemy and just what instructions can I expect to receive so I can inform my people? Van, this is an informal, eyes alone letter to you which I send with deep feeling, after much thought, in the great hopes that you can give me some sound direction and advice.

Dispatched the fol redline (secret):

VANDENBERG FROM STRATEMEYER. Yesterday morning eight F–86s bounced from sun by eight hostile jets, possibly Type 15. We lost one F–86.[54] In the afternoon eight F–86s encountered fifteen plus MiG–15s. Results: six MiG–15s definitely destroyed and one damaged with no friendly loss or damage.

Instructed Nuckols that no publicity would be put out on our F–86 loss, but that he could publicize the six MiG–15 and one probable losses by the enemy in yesterday afternoon's dogfight.

Dispatched the fol memo to CINCFE:

Destruction of Enemy Facilities.
1. I submit the following suggestion for your consideration: That we

---

54. During this fight, Capt Lawrence V. Bach was caught in a tight turning battle and shot down in flames.

immediately launch a psychological warfare campaign warning the enemy that P'yŏngyang, Wŏnsan, Hamhŭng, Hŭngnam will be burned and the Suiho power facility will be destroyed if the Chinese Communist forces continue their aggression. *2.* This threat, <u>coupled with our ability to carry it out</u> [underlining in original], should have a decided effect on the enemy. Loss of these facilities will constitute a major blow to him. *3.* I feel that these targets should be destroyed soon regardless of enemy moves, and that we can strike a double blow by capitalizing on this plan for psychological warfare purposes. G.E.S.

Upon my return to the office from lunch received the shocking news of General Walker's accidental death. Lt. General Ridgway appointed by CINCFE as CG Eighth Army.[55]

Received the fol Op Immediate personal from Vandenberg:

Messages were dispatched on 6 Dec alerting all addees [addressees] to the increased possibility of general war and directing that action to increase readiness without creating an atmosphere of alarm be taken. No intelligence is available which would indicate a greater possibility of general war than existed that date. However, it is obvious that the relaxation of readiness which might be anticipated during the Christmas holiday would invite an opportunity for surprise if an aggressor were to choose this period for the initiation of hostilities. It is therefore necessary that we maintain during Christmas and New Years the same degree of vigilance as has been attained in the past few weeks.

Immediately sent Vandenberg the fol answer:

Reference your dtg 22020/Z message acknowledge. Instructions to all my commanders, subject your signal, dispatched 17 December, and has this date been reiterated as well as quoting to them your signal 222020/Z.

To all my commanders - CG 5th, 13th, 20th, 314th, 19th BW, BOMCOM, COCARCOM, and FEAMCOM dispatched the fol rad in two parts:

PART I. Reference my 4715B, dtd 170848/Z, add thereto entire holiday period to include dusk to 2 January. *PART II.* For your compliance, I quote signal personal Vandenberg to me: "Messages were dispatched on 6 Dec alerting all addees to the increased possibility of general war and directing that action to increase readiness without creating an atmosphere of alarm be taken. No intelligence is available which would indicate a greater possibility of general war than existed at that date. However, it is obvious that the relaxation of readiness which might be anticipated during the Christmas holiday would invite an opportunity for surprise if an aggressor were to choose this period for the initiation of hostilities. It is

---

55. On the morning of Dec. 23, Walker was killed in a vehicle accident near Ŭijŏngbu as he was heading to the front lines to inspect his troops. Ironically, the manner of his death was strikingly similar to that of his World War II commander, Gen. George S. Patton, Jr. When General Collins visited Japan earlier, MacArthur had indicated that he wanted Ridgway to command the Eighth Army in case Walker was lost. Thus, Collins sent Ridgway to the Far East when he was informed of Walker's death. (Schnabel, pp 305-306.)

therefore necessary that we maintain during Christmas and New Years the same degree of vigilance as has been attained in the past few weeks."

SUNDAY
24 DECEMBER
1950

Dispatched fol ltr to Dr. Robert L. Stearns, President, University of Colorado, Boulder, Colorado, SUBJECT: General of the Army Douglas MacArthur.

I want to express my appreciation to you and your group for the service that I know you will render the United States Air Force and for the fine attitude that all of you took in bearing with us in order to secure the data that is so important to your mission. I have a request to make of you personally which is that upon your return to Washington you emphasize, if you agree with me, to those in authority the greatness of Douglas MacArthur. Although he does not have an integrated service staff to work for him, I know of no individual in our armed services today who more correctly utilizes our three armed services as a team than does he. In my opinion his generalship, his leadership, his command ability, and the admiration and loyalty of all of those who work for him are out-standing. Our people should not let the recent reverse on the ground that happened in Korea in any way hurt him professionally. The fact that he was able to denude the Japanese Islands of his occupation forces with alacrity and no hesitation in order to fight in Korea, and his ability as an administrator and Supreme Commander, Allied Powers speak for themselves. I urge this plea and yours, if you agree, be presented for his continued support and backing by the higher officials in our govern-ment. With admiration and my very best wishes. Sincerely, G.E.S.

Annalee and I left for Haneda at 1000 hours to be present when General Walker's remains reach Tokyo. The plane carrying his body is scheduled to land at 1100 hours.

MONDAY
25 DECEMBER
1950

Dispatched the fol Op Im radio, PERSONAL FOR TWINING:

Reur RL-132, 23 December. Greatly appreciate your efforts towards providing especially qualified reconnais-sance and Photo Interpreter personnel. One or two well-qualified civilians referred to will be welcome addition but suggest increasing period of TDY beyond 30 days if practicable. Request reconsideration of non-availability of Major Robert N. Welch[56] who was afforded unique oppor-tunity during first tour of TDY to familiarize himself with conditions here. These requests are submitted in consonance with last sentence your 57526 dated 18 Nov. We need the best available talent and newest ideas to assist us in coping with this problem. Use of camouflage increasing. We require the talent to distinguish between camouflage and deception.

Ok'd for dispatch the first of my SOP radios (to be dispatched every Monday and Thursday morning) via redline to Twining on operations of the F–84s and '86s.

---

56. Welch came to the Far East in August as a photo interpretation specialist and was immediately sent to X Corps to head the Air Section in its G-2 office.

A Thunderjet is towed to a new parking spot.

4th FIW Sabres take off for MiG Alley.

This first rad is as follows:
This is the first of a series of periodic redlines that I will send to you each Monday and Thursday concerning operations of the F–84s and F–86s. *A.* F–84E. *1.* The full capability of the F–84 has not been utilized due to length and condition of runway at K-2 and lack of suitable targets. *2.* The F–84s have not had an air-to-air encounter with enemy acft so no evaluation can be made of the A1-C AN/APG-30 sighting system. *3.* The average combat loads of the F–84s have been 8 rockets with full external fuel tanks plus full .50 cal ammo. Several missions have been flown with two 500# GP bombs, 12 rockets and full external fuel tanks, using JATO. *4.* The accuracy of the bombing, strafing and rocket firing of the F–84's has been superior to that of the F–80s and F–51s. This is due to the A1-C sighting system. *5.* Col Blakeslee[57] the CG of the 27th Ftr Escort Gp feels that if the F–84E had a critical mach comparable to that of the F–86, the F–84E would be similar to the F–86 in air-to-air combat. Understanding here is the F–84F has a critical mach comparable to the F–86. If the F–84F is comparable in all other respects to the F–84E it should prove to be far superior to the F–84E. *6.* To date three F–84 aircraft have been lost. One crashed into a supply cart while strafing. Another crash-landed in friendly territory after an engine failure due to main bearing freezing. Another suffered a collapsed nose gear while taxiing over soft ground. *7.* Four F–84s have received

---

57. Col. Donald J.M. Blakeslee, who had acquired some fame in World War II as the C.O. of the 4th FG.

battle damage. Two received 20 mm hits in tail pipe and tail cone respectively while flying over P'yŏngyang at 2500 feet. The pilots did not know that their acft had been hit until post-flight inspection. Two others received fragment hits in wings and fuselage from their own bombs. *8.* No unusual maintenance problems have been encountered. At the present time 48 F–84s are at K-2, Taegu. The remainder are at Itazuke. All major inspections and repairs are accomplished at Itazuke. *B. F–86. 1.* The F–86s operating from Kimp'o have been used only as CAP. At the present time there are 25 F–86s at Kimp'o. *2.* The F–86 is the only USAF fighter that has been able to cope with the MiG–15 for speed, climb and turn. *3.* Although only a few encounters have taken place between F–86s and MiG–15s it is felt that the F–86 can out-turn the MiG–15. The max speed and critical mach of the F–86 and MiG–15 appear to be nearly the same. *4.* Pilots of the F–86s who have engaged the MiG–15s feel that on several occasions had the F–86 been equipped with the A-1C/AN/APG-30 sighting system MiG–15s that were only damaged could have been destroyed. These pilots also feel that due to the short interval that they are in firing range of the MiG–15's that guns of a larger caliber and greater effective range are absolutely necessary.[58] *5.* Two F–86 acft have been lost. One due to enemy action and one at Johnson AB due to engine failure. *6.* No unusual maintenance problems have been encountered.

Left the office before noon. Played golf with Annalee and the Hickeys. Shot a 90 - consisting of two 45's. Following our game, the Hickey's had dinner with us. General Ridgway landed at 2300 hours, Haneda.

TUESDAY
26 DECEMBER
1950

Received which I consider the best letter of thanks on our close air support. Sent the letter to Nuckols, telling him to buck the original to Partridge, send a copy to Vandenberg, and send copies of same as per his usual SOP distribution.

Ltr dtd 25 December -

Dear General, My delay in writing you has been due to the fact that I have been hospitalized since 5 Dec. As a member of the 2d Infantry Division which fought its way through the encirclement south of Kunu-ri on 30 Nov, I want to express my highest praise for the superior support the Air Force gave our outfit. It is my very definite opinion that had it not been for the closest cooperation and all-out help given us by your close air support we would not have gotten through that block in any order at all. Never before

---

58. This feeling resulted in Project Gun Val. From mid-January to May 1953, the 4th FIW conducted a combat evaluation of a four 20mm-cannon installation in an F–86F instead of the aircraft's normal complement of six .50-caliber machine guns. Eight modified F–86Fs were used for this evaluation, flying more than 365 (284 combat) missions. MiG–15s were sighted 139 times and fired on 41 times. Only 21 of these firings resulted in hits, with 6 MiG–15s claimed destroyed, 3 probably destroyed, and 12 damaged. This was a better ratio of enemy aircraft destroyed or damaged per mission than the 5AF average, but it remained unclear if this was due to the new armament or the skill of the evaluation pilots. A serious side effect of the 20mm installation was the occurrence of compressor stalls when the guns fired. One of the test planes was lost because of this. Despite the evident superiority of the 20mm cannons, the evaluators concluded that the limited firing time (only four seconds) and the occasional compressor stall when firing made the Gun Val installation unsuitable for combat. However, the gun's reliability, high cyclic rate, and muzzle velocity indicated that the 20mm would be an excellent weapon on future fighters. (FEAF Report of the Korean War, Vol. II, pp 173-174.)

have I had metallic links from MG [machine gun] fire drop on my head, nor have I seen napalm splash on the road. The support was that close. That needed close support sealed up the machine gun and mortar fire in the pass which was holding up our vehicular movement on a one way road. I can't be too loud in my praise for your boys who flew over us as darkness approached. I don't mean twilight - I mean darkness. As an example, I recall that just before dark one of your TACP boys, a captain whose name I cannot now recall came to me and asked what he could do. I stopped my jeep in order to get a break in the bumper to bumper column and asked the lad to find out if the Mosquito plane could see a 200 yard gap in the column where the road crossed a railroad track. The answer from the plane was "Roger." I then asked him to plaster the hill due east of the gap. Within four minutes four fighters barreled in all they had and we were able to move again. Please convey to your "little fellers" my deepest appreciation. They materially helped in saving some 8,000 doughboys. Sincerely, Sladen Bradley, Brig Gen, USA, Asst Div Comdr, 2d Inf Div.

To amplify - and correct - my resume radio of yesterday to Twining re operations of F–84s and '86s, dispatched the following:

For Twining from Stratemeyer. This radio in two parts. *PART I.* Para B 4 my V-0509 recommending guns of larger caliber in error. After check, wing and group commanders concur that under conditions encountered to date, higher rate of fire of 50 caliber more desirable than larger caliber with slower rate of fire and do not repeat no recommend change in F–86 guns. *PART II.* I am concerned by publicity on F–86 typified by London UP dispatch 25 Dec stating quote Sabres are more than a match for any jets the Russians are known to have unquote. As reported in my V-0509, relative performance MiG–15 and F–86 very close. I feel such advantage we have had is due mainly to superior US pilotage and gunnery.
1515 O'Donnell called at the office.

Dispatched the following TS redline to Vandenberg:

Reourad AX 4432B Op-Op, 9 Dec 50 and your AFOOP-ZI-59867, 23 Dec 50. I am extremely apprehensive reference our capability for minimum reconnaissance required for any air war that might be precipitated in the Far East. In my opinion, the RB–29s would not be able to live for visual or photo reconnaissance unless escorted by pro-hibitive numbers of fighters. The only other known reconnaissance airplane with any chance of survival and with a radius of action great enough for visual and photo reconnaissance is the RB–45 or the RB–47 if such exists. The lessons of this war so far have shown us that we need almost daily coverage of airfields if we are to successfully destroy the enemy's air capability. Since no additional RB–45s are to be deployed to this theater, I am worried as to just what we should do for this type of reconnaissance.

1000 hours attended General Hickey's briefing for General Ridgway – all GHQ staff, plus Admiral Joy and myself in attendance.

WEDNESDAY   *Received fol signal from Van Meter.*

27 DECEMBER   Unable to accomplish mission owing to absence of
1950   addressee who will be absent for several days. Other
letter was delivered 1600 this date. I will await your
instructions. Address Army & Navy Club. Please forward reply in care
of General Twining.

Dispatched a TS REDLINE TO TWINING.

This rad in two parts. *PART I.* Desire Colonel Van Meter, my courier,
Army-Navy Club, deliver letter to you. *PART II.* I urge my letter with
enclosure be given first opportunity to Vandenberg as one of Joint Chiefs
of Staff. After reading same I'm sure you will agree because of delicacy
of subject my desire to have Vandenberg receive it without delay.

Above refers to my letter under diary date of 23 December 50 which I had
dispatched to CSAF via courier, Colonel Van Meter.

Arrangements made for using the Constellation that brought out Ridgway to
return Mrs. Walker, her son and their sergeant along with General Walker's body
was approved by me and sent to CINCFE.

Weyland held joint FEAF and COMNAVFE meeting and the basis of his
opening remarks were as follows:

1. With the highly successful evacuation of X Corps from Hŭngnam area
and its consolidation with Eighth Army, we are entering upon a new phase
of the Korean War. Since air operations plays such a dominant role, and
since both FEAF and Navy air are involved in the same problem, I thought
it appropriate to get together at this time and chew things over. *2.* I feel that
the previous meetings we held were useful and as far as I know, there are
not major problems or differences of opinion now. *3.* My idea of this meeting is simply to review our joint operating procedures with the view to seeing if we can improve our relationship and liaison, and the smoothness and
efficiency of air operations. *4.* We have no axes to grind, we have no new
or radical ideas to put forth. *5.* Although we are assembled in this rather
resplendant conference room which belongs to the Allied Council, my
thought is that this meeting should be most informal. *6.* Some sort of a
resume of principal topics discussed and conclusions reached may be
useful. If you consider it necessary or desirable, we can turn on a tape
recorder. I would just as soon leave it off. (Recorder was kept in operations
and stenos also took notes. W.) *7.* Colonel Cole[59] made up an agenda of a
few points as a point of departure. I hope all of you will have some additional items to kick around.

THURSDAY   *Fol radnote rcv'd from Van Meter in Washington:*

28 DECEMBER   Ltr addressed to General Vandenberg delivered this date
1950   to General Twining 0830, 27 Dec.

---

59. Lt Col Clifford E. Cole, Chief, Facility Requirements Branch, FEAF.

Dispatched a redline to Twining:

Re MATS Traffic Manual 76-1, 1 Mar 50, which restricts the transportation of pets in AF acft. Anticipating approval, I have in Chief of Staff's name auth General Walker's dog to accompany Mrs. Walker in the acft which is returning General Walker's remains to the ZI. Request confirmation.

Prepared a letter to be handcarried (by myself) to Partridge reinstituting plan for rotation of rated officers (pilots) in order to assure relief for those now in combat, and to provide combat experience for those officers here in FEAF without such experience.

O'Donnell dropped by the office at 1530 hours.

Weyland bucked the fol memo to me - which he stated covered just the highpoints, but "a more complete memo of record under preparation."

28 Dec 50, MEMORANDUM FOR: Vice Commander for Operations, SUBJECT: Navy-Air Force Conference at FEAF Hq on 27 Dec 50.

There follows a brief summary of major discussion points and agreements which were made at the Navy-Air Force Conference, 27 December. (More complete tabulation for purposes of record is being prepared separately from the recording tape and steno notes.)

a. Establishment of Areas to Facilitate Air Coordination: [underlined in original] It was mutually agreed by representatives of FEAF, COMNAVFE, FIFTH AIR FORCE and the 7th Fleet that standard grid blocks (example: BU, CU, etc) would be used whenever area coordination was desirable.

b. Desirability of Weekly Meetings Between Senior COMNAVFE and FEAF Operations and Intelligence Personnel: Navy agreed that meeting was a good idea and the first meeting will be held at FEAF Hq at 1000 hours, 5 Jan 51.

c. COMNAVFE Participation in FEAF Target Planning Committee: Navy did not desire to participate regularly; however, suggested that they attend on an optional basis and that we advise them of scheduled meetings.

d. Integration of Naval Air Coordinators in Tactical Control Systems: Admiral Morehouse agreed to establish naval policy which would permanently place naval officers from COMNAVFE, and the Fleet when available, in the JOC.

e. Daily Air Courier Service Between Tokyo and 7th Fleet: Navy rejected proposal. s/Crabb.

FRIDAY
29 DECEMBER
1950

Received a radio from Twining: "re your redline A 9804 dated 280541Z. This confirms action taken" - which OK'd my clearance for Walker's dog to return with Mrs. Walker in AF Constellation.

I proposed to take up following with General Partridge:

(1) Rotation of rated (pilot) officers for combat experience (see diary entry 28 Dec.);

(2) Present to Partridge his clusters including 7 for the Air Medal and his second cluster on the DFC.

(3) Production line maintenance - particularly for F–51s to get the load off of FEAMCOM. Tsuiki is suggested. Colonel Harvey,[60] his maintenance man, fully qualified. Leave the F–80 job with pylons, etc. at FEAMCOM.

(4) Delegation of authority for making of awards, execution and approval of contracts.

(5) The promotions of Colonel G. L. Meyer and Colonel A. W. Tyer.

(6) Reply to his letter of 15 December covering my idea as to the organization of a troop carrier air division under the Fifth Air Force or directly under me.

(7) The Army is short of photographs for their interpreters to evaluate.

(8) The non-promotion of Lt. Colonel John H. Walls, Jr.[61]

(9) Several items for Merchant - including Distinguished Unit Citations, citations for individual decorations not being properly prepared, and casualty reporting.

(10) The failure of Fifth Air Force to return four (4) kits from Korea back to FEAMCOM (AN/TPS-1B's).

Approved in draft the fol radios (which were dispatched) both Personal Twining from Stratemeyer.

Cite AX 0134C, with info to Fifth AF and FEAF Combat Cargo Command - This rad in 8 parts. *(1)* The temp nature of FEAF's air trans orgn is causing me considerable concern. The current world situation makes it imperative that FEAF's troop carrier avaiation be permanently established. *(2)* FEAF has the fol trp carrier units at the moment: *a.* 374th T.C.Wg, asgd FEAF, with two C–54 sqdns and one C–47 sqdn. *b.* 437th T.C. Wg, asgd FEAF, with 3 C–46 sqdns. *c.* A provisional T.C. Grp with 2 C–46 sqdns. *d.* 314th T.C. Gp, TDY from CONAC, with 96 C–119s. *e.* 61st T.C. Gp, TDY from MATS, with 2 C–54 sqdns. f. 4th T.C. Sq, TDY from MATS, with C–54s. *(3)* Your radios AFOMA-A 58335 dtd 1 Dec 50 and AFOMA-A 59111 dtd 14 Dec 50 auth trp [troop] spaces and pers required to org the Prov Trp Carrier Gp as T/D [table of distribution] unit with 2 crews per C–46. Same rad[io]s provided for 2 1/2 crews per C–54 in 374th Wg and 2 crews per C–46 in 437th Wg. *(4)* In light of recent developments, the advisability of organizing a T/D T.C. gp without a supporting wing has been reexamined. I believe this should be avoided if possible. It is also undesirable to man the 374th and 437th T.C. Wgs with add crews while these wgs are at peace str[ength] except as a temp measure. *(5)* Much of FEAF's airlift capability is being provided by 314th T.C. Gp, 61st T.C. Gp, and 4th T.C. Sq which are not asgd to FEAF. Retention of these units in FEAF in an all out war is not assured. *(6)* To command and con FEAF's trp carrier units, the FEAF Combat Cargo Command Hqs was orgd last Aug. This is a provisional unit commanded by Gen. Tunner. Most of the pers that make up this Hqs are on TDY from the ZI or other theaters. I am convinced that it is nec to permanently est this hqs and gradually replace its TDY pers with pers asgd to FEAF.

---

60. Previously the executive officer of the 374th TCW, Col Marvin M. Harvey had just become Deputy for Maintenance, Fifth Air Force.
61. Walls was 5AF deputy for personnel.

(7) To put FEAF's airlift on a permanent basis I propose: *a.* To activate Hqs and Hqs Sq, FEAF Combat Cargo Command under Col 6 T/O&E L-1005 and to gradually replace TDY pers in this hqs with perm asgd pers. *b.* To reorg the 374th T.C. Wg fr peace to war str with 3 C–54 sqdns and 1 medium sqdn. It is realized that a C–54 sqdn is gained by this action and that C–54s may not be immed avail. *c.* To reorg the 437th T.C. Wg fr peace to war str with 4 C–46 sqdns. The fourth sqdn will be manned and equipped fr the Prov T.C. Gp. *d.* To discontinue the Prov T.C. Gp. *e.* To keep utilization of C–119s at a minimum due to spare part and engine situation for C–119s. *(8)* Your approval of my proposals and auth to activate Hq & Hq Sq, FEAF Combat Cargo Command and reorg the 374th and 437th T.C. Wgs are reqd. If my proposals are approved 430 off and 1200 amn non T/O&E trp spaces may be withdrawn from FEAF.[62]

Cite AX 0134C with info to AIRDEFCOM, SAC, FIFTH AF, TWENTI-ETH AF, and THIRTEENTH AF (also direct personal Twining from Stratemeyer): This rad in four (4) parts. *(1)* FEAF is now entering the 7th month of sustained combat in the Korean War. Combat and supporting units have been going all out twenty-four hrs a day, seven days a week. With few exceptions, FEAF units are still orgnd at peace str. Instead of being orgnd at war str, our units have been augmd [augmented] with add combat crews and with limited maint and armament pers. As a temp measure this was an acceptable solution, but continuation of this solution will result in loss of effectiveness and increased casualties. It is reqd that the fol units be reorgnd immed under the war column of applicable T/O&Es.

8th, 18th, 49th Ftr Bmr Wgs	421, 422, 430 Air Police Sqs
35th, 51st Ftr Intcp Wgs	543d Tac Support Gp, HHS
4th 68th, 339th Ftr AW Sqs	45th, 8th, 162d Tac Rcn Sqs
3d Bomb Wg, Light	465th, 466, 467, 474 Sig Avn Hvy Const Cos.
19th Bomb Wing, Medium	934th Sig Bn (Sep) Tac.

Reorg of the 374th T.C. Wg, Hvy and the 437th T.C. Wg, Medium, will be covered in separate communication fr me. *(2)* It is further reqd that the 4th Ftr Intcp Wg and 27th Ftr-Escort Wg, currently attached to FEAF, be orgn under the war column of applicable T/O&Es. *(3)* It is desired that units joining FEAF in future be orgn at war str prior to arr. *(4)* As a result of reorgn of units listed in Part I at war str, 267 off and 1611 amn Non T/O&E trp spaces may be withdrawn fr FEAF.

Took off from Haneda 1000 hours, flew direct to Chinhae (K-10) and met General Partridge, Colonel Low, the acting group commander as Colonel Wintermute was off on a short holiday, Colonel Pretorious, the South African top

---

62. Except for the addition of the fourth squadron of the 374th TCW, General Stratemeyer's request was approved. The 315th AD was activated and FEAF ComCarCom deactivated on Jan. 25. The two troop carrier wings and an air base group were assigned to the 315th AD, but attached to 5AF for administrative and logistical support except for the assignment and promotion of their personnel. Additionally, the 1st TCG (Prov) was disbanded, its personnel being used to man an additional squadron. The TDY units were attached to the 315th AD for operational control. (Futrell, pp 382-383.)

officer, and Commandant S. B. Theron.[63] K-10 is to my mind the nicest field in Korea although the strip is only 4,200 feet long and they are pushed for parking area. This is being remedied by the engineers and is considered an ideal station for F–51s. One gets a bit of a thrill sliding down a mountain in order to land, but there is ample room. I inspected all the facilities there, everybody appeared to be happy and gave the impression of doing a job. From K-10 flew to K-9; checked on the gasoline situation which has now been remedied although they need another [fuel] tank. I authorized Colonel Gray to go ahead with the installation of this additional tank. He indicated they were ready to go, but did not have authority. The deputy group commander gave General Partridge and me a quick briefing, which should not have been said to me in General Partridge's presence. Nearly everything that he brought out could be remedied in the Fifth Air Force. Although I understand he is a fine officer, he gave a very poor impression.

Met Major McIntyre,[64] the Marine F9F jet squadron commander and he made a tremendously good impression on me. There was a Major Lowe,[65] another Marine, whom I met.

While there, ran into General Ridgway and talked with him a while as well as General Almond and some other officers from X Corps. Departed K-9, flew to K-2, where we landed at 1730 hours and proceeded directly to General Partridge's headquarters where we again met General Ridgway - and all of us listened to the Fifth Air Force briefing.

Discussed all the subject mentioned in my diary of this date (29 December) with General Partridge and arrived at satisfactory solutions for all of them. Had a good dinner; to bed at 10:30 P.M.

SATURDAY 30 DECEMBER 1950

Went with General Partridge to his headquarters, met Colonel Walls and ironed out the intra-theater rotational policy with him, General Partridge, and General Timberlake. At 0900 hours, General Partridge, Timberlake and I attended General Ridgway's briefing at Eighth Army headquarters.

Departed at 1005, flew direct to Tokyo, where we had to do a GCA as there was only a 1/4 mile visibility and practically no ceiling.

Arrived in office about 1400 hours.

Immediately upon my return, got off the following memos to my staff:

I. To Surgeon, Colonel Brothers: From several sources yesterday while in Korea I learned that a flight surgeon is required with each combat squadron and I found that the usual assignment is one flight surgeon for a combat group. Under these conditions, there is very little work being done as a flight surgeon as the surgeon's entire time is taken up with health problems, sanitation, and other medical operations rather than flight surgeon duties. What have we done - or what are we doing - to obtain one flight surgeon per each combat squadron?

II. To Deputy, Personnel (thru VC A&P): Reference my letter to

---

63. Col Curtis S. Low commanded the 18th FBW, while Lt Col Ira F. Wintermute was C.O. of the 18th FBG. Thereon led No. 2 SAAF Squadron.

64. Maj Neil R. McIntyre commanded VMF-311, the only land-based Marine air unit in Korea.

65. This officer is unknown.

General Partridge dated 28 December on intra-theater rotation, as per my approval the attached covers the instructions that General Partridge put into effect today, 30 December. We will conform to this agreement. Note that it is permanent change of station basis and that where training is involved, General Partridge will do that within his wings. The people not in Korea will be furnished as per SSN and/or MOS first, and then General Partridge will release people from Korea. If there is any further information you desire on this intratheater rotation, come in to see me.* [See below.]

III. To Deputy, Materiel - Discussed the production line maintenance question for F–51's with General Partridge and he indicated that he would take it over. He indicated 150 people would be needed. This can be worked out after he designates the place where he will conduct this maintenance. He seemed to favor Komaki over Tsuiki; however, if he can do so because of its proximity to FEAMCOM, he might want to do it at Tachikawa. I indicated to him that FEAMCOM would continue all the work on the F–80's. Come in to discuss this with me at your first opportunity.

IV. While talking with the acting group commander, 35th Fighter Group, and Colonel Gray, the wing commander at K-9, I found that the Australian 77th Fighter Squadron is authorized to fly only 1,000 hours per month. I also found that the two squadrons in the 35th Fighter Group have averaged about 1,500 hours per month. It would appear that the 77th Squadron is not carrying their proportionate share of the load in fighter sorties - as are the U.S. squadrons. This is probably due to the Australian government not having sufficient dollars to allow them to exceed the 1,000 hours per month. It seems to me that if they cannot afford it, then the U.S. government should make up the difference in expense in order that the Australian squadron can carry the same load in fighter sorties that other fighter squadrons carry. It is desired that you discuss this with the proper authority and see what can be done. *(Above directed to Vice Commander, Operations - General Weyland.)*

V. To Deputy, Personnel - Is General Partridge authorized to make battlefield appointments to commissioned officers to airmen? As you know, the Eighth Army, right on the field of battle is authorized to promote warrant officers and non-commissioned officers to grade of second lieutenant. Is General Partridge authorized to do the same thing? If not, I want a signal prepared to Chief of Staff, United States Air Force, for my approval before dispatch, requesting such authority.

VI. To Adjutant General: I find that the UN flags that have been sent to Korea are either too large or of such fine quality that they cannot be flown. Are we furnishing AF stations with a UN flag about the same size as the U.S. storm flag - and if not, what can we do to obtain such flags for our AF stations?

VII. To Deputy, Personnel: I met a Colonel Wilson[66] while at Chinhae (K-10) who was from the 18th Fighter Wing and he indicated that there were still many airmen and fine pilots who had not had an opportunity to

---

66. Lt Col Eugene E. Wilson, the 18th FBG executive officer.

get into combat in Korea. He knew them almost by name and at my suggestion he is preparing a list of officers and airmen which he will send to me through General Partridge in order that they may be rotated to the 18th Group in Korea and people in the 18th transferred back to Clark. Be on the look-out for this letter and keep me advised.

VIII. Dispatched the fol Stratline to CG Fifth Air Force (copy to Banfill): Cite: V 0521 CG - TOP SECRET PERSONAL PARTRIDGE FROM STRATEMEYER. This radio in two parts:

PART ONE (TOP SECRET) We have authority to destroy the following town: P'yŏngyang, Wŏnsan, Hamhŭng, and Hŭngnam. Attacks will be conducted without psychological warfare warnings or publicity. At first opportunity, inform Ridgway.

PART TWO (NEW SUBJECT - SECRET). Discontinue work on the large mosaic that was discussed in your briefing last night and Ridgway's briefing this morning. You are authorized to employ all of your recon as deemed best to suit your needs and that of Eighth Army. Advise Ridgway.

*CG Fifth AF to CG FEAF memo dtd 30 Dec: The fol instructions were given by General Partridge to FAF A-1 in regard to ur ltr of 28 Dec 50, subject: "Intra-Theater Rotation": disregard families. Give me a weekly reading on progress for dispatch to General Stratemeyer. We [underlined in original] will do whatever training is necessary. s/P. (E.E.P.)

SUNDAY   *In answer to the fol two radios I received:*

31 DECEMBER *1)* Personal for Stratemeyer from Nugent. It is requested

1950   that you return Gen. Barcus to the ZI to report back his

                           station here not later than 15 Jan. Please advise his ETD your theater and ETA Langley.

and

2) Personal to Stratemeyer from Twining. Based on recommendations of both Dr. Stearns and Gen. T.D. White, it is my belief that Gen. Glenn Barcus and the group of officers and civilians who have been engaged in an evaluation of the FEAF effort in Korea should plan to terminate their work in the near future and return to the ZI. Will 15 Jan be a suitable target date for their departure from the theater? Please pass to Barcus and relay his reaction. The Chief of Staff is particularly interested in his early return. It has been suggested that you may be in a position to continue the collection of data which would be valuable in an extension of the current evaluation using Col. Tate[67] and resources now available in the Fifth AF. Please give us your reaction to this suggestion.

I dispatched following answer:

Personal for Twining from Stratemeyer. Answering your AFODC 50171 and Nugent's Cite 50240 of 29 December. Barcus and I concur that Barcus and his group of officers and civilians depart theater 15 January.

---

67. Col David A. Tate.

Collection of data for extension of current evaluation will continue, using resources now available in theater.

Got off the fol Priority Msg to Twining:

I understand that Generals T. D. White and Barton Leach have indicated that Colonel Sykes should return to Washington. The Sykes' documentation project for me completed and approved and embodied in material furnished Stearns and Barcus. If Sykes' return is desired, request authority to return him to permanent station departing theater 15 January with Barcus Group. However, a replacement to carry on the Sykes' type of work is required. I suggest Colonel Noel F. Parrish[68] or a colonel of his qualifications.

After sending off the above signal, a radnote came into hqrs which indicated that USAF desired Sykes' return prior to the time I contemplated letting him go. Consequently, *dispatched another message - Personal priority to Twining:*

Reur AFCVC 48719, dtd 29 Dec, see my A 0202C-CG, dtd 31 Dec. Must I return Sykes prior to 15 January? If so, request replacement as specified by me in my A 02020-CG.

MONDAY
1 JANUARY
1951

Dispatched the fol ltr to General O'Donnell via courier:

Dear Rosie - reference our authority to burn and destroy P'yŏngyang, Wŏnsan, Hamhŭng, and Hŭngnam, it is desired that no publicity whatsoever be given out as to these strikes. No reporters or personnel nor members of FEAF Bomber Command will be permitted to ride as observers on these strikes. Make sure that these instructions are strictly adhered to. Best regards.

Got off my weekly ltr to Gill Robb Wilson
Also sent Hugh Baillie a letter of thanks for the play he gave our special news release.

Dispatched the fol rad:

PERSONAL TWINING AND LEMAY FROM STRATEMEYER. Re LeMay's DP2B 13381, dtd 29 Dec 50, personal to Twining and Stratemeyer. A planned program of replacement of all crews of the 98th and 307th Groups should be drawn up and put into effect immediately. These crews have been engaged in continuous operations since August and should be replaced as rapidly as possible. Replacement crews must be in place before returnee crews can be released. Request schedule for forwarding replacements.

TUESDAY
2 JANUARY
1951

In reference to F–80C pylons, General Doyle submitted the fol report-letter, dtd 31 Dec 50, which I bucked to Alkire for his info:

---

68. Colonel Parrish commanded Tuskegee Army Air Field during World War II, and organized and directed the training of those black pilots who became known as the Tuskegee Airmen. From 1948 to 1951, he was Deputy Secretary of the Air Staff. In January 1951, he became Special Assistant to the Vice Chief of Staff, USAF.

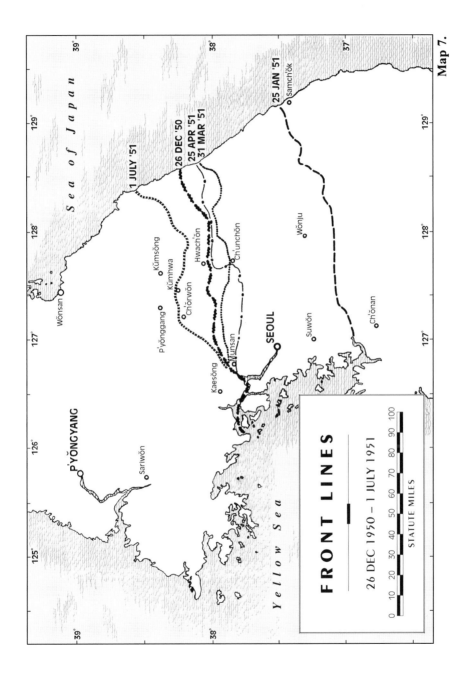

Map 7.

FRONT LINES

26 DEC 1950 – 1 JULY 1951

STATUTE MILES

Progress report on F–80C pylons per your verbal directive as follows:

Aircraft Delivered or RFD [ready for delivery]	Pylon Manhours Expended	Other Manhours Expended
49-548	294	1639
49-693	301	279
49-695	312	278
49-6972	95	248
49-724	300	2330

As you will see, in line with what Alkire told you the other day, the pylons are only a part of the job of putting out combat serviceable airplanes. Best wishes for a successful new year. s/John P. Doyle, etc.

WEDNESDAY 3 JANUARY 1951 General Partridge called at about 1000 hours and stated that today he was evacuating his forward command post in Seoul, that Meyer with his group was leaving Kimp'o and that both fields - K-14 and K-16 - would be evacuated by sundown tonight. All buildings and facilities at both fields would be destroyed as well as supplies, and that later, the runways would be bombed. He indicated that the ground situation was deteriorating and told me that he would send me a Top Secret message, for my eyes only, giving me his estimate of the situation.

General O'Donnell called at 1050 hours and stated that he had 73 B–29's airborne for the strike at P'yŏngyang and that the first two flights had reported in that the visibility was good and the bombing was excellent. I indicated to him that he would keep me informed reference the P'yŏngyang strike which he said he would do.

Korean Minister Kim[69] at 1500 hours came by the office and with him was an American citizen, born in Hawaii, by the name of Walter Jhung. Jhung was in Hawaii at the time Rosie O'Donnell was a captain. Jhung speaks excellent English and his position now is Consultant to the Korean Diplomatic Mission in Japan, with headquarters in Tokyo. He is of Korean ancestry. He is a most unusual fellow.

THURSDAY 4 JANUARY 1951 *Received the fol ltr from Twining in reply to my TS, EYES ONLY, to Vandenberg of 23 Dec which was handcarried to Washington:*

dtd 29 Dec 50, TOP SECRET, EYES ONLY - General Vandenberg will be away for several days, so with your concurrence I had read the "eyes only" letter of December 23 that you addressed to him on the subject of the restrictions placed on your aircraft with regard to the Manchurian border. I will show your letter to him as soon as he returns. I know he shares your concern in this matter, but, at the same time, he cannot change your present directives or approve your recommendations

---

69. Kim Yong-Joo, Chief, Korean Diplomatic Mission to Japan.

that your fighters be permitted to pursue hostile aircraft across the border as such action has been disapproved by the United Nations. Furthermore, the United Nations as of this date have not declared the Chinese Communists "aggressors" in this conflict. It is to be hoped that if and when such steps are taken, some of the restrictions under which you are operating can be removed. Rest assured that you will be kept fully informed of any new developments that will permit the removal of the restrictions now imposed on your operations.

Called on General MacArthur about 1120 hours and showed him the reply from Twining to my letter to Vandenberg enclosing the Partridge letter wherein I requested authority to pursue hostile aircraft into Manchuria, but not attack ground installations. Was there about 20 minutes, and MacArthur's remark, when I showed him the Twining letter was "Well, Strat, that's just a brush-off, isn't it?" To which I replied, "Yes, Sir."

One of the statements made during my visit was this: "Strat, I can't understand why the people back in Washington don't understand the combined use of air power and Navy power. We simply cannot afford to meet the enemy in Asia - or in Europe - on the ground. By the utilization of air power and Navy power, and, in combination, our great potential could be made to be felt."

This is a thought in which I agree with General MacArthur. We have not - and, I'm afraid do not intend to put our strength in the air and on and under the water, but will in all probability divide it three ways and therefore dissipate our effort. I intend to think more along this line and see if I can't arrive at some conclusions in order, maybe, to influence the powers that be.

Again, I left General MacArthur's office with that feeling of great admiration for a great leader and a great man.

Placed the fol mem FOR THE RECORD on file:
subject - RAAF and 35th Group Squadrons Operational Data.

(1) Reference interest in the 77th Squadron (RAAF) and 35th Group's squadrons, the following data is recorded:

    a. Sortie rate per month per a/c on hand in Korea –

(1) RAAF	15.4
(2) 35th Ftr Gp	22.5

    b. Total sorties flown 1 Dec thru 30 Dec –

(1) RAAF	301
(2) 35th Ftr Gp (2 Sqs)	1025 – 512.5 per sq

    c. Average aircraft per day on hand in Korea, 1 Dec thru 30 Dec –

(1) RAAF	19.5
(2) 35th Ftr Gp	45.5 – 22.75 per sq

    d. Flying hours -

(1) RAAF	1000
(2) 35th Ftr Gp Sqs	1500 per squadron
s/G.E.S.	

Dispatched the fol ltr to Vandenberg, subject; FEAF Assistance to the X Corps During Its Crucial Withdrawal:

1. I have had assembled figures to give you a picture of the support given the X Corps by the Far East Air Forces during the period 28 November to 24 December.

2. During the X Corps withdrawal from the Chosin Reservoir area (28 November - 11 December, inclusive), FEAF Combat Cargo Command flew a total of 1608 sorties which airlifted 5286.6 tons of cargo including 14,518 passengers and evacuees. During this same period, Fifth Air Force flew a total of 408 sorties in direct and close support of the X Corps.

3. In support of the evacuation from Hamhŭng (12 December - 22 December, inclusive) which has been greatly publicized as strictly a <u>Navy Show</u> [underlining in original], FEAF Combat Cargo Command flew a total of 555 sorties which airlifted 2999 tons of cargo including 5,504 passengers and evacuees from the beachhead. During the period 12 December to 24 December, inclusive, Fifth Air Force flew a total of 328 sorties in direct and close support of the X Corps.

4. A detailed breakdown, indicating the effort by FEAF Combat Cargo Command from each field, is attached.

   s/G.E.S.

Typical Korean airfield conditions. (Above) A C–46 muscles its way off a muddy, rutted runway. (Below) C–119s waiting to load troops.

Inclosure #1 (to above ltr)

FEAF ASSISTANCE TO THE X CORPS
28 November - 22 December
FEAF Combat Cargo Command

28 Nov - 11 Dec (Incl)	Sorties	Passengers	Cargo*	Evacuees
Into YŎNP'O	538	1953	1947.3	4689
Out of YŎNP'O	612	2240	1662.3	5169
1 Dec - 7 Dec (Incl)				
Into HAGARU-RI	148	462	235.2	—
Out of HAGARU-RI**	142	332	330.7	4377
8 Dec - 10 Dec (Incl)				
Into KOT'O-RI	15	5	6.4	—
Out of KOT'O-RI**	20	23	33.6	312
28 Nov - 12 Dec (Incl)				
Airdrop (1 on 12 Dec)	296	—	1436.3	—
12 Dec - 17 Dec (Incl)				
Into YŎNP'O	73	127	220.8	—
Out of YŎNP'O	461	4444	2763.3	820
17 Dec - 22 Dec (Incl)				
Into JADE (beach strip)	9	10	2.2	—
Out of JADE (beach strip)	11	103	11.8	—

*Cargo figures include passengers and/or evacuees.
**These figures are included in the "Into YŎNP'O" figures shown above.

FRIDAY
5 JANUARY
1951

Nuckols got off the following marble to Vandenberg; which I approved:

PERSONAL PRIORITY VANDENBERG FROM STRATEMEYER. Final operational reports for 3 January show that FEAF aircraft and aircraft under FEAF operational control, namely, ROKs, Australians, South Africans, land-based Marines, and Greeks, flew 965 sorties for new all-time record in Korean conflict. Naval aviation on 3 January flew additional 208 sorties making grand total air effort for day 1173. Above 965 figure has not repeat not been released to press here and suggest you may want to issue statement on this new record.

Instructed my Plans people (Colonel Zimmerman) as follows:

· I am greatly concerned with the apparent method in which our government intends to spend the money recently appropriated for national defense. By that I mean it looks as though they are going to split it three ways - Army, Navy and Air Force.

I am confident that we cannot meet Russia and her satellites - either in Europe or Asia on the ground. I am further confident that our great industrial resources in the United States should build an Air Force and a Navy (to operate both under and on the water). Our great offensive potential with the Air Force - Navy team then could be made to be felt by the enemy. We can whip him with such a team. I do not mean that we should not have an Army. We must, but our Army should be used for defense of our Air Force and Navy bases and for ZI defense and against sabotage.

It is my desire that you prepare a study, developing what I have said above, for my approval. I intend to send it to General Vandenberg.

    s/G.E.S.

General O'Donnell called at 1530 hours.

Dispatched the fol rad to CGs 5th, BomCom, COCARCOM, and FEAMCOM:

Personal from Stratemeyer to Partridge, O'Donnell, Tunner and Doyle. During my conference with General MacArthur this morning I was gratified to be able to report to him that final operational reports for 3 January show that on that date FEAF and FEAF operationally controlled airplanes flew 965 effective sorties, the highest figure thus far in the Korean conflict. PARA. General MacArthur asked me to pass on to you his deep and sincere appreciation for the efforts of all of your personnel that made these sorties possible. Signed George E. Stratemeyer, Lt. General, USAF.

SATURDAY 6 JANUARY 1951

The TOP SECRET - EYES ONLY evaluation which Partridge had told me he was sending me *arrived via hand courier, and is as follows:*

FOR STRATEMEYER FROM PARTRIDGE. For 2 months we have been operating against fresh Chinese Communist Armies augmented by rejuvenated North Korean formations. Over the same period we have been opposed by a Russian equipped air force using aircraft new to this theater. Up to the present time this air force has had no decisive influence on the conflict in Korea and for the purposes of this dispatch will be ignored.

The characteristics of our ground opponents bear careful study. The Chinese appear in overwhelming numbers at critical points, revealing not only large resources of trained manpower but expert, experienced leadership. The individual soldiers are hardy, skilled in night movements and infiltrations, and capable of living and fighting when provided a small amount of logistic support. Their troops capitalize on their lack of vehicles and heavy weapons by utilizing the Korean terrain in such a skillful manner as to embarrass the better equipped UN forces. Lastly, when important objectives are to be secured the Chinese throw in their men with utter disregard of human life, although at other times, camouflage discipline is so good that the effectiveness of our air attacks is minimized. Based on the events of the month of December it is apparent that the enemy can advance at the rate of some four miles a day accomplishing meanwhile one major offensive per thirty-day period. Assuming for the moment that this is his best capability, he should appear opposite the Naktong River in about forty days. Thereafter his progress should be slower but since it is only sixty miles from Taegu to Pusan, two or three additional months should suffice for him to drive us off the penninsula unless unforseen developments occur.

The performance of UN ground forces in attempting to hold the communists on the Imjin River - 38th Parallel line introduces grave doubts as to the capability of our ground army to withstand a well planned attack. Not only did the enemy succeed in probing our lines and in discovering a spot through which troops could pass to infiltrate our rear, but he also made a frontal penetration where we were strongest. Attacking against a position most of which had been in preparation for years and all of which was worked on vigorously since the arrival of our forces on the line in mid-December, the enemy drove over 12,000 yards through our strongest defenses within a few hours. The final outcome of this particular action was plain from the outset.[70]

Short of the line of final defense about Pusan, no well prepared positions exist southeast of the Army's current location. Even the Pusan perimeter is ill-equipped to stop the determined onslaught which has to be expected in due course.

All this background leads up to the question of the future of military operations in Korea. Are we going to make a determined fight or must we withdraw to avoid annihilation. In view of the past record it is my personal belief that evacuation through Pusan will be forced upon us.

This withdrawal can be avoided if the ground armies will make a stand in South Korea although the price in casualties will be heavy. With ever-lengthening lines of communication to support his advancing troops from Manchuria and under constant attrition from ground action and air strikes, the enemy can be whittled down in the course of a few months to a point where offensive ground operations can be resumed. His resources of manpower may be inexhaustible but I refuse to concede that he can train people fast enough to replace even those casualties which can be inflicted upon him by the air force alone provided - and I repeat the provided -that air force is supported by vigorous and determined ground arms.

It is thoroughly understood by me that the decision to fight or get out rests on a high level. My purpose in writing this message is to emphasize that the Air Force cannot wait for that decision. The final announcement will be delayed as long as possible and may come by default. We must start now with the construction and rehabilitation of our air facilities in the northern Kyushu area and be prepared first for the support of an evacuation

---

70. That this defensive line (Line B) was truly strong or had really been under preparation (by the ROKs) for years is a matter of conjecture. After all, the 38th Parallel already had been crossed once by the enemy just a few months earlier. What is not in dispute is that the battle which started on New Year's Eve, quickly became a rout of the UN forces. (Blair, pp 592-603.)

and second for continuation of air war over Korea should that course of action be required.

Weyland has been read into our broad plans and unless I hear further from you we will proceed on detailed preparations.

In order that you may have my own views on what should be done about Korean operations I add them. The UN forces entered this country in support of a principle. To withdraw will lower the prestige of the UN to such a level that the usefulness of the organization will be lost. It would be far better to make the stand here than to avoid the issue. Recognizing that the cost in the present action will be high I feel certain the price will still be small when compared with that of subsequent military operations elsewhere if we pull out now.

Upon receipt of Partridge's TOP SECRET EYES only message, directed it to General Craigie with attached memo:

Attached hereto is a hand-carried, TOP SECRET, message from General Partridge. I have read it carefully and am inclined to agree with every word that the message contains. It is my desire that you study this message and then in consultation with General Weyland (who read it at Taegu), come up with a recommended action.

I approve the construction and rehabilitation of FEAF's air facilities in northern Kyushu and for the purpose as stated by General Partridge.

I also agree with all statements in his last paragraph.

The suggested action in my opinion can be as follows:

(1) Do nothing with reference to the attached message as I am in agreement with General Partridge.

(2) Prepare a paper for my signature to CINCFE covering generally what General Partridge has said, backing up the statements made in his last paragraph.

(3) Boil the attached message down and send it over my signature, EYES ONLY, to General Vandenberg and request instructions from him.
   s/G.E.S.

Dispatched fol priority msg to Vandenberg:

FEAF on Saturday, 6 Jan, flew its 100,000 sortie of Korean conflict. Am releasing to press text of my message to all UN air units who contributed to effort.

To CGS 5th, 13th, 20th, BomCom, Cocarcom, FEAMCOM, C/S ROK AF, Cmdrs of 77th RAAF, No. 2 SAAF, 13th Hellenic Flight, Royal Hellenic AF, with info cy to CSAF, *issued the fol statement via radio:*

PERSONAL FROM STRATEMEYER. During yesterday's (Saturday, 6 January) air operations, the Far East Air Forces flew its 100,000th sortie against the enemy since we initiated combat operations in Korea on 26 June. In the 195 consecutive days, FEAF fighters, bombers and combat transports have carried the air battle to the enemy without let-up. PARA Our fighters have provided the United Nations surface forces with both a greater degree of immunity from air attack and also a more intensive and uninterrupted close air support than has ever before been afforded in modern war. PARA In early weeks of the war, our medium bombers completely neutralized the limited strategic war potential in North Korea. Since then, both by day and by night, our fighters and bombers have constantly interdicted enemy lines of supply and communication in Korea. PARA Our transports, despite adverse conditions, have maintained the flow of supplies for United Nations troops, and have saved countless lives by the prompt aerial evacuation from Korean battlefronts of battle and weather casualties. PARA Ever increasing our daily effort, we have decimated the enemy forces, disrupted his supplies and equipment, and more recently have magnificently supported withdrawals of United Nations forces. PARA. Today we salute the 437 officers and airmen of all our services who have died, were wounded or are missing in air action, and whose efforts contributed to our achievements. Signed George E. Stratemeyer, Lt. General, USAF.

Left the office early for a golf game with Joy.

SUNDAY
7 JANUARY
1951

Upon my arrival at the office found the fol radio AFCVC TS- 6500, from Vandenberg:

As you know the build up of Strategic Air Command is being accelerated at a greatly increased rate placing high priority on requirement for senior and experienced bombardment commanders in SAC. I feel, therefore, that General O'Donnell should be returned to the ZI in the very near future as his services are urgently needed during this build up. As a replacement for O'Donnell I consider General Briggs highly qualified to command the FEAF Bomber Command. Would like to have your comments.

In immediate reply thereto dispatched the fol:

TOP SECRET PERSONAL VANDENBERG FROM STRATEMEYER. Reur AFCVC TS-6504 dtd 6 Jan 51. I approve the return to ZI of Major General Emmett O'Donnell and, like you, consider Brigadier General James E. Briggs fully qualified to command FEAF BOMCOM.[71]

Made copies of both the above signals and sent them out to O'Donnell stating:

I approved your return to the ZI without consulting you because as per enclosed signals realized the necessity for such return.

Dispatched Partridge's TOP SECRET EYES ONLY Evaluation *[underlined in original] (see diary entry 6 Jan 51) to CINCFE - TS and EYES ONLY with following comment from me:*

I am transmitting herewith an EYES ONLY message which I have just received from General Partridge. As you know, I have a great deal of respect for Partridge's sound judgment and analytical abilities. I am sure

---

71. Briggs replaced O'Donnell on Jan. 10.

you also know that Partridge has kept himself thoroughly informed with respect to the ground situation by almost daily personal aerial reconnaissance flights often accompanied by the Commanding General, Eighth Army. I, therefore, have great confidence in his views relative to the status of the air-ground war in Korea and feel that he speaks with considerable authority. I am in complete agreement with his analysis of the overall situation in Korea and with his statement relative to the capabilities of the Air in the event of a determined resistance on the Naktong River or Pusan perimeters. With reference to the construction and rehabilitation of air facilities in northern Kyushu mentioned by Partridge in the middle of page 4, we are proceeding at full speed with this work. Involved in this program are the runway extension of Tsuiki and the construction of winterized tents, mess facilities, latrines and other items at Ozuki.[72] It is requested that these papers be returned to me. s/G.E.S.

Reference the above. General MacArthur returned the papers - quoted is his comment: "Strat, very interesting and represents much sound thought. Thanks for cutting me in. Signed MacA."

Departed Haneda about 1015 hours for Okinawa and Clark. However had to return because of bad engine in staff C–54, returning 8 January 1951 in Stearley's B–17. The staff C–54 remained on Okinawa for engine change.

**MONDAY
8 JANUARY
1951**

Landed Haneda from Okinawa 1437 and proceeded direct to the office. *Dispatched the fol R&R to Alkire (Deputy for Materiel):*

On my trip to Okinawa yesterday, #4 engine vibrated to the point that we almost turned back, however, it was not overheating and not using up oil, so we proceeded on to Kadena. Upon landing, the engine was immediately inspected and was found to contain many filings and everyone recommended pulling the engine. This is the third engine of the four that came over with FEAF staff C–54 and I therefore desire that a special report UR [unsatisfactory report] be submitted for my signature on these three engines. Number 1 engine failed at 170 hours; number 2 engine failed at 153 hours; and number 4 engine failed yesterday at 191 hours. I left instructions at FEAF Flight Section to pull the fourth engine and get a safe one installed.

To the Adjutant General, directed fol R&R:

I find that the airmail delivery to Okinawa has been bad for the last couple of weeks. They are just receiving airmail there that was mailed in the States on 8 December. It is desired that you look into the airmail situation for Okinawa and see that it gets on our inter-island air service - and that it improves. Keep me posted on this matter." (Also sent a cy to VC, A&P.)

---

72. Tsuiki is located in northern Kyushu near the Shimonoseki Strait, while Ozuki is on the other side of the strait on Honshu. Tsuiki was widely used during the war; Ozuki was used only occasionally.

To Deputy, Personnel:

I find from the group commander of the 19th Bomb Group that they are 120 airmen short in their group. How come? I thought we had received sufficient airmen to keep the 19th Bomb Group up to strength. Come in and see me reference this matter. (Cy also to VC, A&P)

To Director Air Installations:

There is a feeling on Okinawa that the Futema air strip can be extended and rehabilitated for much less money than the strip at Naha. Also, that if all the money that has been appropriated - or is to be appropriated for Naha - were put into Futema we would not only have a better strip, but a better living and administrative area. At one time it was thought that there were coral caverns under the runway at Futema in the area where extensions would be built. Borings have been made and to date no caverns have been found. It is desired that you, at your leisure, come in and discuss this with me. I do not want any action taken - I just want to discuss it.

TUESDAY　　*Received the fol TS signal from HQ USAF:*

9 JANUARY　　Authority granted you to issue orders assigning General

1951　　Briggs as CG FEAF BOMCOM (Prov). Please advise
　　　　　　　date General O'Donnell's TDY terminates and his ETA
home station.

I will reply to this signal today after discussing same with General O'Donnell.

1010 hours, General Robertson was in. After our discussion, *dispatched the fol R&R to Deputy, Ops (info & thru VC, Ops):*

Attention is invited to the following quoted signal received by General Robertson from Australia: "Forward a broad rearming plan after discussion with CG FEAF and including his views. Also include recommendations regarding disposal of Mustangs as they become surplus and any additional personnel required during conversion." It is desired that we furnish the data called for in above signal and work closely through Fifth Air Force with the RAAF 77th Fighter Squadron and with General Robertson's headquarters in arriving at the data desired by his government. The first contingent of Meteor-8 jet aircraft will arrive on or about 28 February.[73] It is desired that three senior officers from the 77th RAAF Fighter Squadron, namely, Squadron Leader Cresswell, Flight Lt Harvey, and Flight Lt Murphy,[74] receive operational training with one of our tactical jet squadrons in order to give them the experience necessary for squadron tactical operations. Keep me informed of progress. s/G.E.S.

---

73. The Australians began converting to their new aircraft in April 1951. It soon became evident that the Gloster Meteor F.8, which had been the Allies' first operational jet fighter in World War II, was obsolescent for air-to-air combat with the speedy MiG–15. The plane was, however, well-suited as a fighter-bomber and went on to perform this mission with distinction.
74. Cresswell and Flt Lt Desmond Murphy were the first Australian pilots to fly jets (F–80s) in combat over Korea. Flt Lt Gordon Harvey was later shot down and made a POW.

I discussed with General Hickey this morning the non-approval of our scheduled taking over of the three hospitals - namely, those at Tachikawa, Johnson, and Nagoya and staffing them with Air Force medical personnel. by J.L.C.[75]

General Hume, who happened to be in the hall, was present and indicated that he had approved this and was all for it - as were we - and for the same reasons: i.e., *(1)* Air Force medical people would have a crack at professional duties in hospitals; *(2)* we would be taking a load off the Army medical people; *(3)* based on the original approval by everyone concerned - or at least Japan Logistical Command's non-committal attitude, and *(4)* the fact that the Japan Logistical Command would still control the patients and general administration of the hospitals, we requisitioned the necessary Air Force medical people who are due to arrive within the next six weeks.

General Hickey indicated not only that he believed in it, but we should have done it a long time ago. I told him we couldn't have done this before as Air Force medical people were not available until now.

My reaction is we will take over the three hospitals with Air Force personnel as originally scheduled. (cy of discussion with Generals Hickey and Hume extracted from diary for Col Brothers' info.)

Mr. Don King of Northwest Airlines came by to introduce Mr. Amos Culbert, NW Vice President in Charge of Sales, and Mr. Ferrell, Sales Manager for [Northwest] Orient who is located here in Tokyo, at 1430 hours.

WEDNESDAY
10 JANUARY
1951

Received cy of fol rad:

Ops Immediate, from SAC to FEAF BomCom, info FEAF, CSAF, 15th AF, cite CG 5266, dtd 9 Jan 51 - PERSONAL TO O'DONNELL FROM LEMAY. Ref your BCX 3659, I would like to have Power[76] and you meet in Hawaii and consider in detail our plan for relief of 98 and 307 Medium BWs. We will have planning data aval this week and in view of urgency we all attach to obtaining an early solution to this subj, I suggest a meet 13-14 Jan at Hickam. Recommend you also have on hand representatives from CG FEAF's hq qualified to concur for Stratemeyer in agreements reached. Pressure of work at this end makes meeting at some intermediate sta[ge] mandatory. Please confirm this arrangement promptly.

In reply to above, dispatched the fol:

Ops Immediate, fm CG FEAF, to CG SAC, info V/CSAF, CG BomCom. PERSONAL LEMAY FROM STRATEMEYER. INFO TWINING AND O'DONNELL. O'Donnell leaves his TDY here 16 Jan. I will have representative accompany him for 16 Jan meeting in Hawaii with Power, although I do not anticipate that he will be required to make any decisions for me. Any plans for crew rotation which come out of the O'Donnell-

---

75. The Japan Logistical Command (JLC) had been established on Aug. 24 to administer the logistics support activities of FEC in Japan and to get all supplies from Japan to Korea. In this latter task the JLC functioned as a communications zone command for the Eighth Army. (Schnabel, pp 136-137.)

76. In addition to being SAC's vice commander, Lt Gen Thomas S. Power was SAC's X-Ray commander in Tokyo, in charge of the command's atomic forces in the Far East. A similar command, Zebra, was located in England.

Power meeting will be satisfactory to me, provided they do not violate following: CINCFE's position and, therefore, mine, is that as long as Korean incident lasts we must retain in this theater equivalent of three peace-strength medium groups, plus three Tarzon airplanes and crews. O'Donnell has suggested as a possible means of releasing some additional experience to SAC Z.I. activation program that the above mentioned 90 acft and combat crews be contained in two war strength groups of 45 acft each, thus releasing the overhead of one combat group. I will concur in such a scheme if you desire to do it.

Major General Kim Chung Yul, who commands the Korean Air Force, arrived 1510 hours with his party of 7 officers. General Banfill met him in my stead.

At 1930 hours, had a stag dinner at Mayeda House honoring Major General Kim Chung Yul, Brigadier General Choi Yong Duk, Colonel Kim Chang Kyoo, Lt. Colonel Kim Yong Hwan, Lt. Colonel Han Yong Hoon, Major Chun Myon Sup, Captain Lee Kyoo Sung, and 1st Lt. Lee Sun Yong (Aide de Camp).[77] Other guests present: Generals Craigie, Weyland, Banfill, and Nuckols, and Major Woodruff.

Made the award of the Legion of Merit, Grade of Officer, to Major General Kim Chung Yul.

Dispatched a ltr to General Vandenberg:

Dear Van, Attached hereto is Banfill's current estimate of the short-term courses of Soviet action which would affect FEAF. To my mind, as well as that of Weyland's and Craigie's, this estimate is so worthwhile that I feel it should be forwarded to you personally and for such use as the Air Staff may have for it. I have furnished General MacArthur with a copy for his information. Best regards.

To CINCFE:

Memorandum For General of the Army Douglas MacArthur: The attached estimate prepared by my Deputy for Intelligence, Brigadier General Charles Y. Banfill, I consider of sufficient importance for you to read. I, therefore, sent it to you for your information. s/G.E.S.

Here follows the report, which I sent to both Vandenberg and MacArthur (see above):

PURPOSE: To estimate the short-term courses of Soviet action which would affect the Far East Air Forces.

DISCUSSION:
(1) While the facts of Soviet military potential are not definitely available, it would appear that while Soviet air and naval strength and capability of waging atomic, chemical, and/or bacteriological warfare is vague and inconclusive, the traditional immense strength of the Soviet ground forces has been maintained and in all probability augmented in numbers, materiel and efficiency.

---

77. Choi Yong Duk is probably Ch'oe Yong Tuk, the Assistant Chief of Staff, ROKAF. The other individuals are unidentified.

(2) Dictatorship control permits the launching of a war without warning. For this reason alone, it is impossible to determine the WHERE and the WHEN of future Soviet military action. There is, however, some basis for the determination of the WHAT, HOW and WHY of possible near-term Soviet action based on their well-known practical approach to a problem and their freedom for influence by considerations other than that of strict objectivity in their approach to a solution.

(3) It would be less than realistic not to recognize that the Soviets have matched the air supremacy which we have employed in Korea with tactics which have offset the effectiveness of our air power as presently employed in conjunction with ground operations.

(4) The consequences of the military setbacks to UN forces, since the active participation of CCF in the Korean incident, may be expected to include a vitalization of Communist subversive and guerrilla activities throughout the Far East. It may further be expected that all anti-Communist forces in the Far East may be overcome with doubts and uncertainties as to the merits of adherence to anti-Communist policy. Especially significant are reports from the Military Intelligence Service, Armed Forces, Philippines, which included a comment that the present situation in Korea may ultimately lead to abandonment of smaller Asian countries to Communist domination, and concluded that the Philippines cannot fully accept promises of protection by Western powers. (CINCFE CX 52817, 6 Jan 51). Undoubtedly encouragement will be given to the JCP [Japanese Communist Party] to engage in acts designed to embarrass the occupation forces and the military effort based in Japanese territory.

(5) During the Korean incident the Soviets have been able to assess each of our current military capabilities except the atom bomb. The hasty but relatively complete evacuation of industries from cities such as Mukden, which have been reported with varying degrees of credibility, seems to have been in anticipation of our employment of the atom bomb against Chinese targets. From the Soviet standpoint, such employment would have served two useful purposes: a. It would have afforded an up-to-date opportunity to determine our capability in placing the atom bomb on a specified target, and b. It would crystallize the immense propaganda effort of the Soviets to mobilize world opinion against the user of an atom bomb.

(6) As indicated above, the Soviet capability in atomic warfare is an unknown quantity. It is somewhat difficult to reconcile the immense propaganda effort that the Soviets have exerted against the use of the atom bomb with a real and present availability to them of such a weapon.

(7) The failure of the UN effort in Korea to date should encourage the Soviets to a continuance of their support of satellite nations in dissipating our strength in embarrassing and largely hopeless contests in places of their choosing.

(8) Realism on the part of the Politburo should enable them to conclude that any direct act of aggression on the part of the Soviets will solidify

the current wave of U.S. public opinion which has already arrived at the conclusion that the sole solution to the Communist problem is a war with Russia.

CONCLUSIONS:

(9) Having established in Korea the U.S. reaction to Far East military conquest by satellite forces, (China has not yet been formally branded an aggressor), the USSR and Communist China may well feel the Korean pattern can be continued throughout Southeast Asia.

(10) Present and contemplated expansion through satellite activity precludes the present necessity or desirability of direct Soviet intervention, particularly against areas under U.S. suzerainty, and specifically against Japan and the Ryukyus.

(11) The Soviet Union will continue both to decry use of the atomic bomb, and to lure us into using it in Asia in order that world-wide opinion may be turned against us, while giving the USSR an opportunity to assess the degree of success we are able to achieve with our "ultimate weapon."

(12) Barring presently unforeseen military or political events, and unless or until our atom bomb capability has been neutralized in some manner or dissipated against non-decisive objectives, the USSR probably will not give cause by overt acts of war for its employment against the Soviet Union.

RECOMMENDATION: That the maximum offensive means under FEAF control be concentrated on the defeat of NK and CG [Chinese government?] units in Korea as they constitute the greatest immediate threat to UN combat capabilities.

THURSDAY 11 JANUARY 1951

Received word that CINCFE had approved the transfer of the three hospitals to FEAF control effective 1 April 1951.

Notified Colonel Brothers, FEAF Surgeon (see diary entry under date 9 Jan 51).

FRIDAY 12 JANUARY 1951

Received the fol signal fm USAF (SAC info) cite:

AFPMP-1-T 51023. ...This msg in 3 parts. *PART I.* Ref Part 1 ourad AFPMP-1T-59754 and Part 1 AFOOP-ZI 50682. Subj is repl[acement] plan for 19th B Wg combat crews. 9 crews fr ccts [combat crew training squadron] will fulfill ur repl rqmt for pers <u>VQD</u> (?) [in original] in first increment of B-29 type combat indivs and crews for additional 3 acft. *PART II.* Ref Part 2 ourad AFPMP-1-T 59754. Upon arrival of 9 crews, or at such time as it is deemed advisable, FEAF will ret[urn] 6 crews to SAC and SAC will reasgn 6 crews to the 19 BW. Interchange of crews w/b [will be] on a one-for-one basis, 6 crews per month until FEAF repl rqmt is met. *PART III.* Reasgmt procedure. CG FEAF advise this hq name, grade, SSN, and crew MOS, eta ZI of crew being retd. This hq will obtain from CG SAC sta asgmt and fwd to CG FEAF. For identification purpose, rpt crews by project number, month of ret, and crew number. Indicate project 1929 for returnees and 1929-R for repls. This info w/b included in all orders. Example: Project 1929 Feb-1 indicates B–29 crews being retd from FEAF in Feb, crew number is 1. This hq will obtain repl crew info from SAC and will issue nec repl instructions.

I changed action of above rad to D/P and placed these instructions on the signal for necessary action:

(1) This is our bible re replacement crews for '29s. *(2)* Get copy to 19th Bomb Wing thru Twentieth Air Force. *(3)* When you attend the O'Donnell-Power conference in Hawaii, do not vary from this. *(4)* New crews must arrive prior to departure of ours. G.E.S.

At 1200 hours went over to GHQ Officers' Club and received the Honor Scroll for 1951 for the March of Dimes Campaign from Mrs. Douglas MacArthur.

Colonel Clinton W. Davies[78] had dinner with us at 1900 hours, Mayeda House.

SATURDAY 13 JANUARY 1951 — *Fol signal rcvd from JCS, personal for General MacArthur, #JCS 80925, dtd 12 Jan:*

General Vandenberg and General Collins, Major General Landon USAF, Brigadier General Gaither, USA, Colonel Hutchinson, USA, Colonel McHugh, USAF, Lt. Colonel Larsen, USA and CWO Davis, USA, will arrive Haneda AFB in Constellation AF plane 8610, Hanson, Pilot, at 140630/Z (141503I).[79] No release of this information is to be made until after arrival.

General Vandenberg will stay with me at Mayeda House; General Landon will stay with the Craigies.

At 1500, with The Honorable Kim Yong-joo, Minister, Chief of the Korean Diplomatic Mission in Japan reading the citation in Korean, and Major General Kim Chung Yul translating it into English, I was awarded the Republic of Korea ORDER OF MILITARY MERIT WITH GOLD STAR. Those in attendance, visiting dignitaries of ROK Air Force (see diary entry of 10 January), Minister Kim, his aide, and various and sundry members of the press, television, and news photographers. Also present were my AG (Colonel Toro) and my PIO (General Nuckols).

After the presentation, General Kim presented me with five figure drawings (Korean) entitled "Parade of Fashions."

The citation presented reads as follows:

CITATION In recognition and appreciation of his distinguished leadership, courage, and unyielding determination in the face of heavy odds, I take great pleasure, in accordance with the powers delegated to me by the Constitution of the Republic of Korea, in awarding the ORDER OF MILITARY MERIT WITH GOLD STAR to LIEUTENANT GENERAL GEORGE E. STRATEMEYER, 5A, UNITED STATES AIR FORCE. GENERAL

---

78. Davies had led the 18th FBW and now commanded the 6200th ABW at Clark AB.
79. Maj Gen Truman H. Landon commanded the VII Bomber Command in World War II, and was now Director of Plans, Headquarters USAF; Brig Gen Ridgely Gaither saw action with the 17th Airborne Division in World War II, and was Chief of the Operations Division, G-3, U.S. Army. Hutchinson and Davis are unknown.

General Stratemeyer receives the Republic of Korea Order of Military Merit with Gold Star from Kim Yong-joo, Chief of the Korean Diplomatic Mission in Japan. Maj. Gen. Otto P. Weyland observes the ceremony.

STRATEMEYER distinguished himself by exceptionally meritorious performance of service to the Republic of Korea during the period June 25, 1950 to date. At the outbreak of hostilities, General Stratemeyer established a 24-hour per day air defense of the area of South Korea, and strengthened the existing air defense system for the Far East. He constantly initiated both strategic and tactical air attacks against the aggressors and took the necessary steps to provide for logistical support of air combat units. Under General Stratemeyer's able direction the Far East Air Forces launched and maintained an air offensive that inflicted heavy casualties on the enemy, destroyed great quantities of war materiel and wiped out the military industries engaged in production of war materiel. General Stratemeyer's tactical and strategic concepts and the skill with which he employed the power of the Far East Air Forces were of immeasurable value in stopping the larger enemy forces. He welded into a cohesive striking force the United Nations' air forces which was composed of the United States Air Force, the land-based elements of United States Marine Aviation, the Republic of Korea Air Force, the Royal Australian Air Force, the South African Air Force, and the Royal Hellenic Air Force, and continually directed his units in successful air support of the Pusan perimeter and the subsequent offensive which pushed the enemy to the northern-most boundaries of Korea. Through his outstanding ability and great devotion to duty, General Stratemeyer has made a magnificent contribution to the Republic of Korea, and has brought extraordinary credit upon himself, the Far East Air Forces, the Far East Command, and the United Nations. Signed and sealed - Syngman Rhee, Seoul, December 25, 1950.

Received the fol ltr from Brigadier General G. B. Barth,[80] CG of artillery, 25th Infantry Division, copies of which I had made, and sent with covering letters to Generals Vandenberg and Partridge, and Dr. Stearns.* Also replied to General Barth with an expression of appreciation for his taking the time to write me.

---

80. Brig Gen George B. Barth had been the division's artillery commander since July 1950. Originally intended only to be a temporary replacement for the commander then on leave in the United States, Barth remained with the division until June 1951.

*Ltrs dispatched under date 14 January 1951.

His letter follows:

Dear General Stratemeyer. Thanks for your very fine Christmas letter. I agree that it meant much more than had you sent a card. In the past months we have often marveled at the air support given us by your P–51s and F–80s. Without it I am convinced that we could not have held the Pusan beachhead in the early days. During the breakout the devastating effects of air attack on both personnel and enemy materiel were very evident. At one time during the Chinju offensive in early August the timely support of two flights of yours saved from complete destruction four of my batteries that had been cut off. It is a pity that the pilots who fly these missions remain anonymous to us. I wish there was some way our men could meet them after action. Much thus could be done to establish a spirit of comradeship and appreciation between the air and ground arms of our fighting team. Even though this meeting is not feasible, I know, first hand, that our men appreciate the efforts of your flyers and are enthusiastic in their praise of the quality and quantity of the air support we have received. The strides made in perfecting the technique of the TAC parties have been remarkable. Much of our success has been due to the efforts of Major James F. Sprinkle. Don't take him away from us now because we need him badly but after this war his knowledge should be invaluable to the Air Force in dealing with the vital problems of tactical air support. Thanks again for your letter. Best regards to Mrs. Stratemeyer. s/G. B. Barth.

SUNDAY 14 JANUARY 1951

Turned over to my Adjutant General (Colonel Toro) the award presented to me by the Republic of Korea, signed by Syngman Rhee, President. The regulations require that this be sent to the Air Force for approval for wear. Acceptance must also be obtained from the State Department and Congress. Colonel Toro is taking necessary action.

General Barcus dropped in at 1100 hours to say goodbye and to comment a bit on the report that he will submit to the Chief of Staff, United States Air Force. He stated that, overall, his report would show that the Far East Air Forces from the very beginning have performed superbly and efficiently.

At my request for some of the deficiencies he found, he gave me the following and I have instructed both the Vice Commander for Administration and Plans and Vice Commander for Operations to take the necessary corrective action re these items wherever possible.

General Barcus stated that Colonel Gil Meyers is doing a fine job and is a very fine officer, but a weakness of his is that he retains too much control over the fighters operating for him. General Barcus feels that more targets could be hit if more airplanes could be turned over to the TACPs.

General Barcus also indicated that Colonel Meyers has always had difficulty getting along with the communications officer, and this was true in the Fifth Air Force - first with Colonel Lee and then with Colonel Wagner. He does not know how he (Colonel Meyers) will get along with Colonel Coleman, inasmuch as Coleman has been there for such a short time.

General Barcus believes that the tactical air control parties should be organized into a squadron - which squadron would become a part of the tactical air
control group - as there is now no real command channel for the tactical air
control parties.

General Barcus feels that the pilots detailed to head up the tactical air control parties should remain in their positions longer than three weeks. He stated
that the reason the Marine tactical air control parties were better than ours was
that the Marines usually stayed on this job for at least a year, and further, Marine
radio (ARC-1) was better than that which we used as you could receive as well
as transmit at the same time.

General Barcus stated that upon his return to the ZI he intended to concentrate
on better equipment and a system of training for the tactical air control parties.

I have transmitted to my two vice commanders a copy of this diary entry for
their information and such corrective action as they deem necessary - which can
be accomplished here in FEAF.

General Barcus promised as soon as his report is completed (which will be
around 10 February) that he would send a copy direct to me. This would not
include, however, all the annexes, but would be in narrative form containing a
summary of the conclusions and recommendations.

1000 hours, General Kim (C/S, ROK Air Force) and his group departed
Haneda for Korea.

1200 hours, General Barcus came out to the house for lunch.

1500 hours, Mr. Frank Coniff (INS) with General Nuckols in attendance
dropped by the office. Had a conference with Coniff that lasted about one hour
and talked with him about many things - much of which was off the record. I had
been assured by General Nuckols that everything I said was safe to say to Mr.
Coniff, as General Nuckols indicated that he was one of the best friends we had
in the American press. Mr. Coniff is one of William Randolph Hearst's outstanding
writers and reporters.

Met General Vandenberg at Haneda at 1930 hours. (Those arriving also:
General Collins, USAF, Major General Landon, USAF, Brig. General Gaither,
USA, Col. Hutchinson, USA, Colonel McHugh, USAF, Lt. Col. Larsen, USA
and a CWO Davis, USA, in Constellation AF plane 8610, Hanson, pilot.) Took
him out to the house for light refreshments and then proceeded direct to the
GHQ, FEC Chief of Staff's conference room where we met with General
MacArthur and his senior staff along with General Collins and Admiral Joy.
Generals Craigie and Landon were also present as were General Smith (CIA) and
General Ackerman - the latter two having landed one hour after General
Vandenberg. (Gen Bolling also arrived with CIA Gp.)[81]

The conference lasted until 2330 hours. Went to bed about 0050 hours, 15 Jan.

---

81. Gen Walter Bedell Smith had been Eisenhower's chief of staff during World War II. From Feb. 1946 to Mar.
1949, he was Ambassador to the Soviet Union. After a tour as commanding general of the First Army, he
became Director, CIA, a position he held from Oct. 1950 to Jan. 1953, when he became Under Secretary of
State. Brig Gen John B. Ackerman, a weather officer in World War II, became Chief, Collection Division,
Directorate of Intelligence, USAF, on Dec. 18, 1950. He later held positions with the National Security
Agency and the CIA. Maj Gen Alexander R. Bolling led the 84th Infantry Division in combat during World
War II. In Dec. 1947, he became Deputy Director of Intelligence, U.S. Army, then was Deputy Assistant
Chief of Staff for Intelligence, General Staff of the Army, and in Aug. 1950, became Assistant Chief Of Staff,
Intelligence, U.S. Army.

During the conference with General MacArthur, even after the arrival of the two [members of the] Joint Chiefs of Staff, there was great confusion in everyone's mind - particularly General MacArthur's as to just what directive and mission he had received. To the majority present, except the two [members of the] Joint Chiefs of Staff, a dual mission had been given to General MacArthur which was impossible to carry out.[82]

After much discussion, particularly by the Boss, his mission was clarified and the two Joint Chiefs promised that he would get a clear-cut mission and that where any risks were involved, they as Joint Chiefs, and General MacArthur's superiors, would take full responsibility and not leave it up in the air as presently worded.

At one time during the discussion, I put in my nickle's worth to the fact that even though understrength, I certainly recommended four National Guard divisions be called to active duty and be dispatched here if only for training and recommended that three National Guard fighter groups be sent out here for the defense of Japan. However, I was informed by General Vandenberg that they just did not exist. He stated that he didn't have sufficient fighters to defend his bases in Europe, and to my great surprise, he informed me that the best the British had was about four squadrons of fighters. He further indicated that I had here in the Far East, except for SAC, the fighting units of the United States Air Force.[83]

Personally, I think this is a hell of a state of affairs.

Of course, every effort in the world is being put to remedy this condition and, as stated by General Vandenberg, if we have time, it will be remedied.

It was decided to leave tomorrow for Korea at 1000 hours.

MONDAY 15 JANUARY 1951

General Vandenberg arrived at the office at 0825 hours. He attended the FEAF briefing at 0830 hours.

Major General Lowe, the President's adviser, also stopped by the office enroute to the FEAF Briefing.

With General Vandenberg, after the briefing, departed at 0940 the office for Haneda.

Flew direct to Taegu (accompanied by General Landon and Colonel McHugh) where we were met by General Partridge, and, after a short visit with Colonels

---

82. On Jan. 9, the JCS informed MacArthur that he was to contain the fighting to Korea and defend successive positions while inflicting the greatest possible damage on the attackers. He was also to withdraw from Korea if an evacuation was absolutely necessary to save his men and materiel. The JCS saw the second task as naturally following the first, but MacArthur chose to view them as two incompatible tasks that could not be carried on simultaneously. Thus, Collins and Vandenberg came to Japan to set MacArthur straight. (Schnabel, pp 320-325; "History of the JCS," Vol. III, pp 408-415.)

Because MacArthur claimed that his troops were suffering a serious morale problem, Collins and Vandenberg also travelled to Korea to personally inspect the troops. They found few indications of low morale and, in retrospect, it is obvious that it was not the troops but MacArthur that had the low morale.

83. The Army and the Air Force had been reluctant to mobilize the reserve components in the summer of 1950, in part because it was believed that the fighting in Korea was just a feint and that the reserve forces would be needed elsewhere. Voluntary recalls were tried but proved ineffective, and it soon became apparent that neither service could attain its ambitious augmentation goals without mobilizing reservists and guardsmen. In August 1950, the Air Force began recalling its own reserve units to active duty. When the Air Force obtained approval for a permanent expansion of its force structure in September 1950, select Air Guard units were notified that they would be mobilized in October as a short-term measure. However, the entry of the CCF into the war turned that limited action into a long-term policy response.

Korea was the Air Guard's first war. Overall, some 45,000 guardsmen, approximately 80 percent of the Air Guard's total strength, were placed on active duty during the war. Two of the Air Guard's fighter wings, the 27th FEW and the 136th FBW, served in combat in Korea, while three more wings were assigned to NATO. Other guardsmen served with regular Air Force units in Korea. The remaining 17 Air Guard wings activated

Packard and Murphy[84] (the 27th and 49th jet group commanders), we proceeded in a C–47 to K-9 and met Colonel Gray and Lt. Col. Jack Dale. Went over their problems, talked with a number of pilots, including the Marines and the 77th RAAF, and then proceeded to K-10 where we were met by Colonel Low, wing commander of the 18th Fighter Wing and Commandant Theron, the South African squadron commander. Inspected the base and talked with pilots and officers of the two units, then departed and returned to K-2 where we proceeded immediately to General Partridge's headquarters and attended the briefing. Had dinner with General Partridge. Plans were made for General Vandenberg's trip about the front on 16 January.

TUESDAY 16 JANUARY 1951

We took off early on 16 January and flew direct to the Hwach'ŏn Reservoir [just north of the 38th Parallel], circled the reservoir at low altitude and could see not a single soul. The size of the dam and the uselessness of normal bombing were very apparent. From there we proceeded direct to the advance C–47 strip in front of the 2d Division, landed there and then Generals Vandenberg and Landon and I proceeded by helicopter, piloted by 1st Lt. Barnes, USAF, forward just short of Wŏnju where there was a patrol accompanied by a TACP under the command of Lt. Smith, USAF.[85] We had difficulty finding the forward patrol, so landed at the 9th Regiment command post and was met there by Colonel Messinger,[86] the regimental commander. He stated that he could take us forward to the patrol - which he did. We had to leave General Landon behind.

We landed forward of the patrol and there with Lt. Smith, our TACP commander (who is a pilot from the 49th Fighter Group), listened to his directions to a Mosquito and saw a Mosquito over the hill searching desperately to find the Red Chinese. While we were there, he could locate none.

We then returned to the regimental command post and picked up General Landon, and thence back to the C–47 strip, and thence flew back to K-2.

From here we transferred to the FEAF B–17 and flew direct to Brady Air Force Base where we were met by General Henebry. Had a short talk with him, took a look at the base, and then proceeded to Iwakuni where we were met by Colonel Zoller and his staff; listened to his briefing of the officers for the night missions which was conducted by Major C. C. Hill, my former pilot. General Vandenberg appeared to be extremely well pleased what what he saw - and with the operations of the 3d Bomb Wing.

From there we proceeded to Miho where we met General Sweetser and were given a very hurried trip about the post, General Sweetser talking continuously, explaining his job, the condition of his troops and equipment, and giving us some of the problems faced by the Air Force Reserves. Here, again, General Vandenberg appeared pleased with what he saw.[87]

---

helped the Air Force build up its forces in the continental United States. Unfortunately, because the Air Guard units had been so poorly trained and equipped prior to mobilization, it took many months to prepare them for their active duty responsibilities. (Charles Joseph Gross, *Prelude to the Total Force: The Air National Guard 1943-1969* [Washington, 1985], pp 58-89; "History of the JCS," Vol. III, p 433.)

84. Col John R.Murphy had been the first director of the JOC and had helped organize the tactical air control system in Korea.

85. Lts Barnes and Smith are unidentified.

86. Col Edwin J. Messinger became the 9th's commander in November 1950.

87. Brady AB, then the home of the 437th TCW, was in northern Kyushu. Zoller's 3d BW was based at Iwakuni, in southern Honshu. At Miho, near the city of Matsue, was Sweetser's 452d BG.

*General Vandenberg confers with Maj Gen. William H. Tunner, the FEAF
Combat Cargo Command leader, and Brig. Gen. John P. Henebry, commander
of the 437th TCW.*

From there we took off and proceeded direct to Haneda where we landed
about 2000 hours, went direct to Mayeda House where we bathed and had
dinner. Along with General Vandenberg, General Weyland was our guest.

**WEDNESDAY
17 JANUARY
1951**
_____

Departed Mayeda House for Haneda where we traveled by
air to Johnson Air Force Base and met Colonels Moe Smith[88]
and Johnny Meyer as well as the base commander, Colonel
Clark.[89] Here again, General Vandenberg devoted practically
all his time talking to Johnny Meyer and Colonel Smith and his pilots. We made
a quick trip about the base and proceeded by car to Yokota where we were met by
General Briggs, FEAF bomber commander, his staff and the base commander.
Here again, General Vandenberg had discussions and conference with General
Briggs and his staff, and, after a quick run about the base, noting particularly the
60 steel mat dispersals, we proceeded by car to Tachikawa where we were met by
Colonel Crawford, 314th Wing commander and his executive, Colonel Bott.[90]

Took a quick run about the base. General Vandenberg had a discussion with
Colonel Crawford at which I was not present.

---

88. Col George F. Smith brought the 4th FIW overseas and served as its CO until May 31, 1951.
89. Col Donald L. Clark, former commander of the 3d BW.
90. Stratemeyer probably means the 314th Air Division. Col Troy W. Crawford commanded the 374th TCW, and
    Col Herbert A. Bott led the 374th TCG.

We then proceeded to FEAMCOM where we were met by General Doyle, and while we waited there, due to the time limitations on General Vandenberg, General Doyle took him (Vandenberg) on a quick turn about the post, giving him a good insight into his operations.

We then boarded FEAF staff B–17 and proceeded to Haneda and thence to my headquarters, and thence to the University Club for lunch - Generals Craigie and Weyland being hosts. Besides General Vandenberg, all my senior staff officers were present.

After lunch, General Vandenberg was taken on a shopping tour to Takashimaya.

After shopping, we then proceeded to General MacArthur's conference room, arriving there at 1530. This was the Joint Chiefs' final conference with General MacArthur. Besides the Joint Chiefs (Vandenberg and Collins) and General MacArthur, there were present Admiral Joy, myself, and the senior staff officers in the Far East Command.

Both Generals Vandenberg and Collins gave their reactions to their trip. General Vandenberg praised the Air Force as did General MacArthur. General MacArthur's great statement was "the magnificent performance of the new, tried veteran Far East Air Forces."

General Collins read a long signal that he had dispatched to General Bradley, Chairman of the Joint Chiefs. It was accepted.

Other decisions of minor nature were made by General MacArthur.

The meeting broke up a little after 1700 hours.

General Vandenberg and I then returned to my headquarters to the Allied Council chambers, accompanied by General Nuckols, where General Vandenberg made a superb presentation to the Tokyo correspondents. Many questions were asked, some of which were most embarrassing, but at no time were they embarrassing to General Vandenberg.

His answers, to my mind, were masterful.

After the press conference, General Vandenberg held a meeting with our senior WAF staff officer, Major Deitz.[91]

After that we proceeded to General Craigie's for hurried cocktails, and thence to Mayeda House where we freshened up and had dinner.

Guests being General Landon, General Collins, General Vandenberg, General Craigie and Colonel McHugh.

General Vandenberg and his party, along with General Collins, departed Haneda Air Force Base at 2200 hours.

General Weyland gave several folders to General Vandenberg answering certain questions which he had raised during his visit to FEAF hqrs. *(1)* Information on the employment and status of aircraft flares used in conjunction with night B–26 operations. *(2)* Information concerning the status of helicopter operations in Korea and making recommendations for helicopter augmentation in the form of an organized helicopter squadron for rescue and evacuation purposes. *(3)* Information on the vulnerability of North Korean reservoirs, dams and power facilities. The study indicated that the largest bombs available are not powerful enough to breach these dams.

---

91. Maj Virginia C. Dietz, Administrative Assistant and Chief of Administration, Directorate of Maintenance, FEAF.

In addition the latest FEAF sortie chart for the period November 16 thru December 31 was given to General Vandenberg. This chart shows comparative Navy and Marine Corps sorties also.

THURSDAY 18 JANUARY 1951

0810 hours Partridge called. Among other things we discussed was how obviously gratified General Vandenberg was on what he had seen and also, because it was good news, recounted to Partridge how at lunch yesterday everyone of my staff, including myself, felt about a "third star" for him (Partridge).

Got off a memo to D/Personnel that Colonel Wilson had submitted a letter, coming thru channels, reference the rotation of people between Fifth Air Force and Clark Field. Referred D/P to my R&R same subject, dtd 30 Dec 50. Told him "when this letter arrives and you prepare a draft of our forwarding indorsement, make it for my signature."

To VC, A&P:

There has grown up within the FEAF bases, or it has been ordered by Hq USAF, that when VIP land or take-off from our airdromes, that the fire trucks be out near the landing strip; to escort the VIP into the parking area - or to escort the VIP out from the parking area to the position of warm up. I want this discontinued and if there are any such orders from Hq USAF, I want a letter prepared for my signature requesting that the orders be cancelled - this per General Vandenberg's personal instructions to me on 16 Jan.

Dispatched a ltr of commendation thru General Partridge to Major Leo G. Fradenburg,[92] USAF, Fifth AF Flight Section, and the crew that flew us in the C–47 to the front lines. Told him that CSAF was impressed by his actions and efficiency, to which I added my appreciation for his job that had been well done.

Dispatched the fol memo to General Tunner:

At the suggestion of General Vandenberg, I think it would be to the Air Force's advantage to have a sign placed inside our MATS airplanes - particularly when we bring back for rest in Tokyo the men of the Eighth Army - read somewhat as follows: "The United States Air Force takes great pleasure in providing this air transportation in order that you may enjoy recreational leave in the Tokyo area."
NEW SUBJECT. In the future, it is desired that when requests are made for the use of individual airplanes by Eighth Army commanders and senior Eighth Army staff officers, that such requests be referred to General Partridge or his headquarters for action. I do not repeat not want you to assign any Combat Cargo Command aircraft for the use of individuals outside of your command - except upon General Partridge's request. My reason for feeling so strongly on this subject is, as you may be aware, there are Army commanders who believe operational control of aircraft in the Army areas should be under the Army or Corps commanders.

---

92. Fradenburg was Chief, 5th AF Headquarters Flight Section.

A fine relationship exists between the Commanding General, Eighth Army, and the Commanding General, Fifth Air Force, and I want all of our actions to strengthen that relationship. Therefore, requests for the use of United States Air Force airplanes should be made by General Ridgway to General Partridge. Also, I call your attention to the fact that the Army through the corps down to the divisions have assigned to them L–5s and L–17s for the command's use and use by their staff.

s/G.E.S.

Dispatched a copy of above memo to General Partridge.

Wrote a ltr of thanks to Colonel Edwin J. Messinger, the CO of the 9th Regiment, for taking care of us so capably on 16 January.

Directed my Director, Plans (Colonel Zimmerman) to prepare a letter for my signature as instructed in the fol quoted R&R:

Recently while in Korea and in conversation with Lt. General Matthew B. Ridgway, he made this request: "I would appreciate very much your letting me know how much air support I could expect from our Air Forces in support of the Eighth Army if the Russians came into the war."

I desire that a letter be prepared for my signature to General Ridgway (after a bit of study) which will contain, generally, the following:

1. We could continue to support you all-out and therefore attrite our Air Forces to zero, taking punishment from the Russian Air Force which would result in great casualties for you by the Russian Air Force - and maybe your destruction. If I did this, I'm sure I would be relieved of command of FEAF.
2. We could immediately take on the Russian Air Force all-out, leaving you with very little air support but thereby preventing attacks on your command by the Russian Air Force.
3. We could, dependent upon the situation, go after the Russian Air Force and, at the same time, give to you that air support which at times we could make available.

We would do number three. s/G.E.S.

Received the following signal (Stratline personal from Partridge):

Subject is conversations Ridgway, Smith, Willoughby and Timberlake this date. Ted was requested to present to Smith our requirement for Escape and Evasion program. This was done and Willoughby entered talks to present his side of picture. His repeated statements demonstrated lack of familiarity with details of program. For example he said Parkerton[93] had overall responsibility for project. Charles also named as top man in Korea someone unknown to Timberlake. After listening to Willoughby for some time, Smith appeared to agree that centralized program was needed. He indicated that his Agency would exercise overall direction over the activity and that he would work out details tomorrow. Ted was embarrassed by mis-statements of Willoughby but confined himself to expression of view that difference of opinion existed and that end product

93. Parkerton is unknown.

was nonexistent. Ted expressed my views exactly. Should there be the slightest criticism of his action, I want you to make it clear that he said rather mildly what I would have said had I been present. NEW SUBJECT. Milburn's promotion was approved long ago and will be announced tomorrow.

In answer to the above signal, got off a letter to Partridge - as follows:

Your Stratline of 17 January to me reference the conversations with Smith, and Willoughby by Timberlake received. I am in entire sympathy with your statements and, as a result of my conversations this noon, there could not possibly be the slightest criticism of Ted Timberlake's actions. A last conference was held this morning and all details reference the utilization of CIA have been resolved.

I heard immediately upon my return about Milburn's promotion having been approved ahead of the two that were publicized while we were in Korea.

I can assure you, Earle, that Vandenberg was pleased with everything that he found at every station where he visited and commented most favorably on the fine job that you are doing with the Fifth Air Force.

He also commented favorably on FEAF Bomber Command, Combat Cargo Command, and FEAMCOM - all of which pleased me very, very much.

Thanks for your fine hospitality while we were with you and best regards as always. s/G.E.S.

Had lunch with Banfill and Ackerman. One of the subjects mentioned during lunch was the Earl of Bandon[94] and his being an Air Commodore.

Upon my return to the office, sent a letter to Jack Slessor (Marshal of the Royal Air Force Sir John C.) commending Paddy Bandon for the work he did for me, and just putting in a general plug for him which might be of some assistance to him when the RAF selection board meets re appointments to Air Vice Marshal.

Sent a copy of the above ltr to Paddy Bandon with a personal note enclosing same.

General Tunner checked in at the office. While he was here I emphasized to him the letter I wrote him this AM re airplanes for senior Army individuals would be referred to General Partridge or General Ridgway for decision. He (Tunner) would not furnish aircraft at their individual request.

**FRIDAY
19 JANUARY
1951**

I approved this date the study - "Distribution of the Defense Dollar" (see my directive to Director, Plans, Col Zimmerman, dtd 5 Jan 51), and forwarded same with personal letter to General Vandenberg. All papers in conjunction thereto placed in the office of my Director of Plans for safekeeping.

5:45, Mrs. Strat and I were guests of Lt. General Sir H.C.H. Robertson at cocktails, honoring Joe and Laurna Gascoigne.

---

94. The Fifth Earl of Bandon, Percy Ronald Gardner Bernard, served in Southeast Asia during World War II as AOC of No. 224 Group. After serving from 1961-1963 as Commander, Allied Air Forces, Central Europe, he retired as an Air Chief Marshal.

SATURDAY
20 JANUARY
1951

1500 hours spent about an hour in the dentist's chair. Earlier in the day, met with (in my office) Drs. Williams and Schramm,[95] and another long-hair professor. We discussed psychological warfare and they were reasonably sure that the results of their visit to FEAF are going to pay dividends. They were greatly disturbed though because no one in the highest level in the government was really concentrating on and controlling psychological warfare. I agreed with them 100% and stated that it should be somebody top-side who had a huge stick and used it as Teddy Roosevelt did when he was president. They indicated that they had the very best of cooperation and assistance from all personnel in FEAF.

SUNDAY
21 JANUARY
1951

Read the fol signal, which was received this AM at briefing. The signal quoted the President as underscoring the need for security, and deplored the recent disclosures by individuals of classified material to the press, etc. He also desired that steps be taken to plug any such leaks. USAF, at the end of the President's quoted message stated that "implementing instructions will follow."

As per my directive to Plans (see diary date 18 Jan 51), the following letter was submitted. After making a few revisions, dispatched the fol ltr to General Ridgway:

Dear Matt: *(1)* During my recent visit to Korea while at Partridge's briefing on 15 January 1951 you requested information on the extent of air support the Eighth Army could expect from the Far East Air Forces in the event Russia entered the war. *(2)* There are several possible courses of action. *a.* Continue our present all-out support which would leave the initiative in the air to the enemy, and would probably result in our complete attrition by the Russian Air Force and subsequent great casualties in your command. If I did this, I am sure I would be relieved of command of FEAF. *b.* Attack the Russian Air Force and furnish no support to you which would expose your forces to attrition by numerically superior forces on the ground. *c.* Current CINCFE plans covering the initial phase of a general emergency require FEAF to initiate the maximum practicable air offensive against Soviet controlled air power. Our present plans envisage the maintenance of an adequate air defense in our areas of operation, the mounting of a counter-air offensive against the Russian Air Force, and the providing of direct ground support consistent with requirements and availability. *(3)* Our present maximum rate of tactical air support of your forces will consequently be greatly reduced. However, we will provide you air defense, essential direct air support, and airlift in consonance with requirements and availability. *(4)* Tentative allocations of atomic weapons for employment in retardation of the advance of Soviet forces in the Far East presage attainment of our objectives far earlier than previously expected. *(5)* I assure you, Matt, that you will have

---

95. Dr Frederick Williams was assistant director of the Air University Far East Research Group in Human Resources and head of the Psychological Warfare Research Team. Dr Wilbur Schramm was a member of the latter group. The team was studying propaganda and counterpropaganda techniques and the vulnerability of certain targets to psywar operations.

the requisite air support from our air forces in furtherance of our common mission. Sincerely, s/G.E.S. etc.

1100 hours I pinned the first cluster to the DFC on Colonel Dixon,[96] commander of our RF–80 recon sq, and the DFC on Captain Monaghan.[97] These DFC's were given for extraordinary flight over enemy territory on a special mission for FEAF and CINCFE.

Left the office before noon in order to be out at the golf course by 1230 hours. It was a dusty, dirty, windy day and I almost froze to death on the 17th and 18th holes. My partner was a Mr. Abraham, FEAMCOM, and our opponents were Lt. Stat and Capt. Graham, both of FEAF Hq & Sv Sq.[98]

MONDAY
22 JANUARY
1951

Dispatched the fol signal to Partridge:

Would like to have you consider General Sweetser taking over command of 315th Air Division (Combat Cargo) and General Henebry taking over command of 452d Bombardment Wing (L). It is my opinion that better utilization of services of two officers named would result from such assignments. Let me know your reaction after meeting Wednesday, 24 January.

1430 hours presented the award of Bronze Star to my senior aide, Major Joseph C. E. Paradis, for his exemplary service to me and my command.

General Weyland sent me the fol memo, which I quote in toto:
22 Jan 51, Memorandum for: General Stratemeyer, Subject: Enemy
Casualties.

I believe you will be interested to know that at the GHQ briefing today, General Wright, G-3 GHQ, commented at some length on this subject. He stated that he felt G-3 and G-2 had the best opportunity, through their intimate knowledge of friendly and enemy action, to evaluate the punishment being inflicted on the enemy by UN forces.
He stated that considering the size of enemy forces involved in see-saw action around Wŏnju, the air effort (FEAF and Navy) applied, and the enemy dead counted on the ground in that area, and further applying those factors to the entire front, that in his opinion about 3,000 enemy ground troops were being killed daily by air action, and about 250 were being killed daily by ground force action.
When questioned, he further stated that the 3,000 daily casualties from air action were only those sighted along the front in the open, and did not include the enemy casualties sustained in fighter and light bomber attacks on buildings, or the casualties caused by B–29 attacks on troop concentrations in towns. s/O.P. Weyland, etc.

General Pee,[99] who is the Chinese Military Attache in Washington, called on me at 1030 hours. We had a nice visit talking about our many, many mutual friends.

---

96. Lt Col Jacob W. Dixon, 8th TRS commanding officer.
97. Capt James D. Monaghan.
98. None of these individuals has been identified.
99. Gen Peter T.K. Pee.

1500 hours, Mr. L.L. Brabham, who is the Director of Republic Aviation Corporation's Military Requirements, came in to see me. We had a very fine discussion on the F–84 and the general topic of jet aircraft.

1900 hours, Major General Robert McClure came to dinner at the house.

**TUESDAY
23 JANUARY
1951**

Immediately upon receipt of the news of the aerial victory of the F–84Es over the MiGs, dispatched to Partridge, the fol:

Stratline Personal Partridge from Stratemeyer. Congratulations to you and the 27th Fighter Wing on your great aerial victory over MiGs this date. Will inform Vandenberg and MacArthur.[100]

Later on in the day, when figures were substantiated, sent the following memo to General MacArthur:

This morning, 34 F–84Es met in aerial combat over Korea with 18 to 28 MiG 15s. Results: 5 MiGs destroyed, 2 probably destroyed, and other (number unknown at this time) were damaged. All F–84Es returned to base with no damage. I have advised Vandenberg and congratulated Partridge and the 27th Fighter Wing. s/G.E.S.

*My operational immediate "nickle" to Vandenberg contained above figures and info. Also send an info cy of this rad to LeMay.

Direct quote of radio:

Personal Vandenberg from Stratemeyer, information LeMay. 34 F–84Es met with 18 to 28 MiG–15s this morning. Results: 5 MiGs destroyed, 2 probably destroyed, and others (number unknown at this time) were damaged. There was no damage to our F–84s.

At 0945 hours, Generals Ho and Ho Ying-chin[101] called on me and we discussed conditions in Korea and in China proper.

7:45 P.M. Gave a dinner party in honor of Joe and Laurna Gascoigne.

**WEDNESDAY
24 JANUARY
1951**

Received the fol ltr from Major General Kim Chung Yul, C/S, Korean Air Force, dtd 17 Jan 51:

I wish to extend my appreciation to you on behalf of my staff for having made our visit to Japan exceedingly pleasant and of great interest. We gained much in increasing our knowledge and understanding inasmuch as the functions of air support installations and operations are concerned. I am certain that by understanding both the operations of air support and tactical organizations, it will be of great assistance to us in the improvement of our own air force.

---

100. Eight F–84 strafers (with a top cover of 25 more F–84s) struck the Sinŭiju airfield in a surprise attack. The MiGs, based across the Yalu at Antung, were tardy in taking off. A 30-minute fight between the 33 F–84s and about 30 MiG–15s ensued, with most of the action taking place below 20,000 feet, an advantage for the F–84s. Two MiGs were downed by Lt Jacob Kratt, while another two enemy planes fell to the other F–84s. Three more MiGs were claimed as probables and four as damaged. All of the F–84s returned safely. (Futrell, p 288.)

101. Ho Ying-chin, Chief of the Chinese Military Mission to the U.S.

I must also mention that I have received the photographs and the newspaper you sent, and am deeply gratified to have received them. I must thank you again for the great honor bestowed upon me through your presentation of the Legion of Merit.

We are most grateful for the gracious hospitality shown us, and hope that we may have the opportunity of your favors by being your hosts when you visit Korea again. s/Kim Chung Yul, etc.

8:30, dinner, honoring the Gascoignes; hosts: Senor and Senora del Castillo, at the Spanish Mission.

THURSDAY
25 JANUARY
1951

1st Lt G.M. Edwards called as requested, at 0930 hours. I had his status looked into by my Deputy for Personnel and find that he is due for transfer rotation to Johnson Air Force Base from K-9, Korea. He seems to be a nice youngster.

At 1730 hours, I approved our plan for the utilization of FEAF aircraft in case Russia comes into the war. It appears that the Navy will do nothing but get their carriers out of range of any Russian land-based aircraft.

Our plan is still to be coordinated before final signature with GHQ staff.

FRIDAY
26 JANUARY
1951

Dispatched the fol personal letter to General MacArthur:

Dear General MacArthur. This brief personal note is sent you today, 26 January 1951, to wish you a Happy Birthday and to convey, in some measure, not only my personal heartfelt greetings to you, but also those of the Far East Air Forces.
I know that each of us realizes the great debt we owe you for your leadership and ability, for your wisdom and courage, to name just a few. In other words, you represent to us simply this - a symbol of everything that is America.
We all wish you many, many more Happy Birthdays and continued health and happiness to you and Mrs. MacArthur. Sincerely. s/G.E.S., etc.

In reply to my radnote of 22 January (re assignment of Sweetser and Henebry to suggested new slots), received a reply from Partridge which indicated, in his opinion - and which was concurred in by Tunner - that Henebry was a good choice for the 315th Air Division, and that Sweetser was a good choice for the 452d Bombardment Wing (L).

I went along with the above consensus of opinion, and so informed Partridge and Tunner.

7:15 P.M. Annalee and I went to the Craigies for dinner where we helped Craigie and Weyland celebrate their 49th birthdays.

(See quote of radio exchange between Stratemeyer and Vandenberg re: Sykes, Ferguson and Weyland, under date 30 Jan 51.)

SATURDAY
27 JANUARY
1951

At 0930 hours, Major General Barnes and Dr. Cook[102] came in and paid their respects and we had a nice visit. At 1400 hours, Mrs. Stratemeyer and I lunched with General and Mrs. MacArthur who honored the President's Ambassador-

---

102. Maj Gen Earl W. Barnes was the USAF representative to the WSEG at the Department of Defense. Dr. J. Emory Cook was a WSEG member.

at-Large, Mr. Dulles and his party. Mr. Dulles' party includes Mrs. Dulles, Mr. John M. Allison, Political Advisor (Deputy to Mr. Dulles), Mr. Earl D. Johnson (Ass't Secretary of the Army) and Mrs. Johnson, Major General Carter B. Magruder, Colonel C. Stanton Babcock, Mr. John D. Rockefeller, III, and Mrs. Rockefeller, Miss Doris A. Doyle, and Mr. Robert A. Fearey (State Department and former assistant to Ambassador Grew).[103]

SUNDAY 28 JANUARY 1951

Departed Haneda 0805 hours and flew with General MacArthur aboard SCAP, and accompanying him were Generals Hickey, Whitney, Colonel Canada (his surgeon), a Signal Corps photographer whose name I did not know and his three, long standby correspondent hands - Russell Brines (Associated Press), Howard Handleman (INS), and Earnest Hoberecht (United Press).

Arrived at Suwŏn at 1130 hours where we were greeted by Generals Ridgway and Timberlake, and all of the senior commanders in that immediate area, including Generals Milburn, Van Brunt,[104] Kean, and the British Brigade commander and the Turkish Brigade commander. We immediately proceeded to the CP of the 35th Infantry where General MacArthur learned that the commanding officer, Lt. Colonel Kelleher,[105] had just received notice of his promotion to full colonel. General MacArthur pinned on Colonel Kelleher's eagles.

We were then briefed as to his front line situation, after which we proceeded to the front line by jeep - except for the last quarter mile (about). General MacArthur, Ridgway and another jeep with General Kean proceeded almost to the front lines. The rest of us were required to walk, which did us all a lot of good.

Upon arrival at the front, the enemy lines were pointed out; it was quiet and there were no air, artillery, nor infantry operations.

Stratemeyer, MacArthur, and Lt. Gen. Matthew B. Ridgway, the Eighth Army commander, meet at Suwŏn, January 28, 1951.

---

103. John Foster Dulles was in Japan to obtain the views of MacArthur and Japanese leaders regarding a Japanese peace treaty; an Air Transport Command pilot in World War II, Johnson had been Assistant Secretary of the Army since May 1950; Magruder formerly had been Deputy to the Under Secretary of the Army, and was now assigned to the Office for Occupied Areas, Office of the Secretary of the Army; Babcock was Chief, Government Branch under Magruder; Rockefeller was a special consultant to the Dulles Mission to Japan on Peace Settlement; Doyle was a secretary; Fearey was in the State Department's Office of Northeast Asian Affairs.

104. Brig Gen Rinaldo Van Brunt, I Corps chief of staff. He had held the same position in Milburn's XXI Corps in World War II.

105. Col Gerald C. Kelleher.

However, off to the left, we could hear both air and artillery in operation.

In walking back, as I passed General MacArthur's jeep, his expression was "My God, the commander of the Far East Air Forces is walking and the dough-boys are riding!" General Kean was a bit embarrassed and tried his best to get me to ride back, and I said, "I'll be damned if I will. Since I'm on foot, I will continue on foot."

Everyone enjoyed the exchange of remarks.

We then proceeded to the SCAP at Suwŏn, said goodby to Ridgway and his group, flew out over Inch'ŏn and Seoul, and generally along the front lines, and then direct back to Tokyo.

Arrived Haneda about 1600 hours.

Proceeded direct to the office and finished up some work and then went home.

MONDAY
29 JANUARY
1951

Annalee departed about 1000 hours for a trip of several days to Fuji View.

This evening had a delicious dinner with the Nuckols and a very delightful evening. I imbibed freely - premeditatively!

Earlier in the afternoon, got off my weekly Gill Robb Wilson letter.

TUESDAY
30 JANUARY
1951

Fol radio received by me on 26 Jan:

Personal [from Vandenberg] for Stratemeyer. Cite M 75895, dtd 12 Jan 51. Unable to return Colonel Ferguson or Sykes to duty your headquarters. Letter follows.

In reply to above, I dispatched fol:

Personal Vandenberg from Stratemeyer. Reurad AFCVC 53400. This contrary to our suggested arrangement for return of Weyland. My opinion is that possibly you had not seen above cited message. Sykes needed at this end too.

In the G-2, GHQ, FEC, INTELLIGENCE SUMMARY (Daily), under date of 30 Jan 51, #3065, on page 8, item 3 CONCLUSIONS (under PART IV, G-2 ESTIMATE OF THE SITUATION), in discussing the enemy's capabilities to defend *1)* Han River bridgehead, in view of the fact that 50th CCF Army being used as a covering force, and the enemy been forced into a defensive role, and as the depth of his defensive position south of the Han River is reduced by UN advances, the probability increases that the enemy finds it necessary to execute at least a limited withdrawal, and ... IF THIS BE CORRECT THE COMBAT EFFICIENCY OF THE ENEMY MAY BE ASSESSED AS DEFINITELY WANING. THE MOST PROBABLE CAUSES FOR SUCH A CONDITION CAN BE ATTRIBUTED TO A RISING RATE OF ATTRITION DUE TO HEAVY LOSSES FROM UN GROUND AND AIR ACTION, TO RAVAGE OF DISEASES, COLD WEATHER CASUALTIES, AND, <u>AS A VITAL BASIC CAUSE, TO HIS INABILITY TO LOGISTICALLY SUPPORT ANY OPERATIONS INVOLVING A LONG SUPPLY LINE WHICH CAN BE STRUCK BY AN AGGRESSIVE, EFFICIENT AIR FORCE</u>.

(The italics [*sic*] of quoted matter and underscoring are mine.)

1030 hours this morning in conference with General Tunner I approved his plan for turn-over to be effective by the end of February and further authorized him to depart around 12 February. He will submit a paper to me, Saturday, 3 February, giving in detail his "phase-out" - of himself and his temporary duty officers.

At 0800 hours, I was briefed by General Banfill and Colonel Gould[106] on the study that was sent to the Director of Intelligence, Washington, D.C., on the A bomb targets in the Far East. Every target selected by CINCFE and those selected by us were reviewed and complete data on each was submitted with our recommended list of targets.

At 1000 hours, had a conference with Major Virginia C. Deitz, WAF, and as a result, directed the Adjutant to get out an order appointing her FEAF Director of WAFs. I also instructed her shortly after the first of the month to make a trip to Okinawa, Guam and the Philippines as WAF director and see how the women of the Air Force were getting along. At this writing I have not heard from Vandenberg telling me of his change giving the senior WAF officer her principal MOS as Director of WAFs and a secondary MOS - an assignment in headquarters. This is the reverse of the present orders.

Left the office at noon; played golf and shot a lousy 95. Got some good exercise though and enjoyed it. Played with General McClure, Major Adams and Capt. Graham.

WEDNESDAY 31 JANUARY 1951

Tunner's ADC delivered to me personally Tunner's phase-out statement (including dates on which his TDY personnel were to depart COCARCOM) which I approved. The original I have filed in this headquarters; sent a copy of same to Tunner (which my signed approval).

Received a radio this AM from USAF which states that sample field uniforms being shipped for our testing and a report required on same with our recommendations re: color, design features, warmth, and general comments. Tests be made complete with documentation report and submitted by 1 Mar 51 to AMC.

Bucked above radio to Alkire: 1) Necessary action; *2)* See that these uniforms get direct to General Partridge; *3)* Draw up and issue a directive to Fifth for list; *4)* See that one individual in your shop monitors this project. G.E.S.

The above radio was made up in sufficient copies so that each division and section chief received one.

Attached to *Air Force* Magazine's article (issue of January 1951) entitled "Survival Under Atomic Attack," I sent the following memo to my VC for Adm & Plans: "*(1)* I suggest that we get started on an indoctrination program covering atomic attack for our personnel throughout FEAF. *(2)* Maybe GHQ might want to run it for entire theater. *(3)* I want to do it regardless."

Mr. Thorpe of Scripps Howard Newspapers, a subsidiary of the United Press, visited me at 1430 hours accompanied by General Nuckols. I had quite a

---

106. Lt Col Robert A. Gould, Jr., Intelligence Officer, Director of Air Targets, FEAF.

talk with him which lasted about thirty minutes. Talked a bit off the record, advising him that it was off the record. Anything that he writes will be looked over by General Nuckols prior to publication.

At 1530 hours Colonel Lei[107] (spelling ?) from Taiwan dropped in with General Banfill. He brought some pineapples from General Chou and greetings from the Gissimo and the Madame in Taiwan.

THURSDAY
1 FEBRUARY
1951

Dispatched the fol signal to Vandenberg:

This radio in two parts. *PART I.* I have agreed to a phase-out plan submitted by General Tunner of all officers in 315 Air Division (Combat Cargo) who are here on temporary duty. General Tunner departs for ZI on 10 February. All will have departed except one by 28 February inclusive. *PART II.* NEW SUBJECT. No reply has been received to my A 1974 dated 27 January reference release of Weyland. Will appreciate your decision this matter.

Had lunch with Mr. Earl D. Johnson, Assistant Secretary of the Army, at the Imperial Hotel which I enjoyed very much. Was impressed greatly by Mr. Johnson who is an ex-Air Force officer who had General Tunner as his instructor and General Sweetser as a classmate while attending flying school in 1931.

At 1500 Piper[108] fixed me up with a new plate which I hope is going to be very comfortable.

Had Mr. and Mrs. Ogden (owners of a Siamese cat) to dinner. They brought over a couple of Siamese kittens.

FRIDAY
2 FEBRUARY
1951

Dispatched the fol "personal secret Stratline" to Partridge:

Earl D. Johnson, Assistant Secretary Army, ETD Haneda for Taegu 0700 hours, 3 February. Desire you or Timberlake meet him and extend all possible courtesy by Fifth Air Force. Inform Ridgway. Your information: Johnson World War II Air Force officer and Air Force friend. Completed flying training in 1931. Classmate of Sweetser. His instructor was Tunner, whom he admires greatly.

After dispatching above, got off another Stratline to Partridge:

Remy Stratline A 2215 this date, destination K-13 instead of K-2. ETA 1030 hours, 3 February. Possibly I will accompany.

Received from Vandenberg a signal as follows:

Reference per 2 A 77512 dated 1 February 1951, do not repeat not understand your reference to the release of Weyland. Apparently there is some misunderstanding. Please enlighten me.

In answer, sent the fol:

Reur 53738 dtd 1 February. In USAF's AFCVC 53400, it was stated "unable to return Colonels Ferguson and Sykes to duty your headquarters."

---

107. This individual is unknown.
108. Col Philip F. Piper, a FEAF dental surgeon.

In my A 1974 I stated "this contrary to our suggested arrangement for return of Weyland" as both Weyland and I understood that with promotion of Ferguson and Ferguson's return here, Weyland could then be immediately released which you indicated was desired without delay. We both understood your agreement to promote Ferguson and therefore my A 1974 and my A 77512, paragraph 2.

**SATURDAY
3 FEBRUARY
1951**

Departed Haneda about 0730 with Assistant Secretary for the Army Earl D. Johnson and Major General Carter B. Magruder for Suwŏn in their Constellation. Arrived at 1130 hours where we were met by Generals Ridgway, Milburn, and Partridge. After a short briefing at 25th Division headquarters (General Kean's division), we had lunch as General Kean's guests. General Barth, artillery commander, 25th Infantry Division, was also present. All of us, after lunch, proceeded to the front lines to one of the battalions of the 35th Infantry where quite an artillery dual was taking place. We could see the artillery shells bursting in front of us (which were being fired from our rear) and were also able to see an infantry outfit in attack on the plains below.

While proceeding to the front lines, we passed a stream of transportation going both ways and noticed the close positions of the artillery placement of the Turkish Brigade. If there was ever a target for enemy air strafing, that was it - but because of the Far East Air Forces having eliminated enemy air, they operate with perfect immunity from air strikes. The secretary commented on this and agreed with me that wrong conclusions could probably be drawn from the operations of the infantry.

After returning to the airstrip, General Ridgway and the secretary proceeded to one of the front line regiments of the 2d Division of the X Corps where they watched a regiment in combat which had a perimeter defense; they also visited ground where they saw hundreds of Communist dead - the results of both air strafing and artillery.

During the secretary's absence, Partridge, Milburn, Magruder and I visited and I did some business with Partridge in the Constellation.

We departed about 1730 hours and arrived at Haneda about 2010 hours.

Proceeded direct home and to bed.

**SUNDAY
4 FEBRUARY
1951**

As the result of my conference with Partridge yesterday, instructed my Deputy for Operations via R&R that as soon as we have sufficient '86s with pylons installed so that they can carry napalm or bombs in addition to their exterior tanks, we should bring such a flight to Korea and then rotate the personnel through that flight in order to train the remainder of the 4th Group. He (Partridge) further stated that if the infantry moves up to the Han River that he would station that flight at Suwŏn, K-13, as this would provide a base from which they could operate into North Korea against the MiGs as well as provide quick interceptor airplanes in the forward areas. When do you think at least eight (8) F–86s will have pylons installed?

Also sent an R&R to my IG telling him that Captain Nichols is being wasted by being tied down with too much administrative details and instructed him to take up with Banfill the *(1)* relief of Nichols from OSI; *(2)* his (Nichols) assignment to Fifth Air Force Headquarters; *(3)* the appointment of a new man to head up the OSI in Korea.

In reply to a letter received from Partridge re the subject of "awards," sent him the following:

Your letter of 2 February, reference a re-examination of the AF awards policy as well as that which I have set up for FEAF, came in this morning and I thank you for it. Although I don't agree with you in some instances, I do agree with the intent and overall suggestions that you have made. Because of your letter, I propose to have the subject studied here in my headquarters, and, as a result of that study, a letter will be written by me to the C of S, USAF, recommending some suggested changes in the overall AF policy. I am a believer in generous awards - rather than adopting a niggardly policy. If you will review history, you will find that battles were won by the use of ostrich plumes by Napoleon, medals by other commanders, and pieces of ribbon by MacArthur. As long as I remain in the AF (which won't be long now), my policy will be one of generosity rather than a limited and stingy one. I enjoyed very much my visit with you yesterday and I can assure you that the Assistant Secretary for Army, Mr. Earl D. Johnson, enjoyed every minute of it. He was just "plain-like-a-boy" when we departed. Please tell Matt Ridgway of Mr. Johnson's great gratitude and satisfaction over his treatment yesterday. I have issued instructions re Captain Nichols - if it is possible to do so - and will keep you advised.

Dispatched the fol stratline to Partridge with info personal to Ridgway:

Recurrent reports received here indicate that front line division commanders are not repeat not receiving aerial photographs for their tactical use. It is requested that you inquire into this situation and ascertain whether this situation can be alleviated, if true, with the reconnaissance means at your disposal. Your comments and recommendations requested soonest. Nuckols received the fol radnote from USAF requesting:
The 3 services are being asked by Scripps-Howard for info on award of Silver Stars in Korea. Our info here is 27 awarded by FEAF. Also being asked for citations of awards to Generals Craigie, Weyland, Crabb, Picher, Banfill, Alkire and Colonel Erler given by General Stratemeyer your theater on 14 Dec. Presume these awards were announced in your theater when made. Will be answering queries Tuesday and appreciate your advice on the subject. Common usage as well as the intent of the Regulation have reserved the Silver Star for specific gallantry in action above the call of duty and not for performance of duty over a period of time.

I OK'd Nuckols' reply which was as follows:

Personal for Lennartson[109] from Nuckols. Reur USAF 287, citations requested are contained in FEAF General Order 135, dated 14 December,

---

109. Nils A. Lennartson, Deputy Director, Office of the Director of Public Relations, HQ USAF.

copies of which were forwarded to HQ USAF, Attn: Director Military Personnel, on 2 January 1951. Awards referred to were for gallantry in action on numerous occasions, all above and beyond the call of duty. This gallantry included flights into enemy territory and/or visits to forward airfields into enemy territory and/or visits to forward airfields under ground attack. The flights were made on particularly hazardous missions at a time when tactics and techniques of air operations were in the trial stages. By virtue of these exploratory flights and the first-hand knowledge gained, air operations in Korea greatly increased in effectiveness. AFR 30-14, dated 22 Aug 50, Para 15B, which authorizes Silver Star, makes no mention of quote specific acts of gallantry unquote which you infer is intent of regulation. Announcement of awards was made to press of home town of individuals decorated.

The clothing that USAF said they were sending us for test arrived on the 3d, delivered to Alkire on the 4th, and by the evening of the 4th was enroute to Korea addressed personally to General Partridge.

MONDAY
5 FEBRUARY
1951

In reply to a signal received this AM from Partridge, dispatched the fol to him personally:

Reur OPS 782 of 4 Feb, Part 6. I approve in general your recommended specific action. Directive will be issued this headquarters to 315th Air Division, information copy to you earliest. However, no specific number of C–47 aircraft will be set up solely for the use of Eighth Army. Further, Eighth Army because of short distances involved must use their L–5s and L–17s to maximum utilization. Our directive to 315th Air Division will specify that their mission at K-37 will be to provide necessary air transportation for Ambassador Muccio, President Rhee, General Ridgway, his Army staff, and other agencies with legitimate lift requirements.

Assistant Secretary for the Army Earl D. Johnson attended FEAF briefing with me this AM.

Dispatched the fol signal, attention Major General Truman H. Landon:

During your visit my headquarters, Vandenberg asked me if I had been notified that 452d Bomb Wing (L) and the 437th Troop Carrier Wing had been designated regular units. You indicated that I had not been notified but that I would be upon your return. To date I have received no information on this matter. It would help if they were designated regular units and if I were notified.

To Vandenberg I sent this radio:

You indicated to me, just prior to your departure, that as soon as you returned instructions would issue from your headquarters that each major Air Force command would be directed to appoint their senior WAF officer as Director of WAFs and that this would be her primary MOS [military occupational specialty]. I have received no information to that effect and per instructions from Hq USAF, the Director of WAFs as such is her secondary MOS. Her primary MOS is in another staff position. Effective 1 February, Major Virginia C. Dietz, my headquarters, was appointed Director of WAFs and operates directly under me, but it is still her secondary MOS.

To Partridge, I sent:

Orders are being issued this date transferring Captain Donald NMI Nichols from OSI to Hq Fifth AF. My congratulations to you on securing Captain Nichols for work under your Deputy for Intelligence. Desire you commend Captain Nichols for his outstanding performance of duty as a member of the OSI operating under orders from Hq FEAF.

Mr. Peipgrof of Northwest Airlines called at 1500 hours and indicated that he had heard from Don King who is in Washington and who wanted to know if I would support a request by Northwest Airlines in case of a world war to inaugurate a route - Seattle, Hawaii, Guam, to Tokyo. I told Mr. Peipgrof that I supported nothing, that all I could do was to make recommendations to CINCFE to whom he should inform Don King to address his query. In case it was referred to me, I would recommend it based primarily on keeping all airlines operating into the Far East in case of a war.

Annalee and I attended the farewell cocktail party given by the Gascoignes at 1745 hours at the British Embassy.

At 2000 hours, Annalee and I honored at dinner at Mayeda House the Assistant Secretary for Army Earl D. Johnson and Mrs. Johnson; other guests were: Major General Carter B. Magruder, Generals Weyland and Tunner, Mrs. Picher, General and Mrs. Craigie, General and Mrs. Hickey, and General and Mrs. Allen.

[There was no diary entry for February 6.]

WEDNESDAY and THURSDAY 7-8 FEBRUARY 1951

Departed Wednesday, 7 February, for Clark, ETD [estimated time of departure] Haneda 0750 hours.

Arrived Clark 1600 hours local. Met by General Turner, Colonel Davies, Colonel Wimsatt; received honors and salute, and proceeded direct to General Turner's office where the following subjects were discussed:

(1) General Turner stated that he could not understand why dependents of officers and non-commissioned officers were not permitted to come to Clark. He has 209 sets of quarters vacant. He indicated that he had taken this up with my headquarters some three weeks ago and was informed that it would be discussed with General Hickey and information sent him. I have directed that General Craigie prepare a letter for my signature, covering this subject, personal for General Turner.

(2) General Turner had been requested to submit the name of a colonel, since he was over in that grade, to head up the Air Terminal Group under the 315th Air Division (Combat Cargo). He submitted the name of Colonel Brooks[110] (colored) who is his communications officer and who has performed in a superior manner.

---

110. Brooks' first name is unknown.

General Turner does not want to lose this officer, but he is the only colonel who is considered qualified to head up the Air Terminal Group.

(3) I have directed Deputy for Personnel to write a letter, personal for General Turner, for my signature covering thoroughly the rotational policy for officers assigned to the Thirteenth Air Force. QUESTIONS: *A.* Have all their tours been extended six (6) months - as was done by the Army? *B.* What is the length of tour in the Philippines and will dependents be permitted to accompany newly assigned officers?

(4) I questioned Colonel Wimsatt, the Depot Wing commander at Clark if he could install pylons on the F–80Cs if he had the pylons and drawings. He indicated that he could and since we have some 53 F–80Cs at Clark, it is my desire that action be taken by the Deputy for Materiel to ship to Clark the pylons, drawings, etc., in order that all F–80C aircraft can be equipped with pylons.

(Copies of above extracted and made for Generals Craigie and Alkire and Colonel Merchant.)

Dispatched from the air, Wednesday, 7 Feb, the fol signal to General Craigie, Hq FEAF:

Send fol message to General Picher: I recommend promotion to tempo-rary major of Captain Lawrence R. Lockwood.[111] He has been a captain since '44. Record outstanding. Signed Stratemeyer.

Message was sent at 03355/Z, to ADA, Dai Ichi Bldg.

The fol message was sent to Major General Hickey, C of S, GHQ, 8 Feb, from the air:

Have package aboard for you. My ETA Haneda 1800. Please send transportation for package. Stratemeyer.

Message was sent at 0420/Z, to ADA, Dai Ichi Bldg.

**FRIDAY
9 FEBRUARY
1951**

Partridge returned the photostat cy [copy] of a letter received from a Mr. and Mrs. Ale Spradlin, Revela, Ky, and stated that he had had photostat copies of same made, published, and distributed throughout all echelons of his command. (See diary entry under date of [not entered])

Weyland brought in fol radio from Partridge:

Personal for Stratemeyer from Partridge. In the present situation in Korea it has been found necessary to return the 4th Fighter Wing to Johnson AFB. This results in presence of 2 senior commanders, one of whom is on temporary duty in this command. I am reluctant to continue a command situation in which the senior, Smith, serves in an Air Defense establishment commanded by a junior, Hall.[112] Equally, I am reluctant to suggest that Smith assume responsibility for the Air Defense of Central Japan while he is on temporary duty in the Far East. Smith feels, and I

---

111. Lockwood was a pilot for Stratemeyer.
112. Col, later Brig Gen, George F. Smith commanded the 4th FIW until 31 May 1951
    Col Thomas B. Hall, who formerly led both the 3d BW and the 355th FIW, now commanded the 6142d ABW.

concur, that under the circumstances his presence is no longer essential and that it would be profitable to the AF as a whole to return him to the United States. This will leave Hall in command over the entire central Japan Air Defense establishments the fighter portion of which will consist of 4th Fighter Wing plus other day and night fighter units stationed at Johnson. Request action be initiated with ZI to return Smith to the U.S. without delay so that during critical period of AF expansion his experience and rank may be better utilized.

My immediate reply to Partridge was:

Your 072315Z, CG 32, delivered to me by Weyland. I can't imagine anything worse happening to a wing commander than to be returned to the ZI when he brought his wing out here to fight. In spite of your reluctance to continue Colonel Hall in his position, having Smith as the Fourth Fighter Interceptor Wing commander under him is to my mind not of sufficient importance to make a change. Colonel Smith and his wing are over here on temporary duty status. He is one of our outstanding wing commanders with much service having graduated from the Military Academy in 1928. I have been informed that he does not object to his position and I disapprove any action to relieve him from his wing.

Got off a radio to CSAF as follows:

Personal priority secret Vandenberg from Stratemeyer. Reference your AFCVC 53400, 26 Jan; 53738, 1 Feb; AFPMP 37724, 8 Feb; and my A 1974 CG, 27 Jan; A 77512 CG, 1 Feb; and A 2236 CG, 2 Feb. THIS RADIO IN FOUR PARTS. *PART I.* No reply from you following my last referenced message where I enlightened you. Reference AFCVC 53400, letter just received from Twining which is contrary to my understanding our conversation which contemplated Ferguson's promotion and return to FEAF. *PART II.* Situation here is now such that I am willing to release Weyland immediately for assignment you outlined. *PART III.* As discussed with you, I would like to have Ferguson promoted and his knowledge of tactical air operations available in this hq. I also consider Sykes or a suitable replacement should be returned to complete the project he was on and maintain follow up of the Barcus study here. *PART IV.* Request your decisions on Weyland, Ferguson, and Sykes.

Dispatched to Twining the following:

Light bomb units of my command are severely reduced in combat effectiveness thru lack of aval acft. Present auth[orization] is 112 UE [unit equipment] B–26s. We have recently asked that this be increased to 144 to provide 24 UE acft per sq. This req was based on the fact that the B–26 has proven to be our best day-night support-interdiction weapon. The increase will considerably enhance our combat capabilities. At present we have a total of 110 B–26s in FEAF, of which 16 are ineffective in FEAMCOM. The inflow of repairable B–26s to FEAMCOM will approximately balance deliveries from there. We are losing 6 B–26s per month in operations. Part 6 of your rad AFODA 53865 dtd 3 Feb 51 schedules certain B–26 monthly departures from the ZI and we assume delivery date to combat to be one month later. Plotting these deliveries against the above 6 per month attrition shows that it will be the last part of May 51 before our light bomb units will have aval even the 112 UE acft they are presently auth. Delivery schedules of B–26s must be advanced if our rqmts are to be realistically met. I request that you give this your pers attn to assure that the max aval force is working around the clock to effect delivery of B–26 acft to my combat units.

Cleaned off all accumulated papers on my desk and left the office at 1700 hours sharp.

SATURDAY 10 FEBRUARY 1951

Received the fol rad from Twining:

Reurad AX 2481 D/O dated 8 Feb 51 every effort is being made to expedite the delivery of B–26 aircraft to your theater. You will be advised as to the increase in estimated deliveries that can be expected.

Bucked Tunner's Activities Report - 10 Sept thru 7 Feb - to Partridge and Doyle for their paragraph-by-paragraph comments and expeditious return to me.

In reference to the X Corps staff study, wrote Partridge that

inasmuch as study bogged down (apparently) in GHQ since it has not been referred to me for comment, and since you would have had comments to make on it had it been referred to you officially, desire you submit a copy of the report (which I understand you have) together with the comments you would have made. I intend to forward your comments on to Vandenberg for reference in case the DA brings up the subject in any way.

Returned to Doyle Hickey the letter from Matt Ridgway signed by Allen

...Your recent reply to my letter re "utilization of aircraft for emergency supply purposes" and the attached letter certainly are fair and well thought out, and meet the objections that I presented. (Follows cy of Ridgway letter)

Ltr 8th Army, dtd 8 Feb:

Dear Doyle: The views expressed in your letter of 5 Feb, relative to effective utilization of transport a/c are fully appreciated and I welcome the opportunity to state our case as we see it here. My policy is to utilize airlift and/or airdrop only when no other means of transportation has the capability of delivering supplies to the location by the time they are required. To this end all requests for air supply are thoroughly screened by a central requirement section in the headquarters. This procedure is designed to eliminate use of air supply when any other means will suffice. In spite of the above, some air supply has become a daily essential requirement for several reasons. This is particularly true at present while we are operating well north of operable rail lines in addition to being engaged in moderate combat activities. As you know, the entire rail system over here is barely capable of serving the number of troops in the theater when moderate combat, forward troop movements or sabotage are not involved. When supplies other than the bare minimum are required, means other than rail must be utilized. Every effort is made to use motor vehicles and sealift for this purpose and to build up quantities of supply near the front. Nevertheless we are forced constantly to use some air supply as the only practicable means to meet emergency requirements and to some extent, what I consider "normal" requirements. In order to supplement the limited capabilities of the railroad the maximum use of sea-lift is made. We are now landing some supplies on the west coast at Kunsan, and trans-shipping them north by rail to I and IX Corps supply points. However, the X Corps is located where its units must rely completely upon a single track railroad, motor vehicles or air. While the above is only a brief statement of the problem I believe you will see that some supply by air, under present circumstances at least may be considered a normal and justifiable requirement. You may be assured, however, that we shall continue to work toward further reduction of these requirements to the absolute minimum. Should either you or Strat have any other suggestions on this subject, I would appreciate your views and will do my utmost to conform. Ridgway signed by Allen.

Received the fol rad from Vandenberg:

Reference your A 2551 CG, 9 Feb. I plan to promote Col. Ferguson on the next list and return him to your command before March 1st. General Weyland will return as soon as possible after Ferguson's arrival. He will proceed for temporary duty to this headquarters before assignment to a permanent station. A suitable replacement will be furnished you for Colonel Sykes to complete the project you refer to.

After receipt of the above quoted radio and in reply to a letter I had previously received from Twining on 29 Jan which was concerned with news of the postponement of the Vincent [*sic*, Vinson] congressional inquiry, the study started by Sykes and the Barcus group, and personnel requirements regarding same for FEAF, *I replied as follows:*

Dear Nate: I have just received your letter of 29 Jan bringing me up to date on the outlook for a congressional investigation, and the action underway in USAF Headquarters to monitor the project of the investigation and operations in Korea. I thoroughly agree that we must continue to be prepared for such an investigation, and to give the whole truth, which is that the USAF in the Far East has continuously discharged all its responsibilities to the joint team consistently better than the other members of the team. The establishment of a small Korean Evaluation Group in your headquarters is an excellent method of accomplishing this at your end. I am sure you realize, however, that the basic information must continue to come from this end in such a manner that it can be integrated with the data already delivered in the Stearns and Barcus reports. It was for this purpose that I originally asked for Bart Leach out here, and then got Colonel Sykes who did an outstandingly superior job. I soon realized that one man could not adequately collate and integrate the mass of material which had accumulated, and accordingly recommended that a USAF Evaluation Group be established. The Barcus group was sent out. I had expected that this group would stay on the job until its conclusion and accordingly turned Sykes over to Barcus. Ferguson also helped out. When the Barcus group returned to the ZI, I concurred in sending Sykes and Ferguson back for a short while to assist in preparing for the Congressional investigation; however, I certainly didn't expect to lose them permanently. I expected Sykes to continue on this end the work which he had started. As you suggested, Darrow, Merle Williams, and Kinney[113] (now in GHQ) are extremely competent officers. However, a new officer assigned to this work would be thoroughly entangled for a long time in familiarizing himself with the past efforts of Sykes, Barcus and Dr. Stearns before he could pick up the ball and make a positive contribution to this complex problem. That is the reason I have consistently asked for Sykes' return. I am enclosing a copy of a signal I sent Van yesterday and which bears on this subject. A copy of his reply is attached also which came in this afternoon. His decisions are most gratifying. I will carry on here now to the very best of my ability. I am acutely aware of the gigantic overall tasks you have back there, and thoroughly appreciate the assistance you and all have given me in carrying on my part of the job. Best regards. G.E.S., etc.

Received the fol rad from USAF:

Reurad M 77935 CG dtd 5 Feb 51. *(1)* Barring further change in the international situation, reservists assigned to these units not desiring to remain in the active establishment under available options will be released as nearly in accordance with their desires as a replacement can be made available. In no case will they be held involuntarily beyond 21 months without amendment to present laws. *(2)* The above should not be interpreted as restricting the transfer of personnel into or out of their unit when such action is considered necessary. *(3)* Present planning provides that the 452d Bomb Gp, L, and the 437th TC Gp, M, will retain their status as USAFR units on EAD [extended active duty] until completion of 21 months of active military service at which time personnel will be released or reassigned to regular AF units (17 Bomb Gp, L and 317 TC Gp) in accordance with above stated personnel policy. *(4)* A board of officers (The Matheny Board) was appointed in 1946 for the purpose of reviewing and determining numerical designations of units to be retained in the regular AF. This board listed the following bomb gps, L, and trp car gps (presently inactive) as having priority over all other presently inactive regular and active USAFR units. Therefore, these units will be activated as regular AF units prior to the designation of any active reserve units of the same type as regular AF units.

---

113. Col Don O. Darrow, Director of Plans, FEAF; Col Merle R. Williams, Assistant Director of Operations, FEAF, and in May 1951, executive officer of the 8th FW; probably Col Andrew J. Kinney, who was a member of the Joint Strategic Plans and Operations Group, and later a member of the U.N. Truce Team in Korea.

Bomb	Group	Light	Troop Carrier
47	17	38	317, 313, 315

Mr. L.L. Brabham, Director of Republic Aviation Military Requirements Branch, had lunch with me at Mayeda House. He is due to return to the ZI.

Received a radio that Chidlaw, with party of eight, including Mr. Mundy Peale,[114] are expected to arrive this theater, 5 March.

Annalee attended the Dulles group soiree at the Imperial Hotel late this afternoon.

SUNDAY
11 FEBRUARY
1951

Bucked copies of the following to CSAF and CINCFE in addition to sending General Kean a "thank you" reply.

Subject: Results of Tactical Air Close Support Mission (dated 12 January 1951) thru CG Eighth United States Army in Korea, APO 301 to CG Fifth Air Force, APO 710. *(1)* Interrogation of prisoners captured 10 Jan 51 by the 27th Infantry reveals that the night B–26 raids, using flares to illuminate the enemy area prior to bombing, have been particularly terrifying and have caused their night movements to become much less effective. These prisoners state that their units have been able to move only approximately one-fourth the distance they normally did without the harrassing effect of night missions flown by your command. The 27th Infantry further reports that these missions have been of inestimable value to them. *(2)* The above information is forwarded to you as it is believed that you and the members of your command should receive firsthand information of the result of your efforts, and know how much we of this Division appreciate your service. s/W.B. Kean, Major General, U.S. Army, Commanding 25th Infantry Division, APO 25.

1st Indorsement, subject: Results of Tactical Air Close Support Mission, Hq Eighth U.S. Army Korea (EUSAK) APO 301, 19 Jan 51, to CG, Fifth AF in Korea, APO 970, *(1)* It is with pleasure that General Kean's letter expressing the appreciation of the officers and men of the 25th Infantry Division is forwarded. *(2)* The entire Eighth Army recognizes and is grateful for the magnificent support being rendered by the Fifth AF in the achievement of our common objective. For the Commanding General, s/Leven C. Allen,[115] Major General, U.S. Army, Chief of Staff.

Received word that Colonel Thomas B. Hall, the CO of my 6142d Air Base Wing, has been reported missing on a night mission over the Hŭngnam area.

Annalee and I attended a poker and supper party at the Castillos (Spanish Ambassador to Japan) and had a very, very pleasurable evening.

MONDAY
12 FEBRUARY
1951

Got off a letter of commendation, with copies going to Stearley and Briggs, to Col. Payne Jennings for the superior Tarzon bombing job done yesterday on the bridge at Kanggye. They took two spans out.

---

114. Peale was president and general manager of Republic Aviation.
115. During World War II, Allen was Omar Bradley's chief of staff at Twelfth Army Group. He was now the Eighth Army's chief of staff.

General Sweetser, 1200 hours, to lunch. Annalee had a cheese souffle with all the trimmings, ending up with a chocolate snowball. I never saw anyone enjoy a meal more than Sweetser.

At 1600 hours, made a Mutual Broadcast Tape "question and answer recording" for Mr. Kallsen, MBC.

TUESDAY
13 FEBRUARY
1951

About 1015 hours, General Hobart R. "Hap" Gay called at the office. Had a nice talk and he again praised the AF and stated that not only did he not agree with all the palaver about Marine air being better than USAF, but he said his lst Cav on the ground was just as good as any Marine outfit.

Left the office early at 1100 hours to play golf. Major Adams and I won our match from General McClure and Lt. Graham.

Before leaving the office, signed and dispatched a letter to Van, enclosing a photostat of Hap Gay's letter re air support - and thanks, and gave a thank you letter to Gay, when he came in, for his consideration in letting us know how he feels about our support. His letter to Partridge quoted herewith:

> Hq 1st Cavalry Division, Office of the CG, APO 201, dtd 31 Jan 51 - Dear General Partridge: Upon my departure for a new assignment I wish to thank you and your Fifth AF for the magnificent air support that you have given this division during the past 6 and 1/2 months of combat. I assure, that whatever combat success we have had has been due to no little part to your cooperation and to the gallantry of your intrepid pilots. The 1st Cavalry Division is, and forever will be, grateful. s/Hobart R. Gay, Maj. Gen., USA.

WEDNESDAY
14 FEBRUARY
1951

General Whitney (CINCFE's military secretary) gave me the following press release as issued by CINCFE 13 Feb:

General MacArthur after inspecting the Korean battlefront, this evening commented as follows: "What the future has in store in Korea continues to be largely dependent upon international considerations, and decisions not yet known here. Meanwhile, the Command is doing everything that could reasonably be expected of it. Our field strategy, initiated upon Communist China's entry into the war, <u>involving a rapid withdrawal to lengthen the enemy's supply lines with resultant pyramiding of his logistical difficulties and an almost astronomical increase in the destructiveness of our air power has worked well.</u>[116] <u>In the development of this strategy the 8th Army has achieved local tactical successes through maximum exploitation of the air's massive blows on extended enemy concentrations and supplies</u> [underlining in original] but in the evaluation of these successes sight must not be lost of the enemy's remaining potential for reinforcement and resupply. We must not fall into the error of evaluating such tactical successes as decisively leading to the enemy's defeat just as many erred in assessing our strategic withdrawals in the fact of Communist China's commitment to war as a decisive defeat inflicted upon us.

---

116. Given what had actually happened in Korea, even for MacArthur this is a remarkable example of obfuscation and palliation. MacArthur's statement, however, indicates that the ground commanders had finally gained a greater appreciation of the FEAF interdiction effort and what it could do for them. (Futrell, pp 313-315.)

We are still engaged in a war of maneuver with the object of inflicting as heavy a punishment upon the enemy as possible, striving constantly to keep him off balance to prevent his obtaining and holding the tactical initiative while at the same time avoiding the hazards inherent in his numerical superiority. The concept advanced by some that we should establish a line across Korea and enter into positional warfare is wholly unrealistic and illusory. It fails completely to take into account the length of such a line at the narrowest lateral, the rugged terrain which is involved and the relatively small force which could be committed to the purpose. The attempt to engage in such strategy would insure destruction of our forces piecemeal. Talk of crossing the 38th Parallel at the present stage of the campaign except by scattered patrol action incidental to the tactical situation is purely academic. From a military standpoint we must materially reduce the existing superiority of our Chinese Communist enemy engaging with impunity in undeclared war against us, with the unprecedented military advantage of sanctuary protection for his military potential against our counter attack upon Chinese soil, before we can seriously consider conducting major operations north of that geographic line.

Meanwhile, however, the complete coordination of our land, sea and air forces and the consequent smooth synchronization of their combined operations, with each arm contributing its full part, continues to inflict terrific losses upon the enemy. General Ridgway is proving himself a brilliant and worthy successor to General Walker in command of the 8th Army and with Admiral Struble in command of the Fleet and General Partridge in command of the Air comprise an ideal trio of field commanders. [underlining in original]

Colonel C.A. Mahoney[117] came by the office this PM and among other things mentioned that the Holy Cross nuns at Nagoya were upset because an Air Force officer had approached the Mother Superior and indicated the AF was going to take back the old barracks buildings that K.B. Wolfe had given them in which to run their high school. Wrote a letter to Del Spivey asking him to personally call on the Mother Superior and set their and her mind at peace. Sent a copy of my letter to Del to Pat Mahoney.

Upon my arrival at the office, read the incoming redline from Vandenberg which is as follows:

As you have probably learned by now, the award of the Silver Star to certain members of your immediate staff has caused a great deal of adverse comment back here. In addition, I have been asked for a full explanation of the circumstances surrounding these awards by Chairman Vinson of the House Armed Services Committee. I am sure you recognize from our previous correspondence, my attitude on the award of combat decorations to staff officers not involved in day to day contact with the enemy. My first inclination on learning of these awards was to cancel them. The more I think of it, the more I think that is still the sound thing to do. Before doing it, however, I would like to know how embarrassing such action on

---

117. Mahoney's job is unknown.

my part would be to you. If you feel strongly that these awards should not be cancelled in light of the above, I need by cable your full justification for making these particular awards.

After mulling over my reply to Vandenberg, I took a rough draft of same over to General MacArthur for him to make, as a personal favor to me, whatever comments he felt. After getting his complete backing, *I sent the following reply redline to Vandenberg:*

Reur 144 redline. I have probed my soul as well as precedents in World War II for a valid reason that would cause me to reverse my decision on the award of Silver Stars to staff officers of FEAF. In all sincerity, I am unable to discover any such justification. The awards now being questioned were made for extreme gallantry far beyond the normal call of duty. My staff officers neither were required nor expected to fly combat missions to test newly devised and at that time untested battle tactics. Neither are staff officers required or expected to intentionally expose themselves to ground fire in order to obtain first-hand knowledge that better fitted them for execution of their job. Yet that is exactly what the seven officers who were decorated did. In the early days in Korea, both Craigie and Weyland felt that they had to know themselves just what if any developments or changes could or should be made in our detailed combat operations. They found out the hard way - by flying unescorted B–29 missions, unescorted RB–29 missions, B–26 strafing missions, and tactical control missions in unarmed T–6 aircraft. In the cases of Crabb and Picher, they did essentially the same. It should be noted that Picher was not serving as Inspector General at the time of the act, but instead was one of two Deputies for Operation, alternating 12-hour shifts with Crabb. Our intelligence resulting from long-range reconnaissance left much to be desired and once again a staff officer, Banfill, as Deputy for Intelligence, flew on missions himself to find out at first hand the reasons why. The effectiveness of FEAF's combat operations today, of which I am proud, is due in no small part to the voluntary actions of these officers. I am truly proud of their actions and feel that a piece of ribbon is small recompense for the dangers these senior staff officers eagerly exposed themselves to. The last thing I want to do is reflect in any disparaging way on the value of the Silver Star as an award to be highly prized. Admittedly these officers were not wounded, not shot down and not captured, but they willingly exposed themselves to that hazard, knowing full well the treatment they undoubtedly would receive should they fall in enemy hands. Colonel Thomas B. Hall, one of Fifth Air Force's top officers serving here in Japan, three nights ago flew with a night intruder mission to better qualify himself to perform his duties, and has been missing in action since. Theirs was a calculated risk, carefully thought through, and accepted not in the emotional heat of battle, but in cold logic and reasoning. Staff officers of the Air Force in World War II faced the same difficult solution: should they depend on written reports or should they go to find out for themselves. Many staff officers decided to go and they were suitably rewarded. I feel that the precedent merits continuance.

I have asked General MacArthur, as a personal favor to me, to review these cases and give his professional opinion as to whether the awards were warranted. He has done so, and has given an affirmative opinion in every case. I cannot fail to disagree with the negative implication of your reference to combat decorations to staff officers in day-to-day contact with the enemy. These awards are for personal bravery and are not connected in any way, that I can see, with continuity of contact with the enemy. I have carefully studied the regulations for the award of the Silver Star and can find nothing in these awards which violates either the spirit or letter of the regulation. I consider that I was justified. I do not believe that the slightest attention should be paid to sensation seeking reporters who attack military actions about which they have no intimate knowledge. To do so tends to establish an invisible control over our officers and airmen which cannot fail to be highly jeopardizing. Before you make any final decision to cancel the awards in question, I earnestly suggest that you weigh the additional publicity which might be adverse and, in any event, unwelcome since you feel as you do. The heroism of my staff officers' acts in my estimation remains unquestioned and undiminished.

THURSDAY 15 FEBRUARY 1951

Started snowing late yesterday afternoon and followed by a blizzard that lasted the night.

Came in from Mayeda House to the office via jeep.

Had copies of Vandenberg's incoming redline to me, and my outgoing redline to him with reference my award of the Silver Star to my staff officers, made up and presented each one a copy each of the two radios: - Generals Craigie, Weyland, Crabb, Banfill, Picher, Alkire, and Colonel Erler.*

*Full quotes of radios under diary date 14 Feb 51.

Dispatched the fol personal letter to Kenneth McNaughton[118] (Major General), USAF Director of Training:

It is my opinion that here in the Far East Air Forces we have the finest operational training unit that has ever existed to prepare both combat crews and ground personnel to take their places in fighting units. This applies to all type outfits that I have here in the Far East - including fighter, light bombardment (both day and night), medium bombardment, tactical reconnaissance and aircraft control and warning units. I discussed this with both General Vandenberg and Ted Landon when they were out here and both were in general agreement with this proposal. We, here, feel that there has never been such an opportunity to train under combat conditions as we now have in Korea, Japan and Okinawa. All of our personnel, both ground and air, have encountered new problems and have secured fresh wartime experience which is invaluable to them and to the United States Air Force. Our air crews have flown through all types of weather and, as a result, have gotten exceptionally fine navigational training. The ever-present threat of air interception and the constant subjection

---

118. McNaughton held several training assignments in World War II. He was appointed head of the newly-created Directorate of Training in Aug. 1949.

The weather in Korea during the winter of 1950-1951 was some of the worst on record for that country. Although such weather could hinder operations considerably, it did not always stop them as evidenced by this F–51 (above) taxiing in the snow and the F–86 (below) being uncovered by its well-clothed ground crew.

to ack-ack and small arms ground fire have given these air crewmen combat seasoning which I strongly believe should be spread throughout the United States Air Force. This, of course, applies equally to adjutants, supply officers, maintenance officers and airmen of all grades, who have gained tremendously in field experience. Headquarters, United States Air Force, has helped us to work out a program to exchange our 19th Group crews with SAC, and SAC has arranged to rotate with their ZI units not only the crews, but the entire personnel of the 98th and 307th Groups. We started in December to return for exchange with ZI units, a limited number of fighter and light bombardment crews and your headquarters is now in the process of attempting to expand this program by a further exchange with ZI units. So far, this is all the rotation we have in process. It seems to me that as soon as you are in a position to turn out enough people from your schools and operational training units, and of course after we are up to war strength, the pipeline could well be filled with these graduates and other people who have not had combat experience, headed towarded the Far East, and we in turn, could fill the pipeline back to the ZI with field and combat trained officers and airmen who could be put directly into the new units that are being created in the ZI or into training spots where they could contribute to the expansion. It will be particularly important to place these people where their experience could be used to the best advantage. I certainly recommend that you discuss this with Nugent and Edwards and then with General Twining, and see if we can't set up a pipeline in order to obtain the full benefit of the combat and field service training that is available here in the Far East Air Forces for your newly activated and training units. Best regards., G.E.S., etc.

Early in the morning, received a signal, personal from Twining telling me that USAF had not received a reply to their signal that they had sent on 6 Feb. Upon investigation, we found that the USAF signal had never been received so we had to go back and ask them for it. The radio arrived in quick order and practically the remainder of the afternoon was spent preparing our reply - A 2803 (redline Personal Twining from Stratemeyer) subject of USAF radio and reply was "recommendations for the promotion to temporary major general and brigadier general."

Mesdames Partridge, Timberlake and Katz, who are here in Tokyo for a few days, joined us at Mayeda House with Marian Picher, General Weyland and Colonel Pat Mahoney, and the Overackers, for a Mexican dinner.

FRIDAY
16 FEBRUARY
1951

Nuckols got a "nickle" for the fol radio which I sent to Vandenberg:

Far East Air Force and Australian, South African, Korean and land-based Marine Corps airplanes under FEAF's operational control on 15 February set new high sortie mark of 1,025. Previous high sortie figure was 958 flown on 3 January.

Dispatched the following memorandum to CINCFE:

On 15 February 1951 your Far East Air Forces and Australian, South African, Korean, and land-based Marine Corps airplanes under Far East Air Forces operational control set a new all-time high sortie mark of 1,025. The previous high sortie figure was 958 flown on 3 January 1951. This confirms your recent statement to me that the Far East Air Forces with other United Nations land-based airplanes would pass the thousand sortie mark. I'm proud of this record. s/G.E.S., etc.

Dispatched the fol personal radio to Vandenberg re Weyland's status:

Appreciate action indicated in your AVCVC 5449, dtd 10 Feb 51. Weyland would like some leave, which he deserves, before temporary assignment your headquarters and new permanent station. In order to facilitate this, I intend to release him from FEAF on 22 February as we can get along until Ferguson arrives.

After much mulling and discussion, dispatched the following letter to Curt LeMay:

Dear Curt, I have had suggested to me from many sources, including staff officers, to urge you to make a bombing attack, non-stop, from the United States, utilizing tankers, against a North Korean target.

I realize that you are under an expansion program which includes the activation and training, equipping and manning of new units.

I do feel, though, that such a mission by a squadron of B–29s if it did not interfere too much with your training and expansion, would be well worth the effort.

I do not propose to even suggest it unless you agree that it could be done without interference with your present important expansion and mission. FEAF Bomber Command (Provisional) under Briggs is carrying on beautifully. Your SAC groups are continuing to demonstrate the excellence of their previous training. Pete Jennings of the 19th Group has devoted a lot of personal effort to the Tarzon project and two out of the last three missions with this potential new weapon have been completely successful. The rotation of personnel between the medium bomb groups here in the Far East and SAC Units in the ZI, as agreed upon at the Hawaii Conference, promises to be mutually beneficial to both FEAF and your new groups and will result in an excellent distribution of our newly acquired Korean experience. I am really pleased at the prospect of having a complete turnover of personnel in both SAC groups and turnover of combat crew personnel in the 19th Group.

Would appreciate your comments on above first four paragraphs.

Best regards. Sincerely, G.E.S., etc.

SATURDAY 17 FEBRUARY 1951

Departed Haneda 1000 hours and landed at Taegu at 1400 hours. Was met by Generals Partridge and Timberlake, Colonel Tyer and other senior officers at the base. We went to the office of Colonel Tyer where I told all, expect Generals Partridge and Timberlake to vacate the office and then took up my business with General Partridge. I showed him and let him keep the copy of Vandenberg's signal reference his promotion and that of Weyland. I also gave him a copy of my radio recommendations to Twining reference promotion of officers to major general and brigadier general. I discussed this signal with him and he was very pleased with what I had done.

He said he would give Colonel George Price a good square break at Misawa.

I cautioned him reference General Mark Clark's visit to Eighth Army and told both Timberlake and him to speak up and state exactly how they considered air support should be rendered and who should be in command and control if the subject was raised by General Clark.

I queried General Partridge reference the tactical support paper supposedly sent all over the Army by the X Corps commander. He stated that a copy with his comments had left his headquarters for me.

He confirmed the assignment of Lt Colonel Jack Dale to my headquarters who, in turn, will be assigned to operations.

The following is the new assignment and switch of certain senior Air Force officers within the Fifth Air Force:

a. Colonel George Price to Misawa, vice Colonel Jenkins.

b. Colonel Jenkins to Hq 314th Air Division to be assistant to General Spivey, vice Lawhon.

c. Lawhon to be CG 35th Wing, vice Gray.

d. Gray to Itazuke to be number two to Colonel Jack Price, vice Stratton.

e. Lt. Col. Bull to be area commander, K-2, vice West.

f. West at Nagoya Air Base to be number two to Davasher.

g. Davasher, A-1, 314th Air Division, to be commanding officer, Nagoya Air Base, vice Parker.

h. Parker at 35th Wing to be executive for Lawhon.

i. Colonel Low relieved from command 18th Wing - to Fifth AF Hq, A-1, vice Lt. Col. Walz to be air base CO 67th Wing Photo.

j. Col. T.C. Rogers to command 18th Wing, vice Low.

k. Wintermute relieved as group commander, 18th Group, returns to Philippines while Col. Cox, 18th Wing, appointed group C.O.

l. Colonel McBride to command 35th Fighter Group, vice Jack Dale relieved to go to Hq FEAF from 452d Wing.

m. Col. Dempster to A-3 section, from 452d Wing, Hq Fifth Air Force.

n. LaClare to be exec to Col. Rogers in 18th Wing.[119]

(2 copies made of above extract from CG's diary under date of 17 Feb 51.)

After our business, I inspected all facilities of the 67th Recon Wing, with Col. Karl L. Polifka.[120] Everyone appeared very happy that I had taken the time to review with Colonel Polifka their facilities and to find out for myself the job that he was doing. During the inspection, I talked with the Eighth Army interpreters who are setting up their facilities right next to the Air Force interpreters' buildings which are to be connected by a covered passageway. While talking to these Army interpreters, I learned that in their opinion, which confirms mine, that the front line divisions were not getting photographs of the area in their immediate fronts and they guaranteed to me as soon as they were set up they would get them forwarded via liaison airplanes as that would be one of their responsibilities.

Departed Taegu about 1615 hours and landed at Haneda at 1925 hours.

---

119. Col Jack S. Jenkins previously commanded the 49th FBW; Col Brooks A. Lawhon had been Assistant Vice Commander, 5AF (Rear), then Deputy for Operations, Assistant Deputy for Operations, and Assistant Vice Commander (Japan) before taking command of the 35th FIW on Feb. 18; Col Frederic C. Gray had commanded the 6150th Tac Sup Wg and the 35th FIW; Col Wilbur A. Stratton, before becoming the Itazuke CO, had been the executive officer for the 8th FBW; Lt Col Frederick K. Bull; Col Joseph H. West had previously been 5AF adjutant general; Col Glenn L. Davasher had also been Assistant Vice Commander, 5AF (Adv), Deputy Vice Commander, Deputy for Personnel (Japan), and, again, assistant vice commander; Col Maurice E. Parker had been executive officer, then CO of the 6101st ABG; Col Curtis R. Low; Lt Col Robert W. Waltz; Col Turner C. Rogers was Assistant Deputy for Operations, 5AF prior to assuming command of the 18th FBW; Col Ira A. Wintermute; Col Homer M. Cox; Col William P. McBride had been the commander of the 502d Tac Ctl Gp; Col Kenneth C. Dempster had been the 452d BW's deputy for operations; Col Edward F. LaClare.

120. Polifka was a major figure in the USAF in the field of aerial reconnaissance and his services had been requested by General Stratemeyer. Polifka arrived in the Far East in late January. His command, the 67th Tactical Reconnaissance Wing, was activated on Feb. 25. Unhappily, Polifka was killed on July 1 when his RF–51 was shot down. (Futrell, pp 546–547.)

Prior to my take-off today, the first radio I saw was a signal from Vandenberg which stated that he wanted me to keep Weyland here a little longer inasmuch as he wanted Weyland to receive his third star while still in the war zone, and Vandenberg also said that he had put in for Partridge's third star. I was very very gratified.

In reply dispatched a redline to Vandenberg: "Your RL 154 received and will be complied with. Overjoyed. Both most deserving."

Sent a copy of the Vandenberg redline to General MacArthur with the attached personal note:

Attached hereto is a signal I received from General Vandenberg this morning. I heartily concur in both these promotions as I am sure you do. Sincerely, G.E.S., etc.

Informed that during my absence from the office, General Turner departed for the Philippines. He attended the 8:30 briefing with me prior to my take-off.

SUNDAY 18 FEBRUARY 1951

Got off the following two memos, based on my conversations while at Taegu:

To Deputy, Materiel: I had a good opportunity yesterday, while at Taegu, to see the new napalm mobile mix machine. All of the Fifth Air Force people are most enthusiastic about it; however, I also found that they are short of napalm mix. Everyone present indicated that everything had been done by the people in the Fifth Air Force, and by FEAMCOM, and by you to ship more mix over to them. I am writing this to see if there isn't some additional push that you could give to having an ample supply of this latest napalm mix in Korea and available for the using units?

Vice Commander, Operations: In conference with General Partridge yesterday he made a strong recommendation that we set up some two or three B–29s for night bombing, utilizing the MPQ-2 system and further recommends that 500-pound general purpose bombs be used with VT fuses. We must be careful to not divert too much of our medium bomber effort for this purpose because General Partridge feels, and I agree with him, that our entire effort might be diverted to this type of operations. He feels, and I agree, that we should train our B–29 crews however in this operation and therefore I desire that you take the necessary action.

Received in the mail from Partridge the Army staff studies on TACTICAL AIR SUPPORT with Partridge's covering letter. *Sent the entire folio to Weyland with the following comments:*

Your attention is invited to the attached letter from General Partridge with the four enclosures which is in reply to my letter on 10 February 1951 concerning the X Corps staff study on ARMY TACTICAL AIR SUPPORT REQUIREMENTS. It is desired that you have prepared for my signature a letter of transmittal to General Vandenberg ("Marked Personal For") and include with the papers a copy of my letter of 10 February.

These attached papers should be carefully studied and the letter that you have prepared for my signature again, very definitely should point out that the X Corps study is biased and displays great ignorance.

Reference should also be made to the study prepared by the Eighth United States Army. We must also state in the letter that the two studies referred to were not given to us for comment nor were we, the experts, permitted to offer any advice or to assist in the study. A statement should also be made that we have not secured these studies officially, but since they are so critical of our air support, they should be made available to Hq United States Air Force with our comments, and those of General Partridge, in case either study is used by the Army to detract in any way against the United States Air Force. s/G.E.S., etc.

Dispatched the fol letter to Matt Ridgway:

We have at Taegu in command of the 67th Recon Wing, Colonel Karl L. Polifka. He was sent out here at the United States Air Force's number one man in this specialized field. He is also a real planner and an organizer. While at Taegu yesterday, I discussed many subjects with him reference the use of photography - how it should be used and how the people that you have in the Eighth Army could be used to better advantage for the Eighth Army. I urge at your first opportunity you send word for Polifka to call on you in order that you can gain all possible advantageous information from him. Please, Matt, understand that I am not getting into your business, but I am so impressed with Polifka's ability that I want you to benefit therefrom. He's a team player and I'm confident can be most useful to you as well as to us with some suggestions he will make, if you request him to do so. Best regards. You are doing a great job. s/ G.E.S., etc.

About 1500 hours, Miss Mildred Tsai arrived and brought a very beautiful luncheon set from Hong Kong for me. Mildred was my Chinese interpreter during my duty in China during the last war; she is a most capable and nice young lady. I have made arrangements with SCAP for her to be assigned to my Deputy for Intelligence for duty in Headquarters, FEAF.

As a result of my R&R to VC, Ops, today's date, he sent out, with my approval, the fol rad to CG 5th AF, and CG FEAF BOMCOM, AX 2944 VCO:

This radio in five parts. *PART I.* In the conduct of joint operations, it is occasionally necessary for strategic bombardment aviation to supplement tactical aviation in close support of ground forces by area saturation or carpet bombing close to friendly front lines *(a)* to facilitate a man attack of friendly ground forces against strong enemy defensive positions, or *(b)* under emergency conditions to break up mass hostile attacks which threaten the existence of friendly ground forces. *PART II.* It is desired to further develop techniques and operational procedures for such employment of medium bombers *(a)* to bomb through an overcast, under bad weather conditions, or at night, *(b)* to improve bombing accuracy of areas lacking really unidentifiable aiming points, and *(c)* to achieve greatest possible safety to friendly ground forces. *PART III.* To accomplish the foregoing, it is desired that BOMCOM, in collaboration with Fifth Air Force, conduct tests under combat conditions at night with individual B–29 aircraft bombing with AN/MPQ-2 radar control. Consider the employment of AN/UPN-4 radar beacons as supplementary guidance and safety feature. *PART IV.* If initial test results warrant, increase utilization of B–29s to 2-3 aircraft per night as permitted by primary BOMCOM mission in order to train sufficient number of lead crews in each of our three groups in this technique to permit maximum effort strikes if called for under conditions contemplated in Part I. *PART V.* Desire that CG FEAF BomCom render a final report on this project as soon as possible, and interim reports if appropriate.

MONDAY 19 FEBRUARY 1951

Got off my weekly letter to Gill Robb Wilson. About 1500 hours Messrs Carroll, Lisle and Williams,[121] USAF Civilian Personnel, paid me a visit. Merchant claims they are helping us.

At 1600 hours, Mr. Melvin E. Terrell who heads up the Special Projects Section for Aeronautical Charts, USAF, came in to see me. I directed that he visit all of my four major commands (their headquarters) and also visit K-2 to meet and discuss the Aeronautical Charts Service with Colonel Karl Polifka, commanding the 67th Recon Wing.

Compton Pakenham, *Newsweek*, was over for cocktails and we invited him to stay to dinner. He wants me to attend with him on 15 March, near Nagoya, the primitive ceremonies that are held yearly (the only cult in existence in Japan) in worship of phallic symbols.

TUESDAY 20 FEBRUARY 1951

Yesterday approved dispatch of fol radio to Twining, # A 2981:

This msg in 3 parts. *PART I.* JCS requested CINCFE;s views in regard to CNO's recommendation to JCS that responsibility for security of the Marianas-Bonins and Volcano Islands, as well as opnl control of facilities and local forces thereon, revert to CINCPAC. *PART II.* For your info, CINCFE's views are as fols: *a.* These facilities should not be assumed by cmdr remote fr actual theater of combat opns. *b.* Bases must remain under CINCFE control for the cmds defense in depth, their use as bases for major air opns and the rqmt for a rear area for staging, maint, and re-sup[ply] of combat forces. CINCFE further states his dissatisfaction with present tenuous naval cmd relationships and recmds 7th Fleet and other temporary allocated naval forces be placed directly under him. *PART III.* I strongly concur in CINCFE's views. I must retain under my control Guam as one of my major air bases. In case of world struggle, Tinian and Saipan must remain under CINCFE.

---

121. R.E. Williams, Chief, Overseas Affairs Division, Director of Civilian Personnel, HQ USAF; Thomas D. Lisle worked in the same division; Margaret J. Carroll.

Presented the Bronze Star award to Squadron Leader Jack F. Sach who has been TDY from RAF to my Headquarters for the past year and who has been utilized in hqs as operations analysis officer. A very fine fellow. Told him so in a letter of commendation, copies of which I sent to Slessor in London and to Fogarty in Singapore. Sach is returning to duty with the RAF in England.

Mr. Pakenham came in this PM - had much discussion about the incident of last month when he was stopped on the road from Tachikawa, near Chofu City, by one of Jack Doyle's AP's [air police]. The alleged impoliteness (which I cannot understand as Pakenham, to my mind, is a polished gentleman) re both parties concerned developed into quite a flap. My Hq Provost Marshal indicated that the reason we were unaware of the incident here was that report of the incident went direct to GHQ. Beiderlinden sent over the copy they have in GHQ for me to read; instructed Jack Doyle to look into non-delivery of letters to him from Messrs Pakenham and Mr. Richard Hughes[122] and to send them both a reply. To make sure Doyle had copies of the referred to letters, I sent out copies I had made to him with a covering letter.

WEDNESDAY 21 FEBRUARY 1951

Mr. Pakenham in again this AM - re the incident on the Chofu City road last month.

U.S. Ambassador to the Philippines, Mr. Cowen,[123] called on me this AM. We had a nice chat. As a result of our conversation I sent two memos to my staff, one of which went to my D/I re the preparation of an official letter for my signature to General Turner concerning the need - and necessity - for coordination of various intelligence agency activities; the second memo was sent to D/M for him to look into the possibility of issuing commissary cards to Ambassador Cowan's staff in order to alleviate the high cost of living they undergo in Manila. D/M is to come up with an answer, prepare a letter for my signature, to General Turner.

USAF sent the fol rad:

Reurad MX 79217 D/P, 16 Feb 51. Unable to authorize permanent assignment Col. Edgar W. Hampton. Services of officer are required as soon as possible in Tactical Air Command to assist in organization of newly authorized Troop Carrier Air Force.

I looked at the pictures of Vladivostok area that were taken by the B-45.

Lt. General Tarugaki,[124] an ex-Japanese army officer, in the company of Colonel Coffey[125] (Executive, Personnel), came in to see me. He was very interesting; was a liaison officer in America at Plattsburg Barracks with General Krueger. He knew General Yamauchi[126] and was interested to learn that Yamauchi's widow lived here in Tokyo. I gave him Mrs. Yamauchi's address.

Colonel Ohman came in to see me re going to FEAF BomCom as vice commander. I had to turn him down because Hq USAF disapproved my request for Colonel Hampton on PCS.

---

122. Hughes possibly may be an Australian reporter representing the Kemsley Press.
123. Ambassador Myron M. Cowen, Ambassador Extraordinary and Plenipotentiary of the U.S. to the Philippines since March 1949.
124. Tarugaki is unknown.
125. Col Walden B. Coffey.
126. Probably Lt Gen Masafumi Yamauchi, who commanded a division in Burma during World War II.

General Partridge called and reported that he had had two days of bad luck - reference loss of airplanes. He stated that on the 20th he lost two F–80s, one pilot recovered, the other shot down and lost by ground fire. He also reported that an F4U was taking off from K-9, didn't make it, and in so doing ran into a line of F–51s washing out 7 and damaging one that can be repaired. Later, at K-9, two F–51s collided, both lost. Later, an F–51 airplane returning from a mission could not lower its landing gear and rather than land at K-10, landed at K-9, nosed up - which will require an engine change. Airplane reparable. Five F–80s, returning to K-2, apparently had homer [a radio or homing beacon] trouble and broke out of the overcast not anywhere near the homer, four of them landing on the Naktong River sandbars; one did make it in to K-2.

A MiG–15 is captured on a Sabre's gun camera film at close range.

Early this morning, one B–26 was lost due to a thousand-pound bomb exploding just under the airplane. Airplane was blown to pieces, all crew members lost. Another B–26 left the formation for some reason and has been reported missing.

Grand total of losses for the two days:

9 F–51s lost - - - - -2 damaged

2 B–26s lost

4 F–80s lost

15 airplanes lost - -2 damaged - TOTAL LOSSES.

Things are beginning to go smoothly between Neko-San and Saki-San.[127]

Received fol TS personal Stratemeyer from Col. Erler:

Re is presentation of FEAF FY 52 requirements to panels established to review budgetary submissions. FEAF program activities by location dtd 11 Feb 51, furnished us by Col. Friedman[128] indicates 1 MB [medium bomber] rotational group for Anderson AFB and 1 for Kadena AB.

127. Stratemeyer's recently acquired Siamese cats.
128. Col Robert J. Friedman was in FEAF operational planning.

For your info present USAF plan is to eliminate 1MB rotational group from FEAF deployment and rotate this unit at Hickam which becomes a SAC base. Staging facilities only would be provided at Andersen. This will leave 1 only MB rotational group at Kadena. For your further info plan here is not to provide for any additional facilities at Clark AFB in present budget submission. PARA Request guidance as to further action on these 2 installations. Panels are working towards final recommendations with 25 Feb 51 at target date.

In reply to Erler personal from Stratemeyer stated:

This radio in 5 parts. *PART I.* FEAF program dtd 11 Feb based on and consistent with Part 1, program guidance USAF expansion program Seed Corn dtd 16 Jan prepared by Asst for Programming, Hq USAF. Subj guidance directed by Hq USAF for compliance in preparation FY 51 and FY 52 budget estimates. See Hq USAF msg cite AFABF 52692 dtd 31 Jan. *PART 2.* USAF conversion and equipping program dtd 19 Jan 51 indicates 19th MB Wg permanently deployed Hickam. This and other supporting documents prepared by Hq USAF, to include troop program as of Jan 51, indicate one each SAC rotational gp at Andersen and Kadena. Further indicated is that these units rotate from ZI rpt [repeat] ZI. *PART 3.* Changes stated urad either stem from misunderstanding by panel or from changes made in guidance subsequent departure Friedman from Washington 3 Feb. *PART 4.* Provided guidance changed by Hq USAF recommend fol action your part. Such action clearly indicated by you as taken by direction Hq USAF and not as representing of FEAF rqmts: *(a)* Kadena: Indicate construction rqmts based on activities indicated in program furn you by Friedman. However, increase mil strength of 6332d Air Base Wg from 1881 to 2700. This increase based on 20th AF reviewing this program since your departure. *(b)* Andersen: Review by 20th AF indicated that mil strength for "X" Air Base Gp should be 2500 rather than 1800 as indicated our program. Accordingly if MB wing deployed this station increase population by 700 military. If MB wg not rept not deployed here reduce mil strength this unit from 2500 to 1700 and by 300 civ spaces. *(c)* Under assumption that only one MB wg is deployed to FEAF, if Hq USAF permits choice for MB rotational station, and I urgently hope they do, since I do not want my mediums based right under the gun, indicate Guam as FEAF preference rather than Kadena in which case mil strength of 6332d Air Base Wg remains at 1881 since programmed spaces are already short as stated in sub para (a) above. In either event rqmts for construction at Andersen for other than housing remains unchanged. *PART 5.* Assume your ref to Clark refers to construction rqmts for depot per FEAMCOM recommendation. If this is the case submit your construction rqmts based on populations and activities reflected in FEAF program activities by location furn you prior your departure. Any reduction below these rqmts should be made only by direction of the panel reviewing your program. Advise ASAP.

THURSDAY
22 FEBRUARY
1951

Received the fol radio from Partridge (which I showed to Nuckols for his info):

Following progress report relative to decorations awarded enlisted personnel published in GO this Hq forwarded your info. DFC 40, Soldiers Medal 12, Bronze Star Medal 134, Air Medal 952, Commendation Ribbon 477, Purple Heart 10. Enlisted personnel of this command have been awarded approximately 70 percent of all non-flying decorations. Program has been initiated command-wide to determine those airmen who in the opinion of individual commanders have performed outstandingly. Nominations have been received in this hq and will be screened by my Awards Board of Review. Awards of the Legion of Merit and Bronze Star Medal will be recommended in deserving cases. This program is in addition to other efforts.

1345 lunch at the MacArthurs in honor of General Mark Clark and his staff.[129] I have a very good friend on Clark's staff, Major General Sullivan.[130]

FRIDAY
23 FEBRUARY
1951

Following is a direct quote of a radio, dated 22 February, sent by General MacArthur to Mr. George Djamgaroff, Chairman, Organizational Committee, The 4th Anti-Communist Convention, Hotel Plaza, Room 924, New York, 19 New York:

I have just today received your letter of the 14th, leaving me insufficient time under pressure of my operational duties to prepare a comprehensive statement on so all important a subject as the Communist threat to our free existence. I am heartened, however, to see so representative a group of distinguished Americans join together for the exchange of views on the best means to counter this threat. Communism may no longer intelligently be discussed as an economic, political or social philosophy. Instead, upon the shallow pretense of human betterment, it has become but a means to satisfy a lust for personal power. Freedom has become its very antithesis. For Communism cannot survive in an atmosphere of freedom. Being a struggle for minority rule over the majority it can only gain and hold power through terrorism, subversion and deceit. To secure its purpose it must subdue the soul of man and bring his mind under the paralysis of mortal fear. Thereby it gains its unwilling converts. In its conquest of the world it has challenged the forces of freedom on the battlefields of Asia. Here the issue is drawn and the predatory Communist adventures must be decisively defeated. Otherwise, all of Asia will fall to Communism and with it Communism will gain all of the requirements to the building of a war-making potential without parallel in history in a war-making potential to point at the heart of Europe and America. Our people must awaken to the reality of this threat and resist complacent thinking that Asia is a long ways off. An Asia consolidated under the rule of those who seek to subjugate the world poses a threat at the very

---

129. Clark was in Japan on an inspection trip.
130. Maj Gen Joseph P. Sullivan was chief quartermaster of the 5th Army and 15th Army Group during World
    War II. From Nov. 1949 to June 1952, he was the Army quartermaster.

doorstep of every American home. Let only they who would see freedom perish ignore the potentiality of this threat. Signed MacArthur.

Had copies of the above radio made and sent them to Hugh Baillie, Generals Spaatz and Bradley and Whiting, Harry Bruno, etc.

Mr. Takasumi Mitsui, who is chairman of the Mitsui Foundation, accompanied by Mrs. Sohma, the daughter of Yokio Ozaki, Japan's elder statesman and the donor of the cherry trees to Washington, D.C., stopped by the office to thank me for sending Col. Brothers out to the Tokyo Imperial Hospital to inquire re the condition of Mitsui's son.[131]

Lt. Colonel Jack Dale and I discussed his efficiency reports and pass over. He is to be assigned to FEAMCOM for six months and to my Headquarters, in D/M, for six months.

SATURDAY 24 FEBRUARY 1951

Received the fol ltr from Partridge which contains a quote of a radio he received from Almond:

Dear General Strat: The following message reached my Headquarters yesterday morning. "FM: CG X Corps, TO: CG Fifth Air Force. Cite X4680. Personal for General Partridge from Almond. May I express appreciation from the troops of X Corps as well as from myself for the continued and effective air support rendered us last night and all day today. Nothing is more heartening to the front line soldier than to observe such striking power as was displayed in the X Corps area during this period. Thanks to you and your command for this splendid cooperation. /s/ALMOND"

Even if we can't satisfy all his requests, perhaps we are beginning to impress upon Almond the fact that we are doing our level best to do a first rate job of air support for him. Sincerely, E.E.P., etc. (Partridge ltr dtd 21 Feb 51)

Bucked this letter to Craigie, Weyland and Crabb for their info, and then sent it to AG file for history and record.

Left the office early to play golf at Koganei. Played with Adams versus Captain Graham and General McClure. My score 84!

SUNDAY 25 FEBRUARY 1951

Received the fol radio from Twining, personal Stratemeyer, 55498 AFODA-A:

This msg is in 2 parts. *PART I.* Reurad AX 2481 D/O dtd 8 Feb 51 and ourad 54510 dtd 9 Feb 51. Estimated out schedule of B–26 acft on proj FAF 1SB-57 fols: Jan 10, Feb 16, March 12, April 19, May 19, Jun 18. The above schedule is the AMC estimate based on an "all-out" effort. *PART II.* Reurad A 2301 D/O dtd 3 Feb 51. Based on contents of cited msg foregoing schedule will provide quantity

---

131. Mitsui was head of one of the four largest combines (*Zaibatsu* or "financial cliques") in Japan; the others being Mitsubishi, Yasuda, and Sumitomo. About 15 families constituted the *Zaibatsu* and were very powerful. MacArthur and the Occupation Forces attempted to limit the power of these combines with little success. See D. Clayton James's biography of MacArthur, Vol. III, pp 162-174 for an interesting discussion on the problems of controlling the *Zaibatsu*.

required for increased UE, however, present B–26 crew output is insufficient to meet your requirements and provide the desired rotation. Plans include increasing the B–26 ccts [combat crew training school] output, but due to the lack of B–26 acft equipped for night atk training, the effect of the increased program may not be felt for approx 6 months. Therefore it is not considered advisable to authorize an increase in the UE of your light bomb units at this time. This problem continues under active consideration and if improvement possible you will be advised.

Lunched at the Imperial with Bob McClure, General Ho Ying Chin and General Ho's interpreter, Dr. Tong.

(Dr. Hollington Tong is Chief, Central News Agency; he is sometimes called "Voice of (Nationalist) China.")

Annalee and I had dinner with the Craigies who honored General Weyland. Got off my weekly letter to Gill Robb Wilson.

MONDAY 26 FEBRUARY 1951
Generals Weyland and Crabb, Colonels Darrow, Friedman, and Ausman came into the office at 0945 and assisted in the preparation of a signal to Colonel Erler (back in Washington) who is appearing before the Installations Board. The data sent to him was in reference medium bomb groups and possible depot movement from Clark AFB to Guam or Marianas. Final signal was dispatched about 1130 hours.

General Barnes at Mayeda House for lunch. Dr. Emory Cook was not with him as Dr Cook was spending the day aboard a carrier.

Major Morris came down and briefed me on the Air Proving Ground's papers re the F–86 and F–84. One of the recommendations made by General Boatner[132] was that jet fighter runways should be increased to 9,000 feet. I told Morris that I was opposed to this and that I felt the solution was in the development of Clear-JATO - or some type of catapult should be developed which could be installed at each end of our runways and upon which a jet could taxi and some simplified cocking and firing mechanism installed.

As of this date, current disposition of F–86s in Japan: Johnson, 35; Niigata, 6; Misawa, 8; K-2, 21. TOTAL 70.

On 25 Feb dispatched fol ltr to CINCFE:

(1) The electrical power facilities of North Korea constitute an important target system which has not been subject to destruction by UN forces. *(2)* These facilities have a double significance since they supply Manchuria as well as North Korea with power. Tab A and inclosure thereto indicate the size, productive capacity and distribution of the major power systems of North Korea. The Suiho hydro electric generating plant, alone supplies nearly one-half the available power for key Manchurian centers and approximately three-eighths of the hydro power potential of North Korea. *(3)* Destruction of these facilities will hinder Communist

---

132. Maj Gen Bryant L. Boatner spent much of World War II in key assignments at Wright Field. When the USAF was established in 1947, he became Secretary of the Air Staff. Following stints as Assistant DCS/Personnel and Administration and Assistant Comptroller, he became the commander of the Air Proving Ground in July 1950.

support of the enemy war effort, adversely affect general morale, and reduce the surplus power available to Manchuria. *(4)* Request authority to attack and destroy the North Korean electrical power complex, including the Suiho plant. Destruction can be accomplished without border violation.

TUESDAY 27 FEBRUARY 1951

Colonel Roberts,[133] Dept of Army, Office of the Chief of Ordnance, who is scheduled to leave for the ZI today, came in to see me. He has been in FEAF on TDY as head of the VT [variable-time] fuze mission with our ordnance people. Had a fine talk with him at 1030 hours re VT fuzes - Tarzon and Razon.

Dispatched a personal radio to Vandenberg asking him to OK an SAM [Special Air Mission] airplane to transport Hap Gay, Mrs. Gay and his aides to his new station in San Antonio, Texas, inasmuch as Hap has been a booster for our tactical support given him when he was CG 1st Cav Div. I urged approval.

Directed via R&R to VC Ops and D/Ops to bring D/I into the picture re reconnaissance missions over Manchuria, and also brief me on best method to be used - if need be, if it is deemed desirable, I will go to USAF for additional RB–45s to do the job.

Left the office early and played golf with Major Davison versus Sgt Jennings and General McClure. We got whipped all three ways.

WEDNESDAY 28 FEBRUARY 1951

Annalee left this AM for Kyoto accompanied by Mrs. Picher and General Weyland and my senior aide. She will return Friday.

Upon arrival at the office, Major Lockwood, my pilot on staff C–54, met me and explained that the staff C–54 could not be repaired satisfactorily at FEAMCOM, which made me angry and exasperated. *Immediately dispatched the fol personal radio to Chidlaw:*

> FEAF capabilities have been exhausted attempting to repair fuel leaks in FEAF staff airplane C–54E, 44-9149. This airplane was a lousy one when it was transferred to me from Bolling and TEMCO didn't help.[134] The aircraft can be released for a one time flight to the ZI with the No. 4 auxiliary tank blocked off. I would like to have a high priority project initiated at one of your depots for the complete resealing and repair of the integral fuel tanks or preferably to expedite it (I need it badly) remove wings and install new ones with good tanks, put in new wings, my four good engines and return. The airplane is in good condition otherwise and due to the large amount of work expended I should like to have the same airplane returned to me quickly. If repairs are instituted, repair of the wing will involve removal of outboard wing panels, replacement of rivets and skin in numerous areas, and resealing of all tanks. The center section tanks also require extensive repair and resealing. It is estimated that with a high priority the repairs could be completed within five weeks. I do not want to wait that long. I would like to get this airplane into work as soon as

---

133. Col C.H.M. Roberts, Chief, Ammunitions Branch.
134 . TEMCO was a Texas-based aircraft refurbishing and conversion company.

possible and will appreciate your personal interest in expediting the work and advising me of the depot that will accomplish the repairs or wing change. I need your help.

After briefing, Major Arthur L. Stevens, Jr., who was sent out here from AMC re the napalm mix mission, checked in at the office prior to his departure.

Dispatched the fol personal radio to Twining at Crabb's request for a senior field grade officer to head up Air Defense:

PERSONAL TWINING FROM STRATEMEYER: I have urgent require-ment for a senior field grade officer for assignment to duty as my Direc-tor of Air Defense under my Deputy for Operations. I have thoroughly screened those officers assigned to FEAF who might meet qualifications desired for this position. The only officer within FEAF who meets desired qualifications is assigned as Deputy for Operations, 314th Air Division, the organization which is charged with primary responsibility for air defense of Japanese islands. I cannot transfer this officer from this key spot to my Hq. FEAF is currently planning for the permanent air defense system in the Far East and is in the process of negotiating joint agree-ments with ground and Navy commands for integration of Navy and Army air defense capabilities with that of FEAF. The availability on my staff of an officer with comprehensive background and experience in air defense planning is most essential during this critical period. I have in mind an officer who has had experience on staff of Air Defense Com-mand or Eastern or Western Air Defense Force and who is thoroughly familiar with current Air Force doctrine and planning for air defense. If possible, request one of the following named officers be made available for assignment to my Hq: Edward F. Rector, Colonel; Joseph A. Cun-ningham, Colonel; Edwin F. Carey, Jr., Colonel; Arvid E. Olson, Jr., Colonel.[135] If none of these officers is available, request assignment of an officer of comparable background and experience in air defense.

Upon return from lunch, received news of the near-disastrous fire at Ashiya in which the warehouse which housed spare parts for C–54s and '119s, plus radar equipment, burned. In that warehouse was 50% of the world's supply of '119 spare parts.

THURSDAY 1 MARCH 1951

Dispatched fol operational immediate radio personal to Vandenberg with personal info to Partridge:

Following received from Partridge: "During recent visit General Vandenberg to this hqs and EUSAK hqs, General Vandenberg in personal conversation with General Ridgway indicated availability of new type bomb capable of destroying Hwach'ŏn Dam. Desire information as to whether General Vandenberg was referring to the Tarzon bomb or a newer development. Request information as to par-ticular type bomb and availability as EUSAK desirous of destroying as

---

135. Rector was Chief, Air Defense Division, Office of the DCS for Development, HQ USAF. Both he and Olson had flown with the Flying Tigers in World War II. What positions the other officers held is unknown.

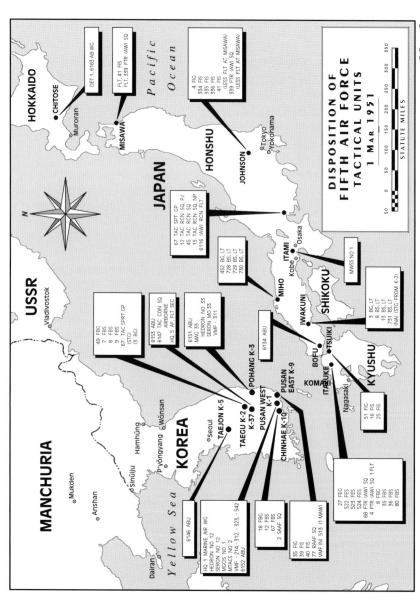

Map 8.

DISPOSITION OF
FIFTH AIR FORCE
TACTICAL UNITS
1 MAR 1951

STATUTE MILES
50 0 50 100 150 200 250 300 350

soon as possible." I recall your discussion with Landon on the possibility of dispatching from SAC a flight of airplanes with block-buster type bombs for dam destruction. I did not hear your discussion with Ridgway. Would appreciate answer to Partridge's query.

Received a very curt letter from Mrs. Walter Simmons whose husband, representative over here of the *Chicago Tribune*, had directed her to write and forward to me a censored copy of one of his releases. My censor had deleted all references to "accurate anti-aircraft" fire over P'yŏngyang and the harrassing qualities the men were experiencing from the wires the Commies had been stretching between mountains, etc. Mrs. Simmons had indicated that her husband thought these deletions were "unnecessary" and "he was not going to consider the Air Force in any future story he might write." I sent Mrs. S a letter of explanation with a copy going to her husband in Korea of why we had made such censorship, and endeavored to placate both. That letter surprised me - it was the damndest, silliest thing I've received in a long time, to say nothing of being a reflection as to the smallness of what I had thought to be a first-class correspondent.

At 3:30 attended the memorial services for Major General Bryant E. Moore[136] (former CG IX Corps, who died of a heart attack following a front-line helicopter crash, on 24 Feb) at the Chapel Center.

FRIDAY
2 MARCH
1951

Upon my arrival at the office, read the radio (following) received from USAF re transportation for Hap Gay, his wife and aides, from the West Coast to San Antonio:

Personal for Stratemeyer from Twining: Concerning transportation Major General Hobart R. Gay arriving San Francisco about 20 March, such transportation is contrary to existing policy unless there is an extenuating circumstance other than that given in your message. Will reconsider if you will provide logical reasons for this transportation. In addition, I am sure you can understand that we are in no position to set a precedent of this kind unless circumstances are unusual.

About 1120 hours, Nuckols came in with the GHQ PIO radio-recorder man and I made the following statement into a tape recorder for the "West Point Tape." (Also bucked a copy of my statement to Courtney Whitney for his info.)

Under the brilliant leadership of West Point's most distinguished son, General of the Army Douglas MacArthur, class of 1903, the Far East Air Forces during the Korean campaign have formed an echelon of the United Nations Command. This closely integrated and coordinated effort with the ground and naval services is giving the world a demonstration of the power which may be mounted only thru operational unification of the combined arms on the battle front. Ever mindful of General MacArthur's oft repeated warning that "THERE IS NO SUBSTITUTE FOR VICTORY" inspired by West Point's great tradition, and impelled by devotion to duty, honor, country, the Far East Air Forces - by round the clock operations is giving our

---

136. Moore had taken command of IX Corps in January. See Blair, *The Forgotten War*, p 727, for details of his death.

actual and potential enemies an insight into the enormous power of which American air might is capable thereby contributing in full measure toward ultimate victory.

Admiral Struble called to invite Annalee and me to lunch aboard the *Missouri* on Thursday, 8 March. I will RSVP later - my plans for next week are not firm as yet.

Bucked the fol copy to Vandenberg of the radio received by Partridge from Ferenbaugh,[137] CG 7th Inf Div, dated 28 Feb 51:

From: CG 7th Inf Div; To: CG EUSAK, CG FAF, thru: JOC: Close air support given this division during period of 24 Feb 1951 to 26 Feb 1951 outstanding. Excellent results of air strikes enabled taking of objectives with minimum casualties. I wish to express my appreciation for superior cooperation of JOC in filling requests for fighter aircraft in numbers sufficient to saturate hill masses. Fine work of Mosquito also worthy of commendation. Sgd Ferenbaugh.

At 6:30, General Craigie and I attended the Top Secret presentation by JSPOG in the Chief of Staff's (FEC) conference room. General MacArthur was present.

SATURDAY, SUNDAY, and MONDAY 3-5 MARCH 1951

Took off Saturday at 1005 hours, 3 March and arrived at Guam 6:00 P.M. Tokyo time, or 7:00 P.M. Guam time which was very embarrassing as we had informed Gilkeson that we would arrive there at 6:00 P.M. and they had been waiting there since that time.

Sunday morning I took the Review for the eight awards that were made. The citations were read over the loudspeakers to the troops, after which I made the presentations. The Review, including the uniforms of the airmen and the band music, were all anyone could wish for. Immediately after the Review, I inspected the entire post including the AMMO outfit and the bomb dump from which they were transferring 10,000 500 lb G.P.s to Japan.

There was no entertainment on my behalf, for which I was grateful.

Spent Sunday afternoon fishing off the end of the island without success, but had a most restful and pleasant time. A Mr. and Mrs. Brown accompanied us as well as three of Gilkeson's staff officers and his WAF lieutenant, Lt. McLaughlin.[138]

Departed Monday morning at 8:00 A.M. for Iwo Jima where I landed at 1206. I was met by the commanding officer, had lunch, and then inspected all facilities at Iwo Jima.

This place has really boomed. All the new buildings will be completed by 20 April. There has been a contract let to remove all old buildings, junk, etc. from the island which will net the government some $109,000 and which will improve the looks of the island.

Departed Iwo at 1:40 P.M., Iwo time, and arrived back in Tokyo at 4:40 P.M. (Tokyo time).

---

137. Maj Gen Claude B. Ferenbaugh became the 7th Division's commander in January.
138. McLaughlin's full name is unknown.

TUESDAY
6 MARCH
1951

Went down to Directorate of Plans office and Colonel Zimmerman gave me a verbal report on his trip to Washington.

His reactions to his visit (although all of the officers in Hq USAF were thinking of the budget and the ZI instead of the Korean War) were good.

He put over his points, including a request from General Twining for a copy of the paper he took back. Apparently all the top-side in USAF are in agreement with our suggestions as to the operations to be continued in Korea.

Got off the weekly Gill Robb Wilson letter.

WEDNESDAY
7 MARCH
1951

Received radio from Hickam that aboard Constellation C-121, the following would land at Haneda today approximately 1300 hours: General Chidlaw, Maj. Gen. Schlatter, Maj. Gen. Stone, Brig. Gen. Early, Col. W. Richardson, Col. A.E. Watson, Col. A.G. Hewitt, Col. K.L. Garrett, Mr. O.L. Johnson, Mr. M.L. Peale and Mr. J.L. Atwood.*[139] They are arriving via Wake.

*Mr. O.L. Johnson, Lockheed Aviation Corp, Mr. Lee Atwood, Pres North Am Avn Corp, and Mr. M.L. Peale, Republic Avn Corp.

Chidlaw party arrived early; they were due at 1406 and got in somewhere around 1350.

We had Gordon and Mary Tweedy[140] to dinner. Also there occurred the damnedest mix-up on transportation that I've had since I arrived here.

THURSDAY
8 MARCH
1951

At the briefing present as my guests were Mr. Earle Cocke,[141] National Commander of the American Legion and two accompanying civilians who are members of his party, and Lt. General B.W. Chidlaw with his party including Generals Stone, Schlatter and Early.

1030 hours I had in my office Col. Simons, Lt. Col. Carmichael (FEAF transportation officer), S/Sgt Switcher[142] (dispatcher for last night), and the Japanese driver reference the tie-up on transportation for Gordon and Mary Tweedy. It is my opinion that this will not happen again.

1400 hours, attended a luncheon at General MacArthur's in honor of Mr. Earle Cocke.

1900 hours attended a dinner party at the Craigies in honor of General Chidlaw and his entire party.

In the morning and in the afternoon, whenever I could be present, I attended the briefings and meetings for General Chidlaw's party in the Deputy for Operations conference room. I feel that a great deal thus far has been accomplished.

---

139. Maj Gen David M. Schlatter, Commander, Research and Development Command; Maj Gen Charles B. Stone, Director of Maintenance, Supply and Services, Office of DC/S Materiel, Headquarters USAF; Brig Gen James F.J. Early, Chief, Supply Division, AMC; Col William L. Richardson; Col Albert G. Hewitt, Deputy Chief, Maintenance Division, AMC. The jobs of the other officers are unknown.
140. These individuals are not identified.
141. Cocke, assistant to the president of Delta Air Lines, was National Commander in 1950-1951
142. Carmichael's and Switcher's full names are unknown.

**FRIDAY
9 MARCH
1951**
_____

Left the office early (1100 hours) to drive with Annalee to Yokosuka where we had lunch as Admiral Struble's guests aboard the *Missouri*. Very pleasant and interesting - but was away from my desk too damn long. Didn't leave the ship until 1600 hours in the afternoon, consequently arrived back at the office about 1730 hours.

**SATURDAY
10 MARCH
1951**
_____

Departed 0730 from Haneda with Chidlaw party (Generals Chidlaw, Schlatter, Stone and Early) and proceeded direct to Hq Fifth Air Force, K-2. Spent the day there. All were pleased with what they saw and found - and especially impressed with the very fine briefings presented by Partridge's staff. Returned to Tokyo and landed about 2130 hours.

**SUNDAY
11 MARCH
1951**
_____

Bucked the fol memos to D/M: (1) In a discussion with General Partridge yesterday, he has about reached the conclusion that the AF should have a depot in Korea. As you know, the Army has a large ammo depot and vehicular overhaul depot in Pusan. It is desired that you look into this and come up with a recommendation as to what we should do. The Fifth Air Force in Korea have many vehicles that are in bad condition. When they turn one into the Army for overhaul, they get none in return - and it's the last they see of the one they turned in. What is our procedure on getting from the Army out requirements in general purpose vehicles? Are we being treated any differently in the issue of transportation vehicles than those that are issued to units in the Army? General Partridge is not happy with the situation. Hundreds of new vehicles come into the port of Pusan apparently, but they all go to the Army. Our T/O&E equipment is not kept up. WHY?

Stratemeyer and Partridge discuss the current situation following the FEAF commander's arrival at Suwŏn.

Memo to D/M #2: General Partridge informed me the Fifth Air Force in Korea, when they go into khaki want three uniforms per man. He has heard that the Army intends to issue only two uniforms per man to the Army personnel. General Partridge wonders if he will be able to get his three. Certainly our AF people need three khaki uniforms and it is hard for me to see how anyone can get by with only two. Make some investigation into this matter and report to me.

To D/O I sent the fol memo: A Captain Butler[143] of the 315th Air Division, who is a C-47 pilot in Korea, has some ideas about napalm bombs for B-29

---

143. Probably Capt Floyd D. Butler, a pilot with the 21st TCS.

use at low altitude. (I refer to General Partridge's present message which contained a query from General Ridgway.) It is desired that you have Captain Butler ordered into this headquarters for questioning and get his mind straightened out on making these reports or suggestions - certainly they should not be made to ground generals. When he gets here and after he has been questioned, I want to see him.

Dispatched the fol personal signal to Vandenberg:

On 16 Feb in your RL 154, you indicated that you wanted Weyland to receive his third star while still here in war zone. Three weeks have now passed. Is it possible to tell me the approximate date Weyland will be returned? I intend to use him in a temporary assignment if time permits with Fifth Air Force reference the JOC and close support to assist in solving an important problem which has arisen. This will take from seven to ten days.

While I was in Korea yesterday, at my request, D/O sent the following radio - PERSONAL CANNON[144] INFO TWINING FROM STRATEMEYER:

PART I. It is my opinion that both FEAF and TAC can acquire material of mutual benefit through a greater degree of coordination, exchange of info and knowledge concerning tac procedures, doctrine, development, and technique of employment of air in the tac role. *PART II.* Since your comd is charged w/the responsibility of developing USAF tac doctrine and procedures and maintaining liaison w/Army field forces, I believe that it would be possible for FEAF to profit considerably by establishing closer liaison and working relationships w/your hq at this time. I am particularly interested in TAC's approach to and solution of the many problems inherent in air-grd opns which might be applied in the Korean War. *PART III.* Conversely, I am sure that you are interested in obtaining all possible info concerning our experiences and difficulties resulting fr our active participation in spt of the 8th Army in Korea. While I realize that many of our experiences here are peculiar to this theater and to the type of war now being conducted in Korea, I feel also that many of them may well have a far reaching influence in future development, plans, and policies related to air-grd opns. *PART IV.* I propose for your consideration the exchange of staff officers between our respective hq and comds on short pds [periods] of TDY on a continuing basis. I have in mind sending sr staff officers, particularly fr FEAF and 5AF Opns, to your hq for pds of 15 days for asgmt to and experience w/your staff and subordinate comds. I would likewise appreciate the opportunity of integrating TAC ops pers into FEAF and 5AF Opns staff for pds of approx 30 days. I believe such an exchange of selected officers would fac[ilitate] the ready exchange of "know how" and experience between our comds. *PART V.* Req your comments and/or concurrence on the merits of the proposal I have outlined.

---

144. Gen John K. Cannon held many important assignments in World War II, including commander 12AF and Air Commander in Chief, Allied Air Forces, Mediterranean. Following the war, he was Commanding General, ATC and the USAFE commander. He had commanded TAC since October 1950.

If you agree that such an exchange of pers will be mutually beneficial, I suggest your making recms [recommendations] to USAF, info to me, w/ a view to initiation of the program ASAP.

Dispatched a short note to Briggs telling him that I do not want Jennings rotated to SAC under our rotational policy. I want to keep him out here indefinitely.

Held the final conference with General Chidlaw and his group at 1500 hours. The general reactions from all of Chidlaw's party and from our people have been very favorable. I know we gained greatly and from conversations with the Chidlaw party, I am confident they likewise secured vast amounts of information which is going to be helpful back at AMC.

At 1930 hours, we gave a dinner party at Mayeda House honoring General Chidlaw and his party.

MONDAY 12 MARCH 1951

Got off a statement to Gill Robb Wilson with copies going to Generals Spaatz and Bradley. Also send copies to Lowell Thomas, George Fielding Eliot, and Dick Howard[145] - cautioning all that it was my "private thinking," they could use it, but it was not attributable to me.

TUESDAY 13 MARCH 1951

Received the fol radio from Vandenberg:

Cite 56784. This concerns your message on return of Weyland and approximate date he may be expected to receive his third star. Expect that his name will be submitted by the President to the Senate Armed Services Committee within next two (2) or three (3) days. Date of approval by the Senate, of course, is uncertain. It usually takes them ten (10) days to three (3) weeks. Suggest therefore that you proceed with your plans to use Weyland on special assignment with the Fifth Air Force. After Weyland's third star has been confirmed, we can return him at your convenience.

After the briefing this AM, the SAAF senior liaison officer, Col Jan Daniel Pretorius called on me in my office and said that when his men heard that the 77th RAAF was converting to jets, their morale took a drop. As a result of our conversation, *dispatched the fol letter to Marshal of the Royal Air Force, Sir John C. Slessor:*

Dear Jack. As you know the 77th Royal Australian Air Force Fighter Squadron is being re-equipped with jet airplanes - the Meteor VIII's. That leaves the other British Commonwealth unit, the South African Air Force Squadron, Number 2, which operate under my control, equipped with F–51s. I have just had a talk with the senior liaison officer, Colonel Jan Daniel Pretorius and he indicated to me that he has suggested back to his Government in South Africa the re-equipping of the 2d Fighter Squadron with the new Vampire Mark Vs.[146] He also indicated to me that the South African Air Force is re-equipping its fighter units with the Vampire Mark V.

---

145. Author, lecturer, adventurer, Thomas had been involved with aviation since the 1920s; Eliot had been writing on military affairs since 1928; Nathaniel Richardson Howard was editor of the *Cleveland Plain Dealer*.
146. The South Africans eventually equipped with F–86s instead of Vampires.

I, therefore, suggest to you that it might be possible in your position as the head of the Royal Air Force to divert as soon as possible to the 2d South African Squadron here in the Far East sufficient new Vampires to equip them in order that they may be tested under combat conditions. This South African fighter squadron contains the cream of the South African Air Force fighter pilots. They were hand picked and are a wonderful group of gentlemen who have been hard at this air fighting in Korea since their arrival. There is no better operational training unit in the world than the United States Far East Air Forces. As you know, Vandenberg is testing out, under my command, besides the F–80, the F–84E, the F–86A, and soon, the F–94A all-weather interceptor. If I am out of turn, Jack, in making this suggestion to you, please understand that it is done to improve our fighting ability out here and to improve the efficiency and better the equipment of the British Commonwealth fighter units operating under my control. Best regards.

Received the fol signal from Cannon: In reference the rad I sent him (see diary entry 11 March)

Reference FEAF Message AX 4663, personal Stratemeyer to Cannon. Enthusiastically concur with the proposal to exchange senior staff officers between this command and FEAF. Request USAF authority and implementing instructions for airlift of personnel to place our officers from this command 30 day TDY FEAF on a continuing basis, officers to be in place FEAF approximately first each month. First increment depart ZI 20 March 51.
(This radio directed to USAF - Twining also)

Captain Butler, of the SAM organization at K-27 in the 315th Air Division, who talked out of turn about the 4,000 pound napalm bomb to be dropped out of a B–29, reported in to me at 1100 hours. I gave him some straight forward fatherly advice - to wit: "sound off all you want to - but to Air Force officers, and when you talk, particularly to senior officers of the Army or Navy, be sure that you know what you are talking about. In the case at hand, you knew nothing about what you said and as a result caused trouble for General Partridge and for me." All in all, it is my opinion that he is a fine young officer and when he found himself in close contact with General Ridgway, he just ignorantly sounded off. I do not want to hurt him.

As a result of Butler's sounding off to Ridgway, on 11 Mar sent the fol personal to Partridge, with info to Briggs and Henebry:

Part I. Extensive tests were conducted at Eglin Field in Oct 45 to determine suitable means of dropping napalm gel as a fire bomb from bomb acft, Proj PL-44-78 dtd 4 Oct 45. The 4000 lb AN-N56 (cap[acity] of 260 gals) and the 2,000 lb AN-M66 (Cap of 86 gals) along with various other type containers were tested. It was concluded that all aval containers for carrying and releasing napalm from bombardment acft at high altitudes were unsuitable for the folg reasons: *(1)* Efficient loads cannot be carried using aimable containers. *(2)* Containers which permitted as efficient bombing load produced cratering and poor functioning, with consequent excessive loss in bomb effectiveness. *(3)* All of the modified containers tested for carrying and releasing napalm gel from other than minimum alt proved inferior to the unstabilized tank released from ftrs at min alt. Further tests conducted in 1947, Proj PL-45-7 18 Aug 47 with B–29s produced the same conclusion as previous tests. To be effective the fire bombs have to be released from 120-200 ft and the vulnerability of this large and unmaneuverable airplane precludes its use at these altitudes. *Part II.* I have previously advised Hq USAF: *a.* That I consider napalm primarily a low altitude weapon due to unsatisfactory cratering characteristics when dropped from high altitudes, *b.* That I do not consider the fire bomb suitable for use in B–29s since they should not be used for low level work. Part III. In view of these facts, please advise me whether you wish further examination of this problem.

In reply to the foregoing, received the folg from Partridge: "Based on information received, no further examination of problem recommended."

WEDNESDAY 14 MARCH 1951

AVM Bouchier brought me a list of questions to answer for Jack Slessor, RAF Chief of Air Force. Referred them to Dir, Installations (thru VC A&P and D/M) for answer and also for them to draft up a letter of transmittal, for my signature, to Slessor. In addition, copies of our questions and answers to Slessor will forward, with a covering letter from me, to Vandenberg.

THURSDAY 15 MARCH 1951

Received good news this AM - *(1)* Clyde L. Brothers, my FEAF staff surgeon recommended for his "first star" and also *received (2) the following radio from Twining:*

The President this date submitted to Senate nominations of Gen. Partridge to Be CG, 5th AF, with rank of lt. general, and Gen. Weyland to be Deputy CG, FEAF with rank of lt. general. Since these appointments are tendered under Section 504, OPA 1947, both officers' stars are pinned to job in which they have been nominated. If they are relieved from these jobs, this law requires that their lt. generalcy be terminated unless they are nominated and confirmed in another designated 3-star position. Therefore, we are issuing order relieving Weyland from assignment TAC and assigning him to your command for duty as Deputy CG and his return to the ZI will be on a TDY basis so he can legally retain his new grade. The C/S desired that Weyland be promoted to 3-stars while he was in your theater and this is the only legal way it could be accomplished. You will also note that Weyland's nomination reads "Deputy CG, FEAF" instead of "Vice Commander for Operations." We designated this position as "Deputy CG FEAF" as it was felt here it would carry more weight for his promotion than his designation as VC for Operations, and since he was to be returned to the ZI in the near future, it would not detrimentally affect your organizational structure. The law with regard to lt. generals, while it is cumbersome administratively, is very specific in the fact that generals and lt. generals who hold their ranks under Section 504, cannot be moved from job to job without nomination by the President and confirmation by the Senate. Return Weyland on TDY at your convenience after appointment. Will advise you further when Weyland's new position is designated and his nomination in this new job is submitted. Upon confirmation in his next position, orders will issue here relieving him from assignment your command will terminate his planned TDY here.

Immediately upon receipt of this radio wrote Earle Partridge the fol letter:

Dear Earle, The attached came in this morning and I'm sure, Earle, you must know how happy and pleased I am with this promotion of yours to lt gen. You have earned this third star in a most difficult command position, and, furthermore, you have lived up to all the traditions that exist in the USAF. Note that this is SECRET because of certain data reference Weyland, and I ask that you place it in your SECRET file. I will give you the information reference yourself over the telephone as soon as possible. Again, my heartfelt congratulations for receipt of one of the most deserving promotions that I know of during my 41 years in service. All good wishes and may everything good continue to come your way. God Bless and long life. Sincerely, G.E.S., etc.

Received the fol ltr from LeMay which I bucked to members of my staff:

I have considered at some length the proposal in your letter of 16 Feb that B–36s, operating directly from bases in the US, bomb a NK target. After weighing all the factors, pro and con, I am convinced that the advantages of such a mission would be greatly outweighed by the disadvantages. The logistics situation would not sustain such a project and also the current program. As you know, we have curtailed our training to be able to build up a small reserve of spare engines for use in the initial months of an emergency. An operation against NK would consume these engines, would require some storage of spare engines in FEAF and would reduce our capability for the main mission. Spare parts and ground handling equipment might have to be diverted into Japan or Okinawa. These items are also in short supply and would have to be taken from bases currently involved in emergency war plans. In SAC we have only 37 B–36s. The remainder are rotating through depots and modification centers. Training and planning are aimed toward keeping our assigned '36s ready for the war missions. You can see from the above why I shy away from diverting any of the '36s to a project of bombing a NK target. I feel certain you will agree we should not attempt it. I am glad to hear that Briggs is doing well and that our units are performing satisfactorily. At any time if deficiencies are exposed in training or equipment, please let me know. We want to benefit, SAC-wide, as much as possible from our experience in FEAF. Warm regards. Sincerely, Curtis LeMay.

We received word that Ted Timberlake, Partridge's vice commander, received notification of his temporary appointment to major general, USAF.

Reference Generals Partridge's and Timberlake's promotions, I called their respective wives and told them about it. Of course, they were both very, very happy.

Received fol reply from Briggs in reply to my ltr of 11 March:

I have your letter of the 11th of March with reference to Colonel Jennings. I had not considered that Colonel Jennings was eligible for rotation to the States under the current SAC plan. Colonel Jennings will, of course, stay in the theater for a full foreign service tour and be rotated only in accordance with FEAF policy. A recommendation for the Legion of Merit for Colonel Jennings is now in your Headquarters. I have included in the citation reference to his superior work in the whole field of command of the 19th Group, rather than refer to the Tarzon project only. Colonel Jennings is submitting a recommendation for the Legion of Merit for Colonel Cannon,[147] Tarzon Project Officer, who, I think, is also deserving.

**FRIDAY
16 MARCH
1951**

General J. T. Cole (Tupper),[148] Chief, Military Assistance Advisory Group to the Thai government and Colonel Ray Schrock, his USAF deputy, reported in this morning. They have a proposition to offer (political) of a Siamese detachment of some six to eight pilots, with their L–4 liaison planes for service in Korea. I turned them over to D/O for discussion and told them to proceed to Korea and find out from General Partridge if he could use the Siamese detachment.

After the briefing, talked a bit with presidential advisor General Lowe and told him that I didn't like the fact that Mr. Cocke (American Legion Commander) in his press conference made no mention of the Air Force. Lowe agreed that Cocke had been remiss and that it would not occur again.

Approved the report submitted by the board I had appointed (6 Feb 51) to look into awards & decorations. Forwarded a copy of this report to General Vandenberg with a covering letter, pointing out to him the lack of uniformity amongst the three services in making awards and decorations to their personnel. Also stated that I felt this matter is one that should be handled at Air Force level.

**SATURDAY
17 MARCH
1951**

Made another trip with MacArthur to Korea. Took off at 0700 hours, landed at Suwŏn at 1100 hours, and departed there for Wŏnju by C–47 aircraft and then proceeded from Wŏnju, some 40 miles forward, to the First Marine Division frontline battalions. The First Marine Division looked fine.

The cushions in the SCAP were most comfortable after that 80 mile ride in a jeep, and I marvelled at General MacArthur who, after his 80-mile ride, and at 71 years, was just as spry, interested, and excited as a youngster. If I'm that good at 71 I will be most grateful.

Flew direct from Wŏnju to Taegu where we met General Partridge and changed from the '47 to SCAP and immediately proceeded home, arriving at Haneda about 1920 hours. All in all it was a fine trip.

---

147. Col Vincent T. Cannon.
148. Brig Gen John Tupper Cole was appointed chief of the Army Section, MAAG, Thailand, in January.

Nuckols, in my name, dispatched the fol radio to Vandenberg:

Personal Vandenberg from Stratemeyer. FEAF mounted greatest effort of Korean war on Friday, March 16th. Revised figures now show 1,123 effective sorties flown, including those of SAAF, RAAF, and land-based Marines.

Nuckols, in my name, dispatched fol congratulatory signal to Partridge:

Personal Partridge from Stratemeyer. Congratulations to you and entire 5th Air Force in again exceeding previous records by mounting 829 effective sorties for Friday's operations resulting in new overall record for FEAF of 1,123 sorties. This new record could not have been accomplished without the enthusiastic participation of all assigned and attached units under your command. Please pass to them my sincere congratulations.

SUNDAY
18 MARCH
1951

Dispatched the fol memorandum to CINCFE:

Friday, 16 March 1951, the Far East Air Forces, including United Nations' units and land-based Marine Corps units operating under our control, set a new all-time high sortie mark of 1,123 sorties. The previous high sortie figure was 1,069 on 8 March 1951. The Navy on 16 March 1951 flew 354 sorties on that date - making a grand total for the day of 1,477 sorties. s/G.E.S., etc.

Dispatched ops immed the fol signal - to CG 8th Army, info CINCFE, CG 5th AF, CG 315th Air Div, and FEAF D/O:

PERSONAL RIDGWAY FROM STRATEMEYER INFORMATION PERSONAL HICKEY, PARTRIDGE, HENEBRY FROM STRATE-MEYER. Radio in three parts. *PART I*. This relates to our conversation 17 March relative to adv notice which FEAF requires to airdrop RCT. I have investigated problem and placed the 315th AD on a semi-alert status today. We desire five days for perfection; however w/ all-out effort, we can prepare for airdrop 2/48 hrs adv notice and give you the seventy C–119s and thirty C–46s at K-2 which are required. *PART II*. In 36 hrs we can provide sixty C–119s and thirty C–46s at K-2, however, do not believe this would meet your rqmts. We naturally prefer as much adv notice as possible to guarantee you a first-class job. *PART III*. During preparatory stand-down and during mission we will be unable to provide you w/front line cargo airdrop; however, will be able to provide your normal A/L [airlift] rqmts.

Busy as hell in the morning, but left the office at 1030 for a game of golf. Had a fine game with General Robertson, Capt. Davison, Admiral Joy - Davison and I took them.

MONDAY   *In reply to Ridgway's signal to CINCFE in praise of*
19 MARCH   *sister services, dispatched the fol to him (Ridgway):*
1951

PERSONAL RIDGWAY FROM STRATEMEYER. Please accept my deep appreciation for your splendid message of 17 March expressing your admiration for the manner in which the sister services have supported the units of your command. No enemy can hope to achieve victory over a team such as we have under the inspired leadership and direction of General MacArthur. It gives me great pleasure and pride to pass on your stimulating message to the units of FEAF.

Dispatched to 5th AF, FEAF BomCom, 20th AF, 315th AirDiv, FEAMCOM, CO FEAF Base with info to CINCFE, COMNAVFE and EUSAK, the following:

It gives me great satisfaction to pass on to you the following message from the CG, Eighth Army, to CINCFE, to which I add my personal congratulations for your continued magnificent performance:

"I wish to express to all members of your command my admiration for the manner in which they have supported combat operations during the past three months. Their courage, tenacity and determination to win over seemingly unsurmountable odds have resulted in the inflicting of severe defeats and exceedingly heavy casualties on the enemy.

"During the next few months enemy action will perhaps bring us even greater challenges than those when were confronted and conquered during the winter and I feel certain that the actions of our combined forces will permit us to emerge victorious.

"I have complete and unswerving confidence in this battle tested team of Army, Navy and Air Force, bound together by mutual respect and confidence - a respect and confidence built upon steadfastness in battle and devotion to one common purpose."

I am confident that under the inspiring leadership and direction of our Commander-in-Chief, General MacArthur, we shall be able to mount in coordination with our sister services, the Army and Navy, the destructive power essential to ultimate victory. s/G.E. Stratemeyer, Lt. Gen., USAF.

Dispatched the following courier signal to CG FEAMCOM:

FEAF units 16 March mounted a new record of 1123 effective sorties. This magnificent effort which was preceded by over 1000 daily sorties last week could not have been accomplished without the sustained support rendered by FEAMCOM since the beginning of hostilities. It gives me great pleasure and pride to forward message received from General Hoyt S. Vandenberg, CSAF, and to add my appreciation for the support FEAMCOM has rendered. Message follows: QUOTE "Personal Stratemeyer from Vandenberg. The effort mounted by FEAF in air operations on March 16th of 1123 effective sorties is most gratifying. Please convey to the commanders, air and ground crews, and others responsible for the splendid achievement my highest commendations for a job well done." UNQUOTE. s/G.E. Stratemeyer, Lt. Gen, USAF.

*To CG 5th AF, FEAF BomCom, 20th AF, and 315th Air Div, with info
to CINCFE, sent the fol:*

It is with great pride that I pass on to you the following message from
General Hoyt S. Vandenberg, CSAF. The ability to launch this massive air
assault is indicative of the high effectiveness of your organization.
(COMGEN FIFTH AF: Pass to CO of following units under your operational control - ROK, SAAF, RAAF, 1st Marine Air Wing. COMGEN
315th AIR DIV: Pass to CO, 13th Royal Hellenic Flight.) Message
follows: QUOTE "Personal Stratemeyer from Vandenberg. The effort
mounted by FEAF in air operations on Mar 16 of 1123 effective sorties
is most gratifying. Please convey to the commanders, air and ground
crews, and others responsible for the splendid achievement my highest
commendations for a job well done." UNQUOTE. Signed G.E. Stratemeyer, Lt. Gen., USAF.

Left the office before noon to visit the 315th Air Division Hq at Fuchu. Was
met by General Henebry. Had a pleasant discussion with him and his VC,
Colonel Childre,[149] in his office. Was then given a very fine briefing in their conference room followed by an average luncheon - by that I mean the food was
average - the company was superior.

Returned to the Meiji Building at 1400 hours.

Part III of my radio to EUSAK on 18 Mar (see diary entry) needed
revision and clarification. *As a result dispatched the fol to EUSAK,
with info to CINCFE, CG 5th AF, and 315th Air Div:*

PERSONAL RIDGWAY FROM STRATEMEYER INFORMATION
PERSONAL HICKEY, PARTRIDGE, AND HENEBRY. This rad in 2
parts. *PART I.* Reour AX 5018 CG PART III, 18 Mar 51, and confirming
telecon Craigie-Hodes, this date, on basis 48 hours advance notice, it is
our present estimate that we may be able to furnish up to 50 tons air drop
per day from D minus 2 through D-Day. To do so will in all probability
disrupt our airlift and other air transport commitments to some extent.
Therefore, if possible, we would appreciate your pre-planning your logistical flow in such a manner as to make air drop unnecessary during this
period. *Part II.* Remember air drop is dependent upon parachutes and
recovery of all chutes in Korea and shipment back to Japan is a must. I
have learned from FEC that chutes are now in short supply. This critical
shortage of cargo chutes will not be alleviated prior to the first of May.

*Dispatched the fol personal to Twining with info to CG 5th AF, 13th
AF, 20th AF, 314th Air Div, AMC, and FEAMCOM:*

Personal Twining from Stratemeyer info Partridge: Subject T-33 aircraft.
Analysis of recent accidents shows increasing number caused by faulty
landing techniques. Several expedients are being adopted in an attempt to
supervise pilots more closely, one being an immediate recheck of all pilots
of dual controlled acft by competent instructors. FEAF now has only 26

---

149. Col Cecil H. Childre became the 315th's commander on Feb. 26, 1952.

T–33s against a requirement for 38 based on 2 T–33s for 17 jet fighter sqdns and 4 T–33s for one tac recon gp. I am well aware of the USAF world-wide shortage of T–33s. However, the requirement for additional dual controlled jet ftrs is nec to maintain a high degree of operational readiness. In addition my particular problem includes *(a)* transitioning F–82 pilots to F–94s in three sqdns, *(b)* transitioning F–51 pilots to jet ftrs when the four sqdns equipped with F–51s convert to jet ftrs, *(c)* refresher check outs for replacement jet pilots from the ZI, *(d)* the fact that when my combat units can spare time for tng they must have the facilities immediately aval. These facts lead me to believe the FEAF requirement for T–33s merits an especially high priority. I urgently request your support in providing 12 T–33s to fulfill my requirements. This signal sent per the last sentence of your radio 57526 of 18 November which I quote: "In the future, bring directly to attention of this office matters such as this which play such an important part in your combat operations."

Approved the fol signal to CINCFE, with info going to CG 5th AF, FEAF BomCom, EUSAK:

This rad in 3 parts. *PART I.* Ref yourad CX 57845, dtd 16 Mar, FEAF is in full agreement with desirability for further dev close air cooperation techniques. Improvements to tactics dev[eloped] in WW II are continually being made by the AF with view to increasing effectiveness and flexibility in employment of air power. Subsequent to the carpet bombing attacks by B–29s in support of 8th Army opns last Aug and Sep, this hq procured from the ZI addl control and safety devices to permit more effective bombing in support of ground opns. Emphasis on recn capabilities of FEAF resulting from the assignment of an AF officer eminently qual in this phase of AF opns and the organization of a rcn wing providing this theater with addl acft and equipment will contribute considerably to the detection of lucrative targets suitable for attack by these more accurately controlled acft. *PART II.* FEAF has in prog[ress] several experiments designed to produce improved control and direction of all types of acft in close support opns. Results of these experiments will be forwarded as soon as any conclusive evidence of effectiveness is determined. *PART III.* Message sent to 5th AF and FEAF BomCom, on 18 Feb 51, relative this subj is quoted herewith for your info: "*PART I.* In the conduct of joint operations, it is occasionally necessary for strategic bombardment aviation to supplement tactical aviation in close support of ground forces by area saturation or carpet bombing close to friendly front lines *(a)* to facilitate a main attack of friendly ground forces against strong enemy defensive positions, or *(b)* under emerg conditions to break up mass hostile attacks which threaten the existence of friendly ground forces. *PART II.* It is desired to further develop techniques and operational procedures for such employment of medium bombers *(a)* to bomb through an overcast, under bad weather conditions, or at night, *(b)* to improve bombing accuracy of areas lacking readily identifiable aiming points, and *(c)* to achieve greatest pos safety to friendly ground forces. *PART III.* To accomplish the foregoing, it is desired that BOMCOM, in collaboration with 5th AF, conduct tests under combat conditions at night with individual B–29 acft bombing with AN/MPQ-2 radar control. Consider the employment of AN/UPN-4 radar beacons as supplementary guidance and safety feature. *PART IV.* If initial test results warrant, increase utilization of B–29s to 2 - 3 acft per night as permitted by primary BOMCOM mission in order to train suff number of lead crews in each of our three groups in this technique to permit maximum effort strikes if called for under conditions contemplated in PART I. *PART V.* Desire that CG FEAF BOMCOM render a final report on this project as soon as possible and interim reports if appropriate."

TUESDAY
20 MARCH
1951

Drafted into final form the following memorandum (official):

Subject: Destruction of Yalu River Bridges. To: CG, 5th AF, CG FEAF BomCom

1. It is desired that the Korean ends of the key bridges over the Yalu River be taken under attack and destroyed, starting at Sinŭiju, as soon as possible utilizing Tarzon bombs. It is desired that careful coordination and planning be effected between FEAF Bomber Command and Fifth Air Force to assure the greatest possible effect with greatest safety to friendly aircraft. Power stations and dams will not repeat not be attacked.

2. Commanding General, FEAF Bomber Command, is directed to plan and execute these attacks to assure optimum success in delivering bombs on the Korean end of these bridges, and will make his bomb runs in a direction to insure greatest accuracy possible and according to best bombardment tactics for precision bombing utilizing the air space essential to success.

3. Fighters of the Fifth Air Force are directed to escort and defend Tarzon aircraft from hostile fighters, and will utilize the air space necessary to accomplish their mission. This authority is limited to the immediate defense of the bombardment aircraft and will not be construed to permit friendly fighters to pursue hostile aircraft beyond distances essential to the immediate protection of the bombers or to attack targets on the ground in Manchuria.

4. No statement relative to these missions, either before or after their execution, will be made without my specific personal clearance. s/G.E.S., etc.

Got off my weekly letter to Gill Robb Wilson, sending copies of same to Generals Spaatz and Bradley.

At about 1030, Colonel Jack Cram,[150] with a letter of introduction from K.B. Wolfe called at the office. After talking with Colonel Cram (USMC), turned him over to D/O. *Sent the fol letter to Partridge re Cram's visit to FEAF:*

Dear Earle, Colonel Jack Cram, United States Marine Corps (Aviation), arrived in my headquarters with a very fine letter of introduction from K.B. Wolfe. Colonel Cram is interested in air support and night operations and has some ideas that might be useful. He is out here to secure all

---

150. Cram, a member of the Marine Corps Equipment Board, was in Korea evaluating the use of jet fighters in close air support.

possible information from us to improve jet operations at night, the equipment used in close support of the ground forces, improve the equipment used by the TACPs, and is interested in the use of electronics in close support at night. PARA It is my personal desire that the Fifth Air Force do everything possible to assist Colonel Cram in his mission, and to gain all possible information from him that will be of assistance to us here in the Far East Air Forces in our close support mission with the ground troops and in all types of night operations. PARA Best regards. Sincerely, G.E.S., etc.

1100 hours, Colonel Edwards, ex-CO of the 91st Strat Recon Sq, came in to pay his respects prior to his departure and brought with him the new commander, Lt. Colonel McCoy.[151] Had a nice visit with both.

At 1500 hours, Colonel Thomas[152] (who was one of the stat[istics] colonels - stat control officers - under Charlie [Charles R.] Landon in Washington) came in and I had a good talk with him. He indicated that everything was well in the Fifth Air Force, BOMCOM, FEAMCOM, and the 315th Air Division insofar as reports in the future were concerned. I am sure he helped us tremendously.

WEDNESDAY 21 MARCH 1951

Upon my arrival at the office this AM, noted the fol radio:

Personal from Twining from Stratemeyer: Reur MSG A4914 OP-PL, 15 Mar 51, because of the limited number of observer spaces available to the entire AF, this hqs has been unable to allocate spaces to FEAF. Available spaces have been allocated to those agencies whose technical or operational functions are considered to indicate a greater or more immediate need to witness the tests.

(This refers to the coming atom bomb tests that are to be held out here in the Pacific shortly.)

Departed 1000 hours for Niigata where I landed and inspected the station; the runways and approaches are excellent - all personnel appear to be on the ball. A wing could be stationed here. Everyone is most enthusiastic about his job and the GCI station and its operation was most impressive. Departed Niigata for Chitose where I was met by both the Army and Air Force commanders. Made a quick survey of this base, including ammunition and fuel dumps. The runway is excellent and can easily be extended - which I was told is being done. Departed for Misawa where I met Colonel George Price and the anti-aircraft commander. After some coffee and donuts inspected one of the anti-aircraft gun enplacements and was amazed at the way these anti-aircraft people have dug in and are ready to fight. They have all their guns laid to be used as artillery as well as anti-aircraft. They need water at their gun enplacements where they have dug in and where they also eat and sleep. Departed Misawa and landed back at Haneda about 1830 hours.

---

151. Lt Col Edward D. Edwards was originally the 31st SRS commander. He remained the squadron commander when the 31st was redesignated the 91st SRS in November 1950. Lt Col Frederic E. McCoy became the squadron commander on Mar. 22, 1951

152. Thomas is unidentified.

THURSDAY
22 MARCH
1951

As a result of my trip to Misawa, bucked an inquiry to Dir Installations re laying pipe out to the four gun enplacements at Misawa. The crews that man these guns eat and sleep out there and at present they have no shower or lavatory facilities.

Approved dispatch of fol personal Vandenberg from Stratemeyer signal:

Ref JCS 2150/11 and CINCFE CX 58087 dtd 20 Mar 51. Inflight refueling experiments on F–80 a/c now being conducted in the ZI may contribute to the solution of the problem in ref messages. Believe also that our D-Day commitments would be much more effectively met if some air refueling capability were furnished this theater now. I strongly urge that at least one KB–29 tanker and six tiptank modification kits for F–80 acft be made available earliest so that we can determine the extent to which this technique can be applied in furtherance of the AF mission in the FE [Far East].

I discussed with Colonel Don Z. Zimmerman this morning the location of the post-treaty CP for FEAF and stated that if CINCFE was to occupy the Dai Ichi Building, I certainly wanted to occupy the Meiji Building.

In Colonel Zimmerman's report as a result of his trip to Washington (which I read in its entirety this morning) two items disturbed me: *(1)* A study had been completed in Washington on the post-treaty Japanese Air Force (a civilian by the name of Mr. Doyle told him this), and *(2)* they (USAF) desired a request from FEAF for the use of chemicals and biologicals in the Korean war.

Dispatched the fol signal to Twining (Personal):

In Colonel D.Z. Zimmerman's written report to me upon his return from Hq USAF, he stated that a paper had been prepared in Hq USAF on the post-treaty Japanese Air Force. Cannot understand why FEAF was not called on to submit recommendations, or at least to comment on the USAF study. We are the occupying Air Force and should be in a better position to submit recommendations to you than anyone else. I would appreciate greatly if a copy could be mailed to me. Comments will then be submitted if desired.

Cleared the fol personal signal to Twining:

In FEAF's rad to USAF cite AX 5165 OP-OP3 dtd 21 Mar 51, I have submitted a detailed statement of our rqmts for C–46/47 type acft. Our min rqmts for C–46/47 acft are considerably greater than the 179 auth by USAF rad AFODA 58717 dtd 8 Dec 50, which is based on AFL 150-10 plus special auth. Changes in FEAF's organization structure and many new tac commitments, such as acft to drop flares for night interdiction and close spt missions, airborne tac air control centers, and transportation of Army corps commanders are not envisioned or provided for in normal auth but nevertheless place a firm rqmt upon FEAF. I am especially concerned over EUSAK's rqmt for 200 tons per day of supplies to be airlifted to forward positions. We have the capability of performing this mission by air drop but this is not an efficient operation, and does not provide for evacuation of the wounded. The spring thaw has made forward air strips unusable for all but C–47 acft, and the anticipated rainy season will cause this condition to continue. Sufficient aviation engr troops are not aval to construct and maintain tac air fields and at the same time construct air fields suitable for C–46, C–119 and C–54 opns in forward areas. Partridge needs all C–47s currently assgd to him for special tac commitments and tac unit spt. Therefore, I feel that we must have addl C–47s to insure that we have the capability of meeting Army rqmts. The attrition of C–46/47 acft has averaged seven acft per month. We have received no replacements since Dec and none are pro[jected]. I consider that my C–46/47 rqmts are rapidly becoming critical, and I req your personal attention and assistance to alleviate this situation, otherwise FEAF may be unable to properly meet all obligations.

Dispatched a long letter to EUSAK thru CINCFE re "Aerial Photographs for EUSAK." Pointed out this ltr evolved from informal reports that we were not giving adequate aerial photographic support to UN ground forces and that I had Partridge run a spot check during a specific period - 13-18 Feb in this case. Presented to addees statistics re photographic prints furnished during that period (I Corps - 2,697; IX Corps - 6,965, and X Corps - 14,070). Also pointed out that period of less than 48 hours elapses from time of request by G-2 Air to time received by requesting commanders. The vast numbers of prints being developed is causing logistic drain and concern to USAF procurement agencies. However, while expenditure rate large, we can increase where needed; however, effective exploitation of photographic effort dependent upon photographic interpretation. We are emphasizing dissemination of interpretation reports rather than distribution of photographs where it is practicable (this results in fewer prints but more readily applicable intelligence). Suggested that addees may wish to examine volume of photos delivered to them in relation to number of photo interpreters available to them. Although FEAF will continue to deliver, suggested that spot checks be run periodically to make sure our efforts not being wasted. (Sent a copy of this letter to Partridge for his info.)

Got off a lengthy letter to Toohey Spaatz which involved specific answers (some furnished by my Intelligence people) to questions presented by him. This letter was classified "secret" and turned same over to my AG for security dispatch to Spaatz.

Entertained General and Mrs. Ho Ying Chin, General and Mrs. Ho Shai-Lai, Miss Mildred Tsai, and Major Paradis at dinner at Mayeda House, at 7:30 P.M.

FRIDAY 23 MARCH 1951

Admiral Towers[153] (Ret) called on me 1000 hours ex-Chief of Naval Aviation and now with PanAm). Our discussion centered around the domestic airline for Japan. Turned him over to Crabb for details.

General Ferguson (Asst D/O) submitted to me the fol MEMO FOR RECORD, dtd 20 Mar, subject: CONFERENCE WITH CG FIFTH

---

153. Adm John H. Towers was now Assistant Vice President, Pan American Airways. In World War II, he had been Commander Air Force, Pacific Fleet, Deputy Commander in Chief, Pacific Areas, and Commander in Chief, Pacific Fleet and Pacific Ocean Areas. In 1919, he commanded the Navy's transAtlantic flight.

AIR FORCE ON 16-17 MARCH, which I quote:

General Weyland, accompanied by the undersigned, visited 5th AF in Korea on 16-17 March at the invitation of CG, 5th AF, to discuss AF policy as it pertains to the current activities of the joint board convened to review 5th AF - 8th Army operational procedures.

Those present at the discussion were General Weyland, General Partridge, Colonel Meyers, and the undersigned. The following topics were dealt with in particular:

1. It was agreed that FM 31-35 and the TAC-AFF Joint Training Directive for Air-Ground Operations should furnish the basis for 5th AF - 8th Army operations and discussions on procedures. Procedures outlined in these documents should be followed unless agreed upon departures therefrom were found necessary by reason of the particular conditions in Korea. It was pointed out that ground force procedures in the air-ground systems varied among all divisions in Korea. The 25th Division is the only one which follows the prescribed doctrine. It is highly desirable that ground units follow a uniform and prescribed procedure.

2. The communications networks for requesting air support and the responsibility for the operation of this net. Discussion on this subject included the fact that in WW II the AF provided this air support request net from division to JOC. Equipment was provided by the tactical AF, and each team at division level was headed by an air liaison officer. Responsibility for getting the battalion and regimental request to division was and still is an Army responsibility. Subsequent to WW II, joint discussions between services led to the recommendation that the Army assume responsibility for air support request communications from the front lines to the JOC. This responsibility was accepted by the Army and they are currently charged with it (see page 74, FM 31-35). In reviewing the joint operations so far in Korea and taking note of the fact that 8th Army was incapable of meeting their commitment to provide these communications at the outbreak of hostilities, it was agreed among those present that, as a negotiating point, the recommendation might be made to USAF that the AF again accept responsibility for the communications required to transmit air requests from the division to the JOC. In this event, however, the Army should retain responsibility for passing such requests from the front lines through Army communications to the division.

3. Since the Korean action began last June, the subject of TACP's, and the number provided by the Marines vs the number furnished by the 5th AF, has been constantly before us. The Marines, being organized for critical amphibious operations, have certain requirements for communications which do not necessarily apply to Army division. For these such situations, the Marines provide one TACP per battalion, one per regiment, and one per division, totaling 13 per division. As soon as this was discovered by adjacent Army units in Korea, the same number of parties were demanded of 5th AF. For reasons already recorded, 5th AF was not capable of providing parties in such numbers except in one or two particular instances. Discussion brought out the fact that the AF is capable of providing sufficient TACP's to meet the average tactical situation. Should an Army division be employed in a tactical situation such as the Marines, i.e., amphibious, then the tactical AF should perhaps furnish at least 13 parties per division. Should 13 TACP's each be present with a large number of ground divisions along a given front, the density of traffic for the limited number of control frequencies would make the system inoperable. However, it was agreed that the AF position in joint discussion would be that a suitable number of TACP's would be provided to insure adequate control of such air power as was available for close support. For our own planning purposes, it was agreed that 4-5 TACP's per division should be adequate.

4. Another proposal recently made by the Army was that they augment the number of TACP's furnished by the 5th AF by equipping Army jeeps with radios and manning them with Army personnel. This proposal led into the subject of whether or not it would be advisable to transfer to the Army the entire responsibility for provision of tactical air control party equipment. (This is the Marine system). Although this suggestion may have some merit, it was finally decided that such an arrangement would threaten AF capability to control aircraft in the battlefield and that relief of responsibility for furnishing jeeps and radios was not sufficient incentive to offset the disadvantages inherent in furnishing large numbers of air-ground radios to the Army.

5. Mosquito aircraft are currently furnished to augment the control of close support strikes furnished by the forward air controllers on the ground. Although the T–6 equipped with long range tank, smoke, rockets, and adequate communications had done exceptionally well, the Army feels that substituting a liaison type for the T–6 would permit landings at division strips and, therefore, permit closer and more careful briefing of the Mosquito pilot on the ground situation. The advantages of this additional briefing are recognized and 5th AF has agreed to an experiment provided 8th Army furnishes the L–19 type plane for the purpose. It was agreed that we must be very careful that influence by the division staff over the Mosquito pilot by this arrangement does not jeopardize control prerogatives.

6. The Army has suggested that their liaison craft be equipped with radios suitable for contacting close support strike formations only to assist them to the target. They are careful to make clear that this proposal is intended only to augment the facilities furnished by the Mosquito planes and that no selection of targets is intended but only to furnish assistance to the pre-selected target. General Partridge felt that he was not prepared to agree to this proposal. The over-riding consideration with respect to the whole Mosquito problem is whether or not such a technique can be employed against any future enemy who has a reasonable number of anti-aircraft weapons and an AF committed to close support. The point was made that we must be careful when committing ourselves to a tactical procedure which has little possibility of existence against a first class enemy to keep in the foreground the fact that the procedure is of interim nature, suitable only under the current conditions of combat. It is our responsibility to keep the Army apprised of this.

Yesterday received the fol signal from LeMay:

In a month or thereabouts I would like to return Briggs for assignment as Rosie O'Donnell's deputy and send you Bob Terrill[154] who now commands

---

154. Brig Gen Robert H. Terrill became FEAF Bomber Command CO on May 23, 1951

the 93d Wg as Briggs' replacement. Terrill is a Brig. Gen., a steady officer with considerable combat experience and with a good record for
having developed and maintained a high order of effectiveness in the 93d.
I am sure you will find him well qualified. Bondley, who returns soon,
will be transferred from O'Donnell's Hq to Spokane for command of the
air div at that place where a general officer is needed. We have worked
out with Briggs certain other changes involving officers in the grade of
colonel. I would appreciate concurrence with this proposal.

My reply to the above, dispatched today, is as follows:

PERSONAL LEMAY from STRATEMEYER: Reference your radio
21 March and your proposal to send Brig. Gen. Bob Terrill here as
replacement for Gen. Briggs, I am fully in accord with your plan. Briggs
has performed a fine and outstanding job out here and I hate to lose him,
but I agree with you that rotation of commanders here is to the best interests of the United States Air Force.

SATURDAY
24 MARCH
1951

Departed 0700 hours with General MacArthur aboard
SCAP. Others accompanying were Generals Hickey &
Whitney, Admiral Joy and Colonel Canada. We flew direct
to the Seoul Municipal Airport where we landed there on the
strip - some 3800 feet long. We were met by Generals Partridge and Ridgway
and proceeded by jeep through Seoul up to Ŭijŏngbu. Enroute we visited the
3d Infantry Division, commanded by General Soule,[155] the 3d Division artillery,
commanded by General Shugg,[156] the Filipino battalion, the 15th Infantry commanded by Colonel Moore,[157] and the Belgian battalion.[158] We witnessed one of
the finest artillery shoots I have ever seen, and in order to visit the Belgian battalion, we paralleled the front lines between the battalion on the front line and
the battalion in reserves, and, particularly on this jeep ride we really witnessed
about all the front line, and immediately-in-rear-of-the-front-line firing that
one could see.

I'll never forget the sight, while at the battalion command post of the 15th
Infantry when an old Korean man carried in on his back a very old Korean
woman whose right hand had been completely blown off. They were quiet, no
fear was on their faces, and the fortitude of these people, to me, is amazing. All
she wanted to know by her expressing and holding the stub of her arm up was
where to go. Two other Koreans who were wounded and a GI went into the
dressing station while we were there.

In World War II, he had trained and led three bomb groups before becoming Assistant Chief of Staff for
Operations, Eighth Air Force in July 1944.

155. 5-foot, 6-inch Maj Gen Robert H. "Shorty" Soule, an ex-paratrooper, had much experience dealing with the Chinese. He served in China for six years in the 1930s and was also a military advisor to Chiang Kai-Shek in 1947.

156. Brig Gen Roland P. Shugg was 3rd Division artillery commander from Oct. 1949 to Sep. 1951, at which
time he became the VI Corps artillery commander.

157. Col Dennis M. Moore was captured on Bataan during World War II. He was relieved as the 15th Infantry
commander in Apr. 1951

158. The Philippine Government supplied a 1,367-man infantry battalion for use in Korea. After an anti-guerilla
operation in South Korea, the battalion was attached to several U.S. divisions for operations. Belgium supplied an infantry battalion, to which was attached a rifle platoon from Luxembourg. These latter units arrived
in Korea on the last day of January and first saw major action in April. (*The History of the United Nations
Forces in the Korean War*, Vol. VI [Seoul, 1977], pp 107-117, 309-328.)

We then proceeded back to Seoul Municipal Airport where we were met by General Partridge, said goodbye to General Ridgway and the other officers and proceeded direct to Haneda where we landed about 1730 hours.

SUNDAY 25 MARCH 1951

Made a broadcast with CBS, in connection with a Mr. Rendell, at Radio Tokyo. Copy of the questions and answers on file in my office. (One question and answer - bottom of page 3, all of page 4 and first 2 lines of page 5 were not given.)

Had a golf game with Annalee and the Davisons; I shot an 85 - Davison shot even par.

MONDAY 26 MARCH 1951

On 24 March, while I was in Korea, Nuckols sent out in my name the info to Vandenberg that I was "delighted to report that FEAF on 23 March mounted total 1220 sorties breaking previous high 1123."

Yesterday cleared the fol personal message to Twining:

Am concerned lest decisions re FEAF rqmts continue under assumption war ends 30 June. This particularly true for acft deliveries. For case in point see your AFODC 53329 dtd 27 Jan. Our opinion that time element and tactical situation such that staff actions affecting this theater must now envisage continuation current opns well beyond July. *PART II.* Realize assumption this nature necessary for certain program and budget actions and note current program documents contemplate return to ZI during first qtr FY 52 of combat units such as 4th and 27th Ftr Wgs, 452d Lt Bmr Wg, etc. We assume these actions will not take place if war continues beyond that date and are projecting rqmts accordingly. *PART III.* Rqst you advise if our assumptions correct. Our rqmts will be re-submitted on basis your reply. However, we consider any action to reduce air potential this theater prior to major change in overall tactical situation as ill-advised.

Also cleared personal radio to Twining re adaptation of type searchlight for infrared use w/night intruder acft. This interim measure only and urged that development programs for infrared equip for night intruder oprs be given max emphasis and as soon as developed, request team of specialists with equip be sent us for opnl test.

On the 25th the fol redline received from Twining:

18th AF (Troop Carrier) being activated 28 Mar with 9 wings including regular active wings and wings now being brought on active duty from reserve components. Van feels that Henebry is ideal choice for CG 18th AF. If selected, Henebry must return immediately. I note that Stearley with splendid operational troop carrier experience is in your command and could be considered for Henebry's replacement. Van willing to promote Henebry upon performance in the 18th AF job. Request your views soonest.

After thinking over the above signal, sent my reply to Twining as follows:

Reurad RL 192 in which you indicated that Henebry was being considered to command 18th Air Force. I am sure Van realizes that I will release anyone whom he needs provided a qualified replacement is furnished me. Henebry is no exception, but before finalizing on him for spot in question, there are several points which I feel duty bound to present to you for consideration. Henebry is without question an outstanding young general officer, particularly in an operational spot such as he now occupies, and I am pleased with the way he is now performing as CG 315th Air Div (Combat Cargo). The 315th Air Div recently underwent a change of command and some reorganization, and I feel that another change would inevitably create concern in the supported ground forces and cause some loss of efficiency. At the present writing General Ridgway holds Henebry in highest esteem. His experience in active troop carrier work, however, is limited to three months command of the 437th Troop Carrier Wing and the brief occupancy of his present spot since Tunner's return to ZI in February. In spite of his excellent record, I believe Henebry lacks the general administrative background which would be invaluable to a commander of a large numbered Air Force particularly a newly activated one with the many administrative problems which are sure to arise. In my opinion, such a background can only be acquired through experience. I strongly recommend that before making so choice an assignment to so junior an officer serious consideration should be given to selecting an individual who already has several years service as a general officer to his credit. I believe we have several general officers in the USAF qualified to command the 18th AF. It would, in my opinion, constitute an injustice to a large number of proven AF generals to select for the job in question a general officer as young and junior as Henebry. In the event it is Van's decision to take Henebry from FEAF, I can handle the situation substantially as follows: Stearley can take over the 315th Air Division with very little difficulty, but I am reluctant to pull him out of his present spot where he commands a numbered AF and put him in command of an air division which we recently decided could be commanded by a brigadier general. On Okinawa there are two medium bomb groups which need support and a tremendously large construction program is being consummated and needs energetic and intelligent direction. The 3 engineer battalions which have been on Okinawa are being moved to Korea and the work on Okinawa is being taken over on contract. This will require extensive and aggressive detailed supervision. The air defense of the installations in Okinawa in itself requires an experienced and stable commander and leader - which Stearley is and has been. I could bring Gilkeson over to Okinawa from Guam. Gilkeson has done an outstanding job on Guam and I would not hesitate to give him the Twentieth. I would then need a forceful brigadier general for the 19th Wing. The present Navy commander, Admiral Hardison, has, at times, proven difficult to cope with. With the Army pulling out of Guam in the immediate future, I consider it essential that you furnish me a strong brigadier general for that spot if Gilkey is moved.[159]

Dispatched the fol personal message to Partridge:

Congressmen O.K. Armstrong and W.J.B. Dorn arrive in theater 27 March at invitation of Air Force Assn.[160] They have particular interest in US Air Force operations. Brig. Gen. Nuckols is project officer and will accompany them during visit to FEAF installations. This message is purely advisory to alert you. Above party will arrive your headquarters, after Armstrong party departs, for several days visit to various installations in Korea. Exact date and time of arrival will be sent you as soon as itinerary is firm with them.

General Armstrong and his party arrived, and called on me at my office. They were and are: Generals Armstrong (the Surgeon General), Schwichtenberg, Colonel Gould, Col Kester, Col. Preston, Colonel Reuter, Colonel Veigel, Lt. Col. Niemi, Lt. Col. Tutor, Lt Col Zeller (AFNC); Col. Byrnes, Col. Campbell, Lt. Col. Nuttall, Lt. Col. Strickland, Major Payne, and Dr. Elmer L. Henderson (President American Medical Assn), Dr. Cortez F. Enloe, Dr. William P. Holbrook, Dr. Russel V. Lee, Dr. John M. Murray, and Dr. Herbert B. Wright.[161]

About 2110 hours, while Mrs. Strat and I were in lounging clothes, viewing a movie, Major General Armstrong called at the house accompanied by Dr. Henderson. Calling at such an hour was embarrassing; Mrs. Stratemeyer was clothed in such a manner that she could not come downstairs, and, to my mind, this unannounced call by Armstrong displayed inconsideration and ignorance on his part.

TUESDAY 27 MARCH 1951

Dispatched a signal to Borum[162] inquiring as to ETD to me of Staff C–54 - it has been in depot there at OCAMA now for 21 days.

At 1430 hours, Congressmen O.K. Armstrong (Rep) and W.J. Bryan Dorn (Dem), accompanied by General Nuckols, called on me. Their mission out here is at their own expense and to inquire into the USAF operations in the Korean War. I made it very plain to them that every facility within FEAF would be made available to them to accomplish their mission. I pointed out that we had already been investigated by the Army and the Navy as to our deficiencies in air support and that for the life of me I could not understand why the Army had not been investigated for their failure as a member of the ground-air support team. They indicated they might look into that themselves.

---

159. 18AF was activated on Mar. 28 with Maj Gen Robert W. Douglas, Jr., as commander.

160. Orlando Kay (O.K.) Armstrong, a Republican from Missouri, was elected to the 82d Congress in Nov. 1950. He was on the Post Office and Civil Service Committee. William Jennings Bryan Dorn, a Democrat from South Carolina, was also elected to the 82d Congress in November. He was on the Expenditures in the Executive Department and the Veterans' Affairs Committees.

161. Maj Gen Harry G. Armstrong was USAF surgeon general; Brig Gen Albert H. Schwichtenberg was Chief, Civil and Military Health Interrelations, Armed Forces Medical Policy Council, Office of the Secretary of Defense; Lt Col Ralph C. Tutor was Director of Medical Staffing and Education, Office of the Surgeon General, HQ USAF; Col Lloyd E. Gould, Lt Col William D. Preston, Col Lester P. Veigel, and Lt Col Osmo I. Niemi were physicians; Col Wayne O. Kester was a veterinarian; Lt Col Walter J. Reuter was a dentist; Lt Col Verena M. Zeller was a nurse; Col Victor A. Byrnes was an ophthalmologist. Dr. Elmer L. Henderson had been president of the American Medical Association since 1947. None of the other officers and doctors have been identified as to their field of expertise.

162. Brig Gen Fred S. Borum, base commander at Tinker AFB, Oklahoma, where OCAMA was located.

I placed General Nuckols on duty with them during their entire stay as project officer.

Mr. Armstrong was a member of the Air Corps in WWI; Mr. Dorn was in the Army Air Forces in WWII.

At about 1515 hours, Mr. Keyes Beech, of the *Chicago News*, accompanied by General Nuckols, called on me for a session re background on AF activities. Had a nice visit and apparently I satisfied him with my answers to all the questions he asked.

At 0930, Annalee and I had dinner with the Dallas Shermans who were honoring Admiral Towers (Ret), who heads up Pan Am.

WEDNESDAY 28 MARCH 1951
Dispatched the fol ltr to CG FAF and CG: FEAF BOM-COM, subject:

Destruction of Yalu River Bridges. 1. I refer to my letter to you, subject: Destruction of Yalu River Bridges, dated 20 Mar 51. 2. Referenced letter is not intended to limit these attacks to the utilization of Tarzon bombs. Commanding General, FEAF Bomber Command, may use GP bombs and such numbers of B–29s as he considers necessary to initiate expeditious destruction of the greatest number of the Yalu bridges in the shortest period of time. 3. All other provisions of referenced letter remain applicable. s/G.E.S., etc.

Also dispatched Stratline to Timberlake and quoted above letter for his info.
General Partridge came in about 1500 hours and the following subjects were discussed with him:

1. The Brigadier General Higgins report to the Chief of Army Field Forces - wherein Partridge agreed with me as to the fineness of the report.[163]

2. He will take immediate action on another follow up on Colonel Tyer's promotion.

3. We decided to bring Colonel Gray from Itazuke to replace General Picher as IG. Gray to arrive in about a week. Picher is to take over Deputy for Personnel this Friday, 30 March.

4. I indicated that the latest Presidential Citation for the 8th Fighter Wing was a bit embarrassing. We came to an agreement that the Unit Presidential Citation in the future would conform to Battle Star periods of time.

5. We discussed the improvement of the Kunsan (K-8) airstrip which will be improved some 9,000 feet, utilizing 2d Battalion of aviation engineers from Okinawa. The 1st Battalion will go to Suwŏn. Col Jack Price supervising the layout with Korean labor.

6. I briefed General Partridge on Congressmen Dorn from South Carolina and Armstrong from Missouri.

---

163. Brig Gen Gerald J. Higgins, a paratrooper with the 101st Airborne Division in World War II, was Director, Army Air Support Center at Ft. Bragg. Because of perceived shortcomings in air support operations, he visited Korea in October and November 1950 to study these operations. His report, issued on Dec. 1, 1950, was generally supportive of the air operations to that date. In his cover letter to the report he stated, "It is my firm conviction that practically all of the personal adverse remarks on air support may be attributed to such lack of information or even misinformation on this subject."[Emphasis in original.] (Ltr, Brig Gen Gerald J. Higgins to Chief of Army Field Forces, 1 Dec 1950, subj: Air Support in Korean Campaign.) Nonetheless, he identified several areas, including communications and training, where improvements were greatly needed.

7. Also briefed him on the Armstrong-Henderson party that will visit FAF bases in Japan and Korea, including Hq FAF.

8. We discussed at great length General Sweetser and decided we would send him to the U.S. to "bird-dog" the securing of sufficient numbers of B–26s for the 452d group, the 3d Bomb Group and the RB–26 recon sq. We anticipate he will be gone some two months.

9. We also discussed the 452d Light Bomb Wing and it was brought out that they were way under strength in airplanes and way over strength in personnel and crews.

10. The question of 12 month's service for the involuntary Reserves was

A spectacular explosion rocks Wŏnsan after a 452d BW(L) Invader's bombs apparently detonated an ammunition dump.

discussed and General Partridge is going ahead with his plan, which I approved, to scatter these involuntary Reserves throughout the FAF so that when their one year is up, it will not immobilize any one unit.

Had a nice visit with William Courtneay, the English reporter, this afternoon and made him an honorary member of FEAF with three FEAF patches.

At 1100 hours, Major Morris[164] came in and presented an entirely different picture reference his desire to leave active duty. Apparently he has a very good compassionate reason. His wife is ill and is not being looked after - and they have five children. I told him that I would on a compassionate basis release him.

---

164. Probably Maj Ray S. Morris.

THURSDAY
29 MARCH
1951

Mr. Stanley Hiller, who is the father of the Hiller who manufactures the Hiller helicopter, paid me a visit at 1100 hours. He is a right nice old boy and I enjoyed visiting with him although he was a bit loquacious.

1530 hours, I pinned the DSM on General Craigie which award was given him as the island commander of Corsica in World War II.

Annalee and I had dinner with the Pichers in their new home and, instead of having bean soup that I expected, we had a chicken curry - and I ate too much.

FRIDAY
30 MARCH
1951

Report received Thursday (yesterday) that Colonel Payne Jennings on a Tarzon bomb mission had lost two engines and was about 300 miles northwest of Okinawa and was returning to base. Last report was that he was at 2,000 feet. Up through this writing we have received no word of the survivors from his airplane although the entire area has been searched by up to 25 airplanes as well as by surface ships. An all-out effort by BomCom will be made 31 March to assist Air Sea Rescue.

Attended a housewarming party given by the Pichers and made that terrible mistake of drinking more than two martinis!

SATURDAY
31 MARCH
1951

Left the office about 1130 hours and played golf yesterday and had an 87. Capt. Muse,[165] USN, and I played Admirals Joy and Ewing. Took a buck from them.

SUNDAY
1 APRIL
1951

Sent Henebry a signal, approving his actions as per following signal received from him:

Personal Stratemeyer from Henebry. Cause of loss of right engine on two C–119 aircraft of 314 Group on 29 March 51 determined to be failure of engine nacelle truss structure. Inspection of all remaining C–119 aircraft discloses same defect in 5 additional aircraft. Causes of failure could occur in flight and may not be detected by thorough inspection prior to take off. Have grounded all C–119 aircraft except for missions of extreme emergency. Expeditious action being taken to procure modification kits from ZI or procure authority for local manufacture of kits.[166]

Got off a strong letter to Twining re my personnel set up, the reasons for my shuffling my staff about (trying to strengthen what I consider a weak link throughout the AF on major command level - Personnel), and requested that Picher not be reassigned until after Korean hostilities.

---

165. Capt George R. Muse was on the COMNAVFE staff.

166. C–119s had been sent initially to Korea for only a short stay and to participate in a single airborne operation. Because of its roominess, however, it became the transport of choice in all phases of airlift, and its stay was extended. There were never enough C–119s to fulfill the requirements imposed on Combat Cargo Command/315th Air Division, and there were never enough men to maintain the aircraft. The double whammy of overuse and lack of maintenance led to soaring out-of-commission rates, and there were several instances where engines actually fell off of C–119s during flight. The C–119 fleet was grounded several times for unsafe conditions, but it was not until the spring of 1952 that newer model C–119s were sent to FEAF.

Had two conferences with Miss Doreen Lonberg[167] - one at 1030 hours and one at 1415 hours. Called General Crabb in and his expert on civilian airline operations into Japan and Okinawa as Doreen was interested in CAT [Civil Air Transport] operating into Okinawa from Formosa. Mr. Burridge[168] of CAT here in Tokyo was present during the afternoon session. They secured, I believe, all possible information that we had. It was fine seeing Miss Lonberg again as she is a most attractive and efficient lady. As a souvenir I gave her one of the geisha girls silver spoons.

MONDAY
2 APRIL
1951

Had the Armstrong-Henderson party to lunch at Mayeda House. Unfortunately, neither General Armstrong nor Dr. Henderson could be present.

General Schwichtenberg (who also couldn't make it to the luncheon) called on me at my office to give his regrets and also brief me a bit as to what he has seen while here.

Dispatched the fol msg which cancelled out a previous radio that I had sent, same subject, to CSAF, CINCFE, CG FAF, 19th Bomb Gp, 98th Bomb Gp, 307th Bomb Gp, FEAF BomCom, 20th AF, 458th RCN Tech Sq, 548th Rcn Tech Sq, Det 2, 67th Tac Rcn Wg, K-2, COMNAVFE:

In furtherance of present Yalu River interdiction program, there is always possibility of accidental bombdrops in neutral territory. Mandatory that special measures be taken to control and limit distribution of strike and reconnaissance photos, taken in connection with interdiction program, to insure that none are inadvertently released to news media or made available to unauthorized sources. Classification of these photos will continue to be in accordance with existing directives pertaining to classification of Korean aerial photography.

TUESDAY
3 APRIL
1951

Departed Haneda aboard SCAP with General MacArthur, Hickey, Whitney and Mr. Paul C. Smith of the *San Francisco Chronicle*, and flew direct to K-18 (Kangnŭng) where we were met by Generals Ridgway and Partridge, and, after a short conference between Generals MacArthur and Ridgway, we proceeded by jeep to the Capital Division Hq on up past the 38th Parallel to Yangyang. Lt General Chung and General Partridge rode in the jeep with me. In my estimation, this was about a 70 mile jeep ride and not nearly as rough as others as the road was much better. We arrived back at Kangnŭng at about 1610 hours and were airborne about 1630. Proceeded direct to Haneda.

During dinner with General MacArthur, aboard the SCAP, I made a statement to him that I could not understand General Marshall's recent statement re General MacArthur's pronouncement. General MacArthur's reply to me is, I think, one for the record: "Why, Strat, that old man has gone nuts." General MacArthur further stated that he could not understand this reaction

---

167. Lonberg was Chennault's wartime secretary and helped recruit personnel for CAT.
168. A. Lewis Burridge had worked for CAT since 1947 and helped negotiate with FEAMCOM the use of CAT aircraft.

in Washington nor the reactions in foreign capitals to his recent statement, and expressed himself as: "It is fantastic."[169]

**WEDNESDAY
4 APRIL
1951**

Colonel Carmichael departed; was very disappointed I didn't get to bid him goodbye.

Signal received that my C–54 would leave Oklahoma City on 3 April (which is 4 April here).

At 1430 Mr. Paul Smith of the *San Francisco Chronicle* visited me for about 35 minutes. We had a talk off-the-record and I indicated to him that I concurred in General MacArthur's strategy and that we couldn't win this war with our hands tied behind us.

At 1400 hours, Miss Follett (of the British Embassy), who works for our communications people, came in and bid me goodbye.

Dispatched a letter to Briggs of BOMCOM, enclosing at the same time a copy of my signal to O'Donnell dated 2 April, and a copy of O'Donnell's reply, dated 2 April. I told Briggs,

I cannot spare Col. Ohman from his present assignment, which is an

---

169. On Mar. 20, the JCS notified MacArthur of the gist of a peace proposal President Truman was preparing to release and requesting MacArthur's recommendations. MacArthur replied that "no further military restrictions" be placed on his command in Korea. He issued on Mar. 24 what he would later label as a "routine communique" and a "military appraisal." MacArthur would claim that his communique had been prepared prior to, not after, receiving the JCS message. (Gen of the Army Douglas MacArthur, *Reminiscences*, New York, 1964, p 387.)

His communique, or "pronunciamento" as one ambassador styled it, exploded like a bomb in Washington and among the other U.N. members fighting in Korea, for it was, in fact, an ultimatum not just to China, but to Truman and the U.N. as well. In it he stated:

"Operations continuing according to schedule and plan.... The enemy's human wave tactics have definitely failed him as our own forces have become seasoned to this form of warfare; his tactics of infiltration are but contributing to his piecemeal losses, and he is showing less stamina than our troops under the rigors of climate, terrain and battle.

"Of even greater significance than our tactical successes has been the clear revelation that this new enemy, Red China, lacks the industrial capacity to adequately provide many critical items essential to the conduct of modern war....

"These military weaknesses have been clearly and definitely revealed since Red China entered upon its undeclared war in Korea. Even under the inhibitions which now restrict the activity of the United Nations forces and the corresponding military advantages which accrue to Red China, it has shown its complete inability to accomplish by force of arms the conquest of Korea. The enemy, therefore, must by now be painfully aware that a decision of the United Nations to depart from its tolerant effort to contain the war to the area of Korea, through an expansion of our military operations to his coastal areas and interior bases, would doom Red China to the risk of imminent military collapse. These basic facts being established, there should be no insuperable difficulty in arriving at decisions on the Korean problem if the issues are resolved on their own merits, without being burdened by extraneous matters such as Formosa or China's seat in the United Nations .

"The Korean nation and people... must not be sacrificed. That is a paramount concern.... [T]he fundamental questions continue to be political in nature and must find their answer in the diplomatic sphere. Within the area of my authority as the military commander, however, it should be needless to say that I stand ready at any time to confer in the field with the Commander-in-Chief of the enemy forces in the earnest effort to find any military means whereby realization of the political objectives of the United Nations in Korea, to which no man may justly take exception, might be accomplished without further bloodshed." (MacArthur, pp 387-388.) In this one "routine communique," MacArthur accomplished three things, all with far-reaching effects: by virtually taunting and challenging the Chinese, he undoubtedly assured their continuing participation in the war; his pronouncement torpedoed Truman's cease-fire, for the President could hardly announce this when his commander in Korea was instead publicly intimating carrying the war to the Chinese mainland; and he added fuel to the smoldering distrust of the U.N. allies about American policy in Korea. ("History of the JCS," Vol. III, pp 468-469.)

It is hard to believe that MacArthur, one of the most political of generals, could be so naive as not to see what he had done. Incidentally, "that old man" George C. Marshall, the Secretary of Defense since Sept. 21, 1950, was just a bit more than 11 months younger than MacArthur

important one to which he has just gone. I am still awaiting a reply from LeMay. In the event no SAC group commander is forthcoming, we will have to furnish him from FEAF or maybe BomCom. Let me hear from you on results of your attempt with SAC to obtain a replacement for Jennings.

Through COMNAVFE sent a personal letter to Major General Field Harris,

USMC, the CG 1st Marine Air Wing, and told him that yesterday, while on a trip to Korea with General MacArthur, I had a fine visit with General Partridge. In the course of our conversation, he expressed in glowing terms the excellence of your daylight close support of ground troops, and, particularly, your night intruder missions. This team play on your part and that of the First Marine Air Wing is most gratifying to me and I wish to add my appreciation and commendation in passing this along to you.

Got off the fol ltr to General Ankenbrandt, Director of USAF Communications:

Your letter of 16 March was greatly appreciated, and I am looking forward to receiving your final reply to Col. Sirmyer's report. There is a great deal of room for organizational as well as technical improvement. The trend towards elimination of the specialist in our staff organization worries me. From the purely personnel side, we must provide comparable opportunity for advancement and career service for all of our people. Organizationally, we should retain or establish those special staff agencies that contain the knowledge required to supervise our variegated activities. Certainly Gen. Van should be able to point his finger to one individual responsible for communications. I have had my staff studying certain relationships and responsibilities in order to assist in finding an acceptable solution. Maybe we will have to revert to the "corps" or "service" system in spite of the fact that it incorporates much duplication of effort and responsibility and may not be as efficient. I hope the USAF will not go to complete integration of the technical fields into the air staff, as this will only tend to aggravate the situation and further weaken our capabilities. Some kind of a compromise solution appears to be answer. I know that you and your staff are doing everything you can to help us. Please keep it up. If there is anything we can do for you in our common effort, do not hesitate to call on us. Best regards.

Dispatched the fol signal to Chidlaw:

Unsatisfactory operation of AN/TPS-1B MTI modification has limited operational employment of this equip in FEAF air defense radar network. FEAMCOM ltr sub "AN/TPS-1B Modification," dtd 21 Mar 51, to your hq outlined this problem in detail. Req that every effort be made to provide a solution. Also req that a qualified technical specialist be placed on TDY with this command if indications are that present difficulty is resulting from lack of technicians qualified in this modification.

Sent CINCFE the fol ltr:

Dear General MacArthur: The forces of the UN Command are exacting such a heavy toll from the enemy that it seems evident he cannot sustain his military opposition indefinitely in the face of these heavy losses. It is futile to attempt to predict when the breaking point will come but that it will come, either militarily or diplomatically there appears no doubt. In the meantime, our operations should be so conducted as to continue to inflict maximum losses on the enemy with minimum loss to friendly forces. From the air point of view, maintenance of this situation becomes increasingly difficult as the land front moves toward the Manchurian border of Korea. With these thoughts in mind, it seems that air action can best assist in the overall effort under the following conditions: *(1)* Enemy LOC's [lines of communication] be of sufficient length to allow effective air interdiction. *(2)* Land action continue to attract enemy forces to the ground front. *(3)* Air and surface forces continue to protect South Korea. *(4)* Minimum length land front consistent with *(7)* below. *(5)* Advantage continue to be taken of the relatively stronger UNC naval surface and air action along the east coast than along the west coast of Korea. *(6)* Disposition of forward air and surface units oriented to approximately face the Manchurian border. *(7)* Disposition of air and surface units beyond the current operating radius of enemy jet aircraft. *(8)* As a prime consideration, so dispose air and surface units to provide best possible conditions for their logistical support. *(a)* Ports as far forward as practicable. *(b)* Best possible rail and highway net to support units in or near the land front. *(c)* Lateral communications across Korea. *(9)* Airfields close to the land front suitable for interceptor, fighter-bomber, transport, intruder, reconnaissance and control aircraft. *(10)* Twenty-four hour, all-weather air operations. *(a)* Increased emphasis on night air operations. *(b)* Radar controlled operations (shoran and AN/MPQ2 for blind bombing) over enemy territory. *(c)* Adequate solid surface runways, taxiways, aprons and dispersal areas. It is my opinion that most, if not all, of the preceding conditions can be fulfilled. The additional aviation engineer battalions being brought into Korea should soon help to alleviate the airfield situation which has been most critical. The addition of Kimp'o to our air base system will be a great help. We need additional airfields in central and western Korea near the land front. Capture of the airfields at Wŏnsan and P'yŏngyang would alleviate the airfield situation as well as provide a port on the east coast. Control of the Seoul-Wŏnsan corridor with its rail line and highways would improve lateral communications and provide the best link in Korea between the east and west coasts. So far, enemy jets have limited their operating radius so that an arc drawn from Antung falls short of this corridor. Continued enemy guerilla activity is one big disadvantage to operations in former enemy territory and our air capabilities against guerillas are limited. I fully recognize the complexity of the problem posed. I submit these thoughts with the realization that other considerations may well alter some of the conditions enumerated or demand others of more importance. Should a strategy along the lines indicated be adopted, the foregoing may provide a partial basis for solution of the problem. Sincerely, s/G.E.S., etc.

THURSDAY
5 APRIL
1951

Alkire brought down and introduced a Mr. C.H. Hahner, representative of the Optical Glass Factory, Bureau of Standards, who is out here collecting Japanese lenses for possible quantity utilization by USAF.

The two congressmen returned to Tokyo and came in to call on me about 1100 hours and expressed their great gratification and thanks for having had a very interesting and informative trip to Korea and my other major command CPs. They have visited every type unit in the Far East Air Forces and have heard briefings and de-briefings. I am sure their trip to the Far East will be most beneficial to the USAF.

Released my #702 press release on USAF helicopter evacuation of both wounded and downed FEAF crews.

Also told UP through my PIO that I had no comment to make on orders received by General MacArthur, but that as an airman I would carry out unquestionably any orders given to me by him.

I rereleased two paragraphs of my interview on 26 March with Mr. Rendell.

FRIDAY
6 APRIL
1951

Dispatched the fol signal, as follows:

From:CG FEAF, To: CG Fifth Air Force (Priority), CG 315th Air Division (Combat Cargo) (Courier), Cite: AX 5876 CG; PERSONAL PARTRIDGE AND HENEBRY FROM STRATEMEYER. I intend to issue following directive. Your comments or recommendations desired soonest. Directive: "Subject: Operational Control of 315th Air Division (Combat Cargo); TO: Commanding General, Fifth Air Force, APO 970, Commanding General, 315th Air Division (Combat Cargo), APO 959. *1*. Effective immediately, the 315th Air Division (Combat Cargo) is placed under the operational control of the Commanding General, Fifth Air Force. *2*. This operational control is limited strictly to operational matters and the Commanding General, 315th Air Division (Combat Cargo) will continue to report direct to this headquarters on all other matters. *3*. This letter directive is issued in order to simplify and place under one individual, the Commanding General, Fifth Air Force, the use of all airdromes in Korea under FEAF control, and to have one senior United States Air Force officer, the Commanding General, Fifth Air Force deal with the Commanding General, Eighth United States Army, on all air matters."

At 1225 I took Mr. William Jennings Bryan Dorn and Mr. O.K. Armstrong, congressmen from South Carolina and Missouri respectively, to call on General MacArthur. General Nuckols accompanied us. As I have stated in other places in this diary, I have always been greatly impressed with anything and everything that General MacArthur has had to say, but today, I have never spent a more inspiring 55 minutes, listening to this great American, nor listened with such interest and admiration as I did this afternoon. Both Messrs Dorn and Armstrong, in my opinion, were so impressed and agreed so wholeheartedly with what General MacArthur had to say that upon leaving they were speechless.

I will try to relate some of General MacArthur's views that he expressed, as follows:

A. He said that the Allied Council could be put out of commission by one signatory serving notice six months in advance; that the Allied Council was nothing more, at present, than a sounding board for Russian propaganda; that the reasons originally for it were instigated by the British.

B. He said that Formosa was the key to the whole Pacific Ocean - that if it fell to the enemy, the Far East line of defense would be pierced; Japan on one hand and the Philippines and Southeast Asia on the other. That under no conditions should Formosa be allowed to fall into the hands of the enemy of the United States of America; that there should be a strong advisory group, headed up by a senior officer, consisting of the three services (Army, Navy and Air Force), placed there without delay - an estimated strength of which could well be 500 officers and 1,000 enlisted men; that the Chinese on Formosa should receive, on a high priority, the equipment necessary for their ground forces and sufficient air and naval equipment to make their Navy and Air Force at least good. That this group, since it is in his area (General MacArthur's) be placed under his command, but that the use of those ground troops and Chinese forces should be left to the Gissimo's discretion; that he would - and has - supported Chiang Kai-Shek even though he was the devil himself because Chiang has always fought Communism.

C. That his directives which prevent him from utilizing the main potential of his air power in going beyond the Yalu River and hitting the Chinese Communists at the roots is simply fantastic.

D. That our dealings with the Russians back in the U.N. and in Washington, has been on the level of treating them as "white men" or Occidentals - whereas they are Orientals, and they think and act as Orientals; that it is impossible to confer or talk with them observing the niceties and dignified confidences that you normally have with Occidentals; that when they come into a conference and insult us, we should not act in the Occidental manner - but deal with them as Orientals (which they are), and call their bluff. That ever since World War II ended in 1945, their whole strategy has been bluff. In Europe, the time Vittles [the Berlin Airlift] took place, in his opinion, an American armored column could have gone straight through to Berlin and, not only would the Russians have let it pass, but they would have played that maneuver down.

E. That Japan industrially, economically - and even spiritually - today is a friend of the United States of America.

F. That for security reasons, Japan should have at least ten ground force divisions, fully equipped; as they cannot afford economically, at this time, a navy or an air force, we would have to supply this for the time being. That as soon as these divisions are equipped and trained, all the American ground forces should be removed from Japan.

G. That, as a result of World War II in the Pacific, our Western Pacific coastline is not now our line of defense - that the Japanese islands, Formosa, and the Philippines - with the 5,000 miles between that line and our West Coast - are our line of defense. Twenty-six miles of water between the British Isles and Europe has served Great Britain - what then does 5,000 miles mean to the security of the United States? Formosa is the key to our present security line, and again, under no conditions should it fall into enemy hands.

H. To my embarrassment, General MacArthur strongly urged both congressmen to respectfully go to Mr. Finletter, General Vandenberg, and Admiral Sherman and fight for my promotion and that of Admiral Joy's for four-star rank. He said so many nice things about FEAF, and me personally, that I will not even record them here.

I. He said that apparently there was a smear campaign going on to get his (MacArthur's) scalp and that in his opinion the leadership of that campaign emanates from London; that every one of his releases, starting from the Formosa release and those reference Korea have been made with the idea of strengthening the pronouncements already made by our government. The only way he can figure the great majority of the press of the world criticizing him is because the Pinks and the Reds within the democracies of the world want to get rid of him, and, again, in his opinion, this stems from England.

J. The Japanese can take all of the cotton grown in America and turn it into cloth and dispose of it in Asia and thereby not only help herself economically, but also the United States as well. That Japan, in his opinion, was more important industrially, and as an ally to the United States of America, than Europe, and that if Japan should fall to Communism, and with their industry and the raw materials of Asia, Europe would fall anyway. That there should be no priority on assistance, arms, and what-have-you in the world. The idea of Europe being always first priority in the present world situation is nonsense - that the State Department's advocacy that the United States of America and world democracies can fight on only one front, namely Europe, is ridiculous. With that policy, we are admitting defeat to the enemy. Russia is disposed on two fronts, and if she can bring about a conflict on two fronts, certainly the world democracies can fight her on two fronts.

K. That we need not fear an attack on Formosa at this time because the weight and numbers of the Chinese armies are now in Manchuria or in Korea.

The above does not contain all the statements made by General MacArthur as some were even too delicate to put in this diary. However, both congressmen reiterated over and over that they agreed with everything that he had said and that upon their return to Washington they would do everything within their power to assist him in the great job that he is doing. Of course, to say the least, I agree.

I invited the congressmen and General Nuckols to lunch at the Union Club with me but the congressmen had a previous engagement - reference their press conference - and could not accept. They asked me to have lunch with them at the Imperial, but because of my diet, I refused and went to the Union Club and had two poached eggs and a glass of tomato juice. General Nuckols did join the congressmen.

**SATURDAY
7 APRIL
1951**

Mr. Clement R. Hurd and Mr. Lawrence Gahn, who are State Department information officers, called in the morning. Hurd was a Plebe at West Point during my tour as an officer and was found in mathematics during his Plebe year.[170] In conversation with them, I let them know that the Voice of America should get its stuff into the satellite countries and into the inside of Russia and let those people know what we

---

170."Found" is a West Point term for a failing grade.

A B–29 of the 19th BG over North Korea.

are doing to help them in their fight against Communism - instead of telling them how the corn grows in Nebraska and how they raise horses in Virginia.

The Sinŭiju railroad bridge was attacked by 23 B–29s, dropping 184 - 2,000 pound bombs. Results at this time are unknown. I hope and pray we got this bridge. We lost a B–29 and all the crew members but the navigator, who was rescued, due to two separate MiG attacks. The fighters and bombers destroyed two MiGs and damaged two.

SUNDAY
8 APRIL
1951

Played golf at 1245 hours at Koganei and Major Davison and I really took Major Adams and Lt. Col. Whitehorn[171] into town. I had an 86.

The dinner party at Mayeda House, honoring Congressmen Dorn and Armstrong, was, in my opinion, a great success. They had a good time and repeated to Mrs. Stratemeyer and me their enjoyment of that dinner. Armstrong and Dorn got in a great political discussion with Annalee, and Mr. Armstrong, just prior to everyone's getting up from the table, stood up and thanked us all for a very delightful evening, etc. Mrs. Strat's reply - before I was able to answer him - was, to my way of thinking, wonderful. She said, "Well, if I get put in jail, will you get me out?" It really flustered Mr. Armstrong and everybody at the table howled.

MONDAY
9 APRIL
1951

Received a copy of a radio (which I call a BELIEVE IT OR NOT) from CINCFE to DA:

Reference DEPTAR msg DA 82893 and CINCFE msg ZX 44186. FEAF has received criteria for award of

171. This officer is unidentified.

Korean campaign stars and Bronze Arrowheads to AF personnel. This fact, coupled with imminent rotation of large numbers of Army combat personnel, make it of utmost importance that Army award service stars and Bronze Arrowheads as soon as possible. On what date can criteria be expected for Army personnel.

For record purposes, I quote the statement released and made last evening by Rep W.J.B. Dorn, D., S.C., just prior to his departure for the States. Follows the UP treatment of his release:

Tokyo, April 9 - (UP) Rep. W.J. Bryan Dorn, D., S.C., left Tokyo's Haneda airport Sunday night on his return to the United States after visiting the Far Eastern command and conferring with General Douglas MacArthur. He said that a lesson learned in World War II and relearned in Korea is that "Air Power is the decisive factor in modern war. Air, single-handedly cannot attain victory, but without air, ultimate victory is impossible." He said his judgment was confirmed by MacArthur in a conference Friday. Another lesson relearned, he said, is that air power must be centrally controlled. He said central control has enabled the Fifth Air Force "to gain and hold the complete air dominance in Korea." But, he said, "this present dominance must not be taken for granted. It is a basic precept that any determined air attack, once launched, cannot be turned back. The best our fighters can do is to blunt the enemy's aerial thrust. Our highly mechanized Army, largely dependent on the roads, presents a tempting target for the Red air commander and his staffers. There is every indication that he is building up a serious air potential. Our ground forces must be prepared and instantly ready to defend themselves against Communist strafing attacks for these attacks can well come and with little advance notice. Air will shoot down many of them, but some will filter through." Dorn paid tribute to the "magnificent" teamwork of MacArthur's land, air and sea forces. He said he planned a detailed report to Congress shortly after his return to Washington.

On 7 April I had sent a letter to Partridge inclosing a clipping from that AM's *Nippon Times* re certain broad and misleading statements re air evaluation of the enemy's air potential. *In reply received today the fol signal from him:*

Stratline personal to Gen. Stratemeyer from Gen. Partridge. Msg in 2 parts. PART I. Ref ur ltr dtd 7 Apr 51 and enclosed clipping, correspondent's dispatch reflects his confusion rather than opinion of this hq. Ltr fol. All intelligence continues to indicate build up of hostile air arm and every effort being made to prepare for eventualities. I have personally warned all my forward commanders plus Ridgway and Chung that they must expect air attack in near future. Active passive measures being pushed toward completion and tested frequently. PART II. Eye-witness account received yesterday, copy being forwarded ur hq, confirms that MiG–15s were being flown and maintained by Russians. Feverish construction activity observed visually and in photos at many North Korean airfields. Believe increased emphasis needed on counter air strokes to keep airfields unserviceable and request for employment of B–29s on this mission has been forwarded.

At 1030 Mr. Raymond Loewy,[172] industrial designer and friend of Mr. Symington[173] called and presented a letter from Mr. Symington written on 1 March. We had a nice visit and he indicated he had no request to make of me - that he was seeing Prime Minister of Japan Shigeru Yoshida[174] next Wednesday and this afternoon had an appointment with Major General Marquat, SCAP's Chief of Economic & Scientific Section.

At 1340 I called on General Hickey, in his office, and as per his request. He showed me the following signal, a copy of which I requested and secured.

Follows a direct quote of this radio:

General Headquarters, Far East Command, Outgoing Message - CofS DOH/re, 9 April 1951. From: CINCFE TOKYO JAPAN, TO: SECRE-TARY OF DEFENSE WASH DC (info JCS)....Priority (SECRET). (C-59497) I earnestly recommend promotion to four star rank of the following officers: Lt. Gen. George E. Stratemeyer, Lt. Gen. Matthew B. Ridgway, Vice Admiral Charles T. Joy, the respective commanders of the air forces, the ground forces in Korea and the naval forces of the Far East Command. These appointments should be relatively simultaneous so as to preserve the coordinated balance and unity of this command. In addi-tion, the following officers are recommended for promotion from two star to three star rank; William M. Hoge,[175] Leven C. Allen, and Doyle O. Hickey respectively, Commanding General, IX Corps, Chief of Staff of Eighth Army and Chief of Staff of Far East Command; and promotion from one star to two star rank of Edwin K. Wright, the Operations Offi-cer of the Far East Command. The distinguished service of all these offi-cers is too well known to require additional comment. It is their brilliant service which has bulwarked our successful operations in the Far East Command. The basic reason, however, for the recommendation for these promotions goes deeper than the individual merits of the officers con-cerned. The positions which they hold must, for maximum efficiency, be clothed with the essential authority and dignity which go with these ranks. Signed, MacArthur. OFFICIAL. K.B. Bush,[176] Brig. Gen., USA, Adjutant General - Copies to CINCFE, CofS(return).

At 1400 hours attended a luncheon at the residence of General and Mrs. MacArthur, the Embassy, in honor of Secretary of Army Frank Pace.

---

172. Raymond F. Loewy was the famous industrial designer who designed a wide variety of items from tooth-paste tubes to automobiles to railroad engines.

173. The first Secretary of the Air Force, Stuart Symington, served in that capacity from Sept. 18, 1947, to Apr. 24, 1950. Prior to World War II, he had been president of Emerson Electric Co., and during the war had made it the largest aircraft armament plant. Prior to becoming Secretary of the Air Force, he had been Asst. Secretary of War for Air. In 1952, he was elected Senator from Missouri.

174. Yoshida was prime minister in 1946-1947 and again from October 1948 to December 1954.

175. Maj Gen William M. Hoge replaced the late Bryant Moore as commander of the IX Corps. During World War II, he had been chief engineer during the construction of the Alcan Highway, led a brigade of combat engineers at Omaha Beach, led the units of the 9th Armored Division which captured the Ludendorff Bridge at Remagen, and commanded the 4th Armored Division.

176. Brig Gen Kenneth B. Bush had been involved with adjutant general activities since 1923. He became FEC adjutant general in 1949, and in July 1950, also assumed additional duty as the UNC adjutant general.

TUESDAY 10 APRIL 1951

General Partridge called at approximately 1040 hours and made the following report to me: (1) A First Marine Air Wing pilot shot down a British fighter this morning in the Wŏnsan area. Major General Field Harris, commander, is very concerned. Every attempt is being made to rescue the downed pilot. (2) The H–19 Sikorsky helicopter has completed its test and General Partridge is recommending the return of the crew, but the retention of the helicopter with the technical representative and possibly some maintenance personnel. I approved this and every effort will be made by FEAF hq to comply with General Partridge's recommendations. (3) General Partridge held a conference with General Sweetser and Colonel Zoller this morning and has concluded that it is desirable to convert the 452d Light Bomb Wing into a night operating unit. I thoroughly approve this and when General Partridge's recommendations arrive FEAF hqs, a strong signal for my signature will be prepared, urging approval, to CSAF, personal Twining from Stratemeyer. (4) A MiG–15 was shot down this morning; the pilot ejected between the North Korean coast and Sinmi-do Island. The airplane was seen to crash in the water and the pilot, with parachute, dropping off shore. General Partridge indicated that he was taking every possible action to recover the pilot and stated that in all probability he would send a request to my Hq to have the Navy make an attempt to salvage and recover the aircraft. (above - copy to each - to VC, D/O, and D/M with notation they were to take necessary action re those items which concerned them.)

General Partridge called at 1550 and reported that he had just received a report from Major General Field Harris, CG 1st Marine Air Wing, that both the damaged British fighters had returned safely to their carriers and that the report he (Partridge) had given me today was incorrect (that a British fighter had been shot down by the Marines.)

General Partridge stated that Captain Donald S. Thomas, who was picked up by a British naval vessel from a junk manned by Korean sympathizers, was now at Fifth Air Force and that last night he had him at his home and listened to Thomas' harrowing experiences for over an hour. He stated that Captain Thomas' story deserved attention and that he (Thomas) did everything as set down in the book for escape and evasion.

General Partridge thinks so highly of Thomas that he recommended that after Thomas' return to the United States (when he returns to duty after his rest and recuperation), he should be put in the business of rescue - that is lecturing, etc. I agree with General Partridge and told him that I though such a recommendation from him, with my endorsement, would be better than for me to institute a letter. General Partridge agreed and will do this.

General Partridge, in his quarters last night, promoted Thomas to captain.

(copy of above extracted from diary and copy each sent to VC, D/O, D/M, and D/I.)

Colonel Aaron W. Tyer, commander of K-2, came out to the house to lunch.

WEDNESDAY 11 APRIL 1951

Captain Thomas, who was recently rescued through the assistance of sympathetic North Koreans and the British Navy, reported to me at 0945 hours and related his entire story from the time he was hit in the air until rescued. Present were Generals Weyland, Craigie, and Nuckols.

His story brought home the importance of the escape and evasion kits.

Two items which Capt Thomas did not have were the gold coins and a proper map of North Korea (where he went down). Further, Captain Thomas indicated that two of the compasses failed to work as did the ballpoint pen. He also indicated that had he had a reasonable supply of South Korean won, he would have eaten much better.

This young man was smart, trusting when he should have been, and he possesses that something which is needed in rescue, and escape & evasion that should be passed on to others.

I have directed that D/I take the necessary action to implement Capt. Thomas' recommendations and to correct the deficiencies now existing in the escape & evasion kits. (above extracted and sent to D/I).

Last night, at my direction, D/I sent out the fol message in my name:

From CG FEAF, To COMNAVFE (Courier): Cite A 85031 CG. Please pass to HMS COCKADE, OP IM. My hearty congratulations and deep appreciation for your rescue. Request that a security restriction be placed on experiences of Lt. Donald S. Thomas. Information concerning same should not be divulged without clearance from me. Signed Stratemeyer, CG, FEAF.

Dispatched the fol msg, personal Twining, Chidlaw and Partridge from Stratemeyer, Cite AX 6114:

Part I. Reourad AX 1224 OP-OP3, dtg 070720Z Jan 51, our let, subj: FEAF Ftr Acft Conversion dtd 13 Jan 51, urad AFODA 53329 dtd 27 Jan 51. As of 7 Apr 51 FEAF had 337 F–80 acft. At curr[ent] attrition rate of 18.3 acft per mo FEAF will be rd [reduced] to UE str[ength] by 1 July 51. If we are to cont[inue] F–80 oprs as at present it is essential that 1 gp of F–80s be converted to F–84s by 1 Jul 51 as reqd previously in ref FEAF rad and ltr. This is in add to 75 F–80s programmed fr AAC [Alaskan Air Command]. *PART II.* The 75 F–84s reqd by 1 July 51 does not consider conversion of FEAF 4 F–51 sqs to F–80s. If conversion of 2 add gps to F–84s reqd in above rad and ltr is not aprd FEAF will be required to cont opn of its 4 F–51 sqs through 1st quarter FY-53. In this event aprx 200 add F–51 attrition will be required during this pd [period]. F–51s are considered unsuitable for indef use in FEAF. *PART III.* Inasmuch as only 2 and 1/2 mos remain before FEAF's F–80 sqs are down to UE str, imm action to initiate conversion of 1 gp of F–80s to F–84s is considered essential. *PART IV.* Req delv of 75 F–80Cs on Project FAF ISF 634 be expedited.

At about 1515 hours, General Nuckols came to my office and stated he had had a flash report that at 0100 hours Washington time, the President has a special message and had called the press to meet with him. At about 1525 hours, Colonel Van Meter telephoned and stated that the President had fired General MacArthur.

The President's orders were as follows:

Order to General MacArthur from the President.

I deeply regret that it becomes my duty as President and the Commander in Chief of the United States Military Forces to replace you as Supreme

Commander, Allied Powers; Commander in Chief, United Nations Command; Commander in Chief, Far East; and Commanding General, U.S. Army Far East.

You will turn over your command, effective at once, to Lt. General Matthew B. Ridgway. You are authorized to have issued such orders as are necessary to complete desired travel to such place as you select.

My reasons for your replacement will be made public concurrently with the delivery to you of the foregoing order, and are contained in the next following message.

Follows the additional statement:

With deep regret I have concluded that General of the Army Douglas MacArthur is unable to give his wholehearted support to the policies of the United States Government and the United Nations in matters pertaining to his official duties.

In view of the specific responsibilities imposed upon me by the Constitution of the United States and the added responsibilities entrusted in me by the United Nations, I have decided that I must make a change of command in the Far East.

I have, therefore, relieved General MacArthur of his commands and have designated Lt. General Matthew B. Ridgway as his successor.

Full and vigorous debate on matters of national policy is a vital element in the constitutional system of our free democracy. It is fundamental, however, that military commanders must be governed by the policies and directives issued to them in the manner provided by our laws and the Constitution. In time of crisis, this consideration is particularly compelling.

General MacArthur's place in history as one of our greatest commanders is fully established. The nation owes him a debt of gratitude for the distinguished and exceptional service which he has rendered his country in posts of great responsibility.

For that reason I repeat my regret at the necessity for the action I feel compelled to take in his case.

To say that I was stunned - and shocked - expresses it lightly. Even this morning (12 April 1951), after an almost sleepless night, I cannot understand why our President could be so wrongly influenced as to remove General MacArthur. To me, it means capitulation of our government and all that it has stood for to our "Pinkish" State Department, the British government, and Moscow. Every Red, regardless of his place in the world, was gleeful at this drastic order.[177]

---

177. To President Truman, MacArthur's March 24 pronouncement was just the latest in a series of challenges to civilian control of the military and to the office of the Presidency. At last fed up with what he perceived as insubordination, Truman decided MacArthur must go. But with MacArthur still enjoying public acclaim, and with an extremely vocal Republican Party looking for ways to damage Truman and the Democrats, the President had to move with care.

Then, on April 5 came the final straw. The month before, the powerful House Republican Minority Leader, Joseph Martin, had written General MacArthur and had enclosed a copy of a speech in which he had vehemently attacked the Administration and its conduct of the war in Korea. MacArthur's reply, in which he stated that his views generally coincided with Martin's, and in which he reiterated his dissatisfaction with Administration policy, contained the provocative statement, "There is no substitute for victory." Martin read MacArthur's letter on the floor of the House on April 5.

[Stratemeyer made this additional entry for Apr. 11 the following day]

Shortly after hearing from President Truman and fired General MacArthur, Admiral Joy and I got together and through Colonel Bunker made an appointment with the General to see him in his office about 1800 hours. We entered through General Hickey's office and General MacArthur greeted us in his same old fine manner. He reviewed some of his actions to clearly show his great attempt to carry out the UN directives and the President's directives to him. He stated that it was beyond him how any one could take exception to his release of 24 March. Joy and I attempted to express our feelings, our shock, and astonishment, but we both did a right poor job, because words were hard to find to express just how we felt. General MacArthur paid us both the very greatest compliments and indicated again his great regret that we both had not received four star rank which we both deserved. He further indicated that in all probability now we would not be promoted. He warned us both to watch our steps because of our loyalty to him and because of the work that we had done for him.

Shortly after this, I arose and we bid him goodbye.

THURSDAY
12 APRIL
1951

41 B–29s and one Tarzon equipped B–29 attacked the Korean side of the Sinŭiju-Antung railroad bridge. Apparently we failed to get the bridge. Score: 8 MiGs destroyed, 7 probably destroyed and 11 damaged; sum total - 25 MiGs. I will send a redline to Vandenberg early tomorrow morning reference this.

Our losses: 3 B–29s lost; 3 B–29s received considerable battle damage and other B–29s damaged due to flak and/or fighters. It looks as though we have another "rubber" bridge which I intend to get.

Also, it looks as though BomCom needs some training.

Flew to Korea, leaving Haneda 1100 and pinned three stars on Earle Partridge. He had his staff lined up and his band, and a right impressive ceremony took place in the field at the air base at K-2, Taegu.

Just prior to departing, I pinned three stars on Weyland in my office.

Dispatched the fol personal signal to Vandenberg:

Weyland duly sworn in and properly equipped with three-star insignia this date. He will depart for temporary duty Washington, ETD 13 April 1700 I, with instructions to report to you personally. I am leaving for Korea immediately to congratulate and pin three stars on Partridge.

Alkire dispatched the fol signal for me to AMC, with info FEAMCOM and FAF:

Personal Chidlaw fr Stratemeyer. This rad in 2 parts. Part 1. I am concerned by the numerous and cont'd failures of the external fuel tanks rels

---

An outraged President Truman now had his reason to fire MacArthur. Meetings with his advisors, including the Joint Chiefs of Staff, garnered a consensus that MacArthur must be dismissed. Unfortunately, because of a leak to a newspaper about the dismissal, the affair was mishandled and MacArthur received word of his firing on April 11 via a press release, not through channels. News of MacArthur's dismissal was received in many quarters with anger, but for Truman the removal of the MacArthur albatross from around his neck was a great relief. ("History of the JCS," Vol. III, pp 505-546; David Rees, *Korea: The Limited War* [New York, 1964], pp 211-220.)

[release] mechanism on the F–86 acft. Trouble was rpt'd in four (4) Johnson Fld UR's [unsatisfactory reports] 51-25, dash 44, dash 54 and dash 58. In add to plug and lead failures the solenoid fails to actuate the rels mechanism. Tanks fail to rels in the air or im after landing, however after acft warms up on the grd the sys functions satisfactorily. Part 2. I feel that an unwarranted opnl hazard is imposed by the unreliability of these units as well as preventing our acft fr engaging enemy acft on even terms. Our efforts to elim these failures have been ineffective to date. This matter is considered of such importance that an im proj should be estb'd to find the cause and elim the malfunctions.

FRIDAY
13 APRIL
1951

Dispatched the fol redline to Vandenberg re yesterday's BOMBCOM effort with accompanying fighter escort over the Sinŭiju-Antung, Korean-side bridges.

Redline Vandenberg fr Statemeyer. *Part 1.* Folg are preliminary repts of the mission against the RR bridge at Sinŭiju 12 Apr: BOMBCOM struck w/1 Tarzon acft and 35 B–29s loaded w/200 pound GP. Ftr cover consisted of aprox 34 F–86s and 54 F–84s. One RB–45 made post-strike photos at 1500/I; photo assessment shows no substantial damage to bridge although most bb [bomb?] patterns were excellent. *Part 2.* Preliminary repts indicated 3 B-29s lost and 7 damaged. No damage to friendly ftrs reptd. *Part 3.* Preliminary repts indicate eny [enemy] losses as fols: B–29s claim 4 MiGs destroyed, 4 probably destroyed and 4 damaged. F–84s claim 3 probables, 3 damaged. F–86s claim 4 destroyed, 4 damaged. Totals: 8 destroyed, 7 probables, 11 damaged, sum total: 26.

General Yoshitoshi Tokugawa, ex lt. general and baron, who is Japan's counterpart of Trenchard and Billy Mitchell, called on me at 1100 hours accompanied by General Banfill and one of Banfill's officer interpreters. Tokugawa began flying in 1910. He is a stoic individual, however, he possesses a sense of humor. I enjoyed my visit with him.

At 1230 hours, had luncheon at the GHQ Officers' Club - luncheon given by Col Pat Mahoney in honor of General Weyland. Pat had all my other general officers to the luncheon as well as some of their ladies -including Annalee, Marian Picher and Mrs. Craigie.

At 1600 hours, we briefed Secretary of the Army Frank Pace, Jr., Mr. Francis Shackelford, Department of the Army Counsellor, and Major General Alonzo P. Fox, of Hq FEC. I was most pleased with the presentations given. Immediately, Mr. Pace by his genial manner and questions produced an informal atmosphere which brought about a serious, but tremendously interesting briefing. I told General Craigie to tell all presentors that I was exceptionally well satisfied.

Attended party given by General and Mrs. Hickey honoring Secretary Pace and his staff at the GHQ Officers' Club.

**SATURDAY
14 APRIL
1951**

Congressman Armstrong returned from Taipei today; leaves for the States tonight.

Dispatched fol:

Personal LeMay and Chidlaw with info personal Twining: *PART I* for LeMay: After recg your 30 Mar 51 ltr which expd [expressed] concern over escort capability of 27th Ftr Escort Wg, I sent my rad AX 6055 CG, dtd 100200Z Apr 51 to Partridge reqg [requesting] his comments. Quote of Partridge reply fols: "Part 1. Ref yourad AX 6055. The 27 Ftr Wg is fully capable of successfully escorting B–29 acft anywhere in Korea fr its pres[ent] loc[ation] at Itazuke by employing staging oprs at K-2 upon compl of the escort. W/the approach of warm wea the rwy at Itazuke is not of sufficient length to permit takeoff w/pylon tanks w/o the use of jato. Chief factor which will lmt the employment of the 27 Wg on escort mission is the shortage of pylon tanks. Only sufficient tanks for 1 more gp mission are aval at this time. I am sure your staff is familiar w/this problem. *Part 2.* Although the F–84E airplane has performed satisfactorily in an escort role, sufficient evidence is aval which indicates that it is out-classed by the MiG–15 fr the standpoint of Mach lmts [limits]. Our fwd based F–86 acft are better suited to perform the counter air and escort missions. *Part 3.* I intend to fully utilize F–84 acft in the escort role whenever conds justify their employment and it is further projected that F–84E acft of the 27 Wg will be utilized in an escort role to a much greater extent upon comp of Kunsan (K-8) airfield which will possess an adequate runway for F-84E escort opns." Part 2 for CHIDLAW. Req info on your ability to prov the 3960 tank sets which are FEAF 120 day rqmt. We can produce tks locally at rate of 2500 per mo[nth] beginning in 90 days. Cost here $400 ea against $783 in ZI. If unable to prov[ide] our rqmts fr ZI req auth be granted to commence local procurement im[mediately].

Cleared the fol rad for dispatch:

PERSONAL VANDENBERG FROM STRATEMEYER. Info LeMay, Briggs, and Chidlaw. Enemy eff[ectiveness] against our med bomr acft has been steadily increasing in recent weeks. Greater aggressiveness on the part of MiG fts, add radar fac[ilities] and greater concentration of heavy AAA guns in the areas of remaining profitable tgts in Korea are contributing factors. On 12 Apr mission against the International bridge at Sinŭiju 3 B–29 acft and 3 crews were lost; two crew members were lost from another crew and 2 add acft received major damage which may result in salvage. In the past 30 days we have lost to both cmbt [combat] and non-cmbt causes 8 B–29 acft and 8 crews. As of 2400 12 Apr the 3 med bomb gps in FEAF had a total of 88 acft asgd of which 13 were out of comm for battle damage and longtime maint. This leaves 75 acft aval for opns, which is 18 short of our authd UE. FEAF had 76 crews against 93 required on that date. *PART II.* We have reqd in our AX 5223 OP-OP3 dtd 22 Mar 51 and AX 6039 OP-OP3 dtd 4 Apr 51 that the SAC gps in FEAF be maintd at 33 acft per gp. We have also requested in our AX 5726 OP-OP3 dtd 2 Apr 51 that SAC be prepared to dispatch on short notice up to 10 B–29s for their units in this theater. I urge your spt in seeing that these requests are met and in assuring FEAF swift deliveries of replacement B–29 acft and crews as required.

Also dispatched the fol letter to the American Embassy for General of the Army Douglas MacArthur. It was delivered to his senior aide, for transmittal to him at 5:16 this evening.

dtd 14 April 1951

Dear General MacArthur,

I humbly want to expressed to you, prior to your departure from Japan, my admiration and wholehearted aggressive support for everything that you have done and stood for - in Japan and for our country.

I completed forty-one years in the Service in both the United States Army and the United States Air Force 1 March 1951. I never, throughout my career, have had a commander who has been as great as you. My hope is that because of my association with you, some of your great competence as a leader and commander will have rubbed off on me. Your greatness, to my mind, is that you give a man a job, you trust him, and you let him alone to do that job.

I assure you that as long as I live, my devotion, affection, and service to you will always remain as staunch as it has been for the past two years during the period I have been the Commanding General, Far East Air Forces, serving directly under you.

I thank you for your signal to the Secretary of Defense re my promotion to four-star rank. This is reward enough for me.

I wish you and Mrs. MacArthur and your son, Arthur, happiness and everything that is good and to your liking in the years ahead. God Bless you all. Admiringly, devotedly, loyally, and sincerely, s/George E. Stratemeyer, Lt General, U.S. Air Force.

SUNDAY 15 APRIL 1951

Colonel Rogers reported to me reference his trip to Australia for Hq USAF. He stated that his mission was successful and he is preparing his report and that now Hq USAF had a job to do reference target folders in coordination with Australia, Great Britain and the United States.

MONDAY 16 APRIL 1951

Mrs. Stratemeyer and I attended the departure this morning of General and Mrs. MacArthur. It was a solemn occasion, but well done by the military and by General and Mrs. MacArthur. General Ridgway masterfully handled himself. My Air Forces were outstanding in their flying — which included F–80s, B–29s and F–86s.

I am to report to General Ridgway at 9:45 hours. Joy is to follow me at 10:00 A.M.

Fol rad received from CINCFE to EUSAK with info to all commands:

Request you give appropriate distribution to the following: "I believe that the fidelity, courage and spirit of the 8th Army and of its equally gallant support naval and air services have set new high standards of achievement in military annals. I would like the 8th Army and the support naval and air services to know how immeasurably proud I am of them, and of the honor of having been privileged to share with them some of their splendid service. In the days ahead I have unbounded faith in this great allied inter-service team under the leadership of its newly arrived, proven combat commander. Signed M.B. Ridgway, Lieutenant General, U.S. Army.

I called on General Ridgway through his chief of staff, General Hickey, at 0945 hours. I was greeted warmly by Ridgway and before he had a chance to speak, I made this statement: that this change has taken place which is none of my official business, that he can depend upon FEAF for the same loyal and conscientious support that was given to General MacArthur, that we had a "team" out here and that my dealing with Admiral Joy as head of the Navy could not be better.

General Ridgway then stated that he knew what a very magnificent job FEAF had done under my leadership and that he was confident that the same loyal and magnificent job would continue. I assured him that it would.

I then strongly urged that he live in the Embassy and that he bring Mrs. Ridgway and his family to Japan - both of which he said he hoped to do. He was concerned about living in the Embassy as he has nothing more than his salary and could not afford it. I then said that since it was the Embassy I was sure funds were available from both the Japanese and American governments to furnish it and make it a livable place.

I then told him very definitely what a great guy Major General Doyle O. Hickey is; he said he knew that, and, with that statement, he wanted me at any time to come to see him and make any recommendations that I saw fit to do on any subject and that the door would be always open for that type of business. I thanked him for this and told him that I intended to do just that - as I had in the past.

We then talked a bit on military subjects: one being the Sinŭiju bridge that FEAF has been unable to knock out so far. I told him that we were studying every possible means to knock this bridge out with the B–29s, the B–26s and by dropping mines. I indicated that it was my opinion that 60 to 70 percent of all personnel and supplies came into North Korea from Manchuria over the Antung-Sinŭiju bridge. I told him that there was no general build-up of the Russian Air Force in Siberia and in Russian territory; however, there was a very definite build-up of Russian aircraft in Manchuria - namely in Mukden, Liao-yang and Antung. He said he was aware of that and that in case the Chinese did come in in force, by air, that he expected the Eighth Army to have to take casualties, but in his opinion, we, FEAF, could within a short period of time knock out that air. I told him we would of course make a great attempt to do just that but unless we can cross the Yalu River and hit them on the three airdromes named above, it would take a long time. He then stated, "Strat, at this time I do not have authority to cross the Yalu River." I said that I knew that, but I felt that if the Chinese Communist Air Force hit the Eighth Army on the ground in strength, he might get such a directive from the Joint Chiefs of Staff - to which he agreed.

The last subject discussed "was I prepared, in case the Russians came in, to immediately counter-attack?" I indicated that I was with all equipment and personnel available - that we keep our plan on that action up-to-date and that each unit down to squadron level knows what its job is to be.

He asked me, in case Russia did attack, would a flash report immediately go to all FEC commands? My answer was that I was sure that was true of FEAF, but that I could not answer him in reference to the other commands, but I was sure such procedure must be in effect. We then shook hands. The meeting was closed with General Ridgway again telling me that he knew he would get our whole-hearted support and he was depending on that—I assured him he was right.

On the way out, I raised the "flash question" [regarding a flash report to FEC commands] with General Hickey and he said he was looking into that and would give Ridgway an answer.

Upon return to my office, I directed General Craigie, my vice commander, to look into the question ("flash question") and to advise me what our procedures are — which I am confident are as follows: that through our aircraft warning set up, the flash report with proper code word would automatically come to FEAF and FEC. (copy of extract of visit to CINCFE given to General Craigie, 16 Apr 51.)

About 1210 hours, General Ridgway returned my call at which time I introduced to him all my key staff except General Picher who had left for lunch.

At 1600 hours, Lt. Colonel Ray[178] (MATS WAF director) called with Major Deitz and Major Bennett[179] (WAF director at Haneda) and we discussed overall general WAF problems and, at present, had to come to the conclusion that we couldn't ask for more WAFs than we can house as set up by minimum requirements. My WAF director, Major Deitz, will discuss the problem with D/M and see if we can't find a solution to secure more WAFs in order to release men to the combat units.

Got off the "dear Gill" weekly letter.

TUESDAY   *Received the fol personal from Partridge:*

17 APRIL   Quoted for your information is part of flash message from
1951   Almond to Van Fleet, dtd 16 Apr 51. "Of significant inter-
                 est in last night's activities was the effective part played by
night air attack and the exhibition of close cooperation between FAF, naval air and my ground troops. Commencing at 142100 hours, 1 B–26 bombing by radar, planted several 100 pounders on a group of enemy reportedly building up just ahead of the 17th infantry. Shortly thereafter, arty placed starshells on the 4 corners of the same area; a C–47 then sowed strings of flares across the marked area, permitting Navy F4Us to strafe with their explosive 20 mm. This devastating performance was repeated periodically until 0330 this morning. The aftermath pleases me, as I am sure it will you ----. This afternoon 10 North Koreans gave up, saying they just could not fight all day and stand bombing all night. The effectiveness of this bombardment was especially gratifying, inasmuch as dense ground haze, coupled with smoke of burning grasslands, had severely restricted employment of close air support during the day." For your information the Marines participated in this attack instead of the Navy.

---

178. Lt Col Elizabeth Ray. In 1961, she became Director of WAF.
179 Maj Joan E. Bennett.

I refused to release the above quoted signal at my briefing this morning as Ned Almond spoiled it all with his last sentence. Apparently he is continuing his emphasis on Marine air.

At 0900 hours, I pinned the Air Medal on Major General Frank E. Lowe, Presidential representative, which he won flying with combat airplanes in order to get information for the President.

Had Lt. Wogan, the son of my classmate, Bugs Wogan, to lunch.

General Stearley came in about 1430 hours and I had rather a long conference with him - Generals Craigie and Picher being present.

At 1530 hours, Mr. Fromm of the *United States News* [*and World Report*] came in with General Nuckols and two secretaries. We then went through a question and answer period - mainly on the build-up of Communist China's air power. This was taken down and after editing will be submitted to me for my approval before released for publication.

At 1630 hours, Mr. Dallas Sherman, PAA head for the Far East, called and asked my advice reference his paying his respects to General Ridgway. I advised him to do so without delay.

Mr. Compton Pakenham came in to see me this morning and told me about the coming *Newsweek* article on Earle Partridge with his picture in color on the front. I told him that I would support him in any way possible for the data in the write-up. He showed me the color film and the picture he intended to use, and I told him I thought it excellent.

WEDNESDAY 18 APRIL 1951   Brigadier General Robert A. McClure, USA, the Army psychological warfare officer in Washington called with two officers from G-2 shop and my psychological warfare officer, Colonel Ambrose,[180] and General Crabb. General McClure is out here in the interest of increasing the activities pertaining to psychological warfare. I told him I was one hundred percent back of it, and that I would support it in every way possible. I did tell him though that the best way to do it was to organize a psychological warfare sq back home with people and equipment, including airplanes, and get it out here. I suggested the use of the P–47 used so efficiently in World War II. I pointed out that we were at the tail end of the line, that our activities in Korea were considered to be a "police action" and that any equipment and personnel to be used out here would necessarily have to be taken from units that were fighting the war. I told him that you "can't have your cake and eat it too," and that unless General Ridgway ordered that I decrease activities that we are now participating in, I could not divert them to psychological warfare. I furthermore told him that I believed one hundred percent in Bonner Fellers article that was published some months ago in *Collier's* Magazine. He stated that he also believed in it.

I further asked him why he didn't control the Voice of America, and he stated that that was a State Department function except in a theater of operations wherein we are at war. I told him that we had some 60,000 American casualties and we were at war here, and I considered this a theater of operations. Upon leaving, he stated that his mission here was to do what he could to

---

180. Lt Col Joseph R. Ambrose.

put impetus in psychological warfare and gain as much information as possible on the subject.

I told him that he had FEAF's wholehearted support. I further arranged to get his two sons who are flying officers on Okinawa up here to be with him next Sunday.

Lt. Robert Leebrick called at 1430 hours; we had a nice visit. He has completed 50 missions. He is staying with the Pullens.

Mr. Earl D. Johnson, Asst Sec of Army, dropped by the office for an informal call. He has returned to the Far East, accompanying Mr. Dulles who arrived here on his mission 16 April 51.

THURSDAY
19 APRIL
1951

Received the fol rad from USAF (also addressed to TAC and SAC with info AMC):

1. It is planned to return the 27th Fighter Wing from FEAF to the ZI starting in June 1951. Unit will deploy by squadrons in June, July and August 1951. *2.* In order to return present combat capability of FEAF it is planned to deploy from the ZI to FEAF the 136th Fighter Bomber Wing now assigned to TAC. Unit will deploy by squadrons in May, June and July 1951. *3.* The following factors will govern preparations of a plan for deployment of these units: *a.* The 27th Fighter Wing will deploy to the ZI less equipment. *b.* Aircraft of the 27th Wing will be retained in FEAF to be utilized by 136th. *c.* The 136th Fighter Wing without aircraft will deploy on an indefinite TDY basis. *4.* Shipping to FEAF of aircraft of 136th and follow on jet aircraft attrition replacements which will be available to FEAF contemplates continuation of F–51 units as now equipped. It will not be possible to support through December 1951 the conversion of your F–51 to jets. Details as to flow of theater reserve and attrition replacement aircraft follows. *5.* Further information concerning these movements will be provided ASAP.

At 0900 hours, General Crabb came in and reported that the cloak and dagger outfit of psychological warfare had utilized our Air-Sea Rescue SB–17s recently on one of their operations and, as a result, when the Tarzon B–29 carrying Pete Jennings and crew went down, some two or three SB–17s were not available to participate in that search. He further informed me that they had another such operation laid on in North Korea and would I provide for it with SB–17s. I informed General Crabb that I absolutely would not --- Air-Sea Rescue is set up to save our pilots, crewmen, and Allied soldiers and airmen. Air-Sea Rescue is an <u>international</u> [emphasis in original] organization and if ever it was determined that we were utilizing this organization as a cover for psychological warfare, it would be most embarrassing to the Air Force and the U.S. government.

I issued a directive to General Crabb that under no conditions would we utilize Air-Sea Rescue personnel and aircraft for psychological warfare. I further stated that if their next movement into North Korea was of sufficient importance to withdraw combat or troop carrier aircraft for the mission, that this would be done, although it must be pointed out that it would lessen the primary mission of the aircraft and personnel to be utilized.

I further pointed out to General Crabb that he would get this information to General McClure with a strong recommendation that equipment and personnel be sent to the Far East Air Forces for use by the psychological warfare organization, that I believed in their mission and wanted to support it, but under no conditions, unless directed by higher authority, would I utilize Air-Sea Rescue. (Copy of above extracted from diary under date of 19 April and sent to D/O, D/I thru VC, with instructions to note and return to CG.)

Dispatched the fol Stratline personal to Briggs and Partridge:

No bridge repeat no bridge over the Yalu River will be attacked when there is possibility of violating the air space over Manchuria. This directive issued in view of CINCFE signal CX 60410 quoted in my AX 6511 dtd 19 April 51. Receipt acknowledgment this stratline desired.

Lunched with Mr. Hodgson[181] of the Australian Diplomatic Mission, honoring Mr. and Mrs. Dulles and the Australian representative in the Philippines, Admiral (Ret) and Mrs. Moore.[182]

**FRIDAY
20 APRIL
1951**

Dr. LeRoy Brothers, the head of the Operational Analyses in Hq USAF, had a conference with me this morning at 1030 hours. I had General Craigie present when Dr. Brothers outlined what his recommendations would be with reference to the utilization of operational analysts in the Far East Air Forces, namely, 4 with the 314th Air Division, 3 with the Fifth Air Force and 2 with Hq FEAF. Although we only have two at present, he indicated he would make every effort to secure the remaining 7 and get them over here.

At 1100 hours, Mr. John Rich of CBS paid me a visit. He likes his work (he was formerly with INS [International News Service]) and is leaving for Korea tomorrow. 1130 hours, Mr. Earl D. Johnson, Asst Sec'y of the Army, and representative of the Department of National Defense [*sic*] with the Dulles Mission, called. We discussed the strength of FEAF in Japan and the construction and build up and beef up of airdromes both in Japan and Okinawa. He indicated he was with the Dulles mission primarily to bring the Defense Department of the U.S. into the picture here in Japan and to impress the people of Japan with the fact that the U.S. forces, particularly air and naval forces, would remain strong in Japan. A picture was taken and an article written by General Nuckols which was submitted to Mr. Johnson for his approval for publication in all Japanese newspapers.

At 1415 hours, Major General Edward P. Parker, Provost Marshal of the Army, called. Present were Colonel Gray, my Inspector General, and Colonel Oge,[183] Provost Marshal of Far East Command.

At 1615 hours, I left my office for Koganei where I celebrated with Mrs. Stratemeyer and her golfing ladies the completion of the gals "Annalee Tournament." Annalee fell and hurt herself; did not rest last night.

Neko-San was returned from the clinic.

---

181. Col William R. Hodgson, Head of the Australian Mission to Japan. He had served previously as Australian delegate to the UN Security Council and as Ambassador to France.
182. Rear Adm George D. Moore, Minister for Australia in the Philippines from 1950-1955.
183. Col Oge's full name is unknown.

In follow up to my radio of 19 April, dispatched the fol ltr to both Briggs of FEAF BomCom and Partridge of FAF:

My signal to you last evening (19 April 1951) directing that the bridges over the Yalu River not be attacked where the air space over Manchuria might be violated, stands for the present. You will, however, continue your training and plans for the attack on the Sinŭiju bridge, the Lin-Chiang bridge, and those other bridges where quantities of supplies are being moved from Manchuria into North Korea. FOR COMGEN FEAF BOMBER COMMAND: When you are satisfied that your training and plans are complete to take out the Sinŭiju railroad bridge, it is desired that you send me a signal to that effect, including the date that you desire to attack, and, at that time, I may be able to obtain clearance to take out the Sinŭiju-Antung railroad bridge. FOR COMGEN FIFTH AIR FORCE: If and when we attack the Sinŭiju-Antung railroad bridge, you will provide all possible fighter escort and cover for the B–29s that it is within your power to furnish. s/G.E.S., etc.

Dispatched an R&R to D/I, with authorization for him to approach and seek assistance from D/O, particularly, Dir of Plans, and asked for answers to questions re the movement and analysis of supplies being brought in from Manchuria into North Korea:

the tonnage and volume that are moved out over the following listed bridges and where the supplies are concentrated: - Antung-Sinŭiju? Ch'angsŏng? the Manp'ojin bridge complex? Lin-Chiang? If the bridges are left in over the Yalu, and the bridges over the Ch'ŏngch'ŏn River are kept out, what is the effect on volume and time on stockpile of supplies in the battle area - if the bridges over the Yalu River are taken out and the only means for moving supplies and people into the battle area would be the putting in and utilization of pontoon bridges - what would be the effect? As I see it, by taking out the Yalu bridges, particularly the Antung-Sinŭiju bridge, we cut down the time & rate at which supplies and personnel can be moved to the battlefront. Is time then an important factor when apparently, under the present mission that CINCFE has, time is not important, as in all probability the utilization of pontoon bridges supplies, munitions and people can be gotten to the battlefront...?

**SATURDAY
21 APRIL
1951**

Departed Haneda 1000 hours; flew to Nagoya where I was met by Generals Spivey and Partridge and was immediately taken to the 314th Air Division hq where I was briefed on the entire air defense set up in Japan, and I was convinced insofar as availability of equipment, personnel, and anti-aircraft artillery, that we are in good shape with the tools we have.

Immediately after the briefing, I made a short talk to all the officers and then proceeded with General Spivey to General Partridge's quarters where we had a delicious luncheon. Immediately after luncheon went to the golf course and had a fine round of golf although I played very poorly. Had a 93.

A remarkable photo of a B–26 low-level attack. Its parafrag bomb has just hit the ground and enemy personnel (one very close to the explosion) can be seen trying to take cover.

After cleaning up in General Spivey's quarters in the hotel, he entertained with cocktails and dinner from which I left about 2120 hours to return to Tokyo. Arrived Haneda 2305 and went directly home to bed.

Two items of business I discussed with Partridge were: *(1)* that I could not send Sweetser back to the U.S. to press for more B–26s and crews in view of Vandenberg's recent directive to me in which he stated he was sending all possible crews and B–26s. However, I did, in view of our conversion from day to night [operations] of the 452d Wing, suggest Sweetser might bird-dog that project and be of help. Partridge will look into this and make recommendations accordingly. *(2)* I agreed with him (Partridge) reference his top secret letter to me re the attack on the Sinŭiju-Antung railway bridge, and I told him that in view of Ridgway's recent directive, my hands were tied; however, I discussed this subject with him and there was a possibility in the not too distant future that I would be given a "green light" on taking it out. If and when that is done, I told him, insofar as the air space over Manchuria is concerned, this would be violated in order to knock MiGs out of the air and protect our bombers.

SUNDAY 22 APRIL 1951 1030 hours Brigadier General Wally Smith[184] came in to see me with Colonel Overacker[185] at which time we read the Presidential Unit Citation for his communications squadron and I presented to him the streamer which he will present in Korea to the commander for use on the organization's guidon.

Left the office at 1700 hours with General Hickey and joined our wives at General Doyle's house where we had a good view of their tulip bed, had cocktails and dinner.

General Kenney arrived at 1555 hours; was met by General Nuckols and taken to my house. We met him when we returned last night.

I went to bed, but I'm sure Annalee talked way into the morning.

MONDAY 23 APRIL 1951 *Signed and dispatched the fol ltr to CINCFE, subject:*

A General Analysis of the Logistic Support of Communist Forces in North Korea.

1. The Commander-in-Chief, Far East, directed in my presence the Chief of Staff, Far East Command, to have FEC staff submit an analysis comparing the probable effect on enemy logistic support of air interdiction at the Yalu River as opposed to interdiction at choke points along the line of the Ch'ŏngch'ŏn River extended roughly parallel to the Manchurian border. I indicated to the Chief of Staff, Far East Command, that I too would submit a report.

2. Based on the current estimate of 60 CCF and NK Divisions in North Korea, the daily requirement for all classes of supplies is 3120 tons. This provides 54 tons of Class I, II, III and V supplies for units in contact and 50 tons for those in reserve area.

3. The lines of communication reaching south from the Yalu River from Lin-Chiang (CB 2629) - Antung (XE 1842) inclusive, have a total maximum estimated daily one-way capacity of 5125 tons, divided between 3,000 tons rail and 2125 tons by truck. These lines of communication will permit the establishment of stockpiles along the general line of Chŏngju-Anju-Yŏngwŏn-Hamhŭng. This line averages 130 miles from the Manchurian border and 90 miles from the present front. The difference between the maximum capacity and daily requirements is 2,005 tons and represents the daily build up potential for stockpiling supplies along the

---

184. Brig Gen Wallace G. Smith, AACS commander from September 1948 to August 1951.
185. Col Charles B. Overacker commanded the 1808th AACS.

line indicated. (See attached map). [Map not in diary.] South of this line the combined rail and highway net has a capacity of 4,000 tons, thereby limiting the rate of build-up in the present battle area.

4. From the standpoint of interdiction, the critical terrain feature is the Yalu River. The rail and highway bridges across this river, wide, and unfordable except in some places between Manp'ojin and Lin-chiang, offer the most promising targets for reducing the flow of supplies. Beginning at Antung, the supply capacity is limited by the rail and road net leading from the south bank of the Yalu and is estimated to be as follows:

> *A.* From Sinŭiju-Ŭiju crossings Rail, 1000 tons; Road, 500 tons;
> *B.* From Ch'ŏngsŏngjin - Sakchu crossing Rail, 1000 tons, Road, 500 tons; *C.* From Chi-An - Manp'ojin complex Rail, 1000 tons, Road, 750 tons; *D.* From Lin-Chiang Road, 375 tons.

5. Rivers south of the Yalu while constituting obstacles, do not present the same interdiction possibilities. The Ch'ŏngch'ŏn River at Sinanju is 800 yards wide, narrowing to 250 yards at Kunu-ri. The depth varies with the season but, with the enemy's demonstrated ingenuity in constructing bridges and fords, it should not be regarded as an obstacle of serious proportions. The presence of stockpiles on the north bank of the Ch'ŏngch'ŏn would merely mean a call on the manpower available to the enemy to move the supplies across the river by boat and "A frame" and would not appreciably delay their forward movement.

6. Assuming that all fixed bridges between Sinŭiju and Lin-Chiang on the Yalu River were taken out, the effect would be to severely restrict the movement of rolling stock between Manchuria and North Korea. The cumulative effect would be to reduce the capacity of the railroads south of the Yalu as rolling stock is destroyed. The feasibility of manhandling single cars across a rail-pontoon bridge is within the bounds of possibility but it is not believed that locomotives could cross the river by this means. Truck traffic would not be appreciably affected by resort to pontoon bridges.

7. Time required to deliver supplies to the point of expenditure is not significant in itself. However, time, combined with distance, exposes these supplies to an attrition rate from air attack directly proportional to the distance over which they must be moved. This distance factor, combined with the limited rail and road-net capacity available, indicates that there is a general line on the Korean Peninsula beyond which a major offensive by the enemy would not be feasible.

8. The time factor is not of particular significance with respect to the movement of a specific item of supply. The rate of delivery of that item will, however, have a direct bearing on the capability of the enemy to sustain either an effective defense or mount an offensive operation. The Italian Campaign was illustrative of the effectiveness of interdiction of communications lines. Tactical air in Italy was able to reduce the flow of supplies to the front to a point where the Germans were unable to maintain their position. Air action has materially reduced the enemy's capability to conduct a full scale of offensive this spring.

9. The following conclusions are based solely upon this general analysis of the logistic support of the enemy in North Korea and should be considered in this light only: *a.* A greater effect upon the logistic support of enemy forces would be obtained by air interdiction at the Yalu River in comparison with interdiction along some other line in North Korea. *b.* It is necessary to continue all forms of interdiction when appropriate opportunities present themselves. *c.* Material shortening of the enemy's present lines of communication would seriously reduce the effect of air interdiction.

10. It is recommended that attacks on the Yalu River bridges be continued as required. s/G.E.S., etc.

General Cannon arrived at 1340 hours and was taken immediately to my quarters, after which he came to my headquarters and was with me the remainder of the day. He will depart tomorrow at 0700 hours to visit the Fifth Air Force in Korea and will return Wednesday evening.

At 1500 hours, Mr. Hudson Fish, managing director of Quantas Empire Airways (Australian) called on me with two other gentlemen.

Generals Kenney and Cannon are staying with us; we had dinner together.

Dispatched the fol ltr to my major commanders - Generals Partridge, Stearley, Turner, Doyle, Henebry, Briggs, Spivey, and Col. Simons, FEAF Base, dtd 23 Apr 51:

Subject: Personal Views of the Commander-in-Chief, Far East Command. To: as noted. *1.* The Chief of Staff, GHQ, FEC, in a letter dated 22 Apr 51 has relayed to me certain basic personal views of General Ridgway in his position as CINCFE. These matters are considered to be of utmost importance and must receive the personal attention of all Far East Air Forces commanders. *a.* Since his arrival, General Ridgway has repeatedly emphasized the frontier nature of the duties of the FEC and the urgent necessity for imbuing our personnel with the habit and mind and way of living essential to troops situated in an area immediately susceptible to armed invasion without warning and at the decision of the enemy. The Commander-in-Chief takes immediate offense at any indication that members of his command are living a normal peacetime garrison existence. An added element of this basic concept is the urgency of time. Time wasted during the accomplishment of our mission here is time irretrievably lost. *b.* During such official visits as the Commander-in-Chief may make to you and to members of your command, the following specific actions are recommended: *(1)* Hold no formal ceremonies, unless they are of extremely short duration and carried out with a very high order of snap and precision. *(2)* If it is desired to have the Commander-in-Chief inspect the troops of the command, have the troops engaged in their normal duties at the time of inspection. *(3)* Hold no cocktail parties or other social or quasi-social functions.[186] *(4)* Long road drives should be excluded, insofar as possible. Light aircraft should be used in making trips to installations which possess only limited landing facilities. *c.* Prior to departure on an inspection visit,

---

186. An interesting recommendation. As noted throughout the diary, General Stratemeyer, and probably most other high-ranking officers in FEC and FEAF, gave or attended many parties.

the Commander-in-Chief desires to have detailed information made available to his Chief of Staff regarding the program and the itinerary. Once he has been apprised of this program and has approved it, he does not desire to have it changed or unexpected events injected into it. *d.* The principal mission of the Commander-in-Chief in visiting his subordinate units is to establish and to maintain a continuing and effective personal contact with his senior commanders. During such visits, he desires to have that commander immediately available to him, so that each may speak to the other with the utmost frankness and completely without reservation. During the greater portion of his visit, the presence of a third party, who might serve to restrain this frank interchange of views, is not desired. *2.* These principles I wholeheartedly indorse and consider precisely appropriate and definitely in keeping with our FEAF mission in this theater. It is my desire that the contents of this correspondence be brought to the personal attention of all Far East Air Forces commanders. I FURTHER DESIRE THAT EACH COMMANDER BE ADVISED THAT I EXPECT FIRM AND DETERMINED COMPLIANCE WITH BOTH THE SPIRIT AND LETTER OF THE POLICIES ANNOUNCED BY OUR COMMANDER-IN-CHIEF. [emphasis in original] s/G.E.S., etc.

TUESDAY
24 APRIL
1951

Follows an extract from a letter received by Nuckols from Sory Smith dated 16 April:

...I love you dearly! Last Friday afternoon, when General Vandenberg and all his staff were on the way to justify the Third Supplemental Appropriation before the House Armed Services Appropriations Sub-Committee, the *Washington Evening Star* that had just hit the stands at 1200 that day carried an eight column banner headline quoting General Stratemeyer on the fact that the air war in Korea was getting rough and liable to pick up some more. As a result of this fine story, plus General Vandenberg's remarks to the committee, the Third Supplemental Appropriation went through the sub-committee in less than 24 hours. This is record time in this town...

Dispatched the fol personal to Partridge (priority):

Recent implementation of Shoran and close cooperation radar bombing opns in Korea has considerably increased our all-weather offensive capabilities. However, the detailed info presently being rece in this Hq as part of the Shoran opns rpt RCS FEAF OP-U1, has indicated that only a small percentage of your total Shoran bombing effort has been evaluated. Effective im this rpt is being terminated and will be replaced by a short weekly narrative rpt of your Shoran and close control radar opns based upon the data obtained by your opns analysis. The problems involved in evaluating individual night missions thru post-strike analysis are realized; however, elect[rical] con[trol] systems must be frequently evaluated to discover system errors which might appear, particularly, when a con sta[tion] is relocated. It is my desire that every effort be made to obtain accurate data on elect con systems which can be used in future USAF planning.

Received a TS redline from Vandenberg, EYES ONLY:

U.S. News & World Report have a story of an interview with you. Information here is that their Tokyo correspondent phoned the story to Washington 16 April. Can you provide immediately the date of your interview in Japan.

Dispatched immediately in reply to Vandenberg's redline my answer which was:

Redline to Vandenberg from Stratemeyer. Reur redline 221 Eyes Only. Interview was on 17 April and after being edited the article was phoned to U.S. by Tokyo correspondent about 1400 hours Tokyo time on 18 April repeat 18 April.

With further reference to the exchange of the above signals (which took place in the small hours of the morning), I received the fol redline from USAF:

Associated Press is quoting General Courtney Whitney, ADVISOP to General MacArthur, that "all senior officers in the Far East, including General Stratemeyer and Admiral Joy, favored the use of Chiang Kai Shek's troops." In answer to inquiries regarding your position on this we are saying no comment. Suggest you may like to handle similarly at your end.

Bucked this radio with my comment of "the chief is right. No comment" to my VC, D/P, D/I, and D/O with action marked to my PIO.

WEDNESDAY 25 APRIL 1951   Nuckols waiting for me in office when arrived this AM. We went over the exchange of redlines that took place between me and CSAF during the small hours of the morning. Immediately after the briefing this AM, Nuckols held a telecon with Sory Smith - transcript of which follows:

FEAF Item #1 - Secret. Re Strat interview *US News*, sole purpose was to protect Air Force from criticism if and when Red air mounts offensive by going on record before hand believed here that we have forestalled any indignation that might otherwise result if ground forces are subject to strafing. Have you read entire text rather than press digest, what are your and other's reactions? I have your confidential radnote No. 400.

USAF Item #1 - Secret (in reply). General reaction here was as you intended. However it was sailing pretty close to wind in controversy of Gen. McA's four points. No criticism yet. Purpose of Gen. Van's redline to Gen. Strat was countermeasure to establish if interview was given before McA incident. This in case we should get hit by press. Or Congress.

FEAF Item #2 - Secret. Absolutely no intention here of entering any political debate on or of taking sides in current controversy. Will abide by your recommendation to avoid Yalu River problem.

FEAF Item #3 - Secret. In view recent efforts to place additional emphasis on bitter nature of air war and seriousness of MiG threat to B–29s was felt here that interview finally given pointed up this subject. Happy to know no criticism as yet and trust will continue. No further items from here.

USAF Item #2 - Secret. Today Courtney Whitney said Gen. Strat favored use of Chinese Nationalist troops. Recommend he decline comment on this and any other of Gen. McA's four proposals.

FEAF Item #4 - Secret. Gen. Strat has never commented on use of Nationalists and feel sure has no intention of doing so.

END OF TELECONFERENCE.

The below two items were given to General Ridgway this morning just prior to our briefing for him: *I.* B–29 (18 daily). Called off training. Priority 18 per day. *(1)* airfields, *(2)* front lines APQ-2 radar, *(3)* Interdiction. *II.* Some not cleared in briefing for communications classification (ACORN).

As a result of our briefing for General Ridgway this morning, and the fine things that he said about the Far East Air Forces, *I have issued the following command letter:*

> Subject: DEFEAT OF COMMUNISM. *1.* General Ridgway visited Headquarters, Far East Air Forces, this morning and was briefed on the missions, facilities, capabilities, operations and plans of the Far East Air Forces. *2.* In his remarks to the assembled group at the conclusion of this briefing, General Ridgway indicated, in a very definite manner, his complete awareness and admiration of the magnificent contributions made by the Far East Air Forces to the war in Korea. He stated that he fully appreciated, and that it was universally recognized, that the Far East Air Forces, in the early days of the war, made it possible for the Eighth Army to stay on the peninsula of Korea. He further went on to say since that time FEAF has contributed in an outstanding manner to our number one task at the moment - the defeat of Communism in Asia. *3.* General Ridgway expressed, in strong terms, his views relative to the necessity for instilling in the hearts and minds of every individual in the Far East Command, first, the will to fight Communism, and second, complete confidence in the ability to defeat it. General Ridgway did succeed, as you know, in instilling in the officers and men of the Eighth Army these essential convictions. *4.* I share completely General Ridgway's belief that we can, on the Peninsula of Korea, defeat Communism in Asia [Emphasis in original]. In order to do this, however, it is essential that every commander, every staff officer, every subordinate commander, in fact every officer, airman, and civilian employee, assigned or attached to FEAF wholeheartedly believe in and preach to others our ability to accomplish this task. I desire that you, at your staff meeting, on your inspections, and in your contacts with subordinate units, preach this essential philosophy at every opportunity.* *5.* If we achieve success in this campaign, as I know we will, Communism throughout the world will have received a terrific jolt. s/G.E.S.

*This letter as written above, but with the added sentence "See that this letter, suitably indorsed by you, reaches each one of your commanders down to and including squadrons," sent to 8 of my major commanders: Partridge, Stearley, Turner, Simmons (Col.), Briggs, Henebry, Doyle, and Spivey.

The above letter went to D/P, D/I, D/O, D/M, D/C, IG, Surg, PIO, JA, AG and Chaplain.

At 1515 hours, Air Commodore Charlesworth came in to bid me farewell.

Dinner with the Sebalds at their home, U.S. House 525. They had a wonderful group of guests and both Annalee and I enjoyed the dinner and the company.

THURSDAY 26 APRIL 1951 We gave a very superior briefing to General Cannon at 0900 hours after which he visited FEAMCOM, lunched there and then visited the 315th Air Division (Combat Cargo). He was delighted with everything he saw and particularly praised General Doyle and the job he was doing. At 1100 hours, Mr. Crump,[187] a Hollywood fellow, visited me with General Nuckols and stated that he was out here to make a picture on air evacuation for the Department of Defense.

We gave a dinner at 7:30 P.M. at Mayeda House in honor of Generals Kenney and Cannon.

FRIDAY 27 APRIL 1951 At 1000 hours had a conference with Major General Chase[188] who is to be the head of the Military Assistance Advisory Group on Formosa. I discussed with him the following individuals: Generalissimo Chiang Kai Shek, the Madame, K.C. Wu, General Chou Chih Jou, Tiger Wan [?], and Son Li Ren [?].[189]

Immediately after the briefing this AM, at General Ridgway's request, went to the Dai Ichi Building for a conference with him. As a result of this conference, dispatched the fol R&R to my Director of Plans, thru Deputy for Operations. General Craigie was also brought in on the discussion of the subject at hand and all three initialed the document Ridgway had given me and which is the inclosure to my R&R:

> General Ridgway desires sufficient data be furnished him by 1500 hours this afternoon for him to reply to attached message from the Joint Chiefs, to include what actions the Far East Air Forces would take to counter the hostile air offensive. The following questions will be answered: *1.* What are the courses of action by Far East Air Forces? *2.* Should we initiate the attack if our Intelligence indicates this enemy air offensive against us is imminent? *3.* Are there alternate courses of action including reconnaissance and photographic coverage of targets? Although I do not believe this message requires any mentioning of an attack by Russia in conjunction with the Chinese against Korea or Japan, or both, General Ridgway indicated that he might want to put into his reply to the Joint Chiefs of Staff what our actions would be in case Russia launched the attack; therefore, I should take with me our Emergency Plan. I also desire to take with me our studies and recommendations reference the use of atomic bombs, to include the targets we have recommended, the forces we have recommended, and the latest information that we have from SAC on this subject. G.E.S.

---

187. Owen Crump was a Hollywood movie producer.
188. Maj Gen William C. Chase commanded the 1st Cavalry Division in World War II and postwar. Following a tour with the Third Army, in Apr. 1951 he was named head of a MAAG to Nationalist China.
189. K.C. Wu was the Governor of Formosa; "Tiger" Wang Shu-ming became C-I-C of the Nationalist AF in 1952; Gen Sun Li-jen was C-I-C of the Nationalist Army in 1951.

Reference the above directive, I reported to General Ridgway at 1500 hours with my recommendations which I read to General Hickey, Admiral Joy, and General Ridgway. Upon my arrival, General Ridgway asked Admiral Joy to read what he had, which he did and which was almost identical with mine except his was in general terms, and mine was in more detail. Mine included the request for authority to reconnoiter certain areas in China and Manchuria and contained much more details. General Ridgway then stated that he liked my message. He then directed General Hickey to take both my recommendations and Admiral Joy's and come up with a signal for his approval and with Joy's and my concurrence and to include in it my recommendation that we immediately be authorized to reconnoiter the listed targets that I submitted.

Admiral Joy then asked if the discussion of dependents returning to the ZI could be raised as General Ridgway had this morning indicated that it was open for discussion. Ridgway said "yes" and Admiral Joy then stated that dependents of people stationed in Japan, regardless of the considered seriousness of the situation, be sent here. Ridgway then looked over at me and I not only stated that I agreed with Admiral Joy but that he had my study on the matter, backed up by General Partridge, with numerous inclosures in which generally I stated that persons in Japan be permitted to bring their dependents over. If that cannot be done, then reduce the tour to 18 months for those people whose dependents are not here. I furthermore pointed out that there were a great number of dependents' houses now vacant in Japan and that because of the type of their construction, that if they were not occupied and cared for, they would disintegrate and fall down, and I urged their occupancy by dependents of people now permanently stationed in Japan.

I then told General Ridgway that I had an expert on atomic bombs and that I had two other officers that were thoroughly familiar with our War Emergency Plan. If he wanted discussion on either or both, we were ready to accommodate him. He indicated that was not necessary this afternoon.

The entire conference was one of understanding, good will, and an earnest attempt to arrive at a coordinated Army, Navy, Air Force reply to the Joint Chiefs of Staff message.

Also, during that conference, General Ridgway asked this question: "Should we include in our reply to the Joint Chiefs of Staff's message that we should hit the airfields in Manchuria prior to an air offensive against our forces in Korea?" My answer immediately was "Yes," that "I would have done it two months ago had authority been granted, that I would do it tomorrow if I had the authority; however, because re the JCS message, our recommendations (as I interpreted it) were limited; therefore, I did not include it."

General Ridgway then asked Admiral Joy his thoughts on the matter and Admiral Joy said he would not make such recommendation, the reason being that he felt it would bring about an all-out submarine offensive against his fleet and that would make his position in the Yellow and Japan Seas untenable because General Ridgway was dependent upon him to supply the people in Korea by boat, and he felt this was not the time to hit the airfields.

General Hickey then spoke up and stated that he was inclined to agree with Admiral Joy that it was an inopportune time to make such a recommendation to the Joint Chiefs of Staff.

I then indicated that I would go along with that recommendation, but reiterated that since I was asked the question by my immediate superior, I, as an airman, would hit them as soon as possible regardless of any enemy offensive.

Dispatched the fol memo to CINCFE:

1. Reference the attached papers requesting my comments in writing on subject: "CINCFE's Concept of His Responsibilities as CINCFE and CINCUNC." My comments are as follows: Your Par. 1. Since information is being furnished to the Department of the Army, it is recommended that information be furnished the Department of the Air Force and Navy Department. Your Par 3b(4). This is the first time I knew of the existence of this limiting directive. Would appreciate a copy of this directive. No further comments. *2.* No further comments. Concur. *3.* Would appreciate a copy of the final signal as dispatched. G.E.S., etc.

At my quarters at 1910 hours, I concurred in draft signal to be dispatched to the Joint Chiefs of Staff reference the signal that is referred to earlier in diary this date. I almost identically followed the draft that I submitted and included all my recommendations as submitted in writing.

General Cannon departed for the ZI 1800 hours.

SATURDAY 28 APRIL 1951 — Came to the office and attended the briefing and immediately left, after seeing General Brothers, for Mayeda House where I immediately went to bed. The stiffness and sorness in my shoulder and neck, which I have been noticing for the last 3 days, has consistently gotten worse.[190] Spent all day in bed.

General Power (SAC) and his retinue arrived 1700 hours. They were met by General Fox (GHQ, FEC) and FEAF's Colonel Trask.

SUNDAY 29 APRIL 1951 — Again, spent the day at home nursing my shoulder and neck muscles. Damned painful. Major General Robert M. Lee[191] arrived Tokyo for a 48-hour stay; enroute to the States from Eniwetok.

At about 1130 hours, Craigie brought out all his papers for signature and action. He also gave me, to the best of his memory, the JCS reply to CINCFE's answer to their original signal, referred to 27 April, which included authorization to make the recon flight after a plan is submitted and approved by CINCFE. Also authorization was delegated to CINCFE to hit bases in Manchuria and China if sufficient time was not available to get JCS authority. In fact, every recommendation that I made to CINCFE to be included in his reply signal was approved.

---

190. It is possible that this condition was the first indication of Stratemeyer's impending heart attack.

191. Lee had been Deputy Commanding General for Operations, 9AF in World War II. In Nov. 1948, he became TAC commander and in Jan. 1950, was also made CO of TG 3.4(AF) of Joint Task Force 3. This organization was responsible for the atomic weapons testing at Eniwetok in April–May 1951. Because this latter job took up all his time, he was relieved as TAC commander in July 1950.

**MONDAY
30 APRIL
1951**

I directed Col Darrow and Colonel Trask to report to JSPOG and work with them on the papers being prepared for approval of General Ridgway and General Power (who is out here representing SAC).[192]

At about 1820 hours, Colonel Darrow reported back with the draft agreement to which I objected as no place in the paper was FEAF mentioned. I suggested two changes which he is working on.

At Sinmak, due to accurate anti-aircraft fire, three F–51s out of four were shot down - one in a strafing run, one following at 1,000 feet and the third following at 3,000 feet. The fourth one pulled out and reported these casualties. The pilot at 3,000 feet bailed out and was immediately captured by the enemy. The first two were casualties as they went in with their airplanes.

This indicates that the Reds must have radar controlled anti-aircraft and great quantities of it. It also indicates that the area about Sinmak is most important. I directed Operations to look into it and see if we couldn't get radar controlled strikes there at night as well as heavy strikes during daylight.

Got off my weekly letter to Gill Robb Wilson.

**TUESDAY
1 MAY
1951**

At 1500 hours, Messrs N.E. Marshall Lindholm (VP Operations), Knut Ros (Operations Representative) and Asbjorn Oyan all of the Scandinavian Airlines System called at the office. Mr. Lindholm brought me a couple of bottles of Aquavit from a Major Stone Christopher.[193]

At 1700 hours, Generals Power and Hickey and I had a conference with General Ridgway at which time he approved the paper that I had concurred in, prepared by General Power and my Plans people, reference the taking over by SAC of all SAC units in FEC on D-Day. The two points that I had put in the paper were most welcome by both Generals Ridgway and Hickey and also concurred in by General Power (SAC representative).

We all concurred that SAC's advanced headquarters in the Far East would automatically come from Hq FEAF BomCom - I mean by that, FEAF BomCom would be SAC's advanced headquarters. The results from this action means for the FEC and FEAF that coordinated action by SAC then would continue as prepared by FEAF in coordination with SAC.

**WEDNESDAY
2 MAY
1951**

General Craigie entertained Admiral Henderson at the Union Club at 1230 hours at lunch. General Picher and I were guests.

At 1745 hours, I was called to General Hickey's office along with Admiral Joy and we were informed that General Ridgway, in an emergency, had set up four offices in the building where he, with his Chief of Staff, and one or two others and where Admiral Joy and myself, with one or two key staff could immediately meet without delay. The code word being HEDGEHOG. No matter where we are or what we are doing, when that word is flashed to us

---

192. Darrow and Trask were preparing a paper on the taking over by the Strategic Air Command of all the SAC units in the Far East Command.

193. Of Swedish-American descent, Christopher had been the only American to work in Britain's MI-9 intelligence unit during World War II. Following the war, he remained in intelligence work.

we are to report to him in the above location immediately. I will inform my VC, General Craigie, of this code word and its meaning in case he must report if I am some distance from my command post.

On 29 Apr received the fol rad from FAF in 3 parts:

PART I. For the past several months FAF has exercised operational control, to a degree, over Marine acft based in Japan and Korea. During this period, it has been necessary to prepare numerous written agreements between this Hq and First Marine Air Wg with respect to responsibilities each command for operation of the several air bases which are being utilized by Marine air units. *PART II.* It is desired that a final and more complete agreement be prepared which will suffice for all phase of Marine operations with which this hq is concerned. In order to accomplish this, clarification of the following points is necessary: *(a)* by what specific authority does FAF exercise operational control over Marine land-based acft? *(b)* What does this operational control consist of? *(c)* Does such control include Marine administrative and/or transport type acft? *(d)* to what extent is FAF responsible for providing base support for Marine units. *PART III.* This hq has no record of previous instructions from FEAF concerning those queries listed above. It is requested that this info be provided so that the present relationship between this command and First Marine Air Wg may be properly determined.

In reply to above Plans drew up the following and it was dispatched with my approval:

To Fifth AF: Reur OPP3705 specific auth for opnl con of Marine land based acft when not in execution of naval missions, delegated to CG, FEAF by CINCFE, AG 370-2 (8 Jul 50) CC, redelegated to CG, Fifth AF by FEAF AX 3101 OP-PL, 22 July 1950. Copies of these documents fwdd [forwarded] w/plan of operation of 1st Marine Air Wing, 10 Aug 50. FAF is not charged specifically w/provg [providing] base spt for Marine units. Assistance is authd and encouraged when w/i [within] your capabilities and considered desirable or in best interest of the overall effort. Extent of spt provd Marine Air units by FEAF now under study this hq w/a [with a] view toward obtaining a commitment for this spt fr COM-NAVFE. Separate instructions will follow ASAP. Operational control as interpreted by this Hq includes assignment of tasks, designation of objectives and authoritative direction necessary to accomplish the mission. It shall be exercised through responsible commanders of the units concerned. It does not include administration, discipline, internal organization, logistic support and training except in such instances as the commander concerned may request assistance.

Partridge forwarded to me an interesting article by a Lynn Landrum, *Dallas News*. From this clipping, the fol letter to Idwal Edwards was evolved to underscore again that the war in Korea, that is called a "police action," is a real war and that thinking at home, which has been mislead by the words "police action," should be slanted differently.

Dear Idwal, It is not my intention to become involved in the controversy on the advisability of extending the war into China.

The purpose of this letter is to show you that we have the opportunity before us to deal such a serious blow to Red China and to Communism in Asia that the controversy may be academic.

Our best educated guess is that the Red Chinese troops now committed, added to those committed in November, constitute about one-half of the trained ground forces of the Red Chinese Army. They were stopped once with terrific losses, and will be stopped again with even more terrific losses. Our strength now will prevent our being pushed into Tsushima Straits.

While it is not possible to separate statistically the North Korean and Chinese losses, the estimated total is 872,000. The total United Nations casualties are high, because of the heavy losses incurred by the ROK divisions during each enemy drive, but even so, the ratio is four to one between Communist and United Nations losses. Subtracting the ROK losses, the ratio is 12 to 1, which is unfair statistically, because the ROKs have done some good fighting.

Here is a breakdown:

NK & CCF		**UNITED NATIONS**	
Casualties	725,500	ROK	141,000
P.O.W.	146,500	US	53,000
	872,000	OTHER (U.N.)	18,000
			212,000

Of course, from a casualty standpoint, the FEAF operation is the most economical. We have killed 100,000 at a cost of 736 casualties.[194]

While a continuation of the war in its present manner appears to be a stalemate as far as holding real estate goes, or terminating the war with a decisive military victory, the continued inflicting of casualties on Chinese and North Korean Communist forces at the present rate must soon result in a decided military setback to Red China and a loss of prestige to Communism throughout Asia. China may have millions of people, but it hasn't enough millions of trained soldiers to continue pouring them into a Korea rathole which probably looks to them even more dismal than it does to us.

This is the happy side of the picture. From my point of view, there is another. The people of the United States, and the members of the Armed Forces who are not out here consider that the Korean operations are minor in nature, perhaps because they are concentrated geographically and, except for the Inch'ŏn landing, consist of slow and labored trips up and down a small peninsula.

The Korean War is not a minor engagement, but a full-scale war. The proof lies in the casualty figures above - 53,000 United States casualties (U.N. less ROKs - 71,000) in ten months. If they continue at the same rate, they will total 63,900 in a year for U.S. alone.

Compare this with the losses in WWII. From Pearl Harbor until the end of 1942 the total U.S. casualties were 58,547 — if attached article by Lynn

194. See Futrell, pp 370-371, for figures through June 1951. These figures were derived from FEC Intelligence Summaries.

Landrum is correct. During this period such major actions took place as Pearl Harbor, Bataan, Corregidor, the battles of the Coral Sea and Midway, the attack on Alaska, our landings on Guadalcanal, the beginning of Eighth Air Force's bombing, and the invasion of North Africa.

I urgently request that you exercise your good office in the Headquarters of United States Air Force and in the joint bodies on which you sit to start a change in the thinking that this is a minor skirmish and that it is not having any lasting effect. All the services need all-out assistance in Korea as long as this is the only place where actual war exists.

I would sure like to have a reply to this with your reactions.

Best regards. s/G.E.S.

THURSDAY 3 MAY 1951

General Partridge came in this morning at 1000 hours and we had present, during my conference with him, Generals Craigie and Picher.

The main subjects discussed were as follows:

The question of airplane shortage and pilot shortage. It was brought out that our stat control reports do not give a true picture on either airplanes or pilots. General Picher indicated that in about 10 days with reports that he has ordered to this headquarters, he can give us a clear picture on the status of pilots and combat crews.

I gave Partridge a copy of the Idwal Edwards letter as well as my letter to him, copy to Spivey, reference the placing of the 314th Air Division directly under this headquarters.

The most important subject discussed was Brigadier General Sweetser. The result of my sending Colonel Gray to the 452d Wing to investigate the situation where some 3 or 4 navigators had refused to fly missions after their having completed 50 was, to my astonishment, the knowledge that Sweetser displayed disloyalty to Partridge and myself and great antagonism to the Regulars, and an all-around general attitude of non-cooperation, and the installation on his wing is of a disgruntled and dissatisfied atmosphere. I further learned, to my astonishment from Partridge that Sweetser, as a combat wing commander, has flown only one sortie. It was brought out that he lacks leadership, loyalty and integrity. I told General Partridge that since General Sweetser was one of his officers, that it was up to him to take the necessary action by tests of his wing, inspection of him by his inspector general, and any other means that he felt necessary to furnish data to me upon which I could base a signal to the CSAF requesting that he remove Sweetser from the Far East Air Forces. I further told General Partridge my inspector general written reports, which I directed he submit to me today, would be referred to him for his use in bringing about the removal of General Sweetser from the Far East Air Forces.[195]

At 1130 General Crabb and Colonel Zimmerman came in and discussed with us (General Turner was also present) the agreement that had been arrived at reference the Far East Air Forces facilities and units on Guam between CINCFE and CINCPAC. I told them that I liked the written agreement and that insofar as

---

195. Sweetser was removed from his command on May 10. FEAF and 5AF records are noticeably reticent about this incident.

I was concerned, it was approved. General Crabb pointed out that CINCPAC's representative and the new Navy Commander on Guam had agreed.

They were a bit worried about the Air Rescue Service because it was felt that the Navy would insist upon taking it over within their command on Guam.

I instructed both Crabb and Zimmerman to fight this.

Generals Partridge and Turner had lunch with me at Mayeda House.

Mr. Bond of the State Department (Tokyo) brought in Mr. Lightner, State Department, who is going to Korea to relieve Mr. Drumwright who is ordered returned to the U.S.[196] I sure poured it on to both of them the great jobs that have been done by Messrs Drumwright and Muccio.

Received the fol rad which CINCFE had sent to DEPTAR [Department of the Army]. Directed that my AG send it out to White at MATS:

Informal information has reached this Hq that MATS is considering the transfer of 1273d Air Transport Sq from Haneda to McChord AFB, Washington, during first quarter fiscal year 1952. It is strongly urged that this move not be made as long as hostilities continue in Korea. There is an ever present and, in fact, increasing possibility of the entry, on a large scale, of enemy air into the Korean war. I consider it of extreme importance that I retain, in this command, the potential increases in air transport operation and maintenance capability which were so vital to this command on the outbreak of hostilities in June 1950. Signed Ridgway.

**FRIDAY
4 MAY
1951**

Admiral Litch,[197] the new Guam Admiral, paid his respects to me this morning, in company with General Craigie. He made quite an impression and I'm sure the relationship on Guam between the Navy, the Air Force and the Army will now be pleasant. God knows it wasn't with the last admiral.

Just received information that Shin Sung Mo has been relieved as Minister of Defense for the Republic of Korea and Chung Huhh has been appointed in his stead.[198]

Dispatched the fol rad to Twining (Personal) and instructed that a copy of same be sent to CINCFE:

Are there available anywhere in ZI or its possessions F–47 aircraft that could be made available to FEAF? It is understood that there are some 25 in National Guard squadron in Hawaii. Even this number would be gratefully received. Info here also indicates some 429 in service with Air National Guard in ZI and 721 in storage. Small arms fire and both light and heavy flak have increased tremendously along enemy MSRs and at main bridges in Korea as well as around their supply areas and airdromes. All here know that F–47 can take it. Our fighter losses to enemy ground fire during past 33 days total 25 F–51s, 13 F–80s and 2 F–84s. Loss rate of F–51 to ground fire

---

196. Niles W. Bond, First Secretary and Consul at Tokyo in the Office of Political Advisor to SCAP; E. Allan Lightner was replacing Everett F. Drumwright as Counselor of Embassy at Seoul.

197. During World War II, Adm Ernest W. Litch commanded the carrier *Lexington*, followed by several carrier divisions. He did not actually report as Commander Naval Forces, Marianas until July 2.

198. Shin Sung Mo was one of three South Korean cabinet officers who were forced to resign when on Apr. 25 they were implicated in a Feb. 12 mass execution of 187 alleged Commmunist collaborators.

per sortie is just under 100% greater than the loss rate of F–80 and almost 6 times greater than the F–84 loss rate during the same period.[199]

SATURDAY
5 MAY
1951

At 0930 hours, General Power and his officers from SAC gave us a briefing on SAC's plans and targets.

At 1100 hours, Mr. Eddie Eagan, Chairman of the New York State Athletic Commission, and Mr. Robert Hall, Director of Athletics, Yale University, called. Mr. Eagan presented a letter from Mr. Harry Bruno. They are leaving tomorrow for Korea and I have arranged with General Timberlake to get them back from Korea leaving there next Friday morning. They will have dinner with Mrs. Stratemeyer and me that evening.

SUNDAY
6 MAY
1951

I saw General Ridgway at 1130 and raised the question of uniform shirts and ties with him and indicated that this policy did not conform to his "frontier offensive against Communism" paper. He agreed with me and called General Hickey in and directed that his order on ties be rescinded.

He also issued orders, per my request, that whenever he visits Korea, a message will go to CG FAF as well as CG 8th Army.

He was further delighted to hear the 1263d Sq at Haneda would stay here until the termination of hostilities in Korea. I originated the request to the JCS which Hickey sent.

CINCFE was interested in the photograph showing the by-pass to the by-pass to the by-pass of the railroad bridges at Sinanju and indicated if this picture could be declassified; he thought it a good one to send to the UN to indicate the determination of the Communists and North Koreans in their war in Korea.

Received the fol rad from Twining:

Your AX 7149 CG (re F–47 a/c, see diary item under date 4 May) has been received and your recommendations will be considered at once as your problem is fully appreciated. Reply will be forthcoming you shortly.

MONDAY and
TUESDAY
7-8 MAY
1951

Departed 0930 hours, 7 May, and flew direct to Suwŏn where I was met by General Partridge and Colonel Schmid,[200] Commander, 4th Fighter Interceptor Wing. Spent about an hour driving around his facilities at Suwŏn. They are making great progress. In addition to setting up facilities for themselves, they are including facilities for the 51st Fighter Wing which eventually will move there from Tsuiki.

Dropped in at K-6, P'yŏngt'aek, where the Mosquito wing is located. Was greeted there by Lt. Colonel Robert A. Trennert who commands the 6147th TAC Group.

Colonel Trennert and his people have done a wonderfully outstanding job in making the base, including the runway, an outstanding one, with everything and anything they could get their hands on. I sure commended him (Trennert).

---

199. No F–47s were ever used in Korea. (See May 11 entry below.)
200. Col Herman A. Schmid did not take actual command of the wing until May 31.

While enroute to Taegu, I discussed with General Partridge which fighter bomber wing should be converted to F–84Es and he designated the 49th which is at Taegu and which will eventually have a 9,000 foot runway at that base.

I then discussed the air defense paper which he commented on and which he is now of the opinion that air defense should be divorced from his responsibility since all Fifth Air Force eventually will be sent to Korea. He stated that he will take the necessary steps to recommend the promotion to Colonel of Lt. Colonel William F. Bull.[201] He also stated that he will be glad to see General Old who is scheduled to arrive at Taegu on Thursday, 10 May.

I discussed at length our feeling that since the B–29s were hitting hostile airdromes that he should put at least a fighter-bomber group on interdiction and he indicated that he was really doing more than that now with fighter bombers (B–26s) and, after listening to his briefing last night, which was a normal one, I am convinced that he is doing a great interdiction.

I discussed with him the "special recon" mission and he stated that up to that time he had not even been briefed on it. He called for Colonel Meyers, but found that Colonel Meyers was back at FEAF on that subject. General Partridge will be briefed in full as soon as Meyers returns.

Attended Partridge's briefing last evening, also talking with General Allen, Van Fleet's Chief of Staff, and gave to Allen my greetings for Van Fleet.[202]

Had dinner with Partridge and Mr. Pakenham (*Newsweek*) who had been there for the past two days. (I brought Mr. Pakenham back to Tokyo with me.)

This morning, 8 May, took off from Taegu at 0800 hours and dropped in at K-1 where the First Marine Air Wing is located and inspected that base accompanied by Generals Harris and Cushman. They have the best base in Korea and I want to emphasize for the record here that the United States Air Force built it for them.

Spent about an hour at K-1 and then took off at 0905 for Tsuiki-could not land at Brady as it was 0 - 0 [zero-zero ceiling and visibility]. Was met at Tsuiki by Colonel Cellini and his group commander and thoroughly inspected the entire base by car. Partridge accompanied me.

Left Tsuiki for Haneda at 1100 hours and landed at Haneda about 1345 hours. Had to do a GCA at both Tsuiki and Haneda.

Upon return to the office, approved dispatch of the fol personal rad to Twining with info personal going to Boatner and Chidlaw:

Ref im reqmt in FEAF for KB–29 drogue tanker w/probe tip tanks for the F–80. Req you advise me ASAP the earliest possible date which you could make tanker and initial supply of tip tanks aval here for use in special classified recon flt which has been directed by CINCFE. I must have this equip to execute mission since it exceeds range capability of present equip.[203]

---

201. Bull's job is unknown.

202. Lt Gen James A. Van Fleet was the new commander of the Eighth Army. During World War II, he had led troops during the Utah Beach landings at Normandy and later rose to command of the III Corps.

203. In the spring of 1952, an air refueling test (named Operation High Tide) was conducted utilizing KB–29M tankers with drogue refueling equipment and F–84E fighters with refueling probes mounted on tip tanks. Along with training missions, several combat missions were flown during this test.

Approved dispatch of fol personal to Vandenberg with info cys to CINCFE, FAF, and 314th AD. This rad coordinated with Gen. Hickey by Craigie:

This rad in 3 parts. *PART I.* Study of results of war gaming recently held by GHQ, FEC for plan for initial air action in the event of hostilities with USSR and Communist China, demonstrates folg min[imum] force augmentation required by FEAF: 6 ftr bmr wgs, 2 ftr intcp wgs, 2 med bm wgs, 2 strat recce sqs, 2 WX recce sqs and corresponding increase in air rsq capability. *PART II.* Above req are result of scaling down original war game estimates. Every effort has been made to produce here a practical min rqmt. *PART III.* CINCFE concurs in my forwarding this info to you.

WEDNESDAY
9 MAY
1951

General Crabb dispatched at my direction the fol memo to CINCFE, ATTN JSPOG:

1. Reference attached draft of radio from CINCFE to DEPTAR for JCS outlining additional force requirements for Fast East Command. *2.* Commanding General, FEAF concurs with the exception of Par. 1c(1)a, which should be deleted in view of recent agreement signed by General Ridgway, General Stratemeyer, and General Power.

I attended the two sessions on atomic bombs given by Colonel Ford and his group at 1000 hours and 1400 hours. It was an excellent presentation.

At 1730 hours, in General Ferguson's office, with practically all the operations senior officers present, we listened to Colonel Polifka's briefing on our contemplated T.S. recon missions.

Dispatched the fol rad, Ops Priority, VC 0165 CG, to CG FAF, 20th AF, 13th AF, 314th AD, BomCom, 315th AD, FEAMCOM and info to CINCFE:

Personal Partridge, Stearley, Turner, Doyle, Spivey, Briggs, Henebry from Stratemeyer and information personal Ridgway from Stratemeyer. This rad in 3 parts. *PART I.* I am fully aware of your efforts to implement my previous directives with respect to preparedness; however, the gravity of situation in FE prompts me to reiterate my concern. Maximum continuing use must repeat must be made of all dispersal facilities available, and auxiliary fields where applicable, to minimize losses resulting from a surprise enemy air attack. *PART II.* FOR SPIVEY. I want prompt action to disperse your aircraft, utilizing Atsugi and Kisarazu as auxiliary air defense fields. Communications and servicing facilities must be provided expeditiously. Niigata should be reoccupied by at least a flight of fighters. *PART III.* TO ALL. Desire you frequently re-examine your overall deployment to insure maximum use of dispersal facilities and fields as they become available. You must continue efforts to improve dispersal within all your local capabilities.

THURSDAY
10 MAY
1951

Received the fol TS, personal from Twining:

Reurad V 0159 OP-PL (dtg 151345Z). Referenced message has been received and will be used for information by the air staff in any further actions on the subject pending receipt of messages from CINCFE and CINCPAC by the JCS.

On 5 May the fol personal for Twining was dispatched:

Reour ad TS 8795. Confer between representatives of CINCPAC and CINCFE concluded 4 May. Fol tentative agreements were reached subject to concurrence of CINCFE and CINCPAC. *a.* Opnl con of units and fac assigned or attached to FEAF in Marianas-Bonin or Volcano Islands remains w/CINCFE. These forces and fac w/b [will be] utilized as directed by CINCFE in support of COMARBODEFCOM for purpose of local defense, disaster relief and civil disturbance missions. Plans for use of FEAF forces in local defense, disaster relief and civil disturbance missions w/b subject to approval by CINCPAC and CINCFE. *b.* CINCPAC w/b responsible for broad policy decns [decisions] concerning mil[itary] con of air traffic in Marianas-Bonins-Volcanoes area. Changes in traffic con procedures affecting tactical air operations of CINCFE force in Marianas-Bonin-Volcano Islands w/b as agreed by CINCPAC and CINCFE. *c.* That CINCPAC has primary responsibility for SAR in Marianas-Bonins-Volcanoes area; that ARS elements attached to FEAF and based in Marianas-Bonins-Volcanoes area remain under opnl con of CINCFE and their non-combat operations, as consonant with their FEAF MISSIONS, be coordinated with CINCPAC's SAR commander in the area as provided in the effective edition of "Search and Rescue Joint Standard Operating Procedures, Pacific." *d.* That CINCFE retain responsibility for Army logistic spt of U.S. Air Force elements under CINCFE in Marianas-Bonin-Volcanoes. It is understood that CINCFE and CINCPAC will each advise JCS of their concurred agreements.

General Power came in to see me at 1000 hours and discussed the following subjects. General Craigie was present.

He had personally investigated all crews - thru their commanders - and there were some cases where gunners had not fired from a B–29 prior to their arrival in the Far East; however, they did bring a piece of paper with them indicating that fact. His criticism was that BOMCOM should have known this and provided for training here before sending them on missions.

He sent the following signal to General LeMay which I concurred in:

PERSONAL LEMAY FROM POWER INFORMATION STEARLEY. I have just returned from Okinawa where I found to my dismay that 307th Wing still operating out of tents. I am referring particularly to briefing rooms, tactical planning and intelligence facilities. I consider this a very inefficient operation due to this factor and in discussing with General Stratemeyer I find that they have requested funds to provide temporary structures but that it has been held up in Hq, USAF. I urgently request that you attempt to break this log jam. Signed Stratemeyer.

(copies of this rad also provided Col Broadhurst[204] who is with General Power and Colonel Erler).

General Power also stated that he was very anxious to obtain radar photos of certain targets which we have scheduled to be taken by the B–45s. I told him that this was a case of obtaining CINCFE's approval and which we hope to obtain from CINCFE during our presentation for him (CINCFE) at 1000 hours tomorrow.

He also stated that he visited the 27th Fighter Escort Wing and that he found the group commander, Colonel Ruddell,[205] had the group well in hand. Further, many of the pilots had flown well over 100 missions and that because of the over-all theater policy of releasing fighter pilots who had flown 100 sorties, morale, although good, was being hurt. He suggested that maybe we could have some 25 pilots from the 136th Fighter Bomber Wing that is scheduled to come out here flown out ahead of their group and place them in the 27th Group in order to reduce the sortie rate. I thought this an excellent idea and directed General Craigie to send such a signal to USAF.

General Power was a bit concerned reference the squadron on Guam not being able to fly suitable profiles and making radar attacks and having the results thereof scored.

I suggested that he utilize cities in Japan for this purpose and he thought that a good idea provided we had the radar communications equipment to place here in Japanese cities to score the radar attacks. He indicated he would investigate this himself.

I directed General Craigie NOT to send our inspector to BOMCOM to look into the proficiency of SAC's replacement crews as I thought General Power had fully covered that in his investigations.

Rcvd fol Ops Imm from 314th AD:

Reference your wire VC 0165 CG. The fol action has been taken: All bases have been directed to comply with your instructions. Flight of 6 F–86Ds has been deployed to Niigata.[206] Hotline communications have been established with Kisarazu Atsugi and with 339 Detachment at Yokota. Ammunition has been stored at Atsugi and Kisarazu. Arrangements are being made for alert shacks at these 2 places. Believe it inadvisable to further deploy limited aircraft from Johnson or Misawa.

On 7 May I approved for dispatch the fol rad drawn up by Ops to CSAF and info BOMCOM & SAC:

Personal Vandenberg from Stratemeyer, info personal Briggs and LeMay: On 14 Dec 50, DEPTAR (JCS) sent CINCFE JCS 98778, advising that 2 med bmr gps were on alert in the ZI for possible deployment to FEC if situation warranted. Req info on availability of these units should an emerg occur or should decision be made to conduct oprs against enemy

---

204. Col Edwin B. Broadhurst, chief of plans for SAC.
205. Col Raymond F. Ruddell had been the wing commander since May 1.
206. There is some doubt that F–86Ds were actually in Japan at this time. According to Marcelle Knaack in her book, *Post-World War II Fighters*, first production deliveries of this radar-equipped all-weather fighter did not begin until March 1951 and the first deployments to FEAF did not occur until the fall of 1953. (Knaack, pp 71-72.)

air in China and Manchuria. Need to know availability for my planning and discussions w/CINCFE.

In reply to above, received the fol PERSONAL FROM VANDEN-BERG this AM:

If a combination of events and emergencies cause a decision by the JCS to commit 2 additional med bomb wings to FEAF, reurad VC 0162 CG, those units could be combat ready in FEAF 10 days after receipt of orders. I think we are agreed however that currently the only reason for any medium bombardment in FEAF, other than the regularly assigned 19th Wing, is to provide a force to be used in case circumstances combine to present profitable targets. On that subject, I feel that your use of bombers in flights of small numbers against many small targets is an expensive and arduous method of achieving small results. I recognize that there will be relatively few targets in your limited area of operation which would warrant mass employment of your medium bombers. Nevertheless, it appears to me that less frequent flights of greater numbers or at least the concentration of your bombing effort in selected areas and the coordination of these attacks with fighter bombers to work over the antiaircraft would offer better protection to crews and airplanes and achieve more effective results. You are again reminded that our replacement capability in aircraft and crews, and your attrition rate combine to limit your rate of operation to an average of 12 sorties per day. Our indications here show your average rate for the past 2 weeks to be 16.5 per day.

Dispatched personal TS message to Vandenberg telling him that I issued instructions to all my commanders with info to CINCFE re his redline RL 232 and quoted in full the text of my message to them (see radio under diary date of 9 May). Also said "Cabell's follow up your signal received. Answer to him same channels dispatched today." (a copy of this signal was sent to my D/I).

Mrs. Strat and Major Paradis, my senior ADC, met Mrs. Ridgway.

At 1500 hours, Mr. Bert Andrews, Washington office of the *New York Herald Tribune* reporter, called on me. I assured him that we would get him around FEAF and urged that he visit in addition to the installations in Korea and the Fifth AF, my other three major commands here in Japan. I wrote Secretary Finletter and told him that we would extend every courtesy and offer every service to Mr. Andrews. (Mr. Andrews came with a letter of introduction from the Secretary.)

At 1600 hours, with Generals Craigie and Crabb, Colonel Polifka present, we listened to Banfill's rehearsal of the presentation he will make tomorrow to General Ridgway on our contemplated recon mission.

At 1130 hours, Lt. Colonel Corey Ford[207] called, accompanied by General Nuckols. He outlined to me the mission he had to carry out, given him by General Van. I assured him he would get the works and asked him to visit all my headquarters besides the Korean installations. I wrote Van a letter (Ford had a letter from General Van to me) and assured him that we would take care of Ford.

---

207. Ford, a well-known author (15 books) and playwright, was working as a reservist at Headquarters, USAF, in public relations. He was in the Far East to gather material for articles on the Air Force in Korea and Japan.

Dispatched the fol personal to Vandenberg:

Appreciate your prompt reply to my rad VC 0162 CG. Will cont to husband resources and utilize same to inflict max casualties on enemy. Realize some B–29 opns here unorthodox under strategic concept, however, am using my aval forces in most eff possible manner to accomplish my present mission of sptg [supporting] Korean grd effort and inflicting max enemy casualties in furtherance of CINCFE's directives to me. I have directed 5AF to undertake major portion of interdiction program in order to make our limited B–29 effort aval for other urgent missions such as neutralization of airfields, destruction of rolling stock and supplies and enemy trp concentrations. Firmly believe we are inflicting extremely heavy casualties on enemy which more than warrant ea sortie expended.

FRIDAY
11 MAY
1951

Dispatched the fol to Vandenberg:

Personal Vandenberg from Stratemeyer. Have reviewed your rad Cite AFODC 59658 and AFCCS TS 8889 and my A 7351 CG and discussed FEAF Bomber Command's sorties capability with Briggs and Power. Based upon logistic support B–29 groups are currently receiving from the ZI, FEAF Bomber Comd has sustained capability of 18 sorties per day provided we are not operating against such targets as the Sinŭiju-Antung bridge. If and when attacks are resumed on the Yalu River bridges loss rate will probably go up and sortie capability will of necessity come down. In the event it was your intention in AFODC 59658 to limit my B–29 operations to an average of 12 sorties per day, request you confirm by return message. My interpretation of subject msg permitted use of B–29s to extent logistic support would permit. I further understood that you were not in position to support more than 12 sorties per day based upon attrition rates cited my rad A 6277 CG. After receiving your TS 8889 I have reread 59658 and am not sure as to your desires. Request clarification.

Sent the fol letter thru channels, official:

Subject: Jet photographic Airplanes and Photographic Interpreters.
THRU: CSAF to: Marshal of the Royal Air Force Sir John Slessor, etc.
We are in great need of modern jet photographic airplanes and more photographic interpreters.
This would be a great opportunity for the Royal Air Force to test a flight of Canberras under field conditions and, in addition thereto, give me some greatly needed assistance.
I strongly recommend that you issue an order and send a flight of Canberras out here for 180 days with about 15 officer P.I.'s with their normal support (draftsmen, plotters, etc.) to work under our Colonel Karl L. Polifka (who worked for you in the Mediterranean and is known to you personally) who runs our reconnaissance wing at K-2 in Korea under Fifth Air Force.
As you know, we have no Royal Air Force units represented with the Far

East Air Forces and here's a great chance for you to get not only needed assistance to me, but to gain great field experience for the Royal Air Force. s/G.E.S., etc.

(copies of this Secret letter went to Generals Partridge & Banfill and Colonel Polifka.)

Met with General Ridgway this morning at 1000 hours re our TS recon missions. Present besides General Ridgway and myself were Admiral Joy and Generals Craigie and Hickey. The presenters were General Banfill and Colonel Polifka.

The presentation to my mind was as fine as I have ever heard. Both Banfill and Polifka inspired confidence and thoroughly knew their subject.

After the presentation, General Ridgway called for comments and questions. Both General Craigie and I urged approval of the three short missions and the B–45 mission and stated that the remaining two would have to wait for the arrival of the tanker due in on or about 1 June.

After asking if there were any further comments, and there were none, General Ridgway then directed the Chief of Staff, FEC, to approve my recommendations, to wit: fly the three short missions and the B–45 mission (for scope photography) at my discretion depending upon the weather.[208]

We have a C-in-C that isn't afraid to make a decision - and he can make it quick. My admiration continues for him - one hundred percent.

Dispatched the fol personal rad to Nugent:[209]

There are many Japanese and civilian employees of FEAF who are paid from non-appropriated funds and who have rendered outstanding service. Example is group of 20 Koreans employed by tactical air control group who accompanied unit from Taegu to Sariwŏn and returned to P'yŏngt'aek and acted as supervisors when under enemy fire. Do not desire to give them military award or Medal of Freedom and believe more suitable to request herewith exception to restriction that Meritorious Civilian Service Award can be given only to civilians paid from appropriated funds, so that in exceptional cases I can award it to foreign civilians in FEAF employ.

Rcvd the fol signal from USAF that had also gone to ADC, CINCAFE, 34d Air Div, Alaskan Air Comd, SAC, and CINCAL:

Ref redline Nr. 232. Any specific immediacies concerning strained relations referred to therein no longer exist.
(Refers to "strained" Far East diplomatic relations.)

Rcvd the fol Personal from Vandenberg:

This answers your AX 7149 of 4 May requesting F–47 a/c to replace F–51s in FEAF. After considering the availability of F–47 the spare parts situation, and the complications which result from an introduction of an additional fighter type in FEAF, we fail to see any appreciable results to

---

208. The nature of these missions is unknown, although the RB–45s did conduct some reconnaissance missions over China and Vladivostok during the war.

209. Lt Gen Richard E. Nugent, Deputy Chief of Staff, Personnel, Headquarters USAF.

be gained by the substitution. It is probably true that the F–47 would confirm its WW II reputation and prove somewhat less vulnerable than the F–51 to small arms fire and light flak, I believe, however, that the disparity between the F–47 and your jet types would be almost as great as the present disparity between the F–51s and jets. It is certain that the F–47 would be far less desirable for aerial combat than the '51, altho this problem is not immediately pressing. The only real solution to your problem is the replacement of F–51s with jet types. You are familiar with the F–80 situation and realize that beginning in December we must meet your attrition in F–80s with F–84s. This replacement will continue to include the replacement of F–51s by jet types as soon as it is physically possible to do so. The a/c situation is critical now and will continue to be so for many months. We are attempting to meet your attrition and, at the same time, improve qualitatively the fighter forces which have been allocated to you. You appreciate that the a/c industry was not in a condition to meet the heavy demands which were made on it beginning last June, and relief will not be felt until Fiscal Year '51 production funds have been converted to a/c. We are continuing heavy pressure to accelerate production. Your morale problem is admittedly difficult. Could you possibly alleviate it by the employment of '51s in a defensive role in Japan and Okinawa? I note that you have three F–80 squadrons of the 51st Group on defense. There would appear to be a somewhat greater risk involved should air attacks actually be launched against these areas. However, it would seem that these areas are not immediately threatened by any heavy concentration of Soviet jet bombers and would not the '51s, which did such a fine job in aerial combat in the last war, be capable of operating successfully against such types as the Tu–4 should they be employed against your rear areas? You, however, are in a better position than I to judge the comparative risk. I am sure in my own mind that your suggestion of using F–47s in place of F–51s which would require a complete substitution from the CCTS [Combat Crew Training School] in the ZI thru the pipeline to your theater, is not a solution.

In reply thereto dispatched the fol reply, personal to Vandenberg:

This rad in 3 parts. *PART I.* Ref yourad AFCCS TS 8907, dtg 101604Z May. Appreciate your consideration my request for F–47s. *PART II.* Desire correct apparent misinformation ref employment of three jet squadrons of the 51st Group. One squadron only assigned air defense mission Okinawa. Remaining two squadrons have been employed continuously in Korean war since 24 Sept 50. *PART III.* In spite of losses, do not now contemplate bringing F–51s to Japan because of their effectiveness in detecting and destroying vehicles.

Ok'd for dispatch the fol personal Twining rad:

Re my VC -164 CG 8 May 51 (see Diary item that date) and your rad Cite TS 8909 10 May 51 and TS 8924 11 May 51. KB–29 drogue tanker with 4 sets probe tip tanks for RF–80A required as soon as possible. Importance of test program at APG is appreciated and acft will be released imm upon compl of mission. Estimated time required in theater will not exceed 15 days. Length of time dependent upon weather and time required to train 2 exceptionally well qualified RF–80 pilots in refueling technique.

Banfill departed for Hq USAF this evening on TDY.

Had 18 guests to dinner at Mayeda house - honored Mr. Eddie Eagen, Director of Athletics for the State of New York, and Mr. Robert Hall, Director of Athletics at Yale University, both of whom are visiting this theater at the suggestion of CSAF.

SATURDAY **12 MAY** **1951**	Dispatched a ltr to Nugent urging him to set up FEAMCOM for a two- star spot. Hq USAF radioed me re the necessity for placing 2 AF field grade officers on TDY to Formosa to provide intermin liaison pending arrival of initial AF increment.

They suggested Col. McComas.[210] Also, CINCFE's hqs bucked an info cy of a radio they had received from MAAG Formosa stating that they were "officially embarrassed by fact that no USAF pers there."

Miss Mildred Tsai, my translator and interpreter during WWII, who recently arrived to work in Hq FEAF from China, had approached me re her visa problems. She wants USA citizenship, but that is not a simple matter as I explained in a letter (which I had my JA draw up) to her yesterday. However, in addition to a To Whom It May Concern letter I gave her (also yesterday), *dispatched the fol ltr to the Head of the Brazilian Diplomatic Mission in Japan, Gastao P. do Rio Branco:*

> Miss Mildred Tsai, born in Shanghai, China, on 20 April 1919, bearer of Chinese Passport Number GV-02990, issued by the Chinese Embassy at Bangkok on 13 September 1950, is presently employed as a translator with my hq here in Tokyo. Miss Tsai arrived in Japan on 17 Feb 51 aboard the *Hai Ming* as a tourist. Subsequently, she received permission from SCAP to remain in Japan as a DAFC employee. Miss Tsai has indicated a desire to go to Brazil upon completion of her employment with this Hq and I understand that she is making application at your office for an entry permit to Brazil. I have taken a personal interest in this case because of the loyal and efficient assistance rendered by Miss Tsai to organizations I have commanded in China during 1945, 1946 and at the present here in Japan. She is a loyal and ardent believer in the democratic way of life and I highly recommend her as a desirable visitor to your country. G.E.S.

Was just briefed by Colonel Friedman; present were Generals Craigie and Crabb and Colonel Zimmerman - re USAF paper on a post-treaty Japan AF and our comments and recommendations thereto. I signed the letter of transmittal and agreed entirely with the paper after about 50 minutes of discussion.

Dispatched a reply radio, to the one I received this AM, telling USAF that Colonel McComas has the very important slot of CO off the 8th Ftr Bomber Group in the FAF and I cannot release him; however, suggested names of two field grade officers will be sent you.

---

210. Col Edward O. McComas had been both the chief of the Combat Operations Division and assistant deputy for operations at FEAF before becoming the 8th FBG's commander in May.

Dispatched the fol personal to Partridge:

The sortie rate of FAF units since the outbreak of hostilities in Korea has been beyond my greatest expectation. The continuing pressure that you have maintained regardless of the movement of units, inclement weather, or darkness has paid off tremendously in destruction of enemy's supplies and has cost him dearly in personnel. The announced policy of C-in-C recently reiterated by the Secretary of Defense is that our principal objective is not so much the acquisition of real estate in Korea but the destruction of supplies and personnel of such magnitude as will ultimately force a political decision. In light of this, it would appear well advised to husband our forces with a view to an extended period of operations. While I have directed that you continue your efforts against various target systems, I at the same time suggest that you consider the periodic standdown of your combat elements on a staggered basis when the ground forces degree of engagement justifies. I appreciate your unmatched efforts to extract the utmost from your units but feel that a slightly lower tempo with emphasis on results rather than on sorties flown may prove prudent in the long run. Please let me have your views on this matter.

SUNDAY
13 MAY
1951

In reply to my long radio to Partridge re the husbanding of his forces (see diary item dtd 12 May) received the fol:

Citing ur A 7416 CG. Appreciate your remarks concerning sustained effort exerted by FAF in Korea. Since with adequate flow of pers and equip from ZI we could continue indefinitely at present rate of operations, it is deducted that these replacements will not be forthcoming. Reduction in daily effort will be initiated in few days after subject can be discussed with wing commanders.

USAF via signal informed me that

...tanker your request with four sets of probe tip tanks for F–80 aboard will arrived FEAF o/a [on or about] 1 June 51. Desire information as to base destination for this aircraft.

Ok'd the fol Stratline to Partridge:

In reporting your recent heavy attack on Sinŭiju, press made many exaggerated and completely unsubstantiated claims for damage inflicted. Your official preliminary estimate was quite properly on the conservative side. This preliminary estimate of one plane destroyed and one damaged on ground is being misunderstood in Washington which reflects unfavorably on USAF. General Marshall made this statement to Senator Cain[211] in Washington yesterday. "In the last few days, we had a highly exaggerated estimate by pilots as to the number of planes destroyed in one bombardment at Sinŭiju. I think they said 35 planes. Actually, the report finally came back to us from photographs and others that one plane was destroyed and one damaged." Suggest you issue well-rounded statement to press, spelling out in some detail evaluated destruction, damage and

---

211. Senator Harry P. Cain of Washington.

casualty figures, as soon as practicable, today if possible. Nuckols will talk to your PIO on this subject.

Received the fol cy of a rad that Van Fleet (CG Eighth Army) sent to his Corps Commanders and the ROK Army, with info to me, CINCFE, FAF, and KMAG, # GX 5-1697 KGOO:

In order to provide maximum air effort for interdiction missions during the present period of loose enemy contact, the fol temporary restrictions on the use of close support aircraft will obtain. Requests will be limited to those for: *(A)* Remunerative targets that cannot be neutralized by weapons available to commanders concerned. *(B)* Column cover for forces making deep penetrations into enemy territory. The foregoing restrictions will be removed by this headquaraters when the appearance of profitable front line targets makes such action desirable.

Upon receipt of the above quoted message, I immediately sent the fol letter to Vandenberg:

Dear Van. Your attention is invited to the attached signal sent by the Commanding General, Eighth Army, to his corps commanders and the ROK Army. This is the first time to my knowledge that such a signal has emanated from the United States Army over here and speaks well for the planning and thinking of Lieutenant General James A. Van Fleet, the present commander. It is my opinion that you might want to file this document with the Stearns and Barcus reports. We are now awaiting "phase two" of the Communist spring offensive, are as alert as possible to his use of air in support of his ground action as well as his hitting us at our air facilities both in Korea and Japan. s/G.E.S.

Squadron Leader Morgan[212] called on me about 0900 hours and, as a result of his call, issued the fol memo to D/O which incorporated these two points:

...Sq Ldr Morgan out here on liaison duty from the RAF, London, is a photographic expert and worked for Colonel Polifka while commanding an RAF photographic sq in the Mediterranean. It would appear to me that during his tour of duty with us until Sq Ldr Adderly[213] comple[te]s his 6-months operational tour, that he, Morgan, specialize on recon, coming up with a report to us on what he has found both good and bad with some recommendations for improvement.... Sq Ldr Adderly is now flying with the 27th Ftr Bomber Group and has flown some 50-odd operational missions in F–84Es. I feel it is now about time for him to switch and get some experience in both the F–80Cs and F–86s, and it is therefore requested that you get out the necessary instructions.

Golf game at Koganei with the Lockwoods and ourselves; I had an 86.

General Brothers, my FEAF Staff Surgeon, admitted to and was operated on at the USAF Hosp FEAMC, for duodenum perforated ulcer. His condition was reported to me to be "satisfactory."

---

212. Morgan is unidentified.
213. Sqdn Ldr Michael C. Adderly.

General Stratemeyer and his principal staff officers, May 1951. Standing, left to right: Brig. Gen. James E. Ferguson, Assistant Deputy for Operations; Maj. Gen. Laurence C. Craigie, Vice Commander, FEAF; General Stratemeyer; Brig. Gen. Darr H. Alkire, Deputy for Materiel. Seated, left to right: Brig. Gen. Jarred V. Crabb, Deputy for Operations; Brig. Gen. Oliver S. Picher, Deputy for Personnel; Brig. Gen. William P. Nuckols, Public Information Officer. Two other members of the staff, Brig. Gen. Charles Y. Banfill, Deputy for Intelligence, and Brig. Gen. Clyde L. Brothers, FEAF Surgeon, were absent when the photo was taken.

**MONDAY
14 MAY
1951**

Because I had heard that Gill Robb Wilson was in Europe and the letters that I have been sending him "personally" weekly have apparently been opened by his assistant (I have received neither the courtesy of a reply to questions raised in those letters nor info from him that he was leaving the States), I had this week's letter addressed to General Spaatz (who has requested they keep coming) and will continue to address these letters to Toohey Spaatz until I have some word of explanation from Mr. Wilson.

Received a signal from Banfill that he must undergo an operation while in Washington upon completion of mission.

At 1000 hours visited the hospital at FEAMCOM to see how General Brothers was progressing. He had a very serious operation, but is coming along fine. After my visit with him, I inspected the hospital with Colonel Jenkins and on my way back to the office, I stopped by for a visit and a cup of coffee with General Doyle.

At 1800 hours, Annalee and I attended a poker party at the Sebalds.

TUESDAY
15 MAY
1951

Received the fol telephonic report on General Brothers' condition — which is good, he spent a quiet night, has gotten up, and is feeling fine.

Rcvd fol personal from Nugent:

The Secretary and C/S have expressed concern over the morale implications incident to the augmentation of forces in your command and have directed a comprehensive study of situation with appropriate recommendations. Believed here that major morale problems involved are those associated with rotation, dependent travel and family housing. In order to insure that your personal views are reflected in our study, I would appreciate participation of qualified representatives from your staff. Request they be ordered TDY this Hq for one week with reporting date 28 May. Believes one personnel officer qualified to represent you from a policy viewpoint and air installation officer with best available information on your housing situation will be adequate. Please acknowledge and advise names of representatives.

My immediate reply was:

Personal Nugent from Stratemeyer. Reur AFPDP 51399, Colonel Walden B. Coffey, from Personnel, and Major Stuart L. Davis,[214] from Materiel, will report Hq USAF 28 May. Both qualified to represent me on policy matters.

0900 hours, had my typhoid shot.

About 1500 hours, Mr. Owen Crump, of Hollywood, who is out here shooting a picture in the interests of the Disabled Veterans' Assoc called on me prior to his departure. His movie will be the "air evacuation from front lines of the wounded men clear back to a hospital in the U.S." Colonel Johnson, General Brothers' assistant, was present. Mr. Crump praised FEAF for all courtesies and facilities offered him.

Received a signal from Nugent in which he said he would find a 2-year spot for Gilkeson in AMC, but that as Gilkey's replacement, could not supply a brigadier general.

In reply thereto (copies of which were mailed to Stearley and Gilkeson, with a cc going to Personnel), I said:

Personal Nugent from Stratemeyer. Reur 51451. I wholeheartedly concur transfer Gilkeson to AMC. I do feel, though, that since you cannot give me a general to replace him, and since we have only 83 percent of authorized strength of colonels, that you should immediately send me as Gilkeson's replacement a senior well-qualified AF colonel with good background in administration and executive ability. I suggest you discuss this with Twining as he is familiar with the problems on Guam where the AF commander has daily contact with a two star admiral and an Army brigadier. We must maintain good relations with our sister services but still maintain an assured position with dignity.

---

214. Davis was in charge of the Facilities Branch, Engineering Division, FEAF.

WEDNESDAY 16 MAY 1951

Received the fol report (FEAF AG No. 19985) signed by Hardman,[215] JOC, Hq Eighth USAK, Office of G-3 Air, APO 301, dtd 29 Apr 51, subject: EXTRACTS OF REPORTS ON NIGHT BOMBING.

1. I US Corps 2 April 1951. On 8 April 51 a warrant officer PW stated that night bombing was more effective than daylight bombing because daylight bombing was aimed mostly at buildings, while the troops hid in foxholes, whereas at night they all come out of their foxholes and move around. *2.* I US Corps 2 April 1951. PW stated that while advancing to CS 5258 his company was subjected to approximately 10 night bombing attacks and as a result lose 3 of their 4 mortars and suffered heavy casualties. *3.* I US Corps 2 April 1951. On 20 Feb 51 PW reported night bombing is very effective. *4.* I US Corps 2 April 1951. On 14 March 51 PW stated he witnessed 20 men in his company killed during 2 recent night bombing attacks. *5.* I US Corps 2 April 1951. POW's reported night bombing caused heavy casualties during meal hours. *6.* I US Corps 2 April 1951. PW stated that supplies and arms were transported from an unknown position; these runs were made once every three to six days DEPENDING UPON THE INTENSITY OF NIGHT AIR ATTACKS [emphasis in original]. *7.* I US Corps 28 April 1951. On 26 April MPQ–2 bombing helped greatly to relieve enemy pressure on the 1st ROK Div. Attacking enemy units were reduced from regimental size to less than battalion strength prior to their attacks. *8.* I US Corps 28 April 1951. The 3rd US Division on 27 April reported that a large hill mass running north and south from Seoul to Ŭijŏngbu was a big threat to friendly forces, as 3 enemy regiments were reported moving south. MPQ–2 bombing reduced the enemy strength to the size of 1 battalion and their attack was easily contained. *9.* I US Corps 28 April 1951. The Chief of Staff, I US Corps, expressed thanks to the Air Force for their maximum effort yesterday. He feels that they are in such a favorable position today only because of their MPQ–2 effort around the clock. *10.* I US Corps 28 April 1951. The 24th RCT was attacked and a penetration was made on 26 April. An MPQ–2 drop was requested. Two B–26s were vectored to the target and dropped their loads less than 1,000 yards from friendly positions. The immediate effect of the drop was that the attack was stopped and the lines were restored. The 25th US Division was also attacked during the night of 26 April and requested an MPQ–2 drop. Friendly elements report the attack stopped immediately. The presence of aircraft over enemy lines at night seems to discourage any ideas of attacking. *11.* Report from IX US Corps on 13 April 1951. A total of 16 B–29s were controlled by MPQ–2 during period 7 March to 10 April. Results are as follows: 1 Army command post destroyed, 1 regimental command post destroyed, 3 supply dumps destroyed, excellent coverage on 27 troop concentrations each averaging 1,000 troops, 2 villages containing troops, supplies and communications destroyed. *12.* Report from IX US Corps on 28 April 1951. At 0341 today one aircraft under MPQ–2 control dropped ten 500 lb bombs on a target through a solid overcast. The pilot reported

---

215. Hardman's full name is unknown.

immediately after the drop there was a secondary explosion, larger than any he had previously witnessed that came up through the overcast. *13.* X US Corps periodic intelligence report No. 170. PW states that the 3d Regt, 15th NK Division was attacked with air burst bombs and his battalion suffered 18 killed and 12 wounded. A PW from the 2d Regt, 15th NK Division states a lone UN plane attacked his unit during night of 27-28 Feb with 5 napalm bombs. PW credits bombing as being uncanny for all bombs scored direct hits on houses containing troops. Casualties unknown. PW from the 1st Regt, 12th NK Division saw 1 UN aircraft attack a group of 100 and inflected heavy casualties. Later, a village in which PW was hiding was effectively attacked by a lone UN airplane.

I bucked a copy of the above EXTRACTS OF REPORTS ON NIGHT BOMBING to Idwal Edwards with this comment:

I inclose a copy of Eighth Army reports attesting to the effectiveness of recent night attacks along the front lines. I feel it necessary, however, to add a few comments and reservations. I cannot help but think that complimentary remarks and the enthusiastic acceptance of our recent efforts in contra-distinction to the repeated complaints with respect to our close support missions of last summer portend a change in overall strategy on the part of Army with respect to the close air support issue. The B–29 effort that we have placed on close air support in recent weeks amounts to about a third of the total daily missions scheduled by Bomber Command. My reason for emphasis on night operations under radar direction and particularly those placed against troops on the battlefield is to develop our capability for all weather close support operations in preparation for the rainy season. It has also proved quite worthwhile in disrupting attacks at night in the recent Chinese Communist drive. You will recall that last summer GHQ directed that I employ all the B–29s on close-in missions until early August (the situation was so critical then that I agreed). About this time, at my request, Opie Weyland persuaded GHQ staff that more profitable targets could be found in the north. Our point was sold. I am concerned lest the current favorable comments are a prelude to a request or a directive that I again place my maximum effort along the front lines with the B–29s regardless of the tactical requirement. This contention gains some support from the fact that GHQ is showing great interest in the bomb loads carried by B–29s (100 - 100 lbs, VT fused G.P.) on the MPQ–2 close support radar strikes and by the fact that there is currently in preparation within G-3 of GHQ a plan to increase air effort on close attacks by B–26s and B–29s. To this, up to a point, I will agree—particularly with the B–26s. General Ridgway has stated to me that our principal objective in Korea is to inflict the maximum casualties on Communist forces with the hope that the toll will ultimately reach such proportions that a political decision will be forced. I accept this view fully and I am directing the use of the forces available to me along these lines; however, I will insist that the selection of targets must be left to me. I recommend, therefore, that you note the attached optimistic and complimentary reports, but bear in mind my views in so doing. Best regards. s/G.E.S.

*Re the same EXTRACTS, I dropped Bill Hoge (CG IX Corps, Major
General William M. Hoge) a letter and stated:*

In the Eighth United States Army, Korea, Office of G-3 Air's report under
date of 29 April 1951, subject: EXTRACTS OF REPORTS ON NIGHT
BOMBING, appears Paragraph 11 which states as follows: (quoted Par.
11 in toto). I am interested to know how you were able to make such a
positive statement, as the above, from your hq on 13 April as I have been
attempting to determine just what the results of our MPQ–2 bombings
are. Was this from PW reports - or from ground recon from your corps?
Hope everything goes well and that you can give me some answer to my
above query. Best regards. s/G.E.S.

*On receipt of the fol quoted signal from Nugent to all commanders,
which stated:*

Selection Board convening 1330 hours 16 May to consider officers for
promotion to temporary MG and BG. Any changes such as deletions,
additions or realignment of your present priority list on file here must be
in to me not later than 0900 hours, 16 May. In the event there are no
changes in your present priority list for promotions, please acknowledge
receipt with negative reply.

I sent the fol answer:

...Change Part I my rad A 2803 CG dtd 151100Z Feb 51 as follows: Maj.
Gen. list: delt [delete] Timberlake. Move Crabb to pos following Doyle.
New Brig. Gen. list: Meyers, Gilbert L., D/O Fifth AF, same pos after
prom. Tyer, Aaron W. CG 49th F-B Wing, Taegu, same pos. Price, George
E., Northern Air Defense area comdr and base CO Misawa, same pos.
Erler, Leo J., Dir Installations, FEAF, same. Gilger, Chester P., VC Twen-
tieth AF, same. Zimmerman, Don A, Dir Plans, FEAF, same. Moorman,
T.S., CO 2143 Air Wea Wg, same. Weltman, John W., enroute ZI frm CG
51st F Wg. Polifka Karl L., CG 67 Tac Recn Wg, Taegu, same. Harvey,
Marvin M., D/M Fifth AF, same. Rogers, Turner C., CG 18 F-B Wg,
Chinhae, same. Lawhon, Brooks A., CG 35 F-I Wg, Pusan, same. Jenk-
ins, Jack S., VC 314 Air Div, same. No change to Part II myrad A 2803
CG. New subj: All lists arranged in order of priority. I particularly and
urgently recm [recommend] prom of Doyle and Crabb to Maj. Gen. and
Meyers, Tyer, George Price, Erler and Gilger to Brig Gen.

In reply to a signal that came in 8 May:

Reurad AX 7190 OP-op3, dtd 5 May 51. *PART I.* Act[ion] is being initiated to reinstate pers snatch pickup project. It appears possible that equip
and pers can be made avail to your command in a relatively short period
of time. Detailed info will be fwdd at an early date. *PART II* . The AMC
has developed a simple long-range tank instal[lation] for the H–19 helicopter utilizing C–47 wing tank. It is understood that the instal can be
accomplished locally with avail materials. Act is being initiated to furn nec
instructions and drawings to your command at the earliest possible date.

Directed dispatch of the fol:

TO SAVILLE[216] FROM STRATEMEYER. Reurad AFDRQ 51055, dtd 8 May 51. I consider both personnel snatch pickup project and long range tank installation for H–19 helicopter of extreme importance. Appreciate your interest and action on these matters. Information, equipment, and personnel for these projects will be more than welcome to this command.

**THURDAY
17 MAY
1951**

General Orders Number 218, this date, issued making the 314th Air Division a subordinate command of the Far East Air Forces (relieved from assignment to Fifth Air Force), to be effective 0001 hours, 18 May 1951.

A group picture of all hqs' generals was taken in the Allied Council Room, including several in color, at 0830 hours.

At 1030 hours, General (Dr.) David Yu (Yu-Tai-Wei)[217] who, during the war was the Minister of Communications under Chiang, called with General Ho Shai Lai. General Yu is enroute to Formosa.

At 1900 hours, Mr. Takahashi paid his second call to try to eliminate this stiff neck and shoulder pain of mine. He has a grip of iron.

Made a tape broadcast of the following message, to be broadcast Armed Forces Day, 19 May 1951, and also released to the papers as Release No. 817:

The unity of purpose of the Armed Forces of the United States in their fight against Communism in Korea is the finest demonstration possible of unification in action. On Armed Forces Day, 1951, in the Far East, the skyfilling throb of airpower overhead, the constant snarl of machine guns in forward positions on the ground, and the majestic roar of naval gunfire speak in unison to say that the three armed services of the United States are in concerted action against the foe.

It is also fitting on this Armed Forces Day to pay tribute to the United Nations forces under the leadership of General Ridgway who are fighting so valiantly in the unified effort against Communism, the common enemy of all free peoples of the world.

**FRIDAY
18 MAY
1951**

General Power brought in Generals Terrill and Briggs and two colonels, at which time General Terrill was introduced.[218]

At 1130 hours, I accompanied General Power to General Hickey's office where General Terrill was introduced to General Hickey and we cleared up a point reference SAC taking over our two bomb groups on D Day.

Mrs. Marge Timberlake and General Willoughby had lunch with us at Mayeda House.

---

216. Maj Gen Gordon Saville, Deputy Chief of Staff/Development, Headquarters USAF.
217. Yu was Special Assistant to the Chinese Ambassador to the United States.
218. Brig Gen Robert H. Terrill relieved Brigadier General Briggs as FEAF BomCom commander on May 23.

1530 hours, Colonel Pretorious came in reference a change in his lodgings from the Maronouchi Hotel to the Imperial Hotel. I turned him over to General Craigie.

At 1800 hours, Annalee and I called on General and Mrs. Ridgway at the Embassy. Present, who also had been invited to call, were the Hickeys, General Willoughby, General Beiderlinden, and Peg Almond.

Dispatched a personal radio to Vandenberg re Lt. [Col.] Corey Ford and stated my case that inasmuch as Ford is to visit corps and division commands, and to facilitate the ease with which he can receive entree, he should receive a spot promotion from CSAF to colonel.

SATURDAY
19 MAY
1951

In reply to USAF rad AFPDC-2 51696, dtd 17 May 51 which stated:

Personal Stratemeyer from Nugent. Reurad A 7535 CG dtd 15 May 51. Orders issuing this date relieving BG Gilkeson from asgmt your command and asgng him as CG, Ogden AMA. Orders will authorize delay enroute not to interfere with reporting date at Ogden on or about 18 June. Gen. Chidlaw desires that Gilkeson be present at Commanders' Conference AMC between 19 and 22 June. If Gilkeson desires more leave after that time, he can work it out with Gen. Chidlaw. I have screened the names of a number of cols. who I felt would be acceptable to you as replacement for Gilkeson, but was unable to obtain their release. Could you possibly utilize Col. Robert W.C. Wimsatt for this duty and we will furnish you a more junior col as replacement for Wimsatt? Please advise if this solution is acceptable to you. Appreciate your early release of Gilkeson.

I dispatched the fol signal to Nugent with info personal to Stearley and Gilkeson, this date, Cite AX 7671 CG:

Reurad AFPDC 251696. Regret your inability to provide senior colonel for Gilkeson. Col. Wimsatt will be utilized for this position. Request one of the following colonels as replacement for Wimsatt: Col. Victor L. Anderson, Col. Carl E. Rankin, Col. Charles E. Jung.[219] Gilkeson's approx ETD is 26 May.

At my direction, the FEAF staff surgeon, prepared the fol "personal to Twining" "Priority" radio, which I OK'd for dispatch:

This radio in VII parts. *Part I*. Shortage of Medical Corps officers becoming more acute to the point where some immediate action must be taken. *Part II*. This command authorized two hundred sixty (260) Medical Corps officers with one hundred twenty-three (123) assigned, eight (8) of whom are residents reported for return to residency training this month. USAF overall rate of physicians is 2.3 per thousand (based on USAF Medical Service Statistical Review for March) where FEAF rate is 1.4 for troops dependent on this command for primary

---

219. Anderson was Chief, Programs and Requirements Office, DCS/Materiel, HQ USAF. Nothing further is known about the other officers

medical support. In computations officers returning for residency training were not included nor were Army medical officers presently serving with FEAF as GHQ FEC has requested return of Army personnel. Not considered is care given Army combat casualties or additional medical responsibility for civilian employees and dependents overseas. *Part III.* Since October 1950 I have been asking General Brothers to obtain one (1) flight surgeon for each squadron in combat. Since approximately 1 January 1951, squadrons have been operating under wartime strength and their Tables of Organization authorize one flight surgeon for each squadron. We have requisitions pending dated as far back as December 1950 which have not been filled and according to present commitments made by your headquarters we will not even be able to maintain our present strength of medical officers. *Part IV.* When I requested transfer of three (3) hospitals to FEAF from Army I was assured USAF medical personnel would be furnished to staff the 3 hospitals. Plans were made in September 1950 to take control and eight (8) months later we still do not have them completely staffed by USAF personnel. Several letters dating as early as September 1950 from the Surgeon General's office definitely stated USAF personnel to staff the hospitals would be available if we could manage the transfer of these facilities. With non receipt of adequate personnel we are not capable of fulfilling our commitment. *Part V.* Because this is the only war zone in the world and because records indicate there are sufficient medical officers available, it not understood why this command must be so short of medical personnel. Based on our information the medical personnel scheduled for this command do not equal expected losses. For instance there are thirty-four (34) medical officers eligible for return to the ZI (separation, rotation or residency) during May, June and July. Replacements we have been promised amount to only twenty-four (24) for same period. With presently assigned medical officers we are approximately fifty percent (50%) staffed with no early replacements enroute which creates a serious situation. In addition our responsibilities and our overall troop strength are increasing. It is also disturbing to note that an officer scheduled for this command there is a definite lack of experienced flight surgeons. *Part VI.* Applications for separation from eligible medical officers were forwarded with approval recommended providing replacements were in place prior to departure yet TWX directives have already been received on three (3) officers of the group to be immediately returned for separation. No replacements could be in place as the applications for separation were not received at your headquarters until approximately ten (10) days ago. *PART VII.* I request that all our outstanding requisitions be immediately filled and the officers start air travel no later than 10 June even though residencies must be slightly shortened, basic training eliminated or no leave given. We will furnish air priority. Likewise replacements for any returnees must be in place prior to release of any medical personnel. I am concerned and urge your help.

Dispatched the fol memo to CINCFE, subj: Eighth Army Support by FEAF:

Reference your message number 191345K, dated 19 May 1951, the following information is submitted:

Last night, 18-19 May, entire effort of FEAF Bomber Command of 11 B–29s was flown on MPQ–2 radar missions in support of Fifth Air Force mission of supporting Eighth Army. Along with this number of B–29s, there were 22 B–26s flown on a similar mission.

Tonight, 19-20 May, our entire effort of 14 B–29s will be flown on MPQ–2 radar missions. There are 21 B–26 MPQ–2 radar missions scheduled by Fifth Air Force for tonight. (Got off 17 B–29s; telephoned Hickey).

The above number of 35 MPQ–2 radar missions to be flown requires very careful scheduling of these sorties because, as you know, they go in individually and, therefore, an increase in the number for tonight was impracticable.

Tomorrow night, 20-21 May, we will attempt to schedule 24 B–29s on the MPQ–2 type of mission if Fifth Air Force can handle through their MPQ–2 stations.

We will continue nightly our maximum effort on this type of mission in support of the Fifth Air Force in its mission of supporting the Eighth Army. s/G.E.S.

General Beiderlinden (ex-G-1 of GHQ) called to say goodbye at 1000 hours.

Attended Mr. Pollack's (Jardine Matheson Co.) cocktail party and then went on to the Hickey's, where we picked them up, and then all went to Yokohama to have dinner with Colonel and Mrs. Scott. (Mr. Pollack secured my jasmine tea (China).)

To bed at midnight—too late.

SUNDAY   Left the office at 1130 hours to play golf.
20 MAY
1951

[Later this day, Gen. Stratemeyer suffered a severe heart attack]

Abbreviations

AAA . . . . antiaircraft artillery

ABN . . . . airborne

A/C or acft . . . aircraft

AC&W . . . . . . aircraft control and warning

act. . . . . active

ADC . . . . Air Defense Command

ADC . . . . aide-de-camp

ADCC. . . . . . . air defense control center

ADCOM. . . . . GHQ Advance Command and Liaison Group

add . . . . additional

adees. . . . . addressees

adv . . . . advance

afld . . . . airfield

AG . . . . Adjutant General

alt . . . . altitude

ammo . . . . ammunition

ARG . . . . air rescue group

ARS . . . . air rescue squadron

asgd . . . . assigned

atk . . . . attack

ATW. . . . . air transport wing

auth . . . . authority or authorize

avail or aval. . . available

Avammo . . . . . aviation ammunition

avgas. . . . . aviation gasoline

AVM . . . . Air Vice Marshal

AW . . . . automatic weapon(s) or all-weather

AWW . . . . air weather wing

BCOF. . . . . . . British Common- wealth Overseas Forces

BFEAF. . . . . . British Far East Air Force

BG . . . . bomb group

BomCom . . . . Bomber Command, FEAF

BS. . . . . bomb squadron

BW . . . . bomb wing

C of S or C/S. . Chief of Staff

CAP . . . . combat air patrol

CAT . . . . Civil Air Transport

cav . . . . cavalry

CBS . . . . Columbia Broadcasting System

CCF . . . . Chinese Communist Forces

CCRAK . . . . . Combined Command Research and Activities in Korea

CCTS . . . . Combat Crew Training School

CG . . . . Commanding General

CincFE. . . . . . Commander in Chief, Far East Command

CincPacFlt . . . Commander in Chief, Pacific Fleet

CincUNC . . . . Commander in Chief, United Nations Command

cmbt . . . . combat

CNO . . . . Chief of Naval Operations

COMGEN	. . . Commanding General	**FBG**	. . . . fighter-bomber group
comm	. . . . communication(s)	**FBS**	. . . . fighter-bomber squadron
ComNavFE	. . Commander Naval Forces Far East	**FBW**	. . . . fighter-bomber wing
comp	. . . . complete	**FEAF**	. . . . Far East Air Forces
con	. . . . control	**FEAMCOM**	. . Far East Air Materiel Command
CONAC	. . . . . Continental Air Command	**FEW**	. . . . fighter-escort wing
CP	. . . . command post	**FIG**	. . . . fighter-interceptor group
CSAF	. . . . Chief of Staff, USAF	**FIS**	. . . . fighter-interceptor squadron
CW	. . . . continuous wave	**FIW**	. . . . fighter-interceptor wing
D/A	. . . . Department of the Army	**FM**	. . . . frequency modulation
D/I	. . . . Deputy for Intelligence	**fol or folg**	. . . . following
D/Ops	. . . . Deputy for Operations	**fr**	. . . . from
dir	. . . . direct(ed)	**frags**	. . . . fragmentation bombs
DIR	. . . . depot inspection and repair	**ftr**	. . . . fighter
Div	. . . . division	**FW**	. . . . fighter wing
dtd	. . . . dated	**fwd(d)**	. . . . . . forward(ed)
EAD	. . . . extended active duty	**GCA**	. . . . ground-controlled approach
eff	. . . . effective/effectiveness	**gnd or grd**	. . . ground
elim	. . . . eliminate	**gp**	. . . . group
Engr	. . . . engineer	**GP**	. . . . general purpose (bomb)
eny	. . . . enemy	**HF**	. . . . high frequency
equip	. . . . equipment/equipped	**HQ or Hqrs**	. . headquarters
Estab or **estb'd**	. . . . establish(ed)	**hwy**	. . . . highway
ETA	. . . . estimated time of arrival	**IG**	. . . . Inspector General
EUSAK	. . . . . . Eighth United States Army in Korea	**im**	. . . . immediate
expd	. . . . expressed	**INS**	. . . . International News Service
fac	. . . . facility(ies)	**JA**	. . . . Judge Advocate
FAF	. . . . Fifth Air Force	**JATO**	. . . . jet-assisted take off
F (AW) S	. . . . fighter (all-weather) squadron	**JOC**	. . . . Joint Operations Center

KMAG	Korean Military Advisory Group		**POW**	prisoner of war
loc	location		**pres**	present
ltr	letter		**proj**	project(s)
M/B	medium bomber		**prov(g)**	provide(ing)
MAG	Marine Air Group		**prov**	provisional
maint	maintenance		**R&R**	routing and record sheet
MARINEX	Marine Express		**RAAF**	Royal Australian Air Force
MATS	Military Air Transport Service		**rad**	radio
MAW	Marine Air Wing		**radnote**	radio note
mg	machine gun		**RAF**	Royal Air Force
mil	military		**RCAF**	Royal Canadian Air Force
mo	month		**RCT**	regimental combat team
msg	message		**rcvd**	received
mvmt	movement		**recon sq**	reconnaissance squadron
nec	necessary or necessity		**ref**	reference
NK	North Korea(n)		**rein**	reinforcement(s)
NKPA	North Korean People's Army		**req or rqst**	request
O	office		**reurad**	re your radio message
opnl	operational		**RFD**	ready for delivery
opns or ops	operations		**ROK**	Republic of Korea
OSI	Office of Special Investigations		**RON**	remain overnight
par	paragraph		**rptd**	reported
pd	period		**rqmts**	requirements
pers	personnel		**rqn**	requisition
PhibGruOne	Amphibious Group One		**RR**	railroad
PIO	public information officer		**RTT**	radio, telephone and telegraphy
pirep	pilot report		**rwy**	runway
POL	petroleum, oil, and lubricants		**SAC**	Strategic Air Command

SCAP . . . . Supreme Commander Allied Powers

SCARWAF . . . Special Category Army Personnel with Air Force

ship . . . . shipment

sit . . . . situation

SK . . . . South Korea(n)

SOP . . . . standing operating procedure

sq, sqdn or sqdr . . . . . . squadron(s)

SRS . . . . strategic reconnaissance squadron

SRW . . . . strategic reconnaissance wing

sta . . . . station

strat . . . . strategic

SYG . . . . Secretary General, UN

T/O&E . . . . . . Table(s) of Organization and Equipment

TAC . . . . Tactical Air Command

tac . . . . tactical

TACC . . . . tactical air control center

TACP . . . . tactical air control party

TCC . . . . tactical control center

TCG . . . . troop carrier group

TCW . . . . troop carrier wing

tech . . . . technical

tgt . . . . target

TOT . . . . time over target

trps . . . . troops

TRS . . . . tactical reconnaissance squadron

TRW . . . . tactical reconnaissance wing

TS . . . . top secret

TSW . . . . tactical support wing

unk . . . . unknown

UR . . . . unsatisfactory report

util . . . . utilize(d)

VC . . . . Vice Chief of Staff

VOCG . . . . . . verbal orders of the commanding general

w . . . . with

w/b . . . . will be

wg . . . . wing

w/i . . . . within

WAR . . . . War Department/ Department of the Army

wea . . . . weather

WRS . . . . weather reconnaissance squadron

ZI . . . . zone of interior

Bibliography

Numerous documents, books, and articles were consulted during the preparation of this work and are listed below. The official documents used can be found in the archives of the Air Force Historical Research Agency (AFHRA) at Maxwell AFB, Alabama. Microfilm copies of these documents are also held in the Air Force History Support Office library at Bolling AFB, Washington, D.C. These documents are filed under series numbers as listed below, with numerous sub-numbers. For example, K720.01 indicates that this is the FEAF history for specific dates as listed in the indexes to the microfilm reels. A sub-number of .052 indicates chronologies; .162, messages; .226, movement orders; etc. Sub-numbers are the same for all series numbers. A finding aid listing all series numbers and sub-numbers is on file at the Air Force Historical Research Agency and at the Air Force History Support Office.

Official Documents and Publications

Far East Air Forces (FEAF) records. AFHRA Series No. K720.

Fifth Air Force records. AFHRA Series No. K730.

FEAF Bomber Command records. AFHRA Series No. K713.

FEAF Combat Cargo Command records. AFHRA Series No. K714.

"An Evaluation of the Effectiveness of the United States Air Force in the Korean Campaign, 25 June - 31 December 1950." (Also known as the Barcus Report.) AFHRA Series No. K168.041-1.

Stearns Mission Report. AFHRA Series No. K168.041-2.

Appleman, Roy Edgar. *South to the Naktong, North to the Yalu: June-November 1950*. Washington: Office of the Chief of Military History, 1961. Vol. 1 of *United States Army in the Korean War*.

Farrar-Hockley, Anthony. *The British Part in the Korean War*. Vol. 1: *A Distant Obligation*. Vol. 2: *An Honorable Discharge*. London: HMSO, 1990-1994.

Field, James A. *History of United States Naval Operations: Korea*. Washington: Director of Naval History, 1962.

Foreign Relations of the United States, 1950. Vol. VII: *Korea*. Washington: GPO, 1976.

Foreign Relations of the United States, 1951. Vol. VII: *Korea and China*. Washington: GPO, 1983.

Futrell, Robert F. *United States Air Force Operations in the Korean Conflict, 25 June-1 November 1950*. USAF Historical Study No. 71. Maxwell AFB, Ala.: Air University, 1951.

United States Air Force Operations in the Korean Conflict, 1 November

1950-30 June 1952. USAF Historical Study No. 72. Maxwell AFB, Ala: Air University, 1955.

The United States Air Force in Korea, 1950-1953. Washington: Office of Air Force History, 1983. Rev. Ed.

Maurer, Maurer. *Aviation in the U.S. Army, 1919-1939.* Washington: Office of Air Force History, 1987.

Mossman, Billy C. *Ebb and Flow: November 1950-July 1951.* Washington: Center of Military History, 1990. Vol. 5 of *United States Army in the Korean War.*

Rearden, Steven L. *The Formative Years, 1947-1950.* Washington: Historical Office, Office of the Secretary of Defense, 1984.

Republic of Korea. *The History of the United Nations Forces in the Korean War.* Vols. I and IV. Seoul: The Ministry of National Defense, 1972-1975.

Sawyer, Robert K. *Military Advisors in Korea; KMAG in Peace and War.* Washington: Office of the Chief of Military History, 1962.

Schnabel, James F. *Policy and Direction: The First Year.* Washington: Office of the Chief of Military History, 1972. Vol. 3 of *United States Army in the Korean War.*

Schnabel, James F., and Robert J. Watson. *The Korean War.* Washington: Joint Chiefs of Staff Historical Division, 1979. Vol. 3 of *The History of the Joint Chiefs of Staff: The Joint Chiefs of Staff and National Policy.*

Taylor, Joe Gray. *Development of Night Air Operations, 1941-1952.* USAF Historical Study No. 92. Maxwell AFB, Ala: Air University, 1953.

Commercial Publications

An, Tai Sung. *North Korea, A Political Handbook.* Wilmington, Del.: Scholarly Resources, Inc., 1983.

Alexander, Bevin. *Korea, the First War We Lost.* New York: Hippocrene, 1986.

Appleman, Roy E. *Disaster in Korea: The Chinese Confront MacArthur.* College Station, Tex.: Texas A&M University Press, 1989.

East of Chosin: Entrapment and Breakout in Korea, 1950. College Station, Tex.: Texas A&M University Press, 1987.

Escaping the Trap: The US Army X Corps in Northeast Korea, 1950. College Station, Tex.: Texas A&M University Press, 1990.

Berger, Carl. *The Korea Knot: A Military-Political History.* Philadelphia: Univ. of Pennsylvania, 1965. Rev. Ed.

Blair, Clay. *The Forgotten War: America in Korea, 1950-1953.* New York: Times Books, 1987.

Collins, J. Lawton. *War in Peacetime: The History and Lessons of Korea.* Boston: Houghton Mifflin, 1969.

Cumings, Bruce. *The Origins of the Korean War*. 2 vols. Princeton, N.J.: Princeton University Press, 1981-1990.

Cumings, Bruce and Jon Haliday. *Korea: The Unknown War*. New York: Pantheon Books, 1988.

Detzer, David. *Thunder of the Captains*. New York: Thomas Y. Crowell Co., 1977.

Dorr, Robert F., and Warren Thompson. *The Korean Air War*. Osceola, Wis.: Motorbooks International, 1994.

DuPre, Col Flint. *U.S. Air Force Biographical Dictionary*. New York: Franklin Watts, 1965.

Fehrenbach, Thomas R. *This Kind of War: A Study in Unpreparedness*. New York: Macmillan, 1963.

Foot, Rosemary. *The Wrong War: American Policy and the Dimensions of the Korean Conflict, 1950-1953*. Ithaca, N.Y., and London: Cornell University Press, 1985.

Gordon, Yefim, and Vladimir Rigmant. *MiG–15*. Osceola, Wis.: Motorbooks International, 1993.

Goulden, Joseph C. *Korea: The Untold Story of the War*. New York: Times Books, 1982.

Halliday, Jon. "Air Operations in Korea: The Soviet Side of the Story." In *A Revolutionary War,* edited by William J. Williams. Chicago: Imprint Publications, 1993.

Hatada, Takashi. *A History of Korea*. Translated by Warren W. Smith and Benjamin H. Hazard. Santa Barbara, Calif.: ABC-Clio Inc., 1969.

Hone, Thomas C. "Korea." In *Case Studies in the Achievement of Air Superiority*, edited by Benjamin Franklin Cooling. Washington: Center for Air Force History, 1994.

Jackson, Robert. *Air War over Korea*. New York: Scribner, 1973.

James, D. Clayton. *The Years of MacArthur*. Vol. III. *Triumph and Disaster, 1945-1964*. Boston: Houghton Mifflin Co., 1985.
       Refighting the Last War: Command and Crisis in Korea. New York: Free Press, 1993.

Lee, Ki-baik. *A New History of Korea*. Translated by Edward W. Wagner and Edward J. Shultz. Cambridge, Mass.: Harvard University Press, 1984.

MacArthur, Gen of the Army Douglas. *Reminiscences*. New York: McGraw-Hill, 1965.

MacDonald, Callum. *Korea: The War Before Vietnam*. London: Macmillan, 1986.

Matray, James I., ed. *Historical Dictionary of the Korean War*. Westport, Conn.: Greenwood Press, 1991.

Millett, Allan R. "Korea, 1950-1953." In *Case Studies in Development of Close Air Support,* edited by Benjamin Franklin Cooling. Washington: Office of Air Force History, 1990.

Nichols, Donald. *How Many Times Can I Die?* Brooksville, Fla.: Brooksville Printing, 1981.

Noble, Harold J. *Embassy at War: An Account of the Early Weeks of the Korean War*. Ed. Frank Baldwin. Seattle: University of Washington Press, 1975.

Odgers, George. *Across the Parallel: The Australian 77th Squadron with the United States Air Force in the Korean War*. London: William Heinemann, 1952.

Rees, David. *Korea: The Limited War*. New York: St. Martin's Press, 1964.

Rothe, Anna, ed. *Current Biography, 1951*. New York: H.W. Wilson Co., 1952.

Simmons, Robert R. *The Strained Alliance: Peking, Pyongyang, Moscow and the Politics of the Korean Civil War*. New York: Free Press, 1975.

Stone, I.F. *The Hidden History of the Korean War*. London: Turnstile Press, 1952.

Stueck, William. *The Korean War as International History*. Princeton, N.J.: Princeton University Press, 1995.

Summers, Harry G., Jr. *Korean War Almanac*. New York: Facts on File, 1990.

Thompson, Annis G. *The Greatest Airlift: The Story of Combat Cargo*. Tokyo: Dai-Nippon Printing Company, 1954.

Truman, Harry S. *Memoirs*. 2 vols. Garden City, N.Y.: Doubleday, 1955-1956.

Vreeland, Nina, et al. *Area Handbook for South Korea*. Washington: GPO, 1975.

Who's Who, 1969-1970. New York: St. Martin's Press, 1969.

Wilson, David. *Lion over Korea: 77 Fighter Squadron RAAF, 1950-1953*. Canberra: Banner Books, 1994.

Articles

"Air Force Trio." *Newsweek*, July 24, 1950.

Almond, Lt. Gen. E.M. (Ret.). "Mistakes in Air-Support Methods in Korea." *U.S. News and World Report*, March 6, 1953.

Bauer, Daniel. "The Pilots That Nearly Started World War Three." *Air Classics*, April 1990.

Bracker, Milton. "Censure Foes List Rally Speakers." *New York Times*, November 29, 1954.

"Citizens Group Asks U.S. to End Red Ties." *New York Times*, February 11, 1957.

Egan, Leo. "13,000 at Garden Vow M'Carthy Aid." *New York Times*, November 30, 1954.

FEAF Bomber Command. "Heavyweights over Korea." *Air University Quarterly Review* 6 (Fall 1953).

"43 on Policy Unit of 'For America.'" *New York Times*, November 14, 1954.

"Gen. George Stratemeyer Dies; Led Air Force in the Far East." *New York Times*, August 11, 1969.

"Gen. Stratemeyer to Retire." *Army-Navy Journal*, October 6, 1951.

Grutzner, Charles. "U.S. F–86 Jet in First Fight Fells Enemy Plane in Korea." *New York Times*, December 18, 1950.

Kihss, Peter. "Petition Drive Set to Back M'Carthy." *New York Times*, November 15, 1954.

Knight, Charlotte. "Air War in Korea." *Air Force*, August 1950.

"Korea Air Chief Deplores Policy." *New York Times*, August 26, 1954.

Leonberg, MSgt. L.B. "To Rest at the Academy." *Airman*, November 1969.

"McCarthy Group Disbands." *Facts on File*, February 10-16, 1955.

"NBC Turns down M'Carthy Request." *New York Times*, November 23, 1954.

"Petitions Oppose Censure." *Facts on File*, November 12-18, 1954.

Quanbeck, Alton H. "My Brief War With Russia." *Washington Post*, March 4, 1990.

Sakamoto, Cpl. Larry. "Navy Flier Doubts Subs Near Korea." *Stars and Stripes* (Pacific Ed.), July 8, 1950.

Stratemeyer, Lt. Gen. George E., USAF (Ret.). "Fourteen Commandments for America Today." *American Mercury*, May 1955.

Straubel, James H. and John F. Loosbrock. "Air Support is a Two-Way Street." *Air Force*, August 1951.

Trussell, C.P. "Senate Unit Cites Korea War Lesson." *New York Times,* January 26, 1955.

Weyland, Otto P. "The Air Campaign in Korea." *Air University Quarterly Review* 6 (Fall 1953).

Zimmerman, Don Z. "FEAF: Mission and Command Relationships." *Air University Quarterly Review* 4 (Summer 1951).

Index

ISBN 0-16-050106-7